Convergence of Industry 4.0 and Supply Chain Sustainability

Muhammad Rahies Khan
Bahria University, Karachi, Pakistan

Naveed R. Khan
UCSI University, Malaysia

Noor Zaman Jhanjhi
Taylor's University, Malaysia

IGI Global
PUBLISHER of TIMELY KNOWLEDGE

A volume in the Advances in Logistics, Operations, and Management Science (ALOMS) Book Series

Published in the United States of America by
IGI Global
Business Science Reference (an imprint of IGI Global)
701 E. Chocolate Avenue
Hershey PA, USA 17033
Tel: 717-533-8845
Fax: 717-533-8661
E-mail: cust@igi-global.com
Web site: http://www.igi-global.com

Library of Congress Cataloging-in-Publication Data

Names: Khan, Muhammad Rahies, 1986- editor. | Khan, Naveed R., 1982- editor. | Jhanjhi, Noor Zaman, 1972- editor.
Title: Convergence of Industry 4.0 and supply chain sustainability / edited by Muhammad Rahies Khan, Naveed Khan, Noor Jhanjhi.
Description: Hershey, PA : Business Science Reference, [2024] | Includes bibliographical references and index. | Summary: "This book explores the integration of Industry 4.0 technology with supply chain management (SCM) sustainability, highlighting its impact on manufacturing and supply chain processes"-- Provided by publisher.
Identifiers: LCCN 2023049127 (print) | LCCN 2023049128 (ebook) | ISBN 9798369313633 (hardcover) | ISBN 9798369313640 (ebook)
Subjects: LCSH: Industry 4.0. | Manufacturing industries--Environmental aspects. | Business logistics--Environmental aspects. | Sustainable development.
Classification: LCC T59.6 .C66 2024 (print) | LCC T59.6 (ebook) | DDC 658.5--dc23/eng/20231122
LC record available at https://lccn.loc.gov/2023049127
LC ebook record available at https://lccn.loc.gov/2023049128

This book is published in the IGI Global book series Advances in Logistics, Operations, and Management Science (ALOMS) (ISSN: 2327-350X; eISSN: 2327-3518)

British Cataloguing in Publication Data
A Cataloguing in Publication record for this book is available from the British Library.

For electronic access to this publication, please contact: eresources@igi-global.com.

Advances in Logistics, Operations, and Management Science (ALOMS) Book Series

John Wang
Montclair State University, USA

ISSN:2327-350X
EISSN:2327-3518

Mission

Operations research and management science continue to influence business processes, administration, and management information systems, particularly in covering the application methods for decision-making processes. New case studies and applications on management science, operations management, social sciences, and other behavioral sciences have been incorporated into business and organizations real-world objectives.

The **Advances in Logistics, Operations, and Management Science** (ALOMS) Book Series provides a collection of reference publications on the current trends, applications, theories, and practices in the management science field. Providing relevant and current research, this series and its individual publications would be useful for academics, researchers, scholars, and practitioners interested in improving decision making models and business functions.

Coverage

- Organizational Behavior
- Networks
- Marketing engineering
- Political Science
- Risk Management
- Computing and information technologies
- Finance
- Decision analysis and decision support
- Operations Management
- Information Management

IGI Global is currently accepting manuscripts for publication within this series. To submit a proposal for a volume in this series, please contact our Acquisition Editors at Acquisitions@igi-global.com or visit: http://www.igi-global.com/publish/.

The Advances in Logistics, Operations, and Management Science (ALOMS) Book Series (ISSN 2327-350X) is published by IGI Global, 701 E. Chocolate Avenue, Hershey, PA 17033-1240, USA, www.igi-global.com. This series is composed of titles available for purchase individually; each title is edited to be contextually exclusive from any other title within the series. For pricing and ordering information please visit http://www.igi-global.com/book-series/advances-logistics-operations-management-science/37170. Postmaster: Send all address changes to above address.

Titles in this Series

For a list of additional titles in this series, please visit: http://www.igi-global.com/book-series/advances-logistics-operations-management-science/37170

Navigating the Coaching and Leadership Landscape Strategies and Insights for Success
Andrew J. Wefald (Staley School of Leadership, Kansas State University, USA)
Business Science Reference • © 2024 • 306pp • H/C (ISBN: 9798369352427) • US $295.00

Strategies for Environmentally Responsible Supply Chain and Production Management
Yanamandra Ramakrishna (School of Business, Skyline University College, Sharjah, UAE) and Babita Srivastava (William Paterson University, USA)
Business Science Reference • © 2024 • 309pp • H/C (ISBN: 9798369306697) • US $275.00

Industry Applications of Thrust Manufacturing Convergence with Real-Time Data and AI
D. Satishkumar (Nehru Institute of Technology, India) and M. Sivaraja (Nehru Institute of Technology, India)
Engineering Science Reference • © 2024 • 353pp • H/C (ISBN: 9798369342763) • US $365.00

Utilization of AI Technology in Supply Chain Management
Digvijay Pandey (Department of Technical Education, Government of Uttar Pradesh, India) Binay Kumar Pandey (College of Technology, Govind Ballabh Pant University of Agriculture and Technology, Pantnagar, India) Uday Kumar Kanike (Independent Researcher, USA) A. Shaji George (Crown University International, Saudi Arabia & Chartered International Da Vinci University, Nigeria) and Prabjot Kaur (Birla Institute of Technology, Mesra, India)
Business Science Reference • © 2024 • 336pp • H/C (ISBN: 9798369335932) • US $395.00

A Critical Examination of the Recent Evolution of B2B Sales
Joel G. Cohn (Everglades University, Boca Raton, USA)
Business Science Reference • © 2024 • 276pp • H/C (ISBN: 9798369303481) • US $255.00

Contemporary Management and Global Leadership for Sustainability
Kannapat Kankaew (International College, Burapha University, Thailand) Shilpa Chaudhary (Lovely Professional University, India) and Sarun Widtayakornbundit (Kasetsart University, Thailand)
Business Science Reference • © 2024 • 324pp • H/C (ISBN: 9798369312735) • US $275.00

Innovation and Resource Management Strategies for Startups Development
Neeta Baporikar (Namibia University of Science and Technology, Namibia & SP Pune University, India)
Business Science Reference • © 2024 • 298pp • H/C (ISBN: 9798369320778) • US $275.00

IGI Global
PUBLISHER of TIMELY KNOWLEDGE

701 East Chocolate Avenue, Hershey, PA 17033, USA
Tel: 717-533-8845 x100 • Fax: 717-533-8661
E-Mail: cust@igi-global.com • www.igi-global.com

Table of Contents

Detailed Table of Contents

This chapter explores the convergence of Industry 4.0 technologies and sustainable supply chain practices, presenting a comprehensive overview of these digital advancements' transformative potential. The chapter begins by defining the intersection between sustainability and Industry 4.0, emphasizing the pivotal role of digital technologies in fostering environmentally and socially responsible supply chains. With clear objectives in mind, the exploration delves into the impact of key digital technologies on responsible supply chain practices. The discussion spans the utilization of the internet of things (IoT) for real-time sustainability monitoring, big data analytics for informed decision-making, and the integration of robotics to enhance ethical manufacturing.

The integration of Industry 4.0 and supply chain sustainability marks the dawn of a new era of innovation and accountability within businesses, bringing technological innovation together with environmental and social responsibilities for the benefit of all. As Industry 4.0 is characterized by the integration of digital technologies, internet of things, and data analytics, it empowers organizations to create smart, connected, and efficient supply chains by harnessing the power of digital technologies. In addition, Industry 4.0 technologies enhance the transparency and traceability of the supply chain. With blockchain technology, for example, it is possible for all transactions and movements within the supply chain to be immutable. By doing so, not only is the authenticity of the sustainable materials ensured, but also fair labor practices are promoted. With consumers becoming increasingly aware of the environmental and ethical implications of their purchases, this transparency facilitates brand trust as well as loyalty among consumers.

The purpose of this chapter is to explore the potential impact of Industry 4.0 on the advancement of supply chain management. The fourth industrial revolution brought potential reform with better performances in SCM sustainability. This study analyses how Industry 4.0 technologies are becoming instruments to advance supply chain performance. A theoretical discussion of systems theory is associated with this research to highlight key approaches of Industry 4.0 for sustainable SCM. Qualitative analysis was used in this research by explaining the primary and secondary data to discuss research problems. This research also used empirical methods to highlight the role of the following technologies for huge performance

The integration of blockchain technology in supply chains has the potential to transform the industry by improving transparency, traceability, and security. This study provides insight into important aspects for data management in blockchains, such as data kinds, collection tactics, integration methodologies, and data input and delivery accountability. Furthermore, it emphasizes the financial ramifications of blockchain adoption, emphasizing the difficulties that small supply chain enterprises confront due to limited resources. Cultural resistance and deeply embedded corporate procedures are investigated as important operational barriers that could stymie blockchain technology adoption. This study emphasizes the significance of building robust governance models and protocols that promote collaboration and compliance among supply chain actors to manage these difficulties. Moreover, the importance of tackling interoperability issues across different blockchain systems to provide seamless information flow within complicated supply chain networks is emphasized.

The goal of this research is to create a decision-making process for sustainable supplier selection and order allocation that is known as Fermatean Fuzzy Sets-Based Decision Making (FFS-DMS). The Improved Salp Swarm Optimization (ISSO) approach is used to pick suppliers and allocate the best order quantities. The suggested FFS-ISSA-DMS technique's viability and efficacy are proven through empirical experiments. With an astounding 99.81% accuracy rate, this method outperforms other models that are already in use in this situation.

This chapter examines the convergence of Industry 4.0 and Pharma 4.0 in the context of healthcare supply chains. It investigates the potential applications of these industrial revolutions to enhance the flexibility, benefits, challenges, and opportunities of healthcare supply chains. This chapter highlights the application of state-of-the-art technology to create intelligent, adaptable, and personalized supply chain systems for the healthcare and pharmaceutical sectors. The literature on "Pharma Industry 4.0" is

Preface

Welcome to this edited reference book, *Convergence of Industry 4.0 and Supply Chain Sustainability*, curated by Muhammad Rahies Khan, Naveed R. Khan, and Noor Zaman Jhanjhi. This collection of research endeavors to illuminate the dynamic interplay between Industry 4.0 and the pursuit of sustainability within supply chain management (SCM).

The genesis of Industry 4.0 in 2011, rooted in the pursuit of accelerated automation in manufacturing, has transformed the global business landscape. Initially driven by the goals of enhanced quality, increased production, and the creation of supportive workplaces, this technological integration has now evolved. Technologies such as the Internet of Things (IoT), blockchain, artificial intelligence, additive manufacturing, and robotics have ushered in a new era, reshaping manufacturing and supply chain operations. Consequently, the imperative for companies to undergo digital transformation has intensified, fueled by the ever-growing necessity for sustainable performance.

Sustainability has emerged as a fundamental prerequisite in the formulation of organizational business strategies, product innovations, and process re-engineering. The United Nations Sustainable Development Goals (UNSDG) 2030 have further underscored this imperative, making it a compulsory consideration for companies at their very core.

In the wake of the COVID-19 pandemic, the incorporation of Industry 4.0 to attain sustainable performance in SCM operations has been prominently featured in both literature and real-world applications. Companies, navigating the challenges posed by the pandemic, have turned their focus towards these emerging technologies to fortify their sustainability initiatives.

Recognizing the timeliness of this intersection between Industry 4.0 and supply chain sustainability, this book, through a carefully curated collection of research, explores the multifaceted dimensions of this integration. It delves into the implementation of Industry 4.0, its implications for sustainable supply chains, and the challenges and opportunities linked with the adoption of Industry 4.0 in SCM.

This book is tailored for a diverse readership, including researchers, scholars, academics, and practitioners in supply chain management, sustainability, industrial engineering, manufacturing, and technology. It is also poised to capture the interest of professionals working in industries that leverage Industry 4.0 technologies. Additionally, governments and organizations keen on understanding the implications of these technologies for supply chain sustainability will find valuable insights within these pages.

Our multidisciplinary approach and comprehensive examination of Industry 4.0 technologies in the context of SCM sustainability make this book an invaluable resource for both academic readers seeking profound research insights and industry professionals in search of practical guidance for adopting sustainable practices.

We extend our gratitude to the contributors whose research has enriched this compilation and hope that this book serves as a beacon guiding readers through the intricate landscape of Industry 4.0 and its profound implications for sustainable supply chain management.

ORGANIZATION OF THE BOOK

Chapter 1: Introduction to Industry 4.0: Understanding the Concept, Evolution, and Key Technologies Shaping Industry 4.0

Authored by Rashmi Mahajan, Meenakshi Singh, Vishwanathan Iyer, Ushmita Gupta, Pritesh Somani, and Nitesh Behare from Balaji Institute of International Business (BIIB), India, this chapter serves as a crucial guide for comprehending the far-reaching changes reshaping industries globally. It delves into core concepts, historical context, and pivotal technologies propelling Industry 4.0. The chapter signifies a fundamental shift in our approach to industrial processes, innovation, and global competitiveness, setting the stage for an enlightening journey into the transformative landscape of the Fourth Industrial Revolution.

Chapter 2: Understanding the Concept, Evolution, and Key Technologies Shaping Industry 4.0

Siriyama Herath and Laksitha Herath from Clark Atlanta University and New York University, respectively, provide a thorough exploration of Industry 4.0's revolutionary paradigm. This chapter explicates the concept, history, and basic technologies that define the Fourth Industrial Revolution. It sheds light on how Industry 4.0 is altering business functions and manufacturing processes, emphasizing the use of networked sensors and cutting-edge software. The chapter also discusses the role of intelligent goods collaborating for decentralized decision-making, showcasing the distinctive features and applications of Industry 4.0 technologies.

Chapter 3: Relationship of Digital Technology Adoption on Sustainability Performance

Written by Ilyas Masudin, Abdul Hakimi, and Dian Restuputri from the University of Muhammadiyah Malang, this chapter explores the critical relationship between digital technology adoption and sustainability performance. Focusing on various sectors, the research delves into the potential of digital technologies to enhance economic competitiveness while promoting sustainability. Examining factors like cost, reliability, quality, energy consumption, and carbon emissions, the chapter emphasizes the need for a systematic approach throughout the product lifecycle. It aims to fill gaps in understanding the mechanisms driving the relationship between digital technology adoption and sustainability performance, providing insights valuable for businesses, policymakers, and industry stakeholders.

Chapter 4: Industry 4.0 Approach in Intelligent Manufacturing: Adoptability of Machine Learning and Challenges

Authored by Archana Sharma and Purnima Gupta from Delhi Technical Campus and IMS-Ghaziabad University Courses Campus, India, this chapter investigates the significant influence of machine learning on the manufacturing business within the Industry 4.0 paradigm. The research analyzes the use of smart sensors, tools, and gadgets to enable smart factories, exploring how machine learning techniques contribute to increased production output and analytical insights. The chapter also provides an analysis of Internet of Things-enabled manufacturing and the strengths and weaknesses of tools used in conventional and unconventional machining processes within an Industry 4.0 context.

Chapter 5: Sustainability in the Digital Age: Harnessing Industry 4.0 Technologies for Responsible Supply Chains

Written by Siva Raja Sindiramutty, Noor Zaman Jhanjhi, Chong Eng Tan, Goh Wei Wei, Norhidayah Hamzah, and Rehan Akbar from various institutions, this chapter explores the convergence of Industry 4.0 technologies and sustainable supply chain practices. Beginning with defining the intersection between sustainability and Industry 4.0, the chapter emphasizes the pivotal role of digital technologies in fostering environmentally and socially responsible supply chains. It delves into the impact of key digital technologies, including the Internet of Things, big data analytics, and robotics, on responsible supply chain practices.

Chapter 6: Integrating Industry 4.0 With Supply Chain Sustainability

Authored by Kasturi Laturkar and Kaustubh Laturkar from Validation Associates LLC and Michigan State University, respectively, this chapter explores the integration of Industry 4.0 and supply chain sustainability. It highlights how Industry 4.0, characterized by digital technologies, the Internet of Things, and data analytics, empowers organizations to create smart, connected, and efficient supply chains. The chapter emphasizes the transparency and traceability enhancements brought by Industry 4.0 technologies, particularly with the use of Blockchain, ensuring the authenticity of sustainable materials and promoting fair labor practices. The transparency facilitated by these technologies fosters brand trust and loyalty among consumers increasingly conscious of environmental and ethical implications.

Chapter 7: Impact of Industry 4.0 Technologies for Advancement of Supply Chain Management (SCM) Sustainability Prospects and Challenges

Mukesh Bharti from Jawaharlal Nehru University delves into the potential impact of Industry 4.0 on the advancement of supply chain management sustainability. This chapter explores how Industry 4.0 technologies, including artificial intelligence, robotics, the Internet of Things, machine learning, big data analytics, blockchain, and additive manufacturing, become instrumental in improving supply chain performance. The study employs qualitative analysis to discuss research problems and uses empirical methods to highlight the role of these technologies in achieving substantial performance improvements in sustainable supply chain management.

Chapter 8: Sustainability Metrics and Measurement in Industry 4.0-Enabled SCM

Authored by Siva Raja Sindiramutty, Noor Zaman Jhanjhi, Chong Eng Tan, Navid Ali Khan, Husin Jazri, and Loveleen Gaur, this chapter delves into the critical intersection of sustainability metrics and measurement in Industry 4.0-enabled supply chain management. The chapter explores the transformative role of Industry 4.0 in SCM and elucidates the importance of sustainability metrics in this context. It emphasizes the alignment of Industry 4.0 SCM with the United Nations' Sustainable Development Goals, showcasing how emerging technologies act as catalysts for achieving these global objectives. The comprehensive elucidation covers key concepts, definitions, and the unique contributions of this research endeavor.

Chapter 9: Ethical and Social Implications of Industry 4.0 in SCM

Azeem Khan, Noor Zaman Jhanjhi, Sayan Kumar Ray, Fathi Amsaad, and R Sujatha contribute to this chapter, critically evaluating the integration of Industry 4.0 technologies within Supply Chain Management. The focus is on examining the ethical and social implications, addressing changes in workforce dynamics, ethical considerations in data-driven operations, and the importance of human-centered designs. Utilizing literature reviews, case studies, and expert opinions, the research provides a comprehensive understanding of ethical considerations, encompassing labor fairness, privacy, dilemmas related to artificial intelligence, and the integrity of data.

Chapter 10: Blockchain Technology in Supply Chain Management Opportunities and Challenges

Authored by Mustafa Khan, Fazeelat Masood, Irum Gul, and Muhammad Khan, this chapter investigates the potential transformation of supply chains through the integration of blockchain technology. It provides insights into data management aspects, including data kinds, collection tactics, integration methodologies, and data input and delivery accountability. The chapter emphasizes the financial ramifications of blockchain adoption and addresses operational barriers such as cultural resistance and entrenched corporate procedures. Furthermore, it highlights the significance of building robust governance models and protocols to manage challenges and ensure collaboration and compliance among supply chain actors.

Chapter 11: Supply Chain Management Using Fermatean Fuzzy-Based Decision Making With ISSOA

Authored by Arunadevi Thirumalraj, Anandhi R J, Revathi V, and Stephe S, this chapter presents a decision-making process known as Fermatean Fuzzy Sets-Based Decision Making (FFS-DMS) for sustainable supplier selection and order allocation. The Improved Salp Swarm Optimization (ISSO) approach is employed to select suppliers and allocate optimal order quantities. The viability and efficacy of the suggested FFS-ISSA-DMS technique are proven through empirical experiments, showcasing a remarkable 99.81 percent accuracy rate that surpasses other existing models. This chapter contributes to the field by offering a robust decision-making process for sustainable supplier selection, adding value to the realm of supply chain management.

Chapter 12: Industry 4.0 or Pharma 4.0? Assessing Suitability, Benefits, Challenges, and Opportunities for Healthcare Supply Chains

Muhammad Khan, Mirza Haq, Mustafa Khan, Arsalan Ghouri, and Raheel Farooqui contribute to this chapter, examining the convergence of Industry 4.0 and Pharma 4.0 in health care supply chains. The chapter investigates potential applications of these industrial revolutions in enhancing flexibility, benefits, challenges, and opportunities in health care supply chains. It reviews the literature on "Pharma Industry 4.0" with a focus on sustainable value creation and research within pharmaceutical supply chains. Addressing issues like counterfeit drugs and non-transparent supply chains, the chapter identifies potential solutions through innovative technologies and practices, contributing valuable insights to the healthcare and pharmaceutical sectors.

Chapter 13: Industry 4.0 Future Trends and Research Directions

Authored by Siva Raja Sindiramutty, Noor Zaman Jhanjhi, Chong Eng Tan, Sei Ping Lau, Lalitha Muniandy, Abdalla Gharib, Humaira Ashraf, and Raja Kumar Murugesan, this chapter delves into the future trends and research directions shaping the landscape of Industry 4.0. It highlights the continued proliferation of the Internet of Things (IoT) and its convergence with artificial intelligence (AI). The chapter emphasizes the role of edge computing in redefining data processing and analytics, promising reduced latency and enhanced decision-making capabilities. The exploration encompasses real-time data analysis, predictive maintenance, adaptive manufacturing, and the importance of addressing interoperability issues across different blockchain systems within complex supply chain networks. This chapter offers a forward-looking perspective, guiding readers through the evolving trends and potential research avenues in the dynamic domain of Industry 4.0.

IN CONCLUSION

As we bring this meticulously curated edited reference book, *Convergence of Industry 4.0 and Supply Chain Sustainability*, to its conclusion, it is with great satisfaction that we reflect on the depth and breadth of insights shared by our esteemed contributors. The journey through the chapters has been a compelling exploration of the transformative dynamics at the intersection of Industry 4.0 and supply chain sustainability.

The initial chapters set the stage by unraveling the foundational aspects of Industry 4.0, capturing its conceptual evolution, and delineating the key technologies that shape this industrial revolution. These foundational insights pave the way for an in-depth understanding of the paradigm shift that extends far beyond technological advancements, influencing the very essence of industrial processes, innovation, and global competitiveness.

As we progress through the chapters, a rich tapestry of knowledge unfolds. From the critical examination of the relationship between digital technology adoption and sustainability performance to the nuanced exploration of machine learning's impact on intelligent manufacturing, each chapter contributes a unique facet to the intricate landscape we seek to comprehend.

The exploration extends further into the realm of ethical considerations, societal implications, and the integration of cutting-edge technologies like blockchain, presenting not only opportunities but also challenges that demand our attention. The emphasis on sustainability metrics, measurement, and the alignment with the United Nations' Sustainable Development Goals underscores the commitment of Industry 4.0 to the broader global agenda of responsible and sustainable practices.

The real-world applications, as exemplified in the examination of health care supply chains, demonstrate the profound impact of Industry 4.0 and Pharma 4.0 on addressing critical issues and enhancing the flexibility and sustainability of these vital systems.

The concluding chapter, outlining future trends and research directions, serves as a beacon guiding us into the uncharted territories that Industry 4.0 will continue to explore. With the proliferation of the Internet of Things, the convergence with artificial intelligence, and the rise of edge computing, the landscape of Industry 4.0 promises a future marked by unprecedented innovation and efficiency.

In closing, we extend our sincere appreciation to all the contributors whose dedication and expertise have enriched this compilation. This book is not merely a collection of chapters; it is a collective journey through the evolving landscape of Industry 4.0 and its profound implications for supply chain sustainability.

May this edited reference book serve as an enduring resource, inspiring further research, discourse, and transformative action in the dynamic realms of Industry 4.0 and sustainable supply chain management.

Muhammad Rahies Khan
Bahria University, Karachi, Pakistan

Naveed R. Khan
UCSI University, Malaysia

Noor Zaman Jhanjhi
Taylor's University, Malaysia

Acknowledgment

The creation of this book, *Convergence of Industry 4.0 and Supply Chain Sustainability*, has been a collaborative effort that wouldn't have been possible without the contributions and support of numerous individuals and organizations.

First and foremost, we extend my deepest gratitude to the contributors of this book, whose expertise, insights, and dedication have enriched its content and made it a comprehensive resource for understanding the intersection of Industry 4.0 and supply chain sustainability. Your passion for innovation and sustainability is truly inspiring.

We are indebted to the researchers, scholars, and practitioners who have paved the way in this field, whose groundbreaking work has laid the foundation for our understanding of the complex dynamics between technology and sustainability in modern supply chains.

We are thankful to the publishers and editorial team for their guidance and support throughout the publishing process, and for their commitment to bringing this important topic to a wider audience.

Last but not least, we are grateful to my family, friends, and colleagues for their unwavering encouragement and understanding during the writing of this book. Your support has been invaluable.

Together, we have endeavored to shed light on one of the most pressing challenges of our time, and we are confident that our collective efforts will contribute to a more sustainable and resilient future for generations to come.

Chapter 1
Introduction to Industry 4.0: Understanding the Concept, Evolution, and Key Technologies Shaping Industry 4.0

Rashmi Mahajan
https://orcid.org/0000-0001-9082-6874
Balaji Institute of International Business, Sri Balaji University, Pune, India

Meenakshi Singh
https://orcid.org/0009-0006-9505-8214
Balaji Institute of International Business, Sri Balaji University, Pune, India

Vishwanathan Iyer
https://orcid.org/0009-0007-1469-2369
Balaji Institute of International Business, Sri Balaji University, Pune, India

Ushmita Gupta
Balaji Institute of International Business, Sri Balaji University, Pune, India

Pritesh Pradeep Somani
https://orcid.org/0000-0002-0039-0358
Balaji Institute of International Business, Sri Balaji University, Pune, India

Nitesh Behare
https://orcid.org/0000-0002-9338-8563
Balaji Institute of International Business, Sri Balaji University, Pune, India

ABSTRACT

The fourth industrial revolution (Industry 4.0) heralds a profound transformation that extends beyond mere technological advancement. The chapter serves as an indispensable guide for comprehending the far-reaching changes that are reshaping industries on a global scale. This chapter embarks on an enlightening journey that delves into the core concepts, historical context, and the pivotal technologies propelling Industry 4.0. It signifies a fundamental shift in our approach to industrial processes, innovation, and global competitiveness.

DOI: 10.4018/979-8-3693-1363-3.ch001

1. DEFINING INDUSTRY 4.0: SIGNIFICANCE AND THE EVOLUTION OF INDUSTRY

1.1 Defining Industry 4.0

The term Industry 4.0 was introduced in 2011 at the Hanover fair in Germany, where it was used for denoting the transformation process in the global chains of value creation.

Industry 4.0 refers to the fourth industrial revolution, which represents a significant shift in the way industries operate and manage their processes. It is characterized by the integration of digital technologies, data-driven decision-making, automation, and the convergence of physical and digital systems. Industry 4.0 encompasses several technological advancements, including the Internet of Things (IoT), artificial intelligence (AI), cloud computing, big data analytics, and cyber-physical systems (Eswaran, et al., 2024).

Industry 4.0 includes business processes in industry that envisage organization of global production networks on the basis of new information and communication technologies and Internet technologies, with the help of which interaction of the production objects is conducted (Pachouri, et al., 2024; Zezulka, Kaczmarczyk, & Schroeder, 2018).

1.2 The Basic Characteristics of Industry 4.0

i. transition from manual labor to robotronics, which ensures automation of all production processes;
ii. modernization of transport and logistical systems, due to mass distribution of unmanned vehicles;
iii. increase of complexity and precision of manufactured technical products, manufacturing of new construction materials due to improvement of production technologies;
iv. development of inter-machine communications and self-management of physical systems, conducted with the help of IoT;
v. application of self-teaching programs for provision of constant development of production systems.

1.3 Significance of Industry 4.0

i. **Improved Efficiency and Productivity for Competitive Edge:** Industry 4.0 technologies enable businesses to streamline their operations, reduce downtime, and increase overall efficiency and productivity.
ii. **Data-Driven Decision-Making leading to better performance:** The abundance of data generated by connected devices and systems allows for informed decision-making and predictive maintenance, optimizing resource allocation and performance.
iii. **Customization and Personalization according to customer preference:** With the help of AI and data analytics, companies can tailor products and services to individual customer preferences, enhancing customer satisfaction.
iv. **Supply Chain Optimization:** Real-time data and connectivity enable better supply chain management, reducing lead times and costs.
v. **Cost Reduction:** Automation and predictive maintenance can lead to cost savings in production and maintenance.

vi. **Innovation and New Business Models:** Industry 4.0 fosters innovation by enabling the development of new products and services, as well as the creation of entirely new business models.
vii. **Global Connectivity and extensive reach:** Businesses can connect and collaborate with partners and customers globally, expanding market reach.

1.4 The Evolution of Industry 4.0

Figure 1. The evolution of industry from 1.0 to 4.0 (https://www.seekmomentum.com/blog/manufacturing/the-evolutionof-industry-from-1-to-4)

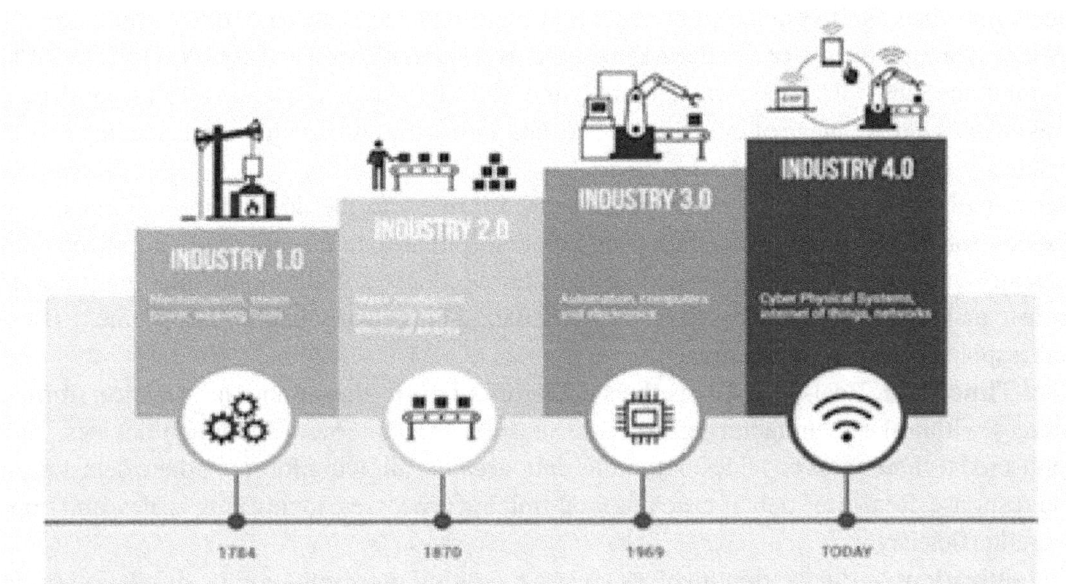

i. **First Industrial Revolution (Late 18th Century- 1760 to 1840):** The first industrial revolution was characterized by the transition from agrarian and craft-based economies to mechanized, factory-based production. Key innovations included the steam engine and mechanized textile production.
ii. **Second Industrial Revolution (Late 19th Century- 1840 to 1960):** The second industrial revolution brought about mass production and electrification. Innovations like the assembly line and the telegraph played a significant role.
iii. **Third Industrial Revolution (Late 20th Century- 1960 to 1990):** The third industrial revolution, often referred to as the Digital Revolution, saw the rise of computers, automation, and digital technologies. It fundamentally transformed industries through the use of computers, the internet, and advancement in communication technologies.
iv. **Fourth Industrial Revolution (21st Century - 1990 to current):** Industry 4.0 builds upon the digital revolution by integrating emerging technologies like 'Internet of Things' (IoT), Artificial Intelligence (AI), use of big data, and automation into industrial processes. It aims to create smarter, more connected, and more efficient industrial systems.

2. KEY CONCEPTS AND PRINCIPLES OF INDUSTRY 4.0

2.1 Fundamental Principles of Industry 4.0

Industry 4.0, often referred to as the fourth industrial revolution, is characterized by the integration of digital technologies into various aspects of industrial processes. Several fundamental principles underpin Industry 4.0 (Annanth, Rao, & Bhaskara, 2021; Karnik, Bora, Bhadr, Kadambi, & Dhatrak), and these include:

i. **Interoperability**: Interoperability is a key principle that emphasizes the ability of different devices, machines, and systems to connect and communicate with each other seamlessly. This is achieved through the use of standardized protocols and interfaces, such as OPC UA (Open Platform Communications - "Unified Architecture") and MQTT (Message Queuing Telemetry Transport). This enables the exchange of information and data across the entire value chain, leading to improved efficiency and productivity.

ii. **Decentralization**: Decentralization in Industry 4.0 refers to the distribution of decision-making and control throughout the manufacturing process. Rather than relying on a centralized command structure, individual components and systems have a degree of autonomy, making it possible for them to make local decisions based on real-time data. This decentralization contributes to flexibility and responsiveness in production.

iii. **Real-Time Data**: Real-time data is the availability of up-to-the-minute information from various sources within the manufacturing process. Sensors, IoT (Internet of Things) devices, and other connected technologies provide continuous data streams, allowing for immediate decision-making and response. Real-time data is crucial for optimizing processes, identifying issues, and improving overall efficiency.

iv. **Virtualization**: Virtualization involves creating a digital representation or simulation of physical processes, systems, and products. This can include virtual models of production lines, products, or entire factories. Virtualization allows for testing and optimizing processes in a risk-free environment before implementing changes in the physical world. It also facilitates the design and prototyping of new products and systems.

v. **Big Data and Analytics**: Industry 4.0 relies on the collection and analysis of large volumes of data generated by connected devices and systems. Big data analytics is used to derive meaningful insights, patterns, and trends from this data, enabling better decision-making, predictive maintenance, and the identification of areas for improvement.

Figure 2. Fundamental principles of Industry 4.0

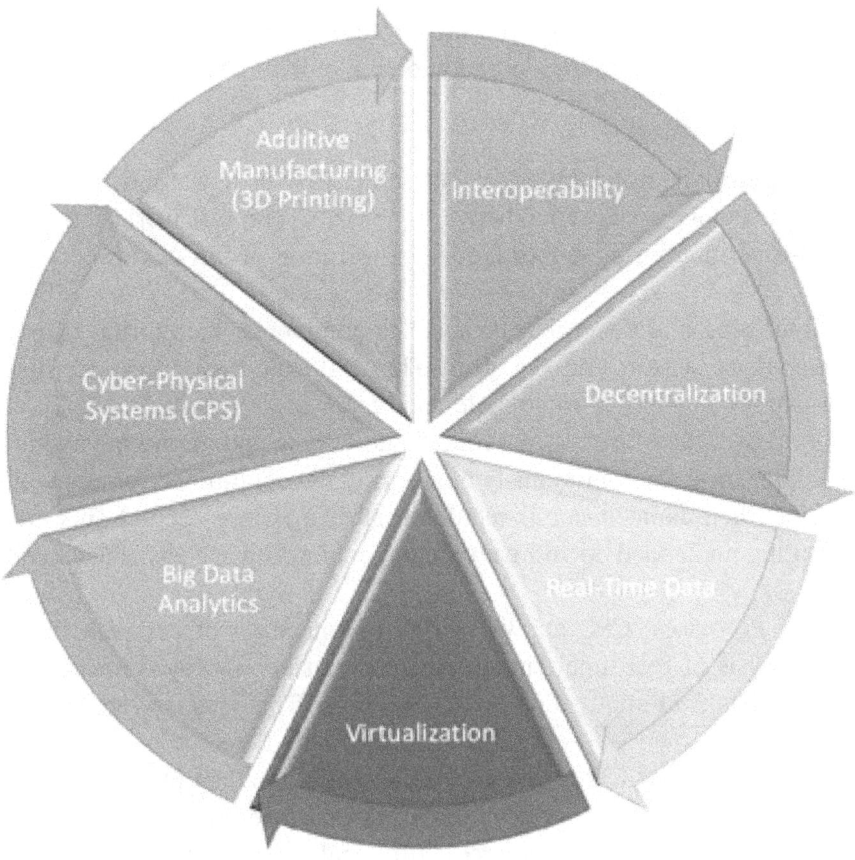

vi. **Cyber-Physical Systems (CPS)**: Cyber-physical systems are integrations of computation, networking, and physical processes. These systems play a central role in Industry 4.0 by connecting the digital and physical worlds. CPS enable real-time monitoring and control of physical processes through a network of interconnected devices and systems.

vii. **Additive Manufacturing (3D Printing)**: Additive manufacturing is a key technology in Industry 4.0, allowing for the production of complex and customized components. This technology enables more flexible and efficient manufacturing processes compared to traditional methods.

These principles collectively contribute to the transformation of traditional industries into smart, connected, and highly efficient systems under Industry 4.0. The integration of digital technologies and the emphasis on connectivity and data-driven decision-making are central to achieving the goals of increased productivity, flexibility, and innovation in manufacturing processes.

2.2 The Transformative Role of Cyber-Physical Systems (CPS)

Cyber-Physical Systems (CPS) play a transformative role in various industries, driving innovation, efficiency, and connectivity by integrating computational elements with physical processes. Some key aspects of the transformative role of CPS are:

i. Integration of Digital and Physical Worlds: CPS integrates the digital and physical components of a system, creating a seamless connection between the virtual and real-world entities. This integration allows for real-time monitoring, control, and optimization of physical processes through digital interfaces.
ii. Real-Time Monitoring and Control: CPS enables continuous monitoring of physical processes through a network of sensors and actuators. This real-time data allows for immediate analysis and decision-making, leading to more agile and responsive systems. Industries can benefit from enhanced control over their operations, reducing downtime and improving overall efficiency.
iii. Predictive Maintenance: By continuously monitoring the condition of equipment and machinery, CPS can predict when maintenance is required before a failure occurs. This proactive approach helps in preventing unplanned downtime, reducing maintenance costs, and extending the lifespan of assets.
iv. Optimization of Processes: CPS allows for the optimization of complex industrial processes. Through the analysis of real-time data, algorithms can be employed to identify inefficiencies, streamline operations, and improve resource utilization. This leads to increased productivity and cost-effectiveness.
v. Flexibility and Adaptability: CPS provides the flexibility to adapt to changing conditions and requirements. With the ability to reconfigure and adjust processes in real-time, industries can respond quickly to market demands, changes in production goals, or unforeseen disruptions.
vi. Enhanced Safety and Security: The integration of digital control in physical processes allows for the implementation of advanced safety measures. CPS can detect anomalies, shut down operations in case of emergencies, and provide a more secure and controlled working environment. However, it's crucial to address cybersecurity concerns to ensure the integrity and safety of these systems.
vii. Innovation and Product Development: CPS facilitates innovation by enabling the rapid prototyping and testing of new products and processes in a virtual environment. This reduces the time and cost associated with traditional trial-and-error approaches, fostering a culture of continuous improvement and innovation.
viii. Supply Chain Optimization: CPS extends its influence beyond the factory floor to optimize the entire supply chain. From inventory management to logistics and distribution, the integration of CPS technologies enhances visibility, coordination, and efficiency across the entire value chain.
ix. Energy Efficiency: CPS can contribute to improved energy efficiency by monitoring and optimizing the consumption of energy in industrial processes. This not only reduces operational costs but also aligns with sustainability goals and environmental considerations.
x. Advanced Robotics and Automation: CPS often integrates with advanced robotics and automation systems, leading to more sophisticated and adaptive manufacturing processes. Robots can work collaboratively with humans, adapting their actions based on real-time data, which enhances overall efficiency and flexibility.

The transformative role of Cyber-Physical Systems lies in their ability to create intelligent, connected, and adaptive systems that bridge the gap between the physical and digital realms. This integration opens up new possibilities for innovation, efficiency gains, and improved decision-making across a wide range of industries.

3. ENABLING TECHNOLOGIES

Several key technologies are propelling Industry 4.0 forward, enabling the transformation of traditional industries into smart, connected, and highly automated systems. These technologies work in synergy to enhance efficiency, productivity, and innovation in manufacturing and related sectors. Here are some of the key technologies driving Industry 4.0 (Pachouri, et al., 2024; Bauer, Hämmerle, Schlund, & Vocke, 2015):

i. Internet of Things (IoT):
   - **Sensor Networks:** Integration of sensors and actuators in machines, devices, and products to collect real- time data.
   - **Connectivity:** Enabling seamless communication and data exchange between physical devices over the internet.

ii. Big Data and Analytics:
   - **Data Collection:** Gathering and processing large volumes of data from various sources, including sensors, machines, and systems.
   - **Predictive Analytics:** Utilizing advanced analytics to extract insights, predict trends, and optimize decision-making processes.

iii. Artificial Intelligence (AI) and Machine Learning (ML):
   - **Predictive Maintenance:** Using AI algorithms to predict equipment failures and schedule maintenance proactively.
   - **Optimization:** Applying machine learning for process optimization, quality control, and resource allocation.

iv. Cloud Computing:
   - **Data Storage and Processing:** Storing and processing vast amounts of data in the cloud, enabling accessibility and scalability.
   - **Collaboration:** Facilitating collaboration and information sharing across geographically distributed teams.

v. Augmented Reality (AR) and Virtual Reality (VR):
   - **Training and Simulation:** Using AR and VR for training purposes, allowing workers to simulate complex tasks in a virtual environment.
   - **Remote Assistance:** Enabling experts to provide real-time guidance to on-site personnel using AR applications.

vi. Robotics and Automation:
   - **Collaborative Robots (Cobots):** Robots working alongside human workers to perform tasks that require precision, speed, and efficiency.
   - **Automated Manufacturing Processes:** Integration of automated systems for tasks such as assembly, welding, and material handling.

vii. Additive Manufacturing (3D Printing):
   - **Prototyping and Customization:** Rapid prototyping and on-demand manufacturing of customized products.
   - **Reduced Waste:** Additive manufacturing techniques often result in less material waste compared to traditional manufacturing methods.

viii. Cyber-Physical Systems (CPS):
   - **Integration of Digital and Physical Systems:** CPS involves the integration of computational algorithms and physical processes.
   - **Real-Time Monitoring:** Real-time monitoring and control of physical processes through interconnected digital systems.

ix. Edge Computing:
   - **Real-Time Processing:** Processing data closer to the source (at the edge) to reduce latency and improve real-time decision-making.
   - **Bandwidth Efficiency:** Minimizing the need to transmit large amounts of data to centralized cloud servers.

x. Block-chain Technology:
   - **Secure Transactions:** Ensuring secure and transparent transactions in supply chain management and digital transactions.
   - **Traceability:** Enhancing traceability in supply chains, reducing the risk of counterfeiting and ensuring product authenticity.

xi. 5G Technology:
   - **High-Speed Connectivity:** Providing high-speed and low-latency connectivity, crucial for the real-time communication required in Industry 4.0.
   - **Wireless Connectivity:** Enabling wireless communication for a wide range of devices, sensors, and machines.

xii. Digital Twins:
   - **Virtual Replicas:** Creating virtual replicas of physical assets, processes, or systems for simulation and analysis.
   - **Predictive Maintenance:** Using digital twins to predict and optimize the performance of physical assets.

xiii. Quantum Computing:
   - **Advanced Computing Power:** Offering unprecedented computing power for solving complex problems and simulations.
   - **Optimization:** Quantum computing has the potential to significantly optimize complex calculations in various industries.

Figure 3. Enabling technologies for Industry 4.0

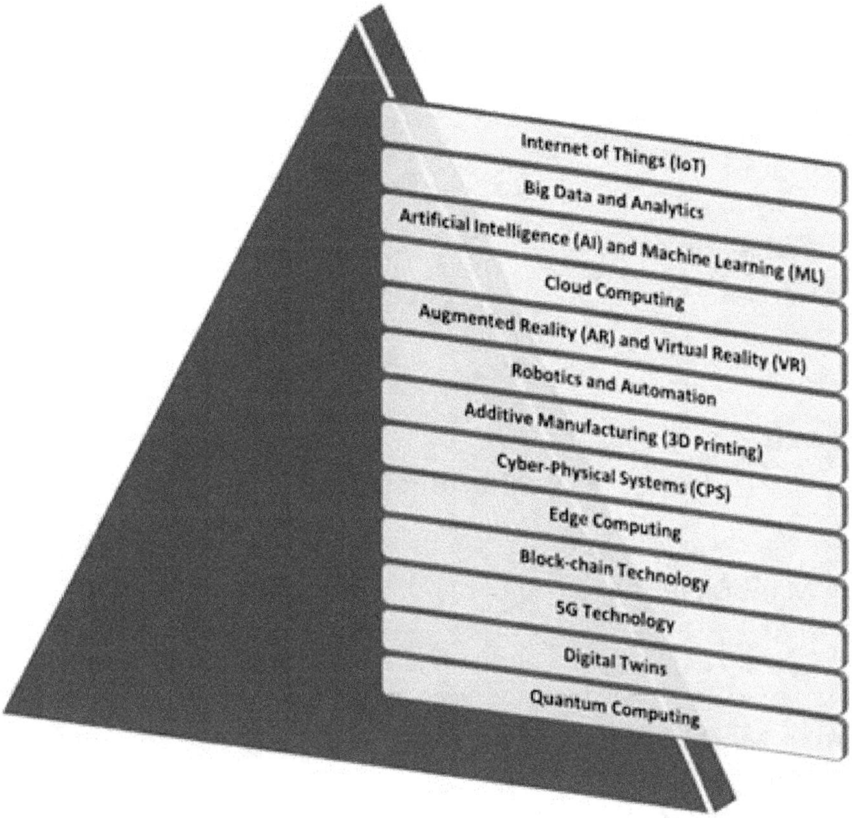

These technologies collectively empower Industry 4.0 by fostering connectivity, data-driven decision-making, automation, and intelligent systems. The ongoing evolution and integration of these technologies contribute to the continuous advancement of Industry 4.0 and its impact on various sectors of the economy.

4. IMPACT OF INDUSTRY 4.0 ON MANUFACTURING, SUPPLY CHAIN, AND LOGISTICS

Industry 4.0 represents the fourth industrial revolution, characterized by the integration of digital technologies, data exchange, and automation in manufacturing. This transformation has profound effects on manufacturing, supply chain, and logistics, leading to increased efficiency, flexibility, and innovation. (Tunca & Cansu, 2019) (Baltacioglu, et al., 2007)Here are some key impacts:

4.1 Manufacturing

Figure 4. Impact of Industry 4.0 on manufacturing

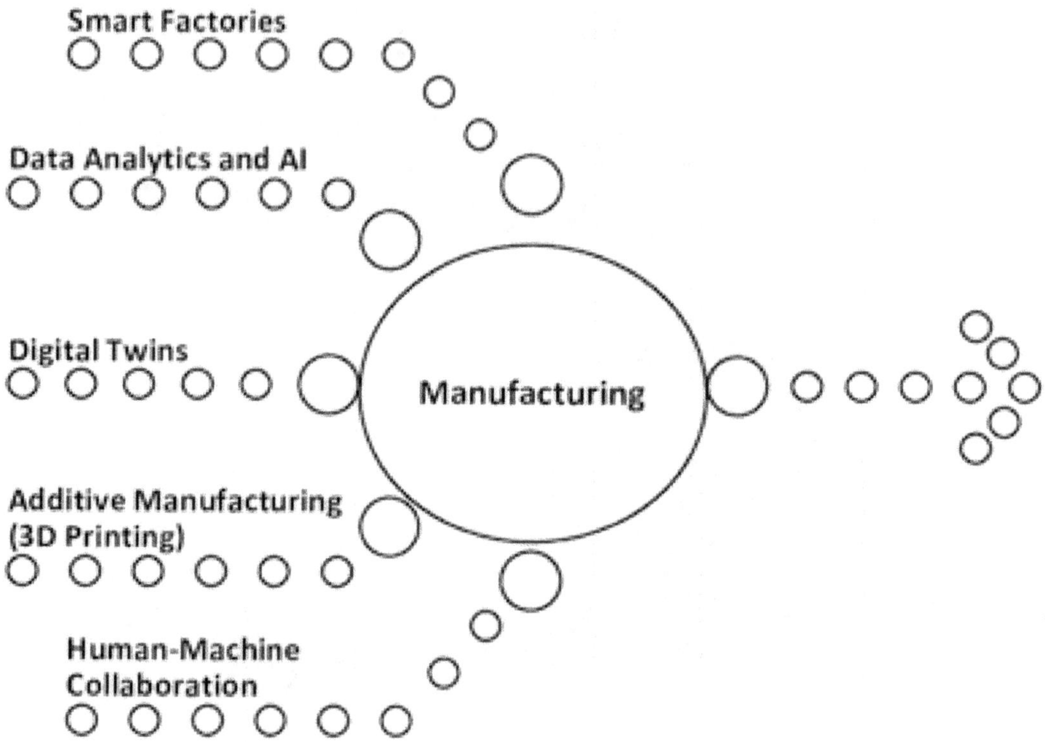

i. Smart Factories:
   - Implementation of IoT (Internet of Things) devices and sensors in manufacturing processes to collect real-time data.
   - Interconnected machines and systems that communicate and collaborate with each other.
ii. Data Analytics and AI:
   - Advanced analytics and artificial intelligence applications for predictive maintenance, quality control, and process optimization.
   - Data-driven decision-making to enhance efficiency and reduce downtime.
iii. Digital Twins:
   - Creation of digital replicas of physical systems to simulate and monitor performance.
   - Enables better understanding, analysis, and optimization of manufacturing processes.
iv. Additive Manufacturing (3D Printing):
   - Adoption of 3D printing for rapid prototyping and customized, on-demand production.
   - Reduces waste and allows for more complex designs.
v. Human-Machine Collaboration:
   - Increased integration of human workers with intelligent machines.

- Collaborative robots (cobots) working alongside humans for tasks requiring precision and efficiency.

4.2 Supply Chain

Figure 5. Impact of Industry 4.0 on supply chain

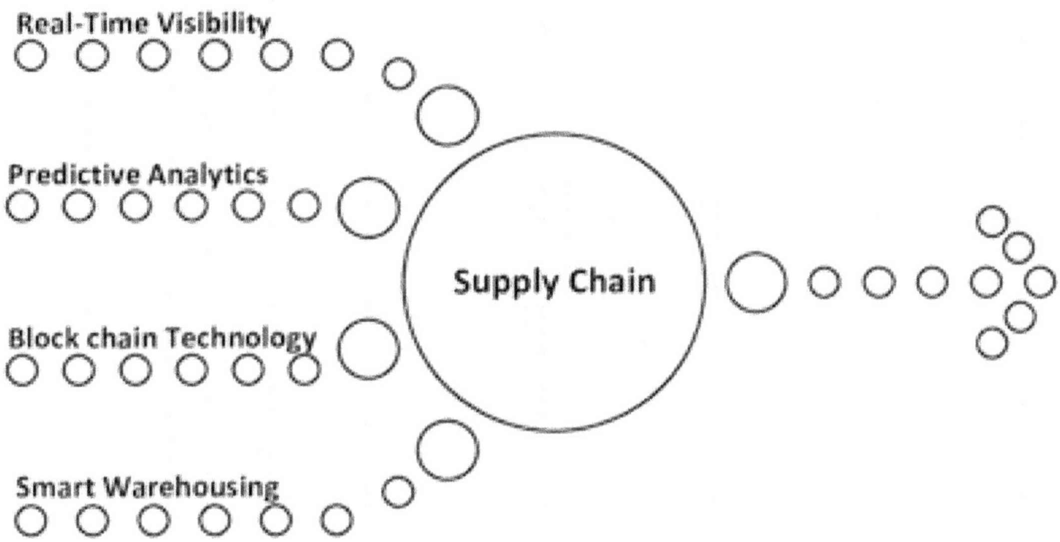

i. Real-Time Visibility:
    - Integration of IoT sensors and RFID technology for real-time tracking of goods in transit.
    - Enhanced visibility across the entire supply chain, leading to better inventory management.
ii. Predictive Analytics:
    - Use of data analytics and machine learning to forecast demand, optimize inventory levels, and improve supply chain planning.
    - Reduction in stock outs and overstock situations.
iii. Block chain Technology:
    - Implementation of block chain for transparent and secure transactions in the supply chain.
    - Enhanced traceability, reducing the risk of counterfeiting and improving accountability.
iv. Smart Warehousing:
    - Automation and robotics in warehouses for efficient order picking and packing.
    - Autonomous vehicles and drones for inventory management.

4.3 Logistics

Figure 6. Impact of Industry 4.0 on logistics

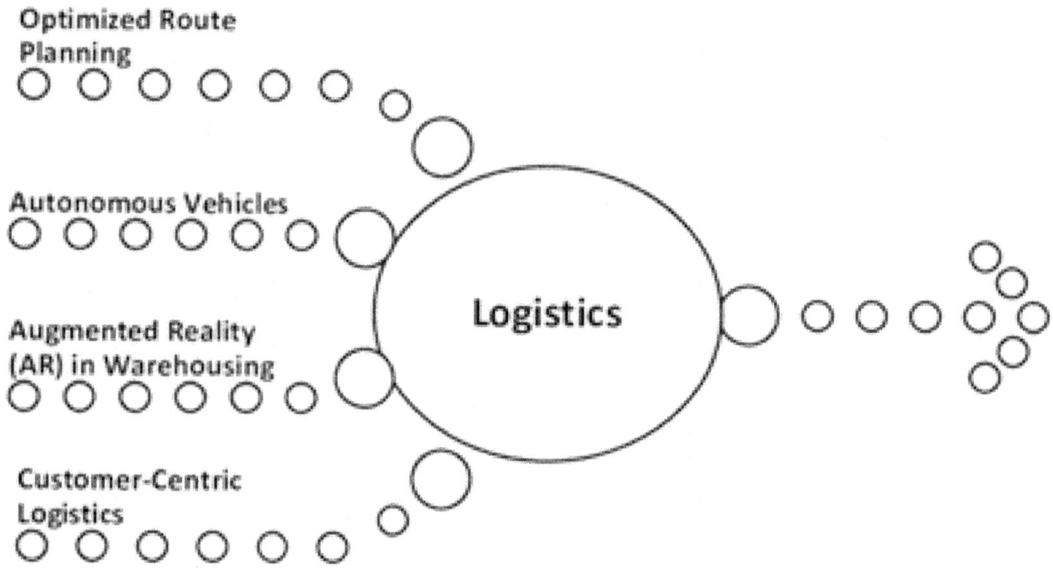

i. Optimized Route Planning:
   - Use of advanced algorithms and data analytics for efficient route planning and optimization.
   - Reduces transportation costs and environmental impact.
ii. Autonomous Vehicles:
   - Adoption of autonomous trucks and drones for last-mile delivery.
   - Improved safety, efficiency, and cost-effectiveness in transportation.
iii. Augmented Reality (AR) in Warehousing:
   - AR applications for order picking, navigation, and inventory management in warehouses.
   - Increases accuracy and speed in fulfilment processes.
iv. Customer-Centric Logistics:
   - Personalized logistics solutions based on customer preferences and demands.
   - Shorter lead times and improved customer satisfaction.

Industry 4.0 is revolutionizing manufacturing, supply chain, and logistics by leveraging digital technologies to create more efficient, adaptive, and interconnected systems. This transformation enhances productivity, reduces costs, and improves overall competitiveness in the global marketplace. However, it also brings challenges, such as the need for a skilled workforce, cybersecurity concerns, and the integration of new technologies into existing systems.

5. THE HUMAN ELEMENT

While Industry 4.0 brings about significant advancements in automation, connectivity, and data analytics, it also introduces profound changes in the role of the human element (Baroroh & Chu, 2022; Liboni, et al., 2019) within the industrial landscape. Here are some key aspects of how Industry 4.0 impacts the human element:

i. Skilled Workforce:
   - **Upskilling and Reskilling:** The adoption of Industry 4.0 technologies requires a highly skilled workforce. Employees need to acquire new skills in data analytics, programming, and digital literacy.
   - **Lifelong Learning:** The dynamic nature of technology means that continuous learning is essential. Employees may need to engage in lifelong learning to stay relevant in their roles.

ii. Human-Machine Collaboration:
   - **Cobots (Collaborative Robots):** Industry 4.0 promotes collaboration between humans and machines. Cobots work alongside human workers, taking on repetitive or dangerous tasks, while humans focus on complex problem-solving and decision-making (Baroroh, Chu, & Wang, 2021, 2022).
   - **Enhanced Productivity:** Human-machine collaboration can lead to increased productivity, efficiency, and improved product quality (Mason, Baines, Kay, & Ladbrook, 2005).

iii. Empowerment Through Data:
   - **Data-Driven Decision-Making:** Employees are empowered by the availability of real-time data. This enables better decision-making and problem-solving, as workers can leverage insights provided by analytics tools (Emmanouilidis, et al., 2019).
   - **Operational Efficiency:** Workers can contribute to process optimization by interpreting and acting upon data insights to improve efficiency.

iv. Innovation and Creativity:
   - **Focus on Creativity:** With routine tasks automated, employees have more time to focus on creative and strategic aspects of their work (Emmanouilidis, et al., 2019).
   - **Innovation Culture:** Industry 4.0 encourages a culture of innovation, where employees are encouraged to contribute ideas and solutions to improve processes and products.

v. New Job Roles:
   - **Emergence of New Roles:** Industry 4.0 creates new job opportunities in areas such as data science, cybersecurity, and AI programming.
   - **Maintenance and Monitoring:** Skilled technicians are needed for the maintenance and monitoring of advanced technologies, ensuring their smooth operation.

vi. Ethical Considerations:
   - **Human-Centric Approach:** As automation increases, there's a growing emphasis on maintaining a human-centric approach. Ethical considerations, such as the impact on employment and societal well-being, become crucial.
   - **Addressing Job Displacement:** Strategies need to be in place to address concerns related to potential job displacement, ensuring a just transition for affected workers.

vii. Cybersecurity Awareness:

- **Cybersecurity Skills:** With increased connectivity, there's a heightened need for cybersecurity skills. Employees must be aware of potential cyber threats and play a role in maintaining the security of interconnected systems.
- **Data Privacy:** Ensuring the privacy of sensitive data is a shared responsibility, requiring employees to adhere to data protection protocols.

viii. Workplace Culture:

- **Adaptability:** A culture of adaptability becomes essential. Employees need to be open to change, continuous learning, and the adoption of new technologies.
- **Collaboration and Communication:** Effective collaboration and communication skills become critical in a workplace where humans and machines interact seamlessly.

In essence, Industry 4.0 transforms the nature of work, requiring a collaborative and adaptable workforce that embraces technology and innovation. The human element remains integral, playing a central role in driving creativity, making ethical decisions, and ensuring the responsible and effective implementation of Industry 4.0 technologies.

6. CHALLENGES AND CONCERNS

While Industry 4.0 offers numerous benefits, its adoption is not without challenges and concerns. Addressing these issues is crucial to ensuring a smooth and responsible transition to the new industrial era. Here are some key challenges and concerns associated with Industry 4.0 (Marta, Arranz, Arroyabe, Fernandez de, & Fernandez de, 2024; Reis, Bastos, Camargo, & Salles, 2024; Arroyabe, Arranz, Arroyabe, Carlos, & Arroyabe, 2024; Masood & Sonntag, 2020):

i. Workforce Displacement:

- **Automation Impact:** The increased use of robotics and automation may lead to job displacement, particularly for workers engaged in routine and repetitive tasks.
- **Reskilling Challenges:** Upskilling the existing workforce to adapt to new technologies can be challenging and may face resistance.

ii. Cybersecurity Risks:

- **Increased Vulnerability:** The higher level of connectivity and data sharing in Industry 4.0 increases the vulnerability to cyberattacks.
- **Data Privacy Concerns:** The collection and use of large amounts of data raise concerns about privacy and the secure handling of sensitive information.

iii. Interoperability Issues:

- **Compatibility Challenges:** Integration of diverse technologies from different manufacturers may lead to interoperability issues.
- **Standardization Needs:** Lack of standardized protocols can hinder seamless communication between various devices and systems.

iv. Cost of Implementation:

- **Initial Investment:** The upfront costs associated with implementing Industry 4.0 technologies, such as IoT devices and smart machinery, can be substantial.

- **ROI Uncertainty:** Organizations may face uncertainty regarding the return on investment (ROI) and the time it takes to realize tangible benefits.

v. Regulatory Compliance:
- **Lack of Clear Regulations:** The rapid pace of technological advancements may outpace the development of regulations, creating uncertainties about compliance requirements.
- **Data Governance:** Ensuring compliance with data protection laws and regulations becomes more challenging with the increased volume and variety of data.

vi. Skills Gap:
- **Shortage of Skilled Talent:** There may be a shortage of workers with the necessary skills in data science, artificial intelligence, and other emerging fields.
- **Educational System Adaptation:** Educational systems may struggle to adapt quickly enough to provide the relevant skills needed for the Industry 4.0 workforce.

vii. Ethical Considerations:
- **Job Quality:** Concerns about the quality of jobs created in the wake of automation and the impact on workers' well-being.
- **Equitable Access:** Ensuring equitable access to the benefits of Industry 4.0 technologies and preventing further societal divides.

viii. Data Overload:
- **Information Overwhelm:** The abundance of data generated by interconnected devices can lead to information overload.
- **Effective Utilization:** Extracting meaningful insights from vast datasets requires advanced analytics capabilities and may pose a challenge.

ix. Environmental Impact:
- **Resource Consumption:** The manufacturing and operation of advanced technologies may lead to increased energy consumption and resource usage.
- **E-Waste Management:** The disposal of outdated or malfunctioning technology components contributes to electronic waste.

x. Dependency on Technology:
- **Single Points of Failure:** Overreliance on interconnected systems can create vulnerabilities and single points of failure.
- **Loss of Manual Skills:** A shift towards automation may lead to a decline in traditional manual skills.

Addressing these challenges requires a collaborative effort from businesses, governments, and educational institutions. It involves developing comprehensive strategies for workforce development, implementing robust cybersecurity measures, fostering regulatory frameworks, and promoting ethical considerations in the deployment of Industry 4.0 technologies. An inclusive and responsible approach is crucial to maximizing the benefits of Industry 4.0 while minimizing its negative impacts.

7. INDUSTRY 4.0 IN PRACTICE, GLOBAL ADOPTION, AND INITIATIVES

Industry 4.0 has been gaining momentum globally, with various countries and industries actively adopting initiatives to integrate advanced technologies into manufacturing and related sectors. Here is an overview of Industry 4.0 in practice, global adoption (Nadeem, Wong, Za, & Venditti, 2024), and some notable initiatives:

i. Germany - Industrie 4.0:
   - **Pioneer of Industry 4.0:** Coined as "Industrie 4.0," Germany has been a pioneer in promoting the fourth industrial revolution.
   - **Initiatives and Standards:** The German government and industry associations have collaborated to establish initiatives and standards promoting the integration of IoT, AI, and automation.

ii. China - Made in China 2025:
   - **Strategic Plan:** China launched the "Made in China 2025" initiative, aiming to become a global leader in high-tech industries, including robotics, AI, and green energy.
   - **Investments:** Significant investments have been made in research and development, fostering innovation in smart manufacturing.

iii. United States - Advanced Manufacturing Partnership (AMP):
   - **Public-Private Collaboration:** The Advanced Manufacturing Partnership is a collaborative initiative between the U.S. government, academia, and industry to accelerate the development of advanced manufacturing technologies.
   - **Smart Manufacturing Institutes:** The U.S. government has established institutes focused on smart manufacturing, such as the Clean Energy Smart Manufacturing Innovation Institute.

iv. Japan - Society 5.0:
   - **Society 5.0 Vision:** Japan's "Society 5.0" vision integrates Industry 4.0 technologies to create a human-centric society.
   - **Robotics and Automation:** Japan is known for its advancements in robotics and automation, with a focus on enhancing industrial processes.

v. South Korea - Manufacturing Innovation 3.0:
   - **Smart Factory Projects:** South Korea has been implementing smart factory projects to enhance manufacturing competitiveness.
   - **Government Support:** The government provides support for the adoption of digital technologies, including AI, IoT, and big data in manufacturing.

vi. European Union - Horizon 2020:
   - **Research and Innovation Program:** The European Union's Horizon 2020 program supports research and innovation in various sectors, including advanced manufacturing and Industry 4.0.
   - **Cross-National Collaboration:** EU member states collaborate on initiatives to drive the adoption of digital technologies in manufacturing.

vii. Singapore - Smart Industry Readiness Index (SIRI):
   - **Framework for Adoption:** Singapore has introduced the Smart Industry Readiness Index, providing a framework to assess and guide companies in the adoption of Industry 4.0 technologies.
   - **Government Support:** The Singaporean government actively supports research, development, and adoption of advanced manufacturing technologies.

viii. India - Make in India and Digital India:

- **Make in India:** The Make in India initiative aims to boost manufacturing, and Industry 4.0 technologies play a significant role in this vision.
- **Digital India:** The Digital India program emphasizes the integration of digital technologies across sectors, including manufacturing.

ix. Global Collaborations - World Economic Forum (WEF):

- **Global Platforms:** The World Economic Forum provides a platform for global leaders to discuss and collaborate on the adoption of Industry 4.0 technologies.
- **International Standards:** Efforts are underway to establish international standards for interoperability and data exchange in smart manufacturing.

x. Corporate Initiatives:

- **Adoption by Multinational Companies:** Many multinational corporations across various industries are actively implementing Industry 4.0 strategies to improve efficiency, reduce costs, and enhance innovation.
- **Investments in Research and Development:** Companies invest in R&D to develop and deploy cutting-edge technologies in their manufacturing processes.

xi. Emerging Technologies:

- **Focus on Emerging Trends:** Industry 4.0 initiatives are increasingly incorporating emerging technologies such as edge computing, 5G, and quantum computing for more robust and efficient operations.
- **Cross-Industry Collaboration:** Collaboration between different industries is becoming more common to leverage combined expertise in implementing advanced technologies.

The global adoption of Industry 4.0 is a dynamic and ongoing process, with countries and industries adapting their strategies to stay at the forefront of technological advancements. Governments, businesses, and research institutions continue to collaborate to overcome challenges and harness the full potential of Industry 4.0 technologies.

REFERENCES

Annanth, K., Rao, A., & Bhaskara, L. (2021, July 23). Intelligent manufacturing in the context of industry 4.0: A case study of siemens industry. *Journal of Physics: Conference Series*, *1969*(1), 012019. Advance online publication. doi:10.1088/1742-6596/1969/1/012019

Arroyabe, M. F., Arranz, C. F., Arroyabe, F., Carlos, J., & Arroyabe, F. (2024). The effect of IT security issues on the implementation of industry 4.0 in SMEs: Barriers and challenges. *Technological Forecasting and Social Change*, *199*, 123051. Advance online publication. doi:10.1016/j.techfore.2023.123051

Baltacioglu, T., Erhan, A., Kaplan, D., Yurt, M., Oznur, K., & Cem, Y. (2007, March). A new framework for service supply chains. *Service Industries Journal*, *27*(2), 105–124. doi:10.1080/02642060601122629

Baroroh, D. K., & Chu, C.-H. (2022, October). Human-centric production system simulation in mixed reality: An exemplary case of logistic facility design. *Journal of Manufacturing Systems*, *65*, 146–157. doi:10.1016/j.jmsy.2022.09.005

Baroroh, D. K., Chu, C.-H., & Wang, L. (2021). Systematic literature review on augmented reality in smart manufacturing: Collaboration between human and computational intelligence. *Journal of Manufacturing Systems*, *61*, 696–711. doi:10.1016/j.jmsy.2020.10.017

Bauer, W., Hämmerle, M., Schlund, S., & Vocke, C. (2015). Transforming to a Hyper-connected Society and Economy – Towards an "Industry 4.0". *Procedia Manufacturing*, *3*, 417–424. doi:10.1016/j.promfg.2015.07.200

Emmanouilidis, C., Pistofidis, P., Bertoncelj, L., Katsouros, V., Fournaris, A., Koulamas, C., & Ruiz-Carcel, C. (2019). Enabling the human in the loop: Linked data and knowledge in industrial cyber-physical systems. *Annual Reviews in Control*, *47*, 249–265. doi:10.1016/j.arcontrol.2019.03.004

Eswaran, K., Kumar, A., & Tamilarasan, K. (2024). Optimal layout planning for human robot collaborative assembly systems and visualization through immersive technologies. *Expert Systems with Applications*, *241*, 122465. Advance online publication. doi:10.1016/j.eswa.2023.122465

Karnik, N., Bora, U., Bhadr, K., Kadambi, P., & Dhatrak, P. (2022, May). A comprehensive study on current and future trends towards the characteristics and enablers of industry 4.0. *Journal of Industrial Information Integration*, *27*, 2022. doi:10.1016/j.jii.2021.100294

Liboni, B., Oranges, L., Cezarino, L., Chiappetta, J., Charbel, J., Garcia, O., ... Nelson, S. (2019). Smart industry and the pathways to HRM 4.0: Implications for SCM. *Supply Chain Management*, *24*(1), 124–146. doi:10.1108/SCM-03-2018-0150

Marta, A., Arranz, C., & Arroyabe, I. (2024). The effect of IT security issues on the implementation of industry 4.0 in SMEs: Barriers and challenges. *Technological Forecasting and Social Change*, *199*, 123051. Advance online publication. doi:10.1016/j.techfore.2023.123051

Mason, S., Baines, T., Kay, J. M., & Ladbrook, J. (2005). Improving the design process for factories: Modeling human performance variation. *Journal of Manufacturing Systems*, *24*(1), 47–54. doi:10.1016/S0278-6125(05)80006-8

Masood, T., & Sonntag, P. (2020). Industry 4.0: Adoption challenges and benefits for SMEs. *Computers in Industry*, *121*, 103261. Advance online publication. doi:10.1016/j.compind.2020.103261

Nadeem, K., Wong, S. I., Za, S., & Venditti, M. (2024). Digital transformation and industry 4.0 employees: Empirical evidence from top digital nations. *Technology in Society*, *76*, 102434. Advance online publication. doi:10.1016/j.techsoc.2023.102434

Pachouri, V., Singh, R., Gehlot, A., Pandey, S., Shaik, V. A., & Abbas, M. (2024, March). Empowering sustainability in the built environment: A technological Lens on industry 4.0 Enablers. *Technology in Society*, *76*, 102427. Advance online publication. doi:10.1016/j.techsoc.2023.102427

Reis, F., Bastos, Camargo, J., & Salles, A. (2024). Industry 4.0: An investigation of benefits and barriers with managers of Brazilian manufacturers adopters. *Journal of Engineering and Technology Management*, *71*. doi:10.1016/j.jengtecman.2023.101786

Tunca, T., & Cansu, Y. (2019). The development of servitization concept in the era of industry 4.0 through SCM perspective. Handbook of Research on Strategic Fit and Design in Business Ecosystems, 593 - 615. doi:10.4018/978-1-7998-1125-1.ch026

Zezulka, A., Kaczmarczyk, M., & Schroeder, B. (2018). Implementing Industry 4.0 in Discrete Manufacturing. *IFAC-PapersOnLine*, *51*(6), 473–478. doi:10.1016/j.ifacol.2018.07.106

Chapter 2
Understanding the Concept, Evolution, and Key Technologies Shaping Industry 4.0

Siriyama Kanthi Herath
Clark Atlanta University, USA

Laksitha Maheshi Herath
New York University, USA

ABSTRACT

One of the most revolutionary paradigms of modern industrial history, Industry 4.0, will be thoroughly explained in this chapter. The fourth industrial revolution's concept, history, and basic technologies are all addressed in this chapter, which also highlights how it will affect other industries such as manufacturing and automated procedures. Industry 4.0, or the "Fourth Industrial Revolution," refers to a revolutionary period that is changing the way companies function and manufacture things. Due to their creative use of networked sensors and cutting-edge software, the intricate machinery and equipment of Industry 4.0, driven by the convergence of digital technology, data-driven processes, and intelligent automation, stand out. Industry 4.0, which encourages a complete, networked strategy in which intelligent goods collaborate for decentralized decision-making, forces businesses to review their strategies. Industry 4.0 creates intelligent, adaptable industrial ecosystems that can be optimized in real time by embracing big data analytics and the internet of things.

1. INTRODUCTION TO INDUSTRY 4.0

The "Fourth Industrial Revolution," also referred to as "Industry 4.0," represents an important shift in how firms perform their operations and produce goods and services. Due to the convergence of digital technology, data-driven processes, and intelligent automation, the industrial environment has undergone

DOI: 10.4018/979-8-3693-1363-3.ch002

tremendous change. The newer, more powerful tools and machines with cutting-edge software and useful networked sensors that can be used to plan, anticipate, adapt, and regulate the social outcome and economic models are what Wang et al. (2016) refer to as the fourth industrial revolution. The fourth industrial revolution in science and technology has altered organizational structures and corporate models, leading to the development of new ones (Vărzaru, 2022). Environmental, Social, and Governance (ESG) reports also contain information on how a firm performs in sustainability and on weaknesses that may negatively affect the company. ESG analysis is likewise multifaceted, wherein the performance of a company is evaluated by existing environmental, social, and governance issues.

1.1 Definition of Industry 4.0

The first three industrial revolutions—automatism, electrification, and mechanization—formed the foundation for this fourth one. This system employs advanced digital technologies from the 3rd Industrial Revolution including biological engineering, physical materials, 3D printing and Artificial Intelligence (Rashid, 2018). Industry 4.0 provides a more through and networked approach where intelligent products can work with similar products, systems and machines to make a smart decentralized decision which also adjust and allow companies the chance to have a reviewed strategic (Chen et al., 2021; Del Sarto et al., 2021). Schwab (2016) claims that because of the fourth industrial revolution's unmatched technological integration, its significance has eclipsed that of earlier periods. Industry 4.0 refers to the incorporation of modern technologies such as big data analytics, artificial intelligence (AI), cyber-physical systems, the Internet of Things (IoT), and others into industrial processes and systems (Masood and Egger (2019). It ushers in a new era in which a record number of computers, systems, and people collaborate to provide data, insights, and efficiency. Industry 4.0 strives to create industrial ecosystems that are highly adaptive, intelligent, and interconnected and capable of real-time optimization of processes. Businesses can give clients a competitive edge by offering them a variety of payment options that are customized based on the asset's performance or current usage, made possible by real-time data collecting (Dewald and Bowen, 2010; Gebhardt et al., 2022).

German academicians Kagermann et al. (2011) coined the phrase "Industry 4.0" to describe how automation, data exchange, and actual optimization of manufacturing processes would shape the German economy in the future. Its foundation is the notion that physical processes can be monitored, managed, and controlled in real time via cyber-physical systems. When the economy shifted to a digital economy, the concept became more important. Industry 4.0 frequently makes use of the Internet of Things (IoT) and cyber-physical systems (CPS) to link individuals, equipment, and other resources with products and services in the real world. A new stage in the growth and evolution of the technology sector has been ushered in by the advancement of computer technology.

The umbrella phrase "Industry 4.0" covers a wide range of ideas, industries, organizational methods, technical developments, and fields. Due to the vertical integration of intellectual product lines, resources, and machinery into adaptable manufacturing technologies as well as their connection into cross-industry value chains that can be streamlined based on different factors like cost, accessibility, and resource consumption (Kagermann et al., 2016), Industry 4.0 is a crucial role model for businesses worldwide.

To create value, Industry 4.0 connects many forms of cutting-edge technology. Cyber-physical systems exhibit high levels of autonomy and independence in decision-making. All throughout the world, digital solutions are becoming more common. People must therefore adapt to the digital environment. Many individuals consider keeping up with technology to be an essential part of staying in business. Digitalization is a useful tool for accelerating ordinary tasks and shortening communication times. Members of Generation Y have already grown up in a culture where knowledge of the significance of IT is prevalent. Older age groups must overcome the challenge of learning new skills. Companies aspire to deploy Industry 4.0 to use IT to boost production and profitability. The global technical and scientific revolution 4.0 is centered on the most recent technological developments of Industry 4.0, including artificial intelligence (AI), big data (BD), blockchain (BC), and cloud computing (CC). Accounting and supply chain management are only two of the numerous sectors already adopting these cutting-edge technologies (Herath & Joshi, 2023; Rikhardsson & Yigitbasioglu, 2018, Milian, et al. 2019). This chapter uses a descriptive review approach, and its contents are outlined in Table 1.

Table 1. Chapter Contents

Section	Contents
Section 1: Introduction to Industry 4.0	• Definition of Industry 4.0 • The significance of Industry 4.0 • The Evolution of Industry 4.0 • Objectives of Industry 4.0
Section 2: The Pillars of Industry 4.0	• Cyber-Physical Systems (CPS) • Internet of Things (IoT) • Big Data and Analytics • Artificial Intelligence (AI) and Machine Learning • Additive Manufacturing • Cloud Computing
Section 3: Key Drivers and Characteristics of Industry 4.0	• Interconnectivity • Internet of Things (IoT) • Big Data and Analytics • Advanced robotics • Artificial Intelligence (AI) • Cyber-Physical Systems (CPS) • Cloud Computing • Virtual and augmented reality (VR/AR) • 3D Printing (Additive Manufacturing) • Promotion of Horizontal and Vertical Integration • Cybersecurity
Section 4: Industry 4.0 in Action	• Smart Factories • Supply Chain Optimization • Healthcare and Industry 4.0 • Healthcare and Industry 4.0 • Smart Cities and Urban Development
Section 5: Challenges and Considerations	• Data Privacy and Security • Workforce Adaptation • Ethical Implications
Section 6: Future Trends and Outlook	• Industry 5.0 • Global Adoption
Section 7: Conclusion and Recommendations	• Conclusion • Recommendations

1.2 The significance of Industry 4.0

With the advent of Industry 4.0, industrial processes will enter a revolutionary period that will profoundly affect many facets of society. Through breakthrough discoveries like nanotechnology and ubiquitous artificial intelligence, it has a profound effect on society, Schwab (2016). This section examines the significance of industrial 4.0 (Figure 1) and the ways it affects many industries and business domains.

Figure 1. Significance of Industry 4.0

Productivity and Efficiency: Industry 4.0 technologies are critical to increasing efficiency and productivity. By reducing waste, simplifying procedures and improving output, businesses can cut costs and gain an advantage in the market. Industry 4.0 increases corporate productivity by decreasing setup times, errors, and equipment downtime (Rocha et al., 2019; El-Sayed et al., 2020). What results from this is improved customer satisfaction, which is translated into more profits. Now, the IoT also gives birth to new forms of employment and economic platforms. According to the study of Raj et al., (2020), Tradition production by manipulating technology towards automation-based Industry 4.0 can retain this productivity level by 45 to 55%. They appear as organizations that are flat, flexible, and flexible in structure; and they routinely offer tailored services to customers which in the long run circumscribe productivity, aided by smart and strong supply networks (Bigdeli et al., 2021; Mubarik et al., 2021).

Innovation: Technological advancement involving AI, IoT, and data analysis has given corporate the tools that can be used for their new thoughts and solutions to problems. This is the innovation that leads to the establishment of new services and businesses that both produce and supply the goods within the market environment. The environment is characterized and improved by the culture of continual adaptation and improvement. After introducing technological changes of Industry 4.0 to their structure, enterprises can improve both their operations and products (Chiarini, 2021; Gebhardt et al., 2022). Such a policy plan will, in turn, lead to enhanced efficiency and cost reduction among businesses, as well as the creation of employment opportunities, thus being the driving force.

Customization: Industry 4.0 has replaced that era of mass production and now is promoting mass customization (Mindas & Bednar, 2016). Businesses can appropriately customize products to meet the preferences of individual consumers, which helps to meet the increasing demand for specialized goods and services.

Global Connectivity: Global connectivity is made possible by the combination of IoT and connected technologies. Global monitoring and control capabilities help businesses make their supply networks more visible and responsive. Conventional business boundaries are reshaped by this interconnection.

Sustainability: Industry 4.0 encourages the use of eco-friendly practices by optimizing resource usage, reducing energy consumption, and mitigating the overall environmental impact (Motlagh et al., 2020). This focus on sustainability aligns with global efforts to create more Eco-conscious industrial processes. Besides productivity improvement, Industry 4.0 is expected to improve sustainability of organizations. Rashid (2018) claims that innovations from the Fourth Industrial Revolution (4IR) could facilitate the attainment of environmental sustainability. The need for green capitalism in promoting sustainable growth has driven the 4IR which could also facilitate the development of a sustainable and resilient supply chain thus enabling countries and businesses to finally realize the circular economy (Acioli et al., 2021; Bag et al., 2021; Mubarik et al., 2021). For example, through the intelligent selection of hazardous materials, previously appropriately recycled, as inputs for 3D printers to manufacture innovative products (Nascimento et al., 2019). The supporters of Industry 4.0 promote intelligent mechanisms of waste management and production channels that focus on the conservation of the environment (Albert, 2020; Bag et al., 2021).

Resilience: The ability of Industry 4.0 technology to adapt makes an industry more resilient to shocks. The adaptability of these systems enables prompt modifications and effective reactions to unexpected events in the handling of pandemics or supply chain problems. Real-time data gathering and analysis is made possible by these technologies, providing the manufacturing system with insightful data (Wang et al., 2022). A deeper look at the technologies and applications covered in the next sections will offer more insights into how Industry 4.0 is transforming a variety of industries, from manufacturing to healthcare and beyond.

1.3 The Evolution of Industry 4.0

In this section, we start a historical journey that explores the intriguing growth of industries from its infancy to the present-day era of Industry 4.0. Understanding this historical trend aids in putting the significance of and revolutionary possibility of Industry 4.0 into context. Industry 4.0 is one of the fundamental ideas, in accordance with Schwab (2016), that is promoting the growth of international trade and the economy. To understand the significance of Industry 4.0, it's essential to consider the historical context of industrial revolutions:

1.3.1 Industry 1.0: The Age of Mechanization (Late 18th Century)

The plot begins during the First Industrial Revolution, also referred to as Industry 1.0. Steam and water-based mechanization were created during this time. Automation of labor-intensive tasks that formerly required manual labor was made possible by significant breakthroughs like James Watt's steam engine. With the growth of factories, mass production became a reality, revolutionizing industries like manufacturing and textiles.

1.3.2 Industry 2.0: The Advent of Electricity and Mass Production (Late 19th Century)

Assembly lines were created, and electricity was widely used during the Second Industrial Revolution, also known as Industry 2.0. Production-related buildings were powered and illuminated using electrical innovations like Nikola Tesla's alternating current system and Thomas Edison's electric light bulb. Henry Ford's decision to begin producing cars on an assembly line is an excellent illustration of the time's emphasis on economy and mass production.

1.3.3 Industry 3.0: The Age of Automation and Computing (Late 20th Century)

Automation, robotics, and computerization were all embraced by the Third Industrial Revolution, or Industry 3.0. The invention of computers and other digital technology led to a global industrial revolution. Companies started employing computer-controlled systems for data management, logistics, and production. At this time, the internet was invented, connecting people from all over the world like never before.

1.3.4 Industry 4.0: The Fourth Industrial Revolution (21st Century)

The previous industrial revolutions were fueled by the heart of technology which are steam engines for the first Industrial Revolution, electricity for the second industry due and computers for the third industrial revolution (Rupp et al., 2021). The beginning of the fourth industrial revolution (Industry 4.0) is said to be the year 2011 according to practitioners and researchers (Mariani & Borghi, 2019; Ozkan-Ozen & Kazancoglu, 2021). This crucial moment initiated the digitalization and interconnectivity of industrial processes via disruptive technologies that enable machines to work together synergistically with not only machines but also humans in a speedy, smart and real-time approach (Agostini & Nosella, 2020; Neumann et al., 2021; Peña & Caruajulca, 2022). During this time, physical and digital technologies were fully integrated, which led to a quantum leap in industrial evolution. The Internet of Things (IoT), artificial intelligence (AI), big data analytics, and greater automation have all combined to form Industry 4.0.

Unlike its predecessors, Industry 4.0 is not limited to a specific industry or sector. Industry, healthcare, agriculture, logistics, and many other human endeavors are impacted. Reactive decision-making has been replaced by predictive and prescriptive analytics, and isolated systems have been replaced by disconnected ecosystems. Mass production has been replaced by mass customization. Industry has endured a remarkable journey of innovation thanks to the human brain and the never-ending search for productivity, efficiency, and advancement. As we delve deeper into the subsequent chapters, we'll study the crucial technologies and applications that influence the Industry 4.0 environment and transform how we live and work in the twenty-first century.

Industry 4.0 performs better than its predecessors due to the seamless integration of the physical and digital worlds. This is an example of the development of intelligent, self-improving systems capable of autonomous decision-making and continuous adaptation to their surroundings. According to Schwab (2016), there are a few key technological characteristics that define Industry 4.0, and technology development is significantly influencing government, business, and industrial growth initiatives. Industry 4.0 operates as a framework encouraging adaptation and agility in response to such shifts, relevant to the scope of industries such as manufacturing, healthcare, and construction (Turner et al., 2021). Companies that can change with the pace of these changes will be the ones that live and prosper in the future. Hence, businesses should invest in the right technologies and capabilities to stay competitive.

1.4 Objectives of Industry 4.0

A thorough understanding of Industry 4.0 necessitates a review of the key factors influencing its dynamics. The most influential factor in Industry 4.0 is the set of factors driving, rather than the separated technology in nature. The Industry 4.0 setting defines key objectives encompassing motivations and achievements, as depicted in Figure 2.

Figure 2. Objectives of Industry 4.0

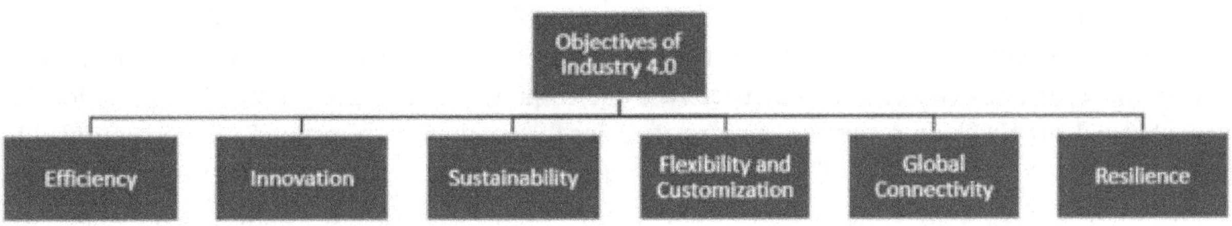

Efficiency: Operational efficiency is at the core of Industry 4.0 developments. For example, reducing waste, improving resource efficiency, and streamlining business processes to enhance efficiency are part of operational efficiency. In Industry 4.0 technologies, enterprises can now operate at the level of efficiency, which was once seen as impractical and unfeasible to accomplish. Businesses can automate procedures, monitor operations in real-time, and make data-driven choices thanks to the integration of cyber-physical systems, AI, and data analytics. A globalized economy benefits from this increased efficiency, since it lowers costs and promotes competitiveness. The Fourth Industrial Revolution has the potential to increase global income levels and elevate the standard of living for everyone, like the previous revolutions (Schwab, 2016).

Innovation: Innovation is essential to Industry 4.0. Digital technology, networking, and data have allowed for the unprecedented development of organizations. Through data-driven insights, businesses can learn about new trends, consumer preferences, and market prospects. AI and machine learning algorithms provide predictive and prescriptive analytics, which also makes it simpler to develop new products, services, and business models. Industry 4.0 encourages a culture of innovation that helps businesses stay ahead of the competition and satisfy customers' changing needs. Automation of physical tasks, planning, control, and information sharing processes improves the efficiency of the supply chain. Automated technologies are widely used by businesses, especially in logistical operations (Ghadge et al., 2020).

Sustainability: As worries about environmental sustainability increase, Industry 4.0 promotes the development of industries that are more environmentally conscious. Industry 4.0 has enormous potential for Sustainable Manufacturing that will allow for better productivity through the optimization of procedures that not only reduce lead times but improve corporate efficiency as well. Sustainable manufacturing is aimed to ensure that the most important principles of sustainable development are achieved in the industrial sphere, contributing to a transition from resource depletion to improving the natural environment and living conditions of citizens (Javaid et al., 2022). Industry 4.0 technology fosters sustainable practices by accelerating processes, using less energy, and creating less trash. IoT sensors, for instance, may track energy use and emissions, enabling companies to take steps to lessen their carbon footprint. Due to an increasing number of environmentally concerned consumers for sustainable goods and services, sustainability is not only a corporate obligation but also a competitive advantage.

Flexibility and Customization: One size fits all production techniques are discouraged by Industry 4.0. Instead, mass customization is encouraged since it makes it possible to modify goods and services to suit the interests of each individual customer. Cyber-physical systems and modern robotics make it simpler to quickly generate customized products. For example, intelligent factories could immediately adjust their production schedules to meet shifting consumer demands in the industrial sector. This flexibility and customization boosts consumer happiness and loyalty. Digital technologies are increasingly used for support of personalization and innovation tendencies of consumers. Lean production paradigm, that emerged thanks to industrial technologies, is being challenged by digitalization, the advances in industry related technologies are usually referred to as Industry 4.0 (Rupp et al., 2021).

Global Connectivity: The atmosphere of Industry 4.0 is characterized by global connectedness. The Internet of Things (IoT) and connected technology have made it possible for businesses to monitor and control operations on a global scale. It is forecasted that as of 2025 there will be more than 75 billion smart devices worldwide (Shehada et al. 2022). Lead times are shortened, and on-time delivery of goods is ensured as supply networks become more responsive and transparent. Global relationship has enhanced supply chain resilience, making it easier for companies to respond to interruptions like pandemics or geopolitical crises. Those organizations that are incapable of promptly responding to the prevailing worldwide shifts do not have chances to survive in the long-term run (Ivanov et al., 2019). Basically, firms need an efficient way to spot and address opportunities promptly.

Resilience: Industry 4.0 admits uncertainty as the base which paves the way towards adaptation. The widespread application of this concept in the industrial age, according to its main purpose is to bring about an architecture, which is uncommon and to apply the Industry 4.0 in the product manufacturing processes and improvement methods for the facilities and distributors to adopt the decision-making and to act correctly and promptly (Javaid et al., 2022). Companies could remain ahead and navigate disruptions that may occur by employing real-time metrics and predictive analytics. Predictive maintenance by means of IoT automation can avoid downtime and prevent accessories from further breaking. The one of Industry 4.0's main goals is the rapidity of the adaption and does this to minimize the accident risks and maintain the business continuous operation. The dawn of an age where man and machine can work together synergistically is crucial for companies. They should promote systems that encourage this kind of collaboration, as it will result in stronger and quicker decisions.

Such inspirational factors and ambitions will serve as the starting point for the overview of the technologies, applications and manifestations developed by Industry 4.0 which will be described in the subsequent chapters. One of the concepts driving this transformation is embedded in the notions of sustainability and ingenuity, efficiency, and adaptability, which can all retrospectively change the course of the industrial sector, as well as general human history.

2. THE PILLARS OF INDUSTRY 4.0

These pillars of Industry 4.0 are generally termed as the 'technical basics' or the 'key technical elements' for the industrial transformation that aligns to the concept of Industry 4.0. The foundation of Industry 4.0 (Figure 3) is aimed to be achieved through the cooperation of these core elements and is considered crucial to meet the expectations of this industrial revolution. The key aspect here is in the core technologies that drive the digital transformation innovation in industries to success. These pillars operate in unison, delivering technological advancements, improvements in the manner organizations do business that are a consequence of the employment of artificial intelligence and data analysis, and creating systems that incorporate Cyber-Physical systems. They suggest ways a company can be very competitive in the market (Li et al., 2020). Profit-making may have a competitive advantage and productivity increase, which can be ensured by contingency of these pillars. Besides that, it does save on operational costs and thus also increases their profitability. The achievements here concern the collection and analysis of vast amounts of information, the emergence of (CPS) and big data is the key either. Failure to do so can hamper the scalability, security, resilience and the efficiency of supply chains in general (Xu & Duan, 2019). \

Figure 3. The pillars of Industry 4.0

The Pillars of Industry 4.0

- Cyber-Physical Systems (CPS): Bridging the Physical & Digital Realms
- Internet of Things (IoT): Connecting the Fabric of Industry 4.0
- Big Data and Analytics: Unleashing the Power of Big Data & Advanced Analytics in Industry 4.0
- Artificial Intelligence (AI) & Machine Learning
- Additive Manufacturing
- Cloud Computing

2.1 Cyber-Physical Systems (CPS): Bridging the Physical and Digital Realms

At the very heart of Industrial revolution 4.0 is Cyber-physical Systems (CPS), a novel engineering paradigm that is the very basis of the 4th industrial revolution. A cyber-physical system is a computer system with the ability to think and understand which is integrated with sensing, computation, control and networking capabilities, and they connected to the Internet and also to each other (Santhi & Muthuswamy, 2023). CPS stands for a crucial transition in our way of thinking and creating relationships with the real and virtual ones.

Defining Cyber-Physical Systems: An advanced, interconnected network that combines computer processing power and techniques with actual physical objects and activities forms the basis of a Cyber-Physical system. To easily link the digital and physical worlds, these systems integrate a variety of technologies, including sensors, actuators, embedded systems, and communication networks (Dang et al., 2023). Making it possible to employ digital intelligence to continuously track, evaluate, and manage physical structures is the main goal of CPS.

The Essence of Real-Time Interaction: A CPS must be able to provide real-time feedback that fosters interaction between a system's physical and digital components for it to be useful. Sensors incorporated into physical objects collect a lot of information about motion, position, temperature, and pressure. In manufacturing, data generated by the sensors e.g. heat, temperature, pressure, moisture, humidity, vibration, friction and movement are constantly recorded to discern the possible trend with the products' performance that would help in bettering the productivity (Santhi & Muthuswamy, 2023). The data is evaluated and understood once it has been moved to digital systems. In response, digital algorithms issue commands that are then sent to actuators to influence or control physical processes. This two-way flow of data and action differentiates CPS from conventional systems.

Key Components of Cyber-Physical Systems: Understanding CPS requires knowledge of the following fundamental components. In the intricate framework of Cyber-Physical Systems (CPS), sensors function as sensory organs, akin to gathering data from the physical world. With these data-drop systems, CPS have at their disposal real-time flowing information, instantaneously transmitting sight and sound from the accident scene. Despite this, actuators are performers, the ones in charge of carrying out digital commands by physically translating them into actions and omissions. Whether it's readjusting the position of a robot arm on the factory floor or regulating drug delivery in life support systems. Actuators are essential to fill the rift between the digital and non-digital worlds within the CPS package. In short, the internal brains of anything physical from light bulbs to smart cars are the Embedded systems which help in the interaction with other cyber physical spaces components. These advanced computer nodes permit hardware, infrastructure, and objects to be linked and perform automated tasks, make decisions, and adapt to quickly changing situations. The intelligent physical world is represented by embedded systems making CPS (Cyber-Physical System) and in consequence, this system is autonomous and adaptive.

The speed of the CPS movement can be realized through fast data communication. These networks are the skeleton which includes sensors, interface systems, and central processing units. The seamless flow of information enables real-time decision-making, ensuring that the entire CPS ecosystem operates cohesively. Whether through wired or wireless connections, communication networks enable the synchronized functioning of CPS components. At the heart of CPS lie Central Processing Units (CPUs), the digital brains responsible for analyzing incoming data, making decisions, and generating commands. CPUs transform raw data into actionable insights, orchestrating the interconnected dance of sensors, actuators, and embedded systems. The computational prowess of CPUs is instrumental in the adaptive and intelligent functioning of CPS across various applications.

Applications of Cyber-Physical Systems: CPS transforms traditional approaches to processes and systems, having a revolutionary effect across a wide range of industries. CPS is integrated into production lines of smart factories in the manufacturing. Lines are optimized based on the data produced. Through the implementation of a Predictive Maintenance and Machine-Coordination CPS, manufacturers may increase output while keeping the downtime rate minimum, also offering a quick response to machinery problems. In healthcare, CPS does a remarkable job in bringing about the changes that directly contribute to medical treatments, care, and overall good prognosis. It provides pathways for using developer tools, in the form of sophisticated medical devices (e.g. personalized treatment), and for facilitating remote healthcare delivery, patterns. The healthcare industry is one of the sectors that is expected to benefit greatly from this growth (Li et al., 2024). For transportation, self-driving vehicles might be one of the primary concepts which the City People association changes the way of traveling by people. Using sensor, connectivity and artificial intelligence, these driving opportunities help maintain a safe and efficient road, which makes them one of the best demonstrations of CPS. As the CPS facilitates the smooth operation of urban planning, traffic management and resource efficiency in the future smart cities, it could create a more comfortable, efficient and sustainable urban environment with these three talents. In the context of agriculture, CPS leads to data-based decision-making, yields optimization, and resource allocation in accurate agriculture scale. The art of this application lays more emphasis on an elaborate and eco-friendly agricultural technology-based farming to keep up with the emerging demands of modern agriculture.

The interconnected functions of sensors, actuators, embedded systems, communication networks, and CPUs will be further clarified in the upcoming chapters. These roles show how these components interact dynamically to create the novel field of cyber-physical systems.

The Role of CPS in Industry 4.0: In the context of Industry 4.0, CPS is the linchpin that orchestrates the transformation of traditional industries into intelligent, interconnected ecosystems. It empowers businesses to achieve unprecedented levels of efficiency, customization, and responsiveness. By merging physical and digital realms, CPS enables companies to monitor and control industrial processes in real-time, predict maintenance needs, and make data-driven decisions, ultimately driving the objectives of Industry 4.0—efficiency, innovation, sustainability, and resilience.

As we navigate through the chapters ahead, the central role of Cyber-Physical Systems will become increasingly apparent, illustrating how this technological marvel continues to shape and redefine industries, revolutionizing the way we live and work in the 21st century.

2.2 Internet of Things (IoT): Connecting the Fabric of Industry 4.0

The term "Internet of Everything" (IoT) was introduced by CISCO to describe the interconnections of people, things, data, and processes, and the Internet of Things has physical "things" inserted with critical sensors (sensing) and being connected to transmit (networking) the gathered data through the internet (Santhi & Muthuswamy, 2023). In the tapestry of Industry 4.0, the Internet of Things (IoT) stands as a prominent thread, weaving together devices, machines, and systems into a seamlessly interconnected digital ecosystem. IoT represents a transformative force that enables the real-time exchange of data and empowers intelligent decision-making. In this section, Industry 4.0's activity with IoT will be assessed, and an image of application and how it impacts industries will be provided.

The recycling of vital data in real time and immediate decision-making is another significant aspect of the World Wide Web of Things. IoT devices can perform multiple functions at once: while they still broadcast data, they also gather data in real time to provide rapid output and equally instantaneous feedback (Barreto et al., 2017). For instance, in a smart factory, you have sensors that are connected to IOT which can detect an impending failure and will initiate maintenance procedure, thus maintaining the optimal production rate and no time lost due to maintenance.

Applications of IoT Across Industries: IoT is the crucial driving force of the Industry 4.0 concept, revealing its orientation to the industry as well as its creative and transformative role in different fields. The IoT goes along the networking of the physical objects, things of different types of equipment and sensors that such objects have through the Internet with the communication among the subjects and the data sharing with the use of the Internet (Ryalat et al., 2023; Tekinerdogan et al., 2023). IoT can help manufacturing at different levels with effective functioning of machines, periodical maintenance or inspections and supply chain optimization that can result in less downtime and increased productivity. Healthcare in the IoT era is transformed into an extensive monitoring system with wearable technologies and remote devices (Dang et al., 2023). The data collected and analysis done is used to personalize and preempt healthcare-giving. In agriculture, the Internet of Things causes the upturn of smart farming by monitoring climatic patterns, farmers' health, and agricultural conditions to offset production. As in case of smart city, the application of IOT in the urban development provides the navigation for the proper planning of city and it can have a major impact on the efficiency of energy, waste management and can improve the traffic flow of city resulting into better quality life and sustainability of urban environment. Furthermore, in logistics, IoT plays a vital role in reshaping the way supply chain management is carried out through the addition of real-time tracking and monitoring of the shipments, the enhancement of transparency, diminish wrong doings and provide visibility throughout the whole supply chain flow. These demonstrate the innovative power and adaptability of IoT technology in the fundamental structure transformation of traditional practice, with clear business and operational transformations concerns across a wide range of industries.

Impact of IoT in Industry 4.0: Within Industry 4.0 where the manufacturing environment being completely data driven due to the industrial internet of things (IoT) which serves as if it's a central nerving system, thus improving our operations and transforming the way we do business - compared to the typical we have known before. IoT allows for real-time data exchange among goods, articles, and logistics, thus avoiding human interference by providing the facility of such level of visibility and control over the data that was never existed earlier (Eslami et al., 2021). The presence of varieties of IoT functions significantly complicated the processes of the industrial sectors and subsequently something changed to the other of a different shade. The sensor is a crucial component behind predictive maintenance, one of the key features of Industry 4.0, as it can not only detect early signs of wear but also can indicate the prevention of such events and proactive maintenance that will help output to be as efficiently higher as it can be. In the cycling of the new IQ (Intelligence Quotient) and networking devices in the Industry 4.0, the Internet of Things plays a role by creating new and better products with greater features and services that can drastically shorten the duration and eventually lower the cost of innovation. This is, furthermore, can target the unique demand of each customer. The information derived from the interconnection of the variously obtained data at this moment of Industry 4.0 brings about those key traits of evidence-based and timely decisions, meaning that companies can come up with timely decisions that make a difference in productivity, efficiency and agility. The IoT powered supply chain revolution opens possibilities to provide greater precision in the operations, as well as the filling of a distributed network networked through the optimization of the entire logistical network, reducing errors and improving delivery efficiency (Ahmed et al., 2021). However, IoT installation does not end there. It can cater for dynamic energy management, thus giving the users to the users to realize low operational and maintenance costs as well as energy efficiency.

The Internet of Things (IoT) is certainly a contributing factor to the Industry 4.0 movement, but you will see more clearly in the following parts how the IoT has infiltrated sectors and set new directions for Industry 4.0. Ii); the universe of data and devices has been created by the Internet of Things (IoT), showcasing the great importance and influence that digital revolution has brought to the working environment.

2.3 Big Data and Analytics: Unleashing the Power of Big Data and Advanced Analytics in Industry 4.0

Data is king in the era of Industry 4.0. The promise of data-driven insights, predictive maintenance, and optimization can only be fully realized by organizations when big data and advanced analytics are integrated. In this section, we set out on a trip to discover how these two forces are transforming Industry 4.0, redefining decision-making, and transforming business operations in an array of industries.

Big Data in Industry 4.0: The huge amount of structured and unstructured data produced by multiple sources in Industry 4.0 are known as "big data." Big Data was originally characterized by the huge volume and exceptional variety of data that comes in an unparalleled velocity (3Vs). The data sources include everything from production equipment, IoT gadgets, and sensors to consumer interactions and supply chain activities. Researchers have added several more characteristics (Vs) to the original 3Vs. As an example, Liao et al. (2014) identified variability and Gandomi and Haider (2015) emphasized Veracity and Value. The essence of big data can be found in its elements that include its speed, variety, veracity and augmentation. For the reasons given below, big data stands out and is an essential component of Industry 4.0:

Volume: A new era of unprecedented volumes and varieties of data creation is being ushered in by Industry 4.0. The volume of data collected is remarkable, especially when IoT-enabled technologies are deployed in smart industrial contexts. These network devices generate gigabytes of data every day, which accumulates into an enormous data bank. The massive volume of data, commonly referred to as "big data," serves as the basis for the discoveries and breakthroughs that drive Industry 4.0's revolutionary potential.

Velocity: Industry 4.0 is characterized by a fast and dynamic data velocity flow. The ability to transmit data in real-time or almost real-time is essential for speedy analysis and decision-making. Because it can assess and respond to data as it is generated, predictive maintenance applications stand to gain a great deal from this high velocity. This helps identify any defects before they worsen. Industry 4.0 systems can react quickly to changing situations because data velocity makes them agile.

Variety: The range of data sources and the uses they support mirrors the kinds of data that Industry 4.0 offers. Data is communicated via the different types of media including text, images, videos, and sensor measurements. It is both a blessing and a curse to have ecology of various formats. In the framework of Industry 4.0, which can be seen as a powerhouse of big data analytics, streams of data characterized by heterogeneity are mixed. This allows businesses to leverage their knowledge from many sources to track subsequent trends, make decisions and understand the context of their business completely.

Veracity: The accurate data makes out the Industry 4.0. Data insights in many cases form the base for decisions that are taken subsequently, they need therefore be completely reliable and trustworthy. The reliability of the data is called veracity, which may affect stakeholders if they do not have enough trust in the information they use to make decisions. It focuses on accuracy and the data itself. The issue of data cleansing methods, verifying procedures and strictly controlling the data environment quality in Industry 4.0 brings us to the solution of this problem. To have precise and trustable intelligence in this age of data analytics is of the greatest asset(s) to most decisions that are strategy oriented.

The characteristics of volume, velocity, diversity, and honesty create the data landscape in the emerging Industry 4.0 environment, highlighting the revolutionary possibilities of this industrial revolution. In order to demonstrate the importance of big data analytics and data governance, we will look at the ramifications of various data properties. To fully exploit the promise of Industry 4.0, several concepts are required.

Advanced Analytics Unleashed: Big data analytics is adopting the advanced algorithmic technique that runs systematically to reveal hidden patterns on the database, interpreting those patterns with the behavior of data and make decisions accordingly (Santhi & Muthuswamy, 2023). Advanced analytics encompasses a spectrum of techniques and technologies that transform raw data into actionable insights. Valuable insights are hidden inside such feedstock data. To find the way to achieve the goal, several analyses like descriptive, inquisitive, predictive, prescriptive, and preemptive are used by industrial sectors (Bihani & Patil, 2014). The potency of advanced analytics lies in its ability to discover patterns, identify trends, and make predictions. Several key facets of advanced analytics within the context of Industry 4.0 include:

Descriptive Analytics: Descriptive analytics is the foundation, providing a retrospective view of historical data. It answers questions like "What happened?" by summarizing and visualizing data.

Diagnostic Analytics: Diagnostic analytics delves deeper, seeking to understand why certain events occurred. It involves root cause analysis and investigates anomalies.

Predictive Analytics: Predictive analytics ventures into the future by forecasting outcomes based on historical data. In Industry 4.0, this is invaluable for predictive maintenance, demand forecasting, and quality control.

Prescriptive Analytics: Prescriptive analytics takes it a step further, providing recommendations on how to optimize processes and achieve desired outcomes. It plays a vital role in decision support systems.

Advanced analytics is a key component of Industry 4.0's innovative environment. Organizations can derive significant value from their data because of its multifaceted approach, which includes diagnostic analytics for root cause analysis, prescriptive analytics for informed decision-making, predictive analytics for future forecasting, and descriptive analytics for historical insights. Businesses need to see patterns, identify trends, and make accurate predictions to manage the challenges presented by the modern industrial period. The continued application of sophisticated analytics will have a significant impact on the future development of industries since it will foster innovation, efficiency, and well-informed decision-making in the fast-paced world of digitalization.

Data-Driven Insights: One of the most transformative aspects of big data and advanced analytics in Industry 4.0 is the generation of data-driven insights. These insights empower organizations to make informed decisions, adapt to changing conditions, and seize opportunities swiftly. In manufacturing, real-time data analysis can detect deviations from quality standards and trigger adjustments in production processes. In logistics, predictive analytics can optimize route planning, reducing delivery times and fuel consumption and in a healthcare system, data-driven insights can assist in disease prediction and personalized treatment plans.

Predictive Maintenance: Another vital technology is augmented (AR) or virtual reality (VR, which involves superimposing digital 3D models on reality, which may be used for assembling huge components or real time technical documentation that is loaded with 3D visualization that is often used for predictive maintenance (Muller, 2019: Muñoz-Saavedra, et al., 2020) The multifaceted nature of predictive maintenance is a great instance of Industry 4.0 where the amalgamation of big data and complex analytics takes place. By constantly collecting information through sensors and doing historical performance data analysis in its turn, predictive maintenance can know about the condition of equipment and foresee its failure. This proactive approach maintains downtime low, brings about reduction of maintenance costs and capitalizes on extending the life of critical assets.

Industry 4.0 is a paradigm shift which blends big data in an intelligent way with analytics that brings data-driven insights to corporate decision-making to speed up the process of taking decisions. This disruptive move generates an impact that hits various sectors, such as manufacturing, logistics, and healthcare, to mention a few. The combination of predictive analytics with real-time data feedback provides a better-quality control of production, as well as a transformation in the way medicine is performed; data-driven insights and not sentiment-based decision-making. By way of example, from the perspective of reputed collusion between work and life, predictive maintenance helps enterprises to obtain indiscriminate machinery failures by tracking promptly and evaluating historic performance data. Being proactive, we have maintenance costs lowered and protected equipment assets over time by their life extension. As agile data-driven insights are the part of Industry 4.0 that provides flexibility, agility and quick decision-making in the face of unexpectedness, they are an essential part of Industry 4.

Optimization Across Industries: The mantra of optimization is dominant in the sector of Industry 4.0, where data analytics alongside big data are regarded as the indispensable helpers to cater to this goal. Optimization activities present themselves in the production processes, the supply chain structure and energy management practices. Through an optimization process, manufacturers try to eliminate waste, boost efficiency, and react to fluctuation in the demands. On the same note, the optimal supply chain aims at boosting stock control, shortening the lead times as well as refining the demand forecasting. Also, energy-sector optimization advantageously uses data to minimize energy consumption and assist in implementing green programs. With the advent of Industry 4.0, the trend demonstrating social coupling between big data, we are getting newer stats in context of sophisticated analytics is obvious.

The collective emerging intelligence in the industry is both powerful enough to adapt rapidly to change and predict outcomes as it unfolds. Indeed, this phase is all about insight-driven decision-making based on data streams at the core of the revolution.

Big data and sophisticated analytics are used by Industry 4.0's optimization thread to combine numerous industries into a massive symphony. Energy efficiency, supply chains, and industrial processes can all be improved. As Industry 4.0 progresses, big data and advanced analytics will progressively converge, producing a synergistic effect that will enable industries to not only anticipate and plan the direction of their operations but also respond swiftly to market developments.

This era of transition and the industries are being built on the superstructure made of data-based insights. Industry 4.0 is built on three pillars: performance, agility, and clairvoyance. For the cross-domain optimization, the big data and intelligent analysis are the perfect combination to make the process simpler However, as the world grows with data and analytics era, the two forever will keep interpreting the world's industries, probably with the sake of growth rather dying out with time.

2.4 Artificial Intelligence (AI) and Machine Learning

It is impossible to emphasize the immense advantages of Machine Learning (ML) and Artificial Intelligence (AI) for Industry 4.0; these are undoubtedly the most important benefits in Industry 4.0. The value of ICT in the contemporary world is evident as this facilitates decision-making at a higher level of intelligence and effectiveness in comparison to experiences. This section will focus on how AI and ML play a crucial role in the coming of the industry, paving the way for revolution, and significantly altering the industrial environment.

Artificial intelligence (AI): Artificial intelligence (AI) is an innovative field that surrounds the creation of intelligent computer systems empowered to perform tasks requiring human intelligence. To illustrate, this area can include solving problems, pattern recognition, interpreting natural language, and decision-making.

Machine learning (ML): The goal of machine learning (ML) as an artificial intelligence discipline is to create a set of statistical models and algorithms which enable computers to not only improve at the activity, but also over time to become more proficient with the input of data. Because it supports many of the capabilities of technology, ML is a crucial part of AI. Applying machine learning (ML) and artificial intelligence (AI) in various fields has various advantages. Thus, integrating AI into operations and procedures within organizations will provide them with a competitive edge (Perifanis, & Kitsios, 2023).

In the era of Industry 4.0, many advantages are furnished with large-scale deployment of AI and ML, which are the core components of relevant solutions. The processing of loads of data with the help of an algorithm generating solutions quicker than before leads to faster response time and better quality of decisions. AI and ML are not only things that make production faster and more efficient, but they also empower the workers to perform complex and repetitive tasks. Automation technology improvement, including Robotic Process Automation (RPA), Cognitive Automation (CA) and Smart Manufacturing to name examples, is the main force behind the tasks that fall under predictive maintenance, customer care and plant monitoring. As a second AI and ML derive the data and insights, these 2 technologies are here to support human decision-making with the application of predictive analytics which is aimed at forecasting future trends and behavioral patterns. Another way to save money is to make wages lower for people working, use predictive maintenance to make machinery working continuously, and just utilize the resource optimally. Moreover, AI and ML help classify data with higher accuracy, for instance, in the process of natural language processing, image recognition and data classification, which helps reduce human error. Last but not the least, if a person can have personalized service, then AI and ML will enable them to make use of the user behavioral models and preferences so that they can customize the unique experiences as per the consumer needs and behavior. At the same time, AI and ML designs let us modify, to optimize processes, by using insights and dampening errors in accuracy.

One of AI's essential abilities is to drive innovation and solve intricate problems that are beyond the capabilities of traditional computing, which are inefficient in doing so efficiently. Using machine algorithms, workflows become improved, and thus new solutions that are unique to a field can be found. Therefore, both research and development are expedited. Apart from that, AI-driven chatbots and virtual assistants are excellent in helping customers with outstanding support and experience that can be attributed to NLP technology. Given that the machine learning models are adaptable, and they can learn from experience, they can deliver great results over time, especially in changing environments where things change per the situations and circumstances. To lace the advantages of AI and ML in risk mitigation, predictive analytics, and risk modeling that assists finance in identifying and mitigating risk proactively is another factor that merits cognizance. This technology not only speeds up treatments but also helps healthcare systems to smoothen the patient's progression, allowing development of new medical approaches and efforts at personalized medicine research. Besides, AI and ML are very useful while designing automized systems which comprise autonomous vehicles and drones. Then, reflecting the use of AI by self-driving cars, these can navigate the roadway and take quick decisions due to the use of AI, which in turn could make transportation safer and more efficient (Saarika et al., 2017). Furthermore, AI-powered drones occur in agriculture, surveillance, and delivery services, offering even higher efficiency and productivity levels.

AI-driven systems enable the development of smart cities, where infrastructure such as traffic lights, waste management, and public transportation can autonomously adapt to changing conditions. Industry 4.0 software wireless networking creates a link between the manufacturing lines, business entities and cross-geographic teams in terms of location, time zone, network and anything else. Smart factories are more scalable if the production line is increased or decreased (Javaid et al., 2022). Although there are many obvious benefits to AI and ML, their effective and equitable application depends on finding answers to problems relating to data privacy, ethics, and potential biases in algorithms. Even if AI solutions can match or even surpass human intellect in some circumstances, such as obtaining, processing, and analyzing huge and complicated data, there are still some scenarios where human intelligence is still necessary (Bolander, 2019; Huang et al., 2019).

The Human-AI Collaboration: Although AI and ML have made great strides in autonomy, it carries an extra note, however: the fact that the human-AI teamwork is primary to Industry 4.0. Humans serve as a bridge between AI systems and the subjective realities through which we live, provide ethical dimension and multifaceted handling that AI cannot. Human-AI synergy introduces a convergence of human wisdom and AI-driven capabilities, which is the dominant factor to enable industries to reach a higher level of the Industry 4.0. Furthermore, AI and ML's integration into society also spark ethical concerns consisting of algorithmic bias, data privacy and accountability. Industries 4.0 experts will inevitably face such complexities, with the goal of ensuring transparency and fairness as responsible development of AI is pursued.

Fascinating the Industry 4.0 progress, the joint AI, ML and human intelligence feedback loop proceeding, the revolution in automation, judgement making and self-exertion level across various companies becomes tangled. Together, these technologies are propelling us toward a new era of innovation and productivity, symbolic of the start of the fourth industrial revolution.

2.5 Additive Manufacturing

3D printing, a term for additive manufacturing, has already made a name for itself as the front-runner of technological innovations that are creating a world without much need for old school manufacturing techniques and leading to an entirely new design paradigm (. Contrary to traditional milling systems, multiple layers of materials are being deposited – this is an additive procedure, not a subtractive one – therefore, new items are being built rather than sculpted or carved. Additive manufacturing is most extensively used for the creation as well as for the manufacture by bulk of design components with such complex geometries that conventional manufacturing process designs those are extremely unreasonable by traditional manufacturing techniques (Gade et al., 2023). Including one of its multiple advantages, additive manufacturing shine in following features, such as crazy customization and complex designs reproduction with droll precision. On the other hand, it decreases the prototyping phase cycle of product development, expediting better refinements through quick production of early designs. An iterative arrangement allows for the setup of the situation in which experiments cannot only bring the development cycle of products to the next level, but also because of the stimulation of innovation. Not only additive manufacturing and improved sustainability, but it does also so by reducing material waste, increasing materials' efficiency, and, especially, by fostering environmentally technologies. Besides that, this achieved localized production and real-time delivery also reduces the requirement for large inventories and makes the supply chain more transparent, which cuts cost and decreases delivery time thus. Through the creation of multidirectional change in the production process procedure, additive manufacturing is revolutionizing both the conceptualization and the production of products. Further developments in technology and materials would allow designers more freedom to explore new designs/shapes, more efficient manufacturing processes, while being more environmentally friendly than other manufacturing processes.

2.6 Cloud Computing

Cloud computing, a fundamental element of the digital transformation era, promises a paradigm shift in the way individuals and organizations use and manage computer resources. Cloud computing is essentially the internet-based provision of various services, such as databases, software, processing power, and storage. A new era of information technology that is more scalable, accessible, and flexible has been brought about by cloud computing.

Cloud computing offers several benefits, including its ability to help businesses cut costs. First, its scalability allows using only needed resources and provides the possibility to vary the resources much more flexibly with peak demand spikes. As a result, companies can manage and reduce their computing resources at the same time, as well as control costs. For those businesses that report volatile workloads over extended periods of time, its dynamic scalability will bring a real benefit (Li et al., 2024). Besides, the pay-as-you-go pricing system makes the economic model more sustainable, helping users avoid allocating large sums of money towards physical infrastructure, as this way they only pay for what they use, reducing the expenses. Furthermore, cloud-based services help to derive global accessibility and contribute to collaborative work across the countries, and in effect teams that are geographically dispersed can efficiently work together. Imposition of such regulations, in turn, leads to the turn of events where remote work is a norm and impedes geographical borders, thus improving the overall productivity. Moreover, cloud providers assemble duplicate data systems in different locations eliminating failures hence has all the operations of high reliability, and the users are guaranteed not to have downtime, but a peace of mind. The significance of service level agreements (SLAs) is expressed through the popularity of uptime guarantees, to solidify the reliability of cloud services. More particularly, flexibility, cost-effectiveness, global accessibility, and reliability are the key features that businesses gain through cloud computing that enables them to stay viable in the ever-changing digital environment.

Because cloud computing offers organizations unparalleled access to scalable, affordable, and cutting-edge computer resources, it has completely changed the IT environment. The cloud will continue to be a game-changer in the digital era if technology develops and has a positive impact on collaboration, corporate operations, and digital innovation.

3. KEY DRIVERS AND CHARACTERISTICS OF INDUSTRY 4.0

This encompasses a broader variety of components that define and impact the overall shift to Industry 4.0. In addition to the technology components that align with the pillars, it considers broader organizational, societal, and economic factors. Potentially important drivers include networking, cloud computing, intelligent robotics, and both horizontal and vertical integration (Figure 4).

Although there are some similarities between the ideas discussed in "The Pillars of Industry 4.0" and "Key Drivers and Characteristics of Industry 4.0," they do not conflict with one another. Although emphasizing distinct aspects, both terms allude to essential elements and concepts associated with the fourth industrial revolution. Industry 4.0's pillars represent its core technologies, but a broader range of technological and non-technology variables are also influencing the movement's salient features and motivations. One way to look at the pillars is as a portion of the entire set of traits and drivers.

Figure 4. Key Drivers and Characteristics of Industry 4.0

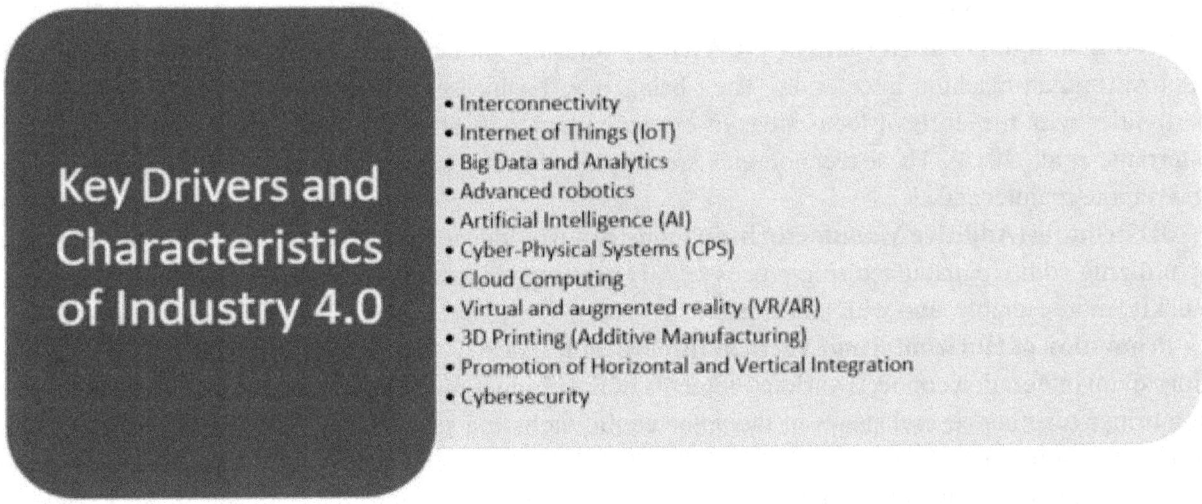

Interconnectivity: The foundation of Industry 4.0 is the seamless interaction of people, machines, sensors, and devices in an industrial setting. Better coordination and decision-making are facilitated by the real-time data exchange and communication made possible by this link.

Internet of Things (IoT): Industry 4.0 would not be possible without the inclusion of IoT devices. Machines and humans might not even be needed for data collected, and human senses can be replaced by electronic sensors, actuators or other devices which can generate digital data (Lu, 2017). Smart devices and sensors gather and disseminate data that offers insights into the supply chain, manufacturing process, and other facets of the industrial ecosystem.

Big Data and Analytics: To manage and analyze the enormous volumes of data produced by networked devices, Industry 4.0 uses big data analytics. By employing this data-driven strategy, businesses can make educated decisions, optimize processes, and spot trends for ongoing improvement (Garcia & Garcia, 2019). For the examination of extensive unstructured, semi-structured, and structured data, Big Data Analysis was employed. This technology aims to present data in an assessable manner (Lu, 2017), enabling the identification of patterns and facilitating decision-making (Pacchini et al., 2019) and serving as a foundation for informed decisions (Sahal et al., 2020).

Advanced robotics: One of the main ideas of Industry 4.0 is robots in manufacturing and other industries. Production can be increased by using intelligent robots with sensors and AI capabilities to complete tasks more quickly, accurately, and efficiently.

Artificial Intelligence (AI): Because AI enables machines and systems to learn, adapt, and act independently, it is a crucial component of Industry 4.0. Machine learning approaches are applied in predictive maintenance, quality assurance, and process improvement.

Cyber-Physical Systems (CPS): Industry 4.0 combines digital and physical processes to build cyber-physical systems. They increase responsiveness and efficiency by monitoring and controlling physical processes with computer-based algorithms.

Cloud Computing: Cloud computing refers to the access of virtual computing services through wireless networks (internet) and visualization of those services by availability of scalable resources through the internet (Garcia & Garcia, 2019). In Industry 4.0, cloud platforms offer the infrastructure required for data processing and storage. This makes remote collaboration, accessibility, and centralized data administration possible.

Virtual and augmented reality (VR/AR): By offering immersive experiences, these technologies improve human-machine interaction. They bring new businesses while providing mass market opportunities with the shifts of focus areas of entertainment, education or training (Gattullo et al., 2019; Interrante et al., 2018). These technologies are employed in the industrial setting for training, support, and remote maintenance.

3D Printing (Additive Manufacturing): Industry 4.0 produces complex and customized components by utilizing additive manufacturing processes. 3D printing makes it possible to create prototypes more quickly, more flexibly, and with less waste.

Promotion of Horizontal and Vertical Integration: Industry 4.0 supports both kinds of integration. Horizontal integration connects various elements of the production process, conversely, vertical integration brings together several stages of the value chain, including suppliers and customers. Industry 4 is about integrating various technologies into all facets of production, including technology communication among digital, physical and biological technologies (Dixon, 2024).

Cybersecurity: The need for robust cybersecurity defense grows with the number of connections. Industry 4.0 emphasizes how important network, data, and system security is to prevent cyberattacks and maintain operational integrity.

Industry 4.0's goal is to create more intelligent, flexible, and productive industrial processes since doing so will boost competitiveness and production. These are Industry 4.0's primary motivators.

4. INDUSTRY 4.0 IN ACTION

Industry 4.0, often called the fourth industrial revolution, is pushing the boundaries of innovation across a range of industries and challenging conventional wisdom. Let's now examine some specific domains where Industry 4.0 ideas are radically altering the landscape.

4.1 Smart Factories

With the advent of smart factories, Industry 4.0 is drastically changing the industrial sector (Dixon, 2024). Conventional manufacturing environments are being replaced by intelligent, networked ecosystems. Industry 4.0 software wireless networking creates a link between the manufacturing lines, business entities and cross-geographic teams in terms of location, time zone, network and anything else. Smart factories are more scalable if the production line is increased or decreased (Javaid et al., 2022). This transformation aims to increase overall operational efficiency, reduce downtime, and optimize production processes through the integration of automation, IoT devices, and real-time data analytics. Smart factories are centers of innovation, flexibility, and data-driven decision-making in addition to being locations of production (Pochiraju, et al., 2019).

4.2 Supply Chain Optimization

Supply chain management is evolving because of Industry 4.0 from a conventional standpoint. Businesses may use blockchain, IoT sensors, and advanced analytics to achieve previously unheard-of levels of supply chain efficiency and transparency. By cutting expenses, reducing interruptions, and leveraging blockchain technology to provide traceability and real-time inventory monitoring, supply chain networks can be made more resilient overall. A blockchain is a distributed electronic ledger making use of cryptographic software algorithms to record and authenticate immutable transactions and/or assets with reliability and anonymity without going through a central authority, also encompassing smart contracts, pertaining to said assets and transactions (Rashid, 2018). By implementation of blockchain architecture, we can ensure data security by data transfer protocols between the stakeholders, which are secure, private, and encrypted (Li & Zhang, 2017).

4.3 Healthcare and Industry 4.0

Assuring the privacy of patient data is considered a major concern within the healthcare industry (Ashan & Siddique, 2022). Digital technologies are being used by Industry 4.0 to improve healthcare (Farahani et al., 2020). The Internet of Things and telemedicine are global technologies that cut beyond national borders. Machine learning and data analytics are used in predictive diagnostics to identify diseases at an early stage.

4.4 Smart Cities and Urban Development

The creation of data-driven, sustainable urban ecosystems, or "smart cities," depends on Industry 4.0. Smart cities optimize resource use, improve public services, and improve quality of life by utilizing connectivity, data analytics, and the Internet of Things. Building robust, flexible, and ecologically sensitive urban settings is the goal of Industry 4.0 concepts like intelligent traffic management and energy-efficient infrastructure. Smart cities can make use of several IoT objects - smart traffic lights, air quality monitors, and noise sensors-all of which can be utilized in controlling respiratory diseases, noise pollution, and traffic accidents (Li et al., 2024) Industry 4.0 is a force that is transforming communities and industries; it is not merely a concept. Industry 4.0 is envisioned as a more inventive, efficient, and sustainable future where innovation and ground-breaking concepts for societal well-being are harmonized. Smart manufacturing, smart cities that are sustainable, improved healthcare, and optimized supply networks are all included in Industry 4.0.

5. CHALLENGES AND CONSIDERATIONS

Significant changes during the Industry 4.0 realization come with technical, human, and cultural challenges, implying the necessity of careful planning (Tortorella et al., 2021). For example, an array of issues and constraints that require due diligence is linked with the adoption of IoT in healthcare (Li et al., 2024). Among these are the fears of data breaches and security concerns (Alazzam, et al., 2022) and interoperability issues (Albouq, et al. 2022). No data privacy and confidentiality concerns should be overlooked, because the movement of sensitive medical records must be done within any invasive procedures performed (Li et al., 2024). Notwithstanding huge potential of personalization and resource efficiency in Industry 4.0, the major challenges remain unsolved (Li, & Duan, 2019; Sen et al., 2018). These challenges include the need for more investment, lack of proper infrastructure, and difficulty in adapting to new technologies. Additionally, there is a need for more research to better understand the implications of Industry 4.0. It will indeed present great challenges, notably gigantic destruction of jobs, when artificial intelligence and cutting-edge robotics dissolve both industrial and service sector jobs (Rashid, 2018). The industrial landscape is shifting due to Industry 4.0, which also brings with it a variety of challenges (Figure 5) that call for careful planning and strategic thinking.

Figure 5. Challenges and Considerations

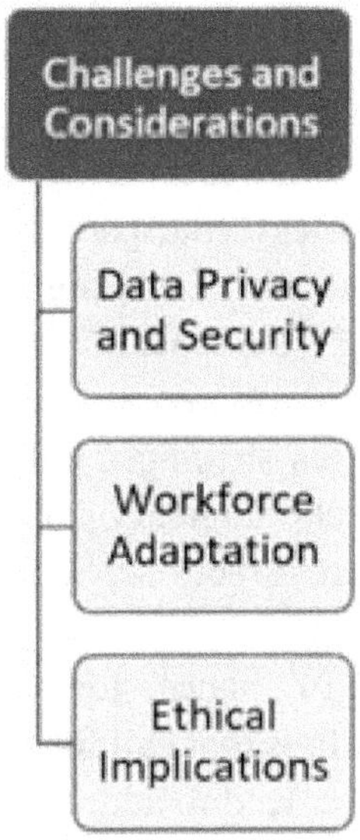

5.1 Data Privacy and Security

Industry 4.0 integrates contemporary technologies, giving rise to a plethora of data and important privacy and security concerns (Chen & Zhang, 2022; Zhao et al., 2022). Critical data must be protected by robust security measures due to the enormous quantity of interconnected systems and devices. To balance security and usability, businesses must use encryption, secure access controls, and comprehensive data governance frameworks. These problems need to be fixed if trust and confidence in the Industry 4.0 digital environment are to be maintained.

5.2 Workforce Adaptation

The rapid advancement of Industry 4.0 technology calls for the need for a workforce that is both tech-savvy and flexible. Employee reskilling and upskilling initiatives are crucial to equipping employees with the competencies needed in a digitally driven company. More than half of the workforce today will be replaced by sophisticated systems and technology by 2025, according to et al. (2020). In addition to providing the necessary training, it is critical to foster a culture of lifelong learning to retain a workforce capable of adapting to the company's constantly changing needs. Organizations should place employees in the first place as automation of repetitive duties by machines will leave people subjected to higher surveillance, more supervision, reduced autonomy, and new imposed uniformed procedures (Cirillo et al., 2021). Companies must adopt new competencies by training employees to improve their skills in abstraction, creativity, decision-making, and socialization (Fantini et al., 2020; Raj et al., 2020). It is not enough; rather focus should be given to their welfare, training, safety and mental health because human beings cannot be redesigned unlike machines and systems (Fantini et al., 2020; Neumann et al., 2021).

5.3 Ethical Implications

The increasing use of automation and artificial intelligence in Industry 4.0 raises moral questions that require serious thought. The integration of artificial intelligence (AI) technologies into business processes and operations has raised questions about privacy, security, safety, transparency, and integrity (Alazzam, et al., 2022; Rahwan, 2018). Issues of fairness, transparency, centralization, and potential impacts to job security are raised as robots become capable of making complicated decisions. Organizations must approach automation ethically, considering the impact on society and ensuring that AI technologies are developed and applied with responsibility, transparency, and equity in mind. A sustainable and socially responsible Industry 4.0 framework requires striking a balance between innovation and moral challenges. To empower people, ensure that technological breakthroughs are in line with moral standards, and gather public opinion to influence future directions, Schwab is in favor of embracing these changes (Schwab, 2016).

Industry 4.0 offers previously unheard-of chances for creativity, productivity, and community development, but it also brings with it difficulties that call for thoughtful and preemptive responses. If we want Industry 4.0 to expand responsibly, we need to address data privacy and security concerns, adjust the workforce to new skill requirements, and discuss the ethical implications of increased automation. As industries take this new course, an integrated strategy that combines technology with moral, human-centered principles will be necessary to maximize the advantages of Industry 4.0 while minimizing its disadvantages.

6. FUTURE TRENDS AND OUTLOOK

Industry 4.0 compels us to consider not just the current situation but also potential future directions and worldwide implications. As you proceed, keep the following in mind:

6.1 Industry 5.0

As Industry 4.0 gained traction, discussions regarding Industry 5.0's potential ascent have already begun. Industry 5.0 prioritizes mutually beneficial partnerships to accomplish its goal of combining humans and robots. Compared to Industry 4.0, which introduced automation and data transfer, Industry 5.0 might emphasize human-machine collaboration more (Dixon, 2024). Instead of taking the place of human talents, this might augment them. Future developments in technology could signal a paradigm shift toward more flexible, compassionate systems that encourage human ingenuity and open hitherto unthinkable possibilities for creativity, invention, and problem-solving.

6.2 Global Adoption

Different nations and industries are adopting Industry 4.0 at different rates. While some countries have jumped at the chance to adopt these technological innovations, others are still adjusting to them. Many variables, such as the state of technology, political agendas, and legal frameworks, affect adoption velocity. However, a worldwide trend is beginning to emerge as more nations become aware of how Industry 4.0 could revolutionize competitiveness, sustainability, and economic development. Future global economies are expected to be more integrated and technologically sophisticated, utilizing Industry 4.0 ideas to foster prosperity and innovation across a range of industries.

The path to Industry 4.0 is dynamic and ever-changing. The future appears to be defined by the continuous infusion of technology into every aspect of human existence, as evidenced by the widespread adoption of Industry 4.0 and the possible rise of Industry 5.0. Industry 5.0 is an evolution of mass customization which began with the ease and efficiency provided by Industry 4.0 technologies, resulting in mass personalization. In this context, it has been termed the personalization revolution (Esben & Østergaard, 2018). The combination of technical innovation and human ingenuity has the potential to drive further evolution of economies, civilizations, and industries in the future by harnessing the revolutionary potential of Industry 4.0 and beyond. This strategy stands out for its creativity, adaptability, and common goal of creating a more linked and intelligent future.

CONCLUSION AND RECOMMENDATIONS

The holistic evaluation of the concept of Industry 4.0, its steps toward development, and its core technologies is intended to highlight the profound implications of these factors, including unprecedented opportunities for creativity and collaboration. Finally, the last paragraph of this chapter will highlight some major importance of Industry 4.0, and it will also include the conclusions of our study. In the first place, we commonly recognize Industry 4.0 era as a new technological epoch which is distinguished with the integration of digital technology, automation and data activation, and it creates an innovative industrial ecosystem which is based on the data processed by the smart industrial systems and devices. As the trajectory of development shows, however, Industry 4.0 goes to refine, data and interconnect sociotechnical networks, it is the culmination of three technological revolutions: from mechanization in Industry 2.0 to automation in Industry 3.0, promulgating an endless refinement path in the quest for ingenuity, effectiveness and connectivity. Our research is regarded as majorly serving the fundamentals of the evolving Industry 4.0 technological sectors such as; additive manufacturing (AM), big data analytics (BD), Internet of things (IoT) and artificial intelligence (AI). Organizations must have a specific, measurable, and integrative mission and vision which is required for implementation of Industry 4.0 to enjoy the preventive effects on performance, as this emphasizes the need to facilitate project management leaders that 4.0 and lead the endeavor in a structured manner (Muller, 2019).

In conclusion, we assume one more time the leading role of Industry 4.0 in global economics. The most impactful effect of this way of thinking is not just the changes on the shop floor, but it also alters industry boundaries and creates an open system which is flexible, data-driven, efficient and imaginative (Santhi & Muthuswamy, 2023). Based on these facts, businesses and agencies are advised to make affirmative steps towards investing in Industry 4.0 technologies and sharing in the benefits of cooperation and coordination among all the industrial stakeholders. Secondly, for effective transformation, supportive policy frameworks should be developed to exploit the full potential of the fourth industrial revolution. Also, upskilling and reskilling programs are imperative to achieving the alignment of the current workforce and the required skills needed to run the Industry 4.0. The key variables discussed in this chapter are displayed in Table 2.

Table 2. Key variables

Advanced Robotics	Intelligent robots with sensors and AI for automating tasks in manufacturing.
Artificial Intelligence (AI)	Computer systems mimicking human intelligence for automation and innovation.
Big Data and Analytics	Processing large datasets for insights and decision-making.
Cloud Computing	Virtual computing services over the internet for scalability and collaboration.
Cyber-Physical Systems (CPS)	Integration of digital and physical processes for monitoring and control.
Cybersecurity	Protecting interconnected systems from cyber threats.
Data-Driven Insights	Informed decisions from analyzing big data.
Horizontal and Vertical Integration	Connecting processes within production and across the value chain.
Internet of Things (IoT)	Interconnected devices collecting and exchanging data for automation.
Pay-as-you-go Pricing and Economic Viability	Flexible pricing model for cost control in cloud computing.
Predictive Maintenance	Anticipating machinery failures to minimize downtime.
Productivity and Efficiency Improvements	Enhancing output and reducing waste in industrial operations.
Real-Time Decision-Making	Rapid analysis and response to data for immediate action.
Scalability and Resource Flexibility	Efficient resource management for varying demands.
Sustainability Practices	Optimizing resource usage and reducing environmental impact.
Technological Integration	Incorporating advanced technologies for improved efficiency and productivity.
Vertical and Horizontal Integration	Coordinating production processes and value chain stages.
Virtual and Augmented Reality (VR/AR)	Immersive technologies for training and maintenance.

REFERENCES

Acioli, C., Scavarda, A., & Reis, A. (2021). Applying Industry 4.0 technologies in the COVID-19 sustainable chains. *International Journal of Productivity and Performance Management*, *70*(5), 988–1016. https://doi.org/10.1108/IJPPM-03-2020-0137

Agostini, L., & Nosella, A. (2020). The adoption of Industry 4.0 technologies in SMEs: Results of an international study. *Management Decision*, *58*(4), 625–643.https://doi.org/10.1108/MD-09-2018-0973

Ahmed, S., Kalsoom, T., Ramzan, N., Pervez, Z., Azmat, M., Zeb, B., & Ur Rehman, M. (2021). Towards supply chain visibility using internet of Things: A dyadic analysis review. *Sensors (Basel)*, *21*(12).

Alazzam, M. B., Alassery, F., & Almulihi, A. (2022). Federated deep learning approaches for the privacy and security of IoT systems. *Wireless Communications and Mobile Computing*, *2022*, 1–7.

Albert, M. J. (2020). The Dangers of Decoupling: Earth System Crisis and the 'Fourth Industrial Revolution.'. *Global Policy*, *11*(2), 245–254.https://doi.org/10.1111/1758-5899.12791

Albouq, S. S., Sen, A. A. A., Almashf, N., Yamin, M., Alshanqiti, A., & Bahbouh, N. M. (2022). A Survey of Interoperability Challenges and Solutions for Dealing With Them in IoT Environment. *IEEE Access : Practical Innovations, Open Solutions*, *10*, 36416–36428.https://doi.org/10.1109/ACCESS.2022.3162219

Ahsan, M. M., & Siddique, Z. (2022). Industry 4.0 in Healthcare: A systematic review. *International Journal of Information Management Data Insights*, *2*(1), 100079. doi:10.1016/j.jjimei.2022.100079

Bag, S., Yadav, G., Dhamija, P., & Kataria, K. K. (2021). Key resources for Industry 4.0 adoption and its effect on sustainable production and circular economy: An empirical study. *Journal of Cleaner Production*, *281*, 125233.https://doi.org/10.1016/j.jclepro.2020.125233

Barreto, L., Amaral, A., & Pereira, T. (2017). Industry 4.0 implications in logistics: An overview. Procedia Manufacturing, 13. DOI: doi:10.1016/j.promfg.2017.09.045, 10.1016/j.promfg.2017.09.045

Bigdeli, Z. A., Kapoor, K., Schroeder, A., & Omidvar, O. (2021). Exploring the root causes of servitization challenges: An organisational boundary perspective. *International Journal of Operations & Production Management, 41*(5), 547–573.https://doi.org/10.1108/IJOPM-08-2020-0507

Bihani, P., & Patil, S. T. (2014). A comparative study of data analysis techniques. *International Journal of Emerging Trends in Technology and Computer Science, 3*(2), 95–101.

Bolander, T. (2019). What do we lose when machines take the decisions? *The Journal of Management and Governance, 23*, 849–867.

Chen, M., Sinha, A., Hu, K., & Shah, M. I. (2021). Impact of technological innovation on energy efficiency in Industry 4.0 era: Moderation of shadow economy in sustainable development. *Technological Forecasting and Social Change, 164*, 120521.

Chen, D., & Zhang, R. (2022). Exploring research trends of emerging technologies in health metaverse: A bibliometric analysis. SSRN Electronic Journal, 5, 1–32.

Chiarini, A. (2021). Industry 4.0 technologies in the manufacturing sector: Are we sure they are all relevant for environmental performance? *Business Strategy and the Environment, 30*(7), 3194–3207.

Cirillo, V., Rinaldini, M., Staccioli, J., & Virgillito, M. E. (2021). Technology vs. workers: The case of Italy's Industry 4.0 factories. *Structural Change and Economic Dynamics, 56*, 166–183.https://doi.org/10.1016/j.strueco.2020.09.007

Dang, V. A., Vu Khanh, Q., Nguyen, V.-H., Nguyen, T., & Nguyen, D. C. (2023). Intelligent Healthcare: Integration of Emerging Technologies and Internet of Things for Humanity. *Sensors (Basel), 23*(9), 4200. https://doi.org/10.3390/s23094200

Del Sarto, N., Cesaroni, F., Di Minin, A., & Piccaluga, A. (2021). One size does not fit all. Business models heterogeneity among Internet of Things architecture layers. *Technology Analysis and Strategic Management, 34*(7), 787–202.

Dewald, J., & Bowen, F. (2010). Storm clouds and silver linings: Responding to disruptive innovations through cognitive resilience. *Entrepreneurship Theory and Practice, 34*(1), 197–218.

Dixon, L. (2024). *Unveiling The Differences Between Industry 4.0 And Industry 5.0.* Retrieved from.https://news.lineview.com/unveiling-the-differences-between-industry-4.0-and-industry-5.0#:~:text=If%20Industry%204.0's%20main,greater%20impact%20in%20innovation%2C%20productivity

El-Alfy, E.-S. M., & Mohammed, S. A. (2020). A review of machine learning for big data analytics: Bibliometric approach. *Technology Analysis and Strategic Management, 32*(8), 984–1005. https://doi.org/10.1080/09537325.2020.1732912

Esben, H., & Østergaard, M.-A. (2018). *Welcome to Industry 5.0.* Retrieved from.https://www.isa.org/intech-home/2018/march-april/features/welcome-to-industry-5-0

Eslami, M. H., Jafari, H., Achtenhagen, L., Carlbäck, J., & Wong, A. (2021). Financial performance and supply chain dynamic capabilities: The Moderating Role of Industry 4.0 technologies. *International Journal of Production Research*, 1–18.

Fantini, P., Pinzone, M., & Taisch, M. (2020). Placing the operator at the centre of Industry 4.0 design: Modelling and assessing human activities within cyber-physical systems. *Computers & Industrial Engineering*, 139.https://doi.org/10.1016/j.cie.2018.01.025

Farahani, B., Firouzi, F., & Chakrabarty, K. (2020). Healthcare IoT. In *Intelligent Internet of Things* (pp. 515–545). Springer.

Gade, S., Vagge, S., & Rathod, M. (2023). A Review on Additive Manufacturing – Methods, Materials, and its Associated Failures. *Advances in Science and Technology Research Journal*, *17*(3), 40–63.https://doi.org/10.12913/22998624/163001

García, S. G., & García, M. G. (2019). Industry 4.0 implications in production and maintenance management: An overview. *Procedia Manufacturing*, *41*, 415–422.

Gattullo, M., Scurati, G. W., Fiorentino, M., Uva, A. E., Ferrise, F., & Bordegoni, M. (2019). Towards augmented reality manuals for Industry 4.0: A methodology. *Robotics and Computer-integrated Manufacturing*, *56*, 276–286.https://doi.org/10.1016/j.rcim.2018.10.005

Gebhardt, M., Kopyto, M., Birkel, H., & Hartmann, E. (2022). Industry 4.0 technologies as enablers of collaboration in circular supply chains: A systematic literature review. *International Journal of Production Research*, *60*(23), 6967–6995.

Ghadge, A., Er Kara, M., Moradlou, H., & Goswami, M. (2020). The impact of Industry 4.0 on supply chains. *Journal of Manufacturing Technology Management*, *31*(4), 669–686. doi:10.1108/JMTM-10-2019-0368

Gandomi, A., & Haider, M. (2015). Beyond the hype: Big data concepts, methods, and analytics. *International Journal of Information Management*, *35*(2), 137–144.https://doi.org/10.1016/j.ijinfomgt.2014.10.007

Herath, S. K., & Joshi, P. L. (2023). Audit Data Analytics: A Game Changer for Audit Firms. *International Journal of Auditing and Accounting Studies*, *5*(1), 29–48. doi:10.47509/IJAAS.2023.v05i01.02

Huang, M. H., Rust, R., & Maksimovic, V. (2019). The Feeling Economy: Managing in the Next Generation of Artificial Intelligence. *California Management Review*, *61*, 43–66.

Interrante, V., Höllerer, T., & Lécuyer, A. (2018). Virtual and Augmented Reality. *IEEE Computer Graphics and Applications*.https://doi.org/10.1109/MCG.2018.02195163

Ivanov, D., Dolgui, A., & Sokolov, B. (2019). The impact of digital technology and Industry 4.0 on the ripple effect and supply chain risk analytics. *International Journal of Production Research*, *57*(3), 829–846.https://doi.org/10.1080/00207543.2018.1488086

Javaid, M., Haleem, A., Singh, R. P., Suman, R., & Santibañez Gonzalez, E. (2022). Understanding the adoption of Industry 4.0 technologies in improving environmental sustainability. *Sustainable Operations and Computers*, *3*, 203–217.

Kagermann, H., Anderl, R., Gausemeier, J., Schuh, G., & Wahlster, W. (Eds.). (2016). *Industrie 4.0 in a Global Context: Strategies for Cooperating with International Partners (acatech STUDY)*. Herbert Utz Verlag.

Kagermann, H., Lukas, W. D., & Wahlster, W. (2011). Industrie 4.0: Mit dem Internet der Dinge auf dem Weg zur 4. industriellen Revolution. VDI nachrichten, 13(11), 2.

Li, Y., Dai, J., & Cui, L. (2020). The impact of digital technologies on economic and environmental performance in the context of Industry 4.0: A moderated mediation model. *International Journal of Production Economics*, *229*, 107777.

Li, C., Wang, J., Wang, S., & Zhang, Y. (2024). A review of IoT applications in healthcare. *Neurocomputing*, *565*, 127017.https://doi.org/10.1016/j.neucom.2023.127017

Li, D. X., & Duan, L. (2019). Big data for cyber physical systems in Industry 4.0: A survey. *Enterprise Information Systems*, *13*(2), 148–169. doi:10.1080/17517575.2018.1442934

Li, C., & Zhang, L. J. (2017). A blockchain based new secure multi-layer network model for Internet of Things. In *Proceedings of the IEEE International Congress on Internet of Things (ICIOT)* (pp. 33–41). IEEE. https://doi.org/10.1109/IEEE.ICIOT.2017.34

Liao, Z., Yin, Q., Huang, Y., & Sheng, L. (2014). Management and application of mobile big data. *International Journal of Embedded Systems*, *7*(1), 63–70.https://doi.org/10.1504/IJES.2015.066143

Lu, Y. (2017). Industry 4.0: A survey on technologies, applications and open research issues. *Journal of Industrial Information Integration*, *6*, 1–10.

Mariani, M., & Borghi, M. (2019). Industry 4.0: A bibliometric review of its managerial intellectual structure and potential evolution in the service industries. *Technological Forecasting and Social Change*, *149*(September), 119752.https://doi.org/10.1016/j.techfore.2019.119752

Masood, T., & Egger, J. (2019). Augmented reality in support of Industry 4.0 - implementation challenges and success factors. *Robotics and Computer-integrated Manufacturing*, *58*, 181–195. doi:10.1016/j.rcim.2019.02.003

Milian, E. Z., Spinola, M. D. M., & De Carvalho, M. M. (2019). Fintech: A literature review and research agenda. *Electronic Commerce Research and Applications*, *34*, 100833.

Mindas, M., & Bednar, S. (2016). Mass customization in the context of Industry 4.0: Implications of variety induced complexity. Industry 4.0, Mass customization, Complexity, Demand, Variety, Advanced industrial engineering. *Industry*, *4*(0), 21–39.

Motlagh, N. H., Mohammadrezaei, M., Hunt, J., & Zakeri, B. (2020). Internet of Things (IoT) and the energy sector. *Energies*, *13*(2), 494.https://doi.org/10.3390/en13020494

Mubarik, M. S., Naghavi, N., Mubarik, M., Kusi-Sarpong, S., Khan, S. A., Zaman, S. I., & Kazmi, S. H. A. (2021). Resilience and cleaner production in Industry 4.0: Role of supply chain mapping and visibility. *Journal of Cleaner Production*, *292*, 126058.https://doi.org/10.1016/j.jclepro.2021.126058

Müller, J. (2019). Assessing the barriers to Industry 4.0 implementation from a workers' perspective. *IFAC-Pap.*, *52*, 2189–2194.

Muñoz-Saavedra, L., Miró-Amarante, L., & Domínguez-Morales, M. (2020). Augmented and Virtual Reality Evolution and Future Tendency. *Applied Sciences (Basel, Switzerland), 10*, 332.https://doi.org/10.3390/app10010332

Nascimento, D. L. M., Alencastro, V., Quelhas, O. L. G., Caiado, R. G. G., Garza-Reyes, J. A., Lona, L. R., & Tortorella, G. (2019). Exploring Industry 4.0 technologies to enable circular economy practices in a manufacturing context: A business model proposal. *Journal of Manufacturing Technology Management, 30*(3), 607–627.https://doi.org/10.1108/JMTM-03-2018-0071

Neumann, W. P., Winkelhaus, S., Grosse, E. H., & Glock, C. H. (2021). Industry 4.0 and the human factor - A systems framework and analysis methodology for successful development. International Journal of Production Economics, 233(November 2020), 107992.

Ozkan-Ozen, Y. D., & Kazancoglu, Y. (2021). Analyzing workforce development challenges in the Industry 4.0. *International Journal of Manpower*.https://doi.org/10.1108/IJM-03-2021-0167

Pacchini, A. P. T., Lucato, W. C., Facchini, F., & Mummolo, G. (2019). The degree of readiness for the implementation of Industry 4.0. *Computers in Industry, 113*, 103125.

Peña, J., & Caruajulca, P. (2022). Industry 4.0 Evolutionary Framework: The Increasing Need to Include the Human Factor. *Journal of Technology Management & Innovation, 17*(3).http://dx.doi.org/10.4067/S0718-27242022000300070

Perifanis, N.-A., & Kitsios, F. (2023). Investigating the Influence of Artificial Intelligence on Business Value in the Digital Era of Strategy: A Literature Review. *Information (Basel), 14*(2), 85. https://doi.org/10.3390/info14020085

Pochiraju, K., Patnaik, A., & Basu, A. (2019). A novel method to optimize energy and productivity in Industry 4.0 enabled smart factories. *Journal of Manufacturing Systems, 53*, 113–124.

Pauceanu, A. M., Rabie, N., & Moustafa, A. (2020). Employability in the fourth industrial revolution. *Economia e Sociologia, 13*(3), 269–283. doi:10.14254/2071- 789X.2020/13-3/17

Rahwan, I. (2018). Society-in-the-loop: Programming the algorithmic social contract. *Ethics and Information Technology, 20*, 5–14.

Raj, A., Dwivedi, G., Sharma, A., Lopes de Sousa Jabbour, A. B., & Rajak, S. (2020). Barriers to the adoption of Industry 4.0 technologies in the manufacturing sector: An inter-country comparative perspective. *International Journal of Production Economics*, 224.https://doi.org/10.1016/j.ijpe.2019.107546

Rashid, A. A. (2018). The Fourth Industrial Revolution impact on the future of sustainable urban development in Malaysia. Urbanice Malaysia. Academia.edu. Accessed from (https://www.academia.edu/36382024/THE_FOURTH_INDUSTRIAL_REVOLUTION_IMPACT_TO_THE_FUTURE_OF_SUSTAINABLE_URBAN_DEVELOPMENT_IN_MALAYSIA).

Rikhardsson, P., & Yigitbasioglu, O. (2018). Business intelligence & analytics in management accounting research: Status and future focus. *International Journal of Accounting Information Systems, 29*, 37–58.

Rocha, C. F., Mamédio, D. F., & Quandt, C. O. (2019). Startups and the innovation ecosystem in Industry 4.0. *Technology Analysis and Strategic Management, 31*(12), 1474–1487.

Rupp, M., Schneckenburger, M., Merkel, M., Börret, R., & Harrison, D. K. (2021). Industry 4.0: A Technological-Oriented Definition Based on Bibliometric Analysis and Literature Review. *Journal of Open Innovation*, *7*(1), 68.https://doi.org/10.3390/joitmc7010068

Ryalat, M., ElMoaqet, H., & AlFaouri, M. (2023). Design of a smart factory based on cyber-physical systems and internet of things towards Industry 4.0. *Applied Sciences (Basel, Switzerland)*, *13*(4), 2156.

Saarika, P. S., Sandhya, K., & Sudha, T. (2017). Smart transportation system using IoT. In *Proceedings of the International Conference on Smart Technologies for Smart Nation (SmartTechCon)* (pp. 1104-1107).

Sahal, R., Breslin, J. G., & Ali, M. I. (2020). Big data and stream processing platforms for Industry 4.0 requirements mapping for a predictive maintenance use case. *Journal of Manufacturing Systems*, *54*, 138–151.

Santhi, R. A., & Muthuswamy, P. (2023). Industry 5.0 or Industry 4.0S? Introduction to Industry 4.0 and a peek into the prospective industry 5.0 technologies. *International Journal of Interactive Design and Manufacturing*, *17*, 947–979.https://doi.org/10.1007/s12008-023-01217-8

Schwab, K. (2016). The Fourth Industrial Revolution: What it means and how to respond. World Economic Forum. Retrieved from https://www.weforum.org/agenda/2016/01/thefourth-industrial-revolution-what-it-meansand-how-to-respond [Accessed September 2023]

Sen, A. A. A., Eassa, F. A., Jambi, K., & Yamin, M. (2018). Preserving privacy in Internet of Things: A survey. *International Journal of Information Technology : an Official Journal of Bharati Vidyapeeth's Institute of Computer Applications and Management*, *10*(2), 189–200.

Shehada, D., Gawanmeh, A., Yeun, C. Y., & Zemerly, M. J. (2022). Fog-based distributed trust and reputation management system for internet of things. *Journal of King Saud University. Computer and Information Sciences*, *34*(10), 8637–8646.

Tekinerdogan, B., Köksal, Ö., & Çelik, T. (2023). System architecture design of IoT-based smart cities. *Applied Sciences (Basel, Switzerland)*, *13*(7), 4173.

Tortorella, G. L., Miorando, R., Caiado, R., Nascimento, D., & Portioli Staudacher, A. (2021). The mediating effect of employees' involvement on the relationship between Industry 4.0 and operational performance improvement. *Total Quality Management & Business Excellence*, *32*(1-2), 119–133.https://doi.org/10.1080/14783363.2018.1532789

Turner, C. J., Oyekan, J., Stergioulas, L., & Griffin, D. (2021). Utilizing Industry 4.0 on the Construction Site: Challenges and Opportunities. *IEEE Transactions on Industrial Informatics*, *17*(2), 746–756. https://doi.org/10.1109/TII.2020.3002197

Vărzaru, A. A. (2022). Assessing the Impact of AI Solutions' Ethical Issues on Performance in Managerial Accounting. [DOI: 10.3390/electronics11142221]. *Electronics (Basel)*, *11*, 2221.

Wang, H., Hu, C., Li, Y., & Tang, J. (2022). Deep reinforcement learning for Industry 4.0: A comprehensive review. *Journal of Manufacturing Systems*, *63*, 429–444.

Wang, S., Wan, J., Zhang, D., Li, D., & Zhang, C. (2016). Towards smart factory for Industry 4.0: A self-organized multi-agent system with big data based feedback and coordination. [DOI: 10.1016/j.comnet.2015.12.017]. *Computer Networks*, 101.

Da Xu, L., & Duan, L. (2019). Big data for cyber physical systems in Industry 4.0: A survey. *Enterprise Information Systems*, *13*(2), 148–169.https://doi.org/10.1080/17517575.2018.1442934

Zhao, R., Zhang, Y., Zhu, Y., Lan, R., & Hua, Z. (2022). Metaverse: Security and Privacy Concerns. arXiv, arXiv:2203.03854.

Chapter 3
Relationship of Digital Technology Adoption on Sustainability Performance

Abdul Qadir Hakimi
University of Muhammadiyah Malang, Indonesia

Ilyas Masudin
https://orcid.org/0000-0002-0153-4560
University of Muhammadiyah Malang, Indonesia

Dian Palupi Restuputri
https://orcid.org/0000-0001-7942-5607
University of Muhammadiyah Malang, Indonesia

ABSTRACT

This chapter explores the relationship between digital technology adoption and sustainability performance. The adoption of digital technologies in various sectors has the potential to enhance economic competitiveness while also promoting sustainability. This study examines the impact of digital technology adoption on sustainability performance by considering factors such as cost, reliability, quality, energy consumption, and carbon emissions. The research emphasizes the need for a systematic approach throughout the entire product lifecycle, including concept development, design, manufacturing, delivery, and supply chain management. The study also highlights the importance of communicating sustainability achievements and commitments in the tourism and hospitality industry. The research aims to fill the gap in understanding the underlying mechanisms and mediating factors that drive the relationship between digital technology adoption and sustainability performance, providing valuable insights for businesses, policymakers, and industry stakeholders.

DOI: 10.4018/979-8-3693-1363-3.ch003

1. INTRODUCTION

Advanced manufacturing leverages emerging technologies to significantly improve both the economic competitiveness of individual manufacturers and the sustainability of the entire industrial sector. With the introduction of new materials and technologies, there is a need for innovative manufacturing processes and sophisticated analytical models to control and optimize various parameters such as cost, reliability, quality, product flexibility, energy consumption, and fossil carbon emissions. The effective integration of advanced manufacturing for sustainability can only be achieved by adopting a systematic approach that encompasses concept development, product design, manufacturing, product delivery, service, as well as forward and reverse supply chain management (Jin et al. 2017).

There is no doubt about the significance of sustainable tourism. Tourism and hospitality companies across the globe are increasingly embracing sustainable practices in their product offerings. However, not all companies effectively communicate their accomplishments and dedication in this field. This study shows Relationship of digital technology adoption on sustainability performance (Tiago et al. 2021). According to Khin and Ho (2019) Emerging digital technologies can be harnessed to create groundbreaking digital products and services, thereby enhancing business performance. These technologies not only enable innovation but also address the existing gaps in the literature concerning the driving factors behind digital innovation and the mediating role of digital innovation in connecting these factors to overall performance (Brunetti et al. 2020).

This research primarily addresses the critical issues of enhancing economic competitiveness in manufacturing through technological innovation, and the imperative of sustainability in various industries, especially in the context of growing environmental and resource-related challenges. The main motivation behind the project is to explore and establish a direct link between the adoption of advanced manufacturing techniques and digital technologies, and their impact on sustainability performance. It seeks to not only optimize manufacturing parameters like cost, reliability, quality, and energy efficiency but also to integrate these improvements into a broader sustainable framework that spans various sectors including tourism, hospitality, business, energy, agriculture, and transportation. A significant part of the motivation is to fill a notable gap in existing research regarding how digital technology adoption can mediate and enhance sustainability performance. The project aims to develop a comprehensive understanding of the factors driving digital innovation and how these innovations can be strategically leveraged for sustainable practices. It also focuses on the necessity for organizations to adapt to the rapid pace and diversity of technological advancements, promoting a mindset of digital transformation that is essential for future resilience and growth. The research is driven by the goal of providing actionable insights and practical guidelines to businesses and policymakers. These insights are aimed at facilitating informed decisions regarding the adoption and integration of digital technologies in sustainability strategies, ultimately leading to a more balanced and resilient future where environmental preservation, economic prosperity, and social well-being coexist harmoniously.

In the realm of digital technology, the pace and diversity of technological advancements are remarkable. New hardware, software, and applications continuously surface, often with unforeseen implications for businesses. Consequently, to effectively harness the potential of digital technology and enhance organizational performance, cultivating a mindset of digital transformation becomes crucial (Li et al. 2021). The strategic plan of the firm regarding digital technology places a strong emphasis on embracing change. This includes selecting platforms that can adapt to technological advancements, encompassing hardware, network, and software standards. Additionally, it involves keeping management informed about valuable options prior to making strategic decisions concerning digital transformation (Lee and Bai 2003).

The concept of 'sustainability' has gained prominence due to environmental pollution, depletion of natural resources, and associated social issues. This has led to the adoption of sustainable practices in various sectors, such as business, energy, agriculture, and transportation. By prioritizing sustainability, society can strive towards a more balanced and resilient future, where environmental preservation, economic prosperity, and social well-being can coexist harmoniously (Nvironment and Erformance 2018). The research gap in understanding the underlying mechanisms and mediating factors that drive the relationship between digital technology adoption and sustainability performance exists. To address this gap, a comprehensive study could investigate the mediating factors that influence the relationship between digital technology adoption and sustainability performance. This study can provide valuable insights to businesses, policymakers, and industry stakeholders, enabling them to make informed decisions regarding the adoption and integration of digital technologies in their sustainability strategies. Additionally, the study can provide actionable recommendations and guidelines for organizations to maximize the sustainability benefits derived from digital technology adoption.

This research delves into the impact of advanced manufacturing, propelled by emerging technologies, on enhancing the economic competitiveness of manufacturers and the sustainability of the industrial sector. It emphasizes the need for new materials and technologies, necessitating innovative manufacturing processes and analytical models to optimize key parameters such as cost, reliability, quality, product flexibility, energy consumption, and fossil carbon emissions. The study advocates for a comprehensive, systematic approach in advanced manufacturing, covering concept development, product design, manufacturing, delivery, service, and supply chain management. Additionally, it examines the role of sustainable practices in tourism and hospitality, particularly how digital technology adoption affects sustainability performance. The research further explores the potential of emerging digital technologies in creating innovative products and services, enhancing business performance, and the need for organizations to embrace a mindset of digital transformation, making strategic decisions about adaptable platforms and standards. It also discusses the importance of sustainability across various sectors, driven by environmental and resource concerns. The study aims to address a research gap in understanding the factors and mechanisms that mediate the relationship between digital technology adoption and sustainability performance, providing insights and recommendations for integrating digital technologies in sustainability strategies for businesses and policymakers.

2. LITERATURE REVIEW

2.1 Digital Technology

The advent of digital technology has brought about a profound transformation in products, services, and operations, giving rise to novel opportunities characterized by convergence and generativity. Digital convergence refers to a fundamental and all-encompassing reshaping of the technical and social information infrastructures that underpin modern society. This reconfiguration is interactive in nature, fostering a dynamic and interconnected landscape where various technologies and social aspects converge to create new possibilities (Koch and Windsperger 2017). The adoption of digital technologies is a multidisciplinary theme that involves various fields, including technology, business, and social sciences (Straub 2009).

Digital technology has revolutionized various aspects of modern life, transforming the way we communicate, work, and access information. One notable impact of digital technology is its role in enhancing communication and connectivity. Platforms such as social media, messaging apps, and video conferencing tools have bridged geographical gaps, enabling instant communication and collaboration across the globe (Nkanu and Okon 2010).This has not only facilitated personal connections but also facilitated business interactions and expanded opportunities for remote work. Digital technology has also opened up new avenues for education and learning. Online courses, virtual classrooms, and educational apps have democratized access to education, allowing individuals to acquire knowledge and skills from anywhere at any time (Lando 2017).

2.2 Sustainability

When an organization or system performs sustainably, it manages and minimizes its negative effects on the environment, society, and future generations while still achieving long-term success. Beyond immediate financial benefit, it emphasizes value creation in a way that is sustainable both economically and ecologically (Zimek and Baumgartner 2017). Corporate sustainable performance (CSP) can be comprehended as an advancement that integrates environmental, economic, and social dimensions (Shahzad et al. 2020).

In order to ensure their survival and achieve long-term sustainability, businesses must actively seek methods to enhance their performance across economic, environmental, and social dimensions. These three performance indicators, namely economic, environmental, and social factors, are commonly referred to as the Triple Bottom Line (3BL). The 3BL is widely recognized as a comprehensive framework for evaluating a firm's sustainability performance, providing a holistic perspective that goes beyond financial considerations alone. By considering economic viability, environmental responsibility, and social impact, organizations can effectively gauge and manage their overall sustainability performance (Wu et al. 2015).

2.3 Digital Technology and Sustainability

Digital technology plays a pivotal role in driving sustainable performance across various sectors, contributing to environmental conservation and resource efficiency. Through advancements in areas such as renewable energy, smart grids, and energy management systems, digital technology enables the optimization of energy consumption and the integration of clean energy sources into the grid (Albach et al. 2015). For instance, the use of data analytics and Internet of Things (IoT) devices allows for real-time monitoring and control of energy usage, leading to more efficient operations and reduced environmental impact (Gupta et al. 2017). Moreover, digital solutions facilitate the development of circular economies by enabling resource tracking, waste reduction, and recycling management through technologies like blockchain and artificial intelligence. By leveraging digital technology, organizations can achieve greater transparency, traceability, and accountability in their supply chains, promoting sustainable sourcing practices and reducing environmental footprint (Ebinger and Omondi 2020). Ultimately, the integration of digital technology with sustainable practices provides opportunities for economic growth while minimizing the ecological footprint and advancing the transition to a more sustainable future (Ness 2008).

Digital technology plays a pivotal role in driving and enabling sustainability efforts across various sectors. It offers numerous opportunities to optimize resource efficiency, reduce waste, and mitigate environmental impacts. Smart grid systems and energy management solutions allow for more efficient energy distribution and consumption, while advanced data analytics and artificial intelligence algorithms enable precise monitoring and optimization of processes. Remote work, virtual meetings, and e-commerce facilitate the adoption of remote work, virtual meetings, and e-commerce, reducing energy consumption and carbon emissions. Digital technologies enhance transparency and traceability in supply chains, promoting ethical sourcing and responsible production practices. By balancing the benefits and challenges, leveraging digital technology in a responsible and sustainable manner can contribute significantly to creating a greener and more inclusive future (Seele 2016).

3. METHODOLOGY

The methodology for the literature review in this research involved a detailed and systematic approach, primarily utilizing the Publish or Perish software, sourced from Google Scholar, to collect a comprehensive range of research journals. Specifically, the selection encompassed 1000 journals published between 2017 and 2023, meticulously chosen to align with the research topic, which focused on "Relationship of digital technology adoption on sustainability performance." This keyword-driven approach ensured that the collected journals were highly relevant to the study's core subject, particularly in the realm of brand strategy.

The Publish or Perish software proved instrumental in this process, as it not only facilitated the retrieval of these journals but also provided crucial bibliometric data such as citation details, authorship, article sources, and abstracts. This information was pivotal in the initial screening and selection of journals pertinent to the examination of brand strategy, as cited by Liao et al. (2018).

Once the journals were selected and retrieved, they were systematically organized and saved in both RIS and Excel (.csv) formats. This dual-format storage was crucial for subsequent processing and analysis. The next critical step involved the Vosviewer software, a specialized tool used for analyzing and visualizing bibliometric networks. By inputting the data collected in RIS format into Vosviewer, the software enabled a detailed and visually engaging analysis of the relationships within the research. This visual representation played a key role in understanding the intricate connections and trends within the vast array of literature, making it easier to identify patterns, key themes, and gaps in the existing research.

The use of Vosviewer software, with its capability to visually map and analyze bibliometric data, added a significant layer of depth and clarity to the literature review process. This methodological approach, combining the comprehensive data collection capabilities of Publish or Perish with the advanced analytical power of Vosviewer, ensured a robust and thorough exploration of the current state of research on the relationship between digital technology adoption and sustainability performance in the context of brand strategy.

4. RESULT AND DISCUSSION

Figure 1. Results of VOSviewer based on keywords

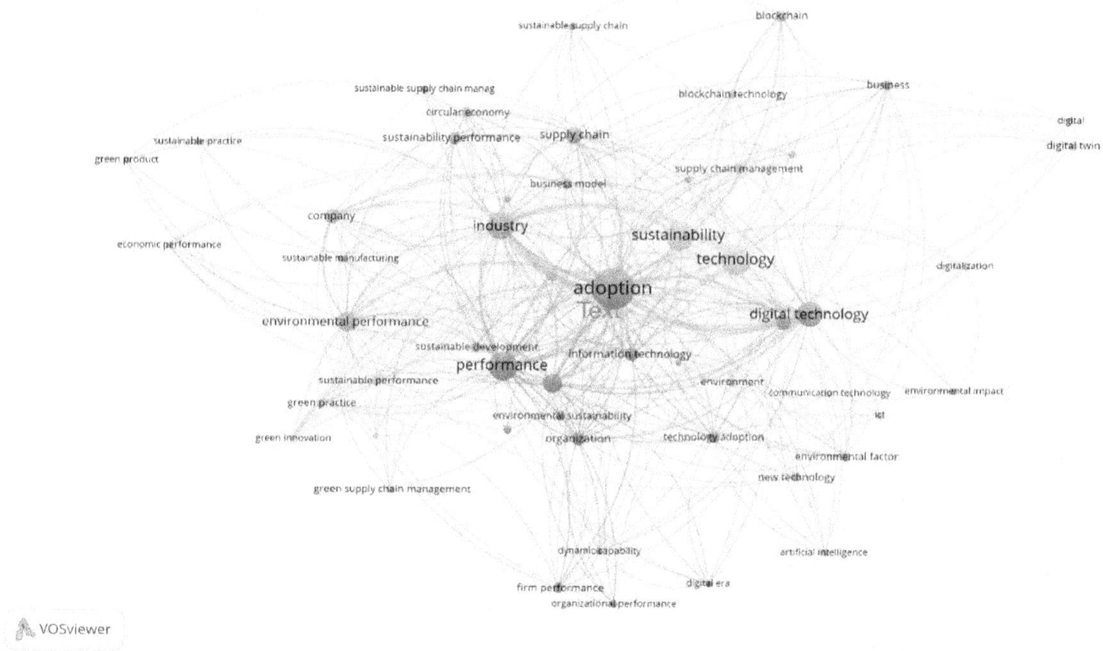

Figure 1 presented above is a bibliometric visualization generated using VOSviewer, which provides an illustrative representation of the interrelationships and thematic clusters within the scope of digital technology adoption and sustainability performance research. Nodes within the network correspond to key terms extracted from a substantial corpus of literature, and their size is indicative of the term's prevalence across the analyzed journals. Edges, or connecting lines, signify the associative strength between terms, with denser lines suggesting more robust connections. At the heart of the network, central terms such as "sustainability," "technology," "adoption," and "performance" emerge as the most prominent concepts, signifying their pivotal role and frequent discussion in the literature. Surrounding these are other significant terms like "supply chain," "environmental performance," and "digital innovation," highlighting the broader discourse on the influence of digital technologies on sustainable practices within supply chains and organizational efficiency. The various colors demarcate distinct thematic clusters, revealing subtopics and specializations within the overarching research domain. This visual analysis not only elucidates the current state of academic discourse but also assists in pinpointing well-established research areas, emerging trends, and potential gaps that warrant further investigation, thereby offering a comprehensive overview of the thematic structure of research at the intersection of digital technology and sustainability within the field of brand strategy.

Figure 2. Results of VOSviewer based on keywords and years

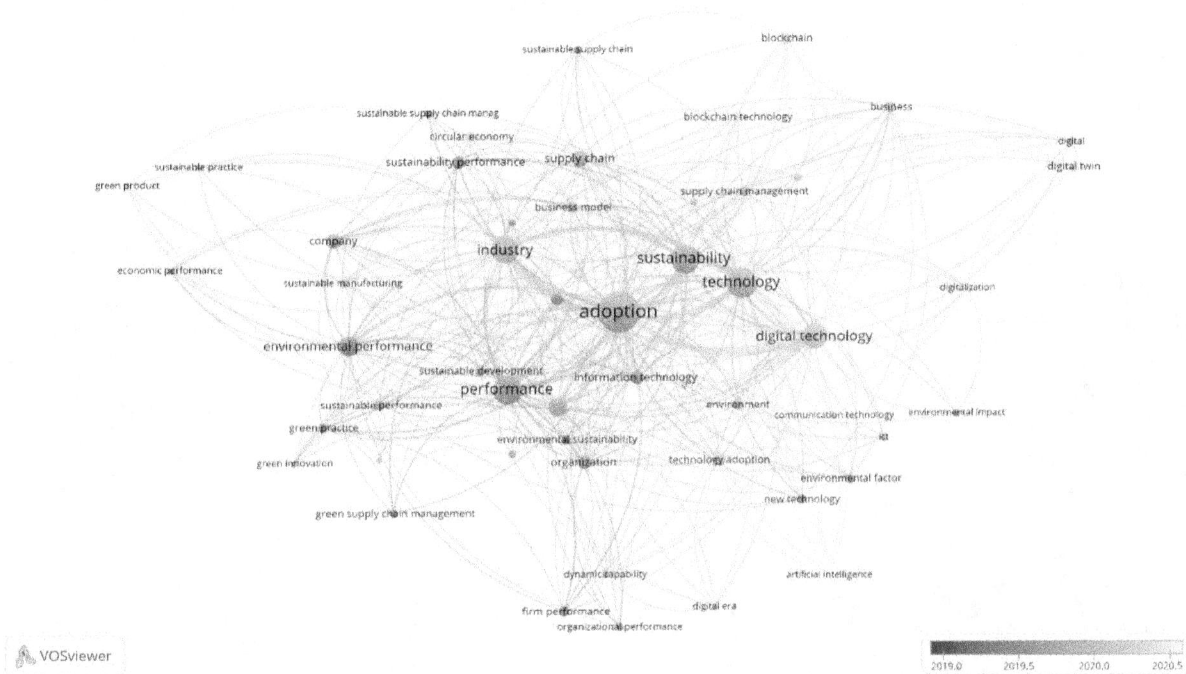

Figure 2 provided bibliometric network map, generated through VOSviewer, offers a visual representation of the scholarly discourse on the intersection of digital technology adoption and sustainability performance, specifically covering literature from the years 2019 to 2020. This timeframe is critical as it captures a period where the intersection of these fields was particularly dynamic, reflecting the latest trends and shifts in research focus. In this map, the size of each node correlates to the term's prominence within the selected years, highlighting the frequency and centrality of keywords in the scholarly conversation during this period.

Key terms such as "sustainability," "technology," "adoption," and "performance" serve as the epicenters of the network, indicating their overarching importance in the literature. The proximity and density of lines connecting these central keywords to others like "supply chain," "environmental performance," and "digital innovation" suggest that these concepts were frequently discussed in conjunction with the core subjects of digital technology and sustainability. The color gradients may indicate the evolution of thematic concentrations over the two years, with certain colors possibly denoting a surge in research attention or a shift in focus at specific points within the timeframe.

The map's ability to visually segregate the keywords into distinct clusters allows for an intuitive understanding of how various research topics were interrelated during this period. It acts as a temporal snapshot, capturing the essence of academic engagement with digital technology and sustainability, and providing a structured overview of the key thematic areas that shaped the research landscape during 2019 and 2020. This visualization is particularly useful for scholars who wish to track the progression of research topics over time, understand the historical context of current trends, and identify areas ripe for future investigation within the realms of digital technology adoption and sustainable performance.

Figure 3. Results of VOSviewer based on density

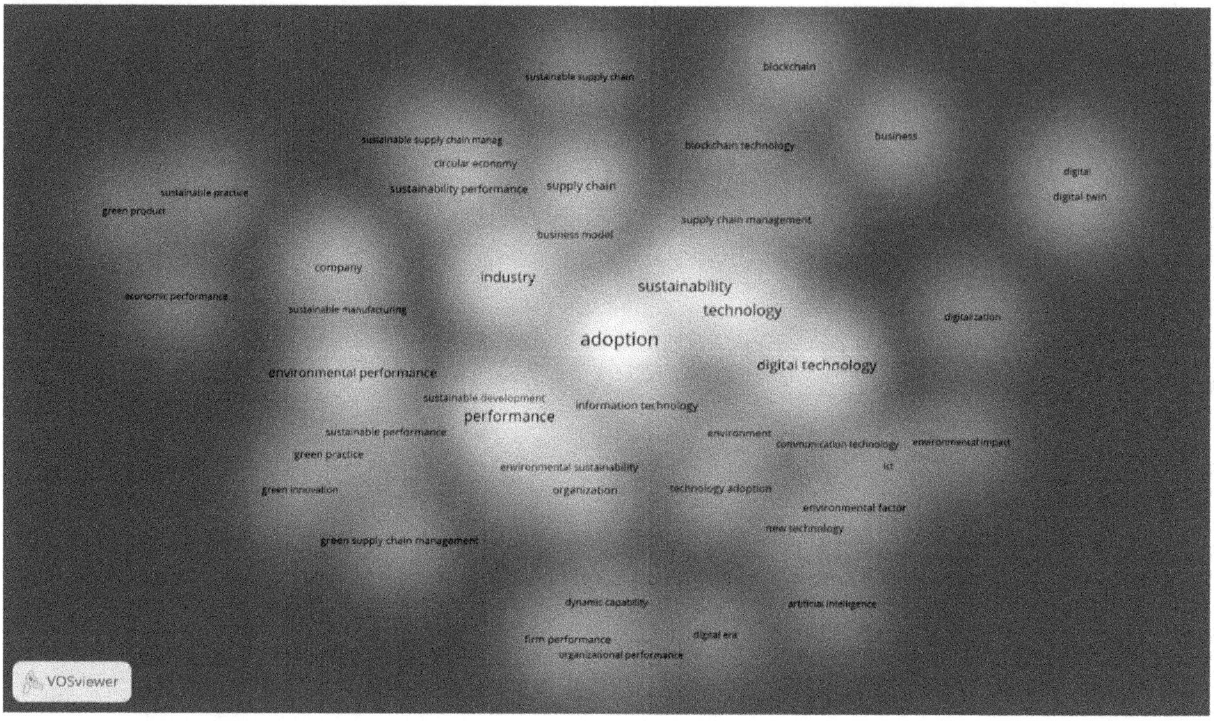

Figure 3 shows the visualization depicted is a density map generated by VOSviewer, offering a compelling insight into the concentration of research themes relating to digital technology adoption and sustainability performance within the scholarly literature. This map, characterized by varying intensities of color, serves as a heatmap to indicate the frequency and co-occurrence of keywords within the body of research analyzed. Prominent clusters illuminated by brighter areas, such as "sustainability," "technology," "adoption," and "performance," signal these terms as focal points of the scholarly discourse. The contiguous spread of color suggests thematic areas with a high density of interconnected research, underscoring their prevalence and importance in the academic exploration of how digital technology contributes to sustainable practices across industries. The gradation from brighter to darker areas represents the spectrum of research intensity, with the most illuminated regions highlighting the most frequently discussed concepts. This visual tool encapsulates the thematic landscape of research, facilitating a nuanced understanding of the areas where academic attention is most concentrated, thereby guiding researchers to key focal points and potential areas ripe for further investigation in the domain of digital technology's role in advancing sustainability.

Table 1. Results of VOSviewers based on clusters

Cluster	Keywords
Cluster1	Digital era, dynamic capability, environmental sustainability, firm performance, information technology, innovation, organization, organizational performance, performance, technology adoption
Cluster2	circular economy, company, economic performance, environmental performance, green product, industry, sustainable development, sustainable manufacturing, sustainable performance
Cluster 3	Adoption, artificial intelligence, business, digital technology, digital transformation, environmental factor, environmental impact, new technology, social media
Cluster4	Communication technology, digital, digital twin, digitalization, environment, ict, sustainability, technology,
Cluster5	Business model, digital platform, social sustainability, supply chain, sustainability performance, sustainability supply chain, sustainability supply chain management
Cluster6	Financial performance, green innovation, green practice, green supply chain management, sustainability performance,
Cluster 7	Block chain, block chain technology, economy, operation, supply chain management,

Table 1 presents the results of a bibliometric analysis using VOSviewer, with a focus on identifying thematic clusters based on keywords associated with digital technology and sustainability. The table categorizes related terms into seven distinct clusters, each representing a different concentration within the research landscape.

Cluster 1 encompasses terms related to the 'Digital era' and includes 'dynamic capability,' 'environmental sustainability,' 'firm performance,' and 'technology adoption.' This cluster signifies a focus on how organizations are evolving in the digital age, enhancing their capabilities, and performing while adopting new technologies for sustainability.

Cluster 2 groups keywords associated with the 'Circular economy,' 'sustainable development,' and 'sustainable manufacturing.' It reflects research on how companies are integrating sustainability into their business operations and the economic impact of these practices.

Cluster 3 gathers terms around 'Adoption' and 'digital technology,' including 'artificial intelligence' and 'digital transformation,' pointing towards the technological advancements organizations adopt and their environmental considerations.

Cluster 4 is themed around 'Communication technology' and 'digitalization,' covering broader technological aspects such as 'digital twins' and 'ICT,' and their relation to 'sustainability.'

Cluster 5 focuses on the 'Business model' aspect, looking at 'digital platforms,' 'social sustainability,' and 'supply chain' management. It reflects on how sustainability is being integrated into business models and supply chain practices.

Cluster 6 is centered on 'Financial performance' and 'green practices,' including 'green innovation' and 'green supply chain management.' This cluster indicates a connection between financial aspects and the adoption of green practices for improved sustainability performance.

Cluster 7 is related to 'Blockchain' technology, indicating its emerging role in 'economy' and 'supply chain management,' highlighting how this technology could potentially transform operations and contribute to sustainability.

Each cluster reveals a specific thematic focus within the broader context of digital technology and sustainability, highlighting the multifaceted nature of research in these areas. These clusters collectively provide a comprehensive overview of the diverse research topics, ranging from technological innovations and their organizational impacts to green practices and their economic implications.

Environmentally sustainable performance refers to the commitment and actions taken by individuals, organizations, and societies to minimize negative impacts on the environment and promote ecological balance. It encompasses a range of practices and initiatives aimed at reducing resource consumption, limiting pollution and waste generation, and preserving natural ecosystems. Achieving environmental sustainability requires adopting strategies such as energy efficiency, renewable resource utilization, waste reduction, sustainable transportation, and responsible land and water management. Organizations committed to environmentally sustainable performance integrate these practices into their operations, supply chains, and product development processes. By embracing sustainability as a core value, they strive to minimize their carbon footprint, conserve natural resources, protect biodiversity, and mitigate climate change. Moreover, environmentally sustainable performance extends beyond individual actions and necessitates collective efforts from governments, businesses, and communities to address global environmental challenges and create a resilient and healthy planet for present and future generations (Yacob, Wong, and Khor 2019).

Previous studies examining the correlation between environmental and economic performance often reached the consensus that a moderate positive relationship exists between these two factors. In several cases, it was also determined that above-average environmental performance does not adversely affect a firm's financial or stock market performance. These findings suggest that organizations can achieve strong environmental performance without sacrificing their financial success, implying a potential alignment between sustainable practices and economic outcomes (Wagner et al. 2002).

A mathematical model based on a data-mining multilayer perceptron artificial intelligence algorithm has demonstrated and validated the relationships and influences between key performance indicators (KPIs) and various organizational problems. This approach facilitates the resolution of existing problems, risk identification, communication, and prevention of future issues by establishing links between each problem and a corresponding KPI. The implementation and monitoring of specific KPIs contribute to a better understanding and identification of potential risks and issues within the system, allowing for timely risk assessment and management. Collaborative efforts and data collection from multiple companies further enhance the trustworthiness and reliability of these predictions (Dumitrascu, Dumitrascu, and Dobrotă 2020).

The pivotal role of information and communication technology (ICT) as a driving force in the present and future era is widely acknowledged and substantiated. It profoundly influences the economic, religious, cultural, legal, and social aspects of nations, particularly in developing countries. Developing nations have long recognized the significance of ICT for sustainable development, In Nigeria, ICT has made a substantial impact on various sectors of the economy, representing a revolutionary advancement of the 21st century. It has facilitated rapid information dissemination, enabled informed decision-making processes, reduced resource and organizational management costs, and created extensive opportunities for information sharing among individuals, businesses, and government institutions. Undeniably, ICT is indispensable for Nigeria's pursuit of sustainable development. Today, ICT has been effectively integrated into the framework of state administration, giving rise to the concept of e-government. The inherent potential benefits of ICT in driving sustainable development in Nigeria are widely recognized and regarded as an imperative paradigm (Nwabueze and Ozioko 2011).

Among the three dimensions of performance, social performance displays the strongest positive correlation with ESG disclosure, followed by environmental performance and then economic performance. The findings also highlight significant positive associations between environmental performance and social performance with economic sustainable performance, indicating the interconnectedness between a company's economic value and its value creation for society. This integration of economic, social, and ecological factors represents a win-win concept. Moreover, the study reveals that all three performance components—economic, environmental, and social—contribute equally to the overall corporate sustainability performance and have causal relationships with one another. A strength or weakness in one component can affect the other components as well. Therefore, when formulating policy reforms, corporations should acknowledge the interdependence between performance components and prioritize the most critical component to enhance the overall corporate sustainability performance. This approach ensures efficient resource allocation, with a primary focus on enhancing corporate sustainability performance (Alsayegh, Rahman, and Homayoun 2020).

Promoting accountability and transparency in disclosing environmental and social strategies within a robust corporate governance system does not impede the pursuit of environmental and social objectives or economic profit. On the contrary, organizations can actively pursue all three goals—economic, environmental, and social performance—in parallel, thanks to the competitive advantages derived from embracing environmental, social, and governance (ESG) responsibilities. These competitive advantages, such as increased efficiency, enhanced competitiveness, reduced operating costs and financial risks, and improved corporate reputation and consumer trust, contribute to elevated levels of corporate sustainability performance (Alsayegh et al. 2020).

Among the three performance dimensions, social performance demonstrates the strongest positive correlation with ESG disclosure, followed by environmental performance and economic performance. The findings also highlight significant positive associations between environmental performance, social performance, and economic sustainable performance, emphasizing the interplay between a corporation's economic value and its contribution to society. This integration of economic, social, and ecological factors represents a mutually beneficial concept. Furthermore, the study reveals that all three performance components—economic, environmental, and social—contribute equally to the overall corporate sustainability performance and exhibit causal relationships with one another. A strength or weakness in one component can impact the others. Therefore, when designing policy reforms, corporations should acknowledge the interdependence between performance components and prioritize the most critical component to enhance overall corporate sustainability performance. This approach ensures efficient resource allocation, with a primary focus on advancing corporate sustainability performance (Asadi et al. 2020).

Environmental sustainability performance is paramount, signifying a commitment by various entities to minimize their ecological footprint, promote ecological balance, and engage in practices that reduce resource consumption, pollution, and waste while preserving natural ecosystems. To achieve such sustainability, strategies encompassing energy efficiency, renewable resource utilization, waste reduction, sustainable transportation, and responsible resource management are integral. Organizations that internalize environmental sustainability integrate these practices into their operational, supply chain, and product development protocols, aiming to reduce their carbon footprint, conserve resources, protect biodiversity, and address climate change. This collective endeavor, extending beyond individual initiatives, calls for collaborative efforts from governments, businesses, and communities to confront global environmental challenges and secure a resilient, healthy planet for current and future generations.

Studies exploring the relationship between environmental and economic performance generally concur on a moderate positive correlation, indicating that environmental stewardship need not compromise financial success, suggesting an alignment between sustainable practices and economic viability. This is reinforced by data-driven mathematical models, such as the multilayer perceptron artificial intelligence algorithm, which elucidates the interplay between key performance indicators (KPIs) and organizational issues, enhancing problem resolution, risk communication, and prevention.

Information and Communication Technology (ICT) is universally recognized as a cornerstone for development, especially in emerging economies. For instance, in Nigeria, ICT has revolutionized multiple sectors, streamlining information dissemination, decision-making, and reducing costs, thus being central to sustainable development and the establishment of e-government.

Moreover, when examining performance dimensions, social performance exhibits the most robust positive correlation with ESG disclosure, followed by environmental and economic performance. The interconnectivity between these dimensions underscores the concept that economic, social, and environmental factors are not mutually exclusive but interdependent, contributing equally to overall corporate sustainability performance. Recognizing this interdependence is crucial for corporations when formulating policy reforms, ensuring that the most critical component is prioritized to enhance sustainability performance efficiently. Promoting accountability and transparency in ESG strategies within corporate governance aligns with achieving environmental, social, and economic objectives, as these strategies can yield competitive advantages such as efficiency, reduced costs and risks, and enhanced reputation, ultimately elevating corporate sustainability performance.

5. CONCLUSION

The adoption of digital technologies in various sectors has the potential to enhance economic competitiveness while also promoting sustainability. Environmental sustainability requires the commitment and actions of individuals, organizations, and societies to minimize negative environmental impacts and promote ecological balance. Studies have shown that there is a positive correlation between environmental and economic performance, indicating that organizations can achieve strong environmental performance without sacrificing financial success. ESG disclosure shows the strongest positive correlation with social performance, followed by environmental performance and economic performance. In driving sustainable development, particularly in developing countries, information and communication technology (ICT) plays a crucial role. Organizations have the ability to pursue economic, environmental, and social performance concurrently, gaining competitive advantages through the adoption of ESG responsibilities. By integrating sustainability as a fundamental value, organizations can make contributions to a resilient and thriving planet while simultaneously achieving their economic objectives.

REFERENCES

Albach, Meffert, Pinkwart, & Ralf. (2015). *Management of Permanent Change—New Challenges and Opportunities for Change Management*. Academic Press.

Alsayegh, M. F., Rahman, R. A., & Homayoun, S. (2020). Corporate Economic, Environmental, and Social Sustainability Performance Transformation through ESG Disclosure. *Sustainability (Basel)*, *12*(9), 3910. Advance online publication. doi:10.3390/su12093910

Asadi, S., OmSalameh Pourhashemi, S., Nilashi, M., Abdullah, R., Samad, S., Yadegaridehkordi, E., Aljojo, N., & Razali, N. S. (2020). Investigating Influence of Green Innovation on Sustainability Performance: A Case on Malaysian Hotel Industry. *Journal of Cleaner Production*, *258*, 120860. doi:10.1016/j.jclepro.2020.120860

Brunetti, F., Matt, D. T., Bonfanti, A., De Longhi, A., Pedrini, G., & Orzes, G. (2020). Digital Transformation Challenges: Strategies Emerging from a Multi-Stakeholder Approach. *The TQM Journal*, *32*(4), 697–724. doi:10.1108/TQM-12-2019-0309

Dumitrascu, O., Dumitrascu, M., & Dobrotă, D. (2020). Performance Evaluation for a Sustainable Supply Chain Management System in the Automotive Industry Using Artificial Intelligence. *Processes (Basel, Switzerland)*, *8*(11), 1–20. doi:10.3390/pr8111384

Ebinger, F., & Omondi, B. (2020). Leveraging Digital Approaches for Transparency in Sustainable Supply Chains: A Conceptual Paper. *Sustainability (Basel)*, *12*(15), 6129. Advance online publication. doi:10.3390/su12156129

Gupta, H., Dastjerdi, A. V., Ghosh, S. K., & Buyya, R. (2017). IFogSim: A Toolkit for Modeling and Simulation of Resource Management Techniques in the Internet of Things, Edge and Fog Computing Environments. *Software, Practice & Experience*, *47*(9), 1275–1296. doi:10.1002/spe.2509

Jin, M., Tang, R., Ji, Y., Liu, F., Gao, L., & Huisingh, D. (2017). Impact of Advanced Manufacturing on Sustainability: An Overview of the Special Volume on Advanced Manufacturing for Sustainability and Low Fossil Carbon Emissions. *Journal of Cleaner Production*, *161*, 69–74. doi:10.1016/j.jclepro.2017.05.101

Khin, S., & Ho, T. C. F. (2019). Digital Technology, Digital Capability and Organizational Performance: A Mediating Role of Digital Innovation. *International Journal of Innovation Science*, *11*(2), 177–195. doi:10.1108/IJIS-08-2018-0083

Koch, T., & Windsperger, J. (2017). Seeing through the Network: Competitive Advantage in the Digital Economy. *Journal of Organization Design*, *6*(1), 6. Advance online publication. doi:10.1186/s41469-017-0016-z

Lando. (2017). *Digital Transformation in Journalism and News Media*. Academic Press.

Lee, G. G., & Rong, J. B. (2003). Organizational Mechanisms for Successful IS/IT Strategic Planning in the Digital Era. *Management Decision*, *41*(1), 32–42. doi:10.1108/00251740310445536

Li, H., Wu, Y., Cao, D., & Wang, Y. (2021). Organizational Mindfulness towards Digital Transformation as a Prerequisite of Information Processing Capability to Achieve Market Agility. *Journal of Business Research*, *122*(February), 700–712. doi:10.1016/j.jbusres.2019.10.036

Ness, D. (2008). Sustainable Urban Infrastructure in China: Towards a Factor 10 Improvement in Resource Productivity through Integrated Infrastructure Systems. *International Journal of Sustainable Development and World Ecology*, *15*(4), 288–301. doi:10.3843/SusDev.15.4:2a

Nkanu, W. O. (2010). Digital Divide: Bridging the Gap through ICT in Nigerian Libraries. *Library Philosophy and Practice*.

Nwabueze & Ozioko. (2011). Information and Communication Technology for Sustainable Development in Nigeria. *Library Philosophy and Practice*.

Seele, P. (2016). Digitally Unified Reporting: How XBRL-Based Real-Time Transparency Helps in Combining Integrated Sustainability Reporting and Performance Control. *Journal of Cleaner Production*, *136*, 65–77. doi:10.1016/j.jclepro.2016.01.102

Shahzad, M., Qu, Y., Zafar, A. U., Rehman, S. U., & Islam, T. (2020). Exploring the Influence of Knowledge Management Process on Corporate Sustainable Performance through Green Innovation. *Journal of Knowledge Management*, *24*(9), 2079–2106. doi:10.1108/JKM-11-2019-0624

Straub, E. T. (2009). Understanding Technology Adoption: Theory and Future Directions for Informal Learning. *Review of Educational Research*, *79*(2), 625–649. doi:10.3102/0034654308325896

Tiago, F., Gil, A., Stemberger, S., & Borges-Tiago, T. (2021). Digital Sustainability Communication in Tourism. *Journal of Innovation and Knowledge*, *6*(1), 27–34. doi:10.1016/j.jik.2019.12.002

Wagner, M., Van Phu, N., Azomahou, T., & Wehrmeyer, W. (2002). The Relationship between the Environmental and Economic Performance of Firms: An Empirical Analysis of the European Paper Industry. *Corporate Social Responsibility and Environmental Management*, *9*(3), 133–146. doi:10.1002/csr.22

Wu, L., Subramanian, N., Abdulrahman, M. D., Liu, C., Lai, K., & Pawar, K. (2015). The Impact of Integrated Practices of Lean, Green, and Social Management Systems on Firm Sustainability Performance-Evidence from Chinese Fashion Auto-Parts Suppliers. *Sustainability (Basel)*, *7*(4), 3838–3858. doi:10.3390/su7043838

Yacob, P., Wong, L. S., & Khor, S. C. (2019). An Empirical Investigation of Green Initiatives and Environmental Sustainability for Manufacturing SMEs. *Journal of Manufacturing Technology Management*, *30*(1), 2–25. doi:10.1108/JMTM-08-2017-0153

Zimek & Baumgartner. (2017). Corporate Sustainability Activities and Sustainability Performance of First and Second Order. *Researchgate.Net*.

Chapter 4
Industry 4.0 Approach in Intelligent Manufacturing:
Adoptability of Machine Learning and Challenges

Archana Sharma
Delhi Technical Campus, Greater Noida, India

Purnima Gupta
IMS-Ghaziabad University Courses Campus, India

ABSTRACT

The machine learning component has significantly influenced the manufacturing business, according to the Industry 4.0 standard. The Industry 4.0 paradigm encourages the use of smart sensors, tools, and gadgets to enable smart factories that continuously collect data on production. Actionable intelligence can be formed by means of ML techniques by dealing with the collected data to increase production output without materially changing the required resources. Additionally, it is now possible to recognize complex production designs owing to machine learning techniques' ability to provide analytical visions, including intelligent and continuous inspection, predictive maintenance, quality improvement, process optimization, supply chain management, and task scheduling. This research presents analysis of internet of things-enabled manufacturing, tools other than machine learning structures used in conventional in addition to unconventional machining processes, and their strengths and weaknesses in an Industry 4.0 context, as well as a perspective on the manufacturing paradigm.

1. INTRODUCTION

In order to translate product concepts and requirements into practical applications for the intended use of the product, manufacturing technology is the embodiment and integration of relevant scientific and engineering aspects into a working whole. To build the product in accordance with the design parameters, the capability of an intelligent manufacturing method has to possess well-being and/or self-control.

DOI: 10.4018/979-8-3693-1363-3.ch004

Researchers who are implementing expert systems have developed the idea of enhancing intelligence. Due to their reliance on symbolic representations of the information and the human expertise needed to successfully encode it, the first attempt at this undertaking through knowledge-based systems and expert systems was insufficient to achieve the necessary level of intelligence. However, the emergence of fuzzy logic systems for modelling uncertainty and human-like reasoning, the acceptance of GA as a global optimization technique for difficult problems, and the expansion of ANN as self-organizing dynamic systems and model-free estimators in the 1980s have all contributed to the realization of intelligent manufacturing systems as a workable idea in the current decade.

The term "Industry 4.0" refers to the latest advancements in manufacturing processes and automation. Industry 4.0 encompasses a wide range of topics, such as data management, manufacturing competitiveness, efficiency in production processes, and production processes. Industry 4.0 encompasses a range of critical enabling technologies, including as digital twins, artificial intelligence, big data analytics, cyber-physical systems, and the Internet of Things, which are essential contributors to automated and digital manufacturing environments. If manufacturing technology is founded on novel knowledge-based applications, it will be crucial to human advancements in the future. Any company needs to utilize all of the knowledge that is available to it. The efficient use of knowledge, from design to production and maintenance, is what this purpose translates into. To achieve this, it is necessary to free and direct the knowledge stored in various organizational modules in a synergistic manner to support integrated engineering and fabrication systems. Manufacturers are not as knowledgeable about the tools and procedures that should be employed. Manufacturers frequently employ their current tools instead of researching the advantages of more advanced intelligent manufacturing approaches. Vendors of intelligent systems can alleviate the dilemma by refining their shells to meet specified specifications for manufacturing applications that succeed. This chapter presents Industry 4.0 enabled manufacturing, analyze the qualities and weaknesses of tools other than machine learning structures utilized across both regular and unconventional machining processes, and provides a perspective on the manufacturing paradigm.

1.1 Sustainable Manufacturing

Its aim is to reduce its detrimental effects on the environment to the point where it can still benefit future generations. If this ambition is to become a reality, research on waste reduction and energy savings must be done. At the very least, the longevity of a product's design and production must be considered. During the design phase, decisions are made that affect the entire lifecycle. Making wise decisions is necessary to reduce a product's environmental impact. How ecologically friendly a product is is greatly influenced by the manufacturing process. The design, use, and planning of contemporary, energy-efficient machine equipment must be carefully considered. The promotion of smart manufacturing is one tactic for fostering sustainable production. Data-driven decision-making is integrated with manufacturing. Sensors collect information from the shop floor, business operations, and manufacturing to provide insights that reduce waste and increase productivity. AI techniques can be utilized to process this data and assist in making the right choices for improved product manufacturing and distribution. Businesses and their entire supply chains will waste less if this knowledge is shared.

1.2 Industry 4.0

The latest manufacturing trend, known as "Industry 4.0," is fueled by various technologies, including the Internet of Things (IoT), cloud platforms, big data, artificial intelligence (AI), deep learning (DL), and machine learning (Kotsiopoulos, T., Loannidis, D., Sarigiannidis, P., & Tzovaras, D. 2021). It aims to optimize products, cut costs, decrease energy excess, and offer valuable information by analyzing data gathered from various manufacturing enterprise-wide aspects. The volume of currently accessible data, also referred to as "big data," has significantly increased for the manufacturing sector (Vassakis, K., Kopanakis, I., & Petrakis, E. 2018). The availability of data on quality presents the possibility of long-lasting changes in procedure and product quality. Due to its enormous dimensions, intricacy, and dynamics, it might also pose problems. The industrial sector has a lot of potential for sustainable transformation due to ongoing developments in mathematics and information technology, notably in machine learning. Smart manufacturing incorporates machine learning practices to handle issues, and selecting the best algorithm is dependent on the pre-processed data (Sarker, I. H. 2021).

"Industry 4.0" represents the fourth manufacturing revolt, in which smart factories that can run more effectively and efficiently are built using automation and data interchange. Machine learning algorithms are essential to Industry 4.0 because they make it possible to analyse massive volumes of sensor-generated data and other devices in the production environment (Angelopoulos et al. 2019). The following are some principles of Industry 4.0 for machine learning algorithms:

Maintenance Planning: Machine learning algorithms are being used to predict equipment failure, which enables maintenance to be carried out before a breakdown takes place. This can decrease downtime and increase the general effectiveness of the equipment (Carvalho, T. P. et al. 2019).

Quality Control: In order to prevent defective products from reaching customers, machine learning algorithms can be used to detect product flaws in real time (Peres, R. S., Barata, J., Leitao, P., & Garcia, G. 2019).

Supply Chain Optimization: Using machine learning techniques, the supply chain could be made more effective by forecasting demand and modifying production plans accordingly. This could increase effectiveness and cut waste (Makkar, S., Solanki, V. K., & Devi, G. N. R., 2020).

Autonomous Systems: Systems that are autonomous can be created using machine learning algorithms that can work without human supervision. This can lower labour expenses and raise security in risky situations (Mallozzi, P. 2017).

Simultaneous Decision Making: The actual data analysis by means of machine learning algorithms enables speedy and well-informed decision-making. This can boost overall effectiveness and lower the chance of mistakes (Skordilis, E., & Moghaddass, R. 2020).

1.3 Machine Learning Algorithms in Industry 4.0

Overall, Industry 4.0's guiding principles for machine learning algorithms centre on exploiting data to enhance operations, reduce waste, and boost efficiency. Manufacturers can build smart factories that function more effectively and economically by using machine learning algorithms to analyze vast volumes of data produced by sensors and other devices. To optimize both conventional and unconventional machining processes in Industry 4.0, machine learning can be deployed. Here's a brief overview of these processes:

Conventional machining methods: It have been used for a while and entail material cleaning using mechanical means such as cutting, drilling, and milling (Melkote, S., et al. 2022).

Unconventional machining methods: It processes besides that, are newer processes that use non-traditional methods where a workpiece should be stripped of material. These processes often involve recent technologies such as lasers, electron beams, and chemical reactions (Yao, Y. L. et al. 2005).

Machine learning (ML), a subcategory of AI that focuses on computers' ability to learn for themselves, is currently employed often in a number of contexts, including those in the entertainment, commercial, and increasingly industrial sectors. Thanks to the wide application and low development barriers of these algorithms, advancements that were previously thought to be impossible to achieve are now becoming a reality in an ever-more digital environment. With the adoption of these technologies across industries, the industrial sector has begun to make money. Due to the current drive for smart manufacturing besides Industry 4.0, ML interest in manufacturing is at an all-time high. However, how much are businesses truly using these generally accepted techniques? The Industry 4.0 standard's machine learning subset has significantly impacted the industrial industry. In order to facilitate smart factories that regularly gather data on production, the Industry 4.0 standard encourages the use of gadgets, intelligent sensors, and machines. ML methods allow the clustering of actionable intelligence with obtained data processing to enhance manufacturing output without any significant change in required resources. A variety of production operations, including predictive intelligence, continuous inspection, quality improvement, supply chain management, process optimization, and task scheduling, can now be supported by intelligent decision support systems thanks to machine learning techniques' ability to deliver predictive insights. This includes the identification of multifaceted manufacturing designs.

Machine learning algorithms can be used to optimise both conventional and unconventional machining processes by analysing data from sensors and other devices to identify patterns and optimise the parameters of the machining process (Ayvaz, S., & Alpay, K., 2021). This could result in increased productivity, decreased waste, and better overall results throughout the production process. Table 1 highlights the evaluation of machine learning algorithms till 2022.

Table 1. Evolution of Machine Learning algorithms

Machine Learning Algorithm	Year of Proposal	Inventor(s)
Random Forest	1999	Leo Breiman
Support Vector Machines (SVM)	1995	Vladimir Vapnik
AdaBoost	1995	Yoav Freund and Robert Schapire
Gradient Boosting Machines (GBM)	1999	Jerome Friedman
K-Nearest Neighbors (KNN)	1991	Aha, Kibler, and Albert
Deep Learning	1965	Alexey Ivakhnenko and Valentin Lapa
Convolutional Neural Networks (CNN)	1980	Kunihiko Fukushima
Recurrent Neural Networks (RNN)	1982	John Hopfield
Generative Adversarial Networks	2014	Ian Goodfellow
Long Short-Term Memory Networks (LSTM)	1997	Sepp Hochreiter and Jürgen Schmidhuber
Deep Reinforcement Learning	2013	Volodymyr Mnih et al.
Capsule Networks	2017	Geoffrey Hinton et al.
Attention Mechanisms	2014	Dzmitry Bahdanau et al.
One-Class Support Vector Machines (OCSVM)	1992	Bernhard Boser, Isabelle Guyon, and Vladimir Vapnik
Adversarial Autoencoders (AAEs)	2014	Ian Goodfellow, Yoshua Bengio, and Aaron Courville
Graph Convolutional Networks (GCN)	2017	Thomas Kipf et al.
Meta-Learning	1993	Jürgen Schmidhuber
Federated Learning	2016	Ian Goodfellow
Transformer Networks	2017	Ashish Vaswani et al.
Contrastive Learning	2006	Yoshua Bengio et al.
Probabilistic Graphical Models (PGMs)	1970	Judea Pearl and Ronald J. Brachman
Self-Supervised Learning	2015	Yann LeCun et al.
Gated Recurrent Units with Attention	2014	Ilya Sutskever, Geoffrey Hinton, and Oriol Vinyals
Continual Learning	1996	Yoshua Bengio et al.
Causal Inference	1988	Judea Pearl

In smart production systems for sustainable manufacturing, energy consumption, systems integration, logistics, environmental services, and other crucial challenges are being improved using AI and ML. The most crucial technique for foretelling and resolving issues in production environments is machine learning (ML). To make informed decisions, you must strike the correct balance between having enough information and not having enough. Data security is a crucial factor in machine learning. Three categories can be used to group ML techniques: supervised, unsupervised, and reinforcement learning.

The goal of the study is to provide a basis for future research by fostering knowledge of ML algorithms and their variants in intelligent manufacturing using industry 4.0. The most advanced machine learning methods for smart manufacturing, such as the aforesaid three categories of ML algorithms, have been analyzed in this research. The first phase of the chapter focuses on the role of machine learning in smart production systems and the various tools applied in intelligent manufacturing. The research in the second phase highlights the problems with how firms can effectively evaluate and select machine learning algorithms for their industry. 4.0 attempts. The benefits and challenges of each method for manufacturing applications have been elaborated and reviewed the performance based on various factors. Further, the last phase of the chapter proposes the solution of a hybrid approach to ML algorithms and how firms can effectively evaluate and select machine learning algorithms for their industry. 4.0 attempts and recommendations for further study

2. INTELLIGENT MANUFACTURING TOOLS

The equipment typically used in intelligent manufacturing is listed below:

- Tools for Neural Net Works Cases
- Uncertain logic
- Gene-based algorithms
- AI

2.1 Scheduling With Neural Network

The building blocks of artificial neural network, also known as neurons, processing elements, etc., share a lot of similarities with their biological counterparts. ANNs are driven by their robustness, fault tolerance, adaptability, and learning capacity and are created to represent networks of actual neurons (i.e., animate brains). The operator can participate in the schedule construction and see how it impacts crucial parameters using an interactive tool for short-term production scheduling with system features and a graphical user interface. This knowledge-based system can respond to delays or unforeseen events in an efficient manner. Neural network approaches are used to correct an erratic schedule and move it closer to a regular or ideal timetable, robustness, fault tolerance, adaptability, and learning capacity and are created to represent networks of actual neurons (i.e., animate brains). The operator can participate in the schedule construction and see how it impacts crucial parameters using an interactive tool for short-term production scheduling with system features and a graphical user interface. If the current schedule does not comply with the restrictions imposed by the production environments, a constraint management subsystem verifies the cause of the conflict and informs the planner so that it can be resolved. This knowledge base system can respond to delays or unforeseen events in an efficient manner. Neural network approaches are used to correct an erratic schedule and move it closer to a regular or ideal timetable.

2.2 Case Based Judgment

This is a tool that is frequently used to interpret process parameters. To interpret the analytical outcomes of the procedure, human experts must be consulted. giving them the chance to use an expert system to enhance the process. Case-based perception presents information as “cases,” or illustrations of prior issues and fixes.

2.3 Software for Intelligent Design and Data Analysis

The expert system generates the best design parameters while abiding by all machine or material constraints. Actually, this is a development of CBR (case based reasoning)

2.4 Chaos Logic

A way to express the language variable in a way that is appropriate for computer processing is to use fuzzy logic systems. Uncertain logic Process control allows for flexibility since the expertise and suggestions of human operators can directly be used to determine process states and control actions. This enables the computerized control of complicated multi-variant processes to make use of real-world operating experience. It provides a mathematical foundation for representing the ambiguities found in human cognitive systems, including thinking and reasoning. The control rule is expressed in language using all the words, such as high, medium, and low.

2.5 Genetic Algorithms

GA is founded on the principles of natural genetics. It aims to locate fresh points in the search area with an anticipated enhanced presentation by utilizing historical information. This is also a tool for arranging a manufacturing line efficiently. The rules of ecological selection and the existence of acceptable species are the foundation of genetic algorithms, also known as adaptive computing. Simply put, a genetic algorithm creates new rules to replace the existing ones that are least useful. These software tools enable users to identify solutions to complicated issues like scheduling a large number of jobs that clash, determining the quickest path between several locations, or simplifying a communications network. As a way to enhance the assembly process of mechanical products while reducing time and expense, the search routine utilised in assembly planning is optimized using genetic algorithms.

3. KEY TECHNOLOGIES OF INTELLIGENT MANUFACTURING

The German Federal Government presented Industry 4.0 in 2014 (Machado, C.G. 2020) as its high-tech industry strategy. Industry 4.0 refers to the recent progress in data substitution and mechanization across manufacturing technologies or activities. Building "smart" factories that can accept new business models, management goals, and dynamic manufacturing scenarios is at the heart of Industry 4.0 (Oztemel, E. 2020). Blockchain technology, virtual reality, augmented and virtual reality, flexible manufacturing systems, artificial intelligence, machine learning, deep learning, IoT, big data analytics, and cloud computing are some of the most important enabling technologies for Industry 4.0 (Borregan-Alvarado, J. 2020; Giallanza, A. 2021). The previous three business transformations were fueled by means of electrification, automation, big data analytics, and IT in business, which increased supply usage and productivity (Zhong, R.Y. 2017). Industry 4.0 is the core technology of CPS, and mass customization is a possibility thanks to its modularity and adaptability in production systems (Kamble, S.S. 2018). Physical objects can be linked by CPS to permit man-machine communication, organization, operations, and supplementary structure functions when they are plugged into an IoT device (Lee, J. et al. 2019). The IoT and CPS interaction makes it easier for real-world and virtual communication by allowing data created by industrial processes and sensor data to be shared (Oborski, P., & Wysocki, P., 2022). While this is going on, other Industry 4.0 technologies support business operations made possible by Industry 4.0. The Industrial IIoT, ML and AI, Data Analytics (DA), Digital Twin (DT), and Cloud Computing (CC) are all taken into consideration as this part assesses a few key concepts and their applications in IM.

3.1 Industrial IoT (IIoT)

IoT is defined as the application of intelligent or digital technologies in fields that make it simple to analyze different system architectures, process information, determine where things are, and address other security concerns. It also has a wider range of connectivity and computing with different platforms, necessitates almost no human interaction, and has several characteristics. Over period, there was indeed a clear assimilation with Industry 4.0, and they had made a distinction between those who, on the one hand, undertake intelligent industrial process with the help of data analytics in order to transform personal and business outcomes and those who, on the other hand, did so in a way that contributed to the IIoT as a whole. So, in summary, we could say that the term IIoT would arise whenever IoT is used in a manufacturing process or for an industrial application (Aberle L 2015, World Economic Forum 2015). Interfaces link different industrial processes and products. such as power grids, sensors that connect to clouds via networks, and engines (Borregan-Alvarado, J.2020, Giallanza, A. 2021). The final goal of this is to optimize the product, beginning with increasing its productivity, efficiency, and overall cost reduction and moving ahead while adjusting to many changes in the contemporary environment.

3.2 Machine Learning and Artificial Intelligence (AI and ML)

Artificial intelligence (AI) is a methodology that employs logic, decision trees, and machine learning to replicate, improve, or maybe entirely replace human intelligence. As unmanned combat vehicles have undergone breakthroughs and developments that easily surpass the most advanced robotics technology, autonomous intelligence systems have come to be recognized as a crucial advancement. (Pan Y 2016, Thramboulidis, K. 2019). A few statistical approaches are used to better a task over time; at this point, ML enters the picture, making it a subset of AI (Wang B 2023). By providing enormous data analysis tools and focusing on the demands for future efficient and sustainable production, deep learning is effective for facilitating the investigation and processing of large industrial data sets. One test that was suggested to evaluate computer communication was the Turing test, which entails a computer, an examiner, and a machine placed in various locations. This test would show the degree of machine intellect. Changes in production that enhance intelligent technologies from strategy to execution are always being driven by automation.(Oztemel E 2010, Wang J 2018, Huang W 2017). The internet of things, cloud computing, and the newest 5G technology are just a few of the current opportunities for AI integration. These advancements would encourage decision-making, the application of new knowledge techniques, and the focus on real-world issues, all of which would significantly advance intelligent manufacturing (Wang L 2019). Therefore, these intelligent behaviors are incorporated into traditional manufacturing systems with the aid of AI and ML, covers all aspects of assessing the product's quality, the production process, and product delivery, Moreover, you should confirm their degree of market competition.

3.3 Data Analytics

Data is now readily available everywhere in a variety of businesses because to the speedy development of the internet and the IoT, which resulted in the big data crisis. Big data is generated by gadgets, sensors, and even social media feeds. The scale of the data required brought up the question of whether IoT could manage the appropriate data at the right time despite expanding IoT capabilities. Data analytics can be used in this situation, which involves using cutting-edge analytic techniques to process large operations and data, particularly in the manufacturing sector (Lee J et al. 2013, Barton D and Court D 2012, Agarwal R and Weill P 2012). The Watchdog Agent, a form of predictive analytics, the product of the Centre for Intelligence Practices And methods, has ensured that almost any handling of enormous data is converted into informative data (Lee J et al 2006, Lee J et al 2014). The cyber-physical system employs the 5S method, which stands for Synchronization, Sensors, Formulation, Service, and Storage as well as in order to reproduce the machine's operating circumstances, knowledge from data-driven analytic algorithms must be combined with practical expertise. Based on computational effectiveness, operational simplicity, investment cost, and additional numerous updates, the data analytics option is chosen.(Brown B, Chui M and Manyika J 2011). By staying with current and innovative technologies and goods more effectively and productively, manufacturers will be able to compete in this analytical process of manufacturing.

3.4 Digital Twin

A system that can calculate, display, and pretend, as well as check system status and control activities, is referred to as a "digital twin." (Tao F et al. 2018, Tao F et al. 2017, Uhlemann T H J 2017, Glaessgen, Edward H, and Stargel D S 2012, Schleich B et al. 2017). Manufacturing systems are capable of detecting material processes, creating DTs in daily life (Wang S. Y., Wan J. F., and Zhang D. Q. 2016), taking real-time data for analysis in a computer simulation from the outside world, and developing wise judgments through routine human interaction and communication. Zheng et al. (Zheng Y, Yang S, and Cheng H. 2019)

3.5 Cloud Computing

The provision of readily available computing resources and data storage that a user can access remotely through a system is known as cloud computing (Liu Y and Xu X 2017, Zhang L. et al. 2014, Wu D et al. 2015, Xu X 2012, Li B H et al. 2010, Tao F 2011). This led to the development of cloud manufacturing, where a system-oriented manufacturing prototype was built up to drastically cut down on resource usage (Tao F et al. 1969, Valilai O F and Houshmand M 2013). Zhong et al. (Zhong R Y et al 2017) and Zhou et al. (Zhou J. et al 2018) evaluated several cloud computing implementations in IM, and The most significant and prepared technology for IM was determined to be cloud computing. On a cloud structure, It is definitely possible to complete anything from processing software to altered company programmers that are set out and expanded for an organization. Because of its increased flexibility, elasticity, cost-cutting, and efficient resource use, cloud computing has gained acceptance in an environment of increasing competition.

4. MACHINE LEARNING ALGORITHMS

4.1 Supervised Learning

Industry 4.0, another name for the fourth industrial revolution, is characterized by an increase in the use of automation, data interchange, and connected devices to enhance manufacturing processes and increase efficiency. Supervised machine learning is a key element of this movement. As a result, manufacturers may optimize their processes and boost production by using supervised ML algorithms to analyses data and predict future events. Within the framework of Industry 4.0, a variety of supervised ML methods, such as neural networks, decision trees, support vector machines, and logistic regression, can be applied. The choice of algorithm will depend on the particular application and the kind of data being analyzed, as each algorithm has pros and cons of its own, which have been mentioned below.

Random Forest: This ML method can be utilized for categorization and regression problems. It operates by creating a huge number of decision trees during the training phase and then determining the class that represents the mean of the regression or classification predictions provided by each individual decision tree. Random Forest's application in Industry 4.0 include problem diagnosis, quality control, and predictive maintenance. A substantial amount of labelled data is required for the RF algorithm to produce results that can be trusted.Kiangala, S. K., & Wang, Z. 2021).

Support Vector Machines: It is an effective supervised learning technique used in prediction purposes. In a high-dimensional space, it creates a hyperplane to separate the classes. SVMs have been widely used in Industry 4.0 applications such as predictive anomaly detection, quality control, and maintenance. (Chamasemani, F. F., & Singh, Y. P. 2011, September).

AdaBoost: A strong classifier is produced by combining several weak classifiers using a collaborative learning technique. It assigns weights to each instance in the training set to give greater weight to the misclassified instances. AdaBoost is used in Industry 4.0 for applications such as fault detection, anomaly detection, and predictive maintenance (Bécue, A., Praça, I., & Gama, J. 2021) (Patil, P. S., Patil, M. S., Tamhankar, S. G., & Patil, S. S. (2020).

Gradient Boosting Machines: In this ML algorithm, it combines multiple weak classifiers to form a strong classifier. It functions by gradually adding more decision trees, with each tree being taught to fix the errors of the one before it. Gradient Boosting Machines are used in Industry 4.0 for applications such as detect cyber-attacks, predictive maintenance, quality control, and anomaly detection (Tran, M. Q. et al. 2021) (Lee, C. Y., Lin, J. Y., & Chang, R. I. 2018).

K-Nearest Neighbors: It is a non-parametric approach that is used for both classification in addition to prediction. It involves finding the k-nearest neighbors of a particular data point and classifying the data point according to the mainstream of the neighbors. Applications of KNN in Industry 4.0 include anomaly detection, quality control, and predictive maintenance. (Hariadhy, R. P., Sutoyo, E., & Pratiwi, O. N. 2021).

Deep Learning: It is a subset of machine learning that employs neural networks to model and solve challenging problems. It has been used in Industry 4.0 for applications such as predictive upholding, quality control, and anomaly detection (Penumuru, D. P., Muthuswamy, S., & Karumbu, P. 2020) (Penumuru, D. P., Muthuswamy, S., & Karumbu, P. 2020).

Convolutional Neural Networks: The main applications of this deep learning platform are image and video analysis. It is predicated on the idea of a convolution operation, which filters input data to extract important features. In Industry 4.0, Convolutional Neural Networks are employed for applications such as visual inspection, quality control, and defect detection (Oborski, P., & Wysocki, P. 2022).

Recurrent Neural Networks: The main application of this family of deep learning models is time-series analysis. Each time step's output is fed back into the next time step's input to make it work. Recurrent Neural Networks are us in Industry 4.0 for applications for example predictive conservation, quality control, and anomaly detection (Rivas, A.et al 2020).

One-Class Sustenance Vector Machines: One-class SVMs are a category of ML algorithms that are used for anomaly detection. They are particularly useful when only one class of data is available for training and the task is to detect outliers. In Industry 4.0, one-class SVMs are suitable for predictive maintenance and fault detection in equipment. (Mahadevan, S., & Shah, S. L. 2009).

Adversarial Autoencoders: Adversarial autoencoders are an assortment of neural networks that are trained to generate data that is similar to a given set of input data. They are particularly useful for data generation and data augmentation tasks. In Industry 4.0, adversarial autoencoders are applicable to produce artificial information for training machine learning models. (Shirazi, H., Muramudalige, S. R., Ray, I., & Jayasumana, A. P. 2020).

Graph Convolutional Networks: The neural network architecture's class is known as convolutional networks and is capable of processing data that is organized into graphs. They are particularly useful for tasks such as predicting node properties or link prediction (Li, Z., et al. 2019). In Industry 4.0, graph convolutional networks are suitable for predictive conservation in industrial equipment or supply chain optimization.

Transformer Networks: Transformer networks are a specific neural network architecture capable of processing time-series data besides text-based sequential data. They are especially beneficial for jobs involving natural language processing, like translation or sentiment analysis. In Industry 4.0, transformer networks can be utilised for predictive maintenance of industrial equipment or for analysing text data from customer feedback (Chen, C., et al., 2023).

Probabilistic Graphical Models: A probabilistic graphic model is a type of ML method that may depict intricate relationships between variables in terms of the probability. They are particularly useful for making decisions in the face of ambiguity or for modeling complex systems. In Industry 4.0, it can be utilized for predictive maintenance, supply chain optimization, or for modeling the behavior of complex manufacturing systems (Sucar, L. E. 2015).

Gated Recurrent Units with Attention: The category of RNNs that are designed to handle sequential data Deep learning employs attention techniques in order to focus only on the input data that is most pertinent to the task at hand. It has been demonstrated that the use of GRUs in conjunction with attention mechanisms is useful for a diversity of sequential data issues, including natural language processing, speech recognition, and time-series analysis (Yuan, J., & Tian, Y. 2019). In Industry 4.0, GRUs can be applied to predictive maintenance, process control, and quality control. When implementing supervised machine learning in a fourth industrial revolution setting, there are various more significant considerations that must be considered along with the algorithm selection. These involve gathering and preparing data, engineering features, choosing and assessing models, and deploying and monitoring. Every machine learning project needs to include methods for gathering and preparing data. The kind and volume of data used will have a substantial impact on the final model's accuracy and dependability. Data may be gathered from sensors, machines, or other connected devices in the Industry 4.0 aspect, and before being used in training, it might need to be cleaned, preprocessed, and transformed.

4.2 Un-Supervised Learning

Unsupervised ML is a kind of ML that focuses on finding data patterns besides relationships without using tagged examples (Angelopoulos, A. et al. 2019). Unsupervised ML algorithms is suitable for Industry 4.0 to assess massive amounts of data collected from sensors, machines, and other connected devices in order to identify patterns and anomalies, group comparable data items together, and derive insights that is suitable for enhancing manufacturing processes and efficiency. Clustering, dimensionality reduction, and anomaly detection algorithms are a few examples of Techniques for unsupervised machine learning that can be used in Industry 4.0(Chen, T., et al 2023).

Each of the algorithms listed below has advantages and disadvantages of its own, and the selection of method will depend on the particular application and the kind of data being analyzed.

Generative Adversarial Networks: This is a specific kind of deep learning algorithm that produces fake data. There are two neural networks in it that compete with one another to produce realistic synthetic data: a generator and a discriminator. Generative adversarial networks are used in Industry 4.0 for applications such as data augmentation and anomaly detection (Terziyan, V., Gryshko, S., & Golovianko, M. 2021) (Peres, R. S., et al. 2021).

Long Short-Term Memory Networks: It is a category of RNN that is used for modelling sequence data. It works by using memory cells to maintain and access data from previous time steps (Mohsen, S., Elkaseer, A., & Scholz, S. G., 2021). Industry 4.0 employs LSTM networks for tasks including anomaly detection, quality assurance, and predictive maintenance.

Capsule Networks: The capsule network is an illustration of a neural network architecture that may control hierarchical interactions between data components. They are particularly useful for object recognition tasks where it's crucial to consider the respective relative positions between object components. Capsule networks have applications in 3D object recognition, image and video analysis, and robotics (Afshar, P., Mohammadi, A., & Plataniotis, K. N. 2018).

Attention Mechanisms: It enables neural networks to concentrate only on the portions of the input data that are most important to the task at hand. They have proven to be successful in a number of tasks, including speech recognition, computer vision, and natural language processing (Soydaner, D. 2022). In Industry 4.0, attention mechanisms are suitable for anomaly detection in sensor data or to monitor equipment for predictive maintenance.

Contrastive Learning: A kind of ML called contrastive learning involves discovering data representations that are tuned for similarity or dissimilarity. For unsupervised learning tasks, it can be extremely helpful, such as clustering or dimensionality reduction (Le-Khac, P. H., Healy, G., & Smeaton, A. F. 2020). In Industry 4.0, contrastive learning is suitable for anomaly detection in sensor data or for optimizing supply chain logistics.

Self-Supervised Learning: In self-supervised learning, the model is trained without any supervision to generate predictions about the input data without any explicit labelling of the data. The model is developed using a sizable dataset with some unsupervised instances, such as forecasting the following frame of a video or filling in a missing part of an image (Doersch, C., & Zisserman,

A. 2017). Industry 4.0 uses self-supervised learning to perform activities like anomaly detection, predictive maintenance, and quality control.

Unsupervised machine learning, which does not require labels or targets, allows manufacturers to discover patterns and relationships in data. Unsupervised ML algorithms can assist manufacturers in increasing efficiency and streamlining their operations by using clustering, data preprocessing, and anomaly detection methods.

4.3 Reinforcement Learning (RL)

Machine learning techniques like reinforcement learning (RL), which prepares agents to make choices based on their environment, are ideal for Industry 4.0 applications. RL algorithms execute actions iteratively while getting feedback as rewards or penalties. This is done in order to maximise the cumulative reward over time. Several Industry 4.0 applications can benefit from the use of RL algorithms, such as supply chain management, process control, and robotics (Kegyes, T., Süle, Z., & Abonyi, J. 2021). The behaviour of robots in a factory, for instance, can be optimised using RL algorithms so that they can learn to navigate challenging surroundings and carry out jobs more effectively.

Deep Reinforcement Learning (DRL): It is indeed an application of artificial intelligence used to make decisions in uncertain circumstances. It works by using trial and error to learn the optimal actions to take in a given environment. DRL is used in Industry 4.0 for uses like robotic autonomy and preventive maintenance (Arulkumaran, K., Deisenroth, M. P., Brundage, M., & Bharath, A. A. 2017).

Continual Learning: A type of ML called "continuous learning" involves training the model on a series of tasks, each of which is learned from a separate dataset. Constructing a model is the goal that performs admirably in every situation, even when additional tasks are gradually added. Continual learning is useful in Industry 4.0, where there are constantly changing environments and new data streams (Pianykh, O. S., et al. 2020). It is suitable for tasks such as predictive maintenance, process control, and quality control.

Causal Inference: Causal inference is one kind of statistical analysis that aims to determine that two random variables are related casually. In Industry 4.0, causal inference is suitable for determining the factors that contribute to a particular outcome, such as equipment failure or production line downtime. This information is subsequently used to optimise processes, improve product quality, and reduce costs. Causal inference is also useful for predictive maintenance and process control (Kuang, K., et al. 2020).

Federated Learning: A type of ML called "federated learning" includes training models on various hardware or software without centralised data storage. It enables machine learning that protects privacy and can be especially helpful in circumstances when data cannot be easily centralised. Federated learning is a tool in Industry 4.0 that is suitable for data analysis from several sensors or for predictive maintenance across various plants (Pham, Q. V., et al., 2021) (Li, T., Sahu, A. K., Talwalkar, A., & Smith, V., 2020). In Industry 4.0 environments, RL possesses the potential to significantly enhance productivity, flexibility, and efficiency. RL algorithms can aid manufacturers in streamlining their processes and boosting their bottom line by enabling agents to learn from their surroundings and adapt to changing situations.All three key categories of machine learning algorithms—supervised, unsupervised, and reinforcement learning—can be applied in Industry 4.0.

In two primary approaches to machine learning, unsupervised learning finds data patterns without explicit labeling, while supervised learning trains the model using a lot of labelled data. While supervised learning excels at process optimization, quality assurance, and predictive maintenance, unsupervised learning is intended for dimensionality reduction, clustering, and anomaly detection. Reinforcement learning creates an autonomous decision-maker depending on its environment, making it the best method for managing robotic arms and optimizing production lines. Reinforcement learning algorithms, however, can be costly to train computationally and require a clearly defined reward function. All ML algorithms have different strengths and weaknesses. Although labelled data is needed, supervised learning is effective for classification and prediction. Anomaly identification and dimension reduction are made easier by unsupervised learning, although assessment can be difficult. Though costly to train, reinforcement learning can improve control. The application and type of data being analysed will determine the algorithm to use. Table 2 illustrates the various machine learning algorithms positive aspects and anomalies.

Table 2. Strength and drawbacks of machine learning algorithms

Machine Learning Algorithm	Strength	Drawbacks
Random Forest	Handles high dimensional datasets	Computationally expensive and can overfit the data
Support Vector Machines	Effective in high dimensional spaces and good at handling non-linear data	Requires careful tuning of parameters and can be sensitive to outliers
AdaBoost	Creates a powerful classifier from weak ones and handles noisy data well	Can be sensitive to outliers and can overfit the data
Gradient Boosting Machines	Good for a diverse array of supervised learning problems and handles missing data well	Can be sensitive to outliers and can overfit the data
K-Nearest Neighbors	Simple and easy to implement and good for small datasets	Can be sensitive to outliers and does not work well with high dimensional data
Deep Learning	for a variety of applications, powerful and adaptable	requires a lot of data, thus it can be expensive to compute.
Convolutional Neural Networks	Recognizes images and videos well, and effectively manages translation invariance	requires a lot of data, thus it can be expensive to compute.
Recurrent Neural Networks	is suitable for sequential data and handles variable-length input well	Can be computationally expensive and difficult to train
Generative Adversarial Networks	Can generate high-quality, realistic data and can learn complex data distributions	Can be difficult to train and prone to mode collapse
Long Short-Term Memory Networks	Good for time series and sequence prediction problems and handles long-term dependencies well	Can be computationally expensive and requires careful parameter tuning
Deep Reinforcement Learning	Effective for decision-making problems, can learn complex policies and handle high-dimensional inputs	requires a lot of training data, which might be expensive computationally.
Capsule Networks	Good at handling complex hierarchical structures, can capture spatial relationships effectively	Limited empirical evidence and not yet widely adopted
Attention Mechanisms	Good at capturing dependencies between inputs, improves model interpretability	Can be computationally expensive and difficult to train
One-Class Support Vector Machines	Good for anomaly detection, handles high-dimensional data well	Requires careful selection of kernel functions and can be sensitive to the choice of parameters
Adversarial Autoencoders	Can generate high-quality, realistic data, good for unsupervised learning	Difficult to train and can be sensitive to the choice of hyperparameters
Graph Convolutional Networks	Good for modeling graph-structured data, can handle variable-size inputs	Limited empirical evidence and not yet widely adopted
Meta-Learning	Can learn new tasks quickly, effective for few-shot learning	Requires a large amount of data and can be computationally expensive
Federated Learning	Enables model training without sharing data, good for privacy protection	Requires a large number of participating devices and can be computationally expensive
Transformer Networks	Good for sequence-to-sequence learning, effective for natural language processing	Can be computationally expensive and difficult to train
Contrastive Learning	Can learn useful representations without labeled data, effective for transfer learning	Requires careful selection of hyperparameters and can be computationally expensive
Probabilistic Graphical Models	Enables probabilistic reasoning and uncertainty quantification, effective for Bayesian inference	Can be computationally expensive and difficult to train
Self-Supervised Learning	Can learn from unlabeled data, good for transfer learning and data augmentation	Requires a large amount of training data and can be computationally expensive
Gated Recurrent Units with Attention	Good at handling sequential data, can learn long-term dependencies	Can be computationally expensive and requires careful tuning of hyperparameters
Continual Learning	Enables learning from non-stationary data, good for lifelong learning	Requires careful selection of regularization techniques and can be computationally expensive
Causal Inference	Enables understanding of causal relationships, effective for decision-making	Requires careful selection of causal models and can be computationally expensive

5. PERFORMANCE REVIEW OF ML ALGORITHMS

High-accuracy prediction and classification jobs benefit from supervised learning, but it also comes with enormous labelling requirements and potential overfitting issues. Unsupervised learning is helpful for tasks involving anomaly detection, clustering, and dimensionality reduction, but it may not be appropriate for jobs involving prediction or classification, and it can be challenging to assess. Reinforcement learning is helpful for control and optimization tasks, but it requires a clearly specified reward function and is computationally expensive to train. In conclusion, each form of ML algorithm in Industry 4.0 offers unique benefits and drawbacks, and the selection of algorithm is based on the particular application and type of data being analysed. Unsupervised learning can manage vast volumes of unstructured data but may struggle with structured data, whereas supervised learning can handle massive amounts of features and data but needs labelled data. Although reinforcement learning can handle problems involving sequential decision-making, it may not be able to adapt well to novel environments. Table 3 elaborates the efficiency of various machine learning algorithms based on various factors.

Table 3. Review on machine learning's effectiveness

Machine Learning Algorithm	Speed	Accuracy	Computation Overhead	Performance Rating
Random Forest	Fast	High	Low	Excellent
Support Vector Machines (SVM)	Medium	High	Medium	Good
AdaBoost	Fast	High	Low	Excellent
Gradient Boosting Machines	Medium	High	Medium	Good
K-Nearest Neighbors (KNN)	Slow	Medium	Low	Fair
Deep Learning	Slow	High	High	Good
Neural networks with convolutions	Slow	High	High	Good
Recurrent Neural Networks (RNN)	Slow	High	High	Good
Generative Adversarial Networks	Slow	High	High	Good
Long Short-Term Memory Networks (LSTM)	Slow	High	High	Good
Deep Reinforcement Learning	Slow	High	High	Good
Capsule Networks	Slow	High	High	Good
Attention Mechanisms	Slow	High	High	Good
One-Class Support Vector Machines	Medium	Medium	Medium	Fair
Adversarial Autoencoders	Slow	High	High	Good
Graph Convolutional Networks	Slow	High	High	Good
Meta-Learning	Slow	High	High	Good
Federated Learning	Medium	High	Medium	Good
Transformer Networks	Slow	High	High	Good
Contrastive Learning	Slow	High	High	Good
Probabilistic Graphical Models	Medium	High	Medium	Good
Self-Supervised Learning	Slow	High	High	Good
Gated Recurrent Units with Attention	Slow	High	High	Good
Continual Learning	Slow	High	High	Good
Causal Inference	Medium	High	Medium	Good

6. PROBLEMS STATEMENT: MACHINE LEARNING ALGORITHMS IN MANUFACTURING PROCESS

Businesses are increasingly looking for methods to integrate machine learning algorithms into their operations as Industry 4.0 continues to revolutionize the manufacturing industry. These algorithms may improve productivity, boost effectiveness, and cut costs in the production process. It can be challenging for organizations to decide which algorithms are the best fit for their unique requirements, though, given the wide variety of algorithms now in use and the constant development of new ones. Implementing and integrating these algorithms with current systems and workflows may also present difficulties. This raises the issue of what the best practices are for integrating these algorithms into business processes, as well as how firms can effectively evaluate and select machine learning algorithms for their industry. 4.0 attempts. How can businesses ensure that these algorithms are providing accurate insights and suggestions while also reducing potential risks like concerns about data privacy and security? Businesses that want to take advantage of Industry 4.0's machine learning processes and maintain their competitiveness in an increasingly digital environment must address these issues.

7. PROPOSED SOLUTION

High-accuracy prediction and classification jobs benefit from supervised learning, but it also comes with enormous labelling requirements and potential overfitting issues. Unsupervised learning is helpful for tasks involving anomaly detection, clustering, and dimensionality reduction, but it may not be appropriate for jobs involving prediction or classification, and it can be challenging to assess. Reinforcement learning is helpful for control and optimization tasks, but it requires a clearly specified reward function and is computationally expensive to train. In conclusion, each form of ML algorithm in Industry 4.0 offers unique benefits and drawbacks, and the selection of algorithm is based on the particular application and type of data being analyzed. Unsupervised learning can manage vast volumes of unstructured data but may struggle with structured data, whereas supervised learning can handle massive amounts of features and data but needs labelled data. Although reinforcement learning can handle problems involving sequential decision-making, it may not be able to adapt well to novel environments.

8. FUTURE SCOPE

Industry 4.0 holds a vast and promising future for machine learning algorithms. Deep learning, convolutional neural networks, generative adversarial networks, and federated learning are several of the top algorithms that have a lot of promise for use in the future. Applications for these algorithms include anomaly detection, quality control, and predictive maintenance, among others. They have demonstrated excellent promise for enhancing operational effectiveness, cutting expenses, and raising overall productivity. These algorithms are anticipated to develop in sophistication, accuracy, and dependability over the next few years as technology and data availability progress, boosting the likelihood of their widespread use in industry 4.0. Support vector machines, random forests, and K-nearest neighbors are examples of the other ML techniques that are anticipated to be employed in Industry 4.0, but to a lesser extent than among the more sophisticated methods. These techniques are well-known and have been extensively used in a diversity of applications, such as problem detection, quality control, and preventative maintenance. However, to effectively investigate and understand data in Industry 4.0, it might be necessary to rely on more sophisticated algorithms, like deep learning and convolutional neural networks. As a result, even though these algorithms will probably continue to play a part in Industry 4.0, their application may be constrained as more sophisticated algorithms gain popularity.

9. CONCLUSION

As more individuals become aware of the fourth industrial revolution, IM is becoming a more significant concept in the development of the modern economy and industry. Since it aids diverse systems and prototypes by merging cutting-edge innovations into conventional production and service prototypes, IM is regarded as a leading perspective for the future in terms of experimentation and application. This research explored the concepts of smart production systems using machine learning with an Industry 4.0 approach. The chapter highlighted the number of ML algorithms developed to handle a variety of issues and applications. Future research will concentrate on improving the efficiency and comprehension of algorithms in intelligent manufacturing processes, as each algorithm has benefits and drawbacks, and the choice of an algorithm depends on the objective and the data at hand. Thus, research analyzed the various ML algorithms' performance with certain factors and proposed the solution of a hybrid approach of supervised and unsupervised learning in intelligent manufacturing, the Industry 4.0 approach. Lastly, it is concluded that to effectively analyze and interpret data in Industry 4.0, it might be necessary to rely on more sophisticated algorithms, like deep learning and convolutional neural networks.

REFERENCES

Aberle, L. (2015). A comprehensive guide to enterprise IoT project success. *IoT Agenda, 1.*

Afshar, P., Mohammadi, A., & Plataniotis, K. N. (2018, October). Brain tumor type classification via capsule networks. In *2018 25th IEEE international conference on image processing (ICIP)* (pp. 3129-3133). IEEE. 10.1109/ICIP.2018.8451379

Agarwal, R., & Weill, P. (2012). The benefits of combining data with empathy. *MIT Sloan Management Review*, *54*(1), 35.

Angelopoulos, A., Michailidis, E. T., Nomikos, N., Trakadas, P., Hatziefremidis, A., Voliotis, S., & Zahariadis, T. (2019). Tackling faults in the industry 4.0 era—A survey of machine-learning solutions and key aspects. *Sensors (Basel)*, *20*(1), 109. doi:10.3390/s20010109 PMID:31878065

Arulkumaran, K., Deisenroth, M. P., Brundage, M., & Bharath, A. A. (2017). Deep reinforcement learning: A brief survey. *IEEE Signal Processing Magazine*, *34*(6), 26–38. doi:10.1109/MSP.2017.2743240

Ayvaz, S., & Alpay, K. (2021). Predictive maintenance system for production lines in manufacturing: A machine learning approach using IoT data in real-time. *Expert Systems with Applications*, *173*, 114598. doi:10.1016/j.eswa.2021.114598

Barton, D., & Court, D. (2012). Making advanced analytics work for you. *Harvard Business Review, 90*(10), 78–83. PMID:23074867

Bécue, A., Praça, I., & Gama, J. (2021). Artificial intelligence, cyber-threats and Industry 4.0: Challenges and opportunities. *Artificial Intelligence Review, 54*(5), 3849–3886. doi:10.1007/s10462-020-09942-2

Bo-Hu, L. I., Lin, Z., Shi-Long, W., Fei, T., Jun-wei, C. A. O., Xiao-dan, J., ... Xu-dong, C. (2010). Cloud manufacturing: a new service-oriented networked manufacturing model. *Computer Integrated Manufacturing System, 16*(1).

Borregan-Alvarado, J., Alvarez-Meaza, I., Cilleruelo-Carrasco, E., & Garechana-Anacabe, G. (2020). A bibliometric analysis in industry 4.0 and advanced manufacturing: What about the sustainable supply chain? *Sustainability (Basel), 12*(19), 7840. doi:10.3390/su12197840

Boyes, H., Hallaq, B., Cunningham, J., & Watson, T. (2018). The industrial internet of things (IIoT): An analysis framework. *Computers in Industry, 101*, 1–12. doi:10.1016/j.compind.2018.04.015

Brown, B., Chui, M., & Manyika, J. (2011). Are you ready for the era of 'big data'. *The McKinsey Quarterly, 4*(1), 24–35.

Carvalho, T. P., Soares, F. A., Vita, R., Francisco, R. D. P., Basto, J. P., & Alcalá, S. G. (2019). A systematic literature review of machine learning methods applied to predictive maintenance. *Computers & Industrial Engineering, 137*, 106024. doi:10.1016/j.cie.2019.106024

Chamasemani, F. F., & Singh, Y. P. (2011, September). Multi-class support vector machine (SVM) classifiers--an application in hypothyroid detection and classification. In *2011 sixth international conference on bio-inspired computing: theories and applications* (pp. 351-356). IEEE.

Chen, C., Liu, C., Wang, T., Zhang, A., Wu, W., & Cheng, L. (2023). Compound fault diagnosis for industrial robots based on dual-transformer networks. *Journal of Manufacturing Systems, 66*, 163–178. doi:10.1016/j.jmsy.2022.12.006

Doersch, C., & Zisserman, A. (2017). Multi-task self-supervised visual learning. In *Proceedings of the IEEE international conference on computer vision* (pp. 2051-2060). IEEE.

Dorsemaine, B., Gaulier, J. P., Wary, J. P., Kheir, N., & Urien, P. (2015, September). Internet of things: a definition & taxonomy. In *2015 9th International Conference on Next Generation Mobile Applications, Services and Technologies* (pp. 72-77). IEEE. 10.1109/NGMAST.2015.71

Giallanza, A., Aiello, G., & Marannano, G. (2021). Industry 4.0: Advanced digital solutions implemented on a close power loop test bench. *Procedia Computer Science, 180*, 93–101. doi:10.1016/j.procs.2021.01.133

Glaessgen, E., & Stargel, D. (2012, April). The digital twin paradigm for future NASA and US Air Force vehicles. In *53rd AIAA/ASME/ASCE/AHS/ASC structures, structural dynamics and materials conference 20th AIAA/ASME/AHS adaptive structures conference 14th AIAA* (p. 1818). Academic Press.

Gyrard, A., Datta, S. K., Bonnet, C., & Boudaoud, K. (2015, August). Cross-domain Internet of Things application development: M3 framework and evaluation. In *2015 3rd International conference on future Internet of Things and Cloud* (pp. 9-16). IEEE.

Hariadhy, R. P., Sutoyo, E., & Pratiwi, O. N. (2021). Application of K-Nearest Neighbor Algorithm for Prediction of Television Advertisement Rating. In *International Conference on Emerging Applications and Technologies for Industry 4.0 (EATI'2020) Emerging Applications and Technologies for Industry 4.0* (pp. 82-91). Springer International Publishing. 10.1007/978-3-030-80216-5_7

Helmiö, P. (2017). *Open source in industrial internet of things: A systematic literature review*. Academic Press.

Huang, W., Shuai, B., Wang, L., & Antwi, E. (2017). Railway container station reselection approach and application: Based on entropy-cloud model. *Mathematical Problems in Engineering, 2017*, 2017. doi:10.1155/2017/8701081

Kamble, S. S., Gunasekaran, A., & Gawankar, S. A. (2018). Sustainable Industry 4.0 framework: A systematic literature review identifying the current trends and future perspectives. *Process Safety and Environmental Protection, 117*, 408–425. doi:10.1016/j.psep.2018.05.009

Kegyes, T., Süle, Z., & Abonyi, J. (2021). The applicability of reinforcement learning methods in the development of industry 4.0 applications. *Complexity, 2021*, 1–31. doi:10.1155/2021/7179374

Kiangala, S. K., & Wang, Z. (2021). An effective adaptive customization framework for small manufacturing plants using extreme gradient boosting-XGBoost and random forest ensemble learning algorithms in an Industry 4.0 environment. *Machine Learning with Applications, 4*, 100024. doi:10.1016/j.mlwa.2021.100024

Kotsiopoulos, T., Sarigiannidis, P., Ioannidis, D., & Tzovaras, D. (2021). Machine learning and deep learning in smart manufacturing: The smart grid paradigm. *Computer Science Review, 40*, 100341. doi:10.1016/j.cosrev.2020.100341

Kuang, K., Li, L., Geng, Z., Xu, L., Zhang, K., Liao, B., Huang, H., Ding, P., Miao, W., & Jiang, Z. (2020). Causal inference. *Engineering (Beijing), 6*(3), 253–263. doi:10.1016/j.eng.2019.08.016

Le-Khac, P. H., Healy, G., & Smeaton, A. F. (2020). Contrastive representation learning: A framework and review. *IEEE Access : Practical Innovations, Open Solutions, 8*, 193907–193934. doi:10.1109/ACCESS.2020.3031549

Lee, C. Y., Lin, J. Y., & Chang, R. I. (2018). Improve quality and efficiency of textile process using data-driven machine learning in industry 4.0. *International Journal of Technology and Engineering Studies, 4*(2), 4–10004.

Lee, J., Azamfar, M., & Singh, J. (2019). A blockchain enabled Cyber-Physical System architecture for Industry 4.0 manufacturing systems. *Manufacturing Letters, 20*, 34–39. doi:10.1016/j.mfglet.2019.05.003

Lee, J., Lapira, E., Bagheri, B., & Kao, H. A. (2013). Recent advances and trends in predictive manufacturing systems in big data environment. *Manufacturing Letters, 1*(1), 38–41. doi:10.1016/j.mfglet.2013.09.005

Lee, J., Ni, J., Djurdjanovic, D., Qiu, H., & Liao, H. (2006). Intelligent prognostics tools and e-maintenance. *Computers in Industry, 57*(6), 476–489. doi:10.1016/j.compind.2006.02.014

Lee, J., Wu, F., Zhao, W., Ghaffari, M., Liao, L., & Siegel, D. (2014). Prognostics and health management design for rotary machinery systems—Reviews, methodology and applications. *Mechanical Systems and Signal Processing*, *42*(1-2), 314–334. doi:10.1016/j.ymssp.2013.06.004

Li, T., Sahu, A. K., Talwalkar, A., & Smith, V. (2020). Federated learning: Challenges, methods, and future directions. *IEEE Signal Processing Magazine*, *37*(3), 50–60. doi:10.1109/MSP.2020.2975749

Li, Z., Liu, Z., Huang, J., Tang, G., Duan, Y., Zhang, Z., & Yang, Y. (2019). MV-GCN: Multi-view graph convolutional networks for link prediction. *IEEE Access : Practical Innovations, Open Solutions*, *7*, 176317–176328. doi:10.1109/ACCESS.2019.2957306

Liu, Y., & Xu, X. (2017). Industry 4.0 and cloud manufacturing: A comparative analysis. *Journal of Manufacturing Science and Engineering*, *139*(3), 034701. doi:10.1115/1.4034667

Machado, C. G., Winroth, M. P., & Ribeiro da Silva, E. H. D. (2020). Sustainable manufacturing in Industry 4.0: An emerging research agenda. *International Journal of Production Research*, *58*(5), 1462–1484. doi:10.1080/00207543.2019.1652777

Mahadevan, S., & Shah, S. L. (2009). Fault detection and diagnosis in process data using one-class support vector machines. *Journal of Process Control*, *19*(10), 1627–1639. doi:10.1016/j.jprocont.2009.07.011

Makkar, S., Devi, G. N. R., & Solanki, V. K. (2020). Applications of machine learning techniques in supply chain optimization. In ICICCT 2019–System Reliability, Quality Control, Safety, Maintenance and Management: Applications to Electrical, Electronics and Computer Science and Engineering (pp. 861-869). Springer Singapore. doi:10.1007/978-981-13-8461-5_98

Mallozzi, P. (2017, May). Combining machine-learning with invariants assurance techniques for autonomous systems. In *2017 IEEE/ACM 39th International Conference on Software Engineering Companion (ICSE-C)* (pp. 485-486). IEEE. 10.1109/ICSE-C.2017.40

Melkote, S., Liang, S. Y., Ozel, T., Jawahir, I. S., Stephenson, D. A., & Wang, B. (2022). A review of advances in modeling of conventional machining processes: From merchant to the present. *Journal of Manufacturing Science and Engineering*, 1–49.

Mohsen, S., Elkaseer, A., & Scholz, S. G. (2021). Industry 4.0-oriented deep learning models for human activity recognition. *IEEE Access : Practical Innovations, Open Solutions*, *9*, 150508–150521. doi:10.1109/ACCESS.2021.3125733

Oborski, P., & Wysocki, P. (2022). Intelligent Visual Quality Control System Based on Convolutional Neural Networks for Holonic Shop Floor Control of Industry 4.0 Manufacturing Systems. *Advances in Science and Technology. The R Journal*, *16*(2), 89–98.

Oztemel, E. (2010). Intelligent manufacturing systems. *Artificial intelligence techniques for networked manufacturing enterprises management*, 1-41.

Oztemel, E., & Gursev, S. (2020). Literature review of Industry 4.0 and related technologies. *Journal of Intelligent Manufacturing*, *31*(1), 127–182. doi:10.1007/s10845-018-1433-8

Pan, Y. (2016). Heading toward artificial intelligence 2.0. *Engineering (Beijing)*, *2*(4), 409–413. doi:10.1016/J.ENG.2016.04.018

Patil, P. S., Patil, M. S., Tamhankar, S. G., & Patil, S. S. (2020). Ensembles of ensemble machine learning approach for fault detection of bearing. *Solid State Technology, 63*(6), 14442–14455.

Penumuru, D. P., Muthuswamy, S., & Karumbu, P. (2020). Identification and classification of materials using machine vision and machine learning in the context of industry 4.0. *Journal of Intelligent Manufacturing, 31*(5), 1229–1241. doi:10.1007/s10845-019-01508-6

Peres, R. S., Azevedo, M., Araújo, S. O., Guedes, M., Miranda, F., & Barata, J. (2021). Generative adversarial networks for data augmentation in structural adhesive inspection. *Applied Sciences (Basel, Switzerland), 11*(7), 3086. doi:10.3390/app11073086

Peres, R. S., Barata, J., Leitao, P., & Garcia, G. (2019). Multistage quality control using machine learning in the automotive industry. *IEEE Access : Practical Innovations, Open Solutions, 7*, 79908–79916. doi:10.1109/ACCESS.2019.2923405

Pham, Q. V., Dev, K., Maddikunta, P. K. R., Gadekallu, T. R., & Huynh-The, T. (2021). Fusion of federated learning and industrial internet of things: a survey. *arXiv preprint arXiv:2101.00798.*

Pianykh, O. S., Langs, G., Dewey, M., Enzmann, D. R., Herold, C. J., Schoenberg, S. O., & Brink, J. A. (2020). Continuous learning AI in radiology: Implementation principles and early applications. *Radiology, 297*(1), 6–14. doi:10.1148/radiol.2020200038 PMID:32840473

Rivas, A., Fraile, J. M., Chamoso, P., González-Briones, A., Sittón, I., & Corchado, J. M. (2020). A predictive maintenance model using recurrent neural networks. In *14th International Conference on Soft Computing Models in Industrial and Environmental Applications (SOCO 2019) Seville, Spain, May 13–15, 2019, Proceedings 14* (pp. 261-270). Springer International Publishing.10.1007/978-3-030-20055-8_25

Sarker, I. H. (2021). Machine learning: Algorithms, real-world applications and research directions. *SN Computer Science, 2*(3), 160. doi:10.1007/s42979-021-00592-x PMID:33778771

Schleich, B., Anwer, N., Mathieu, L., & Wartzack, S. (2017). Shaping the digital twin for design and production engineering. *CIRP Annals, 66*(1), 141–144. doi:10.1016/j.cirp.2017.04.040

Shirazi, H., Muramudalige, S. R., Ray, I., & Jayasumana, A. P. (2020, November). Improved phishing detection algorithms using adversarial autoencoder synthesized data. In *2020 IEEE 45th conference on local computer networks (LCN)* (pp. 24-32). IEEE. 10.1109/LCN48667.2020.9314775

Skordilis, E., & Moghaddass, R. (2020). A deep reinforcement learning approach for real-time sensor-driven decision making and predictive analytics. *Computers & Industrial Engineering, 147*, 106600. doi:10.1016/j.cie.2020.106600

Soydaner, D. (2022). Attention mechanism in neural networks: Where it comes and where it goes. *Neural Computing & Applications, 34*(16), 13371–13385. doi:10.1007/s00521-022-07366-3

Sucar, L. E. (2015). Probabilistic graphical models. *Advances in Computer Vision and Pattern Recognition. London. Springer London., 1.* Advance online publication. 10(978)

Tao, F., Cheng, J., Qi, Q., Zhang, M., Zhang, H., & Sui, F. (2018). Digital twin-driven product design, manufacturing, and service with big data. *International Journal of Advanced Manufacturing Technology, 94*(9-12), 3563–3576. doi:10.1007/s00170-017-0233-1

Tao, F., Zhang, L., Venkatesh, V. C., Luo, Y., & Cheng, Y. (2011). Cloud manufacturing: A computing and service-oriented manufacturing model. *Proceedings of the Institution of Mechanical Engineers. Part B, Journal of Engineering Manufacture*, *225*(10), 1969–1976. doi:10.1177/0954405411405575

Tao, F., Zhang, M., Cheng, J., & Qi, Q. (2017). Digital twin workshop: A new paradigm for a future workshop. *Jisuanji Jicheng Zhizao Xitong*, *23*, 1–9.

Terziyan, V., Gryshko, S., & Golovianko, M. (2021). Taxonomy of generative adversarial networks for digital immunity of Industry 4.0 systems. *Procedia Computer Science*, *180*, 676–685. doi:10.1016/j.procs.2021.01.290

Thramboulidis, K., Vachtsevanou, D. C., & Kontou, I. C. (2019). PuS-IoT: A Cyber-Physical Microservice and IoT-Based Framework for Manufacturing Assembly Systems. *Annual Reviews in Control*, *2019*(47), 237–248. doi:10.1016/j.arcontrol.2019.03.005

Tran, M. Q., Elsisi, M., Mahmoud, K., Liu, M. K., Lehtonen, M., & Darwish, M. M. (2021). Experimental setup for online fault diagnosis of induction machines via promising IoT and machine learning: Towards industry 4.0 empowerment. *IEEE Access : Practical Innovations, Open Solutions*, *9*, 115429–115441. doi:10.1109/ACCESS.2021.3105297

Uhlemann, T. H. J., Lehmann, C., & Steinhilper, R. (2017). The digital twin: Realizing the cyber-physical production system for industry 4.0. *Procedia CIRP*, *61*, 335–340. doi:10.1016/j.procir.2016.11.152

Valilai, O. F., & Houshmand, M. (2013). A collaborative and integrated platform to support distributed manufacturing system using a service-oriented approach based on cloud computing paradigm. *Robotics and Computer-integrated Manufacturing*, *29*(1), 110–127. doi:10.1016/j.rcim.2012.07.009

Vassakis, K., Petrakis, E., & Kopanakis, I. (2018). Big data analytics: applications, prospects and challenges. *Mobile big data: A roadmap from models to technologies*, 3-20.

Wang, B., Tao, F., Fang, X., Liu, C., Liu, Y., & Freiheit, T. (2021). Smart manufacturing and intelligent manufacturing: A comparative review. *Engineering (Beijing)*, *7*(6), 738–757. doi:10.1016/j.eng.2020.07.017

Wang, J., Ma, Y., Zhang, L., Gao, R. X., & Wu, D. (2018). Deep learning for smart manufacturing: Methods and applications. *Journal of Manufacturing Systems*, *48*, 144–156. doi:10.1016/j.jmsy.2018.01.003

Wang, L. (2019). From intelligence science to intelligent manufacturing. *Engineering (Beijing)*, *5*(4), 615–618. doi:10.1016/j.eng.2019.04.011

Wang, S., Wan, J., Zhang, D., Li, D., & Zhang, C. (2016). Towards smart factory for industry 4.0: A self-organized multi-agent system with big data based feedback and coordination. *Computer Networks*, *101*, 158–168. doi:10.1016/j.comnet.2015.12.017

Wu, D., Rosen, D. W., Wang, L., & Schaefer, D. (2015). Cloud-based design and manufacturing: A new paradigm in digital manufacturing and design innovation. *Computer Aided Design*, *59*, 1–14. doi:10.1016/j.cad.2014.07.006

Xu, X. (2012). From cloud computing to cloud manufacturing. *Robotics and Computer-integrated Manufacturing*, *28*(1), 75–86. doi:10.1016/j.rcim.2011.07.002

Yao, Y. L., Cheng, G. J., Rajurkar, K. P., Kovacevic, R., Feiner, S., & Zhang, W. (2005). Combined research and curriculum development of nontraditional manufacturing. *European Journal of Engineering Education, 30*(3), 363–376. doi:10.1080/03043790500114581

Yuan, J., & Tian, Y. (2019). An intelligent fault diagnosis method using GRU neural network towards sequential data in dynamic processes. *Processes (Basel, Switzerland), 7*(3), 152. doi:10.3390/pr7030152

Zhang, L., Luo, Y., Tao, F., Li, B. H., Ren, L., Zhang, X., Guo, H., Cheng, Y., Hu, A., & Liu, Y. (2014). Cloud manufacturing: A new manufacturing paradigm. *Enterprise Information Systems, 8*(2), 167–187. doi:10.1080/17517575.2012.683812

Zheng, Y., Yang, S., & Cheng, H. (2019). An application framework of digital twin and its case study J. *Journal of Ambient Intelligence and Humanized Computing, 10*(3), 1141–1153. doi:10.1007/s12652-018-0911-3

Zhong, R. Y., Xu, X., Klotz, E., & Newman, S. T. (2017). Intelligent manufacturing in the context of Industry 4.0: A review. *Engineering (Beijing), 3*(5), 616–630. doi:10.1016/J.ENG.2017.05.015

Zhong, R. Y., Xu, X., Klotz, E., & Newman, S. T. (2017). Newman, S.T. Intelligent Manufacturing in the Context of Industry 4.0: A Review. *Engineering (Beijing), 2017*(3), 616–630. doi:10.1016/J.ENG.2017.05.015

Zhou, J., Li, P., Zhou, Y., Wang, B., Zang, J., & Meng, L. (2018). Toward new-generation intelligent manufacturing. *Engineering (Beijing), 4*(1), 11–20. doi:10.1016/j.eng.2018.01.002

Chapter 5
Sustainability in the Digital Age: Harnessing Industry 4.0 Technologies for Responsible Supply Chains

Siva Raja Sindiramutty
Taylor's University, Malaysia

Goh Wei Wei
Taylor's University, Malaysia

NZ Jhanjhi
https://orcid.org/0000-0001-8116-4733
Taylor's University, Malaysia

Norhidayah Hamzah
https://orcid.org/0009-0002-2715-001X
Taylor's University, Malaysia

Chong Eng Tan
https://orcid.org/0000-0002-3990-3501
Universiti Malaysia Sarawak, Malaysia

Rehan Akbar
https://orcid.org/0000-0002-3703-5974
Florida International University, USA

ABSTRACT

This chapter explores the convergence of Industry 4.0 technologies and sustainable supply chain practices, presenting a comprehensive overview of these digital advancements' transformative potential. The chapter begins by defining the intersection between sustainability and Industry 4.0, emphasizing the pivotal role of digital technologies in fostering environmentally and socially responsible supply chains. With clear objectives in mind, the exploration delves into the impact of key digital technologies on responsible supply chain practices. The discussion spans the utilization of the internet of things (IoT) for real-time sustainability monitoring, big data analytics for informed decision-making, and the integration of robotics to enhance ethical manufacturing.

DOI: 10.4018/979-8-3693-1363-3.ch005

INTRODUCTION

Definition and Significance

Overview of the Intersection Between Sustainability and Industry 4.0 Technologies

The intersection of sustainability and Industry 4.0 technologies marks a significant turning point in today's industrial landscape. Industry 4.0, characterized by the amalgamation of digital technologies, automation, and data exchange in manufacturing, has the potential to revolutionize traditional industrial practices towards more sustainable and environmentally conscious outcomes (Duan et al., 2024). This report explores the intricate relationship between sustainability and Industry 4.0 technologies, shedding light on critical aspects and their implications. One notable contribution of Industry 4.0 to sustainability lies in resource efficiency. Smart manufacturing processes, enabled by technologies such as the IoT and Artificial Intelligence (AI), allow for real-time monitoring and optimization of resource usage (Haval & Rahman, 2024). This leads to reduced waste, lower energy consumption, and increased efficiency in production systems. Moreover, the adoption of Industry 4.0 aligns with the principles of the circular economy, advocating for the reuse, recycling, and repurposing of materials. By integrating sensors and connectivity into production systems, manufacturers can monitor and manage the entire lifecycle of products, promoting a more sustainable, closed-loop approach (Kazançoğlu et al., 2021; Adeyemo et al., 2019).

Industry 4.0 technologies also enable predictive maintenance through continuous monitoring and analysis of equipment performance. This proactive approach not only enhances operational efficiency but also minimizes downtime and extends the lifespan of machinery, contributing to sustainable resource utilization. Furthermore, the integration of sustainability into Industry 4.0 extends beyond individual factories to encompass entire supply chains. Smart supply chain management, powered by technologies like blockchain and RFID, improves traceability and transparency, aiding companies in making environmentally conscious decisions (Ahmed et al., 2023; Alferidah & Jhanjhi, 2020). Sustainability within the context of Industry 4.0 also prioritizes the workforce. The emphasis on human-centric design in smart factories ensures that technologies enhance worker well-being and productivity, aligning with social sustainability goals (Agote-Garrido et al., 2023; Aljohani, 2023; Alkinani et al., 2021).

In conclusion, the convergence of sustainability and Industry 4.0 technologies holds immense promise for cultivating a more eco-friendly and socially responsible industrial landscape. From optimizing resource efficiency and integrating circular economy principles to enabling predictive maintenance and implementing smart supply chains, Industry 4.0 technologies offer a versatile approach to achieving sustainable development objectives.

Figure 1. Intersection between sustainability and Industry 4.0 technologies (Hassoun et al., 2022)

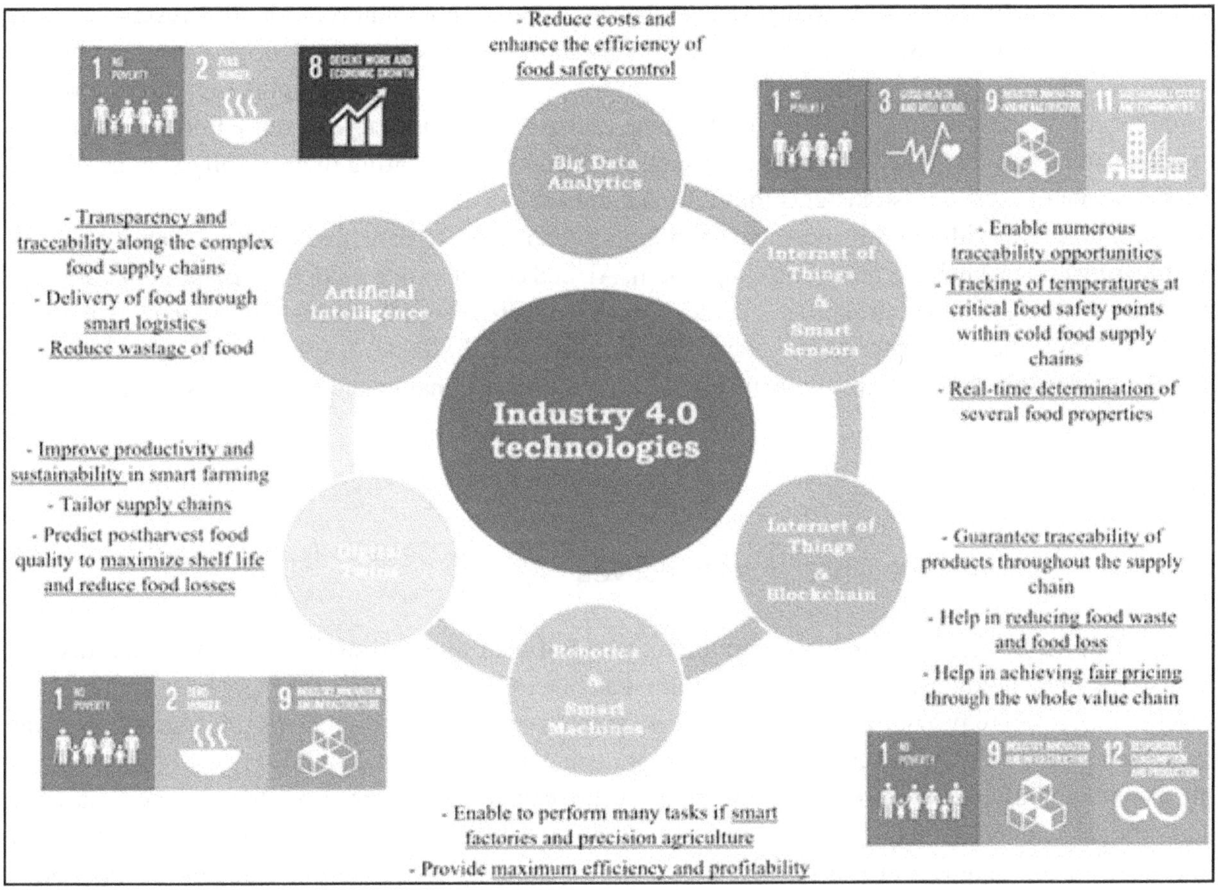

The Transformative Role of Digital Advancements in Fostering Responsible Supply Chain Practices

The advent of digital innovations has emerged as a significant force in reshaping the realm of supply chain management, serving as a linchpin in cultivating ethical business practices. This paradigm shift is propelled not solely by the pursuit of efficiency and cost-effectiveness but also by the escalating emphasis on sustainability and ethical considerations within supply chains. Figure 1 illustrates the intersection of sustainability and Industry 4.0 technologies.

Digital tools such as blockchain, the IoT, and AI are facilitating transparency and traceability across supply chains, ensuring accountability and ethical procurement practices (Tsolakis et al., 2022; Almusaylim et al., 2018). Blockchain, for instance, has played a pivotal role in establishing a decentralized and secure ledger system, furnishing a tamper-resistant record of every transaction, thereby fostering fair labour practices and mitigating the risk of counterfeit products (Rijal & Saranani, 2023). Furthermore, real-time data analytics driven by AI empower supply chain managers to make prompt, well-informed decisions, streamlining processes and curbing waste (Gupta, 2023). This not only enhances operational efficiency but also fosters sustainability by reducing environmental footprints. Digital platforms are fostering collaboration among supply chain stakeholders, creating an ecosystem where information exchange flows seamlessly (Aftab et al., 2022; Brohi et al., 2020). Such collaboration is instrumental in executing responsible sourcing strategies and ensuring supplier compliance with ethical standards. By harnessing these platforms, companies can proactively address issues related to labour conditions, human rights, and environmental impacts within their supply chains. Moreover, the uptake of digital tools for supply chain monitoring and auditing has become indispensable in verifying and enforcing adherence to responsible business practices. These tools aid companies in evaluating their suppliers' adherence to ethical standards and furnish insights for continual enhancement.

The integration of digital advancements into supply chain management heralds a transformative epoch in nurturing ethical business practices. Blockchain, AI, and collaborative platforms assume a pivotal role in fostering transparency, traceability, and accountability across supply chains. As companies increasingly recognize the significance of responsible sourcing, these digital tools offer pragmatic solutions to uphold ethical standards, ultimately contributing to a more sustainable and socially responsible global supply chain.

Objectives

Clear Articulation of the Chapter's Objectives

In this chapter, our main focus is to illuminate the significant intersection between sustainability and Industry 4.0 technologies, highlighting how digital advancements can catalyze responsible supply chain practices. We aim to provide a detailed overview, emphasizing the importance of this convergence and showcasing how Industry 4.0 can drive the development of environmentally and socially conscious supply chains. Initially, we aim to explore how Industry 4.0 technologies, such as the IoT, big data analytics, and robotics, can effectively contribute to establishing sustainable and ethical supply chains. We delve into the practical applications of these technologies, examining their roles in real-time sustainability monitoring, data-driven decision-making, and the promotion of ethical manufacturing practices. Furthermore, our chapter seeks to offer valuable insights by examining responsible supply chain practices enabled by Industry 4.0. This encompasses integrating circular economy principles, optimizing energy usage, and advocating for socially responsible sourcing. Through detailed case studies, our goal is to showcase successful implementations, providing tangible examples of organizations leveraging Industry 4.0 to enhance their supply chain sustainability.

As we navigate through the challenges and opportunities associated with implementing Industry 4.0 technologies, we emphasize strategies for overcoming obstacles and identify innovative opportunities that can drive responsible transformations. Additionally, we shed light on human-centric responsibility in the digital age, addressing ethical considerations and presenting strategies for empowering the workforce within the evolving landscape of Industry 4.0. Ultimately, this chapter aims to serve as a comprehensive guide, inspiring stakeholders to harness the full potential of Industry 4.0 technologies for establishing sustainable and ethical supply chains

Exploration of How Industry 4.0 Technologies Can Be Harnessed for Creating Environmentally and Socially Responsible Supply Chains

The incorporation of Industry 4.0 technologies has emerged as a notable strategy for cultivating environmentally and socially conscious supply chains. Industry 4.0, characterized by the merging of digital technologies with traditional manufacturing processes, offers innovative solutions to tackle sustainability challenges in supply chain management (Srhir et al., 2023; Chauhan & Shiaeles, 2023; Chesti et al., 2020). Through the utilization of technologies such as the IoT, AI, and blockchain, businesses can bolster transparency, traceability, and accountability across their supply chains (Liu et al., 2023). The IoT plays a crucial role in continuously monitoring and optimizing resource usage, thereby curbing waste and reducing energy consumption. AI-driven predictive analytics contribute to efficient demand forecasting, mitigating overproduction and minimizing environmental impact. Moreover, blockchain technology ensures the integrity of social and environmental claims by providing an immutable and transparent ledger for supply chain transactions (Chandan et al., 2023; Diwaker et al., 2019). The adoption of Industry 4.0 technologies also fosters the establishment of circular economies through enhanced product lifecycle management. Smart manufacturing processes facilitate the recycling and reutilization of materials, thereby aiding in waste reduction and lowering ecological footprints (Kusiak, 2023). Additionally, these technologies empower stakeholders within the supply chain to collaborate on sustainability initiatives, promoting a collective approach to social and environmental responsibility (De Oliveira et al., 2023; Fatima-Tuz-Zahra et al., 2020).

The exploration of Industry 4.0 technologies presents a transformative opportunity for cultivating environmentally and socially responsible supply chains. The seamless integration of IoT, AI, and blockchain enhances visibility, efficiency, and collaboration, ultimately fostering sustainable business practices. As industries evolve, the adoption of these technologies becomes increasingly critical for achieving a harmonious balance between economic growth and responsible resource management.

Chapter Contributions

The significance of this chapter lies in its comprehensive examination of the dynamic interplay between sustainability and Industry 4.0 technologies, offering a nuanced perspective on how digital advancements can shape responsible supply chains. To begin with, we provide a robust overview that delineates the importance of the sustainability-industry 4.0 intersection, laying a solid foundation for subsequent discussions. An essential contribution emerges from our in-depth exploration of Industry 4.0 technologies driving responsible supply chains. By dissecting the roles of IoT, big data analytics, and robotics, we furnish practical insights into their applications, supported by real-world examples. This section serves as a comprehensive guide for practitioners and decision-makers seeking to harness these technologies for sustainable and ethical supply chain management.

Furthermore, the chapter delves into specific responsible supply chain practices facilitated by Industry 4.0. Through case studies on circular economy integration, energy-efficient operations, and socially responsible sourcing, we offer tangible examples, providing a pragmatic roadmap for organizations aspiring to embed responsible practices in their supply chains. In addressing challenges and opportunities, the chapter contributes strategic insights into surmounting implementation hurdles, fostering broad adoption, and identifying innovative pathways for responsible transformations. By spotlighting successful implementations across various industries, we distil key takeaways and lessons, enabling readers to grasp the practical implications and potential pitfalls associated with the adoption of Industry 4.0 technologies.

Moreover, the chapter makes a unique contribution by underscoring the human-centric dimension of responsibility in the digital era. Our discussion of ethical considerations and strategies for workforce empowerment adds a crucial layer to the discourse, acknowledging the impact of Industry 4.0 on individuals and communities within the supply chain. In summary, the contributions of this chapter encompass a comprehensive exploration of technology-driven sustainability, offering actionable insights, real-world examples, and strategic considerations to guide stakeholders in fostering responsible supply chains within the evolving landscape of Industry 4.0

Chapter Organization

The chapter unfolds in a meticulously structured manner, aimed at facilitating a coherent and comprehensive examination of sustainability in the digital era through the lens of Industry 4.0 technologies. The organizational framework is meticulously crafted to seamlessly guide readers through various dimensions of responsible supply chains, ensuring a logical progression of insights and information.

The introductory segment serves as the foundation, defining the intersection between sustainability and Industry 4.0, thereby setting the context for subsequent discussions. Clear articulation of the chapter's objectives provides readers with a roadmap for the exploration that follows. The subsequent section, titled "Digital Technologies Driving Responsible Supply Chains," is subdivided into three pivotal sub-sections. Each sub-section zooms in on a specific Industry 4.0 technology—IoT, big data analytics, and robotics—providing detailed analyses of their applications and contributions to responsible supply chain practices. The integration of real-world examples and case studies serves to illustrate the practical implications of these technologies.

Progressing further, the third section, "Responsible Supply Chain Practices Enabled by Industry 4.0," delves into the tangible outcomes resulting from the adoption of Industry 4.0 technologies. It explores various aspects such as the integration of circular economy principles, strategies for energy-efficient operations, and socially responsible sourcing practices. Each sub-section is enriched with insightful case studies to contextualize theoretical concepts within practical settings. The subsequent section, "Challenges and Opportunities," confronts the hurdles and prospects associated with implementing Industry 4.0 for responsible supply chains. It identifies common challenges and offers strategic insights for overcoming them, while also highlighting opportunities for innovation and collaboration to foster positive transformations.

The ensuing section, "Human-Centric Responsibility in the Digital Era," delves into the ethical considerations inherent in Industry 4.0 technologies. It explores their impact on workers and communities within the supply chain, emphasizing strategies for workforce empowerment and well-being amidst digital transformations. The penultimate segment, "Case Studies of Successful Implementations," provides an in-depth analysis of industries that have successfully embraced Industry 4.0 for responsible supply chains. Key takeaways and lessons learned from these implementations are synthesized, offering practical insights for organizations contemplating similar initiatives.

Finally, the chapter concludes with a forward-looking section, "Future Outlook," discussing the ongoing evolution of Industry 4.0 technologies and their implications for responsible supply chains. Anticipated trends and innovations are explored, providing a thought-provoking conclusion to the chapter. In essence, the chapter's organization is meticulously crafted to guide readers through a systematic exploration of sustainability and Industry 4.0, blending theoretical frameworks, practical examples, and strategic considerations to foster responsible supply chains in the digital age.

Figure 2. Drives of digital supply chain

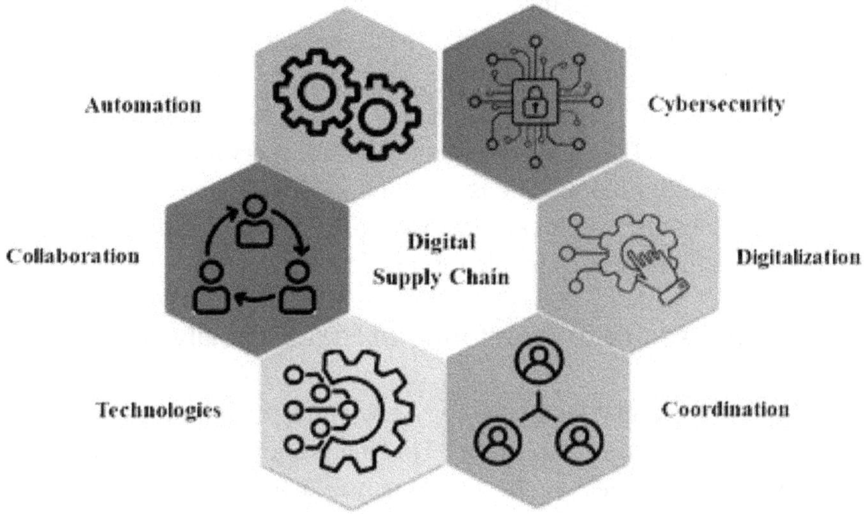

DIGITAL TECHNOLOGIES DRIVING RESPONSIBLE SUPPLY CHAINS

IoT and Real-Time Sustainability Monitoring

The IoT has emerged as a revolutionary technology, triggering significant transformations across various sectors, particularly in sustainability monitoring. IoT-enabled real-time sustainability monitoring is pivotal in tackling environmental issues and advocating for responsible resource management. This segment explores the significance of IoT in enabling real-time sustainability monitoring and its positive influence on environmental preservation. Figure 2 outlines the key drivers behind the digital supply chain revolution.

IoT facilitates the gathering of real-time data from a multitude of sensors and devices, providing valuable insights into environmental conditions. Embedded sensors in infrastructure such as smart grids and waste management systems continuously monitor and transmit data on energy usage, pollution levels, and resource utilization (Mishra & Singh, 2023; Gaur et al., 2021). Immediate access to this data empowers decision-makers to respond promptly to emerging environmental challenges. By incorporating IoT devices into sustainability initiatives, organizations can achieve more effective resource management. For instance, in smart agriculture, IoT-enabled sensors monitor soil moisture, crop health, and weather conditions (Prakash et al., 2023; Gaur, Singh, et al., 2021). This data-driven approach optimizes water usage, minimizes waste, and improves overall crop yield, contributing to sustainable agricultural practices. Moreover, IoT plays a crucial role in reducing the environmental impact of industries. Smart manufacturing systems utilize real-time monitoring to streamline production processes, reduce energy consumption, and lower emissions (Alsudani et al., 2023; Ghosh et al., 2020). This not only enhances operational efficiency but also aligns with environmental sustainability objectives. IoT's ability to provide real-time data aids in the early detection of environmental hazards. For instance, IoT sensors deployed in water bodies can detect changes in water quality, enabling rapid responses to potential pollution incidents (Gunasekaran & Boopathi, 2023; Gopi et al., 2021). Timely interventions based on these alerts help mitigate further damage to ecosystems.

IoT contributes to sustainability not only at an industrial level but also in shaping individual behaviours. Smart home devices connected through IoT enable users to monitor and optimize energy consumption, promoting a more sustainable lifestyle (Renugadevi et al., 2023; Humayun et al., 2022). This interconnected approach fosters collective efforts toward environmental conservation. In conclusion, the integration of IoT into real-time sustainability monitoring is pivotal in addressing environmental challenges. From efficient resource management to early threat detection, IoT empowers individuals and organizations to make informed decisions for a more sustainable future.

Leveraging the IoT for Real-Time Monitoring of Sustainability Metrics

The IoT has emerged as a groundbreaking technology, presenting unparalleled prospects for monitoring and enhancing sustainability metrics in real time. This integration of IoT into sustainability practices empowers organizations to continuously collect and analyze data, enabling informed decision-making towards a greener future. According to findings by Smith et al. (2020), the real-time monitoring capabilities of IoT empower businesses to track and optimize their energy consumption, water usage, and waste generation.

A significant contribution of IoT to sustainability lies in its role in precision agriculture. Sensors embedded in agricultural equipment and fields offer farmers valuable insights into soil moisture, crop health, and weather conditions. This not only improves crop yield but also minimizes resource wastage, as highlighted by Elbaşi et al. (2023). Furthermore, within the domain of smart buildings, IoT devices enable dynamic energy management by adjusting lighting, heating, and cooling systems based on occupancy and environmental conditions (Qayyum et al., 2023). The impact of IoT on waste management is noteworthy. Smart waste bins equipped with sensors notify waste management authorities when they reach capacity, optimizing collection routes and reducing fuel consumption (M. M. Ahmed et al., 2023; Hussain et al., 2019). Additionally, the ability to trace and monitor supply chains in real time assists in identifying inefficiencies and areas for improvement, leading to a reduction in carbon footprints.

However, the integration of IoT in sustainability is not devoid of challenges. Privacy and security concerns, as highlighted by Dhiman (2023), require careful consideration to ensure the responsible and ethical use of data. Moreover, addressing the scalability and interoperability of IoT devices and systems is imperative for widespread adoption and effectiveness (Aitlmoudden et al., 2023; Jhanjhi et al., 2021). The synergy between IoT and sustainability metrics presents a promising avenue for creating a more environmentally conscious and resource-efficient world. Real-time monitoring facilitated by IoT devices empowers businesses and individuals alike to make informed decisions, optimize resource usage, and contribute to a sustainable future. Addressing the associated challenges will be crucial for unlocking the full potential of IoT in realizing global sustainability goals.

Examples of IoT Applications Contributing to Responsible Supply Chain Practices

Real-time Monitoring and Traceability: Utilizing IoT applications allows for real-time monitoring and traceability across the supply chain. For instance, RFID tags and sensors aid in tracking the movement and conditions of goods during transportation (Taj et al., 2023; Kumar et al., 2015). This transparency promotes accountability and facilitates the prompt identification and resolution of potential issues.

Energy Efficiency in Transportation: IoT devices, including smart sensors and GPS trackers, optimize transportation routes and decrease fuel consumption, thereby reducing the carbon footprint of logistics operations (Zadeh et al., 2023). This not only cuts operational costs but also aligns with environmentally conscious practices.

Predictive Maintenance for Machinery: By leveraging IoT-enabled predictive maintenance, companies can minimize downtime and prolong the lifespan of machinery, leading to resource conservation and reducing the necessity for frequent replacements (Kanchana et al., 2024). This approach supports sustainable practices by promoting resource efficiency.

Smart Warehousing: IoT applications in warehouses improve inventory management and diminish waste by offering real-time data on stock levels and expiration dates (Mohamed et al., 2023). This helps prevent overstocking and ensures timely rotation of goods, contributing to responsible resource utilization.

Blockchain for Transparency: Integrating IoT with blockchain technology enhances the transparency and integrity of supply chain data (Sunmola & Burgess, 2023; Lim et al., 2020). This aids in establishing trust among stakeholders and consumers by providing an immutable record of the product journey from origin to destination.

The adoption of IoT applications in supply chain management has emerged as a potent tool for promoting responsible and sustainable practices. From real-time monitoring to predictive maintenance and transparency via blockchain, these technologies foster resource efficiency, reduce environmental impact, and enhance accountability across the supply chain.

Big Data Analytics for Sustainable Decision-Making

Utilizing Big Data Analytics to Inform Sustainable Decision-Making Processes

The integration of big data analytics has become a pivotal tool in shaping sustainable decision-making processes across diverse industries. Big data analytics involves extracting and analyzing extensive datasets to derive meaningful insights, enabling organizations to make well-informed choices aligned with sustainability objectives. This segment delves into the role of big data analytics in shaping sustainable decision-making and its implications for businesses and society.

Firstly, big data analytics facilitates a thorough understanding of environmental patterns and resource consumption. Guan et al. (2023) emphasize that analyzing large datasets enables organizations to pinpoint trends in energy consumption, waste generation, and resource utilization, offering valuable insights for crafting sustainable strategies. Moreover, Lutfi et al. (2023) argue that big data analytics enables real-time monitoring of environmental indicators, allowing for swift adjustments in operational processes to minimize ecological impact. Additionally, big data analytics contributes to supply chain sustainability by optimizing logistics and reducing waste. Research by Al-Khatib (2023) underscores how analytics-driven insights enhance supply chain efficiency, lowering carbon footprints and promoting sustainable practices. This is particularly crucial as businesses increasingly acknowledge the significance of responsible sourcing and ethical supply chain management (Picasso et al., 2021; Muzammal et al., 2020).

The application of big data analytics in sustainable decision-making is also evident in urban planning and development. According to Zadeh and Garay-Rondero (2023), leveraging data analytics assists urban planners in optimizing infrastructure projects, curbing energy consumption, and enhancing overall city sustainability. By integrating data-driven insights, cities can devise and implement policies that tackle environmental challenges while supporting economic growth.

The integration of big data analytics profoundly influences sustainable decision-making processes. From identifying environmental patterns to streamlining supply chains and guiding urban development, the impact of big data on sustainability is undeniable. As organizations strive to balance economic objectives with environmental responsibility, the adoption of big data analytics emerges as a pivotal strategy for informed and sustainable decision-making.

Figure 3. Integrating robotics into manufacturing processes

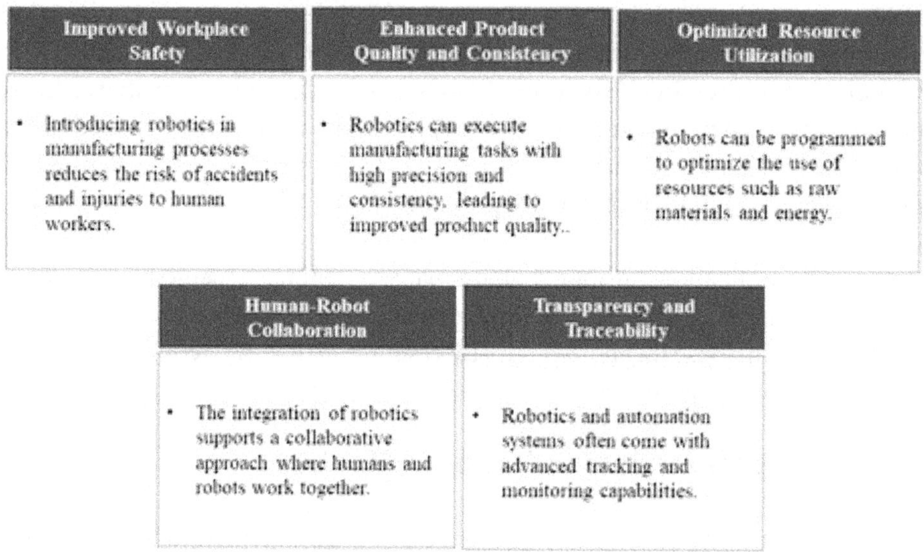

Robotics and Ethical Manufacturing

Integrating Robotics Into Manufacturing Processes to Enhance Ethical and Responsible Production

The integration of robotics into manufacturing processes represents a significant advancement towards fostering ethical and responsible production practices. This technological integration brings forth various advantages, spanning from heightened efficiency to improved safety and minimized environmental impact. As industries progress, the ethical implications of production methods become increasingly pertinent. This section delves into how the inclusion of robotics in manufacturing aligns with ethical considerations, contributing to responsible and sustainable production practices. Figure 3 illustrates the benefits of integrating robotics into manufacturing processes.

One notable advantage of incorporating robotics is the enhanced efficiency and precision in manufacturing processes. Robots can execute repetitive tasks with consistent accuracy, thereby reducing errors and waste along production lines (Gisi, 2024; Sankar et al., 2020). This not only results in higher-quality products but also diminishes the need for rework, subsequently lowering resource consumption and fostering responsible resource management. The introduction of robotics into manufacturing environments also leads to improved worker safety and well-being. Hazardous and physically demanding tasks can be delegated to robots, mitigating the risk of workplace accidents and injuries (Papetti et al., 2022). This ethical approach prioritizes the health and safety of human workers, aligning with responsible production practices.

Manufacturing processes often carry significant environmental footprints. Integrating robotics enables optimized resource utilization, waste reduction, and enhanced energy efficiency, thereby reducing the overall environmental impact (Soori et al., 2023). Ethical production practices necessitate a commitment to environmental sustainability, and the incorporation of robotics supports this commitment by minimizing the ecological footprint of manufacturing activities. Contrary to concerns about job displacement, the integration of robotics also presents opportunities for skills development and job creation. Workers can undergo training to operate and maintain robotic systems, fostering a workforce equipped with expertise in advanced technologies (Fraboni et al., 2023; Singhal et al., 2020). This approach aligns with ethical considerations by promoting continuous learning and adaptation in response to technological advancements.

The integration of robotics into manufacturing processes signifies a crucial stride towards achieving ethical and responsible production. The benefits encompass heightened efficiency and precision, enhanced worker safety, reduced environmental impact, and avenues for skills development and job creation. As industries embrace these technological innovations, it remains imperative to prioritize ethical considerations, ensuring that innovation aligns harmoniously with responsible production practices.

Examples of Sustainable Practices Enabled by Robotic Automation

Robotic automation excels notably in waste reduction, leveraging advanced sensors and sorting capabilities to enhance recycling processes and ensure efficient material separation. According to Chen et al. (2023), this not only boosts the overall recycling rate but also reduces contamination, thereby mitigating the environmental impact of improper waste disposal. Moreover, the application of robots in agriculture has ushered in more sustainable farming practices. Precision weeders and autonomous tractors enable precise resource utilization, leading to decreased pesticide and fertilizer usage, as highlighted in a study by Baweja et al. (2020). This, in turn, promotes soil health, biodiversity, and sustainable food production.

In manufacturing, robotic automation is revolutionizing production lines, enhancing energy efficiency by optimizing energy consumption and operating at peak efficiency. Research by Song et al. (2023) indicates that such practices not only lower operational costs but also diminish the carbon footprint of manufacturing processes. Additionally, the deployment of robots in logistics and transportation has bolstered supply chain sustainability. Autonomous vehicles and drones contribute to more efficient and eco-friendly delivery systems, reducing fuel consumption and alleviating traffic congestion, as outlined in a report by Lv and Shang (2023). This, in turn, fosters cleaner air and lower carbon emissions.

In the healthcare sector, robotic automation has elevated patient care while mitigating the environmental impact. Surgical robots enable minimally invasive procedures, resulting in shorter recovery times and reduced resource usage. Dion et al. (2022) emphasized the positive environmental impact of these technologies, noting the reduction in medical waste and energy consumption in healthcare facilities. The integration of robotic automation across various industries underscores a tangible commitment to sustainable practices. From waste reduction and precision agriculture to energy-efficient manufacturing and green logistics, robots play a crucial role in fostering a more sustainable and environmentally conscious future.

RESPONSIBLE SUPPLY CHAIN PRACTICES ENABLED BY INDUSTRY 4.0

Circular Economy Integration

Implementation of Circular Economy Principles Facilitated by Industry 4.0 Technologies

The integration of principles from the circular economy, bolstered by advancements in Industry 4.0 technologies, has emerged as a groundbreaking strategy for tackling sustainability challenges across diverse sectors. Central to the circular economy is the emphasis on waste reduction and the promotion of resource longevity through strategies like recycling and repurposing. Industry 4.0 innovations, including the IoT and sophisticated data analysis, play a pivotal role in amplifying the efficiency and efficacy of circular economy initiatives.

A critical facet where Industry 4.0 technologies contribute significantly to circular economy endeavours is smart product design. Leveraging IoT-enabled sensors, products can be crafted with features that facilitate easy disassembly and component reutilization (Han et al., 2023; Ananna et al., 2023). This not only extends product lifespan but also enables the recovery of valuable materials, thus mitigating overall environmental impact. Furthermore, within manufacturing contexts, the implementation of predictive maintenance empowered by Industry 4.0 technologies ensures machinery operates optimally, thereby reducing breakdowns and prolonging equipment lifespan (Soori et al., 2023a). This proactive approach diminishes the necessity for frequent replacements, aligning with the circular economy principle of extending product longevity.

Figure 4. Responsible supply chain practices enabled by Industry 4.0

Moreover, data analytics and AI play a crucial role in refining supply chains, improving inventory management, and mitigating overproduction (Mrozek et al., 2020). This not only reduces unnecessary waste but also diminishes resource consumption during production. Additionally, Industry 4.0 technologies facilitate the development of digital marketplaces for pre-owned goods, fostering the concept of product-as-a-service (Attaran et al., 2023; Azam, Dulloo, Majeed, Wan, Xin, & Sindiramutty, 2023). Through such platforms, consumers can access items temporarily, thereby curbing the demand for new products and promoting more sustainable consumption patterns.

Furthermore, blockchain technology ensures transparency and traceability within material supply chains, empowering companies to authenticate the origin and sustainability of resources (Singh et al., 2023). This fosters accountability and encourages the utilization of responsibly sourced materials, aligning with circular economy principles. In summary, the integration of Industry 4.0 technologies is pivotal for advancing circular economy principles. From intelligent product design and predictive maintenance to streamlined supply chains and transparent material procurement, these technologies significantly contribute to fostering a more sustainable and circular approach to resource management. Figure 4 illustrates responsible supply chain practices enabled by Industry 4.0.

Case Studies on Closed-Loop Supply Chain Initiatives

Closed-loop supply chain initiatives have garnered significant attention in recent years as organizations prioritize sustainable and environmentally responsible practices. This section delves into several case studies that showcase successful implementations of closed-loop supply chain strategies. One notable example is Apple Inc.'s commitment to sustainability through its closed-loop supply chain for electronic devices. Apple's recycling program allows customers to return their old devices, facilitating the recovery of valuable materials like aluminium and gold. This initiative not only reduces the environmental impact of electronic waste but also yields cost savings for the company through material reuse (Islam et al., 2023; Azam et al., 2023).

Another compelling case is Unilever, a consumer goods giant, which has integrated closed-loop supply chain practices into its packaging operations. By prioritizing the use of recycled materials for product packaging, Unilever contributes to a decrease in plastic waste and supports a circular economy. This aligns with the company's sustainability objectives and has been lauded for its positive impact on the environment and brand reputation (Shahzad et al., 2023; Azam, Dulloo, et al., 2023). In the automotive industry, Tesla's closed-loop battery recycling program serves as an exemplary case study. Tesla emphasizes the recovery and recycling of materials from old electric vehicle batteries, establishing a circular supply chain for crucial components. This initiative not only mitigates the environmental impact of battery disposal but also bolsters the sustainability goals of the electric vehicle industry (Akram & Abdul-Kader, 2023).

In the fashion industry, H&M distinguishes itself with its closed-loop supply chain approach to textile recycling. Through its "Take Care" initiative, H&M collects used garments from customers and repurposes them into new products. This circular fashion model not only reduces the environmental footprint of the textile industry but also advocates for a more sustainable and ethical approach to fashion production (Abbate et al., 2023; Azam, Tajwar, et al., 2023). Lastly, the pharmaceutical sector presents a compelling case study with Johnson & Johnson's closed-loop approach to medical product packaging. By prioritizing recyclable and sustainable materials, Johnson & Johnson not only meets regulatory requirements but also enhances its corporate social responsibility profile (Kumar et al., 2024; Azam et al., 2023).

These case studies underscore the diverse applications and benefits of closed-loop supply chain initiatives across various industries, highlighting their positive impact on environmental sustainability and corporate profitability. These successful examples offer valuable insights for organizations considering the adoption of similar practices.

Energy-Efficient Operations

Strategies for Optimizing Energy Usage and Reducing the Environmental Footprint

Amid escalating environmental concerns, the quest to optimize energy consumption has become paramount for fostering sustainable lifestyles. This segment delves into pivotal strategies that individuals and organisations can adopt to reduce their environmental footprint through efficient energy practices.

One foundational step is investing in energy-efficient appliances, a move designed to lower overall energy usage (Han, Qamruzzaman, et al., 2023). Modern appliances are engineered to consume less power while maintaining optimal performance. Transitioning to Energy Star-certified devices, for instance, ensures substantial reductions in electricity usage for both households and businesses (Mushafiq et al., 2023). Embracing renewable energy sources stands as a crucial strategy for diminishing reliance on fossil fuels (Ouma, 2023; Sindiramutty, Jhanjhi, Ray, Jazri, Khan, & Gaur, 2024). Solar, wind, and hydroelectric power offer sustainable alternatives that mitigate greenhouse gas emissions linked with conventional energy production. Integrating these sources into our energy repertoire not only combats climate change but also yields long-term cost savings (Aghahosseini et al., 2023; Krishnan et al., 2021).

The incorporation of smart energy management systems enables real-time monitoring and optimization of energy consumption (Ouedraogo et al., 2023; Sindiramutty, 2023). These systems empower users to pinpoint areas of excessive consumption and implement targeted adjustments, leading to more efficient resource utilization. Smart technologies, such as programmable thermostats and energy-efficient lighting, aid in curtailing unnecessary energy expenditures (Hui et al., 2023). Fostering energy-conscious behaviour emerges as a cost-effective and impactful strategy (Roth et al., 2023; Sindiramutty, Jhanjhi, Tan, Khan, Shah, & Gaur, 2024). Simple actions like turning off lights, unplugging devices, and minimizing air conditioning usage contribute significantly to reducing energy consumption. Cultivating awareness and nurturing responsible habits within communities and workplaces can catalyze a collective effort towards sustainability.

Governments play a pivotal role in steering the adoption of eco-friendly practices through policies and incentives (Verma et al., 2023; Wen et al., 2024). Tax credits, subsidies, and regulations that promote energy-efficient initiatives incentivize businesses and individuals to invest in environmentally conscious technologies. By establishing a supportive framework, governments can expedite the transition towards a more sustainable energy landscape. The adoption of strategies for optimizing energy usage is critical for mitigating environmental impact. Through the deployment of energy-efficient appliances, the embrace of renewable energy sources, the implementation of smart energy management systems, the encouragement of behavioural changes, and the formulation of supportive government policies, society can collectively contribute to a greener and more sustainable future.

Technological Solutions Contributing to Responsible Energy Consumption

Amid the urgent call for responsible energy consumption worldwide, technological advancements have emerged as vital catalysts in realizing sustainable and efficient energy practices. This report delves into several state-of-the-art technological solutions that play a pivotal role in promoting responsible energy usage.

The implementation of smart grids and advanced metering systems has transformed the generation, distribution, and consumption of energy (Rind et al., 2023; Sindiramutty, Jhanjhi, Ray, Jazri, Khan, Gaur, et al., 2024). These innovations enable real-time monitoring of energy consumption, empowering both utility companies and consumers to make informed decisions. By optimizing electricity distribution and identifying areas of inefficiency, smart grids significantly contribute to overall energy conservation. Additionally, the integration of IoT devices in energy systems has opened up new avenues for responsible energy consumption (López et al., 2023; Sindiramutty, Jhanjhi, Tan, et al., 2024). Smart sensors and connected devices automate energy-intensive processes, with smart thermostats adjusting heating and cooling based on occupancy, and IoT-enabled appliances operating during periods of lower electricity demand, thus aiding load balancing and promoting energy efficiency.

Advancements in energy storage technologies, including lithium-ion batteries and grid-scale storage solutions, play a crucial role in addressing the intermittency of renewable energy sources (Hasan et al., 2023). These technologies efficiently store excess energy during periods of low demand and release it during peak times, thereby enhancing the stability and reliability of the energy supply. Blockchain technology is revolutionizing energy trading by enabling transparent and decentralized transactions (Yap et al., 2023). Peer-to-peer energy trading platforms built on blockchain facilitate direct transactions between energy producers and consumers, thereby promoting the utilization of locally generated renewable energy and enhancing the overall efficiency of the energy market. The application of AI in energy systems enables predictive analytics and optimization of energy consumption patterns (Olabi et al., 2023; Sindiramutty, Tan, Lau, et al., 2024). AI algorithms analyze historical data to identify trends and make real-time adjustments, thus optimizing energy usage across various sectors, including manufacturing, transportation, and buildings.

Technological solutions stand at the forefront of fostering responsible energy consumption. From smart grids and IoT applications to energy storage technologies, blockchain-enabled trading, and AI-driven optimizations, these innovations collectively contribute to a more sustainable and efficient energy landscape. Embracing and further developing these technologies is essential for achieving global energy goals and mitigating the environmental impact of energy consumption.

Socially Responsible Sourcing

Leveraging Digital Technologies for Socially Responsible Sourcing Practices

In an era dominated by globalization, businesses are increasingly recognizing the importance of socially responsible sourcing practices to uphold ethical standards and meet evolving consumer demands. Leveraging digital technologies strategically has emerged as a fundamental approach for companies seeking to elevate their social responsibility within the supply chain. Technologies such as blockchain, AI, and data analytics play pivotal roles in fostering transparency, traceability, and accountability in sourcing practices (Althabatah et al., 2023).

Blockchain technology has garnered attention for its ability to establish an immutable and transparent ledger of transactions across the supply chain (Kamble et al., 2021). By harnessing blockchain, companies can meticulously track and verify each stage of the production process, ensuring that products are ethically sourced and manufactured. This transparency fosters trust among consumers who increasingly demand information about the origins of the products they purchase. AI emerges as another critical element in socially responsible sourcing. AI-driven algorithms can sift through vast datasets to identify potential risks and unethical practices within the supply chain (Chand et al., 2023). This proactive approach enables companies to address issues such as forced labour or environmental violations before they escalate. Additionally, AI enhances efficiency by automating compliance monitoring, thereby reducing the likelihood of human error. Complementing these technologies, data analytics offers valuable insights into supply chain dynamics. Companies can analyze data to pinpoint areas for improvement, evaluate the impact of sourcing decisions on local communities, and optimize processes to align with social responsibility objectives (Peng et al., 2023; Sindiramutty, Jhanjhi, Tan, Khan, Gharib, & Yun, 2024). The integration of these digital technologies not only promotes ethical sourcing but also contributes to the realization of the Sustainable Development Goals (SDGs) established by the United Nations (UN) (Kulkov et al., 2023). By prioritizing socially responsible sourcing practices, businesses align themselves with global initiatives aimed at creating a more sustainable and equitable world.

The adoption of digital technologies in sourcing practices plays a crucial role in fostering social responsibility within supply chains. Blockchain, AI, and data analytics serve as powerful tools for companies to enhance transparency, traceability, and efficiency, enabling them to meet consumer expectations and contribute to the achievement of global sustainability goals.

Figure 5. Steps to ensuring ethical and fair treatment throughout the supply chain

Code of Conduct	Develop a comprehensive code of conduct that outlines ethical principles and fair treatment expectations for all stakeholders in the supply chain. This code should cover aspects such as labor practices, environmental sustainability, and responsible sourcin
Supplier Audits and Compliance Checks	Implement regular audits and compliance checks to assess whether suppliers adhere to the established ethical standards. This involves evaluating working conditions, wages, environmental practices, and overall compliance with the ethical guidelines set forth in the supply chain
Ethics Training and Awareness	Conduct training programs to educate all participants in the supply chain about ethical practices and fair treatment. This includes employees, suppliers, and any other relevant stakeholders. Raising awareness helps ensure that ethical considerations are integrated into daily operations
Transparency and Traceability	Establish transparent processes and traceability mechanisms that allow for the tracking of products and materials throughout the supply chain. This transparency enables identification of any ethical lapses or unfair treatment, promoting accountability and swift corrective actions.
Whistleblower Mechanism	Implement a whistleblower mechanism that allows individuals within the supply chain to report unethical practices or violations anonymously. This encourages open communication and empowers individuals to speak up without fear of reprisal, fostering a culture of accountability

Ensuring Ethical and Fair Treatment Throughout the Supply Chain

In today's business landscape, maintaining ethical standards and equitable treatment across the supply chain is paramount for fostering sustainable and responsible business practices. The supply chain encompasses a series of interconnected stages, spanning from raw material extraction to the final product reaching consumers. Ethical considerations at each stage are crucial for upholding corporate integrity and promoting a global culture of fairness.

One pivotal aspect of ethical supply chain management is ensuring the fair treatment of labourers. According to Santos (2023), businesses must prioritize the well-being of workers by guaranteeing fair wages, safe working conditions, and compliance with labour laws. Ethical treatment of employees not only meets societal expectations but also enhances brand reputation. Refer to Figure 5 for steps to ensure ethical and fair treatment throughout the supply chain. Environmental sustainability stands as another critical facet of ethical supply chain practices. As emphasized by X. Chen et al. (2023), businesses should aim to minimize their environmental footprint by adopting eco-friendly production methods, reducing waste, and responsibly sourcing materials. Companies that prioritize environmental ethics contribute to the broader goal of combating climate change and conserving natural resources. Transparency is essential for upholding ethical supply chain practices. Companies should provide clear information about their suppliers and manufacturing processes. According to He (2023), transparency fosters trust among consumers, who increasingly demand accountability from the brands they support. Ethical transparency enables businesses to showcase their dedication to fair treatment and responsible sourcing. Global supply chains often traverse diverse cultural contexts, underscoring the importance of cultural sensitivity. As advocated by Senghor et al. (2023), businesses should be mindful of cultural differences and ensure that their practices respect and align with local norms. Cultural sensitivity promotes equitable treatment across borders and mitigates exploitation in diverse international markets.

In conclusion, ensuring ethical and fair treatment throughout the supply chain is not only a moral imperative but also a strategic necessity for businesses. By prioritizing fair labour practices, environmental sustainability, transparency, and cultural sensitivity, companies can cultivate a positive reputation and contribute to a global environment of responsible business conduct.

CHALLENGES AND OPPORTUNITIES

Overcoming Implementation Challenges

Common Challenges in Adopting Industry 4.0 Technologies for Responsible Supply Chains

The incorporation of Industry 4.0 technologies is increasingly vital for improving both the efficiency and sustainability of supply chains. Nonetheless, merging these cutting-edge technologies into responsible supply chains presents several obstacles. One significant challenge stems from the absence of universally accepted frameworks for implementing Industry 4.0 technologies within supply chain operations. This lack of standardized guidelines makes it difficult for companies to align their practices with responsible and sustainable supply chain goals. Consequently, organizations struggle to assess and convey the impact of their Industry 4.0 initiatives on responsible supply chain practices. Another hurdle is the concern over cybersecurity. As companies rely more on interconnected devices and data-driven systems, they become more vulnerable to cyber threats. Safeguarding sensitive supply chain information and preserving data integrity become critical challenges in adopting Industry 4.0 technologies for responsible supply chains.

Moreover, there exists a skills gap in the workforce, which hampers the effective implementation of Industry 4.0 technologies. The rapid pace of technological advancement necessitates a workforce with the requisite skills to operate and manage these sophisticated systems. Insufficient training and education in emerging technologies can impede the successful integration of Industry 4.0 practices, limiting their potential to enhance responsible supply chain management. Furthermore, the substantial initial investment costs associated with Industry 4.0 technologies deter many organizations, particularly smaller ones. The implementation of these technologies requires significant financial resources, and the return on investment may not be immediately apparent. This financial barrier poses a challenge to companies aiming to align their supply chain processes with responsible and sustainable practices. Additionally, regulatory uncertainties complicate the adoption of Industry 4.0 technologies for responsible supply chains. The constantly evolving nature of technology often surpasses regulatory frameworks, leaving organizations uncertain about compliance and ethical considerations.

Addressing these challenges is essential for successfully integrating Industry 4.0 technologies into responsible supply chains. Standardization, cybersecurity measures, workforce development, financial considerations, and regulatory clarity are critical areas that demand attention to unlock the full potential of Industry 4.0 in promoting responsible and sustainable supply chain practices.

Strategies for Overcoming Barriers and Fostering Widespread Adoption

To overcome the hurdles impeding the broad acceptance of Industry 4.0 technologies within responsible supply chains, organizations can implement various tactics. Encouraging collaboration among industry stakeholders stands as a cornerstone. By forging partnerships and forming consortiums, they pave the way for crafting standardized frameworks for Industry 4.0 implementation. This cooperative stance promotes knowledge exchange and presents a unified front to tackle shared challenges, fostering a more cohesive and consistent adoption process. Addressing financial barriers can be achieved through government incentives and grants, particularly targeted at supporting small and medium-sized enterprises (SMEs) in transitioning to Industry 4.0. Governments play a pivotal role in easing the financial burden by offering tax incentives or subsidies, thereby incentivizing responsible supply chain practices.

To combat the shortage of skilled workers, organizations should invest in training programs and educational initiatives. This entails both upskilling current employees and collaborating with educational institutions to design tailored programs suited to the demands of Industry 4.0 technologies. Cultivating a skilled workforce enhances companies' capabilities to effectively implement and manage these advanced technologies. In addressing cybersecurity concerns, organizations must prioritize the establishment of robust cybersecurity protocols. This includes implementing encryption measures, conducting regular security audits, and providing continuous employee training on cybersecurity best practices. A strong cybersecurity foundation is crucial for instilling confidence in the secure utilization of Industry 4.0 technologies.

Overcoming regulatory hurdles requires active engagement with policymakers. Companies should advocate for the development of clear and comprehensive regulatory frameworks that govern the ethical use of Industry 4.0 technologies in supply chains. Active involvement in the regulatory process ensures that guidelines align with responsible supply chain practices. In summary, surmounting the obstacles to adopting Industry 4.0 technologies for responsible supply chains demands a multifaceted approach. Collaboration, financial assistance, workforce development, cybersecurity measures, and engagement with policymakers are essential strategies to foster widespread adoption and ensure the ethical and responsible integration of these technologies.

Opportunities for Innovation

Identifying Opportunities for Innovation in Responsible Supply Chain Practices Through Industry 4.0

In recent years, the incorporation of Industry 4.0 technologies has emerged as a transformative influence, reshaping global supply chain practices to prioritize responsibility and sustainability. This shift in approach presents myriad opportunities for innovation, promoting an ethical and efficient management of supply chains. With Industry 4.0, technologies like the IoT, AI, and blockchain facilitate enhanced traceability and transparency throughout the supply chain. This heightened visibility empowers companies to detect and mitigate potential risks associated with social, environmental, and ethical issues within their supply chains.

A significant area where Industry 4.0 fosters responsible practices is in managing supplier relationships. Smart contracts facilitated by blockchain technology can automate and ensure adherence to ethical standards, promoting fair labour practices and reducing the risk of exploitation. Additionally, IoT devices allow real-time monitoring of working conditions, enabling companies to proactively address any violations of responsible labour practices. This proactive approach not only aligns with ethical considerations but also enhances the overall resilience of the supply chain—another aspect where Industry 4.0 drives responsible innovation is environmental sustainability. Smart sensors and data analytics optimize resource utilization, minimizing waste and decreasing the ecological footprint of the supply chain. By leveraging these technologies, companies can track and analyze environmental impact metrics, making informed decisions to improve sustainability practices. Furthermore, Industry 4.0 facilitates the establishment of circular supply chains by promoting the reuse and recycling of materials. Real-time data analytics help identify opportunities for recycling, reducing dependence on virgin resources. This not only aligns with responsible environmental practices but also improves cost-effectiveness in the long run.

Industry 4.0 presents a promising avenue for innovation in responsible supply chain practices. Integrating IoT, blockchain, and data analytics empowers companies to address social, ethical, and environmental concerns, ultimately fostering a more sustainable and responsible global supply chain.

Collaboration and Partnerships Driving Responsible Transformations

In today's era of responsible business practices, collaboration and partnerships hold significant sway in catalyzing transformative shifts. As businesses increasingly acknowledge the significance of corporate social responsibility (CSR) and sustainability, establishing alliances with a variety of stakeholders becomes essential for effecting meaningful change. This collaborative strategy not only amplifies the reach and effectiveness of responsible initiatives but also fosters the development of a more robust and socially aware business environment.

Figure 6. Smart supply chain management

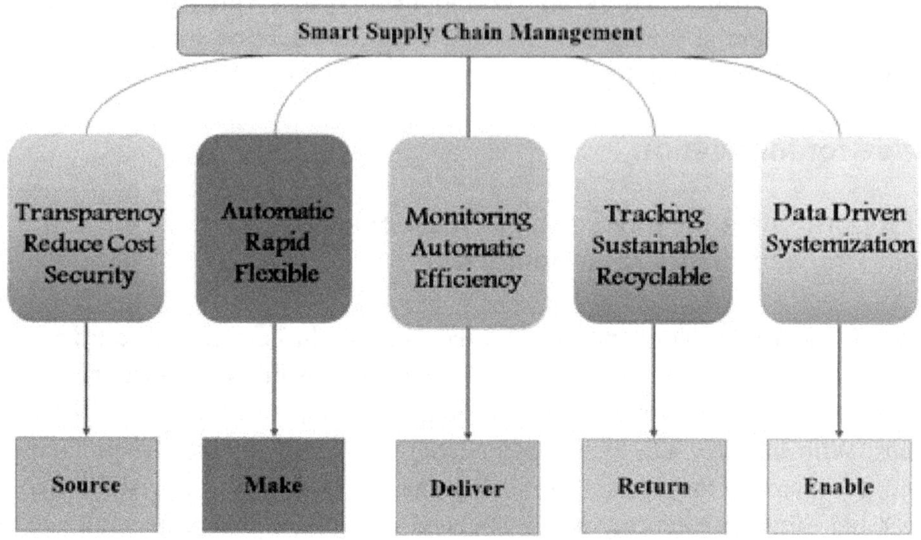

Partnerships between businesses and non-governmental organizations (NGOs) serve as a significant catalyst for promoting responsible transformations. Leveraging their expertise in social and environmental issues, NGOs assist businesses in developing and implementing sustainable practices. These collaborations often yield innovative solutions that tackle societal challenges while promoting positive corporate citizenship. Moreover, industry-wide partnerships play a crucial role in establishing collective standards and best practices. Collaborative efforts, such as industry associations and multi-stakeholder platforms, foster a shared understanding of responsible business conduct and encourage the adoption of common frameworks. This unity streamlines efforts and ensures a more consistent and impactful approach to responsible business practices across the entire sector.

Cross-sector collaborations represent another avenue for driving responsible transformations. By collaborating with governmental bodies, academia, and civil society, businesses gain access to a broader range of resources, knowledge, and perspectives. These partnerships enable the development of comprehensive strategies that address economic, social, and environmental dimensions, leading to more holistic and sustainable outcomes. Furthermore, collaboration within supply chains is essential for promoting responsible transformations. Establishing strong partnerships with suppliers, manufacturers, and distributors facilitates the implementation of ethical sourcing, fair labour practices, and environmental stewardship throughout the entire supply chain. This collaborative approach enhances transparency and accountability, thereby mitigating risks associated with irresponsible practices in the supply chain.

In summary, collaboration and partnerships are integral to driving responsible transformations in the business landscape. Whether through alliances with NGOs, industry-wide initiatives, cross-sector collaborations, or supply chain partnerships, businesses can leverage collective intelligence and resources to create a more sustainable and socially responsible future.

HUMAN-CENTRIC RESPONSIBILITY IN THE DIGITAL ERA

Ethical Considerations

The Human Impact of Industry 4.0 On Workers and Communities Within the Supply Chain

The rise of Industry 4.0, characterized by the integration of advanced technologies such as AI, robotics, and the IoT, has profoundly reshaped the industrial sector. This technological evolution has presented both opportunities and challenges, particularly affecting workers and communities along the supply chain. As industries increasingly adopt automation and digitalization, it is imperative to assess the human implications of these transformations.

Industry 4.0 has ushered in the automation of routine tasks, sparking concerns about job displacement. Workers in traditional manufacturing roles may find themselves replaced by machines capable of performing repetitive tasks more efficiently. Research by Morandini et al. (2023) suggests that this shift towards automation could lead to job losses in certain sectors, underscoring the need for reskilling and upskilling initiatives to help workers adapt to evolving industry demands. Additionally, the introduction of smart technologies in the workplace has influenced the quality of work life for many employees. Pan and Froese (2023) argue that while automation can enhance efficiency, it may also heighten stress levels as workers navigate the challenges of mastering new technologies. Factors like job insecurity and the requirement for continuous learning contribute to a more stressful work environment for some individuals. The ramifications of Industry 4.0 extend beyond individual workers to entire communities reliant on industrial activities. Research conducted by Bai et al. (2023) suggests that the automation of manufacturing processes could lead to the decline of traditional industrial centres, impacting local economies. This shift underscores the necessity for strategic planning to support affected communities and foster alternative economic opportunities. As the workforce becomes increasingly reliant on technology, concerns regarding social inclusion emerge. Fisk et al. (2022) emphasize the importance of addressing the digital divide to ensure that all workers have access to the requisite skills and resources. Neglecting to bridge this gap may exacerbate existing inequalities within the workforce.

While Industry 4.0 offers numerous advantages in terms of efficiency and productivity, its impact on workers and communities within the supply chain cannot be overlooked. To mitigate adverse effects, policymakers and industry leaders must prioritize reskilling initiatives, support affected communities, and promote social inclusion within the evolving industrial landscape.

Ethical Considerations in Implementing Digital Technologies for Responsible Supply Chains

The advent of Industry 4.0, marked by the infusion of digital technologies into manufacturing and supply chain operations, has triggered substantial shifts in the global economic sphere. Despite the gains in efficiency and competitiveness, it's imperative to acknowledge the human dimension impacting workers and communities involved in the supply chain (Agustian et al., 2023). Navigating through this transformative phase requires a thorough examination of how Industry 4.0 shapes the welfare of individuals and communities engaged in production and distribution processes. The adoption of automation, AI, and the IoT has necessitated a reconfiguration of workforce skills (Grabowska et al., 2021). As machines assume routine tasks, workers are compelled to acquire new technical competencies to maintain relevance. This adaptability underscores the need for continuous learning initiatives and skill enhancement programs to sustain competitiveness in the swiftly evolving industrial realm (Achoki, 2023).

While Industry 4.0 holds the promise of heightened efficiency, it also sparks concerns about job displacement due to automation (George & George, 2023). Mundane and repetitive tasks could be overtaken by machines, potentially engendering job insecurity for inadequately skilled workers. Governments and industries must enact policies and initiatives that tackle the socio-economic ramifications stemming from potential job losses and ensure an equitable transition for affected workers (Pavloudakis et al., 2023). The transformative wave ushered in by Industry 4.0 extends beyond individual workers to impact entire communities reliant on specific industries (Santhi & Muthuswamy, 2023). The emergence of smart factories and digital supply chains may reshape the geographical distribution of employment opportunities, influencing patterns of population migration and regional economies. Community leaders and policymakers should take proactive measures to anticipate these changes and foster supportive frameworks for affected regions (Picavet et al., 2022).

In essence, the human repercussions of Industry 4.0 on workers and communities within the supply chain pose a multifaceted challenge necessitating careful deliberation. As technological progress reshapes the industrial landscape, stakeholders must prioritize strategies aimed at mitigating adverse outcomes, thereby ensuring a fair and inclusive transition for the workforce and affected communities (Schuster et al., 2023). By confronting these challenges head-on, we can harness the benefits of Industry 4.0 while safeguarding the well-being of those at its core.

Workforce Empowerment and Well-Being

Strategies for Empowering the Workforce to Contribute to Responsible Practices

In today's ever-changing business environment, nurturing a culture of ethical and sustainable practices is paramount for organizations to thrive responsibly. Central to achieving this objective is the empowerment of the workforce. This report delves into essential strategies that organizations can adopt to empower their employees to actively contribute to responsible practices. Clear and transparent communication stands as a cornerstone. Leaders must effectively communicate the company's values and unwavering dedication to responsible practices. According to insights from Jiang and Shen (2020), transparent communication fosters a collective understanding and imbues employees with a sense of purpose. Regular communication avenues like town hall meetings and internal newsletters serve as vital platforms to keep employees well-informed and engaged.

Another crucial aspect is the implementation of training and educational initiatives. By offering pertinent training on ethical decision-making and responsible conduct, organizations equip their employees with the knowledge and skills necessary to positively impact the company's ethical framework (Daradkeh, 2023). Continuous educational endeavours ensure that employees stay updated on evolving ethical standards and industry benchmarks. Recognition and rewards are also instrumental in motivating employees to embrace responsible practices. As underscored by Pearce and Locke (2023), acknowledging employees for ethical behaviour reinforces the significance of responsible practices within the organizational culture. Incentives such as awards or public acknowledgement inspire employees to consistently make ethical choices in their day-to-day tasks.

Moreover, empowering employees entails fostering a supportive and inclusive workplace culture. Diverse teams, as emphasized by Chukwu (2023), bring forth varied perspectives and insights, thereby contributing to more comprehensive ethical decision-making. By cultivating an inclusive environment, organizations encourage active participation from employees in shaping responsible practices that embrace diverse viewpoints. Furthermore, leaders must lead by example. When executives demonstrate an unwavering commitment to responsible practices, employees are more inclined to follow suit (W. Song et al., 2023). Executives who prioritize ethical decision-making and exemplify responsible behaviour contribute to a positive organizational culture where responsible practices become deeply ingrained in the company's ethos.

Empowering the workforce to contribute to responsible practices encompasses transparent communication, effective training, recognition, the creation of an inclusive culture, and exemplary leadership. Through the implementation of these strategies, organizations can foster a robust ethical foundation that not only benefits the company but also fosters a more responsible and sustainable business environment.

Ensuring the Well-Being of Employees Within the Digitalized Supply Chain

In the rapidly evolving realm of digitalized supply chains, prioritizing the well-being of employees is crucial from both ethical and operational standpoints. This report explores strategies aimed at safeguarding the welfare of workers within digitalized supply chains, recognizing the hurdles posed by technological advancements and advocating for a human-centric approach. Cultivating a culture of adaptability emerges as a pivotal factor. As underscored by Aamer et al. (2022), the digitalization of supply chains frequently necessitates employees to acquire fresh skills and adjust to evolving technologies. Organizations should invest in training initiatives to empower employees, enabling them to navigate the digital terrain with confidence and mitigating potential skill gaps and job-related stressors. Furthermore, prioritizing health and safety protocols within digitalized supply chains is imperative. According to insights from Lamnabhi-Lagarrigue and Samad (2023), the deployment of smart technologies like automation and AI should never compromise the physical well-being of workers. Regular risk assessments, ergonomic considerations, and the provision of protective measures are indispensable to uphold a safe working environment amidst the integration of digital tools.

Moreover, maintaining a healthy work-life balance poses a growing challenge in the context of digitalized supply chains. To address this, organizations can embrace flexible working arrangements and advocate for remote work options. Research by Sharma and Tiwari (2023) underscores the significance of work-life balance in mitigating employee burnout and enhancing overall well-being, even in digitally driven work settings.

Figure 7. The main element in Logistic 4.0 (Kozma et al., 2019)

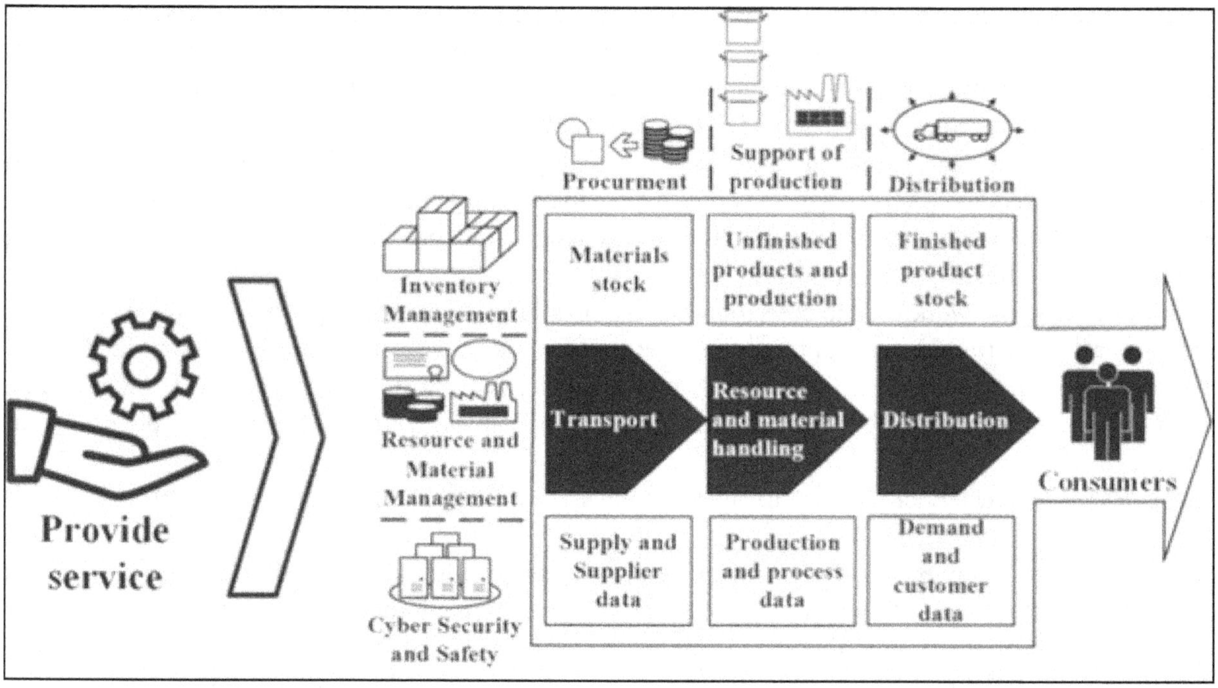

Highlighting mental health support represents another critical facet. The constant connectivity and high-pressure dynamics inherent in digitalized supply chain roles can contribute to stress and burnout. Organizations must implement mental health programs, normalize seeking help, and furnish resources such as counselling services (Everitt & Rundio, 2023). Prioritizing mental well-being not only fosters individual employee welfare but also augments productivity and job satisfaction. Furthermore, fostering a sense of community and camaraderie is paramount. In digitalized supply chains characterized by remote work and virtual collaboration, organizations should invest in team-building initiatives and virtual social interactions. As per insights from Buonomo et al. (2023), a robust sense of community can alleviate feelings of isolation, cultivating a positive work environment and enhancing employee well-being.

Safeguarding the well-being of employees within the digitalized supply chain necessitates a multifaceted approach. By prioritizing adaptability, health and safety, work-life balance, mental health support, and a sense of community, organizations can navigate the challenges of digitalization while safeguarding the welfare of their workforce.

CASE STUDIES OF SUCCESSFUL IMPLEMENTATIONS

Industry Examples

In-Depth Analysis of Industries That Have Successfully Embraced Industry 4.0 for Responsible Supply Chains

The emergence of Industry 4.0 marks a significant transformative phase across multiple industries, fostering the adoption of responsible and sustainable supply chain practices. This comprehensive analysis delves into sectors that have effectively embraced Industry 4.0, highlighting their dedication to fostering responsible supply chains.

The manufacturing sector stands out as a pioneer in incorporating Industry 4.0 technologies like IoT and AI to streamline production processes and mitigate environmental impact (Jan et al., 2023). Smart factories, equipped with interconnected devices, facilitate real-time monitoring, thereby bolstering efficiency and curbing wastage. In the automotive industry, major players have harnessed Industry 4.0 to cultivate responsible supply chains (A. Kumar et al., 2021). Leveraging advanced analytics and automation enables better traceability of raw materials, ensuring the procurement of ethically sourced components and fostering transparency and accountability throughout the supply chain.

Similarly, the healthcare sector has embraced Industry 4.0 to promote responsible supply chains, leveraging technologies such as blockchain and RFID (D. Kumar et al., 2023). These innovations bolster the tracking and authentication of pharmaceuticals, mitigating risks associated with counterfeit drugs and safeguarding patient safety. Industry 4.0 has revolutionized practices within the food and beverage sector, championing sustainability (Hassoun et al., 2022). IoT applications monitor the entire production and distribution chain, guaranteeing food safety and minimizing waste. Real-time data analytics aid in demand forecasting and optimizing inventory management, promoting responsible consumption.

In the electronics industry, Industry 4.0 has played a pivotal role in fostering responsible supply chains (Pessot et al., 2023). The adoption of smart manufacturing processes facilitates resource-efficient operations, thereby reducing electronic waste and promoting material recycling. The successful integration of Industry 4.0 technologies has propelled diverse industries towards the adoption of responsible and sustainable supply chain practices. From manufacturing and automotive to healthcare, food and beverage, and electronics, the utilization of advanced technologies has not only enhanced operational efficiency but also championed ethical sourcing, transparency, and environmental stewardship.

Key Takeaways and Lessons Learned From These Implementations

The successful implementation of Industry 4.0 technologies in various industries for responsible supply chains has yielded key takeaways and valuable lessons that can guide future endeavours.

Enhanced Transparency and Traceability: Industries adopting Industry 4.0 technologies, such as the automotive and healthcare sectors, have experienced heightened levels of transparency and traceability (Vasanthraj et al., 2023). The integration of IoT and blockchain has enabled real-time monitoring and authentication, offering a comprehensive view of the entire supply chain. This increased transparency not only fosters trust among stakeholders but also ensures accountability in sourcing and production processes.

Operational Efficiency and Waste Reduction: The manufacturing and electronics sectors have witnessed significant improvements in operational efficiency through the adoption of smart manufacturing processes (Singh et al., 2022). IoT applications and advanced analytics have allowed for real-time data analysis, optimizing production processes, and minimizing waste. The emphasis on responsible consumption and resource efficiency contributes to sustainable practices within these industries.

Ethical Sourcing and Compliance: A key lesson from the food and beverage sector is the ability of Industry 4.0 to facilitate ethical sourcing and compliance (Hassoun et al., 2023). Through IoT-enabled monitoring, companies can track the entire production and distribution chain, ensuring the sourcing of ethically produced components. This not only aligns with responsible business practices but also helps companies comply with industry regulations and standards.

Improved Risk Management: The integration of Industry 4.0 technologies has empowered industries to enhance risk management strategies. Real-time data analytics and IoT applications enable proactive identification and mitigation of risks within the supply chain (Shah et al., 2021). This not only safeguards against potential disruptions but also fosters resilience in the face of unforeseen challenges, contributing to the overall sustainability of supply chains.

Adaptability and Innovation: Successful Industry 4.0 implementations have showcased the importance of adaptability and a culture of innovation (Soltani et al., 2023). Companies that embrace a mindset of continuous improvement and innovation are better positioned to navigate the complexities of modern supply chains. This adaptability allows industries to stay ahead of evolving trends and challenges, ensuring long-term sustainability. The key takeaways from industries that have embraced Industry 4.0 for responsible supply chains underscore the importance of transparency, operational efficiency, ethical sourcing, risk management, and a culture of innovation. As more sectors embark on their Industry 4.0 journeys, these lessons serve as valuable insights for building resilient and sustainable supply chain practices.

Figure 8. The rise of Industry 4.0 (Raizada, 2023)

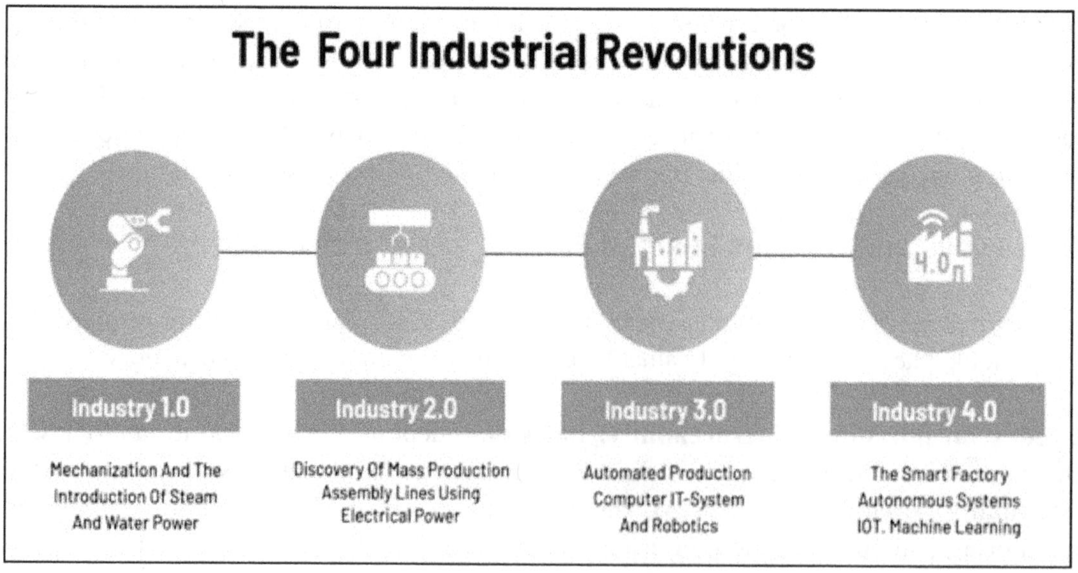

FUTURE OUTLOOK

Evolving Landscape

Discussion on the Ongoing Evolution of Industry 4.0 Technologies and Their Implications for Responsible Supply Chains

The progressive development of Industry 4.0 technologies has sparked significant changes in the global business arena, particularly concerning supply chains. This document aims to shed light on the current status of Industry 4.0 technologies and their impact on promoting ethical supply chains. Industry 4.0, characterized by the integration of digital tools, automation, and data exchange in manufacturing, has seen rapid progress in recent years (Rosário & Dias, 2023). This advancement has given rise to intelligent factories and interconnected supply chain systems. Figure 8 illustrates the evolution of Industry 4.0 from its inception. The integration of Industry 4.0 technologies into supply chain management carries significant implications for ethical business practices. Real-time data analysis enables companies to monitor and streamline their supply chain operations, leading to enhanced efficiency and minimized environmental footprints (Shi et al., 2023). Furthermore, technologies such as the IoT and blockchain enhance visibility and traceability within supply chains. This heightened transparency fosters responsible sourcing and ensures adherence to social and environmental standards, thereby promoting the development of ethical supply chains. However, despite the numerous advantages offered by Industry 4.0, it also presents challenges, particularly in terms of safeguarding data security and privacy (Qahtan et al., 2023). Striking a balance between innovation and ethical considerations becomes imperative to fully harness the potential of these technologies. The ongoing evolution of Industry 4.0 is reshaping supply chains, bringing forth both obstacles and opportunities for ethical business practices. As companies continue to adopt these advancements, it is essential to prioritize ethical principles, ensuring that the benefits of Industry 4.0 are utilized responsibly for the betterment of society and the environment.

Anticipation of Future Trends and Innovations

Forecasting upcoming trends and innovations is essential for organizations to maintain competitiveness and navigate the ever-changing business landscape. This report delves into the importance of anticipating future trends and innovations to equip businesses for the challenges and opportunities that lie ahead.

In today's dynamic world, the business environment is in a constant state of flux. Staying ahead necessitates a proactive approach to identifying emerging trends and innovations before they become widespread (Allal-Chérif et al., 2023). By grasping the dynamics of change, organizations can strategically position themselves to leverage new opportunities and mitigate potential risks. Technological innovation stands out as a primary driver of future trends. Emerging technologies such as AI, quantum computing, and advanced robotics are poised to revolutionize various industries (Zhu et al., 2023). Companies that embrace and integrate these technologies early are likely to gain a competitive advantage.

Anticipating future trends also entails taking into account societal shifts. Changes in demographics, consumer preferences, and social values can profoundly influence market dynamics. Organizations that are attuned to these shifts can tailor their strategies to meet evolving customer needs and expectations. Additionally, there is a growing emphasis on sustainability and environmental concerns. Businesses are increasingly recognizing the significance of adopting eco-friendly practices and products (Reddy et al.,

2023). Anticipating and integrating sustainable practices into business models can not only contribute to environmental well-being but also cater to the demands of an environmentally conscious consumer base.

To effectively navigate the uncertain future, organizations must incorporate trend anticipation into their strategic planning processes. This involves fostering a culture of innovation, continuous learning, and adaptability within the workforce (Achdiat et al., 2022). Moreover, partnerships and collaborations with external stakeholders can offer valuable insights into emerging trends. Anticipating future trends and innovations is a strategic imperative for organizations aiming to thrive in a rapidly changing world. By remaining vigilant, embracing technological advancements, considering societal shifts, and addressing sustainability concerns, businesses can position themselves for success in the evolving marketplace.

CONCLUSION

Summary of Key Findings

Recapitulation of Key Insights Into How Industry 4.0 Technologies Can Harness Responsible Supply Chains

In the concluding chapter, we delve into a recapitulation of the key insights gleaned throughout the exploration of Industry 4.0 technologies and their pivotal role in fostering responsible supply chains. The journey began with an elucidation of the intersection between sustainability and these advanced digital technologies, highlighting their transformative impact on supply chain practices. The outlined objectives guided our investigation into how Industry 4.0 can be harnessed for creating environmentally and socially responsible supply chains. The insights gathered reveal the diverse ways in which digital technologies drive responsible supply chains. From IoT enabling real-time sustainability monitoring to big data analytics informing sustainable decision-making, and robotics enhancing ethical manufacturing, each technological facet contributes uniquely to the overarching goal of responsible supply chain management.

The application of Industry 4.0 technologies enables the integration of circular economy principles, exemplified through case studies of closed-loop supply chain initiatives. Additionally, strategies for energy-efficient operations and socially responsible sourcing practices were explored, showcasing the broad spectrum of positive impacts that can be achieved through digital innovation. Despite the transformative potential, challenges were acknowledged, and strategies were proposed for overcoming implementation hurdles. The chapter also underscores the human-centric responsibility in the digital era, emphasizing ethical considerations and strategies for workforce empowerment and well-being within the digitalized supply chain. Finally, through in-depth case studies of industries successfully embracing Industry 4.0 for responsible supply chains, the chapter concludes with a forward-looking perspective on the evolving landscape. Anticipating future trends and innovations, the recapitulation reinforces the chapter's central thesis — Industry 4.0 technologies are not only catalysts for efficiency and innovation but powerful enablers for the creation of sustainable, ethical, and socially responsible supply chains.

Reinforcement of the Transformative Potential of Digital Technologies for Sustainable and Ethical Manufacturing

In the concluding segment, we emphasize the profound impact of digital technologies on manufacturing, reinforcing their transformative potential for sustainable and ethical practices. Throughout the exploration of Industry 4.0 technologies, a resounding theme emerges — the capacity of digital advancements to revolutionize traditional manufacturing paradigms. The narrative underscores that these technologies extend beyond mere operational enhancements. They are catalysts for a paradigm shift towards sustainability and ethics in manufacturing. By integrating IoT for real-time sustainability monitoring, employing big data analytics for informed decision-making, and incorporating robotics to enhance ethical production, Industry 4.0 technologies offer a holistic approach to responsible manufacturing. The recapitulation emphasizes how these technologies facilitate circular economic integration, exemplified through case studies of closed-loop supply chain initiatives. Furthermore, the outlined strategies for energy-efficient operations and socially responsible sourcing underscore the comprehensive impact of digital innovation on reducing environmental footprints and ensuring ethical treatment throughout the supply chain.

The challenges addressed throughout the chapter do not overshadow the immense opportunities for innovation in responsible supply chain practices. Collaboration and partnerships emerge as key drivers for widespread adoption, showcasing the potential for a collective industry effort toward sustainable and ethical manufacturing. In essence, the chapter reinforces the transformative potential of Industry 4.0 technologies, not merely as tools for operational efficiency but as powerful agents shaping the future landscape of manufacturing. It leaves the reader with a firm conviction that the integration of digital technologies is not just a technological evolution; it is a pivotal force propelling manufacturing into an era defined by sustainability, ethics, and a commitment to responsible global practices.

REFERENCES

Aamer, A. M., Sahara, C. R., & Al-Awlaqi, M. A. (2022). Digitalization of the supply chain: Transformation factors. *Journal of Science & Technology Policy Management*, *14*(4), 713–733. doi:10.1108/JSTPM-01-2021-0001

Abbate, S., Centobelli, P., & Cerchione, R. (2023). From Fast to Slow: An exploratory analysis of circular business models in the Italian apparel industry. *International Journal of Production Economics*, *260*, 108824. doi:10.1016/j.ijpe.2023.108824

Abdulaziz, Q. A., Kaidi, H. M., Masrom, M., Hamzah, H. S., Sarip, S., Dziyauddin, R. A., & Muhammad-Sukki, F. (2023). Developing an IoT Framework for Industry 4.0 in Malaysian SMEs: An analysis of current status, practices, and challenges. *Applied Sciences (Basel, Switzerland)*, *13*(6), 3658. doi:10.3390/app13063658

Achdiat, I., Mulyani, S., Azis, Y., & Sukmadilaga, C. (2022). Roles of organizational learning culture in promoting innovation. *The Learning Organization*, *30*(1), 76–92. doi:10.1108/TLO-01-2021-0013

Achoki, P. M. (2023). Upskilling and reskilling for a VUCA world. *GILE Journal of Skills Development*, *3*(2), 34–52. doi:10.52398/gjsd.2023.v3.i2.pp34-52

Adeyemo, V. E., Abdullah, A., Jhanjhi, N. Z., Supramaniam, M., & Balogun, A. O. (2019). Ensemble and Deep-Learning Methods for Two-Class and Multi-Attack Anomaly Intrusion Detection: An Empirical study. *International Journal of Advanced Computer Science and Applications, 10*(9). Advance online publication. doi:10.14569/IJACSA.2019.0100969

Aftab, J., Abid, N., Cucari, N., & Savastano, M. (2022). Green human resource management and environmental performance: The role of green innovation and environmental strategy in a developing country. *Business Strategy and the Environment, 32*(4), 1782–1798. doi:10.1002/bse.3219

Aghahosseini, A., Solomon, A., Breyer, C., Pregger, T., Simon, S., Strachan, P. A., & Jäger-Waldau, A. (2023). Energy system transition pathways to meet the global electricity demand for ambitious climate targets and cost competitiveness. *Applied Energy, 331*, 120401. doi:10.1016/j.apenergy.2022.120401

Agote-Garrido, A., Gómez, A. M. M., & Lama-Ruiz, J. R. (2023). Manufacturing System Design in Industry 5.0: Incorporating sociotechnical systems and social metabolism for Human-Centered, Sustainable, and Resilient production. *Systems, 11*(11), 537. doi:10.3390/systems11110537

Agustian, K., Mubarok, E. S., Zen, A., Wiwin, W., & Malik, A. J. (2023). The impact of digital transformation on business models and competitive advantage. *Technology and Society Perspectives, 1*(2), 79–93. doi:10.61100/tacit.v1i2.55

Ahmed, M. M., Hassanien, E., & Hassanien, A. E. (2023). IoT-based intelligent waste management system. *Neural Computing & Applications, 35*(32), 23551–23579. doi:10.1007/s00521-023-08970-7

Ahmed, W. A., MacCarthy, B. L., & Ahmed, W. A. (2023). Blockchain-enabled supply chain traceability – How wide? How deep? *International Journal of Production Economics, 263*, 108963. doi:10.1016/j.ijpe.2023.108963

Aitlmoudden, O., Housni, M., Safeh, N., & Namir, A. (2023). A Microservices-based Framework for Scalable Data Analysis in Agriculture with IoT Integration. *International Journal of Interactive Mobile Technologies, 17*(19), 147–156. doi:10.3991/ijim.v17i19.40457

Akram, M. N., & Abdul-Kader, W. (2023). Sustainable Development Goals and End-of-Life Electric Vehicle Battery: Literature Review. *Batteries, 9*(7), 353. doi:10.3390/batteries9070353

Al-Khatib, A. W. (2023). Fostering green innovation: The roles of big data analytics capabilities and green supply chain integration. *European Journal of Innovation Management*. Advance online publication. doi:10.1108/EJIM-09-2022-0491

Alferidah, D. K., & Jhanjhi, N. Z. (2020). Cybersecurity Impact over Bigdata and IoT Growth. *2020 International Conference on Computational Intelligence (ICCI)*. 10.1109/ICCI51257.2020.9247722

Aljohani, A. (2023). Predictive analytics and machine learning for Real-Time supply chain risk mitigation and agility. *Sustainability (Basel), 15*(20), 15088. doi:10.3390/su152015088

Alkinani, M. H., Almazroi, A. A., Jhanjhi, N. Z., & Khan, N. A. (2021). 5G and IoT Based Reporting and Accident Detection (RAD) System to Deliver First Aid Box Using Unmanned Aerial Vehicle. *Sensors (Basel), 21*(20), 6905. doi:10.3390/s21206905 PMID:34696118

Allal-Chérif, O., Climent, J. C., & Berenguer, K. J. U. (2023). Born to be sustainable: How to combine strategic disruption, open innovation, and process digitization to create a sustainable business. *Journal of Business Research, 154*, 113379. doi:10.1016/j.jbusres.2022.113379

Almalki, F. A., Alsamhi, S. H., Sahal, R., Hassan, J., Hawbani, A., Rajput, N. S., Saif, A., Morgan, J., & Breslin, J. G. (2021). Green IoT for Eco-Friendly and Sustainable Smart Cities: Future directions and opportunities. *Mobile Networks and Applications*, *28*(1), 178–202. doi:10.1007/s11036-021-01790-w

Almoaigel, M. F., & Abuabid, A. (2023). Implementation of Cybersecurity Situation Awareness Model in Saudi SMES. *International Journal of Advanced Computer Science and Applications*, *14*(11). Advance online publication. doi:10.14569/IJACSA.2023.01411110

Almusaylim, Z. A., Jhanjhi, N. Z., & Jung, L. T. (2018). Proposing A Data Privacy Aware Protocol for Roadside Accident Video Reporting Service Using 5G In Vehicular Cloud Networks Environment. *2018 4th International Conference on Computer and Information Sciences (ICCOINS)*. 10.1109/ICCOINS.2018.8510588

Alsudani, M. Q., Jaber, M. M., Ali, M. H., Khalil, S., Alkhayyat, A., Kareem, Z. H., & Mohhan, A. R. (2023). RETRACTED ARTICLE: Smart logistics with IoT-based enterprise management system using global manufacturing. *Journal of Combinatorial Optimization*, *45*(2), 57. Advance online publication. doi:10.1007/s10878-022-00977-5

Althabatah, A., Yaqot, M., Menezes, B. C., & Kerbache, L. (2023). Transformative Procurement Trends: Integrating Industry 4.0 technologies for enhanced procurement processes. *Logistics*, *7*(3), 63. doi:10.3390/logistics7030063

Ananna, F. F., Nowreen, R., Jahwari, S. S. R. A., Costa, E., Angeline, L., & Sindiramutty, S. R. (2023). Analysing Influential factors in student academic achievement: Prediction modelling and insight. *International Journal of Emerging Multidisciplinaries Computer Science & Artificial Intelligence*, *2*(1). Advance online publication. doi:10.54938/ijemdcsai.2023.02.1.254

AttaranM.AttaranS.ÇelikB. G. (2023). Digital Twins and Industrial Internet of Things: Uncovering Operational Intelligence in Industry 4.0. SSRN. doi:10.2139/ssrn.4612135

Attiany, M. S., Al-Kharabsheh, S. A., Al-Makhariz, L. S., Abed-Qader, M. A., Al-Hawary, S. I. S., Mohammad, A. S., & Rahamneh, A. A. (2023). Barriers to adopt industry 4.0 in supply chains using interpretive structural modeling. *Uncertain Supply Chain Management*, *11*(1), 299–306. doi:10.5267/j.uscm.2022.9.013

Azam, H., Dulloo, M. I., Majeed, M. H., Wan, J. P. H., Xin, L. T., & Sindiramutty, S. R. (2023). Cybercrime Unmasked: Investigating cases and digital evidence. *International Journal of Emerging Multidisciplinaries Computer Science & Artificial Intelligence*, *2*(1). Advance online publication. doi:10.54938/ijemdcsai.2023.02.1.255

Azam, H., Dulloo, M. I., Majeed, M. H., Wan, J. P. H., Xin, L. T., Tajwar, M. A., & Sindiramutty, S. R. (2023). Defending the Digital Frontier: IDPS and the Battle Against Cyber Threat. *International Journal of Emerging Multidisciplinaries: Computer Science & Artificial Intelligence,* *2*(1). doi:10.54938/ijemdcsai.2023.02.1.253

Azam, H., Tajwar, M. A., Mayhialagan, S., Davis, A. J., Yik, C. J., Ali, D., & Sindiramutty, S. R. (2023). Innovations in Security: A study of cloud Computing and IoT. *International Journal of Emerging Multidisciplinaries Computer Science & Artificial Intelligence*, *2*(1). Advance online publication. doi:10.54938/ijemdcsai.2023.02.1.252

AzamH.TanM.PinL. T.SyahmiM. A.QianA. L. W.JingyanH.UddinH.SindiramuttyS. R. (2023). Wireless Technology Security and Privacy: A Comprehensive Study. Preprints. doi:10.20944/preprints202311.0664.v1

Bai, T., Qi, Y., Li, Z., & Xu, D. (2023). Digital economy, industrial transformation and upgrading, and spatial transfer of carbon emissions: The paths for low-carbon transformation of Chinese cities. *Journal of Environmental Management*, *344*, 118528. doi:10.1016/j.jenvman.2023.118528 PMID:37392691

Baweja, P., Kumar, S., & Kumar, G. (2020). Fertilizers and pesticides: Their impact on soil health and environment. In Soil biology (pp. 265–285). doi:10.1007/978-3-030-44364-1_15

BrohiS. N.JhanjhiN. Z.BrohiN. N.BrohiM. N. (2020). Key Applications of State-of-the-Art Technologies to Mitigate and Eliminate COVID-19. TechRxiv. doi:10.36227/techrxiv.12115596.v2

Buonomo, I., Ferrara, B., Pansini, M., & Benevene, P. (2023). Job satisfaction and perceived structural support in Remote Working Conditions—The role of a sense of community at work. *International Journal of Environmental Research and Public Health*, *20*(13), 6205. doi:10.3390/ijerph20136205 PMID:37444053

Camilleri, M. A., Troise, C., Strazzullo, S., & Bresciani, S. (2023). Creating shared value through open innovation approaches: Opportunities and challenges for corporate sustainability. *Business Strategy and the Environment*, *32*(7), 4485–4502. doi:10.1002/bse.3377

Cassetta, E., Dileo, I., & Pini, M. (2022). Linking external collaborations, eco-innovation and sustainable growth. An empirical analysis on the Italian manufacturing firms. *Industry and Innovation*, *30*(4), 452–479. doi:10.1080/13662716.2022.2109456

Chand, M., Jain, V., & Ajmera, P. (2023). *Data-Driven technologies and artificial intelligence in supply chain: Tools and Techniques*. CRC Press.

Chandan, A., John, M., & Potdar, V. (2023). Achieving UN SDGs in food supply chain using blockchain technology. *Sustainability (Basel)*, *15*(3), 2109. doi:10.3390/su15032109

Chauhan, M., & Shiaeles, S. (2023). An analysis of cloud security frameworks, problems and proposed solutions. *Network (Bristol, England)*, *3*(3), 422–450. doi:10.3390/network3030018

Chen, J., Fu, Y., Lu, W., & Pan, Y. (2023). Augmented reality-enabled human-robot collaboration to balance construction waste sorting efficiency and occupational safety and health. *Journal of Environmental Management*, *348*, 119341. doi:10.1016/j.jenvman.2023.119341 PMID:37852080

Chen, S., Su, Y., Tufail, B., Lam, V. T., Phan, T. T. H., & Ngo, T. Q. (2023). The moderating role of leadership on the relationship between green supply chain management, technological advancement, and knowledge management in sustainable performance. *Environmental Science and Pollution Research International*, *30*(19), 56654–56669. doi:10.1007/s11356-023-26304-x PMID:36920606

Chen, X., Zhou, B., Štilić, A., Stević, Ž., & Puška, A. (2023). A Fuzzy–Rough MCDM Approach for selecting green Suppliers in the furniture Manufacturing industry: A Case Study of Eco-Friendly Material Production. *Sustainability (Basel), 15*(13), 10745. doi:10.3390/su151310745

Chesti, I. A., Humayun, M., Sama, N. U., & Jhanjhi, N. Z. (2020). Evolution, Mitigation, and Prevention of Ransomware. *2020 2nd International Conference on Computer and Information Sciences (ICCIS).* 10.1109/ICCIS49240.2020.9257708

Chukwu, E. (2023, June 16). *Navigating Ethical Supply chains: the intersection of diplomatic management and theological ethics.* https://jurnal.itscience.org/index.php/ijmdsa/article/view/2874

Daradkeh, M. (2023). Navigating the Complexity of Entrepreneurial Ethics: A Systematic Review and Future Research agenda. *Sustainability (Basel), 15*(14), 11099. doi:10.3390/su151411099

De Oliveira, R. T., Ghobakhloo, M., & Figueira, S. (2023). Industry 4.0 towards social and environmental sustainability in multinationals: Enabling circular economy, organizational social practices, and corporate purpose. *Journal of Cleaner Production, 430*, 139712. doi:10.1016/j.jclepro.2023.139712

Dharmayanti, N., Ismail, T., Hanifah, I. A., & Taqi, M. (2023). Exploring sustainability management control system and eco-innovation matter sustainable financial performance: The role of supply chain management and digital adaptability in indonesian context. *Journal of Open Innovation, 9*(3), 100119. doi:10.1016/j.joitmc.2023.100119

DhimanB. (2023). Ethical Issues and Challenges in social Media: A current scenario. *Social Science Research Network.* doi:10.2139/ssrn.4406610

Dion, H., Evans, M., & Farrell, P. (2022). Hospitals management transformative initiatives; towards energy efficiency and environmental sustainability in healthcare facilities. *Journal of Engineering. Design and Technology, 21*(2), 552–584. doi:10.1108/JEDT-04-2022-0200

Diwaker, C., Tomar, P., Solanki, A., Nayyar, A., Jhanjhi, N. Z., Abdullah, A., & Supramaniam, M. (2019). A new model for predicting Component-Based software reliability using soft computing. *IEEE Access : Practical Innovations, Open Solutions, 7*, 147191–147203. doi:10.1109/ACCESS.2019.2946862

Duan, W., Khurshid, A., Khan, K., & Călin, A. C. (2024). Transforming industry: Investigating 4.0 technologies for sustainable product evolution in china through a novel fuzzy three-way decision-making process. *Technological Forecasting and Social Change, 200*, 123125. doi:10.1016/j.techfore.2023.123125

Elbaşi, E., Zaki, C., Topcu, A. E., Abdelbaki, W., Zreikat, A. I., Cina, E., Shdefat, A. Y., & Saker, L. (2023). Crop prediction model using machine learning algorithms. *Applied Sciences (Basel, Switzerland), 13*(16), 9288. doi:10.3390/app13169288

Everritt, M., & Rundio, A. (2023). Mental Health Resources for NCAA Student-Athletes. *Case Studies in Sport Management, 12*(1), 6–10. doi:10.1123/cssm.2022-0016

Fatima-Tuz-Zahra, Jhanjhi, N. Z., Brohi, S. N., Malik, N. A., & Humayun, M. (2020). Proposing a Hybrid RPL Protocol for Rank and Wormhole Attack Mitigation using Machine Learning. *2020 2nd International Conference on Computer and Information Sciences.*

Fisk, R. P., Gallan, A., Joubert, A. M., Beekhuyzen, J., Cheung, L., & Russell–Bennett, R. (2022). Healing the digital divide with digital inclusion: Enabling human capabilities. *Journal of Service Research, 26*(4), 542–559. doi:10.1177/10946705221140148

Fraboni, F., Brendel, H., & Pietrantoni, L. (2023). Evaluating organizational Guidelines for Enhancing Psychological Well-Being, Safety, and Performance in Technology Integration. *Sustainability (Basel), 15*(10), 8113. doi:10.3390/su15108113

Gaur, L., Afaq, A., Solanki, A., Singh, G., Sharma, S., Jhanjhi, N. Z., My, H. T., & Le, D. (2021). Capitalizing on big data and revolutionary 5G technology: Extracting and visualizing ratings and reviews of global chain hotels. *Computers & Electrical Engineering, 95*, 107374. doi:10.1016/j.compeleceng.2021.107374

Gaur, L., Singh, G., Solanki, A., Jhanjhi, N. Z., Bhatia, U., Sharma, S., & Verma, S. (2021). Disposition of youth in predicting sustainable development goals using the Neuro - fuzzy and random forest algorithms. *Human-Centric Computing and Information Sciences*. https://repository.usp.ac.fj/12807/

George, D., & George, A. (2023). Revolutionizing Manufacturing: Exploring the Promises and Challenges of Industry 5.0. Zenodo *(CERN European Organization for Nuclear Research)*. doi:10.5281/zenodo.7852124

Ghasemshirazi, S., Shirvani, G., & Alipour, M. A. (2023). Zero Trust: applications, challenges, and opportunities. *arXiv (Cornell University)*. https://doi.org//arxiv.2309.03582 doi:10.48550

Ghosh, G., Kavita, Verma, S., Jhanjhi, N. Z., & Talib, M. N. (2020). Secure surveillance system using chaotic image encryption technique. *IOP Conference Series. Materials Science and Engineering, 993*(1), 012062. doi:10.1088/1757-899X/993/1/012062

Gisi, P. J. (2024). *The Dark Factory and the future of manufacturing: A Guide to Operational Efficiency and Competitiveness*. Productivity Press. doi:10.4324/9781032688152

Gopi, R., Sathiyamoorthi, V., Selvakumar, S., Ramesh, M., Chatterjee, P., Jhanjhi, N. Z., & Luhach, A. K. (2021). Enhanced method of ANN based model for detection of DDoS attacks on multimedia internet of things. *Multimedia Tools and Applications, 81*(19), 26739–26757. doi:10.1007/s11042-021-10640-6

Grabowska, S., Cagáňová, D., & Saniuk, A. (2021). Knowledge and skills of industrial employees and managerial staff for the industry 4.0 implementation. *Mobile Networks and Applications, 28*(1), 220–230. doi:10.1007/s11036-021-01788-4

Guan, L., Li, W., Cheng, G. Y. M., & Huang, J. (2023). Environmental strategy for sustainable development: Role of digital transformation in China's natural resource exploitation. *Resources Policy, 87*, 104304. doi:10.1016/j.resourpol.2023.104304

Gunasekaran, K., & Boopathi, S. (2023). Artificial intelligence in water treatments and water resource assessments. In Advances in environmental engineering and green technologies book series (pp. 71–98). doi:10.4018/978-1-6684-6791-6.ch004

Gupta, K. (2023, August 16). *Harnessing AI for strategic Decision-Making and business performance optimization*. https://www.ijisae.org/index.php/IJISAE/article/view/3360

Han, Y., Шевченко, T., Yannou, B., Ranjbari, M., Esfandabadi, Z. S., Saidani, M., Bouillass, G., Bliumska-Danko, K., & Li, G. (2023). Exploring how digital technologies enable a circular economy of products. *Sustainability (Basel), 15*(3), 2067. doi:10.3390/su15032067

Han, Y., Qamruzzaman, M., & Kor, S. (2023). Charting a Sustainable Future: The impact of economic policy, environmental tax, innovation, and natural resources on clean energy consumption. *Sustainability, 15*(18), 13591. doi:10.3390/su151813591

Hasan, M., Hossain, S., Mofijur, M., Kabir, Z., Badruddin, I. A., Khan, T. M. Y., & Jassim, E. I. (2023). Harnessing solar Power: A review of photovoltaic innovations, solar thermal systems, and the dawn of energy storage solutions. *Energies, 16*(18), 6456. doi:10.3390/en16186456

Hassoun, A., Bekhit, A. E. A., Jambrak, A. R., Regenstein, J. M., Chémat, F., Morton, J. D., Guðjónsdóttir, M., Carpena, M., Prieto, M. A., Varela, P., Arshad, R. N., Aadil, R. M., Bhat, Z. F., & Ueland, Ø. (2022). The fourth industrial revolution in the food industry—part II: Emerging food trends. *Critical Reviews in Food Science and Nutrition, 64*(2), 407–437. doi:10.1080/10408398.2022.2106472 PMID:35930319

Hassoun, A., Boukid, F., Özoğul, F., Aït-Kaddour, A., Del Castillo, J. M. S., Roohinejad, S., Perestrelo, R., Galanakis, C. M., Bono, G., Bouyahya, A., Bhat, Z. F., Smaoui, S., Jambrak, A. R., & Medina, S. (2023). Creating new opportunities for sustainable food packaging through dimensions of industry 4.0: New insights into the food waste perspective. *Trends in Food Science & Technology, 142*, 104238. doi:10.1016/j.tifs.2023.104238

Hassoun, A., Prieto, M. A., Carpena, M., Bouzembrak, Y., Marvin, H., Pallarés, N., Barba, F. J., Bangar, S. P., Chaudhary, V., Ibrahim, S. A., & Bovo, G. (2022). Exploring the role of green and Industry 4.0 technologies in achieving sustainable development goals in food sectors. *Food Research International, 162*, 112068. doi:10.1016/j.foodres.2022.112068 PMID:36461323

Haval, A. M., & Rahman, F. H. (2024). Application of machine learning techniques and the Internet of Things for smart, sustainable agriculture. *BIO Web of Conferences, 82*, 05021. 10.1051/bioconf/20248205021

He, S. (2023). Do you reap what you sow? Driving mechanism of supply chain transparency on consumers' indirect reciprocity. *Frontiers in Psychology, 14*, 1081297. Advance online publication. doi:10.3389/fpsyg.2023.1081297 PMID:36844304

Hearn, G., Williams, P., Rodrigues, J. H. P., & Laundon, M. (2023). Education and training for industry 4.0: A case study of a manufacturing ecosystem. *Education + Training, 65*(8/9), 1070–1084. doi:10.1108/ET-10-2022-0407

Hrouga, M. (2023). Towards a new conceptual digital collaborative supply chain model based on Industry 4.0 technologies: A conceptual framework. *International Journal of Quality & Reliability Management*. Advance online publication. doi:10.1108/IJQRM-07-2022-0221

Hui, C. K. C. S. H., Dan, G., Alamri, S., & Toghraie, D. (2023). Greening smart cities: An investigation of the integration of urban natural resources and smart city technologies for promoting environmental sustainability. *Sustainable Cities and Society, 99*, 104985. doi:10.1016/j.scs.2023.104985

Humayun, M., Alsaqer, M., & Jhanjhi, N. Z. (2022). Energy optimization for smart cities using IoT. *Applied Artificial Intelligence*, *36*(1), 2037255. Advance online publication. doi:10.1080/08839514.2022.2037255

Hussain, S. J., Ahmed, U., Liaquat, H., Mir, S., Jhanjhi, N. Z., & Humayun, M. (2019). IMIAD: Intelligent Malware Identification for Android Platform. *2019 International Conference on Computer and Information Sciences (ICCIS)*. 10.1109/ICCISci.2019.8716471

IslamM. M.NayemA. I.BristyU. A.EshaS. A. (2023). Approaches to E-Waste Reduction through 4R, Public Awareness, and Design for Sustainability. *Social Science Research Network*. doi:10.2139/ssrn.4458682

Jan, Z., Ahamed, F., Mayer, W., Patel, N., Großmann, G., Stumptner, M., & Kuusk, A. (2023). Artificial intelligence for industry 4.0: Systematic review of applications, challenges, and opportunities. *Expert Systems with Applications*, *216*, 119456. doi:10.1016/j.eswa.2022.119456

Javaid, M., Khan, S., Haleem, A., & Rab, S. (2022). Adoption of modern technologies for implementing industry 4.0: An integrated MCDM approach. *Benchmarking*, *30*(10), 3753–3790. doi:10.1108/BIJ-01-2021-0017

Jhanjhi, N. Z., Humayun, M., & Almuayqil, S. N. (2021). Cyber security and privacy issues in industrial internet of things. *Computer Systems Science and Engineering*, *37*(3), 361–380. doi:10.32604/csse.2021.015206

Jiang, H., & Shen, H. (2020). Toward a relational theory of employee engagement: Understanding authenticity, transparency, and employee behaviors. *International Journal of Business Communication*, *60*(3), 948–975. doi:10.1177/2329488420954236

Kamble, S. S., Gunasekaran, A., Subramanian, N., Ghadge, A., Belhadi, A., & Mani, V. (2021). Blockchain technology's impact on supply chain integration and sustainable supply chain performance: Evidence from the automotive industry. *Annals of Operations Research*, *327*(1), 575–600. doi:10.1007/s10479-021-04129-6

Kanchana, S., Rajan, D., Mahaveerakannan, R., Sagar, K. V. D., Subramanian, P., & Rajakumar, B. R. (2024). Predictive maintenance model using hybrid procedure of improved Quantum Cat swarm optimisation for asset management in industry 4.0. In Lecture notes in networks and systems (pp. 499–515). doi:10.1007/978-981-99-6547-2_38

Karmaker, C. L., Aziz, R. A., Ahmed, T., Misbauddin, S. M., & Moktadir, M. A. (2023). Impact of industry 4.0 technologies on sustainable supply chain performance: The mediating role of green supply chain management practices and circular economy. *Journal of Cleaner Production*, *419*, 138249. doi:10.1016/j.jclepro.2023.138249

Kazançoğlu, Y., Sağnak, M., Kazançoğlu, İ., & Dora, M. (2021). Framework for a sustainable supply chain to overcome risks in transition to a circular economy through Industry 4.0. *Production Planning and Control*, *34*(10), 902–917. doi:10.1080/09537287.2021.1980910

Kozma, D., Varga, P., & Hegedűs, C. (2019). Supply Chain Management and Logistics 4.0 - A Study on Arrowhead Framework Integration. *Proceedings of the 8th International Conference on Industrial Technology and Management (ICITM)*. 10.1109/ICITM.2019.8710670

Krishnan, S., Thangaveloo, R., Rahman, S. B. A., & Sindiramutty, S. R. (2021). Smart Ambulance Traffic Control system. *Trends in Undergraduate Research*, *4*(1), c28–c34. doi:10.33736/tur.2831.2021

Kulkov, I., Kulkova, J., Rohrbeck, R., Menvielle, L., Kaartemo, V., & Makkonen, H. (2023). Artificial intelligence - driven sustainable development: Examining organizational, technical, and processing approaches to achieving global goals. *Sustainable Development (Bradford)*, sd.2773. Advance online publication. doi:10.1002/sd.2773

Kumar, A., Choudhary, S., Garza-Reyes, J. A., Kumar, V., Khan, S. R., & Mishra, N. (2021). Analysis of critical success factors for implementing Industry 4.0 integrated circular supply chain – moving towards sustainable operations. *Production Planning and Control*, *34*(10), 984–998. doi:10.1080/09537287.2021.1980905

Kumar, D., Singh, R., Mishra, R., & Daim, T. U. (2023). Roadmap for integrating blockchain with Internet of Things (IoT) for sustainable and secured operations in logistics and supply chains: Decision making framework with case illustration. *Technological Forecasting and Social Change*, *196*, 122837. doi:10.1016/j.techfore.2023.122837

Kumar, M., Raut, R. D., Mangla, S. K., Chowdhury, S., & Choubey, V. K. (2024). Moderating ESG compliance between industry 4.0 and green practices with green servitization: Examining its impact on green supply chain performance. *Technovation*, *129*, 102898. doi:10.1016/j.technovation.2023.102898

Kumar, T., Pandey, B., Mussavi, S. H., & Jhanjhi, N. Z. (2015). CTHS based energy efficient Thermal Aware Image ALU design on FPGA. *Wireless Personal Communications*, *85*(3), 671–696. doi:10.1007/s11277-015-2801-8

Kusi-Sarpong, S., Gupta, H., Khan, S. A., Jabbour, C. J. C., Rehman, S. T., & Kusi-Sarpong, H. (2021). Sustainable supplier selection based on industry 4.0 initiatives within the context of circular economy implementation in supply chain operations. *Production Planning and Control*, *34*(10), 999–1019. doi:10.1080/09537287.2021.1980906

Kusiak, A. (2023). Smart manufacturing. In Springer handbooks (pp. 973–985). doi:10.1007/978-3-030-96729-1_45

Lamnabhi-Lagarrigue, F., & Samad, T. (2023). Social, organizational, and individual impacts of automation. In Springer handbooks (pp. 61–75). doi:10.1007/978-3-030-96729-1_3

Lim, M., Abdullah, A., Jhanjhi, N. Z., & Khan, M. K. (2020). Situation-Aware Deep Reinforcement Learning link Prediction model for evolving criminal networks. *IEEE Access : Practical Innovations, Open Solutions*, *8*, 16550–16559. doi:10.1109/ACCESS.2019.2961805

Liu, L., Song, W., & Liu, Y. (2023). Leveraging digital capabilities toward a circular economy: Reinforcing sustainable supply chain management with Industry 4.0 technologies. *Computers & Industrial Engineering*, *178*, 109113. doi:10.1016/j.cie.2023.109113

López, O. L. A., Rosabal, O. M., Ruiz-Guirola, D. E., Raghuwanshi, P., Mikhaylov, K., Lovén, L., & Iyer, S. (2023). Energy-Sustainable IoT connectivity: Vision, technological enablers, challenges, and future directions. *IEEE Open Journal of the Communications Society*, *4*, 2609–2666. doi:10.1109/OJCOMS.2023.3323832

Lutfi, A., Alrawad, M., Alsyouf, A., Almaiah, M. A., Al-Khasawneh, A., Al-Khasawneh, A. L., Alshira'h, A. F., Alshirah, M. H., Saad, M., & Ibrahim, N. (2023). Drivers and impact of big data analytic adoption in the retail industry: A quantitative investigation applying structural equation modeling. *Journal of Retailing and Consumer Services, 70*, 103129. doi:10.1016/j.jretconser.2022.103129

Lv, Z., & Shang, W. (2023). Impacts of intelligent transportation systems on energy conservation and emission reduction of transport systems: A comprehensive review. *Green Technologies and Sustainability*, *1*(1), 100002. doi:10.1016/j.grets.2022.100002

McIntosh, O. B., Burnett, A. N., Feldman, I. R., Lamphere, J. A., Reuter, T., & Vital, E. (2023). The role of sustainability knowledge-action platforms in advancing multi-stakeholder engagement on sustainability. *Data & Policy*, *5*, e33. Advance online publication. doi:10.1017/dap.2023.27

Mishra, P., & Singh, G. (2023). Energy Management Systems in Sustainable Smart Cities Based on the Internet of Energy: A Technical review. *Energies*, *16*(19), 6903. doi:10.3390/en16196903

Mohamed, M., Sallam, K. M., & Mohamed, M. (2023). Internet of Things (IoT) in Supply Chain Management: Challenges, opportunities, and best practices. *Sustainable Machine Intelligence Journal, 2*. Advance online publication. doi:10.61185/SMIJ.2023.22103

Mohiuddin, M., Reza, M. N. H., Jayashree, S., Al-Azad, S., & Ed-Dafali, S. (2023). The role of governments in driving industry 4.0 adoption in emerging countries. *Journal of Global Information Management*, *31*(1), 1–31. doi:10.4018/JGIM.323439

Morandini, S., Fraboni, F., De Angelis, M., Puzzo, G., Giusino, D., & Pietrantoni, L. (2023). The impact of artificial intelligence on workers' skills: upskilling and reskilling in organisations. *Informing Science the International Journal of an Emerging Transdiscipline, 26*, 39–68. doi:10.28945/5078

Mrozek, T., Seitz, D., Gundermann, K., & Dicke, M. (2020). *Digital supply chains: A Practitioner's Guide to Successful Digitalization*. Campus Verlag.

Mushafiq, M., Arisar, M. M. K., Tariq, H., & Czapp, S. (2023). Energy Efficiency and Economic Policy: Comprehensive theoretical, Empirical, and policy review. *Energies*, *16*(5), 2381. doi:10.3390/en16052381

Muzammal, S. M., Murugesan, R. K., Jhanjhi, N. Z., & Jung, L. T. (2020). SMTrust: Proposing Trust-Based Secure Routing Protocol for RPL Attacks for IoT Applications. *2020 International Conference on Computational Intelligence (ICCI)*. 10.1109/ICCI51257.2020.9247818

Nyarko, D. A., & Fong, R. C. (2023). Cyber security compliance among remote workers. In Advanced sciences and technologies for security applications (pp. 343–369). doi:10.1007/978-3-031-20160-8_18

Olabi, A., Abdelghafar, A. A., Maghrabie, H. M., Sayed, E. T., Rezk, H., Radi, M. A., Obaideen, K., & Abdelkareem, M. A. (2023). Application of artificial intelligence for prediction, optimization, and control of thermal energy storage systems. *Thermal Science and Engineering Progress*, *39*, 101730. doi:10.1016/j.tsep.2023.101730

Ouedraogo, K. E., Ekim, P. O., & Demirok, E. (2023). Feasibility of low-cost energy management system using embedded optimization for PV and battery storage assisted residential buildings. *Energy*, *271*, 126922. doi:10.1016/j.energy.2023.126922

OumaW. N. (2023). Africa's renewable energy dilemma. *Social Science Research Network*. doi:10.2139/ssrn.4477421

Pan, Y., & Froese, F. J. (2023). An interdisciplinary review of AI and HRM: Challenges and future directions. *Human Resource Management Review*, *33*(1), 100924. doi:10.1016/j.hrmr.2022.100924

Pandey, S., Singh, R. K., & Gunasekaran, A. (2021). Supply chain risks in Industry 4.0 environment: Review and analysis framework. *Production Planning and Control*, *34*(13), 1275–1302. doi:10.1080/09537287.2021.2005173

Papetti, A., Ciccarelli, M., Scoccia, C., Palmieri, G., & Germani, M. (2022). A human-oriented design process for collaborative robotics. *International Journal of Computer Integrated Manufacturing*, *36*(12), 1760–1782. doi:10.1080/0951192X.2022.2128222

Pavloudakis, F., Karlopoulos, E., & Roumpos, C. (2023). Just transition governance to avoid socio-economic impacts of lignite phase-out: The case of Western Macedonia, Greece. *The Extractive Industries and Society*, *14*, 101248. doi:10.1016/j.exis.2023.101248

Pearce, C. L., & Locke, E. A. (2023). *Principles of organizational behavior: The Handbook of Evidence-Based Management*. John Wiley & Sons.

Peng, Y., Ahmad, S. F., Irshad, M. I., Al-Razgan, M., Ali, Y. A., & Awwad, E. M. (2023). Impact of Digitalization on Process Optimization and Decision-Making towards Sustainability: The Moderating Role of Environmental Regulation. *Sustainability (Basel)*, *15*(20), 15156. doi:10.3390/su152015156

Pessot, E., Zangiacomi, A., Marchiori, I., & Fornasiero, R. (2023). Empowering supply chains with Industry 4.0 technologies to face megatrends. *Journal of Business Logistics*, *44*(4), 609–640. doi:10.1111/jbl.12360

Picasso, F. G., Biazzin, C., Paiva, E. L., & Partyka, R. B. (2021). Socially responsible supply chain initiatives and their outcomes: A taxonomy of manufacturing companies. *Supply Chain Management*, *28*(1), 90–106. doi:10.1108/SCM-11-2020-0578

Picavet, M. E. B., De Macedo, L. S. V., Bellezoni, R. A., & De Oliveira, J. P. (2022). How can Transnational Municipal Networks foster local collaborative governance regimes for environmental management? *Environmental Management*, *71*(3), 505–522. doi:10.1007/s00267-022-01685-w PMID:35906346

Pozzi, F. A., & Dwivedi, D. N. (2023). ESG and IoT: Ensuring Sustainability and Social Responsibility in the Digital Age. In Communications in computer and information science (pp. 12–23). doi:10.1007/978-3-031-47997-7_2

Pozzi, R., Rossi, T., & Secchi, R. (2021). Industry 4.0 technologies: Critical success factors for implementation and improvements in manufacturing companies. *Production Planning and Control*, *34*(2), 139–158. doi:10.1080/09537287.2021.1891481

Prakash, C., Singh, L., Gupta, A., & Lohan, S. K. (2023). Advancements in smart farming: A comprehensive review of IoT, wireless communication, sensors, and hardware for agricultural automation. *Sensors and Actuators. A, Physical*, *362*, 114605. doi:10.1016/j.sna.2023.114605

Qahtan, S., Yatim, K., Zulzalil, H., Osman, M. H., Zaidan, A. A., & Alsattar, H. A. (2023). Review of healthcare industry 4.0 application-based blockchain in terms of security and privacy development attributes: Comprehensive taxonomy, open issues and challenges and recommended solution. *Journal of Network and Computer Applications*, *209*, 103529. doi:10.1016/j.jnca.2022.103529

Qayyum, F., Jamil, H., & Ali, F. (2023). A review of smart Energy Management in Residential Buildings for Smart Cities. *Energies*, *17*(1), 83. doi:10.3390/en17010083

Raizada, A. (2023, July 12). From automation to digital transformation: the evolution of Industry 4.0. *Copper Digital*. https://copperdigital.com/blog/industry-4-0-evolution-automation-digital-transformation/

RaneN.ChoudharyS.RaneJ. (2023). Sustainable tourism development using leading-edge Artificial Intelligence (AI), Blockchain, Internet of Things (IoT), Augmented Reality (AR) and Virtual Reality (VR) technologies. *Social Science Research Network*. doi:10.2139/ssrn.4642605

Reddy, K., Chandu, V., Srilakshmi, S., Thagaram, E., Sahyaja, C., & Osei, B. (2023). Consumers perception on green marketing towards eco-friendly fast moving consumer goods. *International Journal of Engineering Business Management*, *15*, 18479790231170962. Advance online publication. doi:10.1177/18479790231170962

Renugadevi, N., Saravanan, S., & Sudha, C. N. (2023). IoT based smart energy grid for sustainable cites. *Materials Today: Proceedings*, *81*, 98–104. doi:10.1016/j.matpr.2021.02.270

Rijal, S., & Saranani, F. (2023). The role of blockchain technology in increasing economic transparency and public trust. *Technology and Society Perspectives*, *1*(2), 56–67. doi:10.61100/tacit.v1i2.51

Rind, Y. M., Raza, M. H., Zubair, M., Mehmood, M. Q., & Massoud, Y. (2023). Smart energy meters for smart grids, an internet of things perspective. *Energies*, *16*(4), 1974. doi:10.3390/en16041974

Rosário, A. T., & Dias, J. C. (2023). How Industry 4.0 and Sensors Can Leverage product Design: Opportunities and challenges. *Sensors (Basel)*, *23*(3), 1165. doi:10.3390/s23031165 PMID:36772206

Roth, L., Lowitzsch, J., & Yildiz, Ö. (2023). Which (co-)ownership types in renewables are associated with the willingness to adopt energy-efficient technologies and energy-conscious behaviour? Data from German households. *Energy Policy*, *180*, 113683. doi:10.1016/j.enpol.2023.113683

Sankar, S., Ramasubbareddy, S., Luhach, A. K., Deverajan, G. G., Alnumay, W. S., Jhanjhi, N. Z., Ghosh, U., & Sharma, P. K. (2020). Energy efficient optimal parent selection based routing protocol for Internet of Things using firefly optimization algorithm. *Transactions on Emerging Telecommunications Technologies*, *32*(8), e4171. Advance online publication. doi:10.1002/ett.4171

Santhi, A. R., & Muthuswamy, P. (2023). Industry 5.0 or industry 4.0S? Introduction to industry 4.0 and a peek into the prospective industry 5.0 technologies. *International Journal on Interactive Design and Manufacturing*, *17*(2), 947–979. doi:10.1007/s12008-023-01217-8

Santos, E. (2023). From Neglect to Progress: Assessing social sustainability and decent work in the tourism sector. *Sustainability (Basel)*, *15*(13), 10329. doi:10.3390/su151310329

Schuster, A., Zoll, M., Otto, I. M., & Stölzel, F. (2023). The unjust just transition? Exploring different dimensions of justice in the lignite regions of Lusatia, Eastern Greater Poland, and Gorj. *Energy Research & Social Science*, *104*, 103227. doi:10.1016/j.erss.2023.103227

Senghor, K., Partelow, S., Herrera, C. G., & Osemwegie, I. (2023). Conflicting governance realities: Aligning historical and cultural practices with formal marine protected area co-management in Senegal. *Marine Policy*, *155*, 105706. doi:10.1016/j.marpol.2023.105706

Shah, H., Gardas, B. B., Narwane, V. S., & Mehta, H. S. (2021). The contemporary state of big data analytics and artificial intelligence towards intelligent supply chain risk management: A comprehensive review. *Kybernetes*, *52*(5), 1643–1697. doi:10.1108/K-05-2021-0423

Shahzad, M., Du, J., & Junaid, M. (2023). Impact of green HRM practices on sustainable performance: Mediating role of green innovation, green culture, and green employees' behavior. *Environmental Science and Pollution Research International*, *30*(38), 88524–88547. doi:10.1007/s11356-023-28498-6 PMID:37438507

Sharma, I., & Tiwari, V. (2023). Modeling the impact of techno-stress and burnout on employees' work-life balance and turnover intention: A job demands-resources theory perspective. *Global Business and Organizational Excellence*, *43*(1), 121–134. doi:10.1002/joe.22206

Shi, H., Feng, T., & Zhu, Z. (2023). The impact of big data analytics capability on green supply chain integration: An organizational information processing theory perspective. *Business Process Management Journal*, *29*(2), 550–577. doi:10.1108/BPMJ-08-2022-0411

Sindiramutty, S. R. (2023). Autonomous Threat Hunting: a future paradigm for AI-Driven Threat intelligence. *arXiv (Cornell University)*. https://doi.org//arxiv.2401.00286 doi:10.48550

Sindiramutty, S. R., Jhanjhi, N. Z., Ray, S. K., Jazri, H., Khan, N. A., & Gaur, L. (2024). Metaverse: Virtual Meditation. In Advances in medical technologies and clinical practice book series (pp. 93–158). IGI Global. doi:10.4018/978-1-6684-9823-1.ch003

Sindiramutty, S. R., Jhanjhi, N. Z., Ray, S. K., Jazri, H., Khan, N. A., Gaur, L., Gharib, A. H., & Manchuri, A. R. (2024). Metaverse: Virtual Gyms and Sports. In Advances in medical technologies and clinical practice book series (pp. 24–92). IGI Global. doi:10.4018/978-1-6684-9823-1.ch002

Sindiramutty, S. R., Jhanjhi, N. Z., Tan, C. E., Khan, N. A., Gharib, A. H., & Yun, K. J. (2024). Applications of blockchain technology in supply chain management. In Advances in logistics, operations, and management science book series (pp. 248–304). doi:10.4018/978-1-6684-7625-3.ch009

Sindiramutty, S. R., Jhanjhi, N. Z., Tan, C. E., Khan, N. A., Shah, B., & Gaur, L. (2024). Securing the digital supply chain cyber threats and vulnerabilities. In Advances in logistics, operations, and management science book series (pp. 156–223). doi:10.4018/978-1-6684-7625-3.ch007

Sindiramutty, S. R., Jhanjhi, N. Z., Tan, C. E., Tee, W. J., Lau, S. P., Jazri, H., Ray, S. K., & Zaheer, M. A. (2024). IoT and AI-Based Smart Solutions for the Agriculture Industry. In Advances in Explainable AI Applications for Smart Cities (pp. 317–351). doi:10.4018/978-1-6684-6361-1.ch012

Sindiramutty, S. R., Tan, C., Lau, S. P., Thangaveloo, R., Gharib, A. H., Manchuri, A. R., Khan, N. A., Tee, W. J., & Muniandy, L. (2024). Explainable AI for Cybersecurity. In Advances in Explainable AI Applications for Smart Cities (pp. 31–97). doi:10.4018/978-1-6684-6361-1.ch002

Sindiramutty, S. R., Tan, C., Tee, W. J., Lau, S. P., Balakrishnan, S., Kaur, S. D. A., Jazri, H., & Aslam, M. (2024). Modern Smart Cities and Open Research Challenges and Issues of Explainable Artificial Intelligence. In Advances in Explainable AI Applications for Smart Cities (pp. 389–424). doi:10.4018/978-1-6684-6361-1.ch015

Sindiramutty, S. R., Tee, W. J., Balakrishnan, S., Kaur, S., Thangaveloo, R., Jazri, H., Khan, N. A., Gharib, A. H., & Manchuri, A. R. (2024). Explainable AI in Healthcare Application. In Advances in Explainable AI Applications for Smart Cities (pp. 123–176). doi:10.4018/978-1-6684-6361-1.ch005

Singh, A., Kumar, V., Verma, P., & Kandasamy, J. (2023). Identification and severity assessment of challenges in the adoption of industry 4.0 in Indian construction industry. *Asia Pacific Management Review*, *28*(3), 299–315. doi:10.1016/j.apmrv.2022.10.007

Singh, A., Kumar, V. R. P., Irfan, M., Mohandes, S. R., & Awan, U. (2023). Revealing the Barriers of blockchain technology for supply chain transparency and sustainability in the construction industry: An application of Pythagorean FAHP methods. *Sustainability (Basel)*, *15*(13), 10681. doi:10.3390/su151310681

Singh, A., Madaan, G., Hr, S., & Kumar, A. (2022). Smart manufacturing systems: A futuristics roadmap towards application of industry 4.0 technologies. *International Journal of Computer Integrated Manufacturing*, *36*(3), 411–428. doi:10.1080/0951192X.2022.2090607

Singhal, V., Jain, S. P., Anand, D., Singh, A., Verma, S., Kavita, Rodrigues, J. J. P. C., Jhanjhi, N. Z., Ghosh, U., Jo, O., & Iwendi, C. (2020). Artificial Intelligence Enabled Road Vehicle-Train Collision Risk Assessment Framework for Unmanned railway level crossings. *IEEE Access : Practical Innovations, Open Solutions*, *8*, 113790–113806. doi:10.1109/ACCESS.2020.3002416

Soltani, S., Maxwell, D., & Rashidi, A. (2023). The State of Industry 4.0 in the Australian Construction Industry: An examination of industry and academic point of view. *Buildings*, *13*(9), 2324. doi:10.3390/buildings13092324

Song, W., Ma, Y., Fan, X., & Peng, X. (2023). Corporate environmental ethics and employee's green creativity? The perspective of environmental commitment. *Corporate Social Responsibility and Environmental Management*, *30*(4), 1856–1868. doi:10.1002/csr.2459

Song, Y., Li, Y., & Liu, T. (2023). Carbon asset remolding and potential benefit measurement of machinery products in the light of lean production and low-carbon investment. *Technological Forecasting and Social Change*, *186*, 122166. doi:10.1016/j.techfore.2022.122166

Soori, M., Arezoo, B., & Dastres, R. (2023a). Internet of things for smart factories in industry 4.0, a review. *Internet of Things and Cyber-Physical Systems*, *3*, 192–204. doi:10.1016/j.iotcps.2023.04.006

Soori, M., Arezoo, B., & Dastres, R. (2023b). Optimization of energy consumption in industrial robots, a review. *Cognitive Robotics*, *3*, 142–157. doi:10.1016/j.cogr.2023.05.003

Srhir, S., Jaegler, A., & Montoya-Torres, J. R. (2023). Introducing a framework toward sustainability goals in a supply chain 4.0 ecosystem. *Journal of Cleaner Production*, *418*, 138111. doi:10.1016/j.jclepro.2023.138111

Sunmola, F., & Burgess, P. (2023). Transparency by design for Blockchain-Based supply chains. *Procedia Computer Science*, *217*, 1256–1265. doi:10.1016/j.procs.2022.12.324

Taj, S., Imran, A. S., Kastrati, Z., Daudpota, S. M., Memon, R. A., & Javed, A. (2023). IoT-based supply chain management: A systematic literature review. *Internet of Things : Engineering Cyber Physical Human Systems*, *24*, 100982. doi:10.1016/j.iot.2023.100982

Tian, L., & Wang, Q. (2024). Improving mineral mining enterprises environmental performance through corporate social responsibility practices in China: Implications for minerals policymaking. *Resources Policy*, *88*, 104442. doi:10.1016/j.resourpol.2023.104442

Tsolakis, N., Schumacher, R., Dora, M., & Kumar, M. (2022). Artificial intelligence and blockchain implementation in supply chains: A pathway to sustainability and data monetisation? *Annals of Operations Research*, *327*(1), 157–210. doi:10.1007/s10479-022-04785-2 PMID:35755830

Vasanthraj, K., Kaur, A., Potdar, V., & Agrawal, H. (2023). Industry 4.0 adoption in food Supply Chain to Improve Visibility and Operational Efficiency—A content analysis. *IEEE Access : Practical Innovations, Open Solutions*, *11*, 73922–73958. doi:10.1109/ACCESS.2023.3295780

Verma, N. S., Kuldeep, D. K., Chouhan, M., Prajapati, R., & Singh, S. K. (2023). A review on Eco-Friendly pesticides and their rising importance in sustainable plant protection practices. *International Journal of Plant and Soil Science*, *35*(22), 200–214. doi:10.9734/ijpss/2023/v35i224126

Wen, B. O. T., Syahriza, N., Xian, N. C. W., Wei, N., Shen, T. Z., Hin, Y. Z., Sindiramutty, S. R., & Nicole, T. Y. F. (2024). Detecting cyber threats with a Graph-Based NIDPS. In Advances in logistics, operations, and management science book series (pp. 36–74). doi:10.4018/978-1-6684-7625-3.ch002

Yap, K. Y., Chin, H. H., & Klemeš, J. J. (2023). Blockchain technology for distributed generation: A review of current development, challenges and future prospect. *Renewable & Sustainable Energy Reviews*, *175*, 113170. doi:10.1016/j.rser.2023.113170

Zadeh, S. B. I., & Garay-Rondero, C. L. (2023). Enhancing Urban Sustainability: Unravelling Carbon Footprint Reduction in Smart Cities through Modern Supply-Chain Measures. *Smart Cities*, *6*(6), 3225–3250. doi:10.3390/smartcities6060143

Zadeh, S. B. I., Pérez, M. D. E., Gutiérrez, J. S. L., & Fernández-Sánchez, G. (2023). Optimizing smart energy infrastructure in smart ports: A Systematic Scoping Review of carbon Footprint Reduction. *Journal of Marine Science and Engineering*, *11*(10), 1921. doi:10.3390/jmse11101921

Zarei, H., Rasti–Barzoki, M., Altmann, J., & Egger, B. (2023). Cooperation, coordination, or collaboration? A structured review of buyers' partnerships to support sustainable sourcing in supply chains. *Environmental Science and Pollution Research International*, *30*(31), 76491–76514. doi:10.1007/s11356-023-27541-w PMID:37280495

Zhu, S., Yu, T., Xu, T., Chen, H., Dustdar, S., Gigan, S., Gündüz, D., Hossain, E., Jin, Y., Lin, F. H., Liu, B., Wan, Z., Zhang, J., Zhao, Z., Zhu, W., Chen, Z., Durrani, T., Wang, H., Wu, J., ... Pan, Y. (2023). Intelligent Computing: The latest advances, challenges, and future. *Intelligent Computing*, *2*, 0006. Advance online publication. doi:10.34133/icomputing.0006

Chapter 6
Harmonizing Innovation – Bridging Industry 4.0 with Supply Chain Sustainability

Kasturi Laturkar
https://orcid.org/0000-0002-4985-909X
Validation Associates LLC, USA

Kaustubh Laturkar
https://orcid.org/0000-0002-2643-3942
Michigan State University, USA

ABSTRACT

The integration of Industry 4.0 and supply chain sustainability marks the dawn of a new era of innovation and accountability within businesses, bringing technological innovation together with environmental and social responsibilities for the benefit of all. As Industry 4.0 is characterized by the integration of digital technologies, internet of things, and data analytics, it empowers organizations to create smart, connected, and efficient supply chains by harnessing the power of digital technologies. In addition, Industry 4.0 technologies enhance the transparency and traceability of the supply chain. With blockchain technology, for example, it is possible for all transactions and movements within the supply chain to be immutable. By doing so, not only is the authenticity of the sustainable materials ensured, but also fair labor practices are promoted. With consumers becoming increasingly aware of the environmental and ethical implications of their purchases, this transparency facilitates brand trust as well as loyalty among consumers.

INTRODUCTION

There is no doubt that the industries today are undergoing a profound transformation, one that is characterized by the fusion of cutting-edge technologies, digital connectivity, and a growing concern for sustainability and social responsibility. There are numerous aspects of this revolution that have been brought together under the banner of Industry 4.0, the fourth industrial revolution that heralds a new

DOI: 10.4018/979-8-3693-1363-3.ch006

era of manufacturing and operations across the globe. There is currently a growing emphasis on supply chain sustainability in the global business landscape due to heightened environmental awareness, shifting consumer preferences, and stringent regulatory requirements.

Industry 4.0, often known as the "smart factory" or the "digital factory," represents a dramatic departure from the traditional manufacturing methods that have been used in the past (Abulibdeh et al., 2024). It represents a convergence of digital technologies and physical systems, which culminates in the creation of an industrial ecosystem that is highly interconnected and data-driven. There are many key elements that make up Industry 4.0, such as the Internet of Things (IoT), artificial intelligence (AI), big data analytics, automation, additive manufacturing, and several others. Together, these technologies have enabled the industrial sector to achieve levels of precision, agility, and adaptability that had previously been inconceivable in the industrial sector.

Industry 4.0 is a constellation of cutting-edge technologies that are at the core of the current industrial complex. It is easy to see that the Internet of Things (IoT), artificial intelligence (AI), big data, automation, and additive manufacturing are just some of the stars in this digital galaxy that the world lives in today (Ghobakhloo, 2020). The combination of these components, when integrated into industrial processes, has the power to create what is referred to as a "smart factory," or a factory that is not just efficient, but also intelligent. As they make decisions, they self-optimize, and they communicate in real time, in conjunction with each other. However, Industry 4.0 isn't limited to manufacturing alone; it extends its influence into logistics, services, and beyond, facilitating a future where innovation and efficiency go hand in hand, creating a connected world in which human ingenuity and technology intersect in a way that has never been seen before (Hofmann et al., 2019)

Alternatively, supply chain sustainability focuses on the ethical, environmental, and economic aspects of the sourcing, production, and distribution processes involved in the supply chain (Bag et al., 2018). In a nutshell, it represents a fundamental shift in the way companies view their obligations towards the planet and society about their corporate social responsibility. For a supply chain to be sustainable, it must minimize its environmental impact, reduce waste, ensure ethical sourcing, and promote social well-being throughout the whole process of production and distribution (Birkel & Müller, 2021). It is believed that the effectiveness of this approach will be strengthened by values such as corporate social responsibility, environmental stewardship, and long-term economic viability, which are the pillars of this approach.

The goal of this chapter is to embark on an exploration of the dynamic intersection between Industry 4.0 and the sustainable management of supply chains. It is imperative to examine how the fusion of these two paradigm-shifting concepts is shaping the modern business landscape and paving the way for a more efficient, eco-conscious, and ethically responsible industrial future.

The convergence of Industry 4.0 and supply chain sustainability is poised to shape the future of industries and businesses. It represents a fascinating frontier where the forces of innovation, efficiency, and responsibility combine to create the kind of industrial landscape that is sustainable and prosperous in the long run (Bag et al., 2018). As the industries navigate this transformative journey, it is important to remain vigilant in addressing the challenges as well as embracing the myriad opportunities presented by this dynamic integration in order to make the most of this transforming process.

OVERVIEW OF INDUSTRY 4.0

At its core, Industry 4.0 seeks to optimize industrial processes, enhance decision-making, and drive operational efficiency through digitalization and connectivity. The term "Industry 4.0" itself implies a sequential progression through four industrial revolutions, beginning with the mechanization of manual labor (First Industrial Revolution), transitioning to mass production through steam power and electricity (Second Industrial Revolution), then evolving to computerization and automation (Third Industrial Revolution)(Popkova et al., 2019). As a logical next step, Industry 4.0 incorporates the following key components:

Internet of Things (IoT)

A cornerstone of Industry 4.0, the Internet of Things (IoT) represents a paradigm shift in the way physical objects, machines, and devices connect and communicate (Holtschulte, 2022). These interconnected "things" are embedded with sensors and communication capabilities, enabling seamless collection and exchange of data in real-time. By bridging the physical and digital realms, IoT fosters unprecedented levels of connectivity and intelligence within industrial processes.

IoT plays a pivotal role in creating a transparent and responsive supply chain ecosystem. In the supply chain, sensors continuously monitor and transmit data on parameters such as temperature, humidity, location, and energy consumption (Manavalan & Jayakrishna, 2019). Organizations can track the environmental impact of their supply chain activities in real time and make informed decisions to enhance sustainability. Agricultural IoT sensors, for example, can monitor soil conditions, optimize irrigation, and minimize water usage, reducing operational costs and preserving the environment (Kamble et al., 2020).

Artificial Intelligence (AI) and Machine Learning

AI extends the capabilities of interconnected systems by using algorithms and software designed to analyze data, predict outcomes, and adapt to changing conditions (Rath et al., 2021). In this technological evolution, machine learning, a subset of AI, plays a crucial role in empowering systems to improve their performance without explicit programming. In the realm of supply chain sustainability, AI and Industry 4.0 symbiotically work together to create intelligent, self-optimizing processes.

As IoT devices and sensors generate vast datasets, machine learning algorithms become adept at recognizing patterns and correlations that may elude traditional programming approaches. AI technologies can analyze historical and real-time data to identify inefficiencies, anticipate disruptions, and suggest strategies for reducing environmental impact in the context of supply chain sustainability (Cioffi et al., 2020). An important aspect of sustainable supply chain management is the use of predictive analytics powered by machine learning to forecast demand fluctuations.

Big Data and Analytics

In today's supply chain, big data and analytics play a pivotal role in advancing sustainability, ushering in a world of data-driven insights that empower organizations to make informed decisions, optimize processes, and minimize the impact they have on the environment. From resource efficiency to ethical sourcing, harnessing the power of big data and analytics in the complex web of global supply chains offers a multitude of benefits that can be beneficial in a wide range of areas (Hlophe & Maharaj, 2023).

There is no doubt that one of the biggest advantages of big data in supply chain sustainability is the ability to gather, process, and analyze vast amounts of data from a wide variety of sources. Data from IoT devices, sensors, suppliers, transportation, and even external factors such as weather patterns are part of this process (Bag et al., 2020). In addition to providing a comprehensive view of the entire supply chain, the amalgamation of these data allows organizations to identify inefficiencies, track the environmental metrics associated with each phase of the process, and determine the carbon footprint associated with each one.

Robotics and Automation

Robotics and automation are proving to be transformative forces in the realm of supply chain sustainability, as they offer solutions that improve efficiency, reduce the environmental impact, as well as contribute to responsible business practices (Attaran, 2020). Due to the incorporation of robotics and automation technologies into supply chain operations, established processes are being reshaped, resource utilization is being optimized, and sustainability goals are being advanced.

Robotics can improve supply chain sustainability in several ways, including automating repetitive, labor-intensive tasks. It is possible to handle material handling, sorting, and packaging with precision and efficiency by using automated systems such as robotic arms and autonomous vehicles (Sanders et al., 2019). The result of this is not only an increase in overall operational speed but also a reduction in the reliance on manual labor, which has a negative impact on the environment and on social issues.

Virtual Reality (VR) and Augmented Reality (AR)

These technologies have the potential to revolutionize supply chain sustainability. VR and AR make supply chains more efficient, transparent, and eco-friendly by improving communication, improving training, and optimizing operations (Zhao et al., 2019).

Training and simulation are key applications of VR and AR in supply chain sustainability. Simulations provide warehouse staff, drivers, and logistics professionals with immersive and realistic training experiences. Not only does this improve the skills of the workforce, but it also reduces the need for physical training environments, reducing carbon emissions and resource consumption associated with travel.

While AR overlays digital information onto the physical world, it provides real-time insights and guidance (Rejeb et al., 2021). Warehouse workers can use AR to locate items, optimize picking routes, and reduce errors. Consequently, energy is saved, and operational costs are reduced, as well as the time spent searching for products is minimized.

SUPPLY CHAIN SUSTAINABILITY AT A GLANCE

Often referred to as sustainable supply chain management, supply chain sustainability ensures long-term viability, ethical practices, and minimal harm to society and the environment by managing the environmental, social, and economic impacts of a supply chain holistically (Martins & Pato, 2019). Maintaining economic success while addressing environmental and social concerns is part of a responsible and sustainable supply chain. Figure 1 illustrates some of the key principles of sustainable supply chain management with a more detailed discussion in the following section.

Environmental Responsibility

Companies aiming to align their operations with global environmental goals have increasingly focused on supply chain sustainability to meet the growing imperative for environmentally responsible practices. Reduced environmental impact within supply chain operations includes initiatives to minimize waste, conserve resources, and reduce carbon emissions. In order to fulfill this commitment, companies must adopt and implement eco-friendly practices across all aspects of their supply chains (Hong & Guo, 2019).

In order to minimize the ecological footprint of supply chains, transportation strategies must be rethought. To reduce emissions associated with the movement of goods, companies are increasingly investing in energy-efficient transportation modes, such as electric or hybrid vehicles. Additionally, optimizing logistics and using route planning technologies contribute to more efficient transportation, which ultimately reduces shipping and distribution's environmental impact.

Material Sourcing and Fair Labor Practices

Conscientious sourcing of raw materials and components that comprise the foundation of products is an important dimension of supply chain sustainability. Responsible and humane practices are highly valued by companies committed to ethical sourcing. In order to meet this commitment, suppliers are meticulously screened to ensure they adhere to a range of ethical standards, including fair labor conditions, fair treatment of workers, and responsible resource utilization (Negri et al., 2021).

In order to ensure ethical sourcing, fair labor conditions must be verified and guaranteed. The process involves assessing the workplace environments within the supply chain and ensuring that employees are treated ethically, provided with safe working conditions, and compensated fairly. It is common for ethical sourcing initiatives to involve auditing supplier facilities, promoting transparency, and collaborating with suppliers who adhere to international labor standards.

Transparency and Traceability

A key principle of supply chain sustainability is transparency, which requires companies to provide accurate and comprehensive information about the origins of their products and the suppliers they work with. There is an increasing awareness among consumers and stakeholders that the products they purchase align with ethical, social, and environmental standards. Transparency is driven by traceability, which enables the tracking of a product's journey from source to consumer, fostering accountability and ensuring ethical compliance at every stage (Laturkar & Laturkar, 2023a).

In the context of supply chain sustainability, transparency is more than just disclosing information; it involves sharing insights into suppliers, manufacturing processes, and distribution channels (Ebinger & Omondi, 2020). It is expected that companies will disclose their sourcing practices, manufacturing methods, and social and environmental impact. A transparent reporting system allows stakeholders to make informed decisions, align their values with their consumption choices, and hold companies accountable for their sustainability commitments.

Financial Viability

Sustainable practices should not compromise a company's financial health in the name of environmentally and socially responsible practices. As a responsible corporate entity, a thriving company endeavors to strike a harmonious balance between economic profitability and sustainable operations.

A comprehensive understanding of economic viability is required when designing sustainability strategies within the supply chain. Ethical sourcing, transparency, and traceability are integral components of a financially sustainable business model in addition to contributing to environmental and social responsibility. Economic viability is not only about mitigating risks and reducing costs, but also about identifying opportunities for innovation, efficiency, and long-term sustainability (Kusi-Sarpong et al., 2019).

Companies are encouraged to view sustainability as an investment rather than a cost when seeking an economically viable supply chain. Environmentally friendly and socially responsible practices can lead to operational efficiencies, cost savings, and enhanced brand value for forward-thinking organizations. By optimizing energy consumption, reducing waste, and maximizing resource utilization, sustainable practices can yield tangible economic benefits.

Adherence to Regulations and Standards

To ensure supply chain sustainability, it is essential to adhere to local, national, and international regulations. Regulatory frameworks provide a structured foundation for responsible business conduct within the supply chain, shaping ethical, social, and environmental practices. Environmental protection laws, labor standards, and product safety requirements are all part of the commitment to compliance (Saeed & Kersten, 2019).

Environmental protection laws are an important aspect of supply chain sustainability, guiding companies in minimizing their ecological footprint and promoting responsible resource management. The use of sustainable sourcing practices, waste disposal, and emissions regulations must be followed. In order to mitigate adverse environmental impacts, conserve biodiversity, and contribute to broader efforts to combat climate change, companies must integrate environmental compliance into their operations.

In ethical sourcing, labor standards emphasize fair and humane treatment of workers throughout the supply chain. In order to ensure safe working conditions, fair wages, and fundamental labor rights, local and international labor regulations must be followed. In addition to complying with legal requirements, responsible labor practices contribute to the well-being and dignity of workers, fostering an equitably respectful workplace.

Resource Efficiency

Supply chain sustainability relies heavily on efficient use of resources. By minimizing waste, optimizing resource consumption, and promoting recycling and reuse, this principle seeks to reduce supply chain environmental impacts. Resource efficiency contributes not only to environmental stewardship, but also to operational resilience and economic viability for companies (Diaz Lopez et al., 2019).

Waste minimization is an essential aspect of resource efficiency. Throughout the product lifecycle, companies are encouraged to prioritize reducing excess materials, packaging, and energy. Waste minimization strategies include designing products with durability in mind, optimizing packaging solutions, and implementing circular economy principles that emphasize reuse and recycling of materials, from manufacturing processes to distribution to end-of-life considerations.

Managing materials, energy, and utilities throughout the supply chain is key to optimizing resource consumption. Implementing technologies and practices that improve energy efficiency, reduce water usage, and minimize the environmental footprint is part of this process. Lifecycle assessments help companies identify opportunities for improvement, adopt sustainable sourcing practices, and continuously monitor and optimize resource consumption.

Continuous Improvement

Sustainability is not a static goal, but a dynamic and ongoing process that demands continuous improvement. Sustainable supply chain practices are not only encouraged, but increasingly obligated, as companies must set ambitious targets, monitor their performance rigorously, and take proactive corrective actions to elevate and refine them over time. In order to keep up with evolving industry standards, technological advancements, and environmental and social issues, an iterative approach is essential.

A foundational step toward sustainability is setting targets. Companies should set clear, measurable, and time-bound goals that align with their overall environmental, social, and governance (ESG) objectives (Heizer et al., 2020). In addition to reducing carbon footprints, reducing waste, promoting ethical sourcing, and promoting circular economies, these targets may encompass a range of sustainability dimensions. As a result of defining these objectives, companies provide stakeholders with a roadmap to track their progress and hold them accountable for their sustainability efforts.

Sustainability in supply chain management relies heavily on monitoring performance. It is essential that companies implement robust monitoring and reporting mechanisms that provide transparent insight into their sustainability metrics. By leveraging technology, data analytics, and key performance indicators (KPIs), companies can systematically assess their environmental impact, social responsibility, and overall sustainability performance (Diaz Lopez et al., 2019). By monitoring in real-time, companies can identify areas for improvement and respond promptly to emerging challenges.

Risk and Mitigation

Supply chain sustainability risks must be identified and mitigated to navigate the complexities of a rapidly changing global environment (Xu et al., 2019). As part of this proactive approach, strategies are devised to address disruptions that may compromise the supply chain's ability to operate sustainably, in addition to recognizing potential challenges. Sustainability risks can come from a variety of sources, including natural disasters, geopolitical conflicts, regulatory changes, and shifts in consumer preferences.

Effective sustainability risk identification requires anticipating and preparing for disruptions. In order to ensure a sustainable supply chain, companies should conduct thorough risk assessments that consider both immediate and long-term threats (Pournader et al., 2020). Natural disasters, such as hurricanes, floods, or earthquakes, can disrupt production and transportation networks, while geopolitical conflicts can affect access to essential resources. Companies can fortify their supply chains against these contingencies by conducting comprehensive risk assessments.

Sustainable supply chain management involves addressing the environmental and social implications of risks. Supply chain sustainability can be significantly affected by climate change-related risks, such as extreme weather events and resource scarcity. It is important for companies to assess their vulnerability to climate-related risks, develop resilience strategies, and explore opportunities for adaptation, such as diversifying their sourcing locations or investing in renewable energy.

In addition to minimizing negative impacts, supply chain sustainability involves creating positive outcomes, including fostering ethical practices, improving brand reputations, and contributing to a more environmentally and socially responsible business environment. Consumers, investors, and regulators increasingly value companies that embrace these principles in the modern business landscape.

Figure 1. Key principles of supply chain sustainability

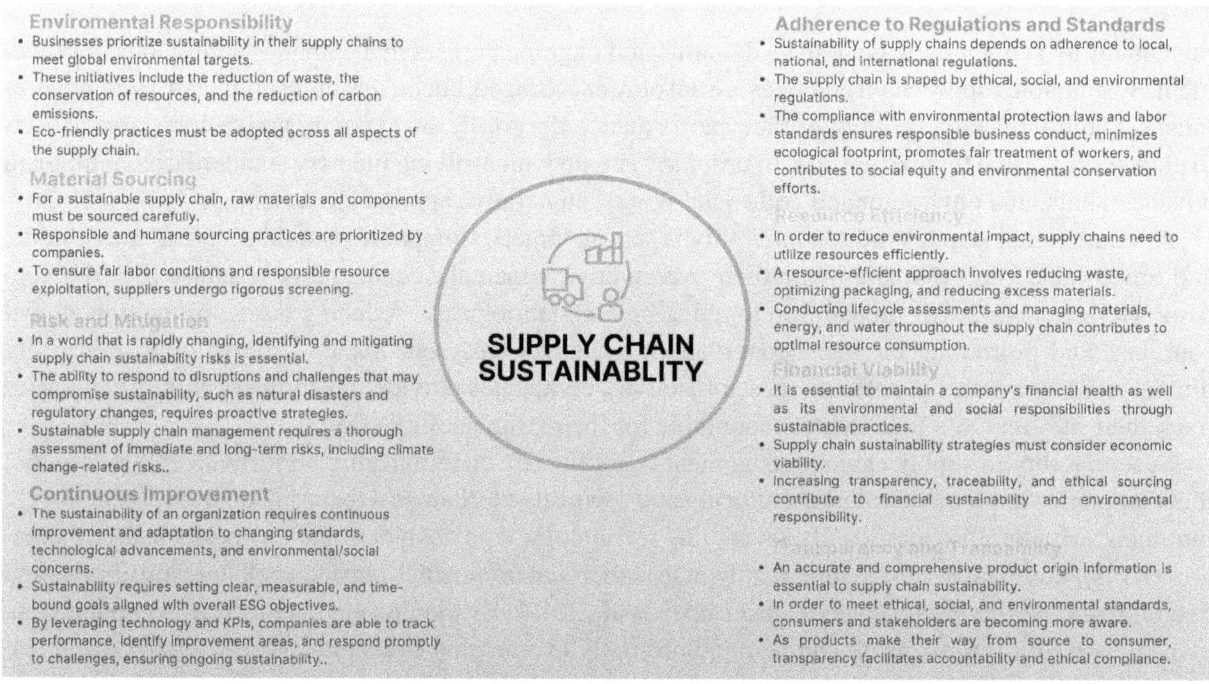

BENEFITS OF INDUSTRY 4.0 AND SUPPLY CHAIN SUSTAINABILITY

Business leaders increasingly recognize the importance of integrating Industry 4.0 with supply chain sustainability in the 21st century. Two pivotal aspects of the evolving business landscape are Industry 4.0, which combines digital technologies with traditional industrial processes, and supply chain sustainability, which focuses on environmental, social, and economic responsibility. As a result of their integration into supply chain management, companies, society, and the environment benefit in multiple ways, as shown in Figure 2, with a more detailed discussion in the following section:

Efficiency and Cost Reduction

The pursuit of efficiency and cost reduction drives Industry 4.0 integration with supply chain sustainability. Industry 4.0 technologies, such as the Internet of Things (IoT), big data analytics, automation, and artificial intelligence (AI), facilitate real-time supply chain monitoring and optimization (Laturkar

& Laturkar, 2023b; Liu & De Giovanni, 2019). Companies can identify inefficiencies, streamline operations, and ultimately reduce costs through this transformative approach.

With Industry 4.0, companies have unprecedented visibility into their supply chain dynamics thanks to real-time monitoring. IoT sensors enable businesses to precisely track the location and condition of goods in transit (Toktaş-Palut, 2022). Through this capability, shipping routes can be optimized, delays can be minimized, and overall logistics efficiency can be improved. Using sensors on shipping containers, for instance, ensures that perishable goods are transported in optimal conditions. As a result, operational efficiency is improved as well as cost savings are realized.

Real-time monitoring is further enhanced by the use of big data analytics. Companies gain actionable insights into performance, demand patterns, and potential areas for improvement by processing and interpreting vast datasets generated throughout the supply chain. The use of predictive analytics, enabled by AI, allows supply chain disruptions to be anticipated and inventory management to be optimized. Data-driven decision-making improves operational excellence, mitigates risks, and enhances decision-making.

Reducing Environmental Impact

Industry 4.0 offers a compelling solution to mitigate the impact of supply chains when it comes to environmental sustainability. Industry 4.0, with its data-driven and precision control capabilities, adeptly facilitates sustainability by minimizing waste and resource consumption. The use of artificial intelligence (AI) and machine learning can enable companies to orchestrate a paradigm shift in their operations, allowing them to significantly reduce energy consumption, lower emissions, and minimize waste production (Javaid et al., 2022).

With AI and machine learning algorithms, supply chains can be controlled at a granular level. With these technologies, companies can make informed decisions based on real-time data, leading to enhanced efficiency and resource utilization. Predictive analytics, one of the hallmarks of AI, allows companies to adjust production levels and inventory management, preventing overproduction.

Industry 4.0 emphasizes precision control in manufacturing processes. The use of AI-driven systems can optimize machine settings and production parameters so that resources are used as efficiently as possible (Oláh et al., 2020). Furthermore, this level of control contributes to a substantial reduction in energy consumption, an important aspect of environmental sustainability.

Transparency and Accountability

Transparency, traceability, and adherence to ethical and environmental standards are fundamental to supply chain sustainability. By providing end-to-end visibility within the supply chain, Industry 4.0 facilitates these fundamental principles. From origin to destination, stakeholders can track products and materials seamlessly with real-time data and analytics (M. Sharma et al., 2021).

With this heightened visibility, responsible sourcing, fair labor practices, and strict adherence to environmental standards can be verified. Using Industry 4.0 technologies, companies can trace the origins of raw materials, ensuring they come from suppliers who follow ethical and sustainable practices (Chauhan et al., 2022). Through real-time monitoring, businesses can ensure that fair labor practices are maintained and that workers are treated ethically throughout the production process.

Further, Industry 4.0 plays a crucial role in addressing environmental concerns within the supply chain. By tracking and analyzing data in real-time, environmental standards can be adhered to more effectively. Monitoring and optimizing energy consumption, waste generation, and emissions can help companies achieve sustainability goals. Consumers, regulatory bodies, and advocacy groups can be assured that companies are actively mitigating their ecological impact by this transparency.

Resilience and Risk Mitigation

Bringing together Industry 4.0 and supply chain sustainability can enhance supply chain resilience and mitigate risks. With the frequency of disruptions increasing, from natural disasters to geopolitical shifts and global pandemics, it is imperative to build a resilient supply chain. As supply chains become more agile, responsive, and resilient to disruptions, Industry 4.0 technologies play an increasingly important role.

Technologies like Industry 4.0 facilitate agility in responding to unforeseen challenges. Data analytics, a hallmark of Industry 4.0, allows companies to identify disruptions in real-time. Whether it's a natural disaster affecting transportation routes or a sudden shift in market demand, companies can use this real-time insight to reroute supplies, adjust production schedules, or implement other responsive measures (Marinagi et al., 2023). As a result of this adaptability, the supply chain can more effectively address challenges associated with climate change and other sustainability-related concerns.

Furthermore, Industry 4.0 enhances the predictive capabilities of supply chains, contributing to risk mitigation. As part of Industry 4.0, machine learning algorithms analyze vast datasets to identify patterns and trends (Ivanov & Dolgui, 2021). With predictive analytics, companies can anticipate potential disruptions, enabling proactive risk mitigation. Whether it's diversifying sourcing locations or creating contingency plans for climate-related events, Industry 4.0 technologies enable supply chains to be better prepared and resilient during uncertain times.

Social Responsibility

Responsible business practices include ethical treatment of workers, fair labor conditions, and community engagement in the supply chain. Monitoring and verifying compliance with these ethical principles can be done with the help of Industry 4.0 technology, further reinforcing the commitment to a responsible and sustainable supply chain (M. Sharma et al., 2021).

Blockchain technology is one innovative application of Industry 4.0 that ensures fair labor practices. The blockchain is a decentralized and transparent ledger that securely records every supply chain transaction. Using blockchain for labor conditions and wages, stakeholders will have real-time visibility into the conditions under which products are manufactured, ensuring a clear, immutable record. Transparency in the supply chain not only ensures fair labor standards, but also deters unethical labor practices.

A business's commitment to social responsibility is demonstrated through the integration of Industry 4.0 with supply chain sustainability. Using technology to monitor and authenticate ethical practices can help companies build trust with consumers, investors, and other stakeholders (Bag et al., 2018). Industry 4.0 offers a way for businesses to demonstrate their commitment to fair labor conditions and ethical treatment of workers, which is particularly important to socially conscious consumers.

Long-Term Viability

Industry 4.0 and supply chain sustainability go beyond immediate business benefits to ensure long-term sustainability. When sustainability is not prioritized within supply chains, it can lead to reputational damage, legal repercussions, and operational disruptions. A company needs to integrate Industry 4.0 in order to remain relevant, competitive, and resilient in a world where sustainability is increasingly valued.

A damaged reputation can have profound and lasting effects on a company. In the globalized economy, news of unethical practices, environmental negligence, or social irresponsibility can spread rapidly, affecting consumer perceptions and trust (Bag et al., 2018). Using Industry 4.0 technologies, companies can monitor and verify sustainability practices in real-time, demonstrate transparency, and safeguard their reputation by proactively addressing issues.

Neglecting sustainability can also have legal ramifications. Non-compliance with regulations around environmental, social, and governance (ESG) issues can lead to legal penalties and fines. By providing a transparent and traceable record of compliance with sustainability standards, Industry 4.0 becomes a strategic asset in mitigating legal risks. Using these technologies, companies can ensure compliance with evolving regulatory frameworks by leveraging data-driven insights (Mastos et al., 2020).

Competitive Advantage

A competitive advantage can be gained by integrating Industry 4.0 and supply chain sustainability. With consumers becoming increasingly aware of environmental and social concerns, businesses that demonstrate their commitment to these issues gain a distinct advantage over their competitors.

There is a growing trend among consumers to support companies that prioritize sustainability in their operations. Integrating Industry 4.0 technologies into sustainability goals positions businesses as leaders in responsible and forward-looking practices (Luthra et al., 2020). In addition to differentiating them in the market, this also appeals to a growing segment of consumers who are willing to pay a premium for products and services aligned with their ethical and environmental values.

A unique value proposition is offered by Industry 4.0 integration for businesses. Beyond operational efficiency and risk mitigation, it also serves as a powerful marketing tool. As a result of Industry 4.0, companies can leverage their sustainability initiatives to communicate a compelling story to consumers (Koh et al., 2019). By combining transparency about sustainable practices with technological sophistication of Industry 4.0, a narrative of innovation, responsibility, and environmental stewardship is created.

Regulatory Compliance

Supply chain sustainability is also dependent on regulatory compliance. As global challenges such as climate change and social inequity arise, governments and international bodies are increasingly imposing stricter environmental and social regulations. As regulations evolve, integrating Industry 4.0 into supply chain sustainability initiatives will assist companies in complying more efficiently (Ghadge et al., 2020).

Various environmental impact metrics can be monitored and reported using Industry 4.0 technologies, particularly data analytics. These include energy consumption, greenhouse gas emissions, waste generation, and water usage. Using real-time data insights, companies can ensure compliance with required standards without incurring significant administrative costs or manual labor (Luthra et al., 2020).

Data analytics platforms, for instance, can collect and analyze data continuously from different stages of the supply chain. It facilitates accurate reporting to regulatory bodies by allowing companies to precisely measure and monitor their environmental performance. In addition to simplifying compliance, Industry 4.0 also helps companies stay ahead of regulatory changes, adapting their strategies accordingly.

As a result, integrating Industry 4.0 with supply chain sustainability is crucial. By using it, companies can improve efficiency, reduce costs, reduce environmental impact, ensure transparency and accountability, build resilience, and meet their social and ethical obligations. In a market that values sustainability, facilitates regulatory compliance, ensures long-term viability, encourages innovation, and optimizes resource use, businesses can gain a competitive advantage through this integration. In addition to being beneficial to businesses, Industry 4.0 and supply chain sustainability represent a strategic approach that is also pivotal to creating a more sustainable and responsible world. Embracing these two critical elements becomes a cornerstone of businesses' success as they navigate the complex challenges of the 21st century.

Figure 2. Benefits of using Industry 4.0 technologies for supply chain sustainability

CHALLENGES OF INDUSTRY 4.0 FOR SUPPLY CHAIN SUSTAINABILITY

Supply chain sustainability is a promising endeavor, but it comes with its own challenges and barriers. Organizations often face obstacles when trying to integrate these two essential components of modern business operations. It is critical to understand these challenges in order to develop effective strategies for overcoming them and reaping the benefits of sustainable and technologically advanced supply chains.

Initial Investment Costs

Integration of Industry 4.0 with supply chain sustainability is hindered by the high upfront costs associated with these technologies. Industry 4.0 technologies, such as IoT sensors, AI-powered analytics, and automation systems, require significant investments in both hardware and software infrastructure. A significant capital investment may also be required as part of sustainability initiatives, such as switching to renewable energy sources or implementing responsible sourcing practices.

The initial financial outlay required to integrate Industry 4.0 technologies and sustainability initiatives can be prohibitive for many organizations, especially small and medium-sized enterprises (SMEs). Business owners face a significant financial challenge because of the multifaceted nature of these investments and the need for specialized expertise in implementing and managing them (Caiado et al., 2022). Industry 4.0 adoption can be hindered by reluctance to allocate such substantial resources upfront.

Additionally, the return on investment (ROI) for these initiatives may not be immediately apparent, adding to the hesitation. Organizations may struggle to justify the initial high costs to stakeholders, particularly when focusing on short-term financial metrics, despite the long-term benefits of operational efficiency, risk mitigation, and market competitiveness.

Data Security and Privacy

As Industry 4.0 relies heavily on data, concerns about data security and privacy can arise due to the extensive collection, analysis, and transmission of sensitive information. Data in supply chains includes product details, customer information, and operational data. Integrating Industry 4.0 with supply chain sustainability requires safeguarding this wealth of data against cyber threats, unauthorized access, and breaches (Kumar et al., 2020).

Cybersecurity becomes more important with the expansion of Industry 4.0 technologies, including IoT devices and interconnected systems. As smart devices are interconnected and data is transmitted between them, malicious actors may exploit potential vulnerabilities. Data breaches in the supply chain may result in reputational damage and financial loss, ranging from compromised intellectual property to the exposure of sensitive customer information.

The challenge is further compounded by compliance with data protection regulations. In Europe, the General Data Protection Regulation (GDPR) and the Health Insurance Portability and Accountability Act (HIPAA) require that personal and sensitive information be collected, stored, and transmitted in accordance with strict guidelines. Building trust with customers and stakeholders requires compliance with these regulations in addition to being a legal imperative.

Lack of Expertise and Skills

Supply chain sustainability requires a skilled workforce with expertise in emerging technologies to successfully integrate Industry 4.0. In many organizations, it is difficult to find or develop the talent required to implement and manage these advanced technologies. Recruiting and training specialized professionals in areas such as data analytics, the Internet of Things (IoT), and sustainability can be time-consuming and costly.

An integrated approach to Industry 4.0 and supply chain sustainability requires skills in technology, data science, environmental science, and business acumen. Competent professionals are in high demand due to this convergence, which results in a competitive talent landscape (Caiado et al., 2022). Often, organizations face a race to attract individuals with knowledge of both industry 4.0 technology and sustainable supply chain practices.

The dynamic nature of technology means that the skill sets required for Industry 4.0 are constantly evolving. Keeping up with technological advances and industry best practices requires continuous learning and upskilling. Investments in employee development are crucial for maintaining a workforce capable of harnessing the full potential of Industry 4.0 technologies and aligning them with sustainability goals.

Regulatory Compliance

Organizations seeking to integrate Industry 4.0 with supply chain sustainability face a complex web of environmental, social, and data privacy regulations. Regulations spanning local, national, and international levels require a deep understanding of legal frameworks in order to comply. Supply chain sustainability efforts become more complex when companies operate across multiple regions.

It is possible for environmental regulations to differ widely from one jurisdiction to another, affecting areas such as waste disposal, emissions control, and resource extraction. Supply chain practices must be aligned with regional legal requirements by staying abreast of evolving environmental standards. A comprehensive understanding of diverse socio-legal landscapes is also required because social regulations regarding labor practices, human rights, and community engagement differ globally (Furstenau et al., 2020).

Data privacy regulations, such as the General Data Protection Regulation (GDPR) in Europe, add to the complexity (Kumar et al., 2020). Since Industry 4.0 involves extensive data collection and sharing, organizations must adhere to data protection laws. Compliance with these regulations is essential for safeguarding customer and operational data and avoiding legal repercussions.

Supplier Collaboration

Multiple partners and suppliers are involved in supply chains, making them inherently complex. As a result of the diversity of these partners, integrating sustainability practices and Industry 4.0 technologies can be a significant challenge. Various suppliers may show different levels of commitment to sustainability or have different technological capabilities, emphasizing the importance of establishing collaborative relationships and standards.

Sustainability requires alignment not only within the focal organization, but also across the entire supply chain. Setting clear expectations and standards for sustainable practices ensures that all partners are on board with the overarching goals. In order to foster a collective commitment to sustainability across the supply chain, collaborative initiatives such as joint sustainability programs and shared best practices are essential (Kunkel et al., 2022).

The integration of Industry 4.0 technologies requires a common technological foundation and interoperability standards. Since each partner may have different technological capabilities and systems, fostering collaboration requires establishing protocols for data sharing, communication, and technology adoption. In order to ensure a cohesive and interconnected supply chain ecosystem, a standardized framework could be developed to enable seamless integration of diverse technologies.

Measurement and Reporting

In order to ensure progress and compliance with sustainability goals, organizations need robust measurement and reporting mechanisms. In order to accomplish this, key performance indicators (KPIs) related to sustainability need to be developed and effective data collection and reporting systems implemented

(Yadav et al., 2020). Tracking and reporting sustainability efforts, however, requires selecting the right metrics and systems, as well as ensuring data accuracy.

Setting meaningful KPIs is a crucial first step. An organization's sustainability KPIs should align with its overall goals and provide insight into its environmental, social, and economic impacts. Carbon footprint, water usage, ethical sourcing percentages, and waste reduction metrics are a few examples. Internally and externally, these indicators serve as benchmarks for assessing progress and communicating performance.

It is equally important to implement a robust data collection system. IoT sensors and data analytics can play a key role in automating the collection of sustainability-related data with Industry 4.0 technologies. These technologies enable real-time monitoring and provide accurate and detailed information continuously. Through the integration of these technologies into the supply chain, organizations can track sustainability metrics at various stages, from raw material sourcing to end-product delivery.

Sourcing Sustainable Materials

In industries with complex supply chains and limited eco-friendly alternatives, sourcing sustainable materials can be challenging. A sustainable supply chain can be more expensive, and organizations may struggle to find suppliers who meet their ethical and environmental standards. Business owners seeking to reduce their environmental impact and meet consumer demands must shift toward sustainable sourcing despite these challenges. Procuring sustainably sourced materials has benefits beyond environmental stewardship, including reputational gains, risk mitigation, and long-term cost savings (Yadav et al., 2020).

To overcome sustainable sourcing hurdles, businesses can establish strong partnerships with suppliers who adhere to ethical and eco-friendly practices. A collaboration built on trust and transparency facilitates open communication about sustainability goals, ensuring that both parties are committed to responsible sourcing.

Moreover, organizations can explore innovative technologies and methodologies that improve visibility and traceability within their supply chains. Using blockchain technology, for example, businesses can trace the origins of raw materials and verify the sustainability claims of suppliers through transparent and immutable records of transactions. As a result, not only are regulatory requirements met, but consumers and stakeholders also feel more confident.

Return on Investment (ROI)

For businesses to demonstrate the return on investment (ROI) of integrating Industry 4.0 with supply chain sustainability, they must use a comprehensive and multifaceted measurement approach. Despite the difficulties in quantifying immediate financial benefits, it is important to recognize the broader impacts on brand reputation and long-term sustainability (Akbari et al., 2023).

Increasing efficiency and optimizing processes can reduce operational costs. With Industry 4.0 technologies, such as Internet of Things (IoT) sensors and data analytics, supply chain activities can be monitored in real time. By increasing visibility, demand forecasting, inventory management, and production planning can be more precise. Organizations can realize significant cost savings over time by minimizing waste, reducing lead times, and improving resource allocation.

Enhancing supply chain resilience is another important aspect. By using Industry 4.0 technologies, companies are able to create agile and adaptive supply chains that are capable of responding to unforeseen disruptions. It is important to be able to adapt quickly to changes in demand, supply, or external factors in order to avoid costly disruptions and downtime. In spite of the fact that these benefits might not yield immediate financial returns, they have a significant impact on risk mitigation and long-term supply chain stability.

The integration of Industry 4.0 with supply chain sustainability is a complex and multifaceted process. To realize the benefits of sustainability and innovation, organizations must overcome common challenges and barriers. To address these challenges, companies should invest in employee training, collaborate with suppliers, and commit to continuous improvement. Businesses that successfully navigate these obstacles can position themselves as leaders in a rapidly evolving business landscape that emphasizes both technology-driven efficiency and sustainability.

INDUSTRY 4.0 AND SUPPLY CHAIN SUSTAINABILITY CASE STUDIES

Integrating Industry 4.0 with supply chain sustainability represents a pivotal step for modern businesses seeking efficiency, innovation, and ethical responsibility. Several companies across various industries have successfully navigated this integration, demonstrating how it can result in positive outcomes. The following section elucidates some real-world examples of organizations that are effectively implementing Industry 4.0 technologies in their supply chains

Siemens

Industry 4.0 integration with supply chain sustainability exemplifies Siemens' forward-thinking approach to industrial manufacturing. Utilizing cutting-edge technologies such as digital twins, the Internet of Things (IoT), and data analytics demonstrates their commitment to minimizing environmental impact while optimizing processes.

Siemens has greatly benefited from the implementation of digital twins (A. Sharma et al., 2022). In real-time, they can simulate and analyze physical products and processes by creating virtual replicas. Siemens is able to identify inefficiencies quickly and implement targeted improvements as a result of this dynamic approach. Through real-time monitoring of production processes, Siemens can optimize the use of energy and raw materials. Reducing waste and emissions not only improves operational efficiency, but also contributes to sustainability.

Siemens' capabilities are further enhanced by the IoT by creating a network of interconnected devices that collect and share data. As a result, supply chains become more responsive and adaptive. In order to prevent breakdowns and minimize downtime, sensors can monitor equipment's condition. Furthermore, this proactive approach contributes to resource efficiency and sustainability in addition to ensuring operational continuity.

Unilever

A global leader in consumer goods, Unilever has demonstrated a commitment to responsible sourcing and waste reduction through Industry 4.0 technologies. Unilever pioneered a transparent and traceable supply chain for critical raw materials like palm oil and tea through blockchain technology (Khan et al.,

2023). The innovative use of blockchain not only provides visibility into raw materials' origins but also enables responsible sourcing practices throughout the supply chain to be verified and authenticated.

Unilever's Industry 4.0 strategy also includes the use of IoT sensors (Götz & Jankowska, 2020). Unilever can track and manage the conditions of their products throughout the supply chain journey by implementing real-time monitoring during transportation. In addition to preventing loss and damage, this proactive approach enhances the quality of the product as a whole. As a result of these measures, Unilever's sustainability goals are aligned with its operational efficiency goals.

The Sustainable Living Plan underscores Unilever's commitment to sustainability (Stanley et al., 2022). From sourcing raw materials to reducing environmental impact, this comprehensive plan outlines specific objectives and indicators. Unilever embeds sustainability into their corporate strategy to guide decision-making and ensure a holistic approach to responsible business.

Patagonia

Industry 4.0 technologies have been successfully integrated into Patagonia's supply chain to advance sustainability. As a result of the company's proactive use of data analytics, the company is able to meticulously monitor and reduce water and energy consumption during the manufacturing process.

For example, Patagonia optimizes dyeing processes, one of the most resource-intensive steps in garment production (Dolzhenko & Churakova, 2022). By analyzing data, they have identified areas for improvement and implemented changes that significantly reduce water usage. In addition to aligning with their sustainability goals, this serves as a testament to the transformative power of Industry 4.0.

Patagonia emphasizes the importance of extending the lifespan of its products beyond the manufacturing stage. By encouraging customers to return used items for repair or recycling, the company actively promotes repair and recycling initiatives. Using a circular approach to product lifecycle management aligns with the principles of a circular economy, where products are designed to be recyclable and sustainable (Erhun et al., 2021). Patagonia encourages a shift away from traditional linear production and consumption models by encouraging a culture of repair and reuse.

Nestlé

Nestlé has integrated Industry 4.0 technologies with supply chain sustainability to reinforce responsible sourcing and minimize environmental impact. A key element of their approach is the use of blockchain technology to trace the origins of ingredients. Besides providing unprecedented transparency to consumers, this also serves as a robust tool for verifying ethical and sustainable practices in raw material sourcing.

Nestlé can track and trace ingredients through the supply chain using blockchain technology (Bhattacharya, 2023). As a result, they can address critical issues like deforestation and unfair labor practices promptly. Nestlé's commitment to responsible and ethical business practices is reflected in an agile and responsive supply chain.

Sustainability goes beyond Nestlé's commitment to transparency in sourcing. They take a holistic approach to minimizing their environmental footprint by actively reducing waste and energy consumption in their operations. Across all aspects of manufacturing and supply chain management, Industry 4.0 emphasizes efficiency and optimization.

Coca-Cola

Coca-Cola Company has successfully incorporated Industry 4.0 technologies into its bottling and distribution processes to enhance sustainability. With data analytics and the Internet of Things (IoT), Coca-Cola optimizes logistics to reduce fuel consumption and emissions. Monitoring transportation conditions in real time allows the company to make informed decisions, minimizing environmental impact (Thakur, 2021).

Using data analytics, Coca-Cola can streamline its supply chain, ensuring efficient routes and reducing unnecessary energy use. Furthermore, this aligns with the company's commitment to environmental stewardship. Through the integration of IoT devices, vehicle performance can be monitored, resulting in proactive maintenance and reducing the carbon footprint of the distribution network.

To address the global problem of plastic waste, Coca-Cola places a great deal of emphasis on sustainable packaging solutions. "World Without Waste" reflects the company's commitment to collecting and recycling every bottle and can it sells. Additionally, this initiative underscores Coca-Cola's commitment to the entire lifecycle of its products while aligning with global efforts to minimize packaging's environmental impact.

A variety of real-world examples illustrate how Industry 4.0 can be applied to supply chain sustainability in several industries. Technology and sustainability can be integrated in a wide variety of industries, from industrial manufacturing to consumer goods and energy management. Throughout these organizations, sustainability has become a core component of their business strategies, demonstrating the transformative potential of Industry 4.0 in achieving sustainable supply chains.

FUTURE TRENDS

Integrated Industry 4.0 with supply chain sustainability will be marked by advanced technologies, innovative strategies, and a heightened commitment to environmental and social responsibility. The use of artificial intelligence (AI) and machine learning in supply chain management is a significant trend on the horizon. By analyzing vast datasets and extracting actionable insights, these technologies are revolutionizing decision-making processes. Predictive analytics will be enhanced by AI, allowing businesses to anticipate fluctuations in demand, optimize inventory levels, and minimize waste (Bag et al., 2018). Learning from historical data and refining supply chain strategies will continue to evolve machine learning algorithms.

Another emerging trend in integrating Industry 4.0 with supply chain sustainability is that of digital twins, which are virtual replicas of physical processes or products (Kamble et al., 2022). With these digital representations, production processes can be monitored and analyzed in real-time, providing a comprehensive view of the entire supply chain. Businesses can enhance resource utilization and reduce environmental impact by creating digital twins of their operations to simulate and optimize processes, identify inefficiencies, and make data-driven decisions.

Supply chains will increasingly rely on blockchain technology to ensure transparency and traceability (Esmaeilian et al., 2020). Blockchain can be used to verify the authenticity of sustainability claims because of its decentralized and secure nature. Blockchain can be used by companies to create an immutable record for every step in the supply chain, from raw material sourcing to manufacturing and distribution. Furthermore, consumers are increasingly demanding visibility into the ethical and environmental practices of the products they purchase, which enhances accountability.

Supply chain operations will become more sophisticated with the deployment of Internet of Things (IoT) devices, enabling real-time monitoring and communication (Laturkar & Laturkar, 2023b). 5G networks will enable these devices to transmit and receive data at unprecedented speeds, enabling more responsive and agile supply chain management. IoT devices will continue to optimize transportation, reduce spoilage, and enhance supply chain efficiency with temperature and humidity sensors and GPS tracking.

The importance of sustainability metrics as key performance indicators (KPIs) will likely increase in the future (Marinagi et al., 2023). Business practices are increasingly integrating environmental, social, and governance (ESG) factors. Companies will be held accountable for meeting specific targets related to carbon emissions, waste reduction, and responsible sourcing as part of their corporate strategies. Businesses will seek to minimize their environmental footprint as they implement circular economy principles (Bhattacharya, 2023). The design of products will increasingly emphasize recyclability and reusability, leading to closed-loop systems where materials are continually reused. To reduce packaging waste, companies will collaborate with suppliers to source recycled materials.

A technologically advanced, transparent, and environmentally conscious supply chain landscape will result from integrating Industry 4.0 with supply chain sustainability. Digital twins, blockchain, IoT, and circular economy principles will collectively reshape how companies manage their supply chains. In embracing sustainability as a core component of corporate strategy, businesses will enhance operational efficiency and contribute meaningfully to global efforts towards a more sustainable and responsible future.

CONCLUSION

Overall, the integration of Industry 4.0 and supply chain sustainability represents a transformative paradigm for business operations in the future. Synergies between Industry 4.0 technologies and sustainable supply chain practices are transforming how companies operate, make decisions, and respond to the evolving demands of a conscientious global market as technology advances.

A cornerstone of the evolution of supply chain sustainability is the adoption of artificial intelligence and machine learning. In addition to optimizing processes, predicting demand fluctuations, and enhancing overall efficiency, these technologies enable businesses to navigate complexities with unprecedented precision. AI and machine learning are expected to streamline operations and contribute significantly to waste reduction, resource efficiency, and carbon reduction in the future.

Supply chain processes can be monitored and simulated in real-time using digital twins. By enhancing visibility, inefficiencies can also be identified and rectified more quickly. By creating virtual replicas of their operations, businesses can minimize their environmental impact and achieve sustainability goals. In the face of dynamic market conditions, the digital twin concept enables an important level of agility and adaptability.

The decentralized and transparent nature of blockchain technology ensures the verifiability of claims related to responsible sourcing and sustainable practices. Blockchain provides a secure and immutable record of the journey from raw material extraction to the final product, as consumers demand greater authenticity and ethical considerations in their purchase decisions. In addition to building trust, this also holds companies accountable for their sustainability commitments.

With the advent of 5G networks and the Internet of Things (IoT), real-time monitoring and communication within supply chains will be revolutionized. As a result of enhanced connectivity and speed, businesses will be able to react quickly to changes, optimize operations, and reduce waste. Sustainable supply chain management relies on data-driven decision-making processes enabled by IoT devices.

Corporate performance measurement will increasingly include sustainability metrics. Sustainability goals will be integrated into corporate strategies as businesses align themselves with environmental, social, and governance (ESG) criteria. In addition to demonstrating a growing societal consciousness, this shift also positions sustainability as a strategic imperative rather than just a compliance issue.

In the future, circular economy principles, such as recyclability, reusability, and responsible product design, will become increasingly important. Companies are recognizing the importance of reducing their environmental impact while also actively contributing to a circular and regenerative system. Businesses committed to closing the loop on resource use will succeed through collaboration with suppliers and innovative packaging and materials.

As a result of the integration of Industry 4.0 with supply chain sustainability, businesses are moving toward a future of technological innovation and environmental responsibility. In addition to enhancing operational efficiency, this holistic approach aligns businesses with the values of increasingly conscious consumers. Companies at the forefront of integrating Industry 4.0 with sustainability are not only adapting to change, but actively shaping a world where economic success and environmental stewardship are intertwined.

REFERENCES

Abulibdeh, A., Zaidan, E., & Abulibdeh, R. (2024). Navigating the confluence of artificial intelligence and education for sustainable development in the era of industry 4.0: Challenges, opportunities, and ethical dimensions. *Journal of Cleaner Production*, *437*, 140527. doi:10.1016/j.jclepro.2023.140527

Akbari, M., Kok, S. K., Hopkins, J., Frederico, G. F., Nguyen, H., & Alonso, A. D. (2023). The changing landscape of digital transformation in supply chains: impacts of industry 4.0 in Vietnam. *International Journal of Logistics Management*. https://doi.org/ doi:10.1108/IJLM-11-2022-0442/FULL/XML

Attaran, M. (2020). Digital technology enablers and their implications for supply chain management. *Supply Chain Forum: An International Journal, 21*(3), 158–172. 10.1080/16258312.2020.1751568

Bag, S., Telukdarie, A., Pretorius, J. H. C., & Gupta, S. (2018). Industry 4.0 and supply chain sustainability: Framework and future research directions. *Benchmarking*, *28*(5), 1410–1450. doi:10.1108/BIJ-03-2018-0056

Bag, S., Wood, L. C., Xu, L., Dhamija, P., & Kayikci, Y. (2020). Big data analytics as an operational excellence approach to enhance sustainable supply chain performance. *Resources, Conservation and Recycling*, *153*, 104559. doi:10.1016/j.resconrec.2019.104559

Bhattacharya, A. (2023). Achieving sustainability in supply chain operations in the interplay between circular economy and Industry 4.0. *Production Planning and Control*, *34*(10), 867–869. doi:10.1080/09537287.2021.1981032

Birkel, H., & Müller, J. M. (2021). Potentials of industry 4.0 for supply chain management within the triple bottom line of sustainability – A systematic literature review. *Journal of Cleaner Production*, *289*, 125612. doi:10.1016/j.jclepro.2020.125612

Caiado, R. G. G., Scavarda, L. F., Azevedo, B. D., Nascimento, D. L. de M., & Quelhas, O. L. G. (2022). Challenges and Benefits of Sustainable Industry 4.0 for Operations and Supply Chain Management—A Framework Headed toward the 2030 Agenda. *Sustainability, 14*(2), 830. doi:10.3390/su14020830

Chauhan, S., Singh, R., Gehlot, A., Akram, S. V., Twala, B., & Priyadarshi, N. (2022). Digitalization of Supply Chain Management with Industry 4.0 Enabling Technologies: A Sustainable Perspective. *Processes, 11*(1), 96. doi:10.3390/pr11010096

Cioffi, R., Travaglioni, M., Piscitelli, G., Petrillo, A., & De Felice, F. (2020). Artificial Intelligence and Machine Learning Applications in Smart Production: Progress, Trends, and Directions. *Sustainability, 12*(2), 492. doi:10.3390/su12020492

Diaz Lopez, F. J., Bastein, T., & Tukker, A. (2019). Business Model Innovation for Resource-efficiency, Circularity and Cleaner Production: What 143 Cases Tell Us. *Ecological Economics*, *155*, 20–35. doi:10.1016/j.ecolecon.2018.03.009

Dolzhenko, I. B., & Churakova, A. A. (2022). Environmental Responsibility of Fashion Industry Multinational Corporations (MNCs) in the Context of Industry 4.0. *Industry 4.0: Fighting Climate Change in the Economy of the Future*, 79–89. https://doi.org/ doi:10.1007/978-3-030-79496-5_7/COVER

Ebinger, F., & Omondi, B. (2020). Leveraging Digital Approaches for Transparency in Sustainable Supply Chains: A Conceptual Paper. *Sustainability, 12*(15), 6129. doi:10.3390/su12156129

Erhun, F., Kraft, T., & Wijnsma, S. (2021). Sustainable Triple-A Supply Chains. *Production and Operations Management*, *30*(3), 644–655. doi:10.1111/poms.13306

Esmaeilian, B., Sarkis, J., Lewis, K., & Behdad, S. (2020). Blockchain for the future of sustainable supply chain management in Industry 4.0. *Resources, Conservation and Recycling*, *163*, 105064. doi:10.1016/j.resconrec.2020.105064

Furstenau, L. B., Sott, M. K., Kipper, L. M., MacHado, E. L., Lopez-Robles, J. R., Dohan, M. S., Cobo, M. J., Zahid, A., Abbasi, Q. H., & Imran, M. A. (2020). Link between Sustainability and Industry 4.0: Trends, Challenges and New Perspectives. *IEEE Access : Practical Innovations, Open Solutions*, *8*, 140079–140096. doi:10.1109/ACCESS.2020.3012812

Ghadge, A., Er Kara, M., Moradlou, H., & Goswami, M. (2020). The impact of Industry 4.0 implementation on supply chains. *Journal of Manufacturing Technology Management*, *31*(4), 669–686. doi:10.1108/JMTM-10-2019-0368

Ghobakhloo, M. (2020). Industry 4.0, digitization, and opportunities for sustainability. *Journal of Cleaner Production*, *252*, 119869. doi:10.1016/j.jclepro.2019.119869

Götz, M., & Jankowska, B. (2020). Adoption of industry 4.0 technologies and company competitiveness: Case studies from a post-transition economy. *Foresight and STI Governance*, *14*(4), 61–78. doi:10.17323/2500-2597.2020.4.61.78

Heizer, J., Render, B., & Munson, C. (2020). *Operations management : sustainability and supply chain management.* https://thuvienso.hoasen.edu.vn/handle/123456789/12793

Hlophe, M. C., & Maharaj, B. T. (2023). From Cyber–Physical Convergence to Digital Twins: A Review on Edge Computing Use Case Designs. *Applied Sciences (Basel, Switzerland)*, *13*(24), 13262. doi:10.3390/app132413262

Hofmann, E., Sternberg, H., Chen, H., Pflaum, A., & Prockl, G. (2019). Supply chain management and Industry 4.0: Conducting research in the digital age. *International Journal of Physical Distribution & Logistics Management*, *49*(10), 945–955. doi:10.1108/IJPDLM-11-2019-399

Holtschulte, A. (2022). Interaction of the IoT with Other Technologies. *Management for Professionals*, (Part F353), 125–147. doi:10.1007/978-3-030-89408-5_5

Hong, Z., & Guo, X. (2019). Green product supply chain contracts considering environmental responsibilities. *Omega*, *83*, 155–166. doi:10.1016/j.omega.2018.02.010

Ivanov, D., & Dolgui, A. (2021). A digital supply chain twin for managing the disruption risks and resilience in the era of Industry 4.0. *Production Planning and Control*, *32*(9), 775–788. doi:10.1080/09537287.2020.1768450

Javaid, M., Haleem, A., Singh, R. P., Suman, R., & Gonzalez, E. S. (2022). Understanding the adoption of Industry 4.0 technologies in improving environmental sustainability. *Sustainable Operations and Computers*, *3*, 203–217. doi:10.1016/j.susoc.2022.01.008

Kamble, S. S., Gunasekaran, A., & Gawankar, S. A. (2020). Achieving sustainable performance in a data-driven agriculture supply chain: A review for research and applications. *International Journal of Production Economics*, *219*, 179–194. doi:10.1016/j.ijpe.2019.05.022

Kamble, S. S., Gunasekaran, A., Parekh, H., Mani, V., Belhadi, A., & Sharma, R. (2022). Digital twin for sustainable manufacturing supply chains: Current trends, future perspectives, and an implementation framework. *Technological Forecasting and Social Change*, *176*, 121448. doi:10.1016/j.techfore.2021.121448

Khan, M. R., Khan, M. R., & Nallaluthan, K. (2023). Blockchain Supply Chain Management and Supply Chain Sustainability. *Management for Professionals*, (Part F539), 155–180. doi:10.1007/978-981-99-0699-4_10

Koh, L., Orzes, G., & Jia, F. (2019). The fourth industrial revolution (Industry 4.0): technologies disruption on operations and supply chain management. *International Journal of Operations and Production Management, 39*(6/7/8), 817–828. https://doi.org/ doi:10.1108/IJOPM-08-2019-788/FULL/PDF

Kumar, R., Singh, R. K., & Dwivedi, Y. K. (2020). Application of industry 4.0 technologies in SMEs for ethical and sustainable operations: Analysis of challenges. *Journal of Cleaner Production*, *275*, 124063. doi:10.1016/j.jclepro.2020.124063 PMID:32921931

Kunkel, S., Matthess, M., Xue, B., & Beier, G. (2022). Industry 4.0 in sustainable supply chain collaboration: Insights from an interview study with international buying firms and Chinese suppliers in the electronics industry. *Resources, Conservation and Recycling*, *182*, 106274. doi:10.1016/j.resconrec.2022.106274

Kusi-Sarpong, S., Gupta, H., & Sarkis, J. (2019). A supply chain sustainability innovation framework and evaluation methodology. *International Journal of Production Research, 57*(7), 1990–2008. doi:10.1080/00207543.2018.1518607

Laturkar, K., & Laturkar, K. (2023a). *A Blockchain-Based Approach to Revolutionizing Healthcare.*, doi:10.4018/978-1-6684-6509-7.ch003

Laturkar, K., & Laturkar, K. (2023b). *Internet of Things: Architectures.* Applications, and Challenges., doi:10.4018/978-1-6684-8145-5.ch023

Liu, B., & De Giovanni, P. (2019). Green process innovation through Industry 4.0 technologies and supply chain coordination. *Annals of Operations Research,* 1–36. doi:10.1007/s10479-019-03498-3

Luthra, S., Kumar, A., Zavadskas, E. K., Mangla, S. K., & Garza-Reyes, J. A. (2020). Industry 4.0 as an enabler of sustainability diffusion in supply chain: An analysis of influential strength of drivers in an emerging economy. *International Journal of Production Research, 58*(5), 1505–1521. doi:10.1080/00207543.2019.1660828

Manavalan, E., & Jayakrishna, K. (2019). A review of Internet of Things (IoT) embedded sustainable supply chain for industry 4.0 requirements. *Computers & Industrial Engineering, 127*, 925–953. doi:10.1016/j.cie.2018.11.030

Marinagi, C., Reklitis, P., Trivellas, P., & Sakas, D. (2023). The Impact of Industry 4.0 Technologies on Key Performance Indicators for a Resilient Supply Chain 4.0. *Sustainability, 15*(6), 5185. doi:10.3390/su15065185

Martins, C. L., & Pato, M. V. (2019). Supply chain sustainability: A tertiary literature review. *Journal of Cleaner Production, 225*, 995–1016. doi:10.1016/j.jclepro.2019.03.250

Mastos, T. D., Nizamis, A., Vafeiadis, T., Alexopoulos, N., Ntinas, C., Gkortzis, D., Papadopoulos, A., Ioannidis, D., & Tzovaras, D. (2020). Industry 4.0 sustainable supply chains: An application of an IoT enabled scrap metal management solution. *Journal of Cleaner Production, 269*, 122377. doi:10.1016/j.jclepro.2020.122377

Negri, M., Cagno, E., Colicchia, C., & Sarkis, J. (2021). Integrating sustainability and resilience in the supply chain: A systematic literature review and a research agenda. *Business Strategy and the Environment, 30*(7), 2858–2886. doi:10.1002/bse.2776

Oláh, J., Aburumman, N., Popp, J., Khan, M. A., Haddad, H., & Kitukutha, N. (2020). Impact of Industry 4.0 on Environmental Sustainability. *Sustainability, 12*(11), 4674. doi:10.3390/su12114674

Popkova, E. G., Ragulina, Y. V., & Bogoviz, A. V. (2019). Fundamental differences of transition to industry 4.0 from previous industrial revolutions. *Studies in Systems. Decision and Control, 169*, 21–29. doi:10.1007/978-3-319-94310-7_3/COVER

Pournader, M., Kach, A., & Talluri, S. (2020). A Review of the Existing and Emerging Topics in the Supply Chain Risk Management Literature. *Decision Sciences, 51*(4), 867–919. doi:10.1111/deci.12470 PMID:34234385

Rath, M., Satpathy, J., & Oreku, G. S. (2021). Artificial Intelligence and Machine Learning Applications in Cloud Computing and Internet of Things. *Artificial Intelligence to Solve Pervasive Internet of Things Issues*, 103–123. doi:10.1016/B978-0-12-818576-6.00006-X

Rejeb, A., Keogh, J. G., Wamba, S. F., & Treiblmaier, H. (2021). The potentials of augmented reality in supply chain management: A state-of-the-art review. *Management Review Quarterly*, *71*(4), 819–856. doi:10.1007/s11301-020-00201-w

Saeed, M. A., & Kersten, W. (2019). Drivers of Sustainable Supply Chain Management: Identification and Classification. *Sustainability, 11*(4), 1137. doi:10.3390/su11041137

Sanders, N. R., Boone, T., Ganeshan, R., & Wood, J. D. (2019). Sustainable Supply Chains in the Age of AI and Digitization: Research Challenges and Opportunities. *Journal of Business Logistics*, *40*(3), 229–240. doi:10.1111/jbl.12224

Sharma, A., Kosasih, E., Zhang, J., Brintrup, A., & Calinescu, A. (2022). Digital Twins: State of the art theory and practice, challenges, and open research questions. *Journal of Industrial Information Integration*, *30*, 100383. doi:10.1016/j.jii.2022.100383

Sharma, M., Kamble, S., Mani, V., Sehrawat, R., Belhadi, A., & Sharma, V. (2021). Industry 4.0 adoption for sustainability in multi-tier manufacturing supply chain in emerging economies. *Journal of Cleaner Production*, *281*, 125013. doi:10.1016/j.jclepro.2020.125013

Stanley, A. O., Ovie, E. A., Ughovero, B. A., & Ijoyah, C. T. (2022). Sustainable Production Strategy and Product Availability: A Study of Unilever Nigeria PLC. *Lafia Journal of Economics and Management Sciences, 7*(1), 44–65. https://lajems.com/index.php/lajems/article/view/201

Thakur, A. (2021). Supply Chain Sustainability in Food and Beverage Industry. In Driving Innovation and Productivity Through Sustainable Automation (pp. 173–189). doi:10.4018/978-1-7998-5879-9.ch008

Toktaş-Palut, P. (2022). Analyzing the effects of Industry 4.0 technologies and coordination on the sustainability of supply chains. *Sustainable Production and Consumption*, *30*, 341–358. doi:10.1016/j.spc.2021.12.005

Xu, M., Cui, Y., Hu, M., Xu, X., Zhang, Z., Liang, S., & Qu, S. (2019). Supply chain sustainability risk and assessment. *Journal of Cleaner Production*, *225*, 857–867. doi:10.1016/j.jclepro.2019.03.307

Yadav, G., Luthra, S., Jakhar, S. K., Mangla, S. K., & Rai, D. P. (2020). A framework to overcome sustainable supply chain challenges through solution measures of industry 4.0 and circular economy: An automotive case. *Journal of Cleaner Production*, *254*, 120112. doi:10.1016/j.jclepro.2020.120112

Zhao, H., Zhao, Q. H., & Ślusarczyk, B. (2019). Sustainability and Digitalization of Corporate Management Based on Augmented/Virtual Reality Tools Usage: China and Other World IT Companies' Experience. *Sustainability, 11*(17), 4717. doi:10.3390/su11174717

Chapter 7
Impact of Industry 4.0 Technologies for Advancement of Supply Chain Management (SCM) Sustainability:
Prospects and Challenges

Mukesh Shankar Bharti
https://orcid.org/0000-0002-3693-7247
Jawaharlal Nehru University, India

ABSTRACT

The purpose of this chapter is to explore the potential impact of Industry 4.0 on the advancement of supply chain management. The fourth industrial revolution brought potential reform with better performances in SCM sustainability. This study analyses how Industry 4.0 technologies are becoming instruments to advance supply chain performance. A theoretical discussion of systems theory is associated with this research to highlight key approaches of Industry 4.0 for sustainable SCM. Qualitative analysis was used in this research by explaining the primary and secondary data to discuss research problems. This research also used empirical methods to highlight the role of the following technologies for huge performance improvement in the SCM, for example, artificial intelligence, robotics, the internet of things (IoT), machine learning, big data analytics (BDA), blockchain, and additive manufacturing.

INTRODUCTION

Industry 4.0 relies heavily on information technology to transform traditional manufacturing into a more connected, efficient, and intelligent system, ultimately driving advancements in productivity, quality, and agility in industrial processes (Esmaeilian et al., 2016). Industry 4.0 aims to create smart factories where intelligent systems and technologies collaborate seamlessly. This includes smart production lines, predictive maintenance systems, and flexible manufacturing setups. Industry 4.0 places a strong emphasis

DOI: 10.4018/979-8-3693-1363-3.ch007

on cybersecurity to protect sensitive data and ensure the integrity of industrial processes (Stock & Seliger, 2016). The incorporation of sustainability into production and consumption processes aligns with global initiatives, such as those set by the United Nations for sustainable development. Sustainability in supply chains involves considering environmental, social, and economic factors to mitigate the negative impact on the ecosystem. This includes addressing issues related to resource use, waste generation, and transportation practices. It is an insightful overview of Industry 4.0 (I40) technologies and their applications in various processes of manufacturing, logistics, and supply chain (SC). The advanced digital technologies which can be mentioned - such as big data analytics (BDA), artificial intelligence (AI), machine learning (ML), internet of things (IoT) and sensors, blockchain technology (BCT), robotic systems (RS), cloud computing (CC), cyber-physical systems (CPS), additive manufacturing (AM) /3D printing (3D), virtual reality (VR), augmented reality (AR), autonomous vehicles (AV), and drones- have indeed transformed industries (Akhtar, 2022).

Industry 4.0 technologies offer a suite of tools and approaches that, when integrated into the supply chain, can lead to significant improvements in efficiency. By leveraging these technologies, organizations can create more agile, responsive, and streamlined supply chain processes, ultimately enhancing their overall competitiveness in the marketplace. Internet of Things (IoT) and sensors enable real-time tracking of goods, inventory, and equipment throughout the supply chain. This visibility helps in optimizing processes and making informed decisions promptly. Big Data Analytics allows organizations to analyze large datasets, extract valuable insights, and make data-driven decisions. This can lead to more accurate demand forecasting, inventory management, and resource allocation. Robotic Systems (RS) and automation technologies can streamline routine tasks such as picking, packing, and sorting in warehouses. This not only reduces the need for manual labor but also enhances the speed and accuracy of these processes. Additive Manufacturing (AM) or 3D printing can revolutionize production processes by allowing on-demand and localized manufacturing. This can lead to reduced lead times and more efficient use of resources. Cloud Computing (CC) facilitates seamless collaboration among supply chain partners. It enables real-time sharing of information, documents, and updates, fostering better communication and coordination. Cyber-Physical Systems (CPS) and connectivity between machines enable a more integrated and interconnected supply chain. This connectivity ensures that different components of the supply chain operate in sync, minimizing delays and disruptions.

Blockchain Technology (BCT) ensures a secure and transparent record of transactions and movements within the supply chain. This enhances traceability, allowing organizations to identify and address issues quickly. IoT and AI can be employed for predictive maintenance of equipment and machinery. By anticipating when maintenance is needed, organizations can reduce downtime and extend the lifespan of assets. Technologies such as drones and autonomous vehicles provide opportunities for remote monitoring and control of supply chain activities. This can lead to more efficient and flexible logistics operations. AI and ML algorithms can optimize resource allocation, from inventory levels to transportation routes. This efficiency contributes to cost reduction and a more sustainable use of resources.

Sustainability is indeed a multi-dimensional concept that goes beyond just economic considerations. It involves balancing economic, environmental, and social aspects to ensure the long-term viability and responsibility of a business. The primary goal of a commercial enterprise is typically economic sustainability, aiming to generate profits over the long term. This involves effectively managing costs and revenues in various aspects of the business, including sourcing, production, and distribution of goods and services. Economic sustainability is achieved through a careful balance between costs and revenues. Businesses need to optimize their operations to ensure that the costs associated with sourcing, production, and distribution are effectively managed, allowing for sustained profitability. Businesses are increasingly acknowledging their role in mitigating climate change. This involves adopting practices that reduce carbon emissions, minimize resource consumption, and promote the use of sustainable and eco-friendly technologies. While economic and environmental aspects are crucial, the social dimension of sustainability is also essential. This includes considerations for fair labor practices, community engagement, diversity and inclusion, and ethical business conduct (Kamble et al., 2018). Social sustainability extends to promoting equity and social integration within communities. Businesses play a role in fostering inclusive practices and contributing positively to the communities in which they operate. The adoption of Industry 4.0 technologies is positioned as a means to achieve long-term sustainability goals by addressing resource use, waste, pollution, and social aspects within manufacturing companies. Social sustainability extends to promoting equity and social integration within communities.

REVIEW OF LITERATURE AND THEORETICAL BACKGROUND

Industry 4.0 brought a meaningful revolution in the sector of manufacturing and easing the work of industry, and human's economic and social development are deeply rooted through invention of new technology. Sustainable development involves the integration of sustainable practices both in production and consumption. This means not only producing goods and services in environmentally and socially responsible ways but also ensuring that the way individuals and societies consume is mindful of long-term ecological and social impacts (Akenji & Bengtsson, 2014). The sustainable supply chain management takes into account goals from all three dimensions of sustainable development: economic, environmental, and social. This implies a comprehensive approach that considers the impact of supply chain activities on financial performance, the environment, and societal well-being (Mardani et al., 2020). Industry 4.0, driven by CPS, IoT, and big data analytics, introduces a paradigm shift in how companies manage their supply chains. The emphasis on data accessibility and real-time information contributes to efficiency, cost-effectiveness, and the ability to offer more personalized products and services, marking a significant evolution in the way businesses operate within the industrial landscape. These technologies, namely Cyber-Physical Systems (CPS), the Internet of Things (IoT), and big data analytics, are integral to Industry 4.0. They contribute to the connectivity and intelligence of systems, enabling a more advanced and efficient industrial landscape. The integration of CPS, IoT, and big data analytics facilitates data accessibility and real-time information. This is a fundamental shift from traditional supply chain models, providing companies with up-to-the-minute insights into their operations (Gottge et al., 2020; Mardani et al., 2020).

Industry 4.0 refers to the fourth industrial revolution and represents a paradigm shift in manufacturing and production processes. The term was coined in Germany as part of a high-tech strategy to promote the computerization of manufacturing. It was introduced at the Hannover Fair in 2011. Industry 4.0 aligns with sustainability objectives by promoting resource efficiency, waste reduction, and environmentally conscious practices. The data-driven insights from IoT can help identify areas for improvement in energy consumption, material usage, and overall resource utilization. Industry 4.0, with its focus on automation and IoT, transforms traditional manufacturing into a highly interconnected and data-driven ecosystem. This integration not only improves efficiency and productivity but also contributes to sustainability goals by optimizing resource usage and reducing environmental impact within supply chains (Legenvre et al., 2020; Naseem & Yang, 2021).

Industry 4.0 technologies, including the Internet of Things (IoT), data analytics, and advanced sensors, enable real-time monitoring and analysis of the supply chain. This real-time information allows for dynamic decision-making, better demand forecasting, and enhanced overall supply chain efficiency. Industry 4.0 fosters the integration and connectivity of various elements in the production processes. Machines, devices, and systems communicate and collaborate seamlessly, leading to a more interconnected and coordinated manufacturing environment. Through the use of smart technologies and data-driven insights, manufacturers can tailor their processes to meet specific customer demands. This level of customization extends not only to the products being manufactured but also to the services provided along the entire supply chain. The interconnected nature of Industry 4.0 technologies provides enhanced visibility and traceability throughout the supply chain. Industry 4.0 technologies are driving a paradigm shift in manufacturing and supply chain management by enabling real-time optimization, fostering interconnected production processes, and facilitating customization to meet the evolving needs of the market (Bag et al., 2021; Bányai, 2018; Beier et al., 2020; Birkel & Hartmann, 2019a).

The role of digitalization in sustainable supply chain collaboration (SCC) is a multifaceted and evolving area of study. Scholars across various disciplines, including supply chain management, sustainability, and information technology, are actively exploring the impacts, risks, and opportunities associated with the digital transformation of supply chains, particularly in the context of the Global North. Digitalization enables collaborative supply chain models where partners share information and work together to achieve common sustainability objectives. This collaborative approach can lead to improved coordination, reduced waste, and enhanced overall sustainability performance (Bag et al., 2020). Collaboration on sustainability in the supply chain involves concerted efforts by firms to address environmental, social, and economic impacts throughout the entire value chain. Various collaborative models and strategies have emerged to enhance sustainability practices (Sellitto et al., 2019). In the global value chains (GVC) literature, the implications of digitalization for production geography across the globe are a subject of considerable attention and analysis. Digitalization, driven by advances in information technology and communication, has profoundly influenced the organization and dynamics of global production networks (Laplume et al., 2016; Organization, 2017).

Governance of value chains for environmental sustainability in the Global South involves the coordination of various actors, policies, and practices to ensure that economic activities contribute to sustainable development while minimizing negative environmental impacts. The Global South refers to developing and emerging economies, and the governance of value chains in this context faces specific challenges and opportunities. The governance of value chains in the Global South often requires inclusive structures that involve multiple stakeholders, including governments, businesses, local communities, and non-governmental organizations (NGOs). The governance of value chains for environmental sustainability in the Global South requires a holistic, co-operative and collaborative approach. It involves the integration of policies, regulations, capacity building, and community engagement to promote sustainable practices throughout the value chain. This approach aims to balance economic development with environmental conservation and social well-being. Governance structures in the Global South need to encourage the adoption of green supply chain management practices. This involves integrating environmental considerations into the entire supply chain, from sourcing raw materials to production, distribution, and disposal (Achabou et al., 2017; Golini et al., 2018).

Industry 4.0 is indeed a strategic initiative that originated in Germany and has since become a global framework for the transformation of manufacturing and industrial processes. The term was first introduced at the Hannover Fair in 2011, representing the fourth industrial revolution. Germany's adoption of Industry 4.0 was part of a broader high technology plan aimed at enhancing the country's industrial capabilities. The initiative sought to leverage cutting-edge technologies to improve efficiency, productivity, and competitiveness in the manufacturing sector. The overarching goal of Industry 4.0 is to create an intelligent environment within manufacturing and industrial settings. This involves the use of smart technologies, real-time data analytics, artificial intelligence, and machine learning to enable more adaptive, responsive, and efficient operations. While originating in Germany, the concept of Industry 4.0 has gained global recognition and has been embraced by industries worldwide. It has become a guiding framework for digital transformation and smart manufacturing initiatives in various countries (Luthra et al., 2020; Mastrocinque et al., 2022).

METHODS AND MATERIALS

To qualitatively analyze the current developments in smart supply chain management sustainability and study the impacts of Industry 4.0 and related ICT (Information and Communication Technology) technologies, an integrated approach involving in qualitative method is employed. An empirical study explores trends in the adoption of Industry 4.0 technologies, such as IoT (Internet of Things), AI (Artificial Intelligence), blockchain and data analytics in manufacturing processes. supply chain. Certainly, conducting a systematic review of academic and practice literature on the impacts of Industry 4.0 technologies on smart supply chains, with a focus on big data, Internet of Things (IoT), cyber-physical systems, blockchains, and 3D printing, involves several key steps. Use combinations of keywords such as "supply chain," "logistics," "inventory," "sourcing," "pricing," "supply network," with each of the technologies (big data, machine learning, IoT, cyber-physical systems, blockchains, 3D printing).

The comprehensive and consistent understanding of the smart supply chain concept can be established, capturing the various stages, drivers, technologies, applications, and characteristics associated with this evolving paradigm. This holistic view can guide both academic research and industry practices toward a more standardized and integrated approach to smart supply chains. Ensuring compliance with transportation regulations and standards, especially when adopting emerging technologies such as autonomous vehicles. Smart logistics and transportation are integral components of a modern and efficient supply chain. By leveraging smart technologies, organizations can achieve greater visibility, optimize operations, and respond more effectively to the dynamic demands of the market. The integration of these smart drivers contributes to a more intelligent and responsive supply chain ecosystem (Act RAMI, 2014; Barreto et al., 2017; Zhang et al., 2023). Smart drivers of supply chains, including smart logistics, smart warehouses and transportation, play a crucial role in enhancing efficiency, visibility, and responsiveness within the supply chain. These smart drivers leverage advanced technologies to optimize processes and improve overall supply chain performance (Liu et al., 2018). Using predictive analytics to anticipate future trends, demand fluctuations, and potential disruptions, enabling proactive decision-making. Adapting to and integrating emerging technologies that contribute to the evolution of the smart supply chain, such as IoT, blockchain, and advanced analytics. The focus on collaboration, sustainability, and continuous improvement aligns with the evolving expectations and requirements of modern supply chain practices.

Figure 1. Intelligent supply chain management in Industry 4.0: A hierarchical framework for intelligent supply chain management (https://link.springer.com/article/10.1007/s10479-022-04689-1/figures/1)

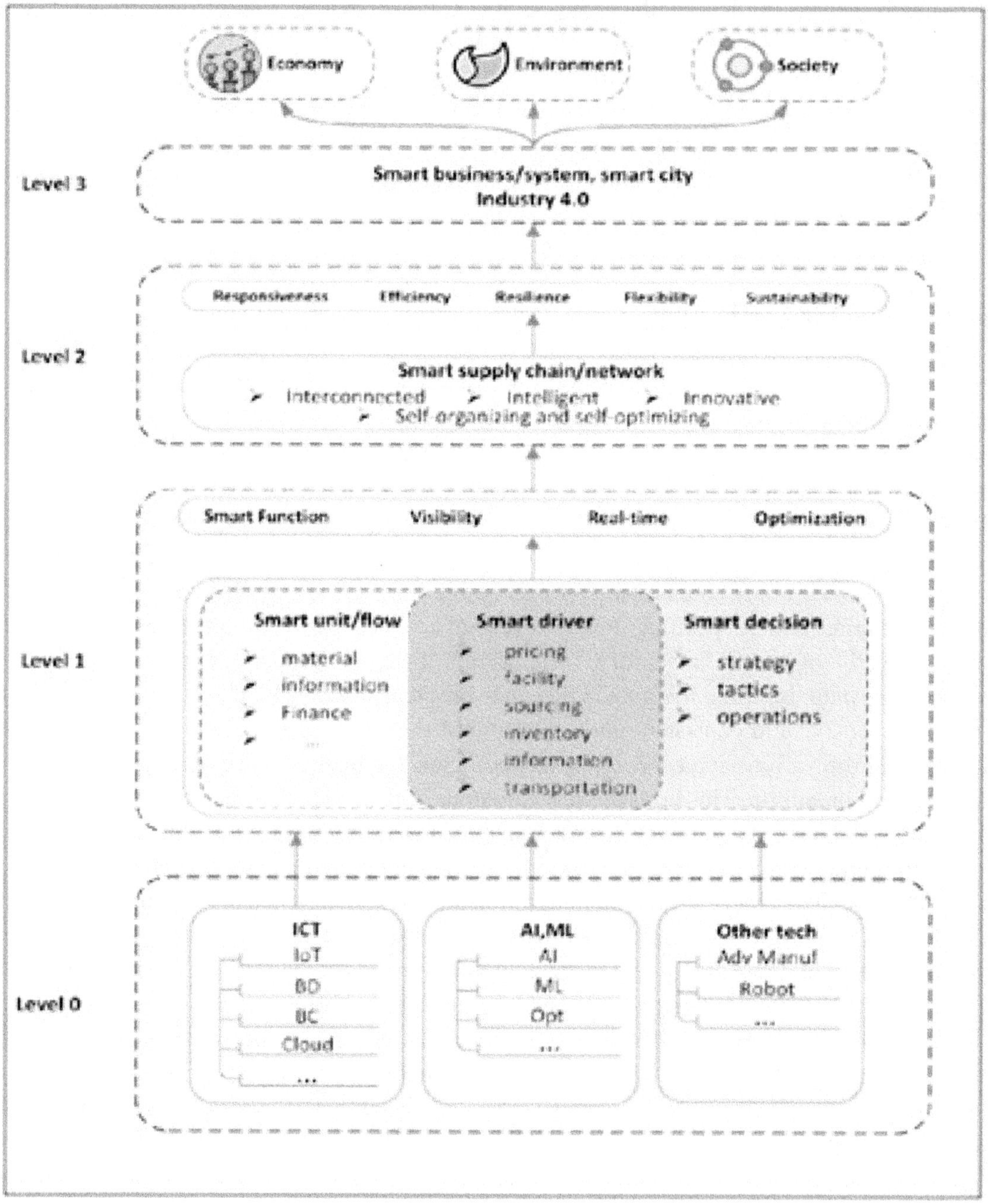

We present a multi-level smart supply chain framework as in Figure 1. The smart supply chain hierarchy also reflects the different stages and scopes of SCM to which ICT, AI and ML and other technologies are applied. This multi-level framework illustrates a holistic approach to smart supply chain sustainability, incorporating various technologies and strategies at different stages and scopes of supply chain management. It allows for a dynamic and integrated system that responds to the complexities and challenges of modern supply chain operations.

It appears that Level 1 in smart supply chain framework represents the initial stage where Information and Communication Technology (ICT) and Artificial Intelligence (AI) are applied to enhance specific aspects of the supply chain. This level focuses on improving a single driver, flow, partner, or level within the supply chain, whether it be operational, tactical, or strategic. Level 1 serves as a foundational step, allowing organizations to gain experience and benefits from applying smart technologies in a focused manner before expanding to broader and more integrated approaches in higher levels of the smart supply chain framework. Level 2 represents a sophisticated stage in the evolution of a smart supply chain, where the integration of intelligence, self-organization, and optimization across all aspects of the supply chain contributes to superior performance in key dimensions. This level aims to create a smart supply chain that is not only intelligent but also self-organizing, capable of reconfiguring and self-optimizing in response to environmental changes and shifts in business goals.

Level 3 signifies the evolution of the smart supply chain from a focused, internally integrated system to an externally aligned and industry-transformative entity. It showcases the strategic importance of the smart supply chain in shaping and supporting the larger business ecosystem. Level 3 in the smart supply chain framework represents the highest level, where the smart supply chain is not only integrated and intelligent but is also aligned with and supports the broader smart business, system, or industry. This level emphasizes the ultimate goal of the smart supply chain, which is to match and support the overarching business strategy, facilitate the implementation of Industry 4.0 principles, and contribute to achieving economic, environmental, and social goals. The smart supply chain is closely aligned with and supports the overall business strategy, contributing to the achievement of business goals and objectives. The supply chain is designed and implemented in alignment with the principles of Industry 4.0, incorporating advanced technologies, connectivity, and intelligence. The smart supply chain actively contributes to achieving economic, environmental, and social sustainability goals, reflecting a commitment to triple bottom line performance.

SUPPLY CHAIN MANAGEMENT UNDER INDUSTRY 4.0

Combining Industry 4.0 technologies with supply chain management (SCM) indeed poses challenges, but it also offers transformative opportunities. Implement a digital thread that seamlessly connects the entire product lifecycle from design to end-of-life, integrating real-world data through digital twins. Leverage digital twins for real-time monitoring, simulation, and optimization of physical processes, enhancing visibility and decision-making across the supply chain. Utilize blockchain to establish a decentralized and secure ledger for transparent and traceable transactions across the supply chain. Enhance trust and reduce the risk of fraud by using blockchain for end-to-end visibility, secure data sharing, and ensuring the integrity of transactions. Harness edge computing to process and analyze data closer to the source, reducing latency and enabling real-time decision-making. Implement edge devices for on-site data processing, improving responsiveness and reducing the burden on centralized systems. Apply artificial intelligence (AI) for predictive analytics to forecast demand, identify potential disruptions, and optimize supply chain planning. Leverage machine learning algorithms to analyze historical and real-time data, enabling proactive decision-making and minimizing risks. Combining Industry 4.0 technologies with supply chain management requires a holistic approach that considers technological, organizational, and cultural aspects. These thoughts, principles, and techniques can guide organizations in designing innovative and adaptive supply chain strategies to meet the challenges and opportunities presented by Industry 4.0. The key is to foster a culture of innovation, agility, and continuous improvement, ensuring that the integration of advanced technologies contributes positively to the overall goals and sustainability of the supply chain (Zhang et al., 2023).

Ghobakhloo (2018) explains the principles of strategically adopting Industry 4.0 technologies in the manufacturing industry, with a focus on 3D printing, involves a set of guiding principles and a keen awareness of evolving technology trends. The integration of digital technologies and the embrace of innovative practices such as 3D printing contribute to the transformation of manufacturing processes, making them more efficient, flexible, and sustainable. This strategic approach positions manufacturers to stay competitive in the dynamic landscape of Industry 4.0. 3D printing fundamentally transforms the product design and manufacturing landscape by offering unparalleled flexibility, efficiency, and innovation. It not only accelerates the design iteration process but also opens up new avenues for customization, sustainability, and cost-effectiveness in manufacturing. 3D printing allows for the creation of fully assembled and integrated components in a single printing process. This reduces the need for post-production assembly, saving time and potentially enhancing the structural integrity of the final product (Berman, 2012).

Blockchain technology holds significant promise for revolutionizing supply chain operations, offering transparency, security, and efficiency. However, several barriers hinder its widespread adoption, indicating that blockchain-led supply chain management (SCM) is still in the early stages of development. The absence of standardized protocols and frameworks for blockchain in the supply chain is a significant challenge. Different stakeholders in the supply chain may use incompatible blockchain systems, hindering seamless integration and interoperability. ack of standardization limits the ability to create a unified and interconnected blockchain network across the entire supply chain, reducing the effectiveness of the technology. Blockchain networks, especially public blockchains like Bitcoin and Ethereum, face scalability challenges. As the number of transactions increases, the processing time and costs rise, impacting the efficiency of supply chain operations. Limited scalability can impede the ability of blockchain to handle the vast number of transactions that occur in complex and extensive supply chain networks, limiting its applicability. while blockchain holds great promise for transforming supply chain operations, there are significant barriers to overcome. Addressing issues related to standardization, scalability, legacy system integration, and regulatory uncertainty is crucial for advancing blockchain-led supply chain management. Additionally, the technology is still evolving, and broader industry adoption is likely to occur as blockchain matures and stakeholders gain a deeper understanding of its benefits and challenges (Saberi et al., 2019).

Furthermore, cloud computing technology and developing simulation methods play crucial roles in enhancing the effectiveness and efficiency of supply chain integration, design, and operations. Cloud computing provides a centralized platform for real-time collaboration among supply chain participants. Stakeholders, including suppliers, manufacturers, distributors, and retailers, can access and share data seamlessly. Cloud platforms enable the centralization of supply chain data, making it accessible to authorized parties from anywhere. This facilitates improved visibility into inventory, demand, and other critical factors. Cloud solutions offer scalability, allowing supply chain participants to adapt their computing resources based on demand fluctuations. This flexibility is crucial for handling variations in supply and demand. Cloud computing reduces the need for individual organizations to invest in and maintain extensive IT infrastructures. Participants can leverage cloud services on a pay-as-you-go model, optimizing costs. Cloud computing and simulation methods offer powerful synergies for enhancing supply chain integration, design, and operations. The real-time collaboration, data centralization, and scalability provided by cloud computing complement the risk assessment, optimization, and continuous improvement capabilities of simulation. As technology continues to advance, the integration of cloud-based solutions and simulation tools will likely play a pivotal role in shaping agile, resilient, and optimized supply chains (Gunal & Karatas, 2019; Manuel Maqueira et al., 2019).

A cloud-based Life-Cycle Assessment (LCA) platform can significantly contribute to the assessment of environmental footprints and resource management within a green supply chain. This platform integrates cloud computing capabilities with LCA methodologies to provide real-time insights, collaboration, and decision support for sustainable and environmentally friendly supply chain practices. By leveraging the capabilities of a cloud-based LCA platform, supply chain participants can proactively manage their environmental footprints, make informed decisions, and collectively contribute to building a greener and more sustainable supply chain ecosystem (Xing et al., 2016).

Designing a cyber-physical production network for a new virtual enterprise involves strategic partner selection decisions and leveraging IoT for an effective sourcing process within the supply chain. This approach aligns with Industry 4.0 principles, emphasizing the integration of digital technologies for enhanced efficiency and connectivity. Designing a cyber-physical production network with strategic partner selection and leveraging IoT for the sourcing process aligns with Industry 4.0 principles. This approach fosters a connected and efficient supply chain ecosystem, promoting transparency, collaboration, and resilience. As technology continues to advance, companies embracing these strategies are better positioned to adapt to dynamic market conditions and achieve sustainable and competitive advantages in their virtual enterprise production networks (Ben-Daya et al., 2019; Bharti & Bharti, 2022; Mladineo et al., 2017).

When implementing the Internet of Things (IoT) in supply chain and organizational contexts, establishing trust and facilitating information sharing are critical for realizing the full benefits of IoT technologies. IoT enables real-time monitoring and tracking of assets, inventory, and processes, providing unprecedented visibility across the supply chain. It has improved decision-making, increased operational efficiency, and better responsiveness to changes and disruptions. IoT fosters collaboration by facilitating seamless communication and information exchange among supply chain partners and within organizations and enhanced coordination, reduced lead times, and increased overall efficiency in the supply chain. IoT technologies support the optimization of supply chain processes, including inventory management, demand forecasting, and logistics. The successful implementation of IoT in supply chain and organizational contexts requires a balanced approach that maximizes the benefits while mitigating potential risks. By prioritizing trust-building initiatives, implementing robust security measures, and fostering a culture of responsible data handling, organizations can navigate the challenges associated with IoT and create a foundation for a more connected and efficient ecosystem. The decision to adopt IoT in the supply chain and organizational processes involves a delicate balance between costs, revenues, and operational efficiency (Birkel & Hartmann, 2019b; Sun et al., 2020).

STRATEGIC NETWORK AND SCM

The advent of new technologies, including the use of big data, has indeed brought both opportunities and challenges to the supply chain network design process. Employing a big data approach can play a crucial role in improving data acquisition, enhancing data quality, and aiding in the estimation of important parameters, thus contributing to more informed and effective network design decisions. Big data technologies provide tools for cleansing, validating, and enriching datasets, leading to higher data quality. Big data enables the processing and analysis of real-time data streams, offering immediate insights into supply chain operations. Real-time insights enhance decision-makers' ability to respond promptly to changes, disruptions, and unforeseen events, thereby improving the agility of the supply chain network. While acknowledging the challenges, the effective use of big data in the supply chain network design process offers immense potential for improving decision-making, increasing efficiency, and enhancing overall supply chain performance. By carefully navigating the challenges and leveraging the opportunities presented by big data, organizations can gain a competitive edge in designing and optimizing resilient, agile, and efficient supply chain networks (Zhao et al., 2017).

Blockchain linkage in the supply chain not only enhances transparency and efficiency in recording activities but also plays a crucial role in supporting environmentally friendly manufacturing process designs. By leveraging blockchain for traceability, data integrity, and sustainability verification, organizations can promote responsible practices and contribute to a more eco-friendly and socially responsible supply chain. Smart contracts can be programmed to automatically trigger incentives for manufacturers adopting environmentally friendly practices. This incentivization mechanism encourages sustainable behavior throughout the supply chain. Indeed, the use of blockchain technology in the supply chain can have a transformative impact on recording intra- and inter-organizational activities and contribute to environmentally friendly manufacturing process designs. The secure and tamper-resistant nature of blockchain helps in reducing fraud and errors in recording and verifying activities. This is crucial for maintaining the integrity of the supply chain data (Kouhizadeh & Sarkis, 2018).

The advent of Industry 4.0 technologies has ushered in a new era of production strategies, necessitating a paradigm shift in supply network design, manufacturing processes, system integration, and overall control. The key characteristics of these strategies include high customization, sustainability, integration of complex systems, and the establishment of resilient and digital manufacturing networks. Industry 4.0 technologies enable mass customization, responding to individual customer demands. Supply network designs become more dynamic to accommodate the personalized production of goods. Industry 4.0 technologies are driving a revolution in production strategies, emphasizing customization, sustainability, integration, and resilience. Supply network designs are evolving to be more flexible and dynamic; manufacturing processes are becoming environmentally conscious and data-driven, complex systems are seamlessly integrated, and manufacturing networks are transitioning into digitized, resilient ecosystems. These advancements are reshaping the landscape of industrial production, enhancing efficiency, sustainability, and adaptability to meet the demands of a rapidly changing global market (Panetto et al., 2019).

The integration of big data-based decision support technologies and cloud computing has become instrumental in reshaping the design and control of manufacturing supply chain networks. Big data enhances visibility across the entire supply chain, from suppliers to end customers. Big data analytics optimize inventory levels by considering factors such as demand variability, lead times, and supplier performance. Cost Reduction: Efficient inventory management contributes to cost reduction and ensures that resources are utilized optimally. The synergy between big data-based decision support technologies and cloud computing is a powerful force in modern supply chain management. By harnessing the capabilities of big data analytics for decision support and leveraging the cost efficiency, resilience, and flexibility of cloud computing, organizations can enhance the design, control, and overall efficiency of their manufacturing supply chain networks. This integrated approach contributes to adaptability, responsiveness, and competitiveness in today's dynamic business environment (Sundarakani et al., 2021).

Meanwhile, the integration of 3D printing into supply chain services is indeed a significant development that can transform the landscape of logistics and manufacturing. 3D printing allows for on-demand manufacturing of products, eliminating the need for extensive warehousing and reducing the costs associated with inventory management. Supply chain service companies can offer more flexible and responsive solutions to their clients, producing goods as needed rather than maintaining large stockpiles. Supply chain service companies can facilitate the quick development and testing of prototypes, speeding up the product design and development cycle and enabling customization according to client requirements. 3D printing enables the production of parts and products with shorter lead times compared to traditional manufacturing methods. Supply chain service providers can offer faster delivery times, contributing to overall efficiency and meeting the demands of time-sensitive industries. The integration of 3D printing into the services of logistics providers opens up a realm of opportunities for more agile, responsive, and sustainable supply chain solutions. By embracing this technology and forming strategic partnerships, logistics companies can position themselves at the forefront of innovation in the evolving landscape of manufacturing and logistics (Eyers et al., 2019).

This study has identified 18 challenges into four main dimensions of challenges Organizational challenges; Legal and ethical issues; Strategic challenges and Technological challenges. Organizational challenges are crucial for the successful implementation and sustainability of Industry 4.0 practices in the supply chain. Organizations need to carefully plan and allocate resources to support the implementation and ongoing maintenance of Industry 4.0 technologies. organizational challenges will contribute to the successful adoption and sustainability of Industry 4.0 practices in the Indian manufacturing sector, ultimately enhancing the efficiency and competitiveness of the supply chain. Effective leadership is critical during periods of organizational transformation. Leaders need to guide the organization through changes, inspire employees, and align the workforce with the strategic goals of Industry 4.0. Top management plays a pivotal role in driving organizational change. Their active involvement and commitment to Industry 4.0 initiatives can set the tone for the entire organization. This includes providing resources, setting clear goals, and communicating the strategic vision for Industry 4.0 sustainability (Luthra & Mangla, 2018).

Warehouse 4.0 systems are emphasizing their heavy reliance on internet-connected devices like IoT (Internet of Things), GPS (Global Positioning System), and a continuous supply of electricity. The companies can reduce the risk of disruptions in Warehouse 4.0 systems and minimize the impact on the entire supply chain network. Proactive measures, robust contingency planning, and a focus on technology resilience contribute to the overall stability and success of Warehouse 4.0 implementations (Aravindaraj & Rajan Chinna, 2022; Nantee & Sureeyatanapas, 2021). The presence of fragmented warehouses, especially in small and medium-sized enterprises (SMEs), can impede the seamless integration of Industry 4.0 technologies. Strategy: Encourage collaboration and integration efforts within the industry. Initiatives that promote the sharing of best practices and standardization can help streamline the adoption of Industry 4.0 across various warehouse setups. Insufficient focus on customer engagement in the supply chain may hinder the adoption of technologies that enhance customer experiences. Strategy: Educate businesses about the benefits of improved customer engagement through Industry 4.0. Emphasize the use of data analytics and customer relationship management tools to optimize supply chain processes and enhance customer satisfaction. It is possible to accelerate the adoption of Industry 4.0 practices in warehouses across developing countries like India. This, in turn, can contribute to increased efficiency, sustainability, and competitiveness in the supply chain (Binos & Bruno, 2021; Srhir et al., 2023).

FINDINGS

The insights from reports like the one from Capgemini underscore the potential of Industry 4.0 technologies to optimize and revolutionize value chains across industries. As businesses continue to embrace these technologies, there is a growing focus on reimagining and improving various aspects of production and supply chain management for increased efficiency and competitiveness. the emergence of Industry 4.0 technologies has been a significant focus for researchers and industries alike, driven by the potential for transformative changes in operational efficiency and value chain optimization. The report by Capgemini which has been showing that likely highlights the various ways in which Industry 4.0 technologies can contribute to optimizing operations across value chains. Industry 4.0 technologies, such as IoT and advanced analytics, enable organizations to collect and analyze vast amounts of data from various points in the value chain. Data-driven insights empower businesses to make more informed and timely decisions, leading to enhanced operational efficiency. Integration of Industry 4.0 technologies improves visibility into the entire supply chain, from raw material sourcing to end-product delivery. Real-time tracking and monitoring of assets, inventory, and production processes contribute to greater transparency and control (Agrawal et al., 2022).

The integration of Industry 4.0 technologies with a focus on human and environmental dimensions to prioritize sustainability in business development. Supply Chain 4.0 acknowledges the importance of human involvement and expertise in the supply chain process. It recognizes that technology should augment human capabilities rather than replace them. It is focusing on the employee well-being, skill development, and collaboration are integral components of a human-centric approach in the context of Supply Chain 4.0. Supply Chain 4.0 incorporates environmentally sustainable practices as a core principle. This involves reducing waste, optimizing energy consumption, and minimizing the ecological footprint of supply chain operations. Supply Chain 4.0 represents a holistic and forward-looking approach that integrates Industry 4.0 technologies with a strong commitment to human well-being and environmental stewardship. By making sustainability a core element of business development, organizations can contribute to a more resilient, responsible, and future-ready global supply chain ecosystem (Cañas et al., 2020).

This study points outs that a comprehensive perspective on the synergy between Supply Chain 4.0 and Industry 4.0 technologies. The integration of these technologies indeed empowers the supply chain through enhanced data capabilities, cooperation, and synchronization across digital networks, software, and hardware. The implementation of Industry 4.0 technologies enables better monitoring and optimization of energy consumption within the supply chain. Advanced analytics and smart systems contribute to cost efficiency by identifying areas for improvement and resource optimization. Industry 4.0 technologies provide tools for better customer relationship management and personalized services. Improved visibility, faster response times, and customization capabilities contribute to higher customer satisfaction. The interconnected nature of Industry 4.0 technologies ensures real-time data sharing across the supply chain. Transparency and flexibility in information flows allow for quick adjustments to changing market conditions and operational requirements. These benefits collectively contribute to the overarching goal of Supply Chain 4.0, which is to create a more efficient, adaptive, and sustainable supply chain ecosystem. The integration of Industry 4.0 technologies aligns with the principles of Supply Chain 4.0, fostering collaboration, data-driven decision-making, and a customer-centric approach. As industries continue to leverage these technologies, the potential for innovation and positive impact on both business operations and global sustainability goals becomes increasingly evident. Market Disintermediation and Sustainable Manufacturing: Industry 4.0 facilitates direct communication and collaboration between suppliers and consumers, reducing the need for intermediaries. Sustainable manufacturing practices, supported by Industry 4.0, contribute to environmentally friendly production processes and supply chain operations (Büyüközkan & Göçer, 2018; Chan et al., 2018; Greif et al., 2020; Hofmann & Rüsch, 2017; Lezoche et al., 2020; Raj et al., 2022).

CONCLUSION

The chapter points out that supply chain management under Industry 4.0 is multifaceted, exploring the implications of digital technologies on various aspects of the supply chain. As Industry 4.0 continues to evolve, researchers are focusing on understanding the challenges, opportunities, and best practices for effectively implementing and managing advanced technologies in supply chain operations. The goal is to create more agile, resilient, and efficient supply chains capable of thriving in the dynamic and interconnected global business environment. Supply Chain 4.0 not only enhances the efficiency of supply chain operations but also aligns with broader sustainability goals. The integration of Industry 4.0 technologies in supply chain processes provides the tools and insights needed to create more environmentally friendly, socially responsible, and economically efficient supply chain ecosystems. This harmonization of sustainability challenges is crucial for businesses seeking to thrive in an era where responsible and sustainable practices are increasingly valued by consumers and stakeholders.

The outlined research directions underscore the dynamic nature of smart supply chains and the need for comprehensive exploration across various dimensions. Future research efforts should not only deepen our understanding of technology impacts but also emphasize practical applications, industry collaboration, and the ethical considerations associated with the evolving landscape of smart supply chain management. Addressing these aspects will contribute to the development of resilient, efficient, and socially responsible supply chain practices in the era of Industry 4.0. Industry 4.0 fosters collaboration among stakeholders within and beyond the organization. Impact on Sustainability: Collaborative platforms and digital networks enhance communication with suppliers, customers, and other stakeholders. Engaging stakeholders in sustainability initiatives promotes shared responsibility and supports the achievement of corporate sustainability values. By understanding and leveraging these attributes and capabilities, organizations can harness the power of Industry 4.0 technologies to drive corporate sustainability values. The integration of these technologies aligns with the broader goals of environmental responsibility, social accountability, and economic efficiency, contributing to a more sustainable and resilient business ecosystem.

Finally, the convergence of Sustainable Supply Chain 4.0 and Industry 4.0 technologies presents a transformative opportunity for businesses to reorient their strategies toward sustainability. By leveraging these emerging topics, companies can not only improve operational efficiency but also contribute positively to environmental, social, and economic sustainability, aligning with the growing expectations of conscious consumers and stakeholders. The future research directions not only contribute to the academic understanding of Industry 4.0 in supply chains but also offer practical insights for businesses and policymakers aiming to navigate the complex landscape of technology integration and sustainability. The interdisciplinary nature of these approaches reflects the multifaceted impact of Industry 4.0 on economic, environmental, and social dimensions, highlighting the need for holistic and data-driven research methodologies. Consideration: The dominance of Blockchain and IoT in the literature might suggest a gap in the exploration of other emerging technologies like artificial intelligence and data analytics. Suggestion: Encourage future research to explore the roles and impacts of diverse technologies, including artificial intelligence and data analytics, within the context of Supply Chain 4.0 and sustainability. This could provide a more comprehensive understanding of the technological landscape.

REFERENCES

Achabou, M. A., Dekhili, S., & Hamdoun, M. (2017). Environmental Upgrading of Developing Country Firms in Global Value Chains. *Business Strategy and the Environment, 26*(2), 224–238. doi:10.1002/bse.1911

Act, R. A. M. I. (2014). *Revitalize American manufacturing and innovation act of 2014*. Retrieved from https://www.congress.gov/bill/113th-congress/house-bill/2996

Agrawal, R., Wankhede, V. A., Kumar, A., Luthra, S., & Huisingh, D. (2022). Progress and trends in integrating Industry 4.0 within circular economy: A comprehensive literature review and future research propositions. *Business Strategy and the Environment, 31*(1), 559–579. doi:10.1002/bse.2910

Akenji, L., & Bengtsson, M. (2014). Making Sustainable Consumption and Production the Core of Sustainable Development Goals. *Sustainability (Basel), 6*(2), 513–529. doi:10.3390/su6020513

Akhtar, M. (2022). Industry 4.0 Technologies Impact on Supply Chain Sustainability. In Recent Advances and New Perspectives in the Industry 4.0 Era. IntechOpen. doi:10.5772/intechopen.102978

Aravindaraj, K., & Rajan Chinna, P. (2022). A systematic literature review of integration of industry 4.0 and warehouse management to achieve Sustainable Development Goals (SDGs). *Cleaner Logistics and Supply Chain, 5*, 100072. https://doi.org/https://doi.org/10.1016/j.clscn.2022.100072

Bag, S., Telukdarie, A., Pretorius, J. H. C., & Gupta, S. (2021). Industry 4.0 and supply chain sustainability: Framework and future research directions. *Benchmarking, 28*(5), 1410–1450. doi:10.1108/BIJ-03-2018-0056

Bag, S., Wood, L. C., Xu, L., Dhamija, P., & Kayikci, Y. (2020). Big data analytics as an operational excellence approach to enhance sustainable supply chain performance. *Resources, Conservation and Recycling, 153*, 104559. doi:10.1016/j.resconrec.2019.104559

Bányai, T. (2018). Real-Time Decision Making in First Mile and Last Mile Logistics: How Smart Scheduling Affects Energy Efficiency of Hyperconnected Supply Chain Solutions. *Energies, 11*(7), 1833. doi:10.3390/en11071833

Barreto, L., Amaral, A., & Pereira, T. (2017). Industry 4.0 implications in logistics: An overview. *Procedia Manufacturing, 13*, 1245–1252. doi:10.1016/j.promfg.2017.09.045

Beier, G., Ullrich, A., Niehoff, S., Reißig, M., & Habich, M. (2020). Industry 4.0: How it is defined from a sociotechnical perspective and how much sustainability it includes – A literature review. *Journal of Cleaner Production, 259*, 120856. doi:10.1016/j.jclepro.2020.120856

Ben-Daya, M., Hassini, E., & Bahroun, Z. (2019). Internet of things and supply chain management: A literature review. *International Journal of Production Research, 57*(15–16), 4719–4742. doi:10.1080/00207543.2017.1402140

Berman, B. (2012). 3-D printing: The new industrial revolution. *Business Horizons, 55*(2), 155–162. doi:10.1016/j.bushor.2011.11.003

Bharti, M. S., & Bharti, S. S. (2022). The EU Public Diplomacy in the Time of Virtual Reality: Political, Social and Economic Implications. In B. Olbrych (Ed.), *Life in Virtual Reality, Chances and dangers* (Vol. 2, pp. 13–25). Akademia Handlowa Nauk Stosowanych w Radomiu.

Binos, T., Bruno, V., & Adamopoulos, A. (2021). Intelligent agent-based framework to augment warehouse management systems for dynamic demand environments. *AJIS. Australasian Journal of Information Systems, 25*. Advance online publication. doi:10.3127/ajis.v25i0.2845

Birkel, H. S., & Hartmann, E. (2019a). Impact of IoT challenges and risks for SCM. *Supply Chain Management, 24*(1), 39–61. doi:10.1108/SCM-03-2018-0142

Birkel, H. S., & Hartmann, E. (2019b). Impact of IoT challenges and risks for SCM. *Supply Chain Management, 24*(1), 39–61. doi:10.1108/SCM-03-2018-0142

Büyüközkan, G., & Göçer, F. (2018). Digital Supply Chain: Literature review and a proposed framework for future research. *Computers in Industry, 97*, 157–177. doi:10.1016/j.compind.2018.02.010

Cañas, H., Mula, J., & Campuzano-Bolarín, F. (2020). A general outline of a sustainable supply chain 4.0. *Sustainability (Basel), 12*(19), 1–17. doi:10.3390/su12197978

Chan, H. K., Griffin, J., Lim, J. J., Zeng, F., & Chiu, A. S. F. (2018). The impact of 3D Printing Technology on the supply chain: Manufacturing and legal perspectives. *International Journal of Production Economics, 205*, 156–162. doi:10.1016/j.ijpe.2018.09.009

Esmaeilian, B., Behdad, S., & Wang, B. (2016). The evolution and future of manufacturing: A review. *Journal of Manufacturing Systems, 39*, 79–100. doi:10.1016/j.jmsy.2016.03.001

Eyers, D., Lahy, A., Wilson, M., & Syntetos, A. (2019). 3D Printing for Supply Chain Service Companies. In P. Wells (Ed.), *Contemporary Operations and Logistics: Achieving Excellence in Turbulent Times* (pp. 61–79). Springer International Publishing. doi:10.1007/978-3-030-14493-7_5

Ghobakhloo, M. (2018). The future of manufacturing industry: A strategic roadmap toward Industry 4.0. *Journal of Manufacturing Technology Management, 29*(6), 910–936. doi:10.1108/JMTM-02-2018-0057

Golini, R., De Marchi, V., Boffelli, A., & Kalchschmidt, M. (2018). Which governance structures drive economic, environmental, and social upgrading? A quantitative analysis in the assembly industries. *International Journal of Production Economics, 203*, 13–23. doi:10.1016/j.ijpe.2018.05.021

Gottge, S., Menzel, T., & Forslund, H. (2020). Industry 4.0 technologies in the purchasing process. *Industrial Management & Data Systems, 120*(4), 730–748. doi:10.1108/IMDS-05-2019-0304

Greif, T., Stein, N., & Flath, C. M. (2020). Peeking into the void: Digital twins for construction site logistics. *Computers in Industry, 121*, 103264. doi:10.1016/j.compind.2020.103264

Gunal, M. M., & Karatas, M. (2019). Industry 4.0, Digitisation in Manufacturing, and Simulation: A Review of the Literature. In M. M. Gunal (Ed.), *Simulation for Industry 4.0: Past, Present, and Future* (pp. 19–37). Springer International Publishing., doi:10.1007/978-3-030-04137-3_2

Hofmann, E., & Rüsch, M. (2017). Industry 4.0 and the current status as well as future prospects on logistics. *Computers in Industry*, *89*, 23–34. doi:10.1016/j.compind.2017.04.002

Kamble, S. S., Gunasekaran, A., & Gawankar, S. A. (2018). Sustainable Industry 4.0 framework: A systematic literature review identifying the current trends and future perspectives. *Process Safety and Environmental Protection*, *117*, 408–425. doi:10.1016/j.psep.2018.05.009

Kouhizadeh, M., & Sarkis, J. (2018). Blockchain Practices, Potentials, and Perspectives in Greening Supply Chains. *Sustainability (Basel)*, *10*(10), 36–52. doi:10.3390/su10103652

Laplume, A. O., Petersen, B., & Pearce, J. M. (2016). Global value chains from a 3D printing perspective. *Journal of International Business Studies*, *47*(5), 595–609. doi:10.1057/jibs.2015.47

Legenvre, H., Henke, M., & Ruile, H. (2020). Making sense of the impact of the internet of things on Purchasing and Supply Management:A tension perspective. *Journal of Purchasing and Supply Management*, *26*(1), 100596. doi:10.1016/j.pursup.2019.100596

Lezoche, M., Hernandez, J. E., & Alemany Díaz, M. del M. E., Panetto, H., & Kacprzyk, J. (2020). Agri-food 4.0: A survey of the supply chains and technologies for the future agriculture. *Computers in Industry*, *117*, 103187. https://doi.org/https://doi.org/10.1016/j.compind.2020.103187

Liu, X., Cao, J., Yang, Y., & Jiang, S. (2018). CPS-Based Smart Warehouse for Industry 4.0: A Survey of the Underlying Technologies. *Computers*, *7*(1), 13. doi:10.3390/computers7010013

Luthra, S., Kumar, A., Zavadskas, E. K., Mangla, S. K., & Garza-Reyes, J. A. (2020). Industry 4.0 as an enabler of sustainability diffusion in supply chain: An analysis of influential strength of drivers in an emerging economy. *International Journal of Production Research*, *58*(5), 1505–1521. doi:10.1080/00207543.2019.1660828

Luthra, S., & Mangla, S. K. (2018). *Evaluating challenges to Industry 4.0 initiatives for supply chain sustainability in emerging economies*. University of Plymouth. Retrieved from https://pearl.plymouth.ac.uk/bitstream/handle/10026.1/11498/SKM%20-%20Industry%204.0%20paper%20-accepted%20version.pdf;jsessionid=3560FDCF3EBDFCCB25D47A113EF5F29E?sequence=5

Manuel Maqueira, J., Moyano-Fuentes, J., & Bruque, S. (2019). Drivers and consequences of an innovative technology assimilation in the supply chain: Cloud computing and supply chain integration. *International Journal of Production Research*, *57*(7), 2083–2103. doi:10.1080/00207543.2018.1530473

Mardani, A., Kannan, D., Hooker, R. E., Ozkul, S., Alrasheedi, M., & Tirkolaee, E. B. (2020). Evaluation of green and sustainable supply chain management using structural equation modelling: A systematic review of the state of the art literature and recommendations for future research. *Journal of Cleaner Production*, *249*, 119383. doi:10.1016/j.jclepro.2019.119383

Mastrocinque, E., Ramírez, F. J., Honrubia-Escribano, A., & Pham, D. T. (2022). Industry 4.0 enabling sustainable supply chain development in the renewable energy sector: A multi-criteria intelligent approach. *Technological Forecasting and Social Change*, *182*, 121813. doi:10.1016/j.techfore.2022.121813

Mladineo, M., Veza, I., & Gjeldum, N. (2017). Solving partner selection problem in cyber-physical production networks using the HUMANT algorithm. *International Journal of Production Research*, *55*(9), 2506–2521. doi:10.1080/00207543.2016.1234084

Nantee, N., & Sureeyatanapas, P. (2021). The impact of Logistics 4.0 on corporate sustainability: A performance assessment of automated warehouse operations. *Benchmarking*, *28*(10), 2865–2895. doi:10.1108/BIJ-11-2020-0583

Naseem, M. H., & Yang, J. (2021). Role of Industry 4.0 in Supply Chains Sustainability: A Systematic Literature Review. *Sustainability (Basel)*, *13*(17), 9944. doi:10.3390/su13179544

Organization, W. T. (2017). *Global Value Chain Development Report 2019*. WTO. doi:10.30875/6b9727ab-en

Panetto, H., Iung, B., Ivanov, D., Weichhart, G., & Wang, X. (2019). Challenges for the cyber-physical manufacturing enterprises of the future. *Annual Reviews in Control*, *47*, 200–213. doi:10.1016/j.arcontrol.2019.02.002

Raj, P. V. R. P., Jauhar, S. K., Ramkumar, M., & Pratap, S. (2022). Procurement, traceability and advance cash credit payment transactions in supply chain using blockchain smart contracts. *Computers & Industrial Engineering*, *167*, 108038. doi:10.1016/j.cie.2022.108038

Saberi, S., Kouhizadeh, M., Sarkis, J., & Shen, L. (2019). Blockchain technology and its relationships to sustainable supply chain management. *International Journal of Production Research*, *57*(7), 2117–2135. doi:10.1080/00207543.2018.1533261

Sellitto, M. A., Hermann, F. F., Blezs, A. E. Jr, & Barbosa-Póvoa, A. P. (2019). Describing and organizing green practices in the context of Green Supply Chain Management: Case studies. *Resources, Conservation and Recycling*, *145*, 1–10. doi:10.1016/j.resconrec.2019.02.013

Srhir, S., Jaegler, A., & Montoya-Torres, J. R. (2023). Uncovering Industry 4.0 technology attributes in sustainable supply chain 4.0: A systematic literature review. *Business Strategy and the Environment*, *32*(7), 4143–4166. doi:10.1002/bse.3358

Stock, T., & Seliger, G. (2016). Opportunities of Sustainable Manufacturing in Industry 4.0. *Procedia CIRP*, *40*, 536–541. doi:10.1016/j.procir.2016.01.129

Sun, L., Zhao, Y., Sun, W., & Liu, Z. (2020). Study on supply chain strategy based on cost income model and multi-access edge computing under the background of the Internet of Things. *Neural Computing & Applications*, *32*(19), 15357–15368. doi:10.1007/s00521-019-04125-9

Sundarakani, B., Kamran, R., Maheshwari, P., & Jain, V. (2021). Designing a hybrid cloud for a supply chain network of Industry 4.0: A theoretical framework. *Benchmarking*, *28*(5), 1524–1542. doi:10.1108/BIJ-04-2018-0109

Xing, K., Qian, W., & Zaman, A. U. (2016). Development of a cloud-based platform for footprint assessment in green supply chain management. *Journal of Cleaner Production, 139*, 191–203. doi:10.1016/j.jclepro.2016.08.042

Zhang, G., Yang, Y., & Yang, G. (2023). Smart supply chain management in Industry 4.0: The review, research agenda and strategies in North America. *Annals of Operations Research, 322*(2), 1075–1117. doi:10.1007/s10479-022-04689-1 PMID:35531562

Zhao, R., Liu, Y., Zhang, N., & Huang, T. (2017). An optimization model for green supply chain management by using a big data analytic approach. *Journal of Cleaner Production, 142*, 1085–1097. doi:10.1016/j.jclepro.2016.03.006

ADDITIONAL READING

Ben-Daya, M., Hassini, E., Bahroun, Z., & Banimfreg, B. H. (2020). The role of internet of things in food supply chain quality management: A review. *The Quality Management Journal, 28*(1), 17–40. doi:10.1080/10686967.2020.1838978

De Vass, T., Shee, H., & Miah, S. J. (2021). Iot in supply chain management: A narrative on retail sector sustainability. *International Journal of Logistics, 24*(6), 605–624. doi:10.1080/13675567.2020.1787970

Dutta, P., Chavhan, R., Gowtham, P., & Singh, A. (2023). The individual and integrated impact of Blockchain and IoT on sustainable supply chains:a systematic review. *Supply Chain Forum: An International Journal, 24*(1), 103–126. 10.1080/16258312.2022.2082851

El Kihel, Y., Zouggar Amrani, A., Ducq, Y., Amegouz, D., & Lfakir, A. (2023). Methodology combining industry 4.0 technologies and KPI's reliability for supply chain performance. *International Journal of Computer Integrated Manufacturing, 36*(8), 1128–1152. doi:10.1080/0951192X.2022.2162605

Gupta, S., Modgil, S., Gunasekaran, A., & Bag, S. (2020). Dynamic capabilities and institutional theories for Industry 4.0 and digital supply chain. *Supply Chain Forum: An International Journal, 21*(3), 139–157. 10.1080/16258312.2020.1757369

Jackson, A., Spiegler, V. L. M., & Kotiadis, K. (2023, February 22). Exploring the potential of blockchain-enabled lean automation in supply chain management: A systematic literature review, classification taxonomy, and future research agenda. *Production Planning and Control*, 1–20. doi:10.1080/09537287.2022.2157746

Le, P.-L., & Nguyen, D.-T. (n.d.). Exploring Lean Practices' Importance in Sustainable Supply Chain Management Trends: An Empirical Study in Canadian Construction Industry. *Engineering Management Journal*, 1–26. doi:10.1080/10429247.2023.2187608

Maheshwari, S., Gautam, P., & Jaggi, C. K. (2021). Role of Big Data Analytics in supply chain management: Current trends and future perspectives. *International Journal of Production Research, 59*(6), 1875–1900. doi:10.1080/00207543.2020.1793011

Zekhnini, K., Cherrafi, A., Bouhaddou, I., Benabdellah, A. C., & Raut, R. (n.d.). A holonic architecture for the supply chain performance in industry 4.0 context. *International Journal of Logistics Research and Applications*, 1–28. doi:10.1080/13675567.2021.1999912

KEY TERMS AND DEFINITIONS

Industry 4.0: Industry 4.0 relies heavily on information technology to transform traditional manufacturing into a more connected, efficient and intelligent system, ultimately leading to advances in productivity, quality and agility in industrial processes. Industry 4.0 has reinvented the way companies design, manufacture and distribute their products. Technologies such as the Industrial Internet of Things (IIoT), cloud connectivity, artificial intelligence and machine learning are now deeply embedded in the manufacturing process.

Supply Chain Management: At the most fundamental level, supply chain management (SCM) is the management of the flow of goods, data and finances related to a product or service, from the acquisition of raw materials to delivery from the product to its final destination. Supply chain management (SCM) is the management of the flow of goods and services, including all processes of transforming raw materials into final products.

Chapter 8
Sustainability Metrics and Measurement in Industry 4.0-Enabled SCM

Siva Raja Sindiramutty
Taylor's University, Malaysia

Navid Ali Khan
Taylor's University, Malaysia

NZ Jhanjhi
https://orcid.org/0000-0001-8116-4733
Taylor's University, Malaysia

Husin Jazri
https://orcid.org/0009-0005-3940-2351
Taylor's University, Malaysia

Chong Eng Tan
https://orcid.org/0000-0002-3990-3501
Universiti Malaysia Sarawak, Malaysia

Loveleen Gaur
https://orcid.org/0000-0002-0885-1550
University of the South Pacific, Fiji

ABSTRACT

The rapid advancement of Industry 4.0 technologies has ushered in a new era of supply chain management (SCM) that places sustainability at its core. This chapter goes deep into the critical intersection of sustainability metrics and measurement in Industry 4.0-enabled SCM, exploring the dynamic landscape where cutting-edge technology meets environmental, social, and economic responsibility. Beginning with an introduction to Industry 4.0's transformative role in SCM, the authors elucidate the importance of sustainability metrics in this context. The research's scope and objectives are outlined, emphasizing the need to decipher the intricacies of sustainability measurement in an Industry 4.0 ecosystem. The authors provide a comprehensive elucidation of key concepts, definitions, and the unique contributions of this research endeavour. A central focus of this chapter is the alignment of Industry 4.0 SCM with the United Nations' Sustainable Development Goals (SDGs), illuminating how emerging technologies can act as catalysts for achieving these global objectives.

DOI: 10.4018/979-8-3693-1363-3.ch008

1. INTRODUCTION

1.1 Overview of Industry 4.0 and Its Role in Sustainable Supply Chain Management (SCM)

Industry 4.0, often referred to as the Fourth Industrial Revolution, marks a transformative period in manufacturing and supply chain management. This significant shift is being propelled by advanced technologies, including the Internet of Things (IoT), artificial intelligence (AI), big data analytics, and automation. Industry 4.0 is fundamentally altering how businesses operate and oversee their supply chains, and it plays a pivotal role in advancing sustainability within supply chain management. In this chapter, we will provide an overview of Industry 4.0 and delve into its critical role in sustainable supply chain management. Industry 4.0 represents the convergence of physical production and digital technologies. It brings together cyber-physical systems, the Internet of Things, cloud computing, and cognitive computing to establish intelligent, interconnected factories and supply chains (Pivoto et al., 2021; Aadil et al., 2021). This integration facilitates real-time data collection and analysis, empowering more informed decision-making and elevating operational efficiency. Industry 4.0 has evolved into a global phenomenon, with businesses spanning various industries embracing its principles to maintain competitiveness and adapt to evolving market demands (Kagermann, 2014; Ali et al., 2022).

Industry 4.0 plays a pivotal role in advancing sustainable supply chain management primarily through improved transparency and traceability. The utilization of IoT sensors and RFID tags facilitates real-time tracking of goods and materials across the supply chain (Unhelkar et al., 2022). This heightened transparency empowers better control over the ecological consequences of supply chain activities by pinpointing inefficiencies and waste, ultimately resulting in a reduction in carbon footprints. Industry 4.0 technologies, such as AI-driven predictive maintenance and machine learning, play a crucial role in averting equipment breakdowns and minimizing resource wastage (Matin et al., 2023). By identifying potential issues before they escalate, companies can extend the lifespan of their machinery, reducing the need for replacements and conserving resources while minimizing waste. Using data analytics and digital twin technology, companies can fine-tune product design with sustainability in mind (He & Mao, 2023; Almusaylim & Jhanjhi, 2018). Digital twins simulate the entire product life cycle, enabling businesses to make eco-friendly choices regarding materials, manufacturing processes, and energy consumption. This approach aligns with the principles of the circular economy and diminishes the environmental impact of products. Smart factories driven by Industry 4.0 technologies are meticulously designed to optimize energy consumption (Singh et al., 2022; Ananna et al., 2023). AI algorithms and IoT sensors analyze energy consumption patterns and make real-time adjustments to reduce waste. This not only results in lower operational costs but also contributes to a decrease in greenhouse gas emissions. The interconnected nature of Industry 4.0 supply chains enhances adaptability and responsiveness to market shifts (Korucuk et al., 2023). By closely monitoring fluctuations in demand and supply, businesses can mitigate overproduction and excess inventory, leading to less waste and more efficient resource utilization. Industry 4.0 fosters collaboration among supply chain partners by enabling the sharing of data and insights (Pfaff, 2023; Azam, Dulloo, Majeed, Wan, Xin, & Sindiramutty, 2023). This collaborative approach promotes sustainable practices by encouraging partners to align their efforts toward common environmental objectives and reduce unnecessary transportation and packaging. Figure 1 show all the goals which proposed and launched in 2016

In summary, Industry 4.0 is fundamentally reshaping supply chain management by harnessing cutting-edge technologies to advance sustainability. Through increased transparency, predictive maintenance, eco-conscious product design, energy efficiency, adaptability, and collaboration, companies can reduce their environmental impact and play a crucial role in responsible resource management. In a world where challenges like climate change and resource scarcity are growing, embracing Industry 4.0 principles becomes increasingly vital for businesses striving to establish sustainable supply chains.

Figure 1. Sustainable Development Goals

1.2 Importance of Sustainability Metrics and Measurement in Industry 4.0 SCM

Sustainability metrics and measurement play a crucial role in assisting organizations in making well-informed decisions concerning their supply chains (Singh, Kumar, et al., 2022). By quantifying various sustainability factors such as carbon emissions, resource consumption, and waste generation, businesses can pinpoint areas that require improvement, optimize their operational processes, and decrease their environmental impacts (Fang et al., 2023; Alshammari, et al., 2017). These insights, derived from data, empower proactive decision-making and contribute to the promotion of sustainability within supply chain management. Research indicates that adopting sustainable practices can yield long-term cost savings (Wang et al., 2023). Sustainability metrics enable companies to monitor aspects like energy efficiency, waste reduction, and material usage. By identifying inefficiencies and taking corrective actions, organizations can lower their operational expenses while simultaneously reducing their ecological footprint (Attaoui, 2023; Humayun et al., 2022). Furthermore, the effective use of sustainability metrics and measurements has a positive influence on stakeholder relations. Customers, investors, and regulatory bodies are increasingly demanding transparency and accountability concerning sustainable practices. By showcasing their dedication through reliable metrics, companies can establish trust and enhance their brand image, ultimately attracting a larger customer base and more investors (Sarpong et al., 2023; Humayun et al., 2020; Wen et al., 2024).

In an era characterized by increasingly stringent environmental regulations, the importance of accurate sustainability metrics cannot be overstated. They are pivotal for ensuring legal compliance, as failure to meet sustainability standards can result in not only financial penalties but also significant damage to a company's reputation. Therefore, companies must adopt comprehensive measurement systems that can guarantee adherence to evolving regulatory frameworks. Sustainability metrics also play a crucial role in identifying and mitigating supply chain risks (De Lima & Seuring, 2023; Jabeen., et al 2023). Challenges such as climate change, resource scarcity, and social disruptions pose substantial risks to supply chains. By quantifying and assessing these risks, businesses can develop strategies to enhance their resilience and adaptability, thereby ensuring the continuity of their operations (Ishak et al., 2023; Khan et al., 2020). Furthermore, companies that prioritize sustainability often gain a competitive edge in the market. Sustainability metrics allow organizations to distinguish themselves, making them more appealing to environmentally conscious consumers and potential partners. Additionally, they can establish collaborations with suppliers who share their sustainability goals, thereby creating a competitive advantage within the supply chain. The integration of sustainability metrics into Industry 4.0 supply chain management contributes significantly to long-term business viability (Rayar & Kumar, 2023; Sindiramutty, Jhanjhi, Tan, Khan, Shah, & Gaur, 2024). In the face of escalating global challenges such as climate change and resource depletion, companies that invest in sustainable practices are better positioned to thrive in a rapidly changing world. By measuring and continuously improving their sustainability performance, organizations ensure their continued existence and success.

In summary, the incorporation of sustainability metrics and measurement systems within Industry 4.0 supply chain management is imperative for contemporary businesses. These metrics yield a multitude of advantages, encompassing enhanced decision-making, cost efficiency, stakeholder contentment, adherence to regulations, risk mitigation, competitive edge, and enduring sustainability. In the present landscape, where environmental awareness prevails, companies must place sustainability at the forefront of their strategies and employ metrics to monitor and elevate their performance.

1.3 Scope and Objectives Research

Scope:

This chapter serves as a foundational pillar for the entire book, delineating the boundaries within which the research operates. It encompasses a comprehensive exploration of sustainability metrics and measurement practices, specifically tailored to the realm of Industry 4.0-enabled SCM. The scope extends across various dimensions of sustainability, encompassing environmental, social, and economic aspects. It examines the integration of cutting-edge technologies, such as the Internet of Things (IoT) and big data analytics, in the pursuit of sustainable supply chains. Moreover, it delves into the assessment of Industry 4.0's alignment with the United Nations' Sustainable Development Goals (SDGs) and its role in advancing these global objectives.

Objectives:

- To elucidate the significance of integrating sustainability metrics into Industry 4.0-enabled SCM, highlighting the need for a holistic approach that considers environmental, social, and economic dimensions.
- To explore the alignment of Industry 4.0 technologies with the United Nations' Sustainable Development Goals (SDGs) and elucidate how these technologies can be harnessed to contribute to SDG achievement.
- To identify and discuss key performance indicators (KPIs) relevant to sustainability in SCM, emphasizing the integration of Triple Bottom Line (TBL) metrics for a comprehensive assessment.
- To investigate the data collection and management strategies required to facilitate real-time sustainability measurement, while also addressing challenges related to data integration, interoperability, security, and privacy.
- To delve into methodologies such as Life Cycle Assessment (LCA) and environmental footprinting, elucidating their application in evaluating and improving environmental sustainability within Industry 4.0-enabled SCM.
- To assess social impacts across the supply chain, emphasizing fair labour practices, diversity and inclusion, and community engagement, while also exploring economic sustainability metrics and their relevance.
- To examine the infusion of sustainability into innovation and R&D processes, emphasizing responsible design and sustainable product development, and to measure the impact of such innovations on SCM.
- To elucidate standards, frameworks, and strategies for reporting and communicating sustainability performance to stakeholders in a transparent and integrated manner.
- To provide insights into future trends and research directions, including the evolving landscape of Industry 4.0 technologies, advancements in data analytics and AI, circular economy principles, and the need to address existing gaps and challenges in sustainability metrics within Industry 4.0-enabled SCM.

In summary, this research chapter aims to comprehensively explore the multifaceted realm of sustainability metrics and measurement within the dynamic landscape of Industry 4.0 SCM, offering valuable insights for researchers, practitioners, and policymakers seeking to navigate and leverage this transformative paradigm.

1.4 Key Concepts and Definitions

1. **Industry 4.0:** Industry 4.0, also known as the Fourth Industrial Revolution, represents the integration of advanced digital technologies, such as IoT, artificial intelligence, big data analytics, and automation, into manufacturing and supply chain processes. It aims to create smart, connected, and highly efficient systems.
2. **Sustainable Supply Chain Management (SCM):** Sustainable SCM involves the incorporation of environmental, social, and economic sustainability principles into supply chain operations. It seeks to minimize the environmental impact, promote ethical practices, and enhance long-term economic viability.

3. **Sustainability Metrics:** Sustainability metrics are quantitative and qualitative measures used to assess the performance of supply chain processes in meeting sustainability objectives. These metrics include indicators related to environmental impact, social responsibility, and economic efficiency.
4. **Key Performance Indicators (KPIs):** KPIs are specific metrics used to evaluate the success of an organization or system in achieving its strategic goals. In the context of sustainable SCM, KPIs measure performance in areas such as carbon emissions, waste reduction, social equity, and cost-effectiveness.
5. **Triple Bottom Line (TBL):** The Triple Bottom Line approach evaluates an organization's performance based on three dimensions: people (social), planet (environmental), and profit (economic). It serves as a framework for considering sustainability in decision-making.
6. **Internet of Things (IoT):** IoT refers to the interconnected network of physical devices and objects embedded with sensors, software, and connectivity. In SCM, IoT enables real-time data collection and analysis for improved visibility and decision-making.
7. **Big Data Analytics:** Big data analytics involves the use of advanced data processing techniques to analyze large and complex datasets. In the context of sustainability, it helps uncover insights for better resource management and environmental impact reduction.
8. **United Nations' Sustainable Development Goals (SDGs):** The SDGs are a set of 17 global goals established by the United Nations to address various global challenges, including poverty, inequality, climate change, and responsible consumption. They serve as a framework for assessing the impact of Industry 4.0 SCM on broader societal and environmental objectives.
9. **Life Cycle Assessment (LCA):** LCA is a systematic methodology used to evaluate the environmental impacts of a product or process throughout its entire life cycle, from raw material extraction to end-of-life disposal.
10. **Circular Economy:** The circular economy is an economic model that aims to minimize waste and resource depletion by promoting product reuse, recycling, and sustainable design. It is increasingly important in sustainable SCM.

1.5 Research Contribution

The research contribution of this book chapter lies in its comprehensive exploration of the intersection between Industry 4.0-enabled Supply Chain Management (SCM) and sustainability metrics and measurement. In an era characterized by rapid technological advancements and growing concerns about environmental, social, and economic sustainability, this chapter addresses a critical need for guidance and understanding.

First and foremost, this chapter sheds light on the evolving landscape of Industry 4.0 and its pivotal role in reshaping the way supply chains operate. It delves into the specifics of how Industry 4.0 technologies, such as IoT, Big Data analytics, and AI, are revolutionizing SCM, making it more efficient, responsive, and adaptable. By highlighting the significance of Industry 4.0 in SCM, the chapter lays the foundation for its subsequent discussions. Furthermore, the research contribution can be identified in its meticulous examination of sustainability metrics and measurement within the context of Industry 4.0 SCM. It goes beyond theoretical concepts by providing practical insights into defining and implementing key performance indicators (KPIs) for environmental, social, and economic sustainability. This aspect equips readers with actionable knowledge to assess and improve the sustainability performance of their supply chains. The chapter also makes a valuable contribution by emphasizing the alignment of Industry

4.0 SCM with the United Nations' Sustainable Development Goals (SDGs). It explores how Industry 4.0 technologies can be harnessed to advance progress towards these global sustainability objectives, making a compelling case for the integration of sustainability principles into SCM strategies.

Overall, this chapter's research contribution extends to its examination of data collection and management challenges, life cycle assessment, social impact measurement, economic sustainability evaluation, sustainable innovation integration, reporting standards, and future trends. It serves as a holistic guide for academics, researchers, practitioners, and policymakers seeking to navigate the complex terrain of Industry 4.0-enabled SCM with a keen focus on sustainability, fostering a deeper understanding of how these areas intersect and offering actionable insights for creating more sustainable and resilient supply chains in the digital age.

2. SUSTAINABLE DEVELOPMENT GOALS (SDGS) AND INDUSTRY 4.0 SCM

The United Nations' Sustainable Development Goals (SDGs) are a universal call to action to end poverty, protect the planet, and ensure prosperity for all by 2030 (United Nations, 2015; Azam, Dulloo, Majeed, Wan, Xin, Tajwar, et al., 2023). These 17 interlinked goals cover a wide range of social, economic, and environmental issues, and they have significant relevance to Supply Chain Management (SCM) practices worldwide. In this section we will explore the understanding of the UN's SDGs and their relevance to SCM, highlighting their interconnectedness and the role SCM plays in contributing to the achievement of these global goals. The SDGs are a continuation of the Millennium Development Goals (MDGs) and represent a more comprehensive and integrated approach to sustainable development. Each goal is accompanied by a set of specific targets and indicators, providing a clear roadmap for action (United Nations, 2015). For example, SDG 2 aims to "end hunger, achieve food security and improved nutrition, and promote sustainable agriculture," while SDG 13 focuses on "taking urgent action to combat climate change and its impacts."

2.1 Relevance to Supply Chain Management

SDG 12 - Responsible Consumption and Production: Supply Chain Management (SCM) can play a crucial role in achieving responsible consumption and production by optimizing resource utilization. This encompasses efficient inventory control, minimizing excessive production that leads to waste, and embracing practices like lean manufacturing. Furthermore, SCM can promote eco-friendly approaches by sourcing materials from sustainable suppliers, ensuring proper waste disposal, and advocating for product recycling or remanufacturing (Dharmayanti et al., 2023). The adoption of circular supply chain models can further contribute to more sustainable production and consumption (Saccani et al., 2023).

SDG 8 - Decent Work and Economic Growth: Supply chain managers hold a pivotal position in ensuring decent work and fostering economic growth through the implementation of ethical labour practices. This includes ensuring fair wages, maintaining safe working conditions, and adhering to labour laws throughout the supply chain (Rayhan & Gross, 2023). Ethical sourcing is also crucial, as supply chain managers can collaborate with suppliers who treat their employees fairly and provide decent working conditions (De Souza Miguel & Tonelli, 2022).

SDG 13 - Climate Action: Supply chains significantly contribute to greenhouse gas emissions. SCM can mitigate this impact by optimizing transportation routes to reduce emissions, embracing renewable energy sources for facilities and transportation, and adopting green logistics practices such as employing fuel-efficient vehicles (Guo, 2023). Additionally, supply chain managers can work towards waste reduction and the promotion of recycling, thereby reducing the carbon footprint of their operations.

SDG 6 - Clean Water and Sanitation: Effective water management within SCM can contribute to clean water and sanitation efforts. This entails monitoring and minimizing water usage in manufacturing processes, responsibly disposing of wastewater, and collaborating with suppliers to encourage water conservation practices in their operations (Nova, 2023).

SDG 7 - Affordable and Clean Energy: Supply chains can align with this goal by embracing clean and renewable energy sources. This involves utilizing solar or wind power for warehouses and transportation and implementing energy-efficient technologies in supply chain operations. By reducing energy consumption and transitioning to clean energy sources, supply chains can support affordable and clean energy for all (Pata et al., 2023).

SDG 16 - Peace, Justice, and Strong Institutions: Ethical supply chain practices, including anti-corruption measures and fair trade, foster good governance and contribute to the development of strong institutions (Joseph et al., 2022). SCM can ensure that supply chain transactions are transparent, equitable, and free from corruption, thus advancing peace, justice, and strong institutions.

SDG 5 - Gender Equality: Supply chain leaders can promote gender equality by nurturing diversity and inclusivity within their organizations. This entails advocating for equal opportunities for all genders, addressing gender pay disparities, and providing training and support to advance the careers of women in supply chain roles (Kelling & Lawan, 2023).

SDG 9 - Industry, Innovation, and Infrastructure: SCM innovation can lead to more efficient and resilient supply chains. For example, the adoption of advanced technologies such as blockchain for supply chain transparency or the Internet of Things (IoT) for real-time monitoring can enhance supply chain operations. Innovation also includes finding novel ways to reduce waste and enhance sustainability within the supply chain (Duarte et al., 2023).

SDG 1 - No Poverty: Supply chains can contribute to poverty alleviation by creating equitable employment opportunities throughout the supply chain. This encompasses providing fair wages, particularly in developing countries, and offering job training and development opportunities for workers within the supply chain (Kanhaiya, 2023).

SDG 3 - Good Health and Well-being: SCM plays a critical role in the reliable and efficient distribution of healthcare products, including medicines, vaccines, and medical equipment. Timely and reliable supply chain management ensures the availability of essential healthcare products when needed, thereby contributing to good health and well-being (Lubag et al., 2023).

The United Nations' Sustainable Development Goals provide a comprehensive framework for addressing global challenges, and supply chain management plays a pivotal role in achieving many of these goals. Companies that integrate the principles of sustainability, responsibility, and ethical practices into their supply chains contribute significantly to the global effort to attain the SDGs by 2030. As such, understanding and actively pursuing these goals is not only a moral imperative but also a smart business strategy in today's interconnected world.

Figure 2. KPI measurement

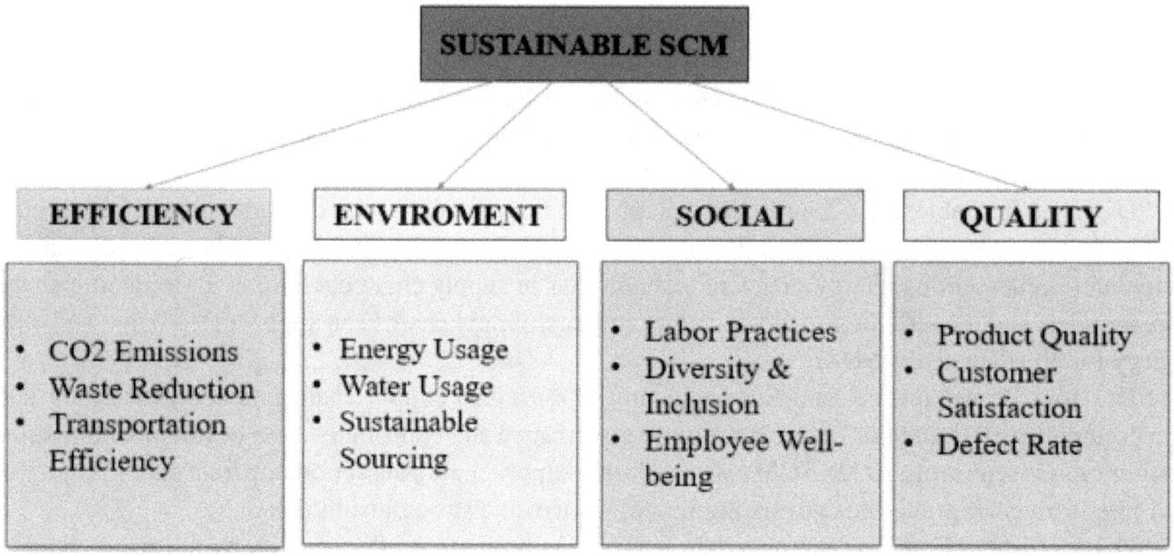

3. KEY PERFORMANCE INDICATORS (KPIS) FOR SUSTAINABLE SCM

3.1 Defining Relevant KPIs for Environmental Sustainability

Businesses, governments, and individuals are increasingly recognizing the importance of adopting sustainable practices to protect our planet for future generations. To effectively measure and track progress toward environmental sustainability goals, it is crucial to define and utilize Key Performance Indicators (KPIs). This report explores the significance of relevant KPIs in monitoring and achieving environmental sustainability objectives, emphasizing their role in guiding decision-making and highlighting the most widely recognized KPIs in this context Figure 2 shows KPI measurement..

KPIs are quantifiable metrics used to evaluate an organization's performance. In the realm of environmental sustainability, KPIs serve as compasses, guiding stakeholders towards a greener future (Ependi et al., 2023; Lee et al., 2021). These metrics enable organizations to assess their environmental impact, set targets, and monitor progress over time, ultimately promoting transparency and accountability (Rivera et al., 2023). The carbon footprint is a measure of the total greenhouse gas emissions produced directly or indirectly by an organization's activities. This includes emissions from energy use, transportation, manufacturing, and more. By calculating their carbon footprint, organizations can identify areas where emissions are highest and take steps to reduce them (Kiehle et al., 2023; Muzammal et al., 2021). This might involve using energy-efficient technologies, shifting to renewable energy sources, or optimizing transportation methods. Energy consumption KPI tracks the amount of energy an organization uses across its operations. It encompasses electricity, natural gas, and other energy sources (Geiberger et al., 2023; Ponnusamy et al., 2022). Monitoring energy consumption helps organizations identify opportunities to reduce energy waste, lower costs, and adopt cleaner energy options like solar or wind power (Minoofar et al., 2023; Azam, Tajwar, Mayhialagan, Davis, Yik, Ali, et al., 2023). This KPI measures the volume of water an organization consumes. Water is a finite and vital resource, so responsible management is crucial. By tracking water usage, organizations can implement strategies to reduce waste, improve water efficiency, and prevent pollution of local water sources. Waste generation KPI evaluates the quantity and types of waste produced by an organization (Voukkali et al., 2023; Shankar et al., 2020). This metric encourages practices such as recycling, composting, and waste reduction initiatives (Voukkali et al., 2023). Reducing waste not only minimizes environmental impact but also often leads to cost savings through reduced disposal expenses. Biodiversity conservation KPIs assess how an organization's activities affect local ecosystems and wildlife (Tschentscher et al., 2023; Seong et al., 2021). It encourages companies to consider the ecological impact of their operations and adopt practices that protect and enhance biodiversity, such as habitat restoration or sustainable land use. A sustainable supply chain KPI evaluates the environmental sustainability of an organization's suppliers and the transportation and logistics involved in its supply chain (Adwiyah et al., 2023; Ullah et al., 2021). This metric encourages responsible sourcing, ethical labour practices, and efforts to reduce the carbon footprint of goods and services throughout the supply chain.

REA KPIs measure the proportion of renewable energy sources in an organization's energy mix (Buonomano et al., 2023; Illah et al., 2021b). A higher REA indicates a commitment to using clean and sustainable energy sources like solar, wind, or hydropower. This not only reduces carbon emissions but also contributes to a more resilient and sustainable energy system. Sustainable packaging KPIs assess the materials, designs, and practices related to an organization's packaging (U. P. Singh, 2023; Azam, Tan, Pin, Syahmi, Qian, Jingyan, et al., 2023). It encourages the use of eco-friendly materials, reduction of single-use plastics, and designs that facilitate recycling or reuse. Sustainable packaging helps reduce waste and environmental pollution. Emissions intensity KPI normalizes greenhouse gas emissions against a specific metric, such as production output, revenue, or some other relevant factor (Crona et al., 2023; Sindiramutty, Jhanjhi, Tan, Khan, Gharib, & Yun, 2024). This allows organizations to assess how efficiently they are using resources and emitting greenhouse gases. Lowering emissions intensity demonstrates a commitment to reducing environmental impact while maximizing productivity. Sustainability reporting KPIs assess the quality and transparency of an organization's sustainability reports (Sebrina et al., 2022; Krishnan et al., 2021). These reports disclose environmental impacts, actions taken to mitigate them, and progress toward sustainability goals. Effective reporting promotes accountability and engagement with stakeholders, including investors, customers, and the wider community.

In conclusion, defining relevant KPIs for environmental sustainability is imperative in the global pursuit of a greener future. These metrics, drawn from authoritative sources, serve as essential tools for organizations and governments to assess their environmental performance, set ambitious goals, and track progress. By focusing on KPIs such as carbon footprint, energy consumption, and waste generation, stakeholders can make informed decisions that align with their sustainability objectives (ANSI, 2021). These KPIs not only facilitate responsible environmental stewardship but also enhance transparency and accountability, fostering a collective effort to protect the planet for generations to come.

3.2 Social Impact KPIs in Industry 4.0 SCM

The integration of Industry 4.0 technologies, including robots and automation, is transforming the workplace landscape by shifting physically demanding and repetitive tasks to machines (Kumar et al., 2023; Sindiramutty, 2023). This shift not only reduces the risk of workplace injuries but also promotes the overall well-being of employees. Workers can now redirect their efforts toward more intellectually stimulating and less physically strenuous tasks, potentially leading to higher job satisfaction and improved mental health. While the adoption of automation and AI can raise concerns about job displacement, Industry 4.0 also presents opportunities for employees to acquire new skills and transition into roles that demand creativity, problem-solving, and technical expertise (Khang et al., 2023; Manchuri et al., 2024). Companies should prioritize investments in training and development programs to facilitate this transition. Industry 4.0 facilitates the more efficient utilization of resources and energy. For example, predictive maintenance based on IoT data can significantly reduce machine downtime and energy wastage. This contributes to sustainable practices by curbing resource consumption and emissions, aligning with environmental objectives and societal expectations (Bach et al., 2023; Sindiramutty, Jhanjhi, Ray, Jazri, Khan, & Gaur, 2024). Blockchain technology and IoT sensors provide real-time visibility into supply chain processes (Reddy et al., 2023). This transparency empowers companies to identify and address ethical concerns, such as child labour or environmental violations, within their supply chains. It also fosters trust among consumers and stakeholders who prioritize responsible sourcing. Industry 4.0 tools play a pivotal role in enabling real-time communication and collaboration with various stakeholders (Debnath et al., 2023). For instance, suppliers can provide immediate updates on inventory levels, leading to more efficient inventory management. This heightened collaboration not only enhances efficiency but also fosters trust and accountability within the entire supply chain ecosystem.

In the era of Industry 4.0, as data becomes increasingly pervasive, safeguarding sensitive information becomes a paramount concern (Begum, 2023; Humayun et al., 2020b). Data breaches can have profound social and economic consequences. Therefore, it is imperative to implement robust data privacy and security measures to shield against cyber threats and preserve consumer trust.

Promoting diversity within organizations is a social responsibility that Industry 4.0 can facilitate. This technological advancement presents opportunities to attract a more diverse workforce. Diverse teams are known to be more adept at generating innovative solutions and catering to a broad spectrum of customer needs, ultimately enhancing a company's social standing and adaptability. Industry 4.0 technologies also enable companies to trace the origins of raw materials and products (Hayat et al., 2023; Verna et al., 2021). This traceability ensures that products originate from suppliers who uphold ethical and social responsibility standards. Ethical sourcing aligns with consumer expectations for responsible business practices. As companies embrace Industry 4.0, they often generate job opportunities within their local communities, both directly and indirectly (Zhong & Cheol, 2023; Humayun et al., 2020c). This job creation can foster economic development in the regions where these businesses operate, thereby improving the quality of life for residents and contributing to social well-being. Moreover, Industry 4.0 empowers companies to offer personalized products and services, respond promptly to customer inquiries, and deliver an overall enhanced customer experience. High levels of customer satisfaction not only drive business success but also bolster a company's social reputation and standing in the community.

Integrating these Key Performance Indicators (KPIs) into daily business operations and decision-making processes can empower organizations to adopt a more environmentally responsible stance. Consistently measuring and monitoring these metrics allows organizations to pinpoint areas that require enhancement, establish clear objectives for decreasing their environmental footprint, and showcase their dedication to sustainability to stakeholders and the wider public. It's important to recognize that these KPIs offer benefits that extend beyond environmental protection. They also play a crucial role in improving overall operational efficiency, cutting costs, and meeting the escalating demand for sustainable products and practices.

3.3 Economic Sustainability Metrics and Measurement

Ensuring economic sustainability holds immense importance within the broader concept of overall sustainability. It involves securing the lasting viability of economic systems, all while taking into account environmental and social considerations. To achieve responsible resource allocation, foster economic growth, and promote equitable development, it is vital to measure and continuously monitor economic sustainability (Smith et al., 2019). In this report, we delve into essential economic sustainability indicators and evaluation techniques, elucidating their significance and real-world utility.

3.3.1 Metrics for Economic Sustainability

Gross Domestic Product (GDP) serves as a widely adopted measure of a nation's total economic output. However, its application has inherent limitations, as it does not encompass critical factors such as income distribution, environmental repercussions, or the overall welfare of a population (Nugroho, 2023). Criticisms often revolve around its inability to provide a comprehensive view of economic sustainability. Figure 3 shows economic sustainability metrics.

Figure 3. Economic sustainability metrics

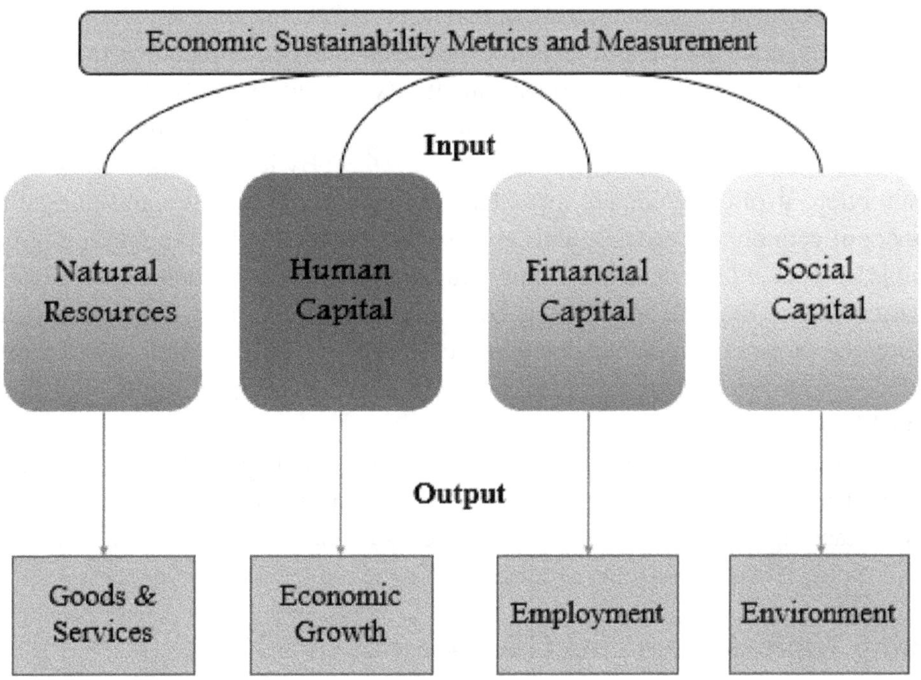

Several alternative metrics, including the Gini coefficient and income distribution indices, concentrate on evaluating income disparities within a society. These metrics offer valuable insights into whether economic growth extends its benefits equitably across all segments of the population or predominantly favours a select few, thereby fostering more inclusive and sustainable economic development. The Human Development Index (HDI), on the other hand, extends its scope beyond income by amalgamating income, health, and education indicators (H. Wang et al., 2023). In doing so, it offers a more comprehensive perspective on development and well-being, acknowledging that economic sustainability ought to encompass enhancements in the overall quality of human life. Environmental sustainability metrics play a pivotal role in ensuring that economic activities are conducted sustainably (Niyommaneerat et al., 2023; Sindiramutty, Jhanjhi, Ray, Jazri, Khan, Gaur, et al., 2024). Metrics such as the Ecological Footprint gauge the ecological demands placed by humans on the Earth's resources, while the Environmental Performance Index evaluates how effectively nations manage their environmental challenges. Resource Efficiency Metrics assess the prudent utilization of resources like energy and water in economic endeavours (Hegab et al., 2023). Enhanced resource efficiency not only curtails wastage but also reduces costs, making a substantial contribution to sustainability.

3.3.2 Measurement Approaches

Composite indices are designed to amalgamate multiple metrics into a unified index, offering a more holistic evaluation of economic sustainability (Charfeddine & Umlai, 2023). A notable example is the Sustainable Development Goals (SDG) Index, which combines a range of indicators about economic, social, and environmental sustainability to gauge progress toward global sustainability objectives. The Time-Series Analysis approach entails the examination of economic data across time, enabling the identification of trends and patterns (Achibane & Errahoui, 2023; Sindiramutty, Jhanjhi, Tan, Tee, Lau, Jazri, et al., 2024). This method aids policymakers and analysts in comprehending the influence of policies, economic cycles, and external events on sustainability indicators. It also serves to unveil whether sustainability is on an ascending or descending trajectory over time. Input-output analysis delves into the flow of resources within an economy (Lenzen et al., 2023). By identifying sectors with substantial resource consumption, it offers guidance for enhancing resource efficiency and mitigating the environmental impact of economic activities. This approach is invaluable for pinpointing opportunities to foster sustainable practices. Integrated Environmental and Economic Accounting (SEEA) represents a framework that quantifies the interconnections between economic and environmental data (Huang & Yu, 2023). It provides a more comprehensive comprehension of how economic endeavours impact the environment and how environmental shifts influence the economy. Such insights play a pivotal role in shaping sustainable policy initiatives.

The collection of data through surveys and social research is indispensable for gaining insights into public attitudes and behaviours concerning economic sustainability. This information equips policymakers with an understanding of the preferences and concerns of the populace, which can prove pivotal in the formulation of effective sustainability strategies.

3.4 Integrating Triple Bottom Line (TBL) Metrics in SCM

Supply Chain Management (SCM) holds a pivotal role in contemporary business operations, extending its influence well beyond financial considerations. In the pursuit of long-term sustainability and ethical business conduct, the integration of Triple Bottom Line (TBL) metrics into SCM has become an imperative practice. TBL encompasses three key dimensions: economic, social, and environmental, providing a comprehensive framework for evaluating a company's performance. Incorporating TBL metrics into SCM necessitates a shift in focus from mere cost reduction to the creation of holistic value (Yosef et al., 2023; Jhanjhi et al., 2015). Businesses can achieve this by considering factors such as the total cost of ownership (TCO), return on investment (ROI), and supply chain profitability. This approach enables companies to optimize their financial performance while simultaneously mitigating risks. Within the social dimension of TBL in SCM, the emphasis is on ethical and socially responsible practices (Yosef et al., 2023). Companies must actively monitor and enhance labour conditions, promote diversity and inclusion, and engage with their communities throughout the supply chain. Socially responsible SCM not only elevates a company's reputation but also fosters trust among employees and stakeholders. Environmental sustainability lies at the heart of TBL metrics in SCM (Khan et al., 2022; Sindiramutty, Tan, Lau, Thangaveloo, Gharib, Manchuri, et al., 2024). Firms are expected to curtail their carbon footprint, champion resource efficiency, and embrace principles of the circular economy. Compliance with environmental regulations and the adoption of eco-friendly practices can lead to cost savings and risk mitigation.

The implementation of TBL metrics in SCM may face resistance due to the absence of standardized measurement tools and the intricacies of multi-dimensional assessment (Huffman et al., 2023). Nevertheless, businesses that successfully integrate TBL metrics gain a competitive edge by fostering innovation and strengthening relationships with stakeholders. Embracing TBL metrics in SCM is essential for companies aspiring to thrive in a world increasingly conscious of environmental and social responsibilities. By concurrently addressing the economic, social, and environmental dimensions, companies can enhance their overall performance and contribute to a more sustainable future.

4. DATA COLLECTION AND MANAGEMENT FOR SUSTAINABILITY METRICS

4.1 Leveraging IoT and Big Data for Sustainable SCM

Supply Chain Management (SCM) has undergone significant evolution in recent years, driven by the integration of emerging technologies such as the Internet of Things (IoT) and Big Data analytics. This section delves into the transformative impact of these technologies on SCM practices, resulting in more efficient and sustainable operations.

IoT, characterized by its network of interconnected devices and sensors, plays a central role in the realm of SCM (Atta et al., 2023). Placing IoT devices along the supply chain facilitates real-time tracking of product locations and conditions (Soori et al., 2023). This heightened transparency empowers better decision-making, reduces wastage, and optimizes the utilization of resources, thereby making significant contributions to sustainability objectives. Complementing IoT, Big Data analytics processes the vast troves of data generated by sensors and various other sources (Rani et al., 2023). This capability enables predictive maintenance, demand forecasting, and route optimization. Harnessing these capabilities empowers companies to diminish their carbon footprint, curtail energy consumption, and mitigate emissions. The synergy between IoT and Big Data also bolsters supply chain resilience. Real-time data analysis aids in the early detection of disruptions and the swift implementation of corrective measures (Chen et al., 2022). This minimizes the adverse effects of disruptions, fortifying supply chains and rendering them more robust and sustainable. Furthermore, IoT and Big Data contribute significantly to ethical sourcing and transparency. IoT-enabled traceability enables consumers to authenticate the authenticity and origins of products (Ismail et al., 2023). This assures that sustainable and ethical practices are adhered to across the entire supply chain, aligning with the growing concerns of today's environmentally conscious consumers.

In conclusion, the integration of IoT and Big Data within SCM is pivotal for attaining sustainability objectives. These technologies enhance visibility, streamline processes, fortify resilience, and uphold ethical sourcing. As companies continue to adopt and innovate in this domain, they not only reduce their environmental footprint but also meet the escalating demand for sustainability in today's marketplace.

4.2 Data Integration and Interoperability Challenges in Industry 4.0 SCM

One of the primary hurdles in achieving data integration and interoperability lies in the wide array of data formats and systems utilized throughout the supply chain (Gavai et al., 2023). This diversity often leads to incompatibility issues, obstructing the smooth exchange of data among various stakeholders. Moreover, the growing volume and speed at which data is generated by IoT devices exacerbates this challenge. Another critical consideration pertains to data security and privacy. With the increased sharing of data among supply chain partners, safeguarding the confidentiality and integrity of sensitive information becomes of utmost importance. Balancing data security with the imperative of interoperability presents a complex conundrum. Real-time data synchronization is a fundamental requirement for effective supply chain management, but attaining it remains a formidable task (Li et al., 2023). Delays in data exchange can result in inefficiencies and missed opportunities for timely decision-making, with this issue becoming particularly pronounced in the context of global supply chains. Vendor lock-in poses a recurring problem within Industry 4.0 supply chain management, where companies become overly reliant on specific technology providers (Yenugula et al., 2023; Sindiramutty, Tan, Tee, Lau, Balakrishnan, Kaur, et al., 2024). This dependence can impede interoperability and hinder the flexibility needed to adapt to evolving business demands. Standardization plays a pivotal role in achieving interoperability. In the absence of standardized data formats and communication protocols, different systems struggle to communicate seamlessly. Establishing and adhering to industry-wide standards becomes imperative. Furthermore, grappling with the sheer volume of data generated within Industry 4.0 supply chain management is an imposing challenge (Meier et al., 2023). Without efficient data governance strategies in place, organizations can find themselves overwhelmed by the deluge of data, making it difficult to extract meaningful insights. Overcoming these challenges necessitates a collaborative approach involving industry stakeholders. Industry consortia and partnerships play a vital role in developing common standards and best practices.

In conclusion, the impediments related to data integration and interoperability pose significant barriers within the realm of Industry 4.0 supply chain management. These obstacles encompass issues such as data format disparities, security considerations, synchronization dilemmas, vendor dependency, standardization imperatives, data management complexities, and the imperative for collaborative efforts. Addressing these challenges is essential for harnessing the full potential of Industry 4.0 in the domain of supply chain management. Figure 4 shows Data Integration and Interoperability Challenges in Industry 4.0 SCM.

Figure 4. Data integration and interoperability challenges in Industry 4.0 SCM

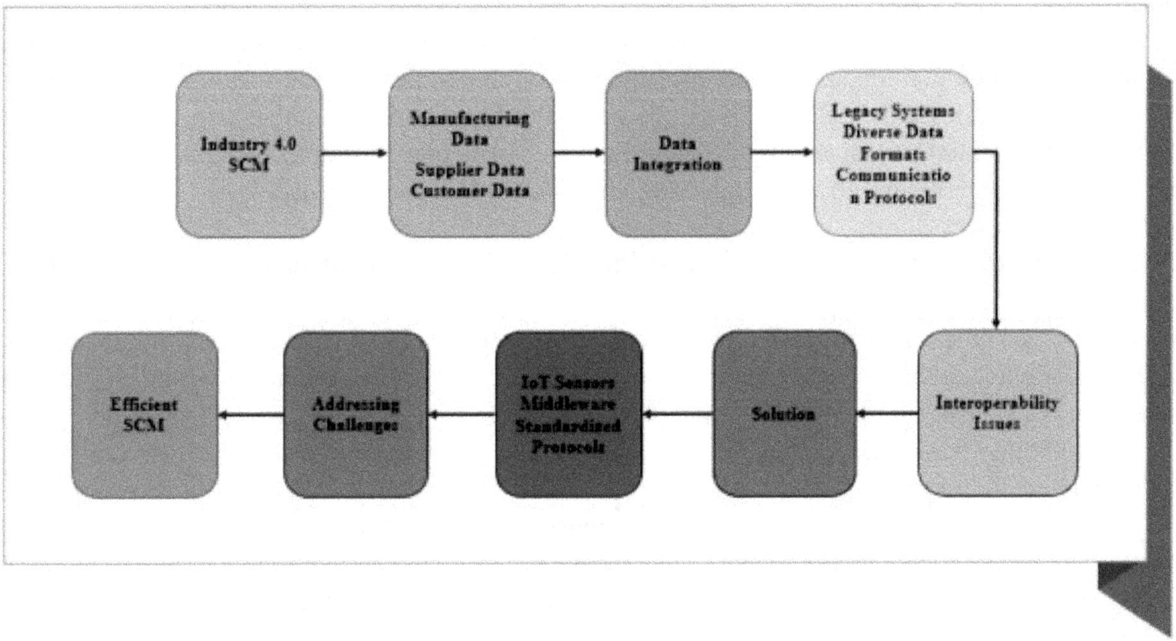

4.3 Real-Time Data Analytics for Continuous Performance Monitoring

Real-time data analytics has emerged as a pivotal resource for organizations spanning various industries, empowering them with the capacity for continuous performance monitoring and well-informed decision-making. This approach harnesses the capabilities of advanced analytics and contemporary technologies to process and scrutinize data in real-time as it's generated, delivering immediate insights and advantages.

Organizations benefit from real-time data analytics by tracking performance metrics at the moment, ensuring they maintain competitiveness and adaptability in swiftly evolving markets (Ramdurai, 2020). Through the continuous monitoring of key performance indicators (KPIs), businesses can promptly detect and address issues, capitalize on opportunities, and fine-tune their operations. This methodology facilitates proactive decision-making and the ability to swiftly respond to shifting circumstances. One notable application of real-time data analytics is evident in e-commerce, exemplified by companies like Amazon, which employ it to monitor website traffic, sales, and customer behaviour in real-time (Widodo & Napitupulu, 2023; Jhanjhi et al., 2021). In healthcare, real-time analytics plays a crucial role in patient monitoring, enabling timely interventions and enhancing patient outcomes (AlAdwani & ALSiyabi, 2023). The financial sector benefits from fraud detection systems that employ real-time data analysis to instantly identify suspicious transactions. Furthermore, real-time data analytics supports predictive maintenance in manufacturing, curtailing downtime and maintenance expenses by analyzing equipment sensor data in real time (Sivaraman et al., 2023). In transportation, it facilitates real-time route optimization, augmenting efficiency and reducing fuel consumption. Additionally, real-time analytics proves indispensable in disaster management, facilitating swift responses to emergencies by analyzing data from diverse sources. To effectively implement real-time data analytics, organizations must make investments in robust data infrastructure (Schneider et al., 2022) and embrace cutting-edge tools and technologies, including stream processing frameworks like Apache Kafka. Additionally, they should prioritize data security and compliance and establish sound data governance practices.

In conclusion, real-time data analytics has solidified its position as a cornerstone of modern business operations, enabling continuous performance monitoring and agile decision-making. Its applications span various industries, encompassing e-commerce, healthcare, finance, manufacturing, and beyond. To unlock its full potential, organizations must commit to infrastructure development, technology adoption, and robust data governance, all while upholding data security and compliance.

4.4 Data Security and Privacy Considerations in Sustainability Measurement

The significance of sustainability measurement has garnered substantial attention across diverse industries. This heightened interest is a response to the urgent necessity of addressing environmental, social, and economic challenges. However, as organizations collect and analyze extensive datasets to evaluate their sustainability performance, they must give paramount importance to data security and privacy to shield sensitive information.

To safeguard sustainability data, organizations must fortify data storage and transmission to prevent unauthorized access (Rathod, 2023). The implementation of robust encryption techniques and access controls is pivotal in this regard (Wasumwa, 2023; Sindiramutty, Tee, Balakrishnan, Kaur, Thangaveloo, Jazri, et al., 2024). The repercussions of data breaches can be severe, ranging from legal consequences to damage to reputation. Employing anonymization and pseudonymization techniques is also imperative (Kanwal et al., 2023). By removing personally identifiable information, organizations can conduct sustainability assessments while preserving individuals' privacy, thereby complying with privacy regulations such as GDPR and CCPA. Transparency within organizations is equally critical. Companies should openly communicate their data collection and usage practices to stakeholders. This transparency fosters trust and ensures that individuals are well-informed about how their data is utilized (Ueda et al., 2023). Regular data audits and risk assessments should be carried out to pinpoint vulnerabilities and compliance gaps, allowing organizations to proactively address security and privacy concerns. Moreover, sustainable measurement data should be aggregated and analyzed according to legal requirements. Companies must remain abreast of evolving data protection regulations and adjust their practices accordingly.

In conclusion, as sustainability measurement takes on an increasingly integral role in organizational functions, considerations of data security and privacy should be front and centre. Employing robust encryption, access controls, and anonymization techniques, while maintaining transparency and compliance with evolving privacy regulations, is paramount. Conducting regular audits and risk assessments is vital to ensure the safeguarding of sensitive sustainability data. By adhering to these principles, organizations can strike a harmonious balance between measuring sustainability and protecting data privacy, an essential endeavour in today's data-driven landscape.

5. LIFE CYCLE ASSESSMENT (LCA) AND ENVIRONMENTAL FOOTPRINTING

5.1 Understanding LCA and Its Application in Industry 4.0 SCM

One of the tools gaining increasing prominence in the realm of sustainability assessment is the Life Cycle Assessment (LCA). LCA stands as a comprehensive methodology that thoroughly evaluates the environmental impacts associated with a product or process throughout its entire life cycle, spanning from resource extraction to disposal (Saleem et al., 2023).

LCA offers a holistic perspective on environmental impacts, aiding industries in making well-informed decisions toward sustainability (Barbhuiya & Das, 2023). Within the context of Industry 4.0 Supply Chain Management (SCM), which incorporates digital technologies such as IoT, AI, and data analytics into supply chain operations (Liu et al., 2023), LCA plays a pivotal role. It empowers businesses to assess the environmental footprint of their products and subsequently optimize their supply chain processes accordingly. A critical facet of LCA involves the assessment of carbon emissions. By quantifying emissions at every stage of a product's life cycle, companies can pinpoint areas for improvement and reduce their carbon footprint (Shabir et al., 2023). This aligns with the global imperative to combat climate change, as underscored in the Paris Agreement. Moreover, LCA supports resource optimization. It enables companies to identify phases that are resource-intensive and explore alternative approaches. This can result in cost savings and more efficient resource utilization, a particularly crucial aspect within Industry 4.0 SCM, where resource management is paramount (Wang et al., 2016). Additionally, LCA promotes transparency and eco-labelling, assisting consumers in making informed choices (Nguyen et al., 2023). In the context of Industry 4.0 SCM, where consumers increasingly demand sustainable products, this can serve as a valuable marketing strategy. Furthermore, LCA can play a supportive role in decision-making within the circular economy paradigm, where products are designed with the intent of reuse, recycling, or remanufacturing (Saidani et al., 2023). This circular approach aligns harmoniously with the sustainability objectives of Industry 4.0 SCM. Figure 5 shows LCA.

In conclusion, LCA stands as a potent tool that seamlessly aligns with the objectives of Industry 4.0 SCM. By encompassing the entire life cycle of products, evaluating their environmental impacts, and promoting sustainable practices, LCA contributes significantly to the pursuit of a more environmentally friendly and efficient supply chain. As businesses continue to embrace Industry 4.0 technologies, the integration of LCA into their operations will become increasingly essential in achieving sustainability goals and maintaining competitiveness in the global market.

5.2 Conducting Environmental Footprinting for Products and Processes

Environmental footprinting stands as an indispensable tool for the evaluation of the environmental consequences associated with products and processes. It empowers us to quantify and comprehend the resources consumed and emissions generated throughout a product's entire life cycle. This report delves into the significance of environmental footprinting, its methodologies, and its role in advancing sustainability.

Diverse methodologies and tools are deployed to execute environmental footprint assessments, with the Life Cycle Assessment (LCA) methodology, as outlined in ISO 14040 and ISO 14044 (Chohan et al., 2023), being a widely adopted approach. LCA evaluates environmental impacts spanning from the extraction of raw materials to production, distribution, usage, and eventual disposal phases. In parallel, the Carbon Footprint Standard concentrates specifically on greenhouse gas emissions. Environmental footprinting serves the crucial purpose of enabling informed choices for businesses and consumers alike. It furnishes a comprehensive overview of a product's environmental footprint, facilitating sustainable decision-making (Saleem et al., 2023b). Additionally, it motivates companies to reduce their environmental impact through innovative practices and efficient resource utilization. Such efforts can result in reduced energy consumption, minimized waste generation, and lowered greenhouse gas emissions. This practice plays an instrumental role in tackling global environmental challenges by supporting international agreements like the Paris Agreement, through the provision of essential data on carbon emissions (Saqib et al., 2023). Furthermore, it assists governments and organizations in formulating and achieving ambitious sustainability objectives. Given the growing environmental consciousness among consumers, environmental footprint labels can serve as guiding markers for their choices (Nydrioti & Grigoropoulou, 2022). Studies indicate that eco-labels wield influence over purchasing decisions (A. Kumar & Basu, 2023). Environmental footprinting empowers consumers to select products with diminished environmental impacts. Despite its manifold benefits, environmental footprinting confronts certain challenges, including data availability and methodological intricacies (Chu et al., 2022). Nonetheless, ongoing research endeavours and standardization initiatives are aimed at surmounting these obstacles. The path forward encompasses the integration of social and economic facets into footprint assessments to yield a more comprehensive view of sustainability (Weidema et al., 2009).

In conclusion, environmental footprinting assumes a pivotal role in the evaluation and mitigation of the environmental repercussions linked to products and processes. Its methodologies, including LCA and carbon footprinting, provide invaluable insights into sustainability. Through the empowerment of consumers, the influence on corporate practices, and the contribution to global sustainability objectives, environmental footprinting stands as a linchpin in addressing environmental challenges.

Figure 5. Life cycle assessment

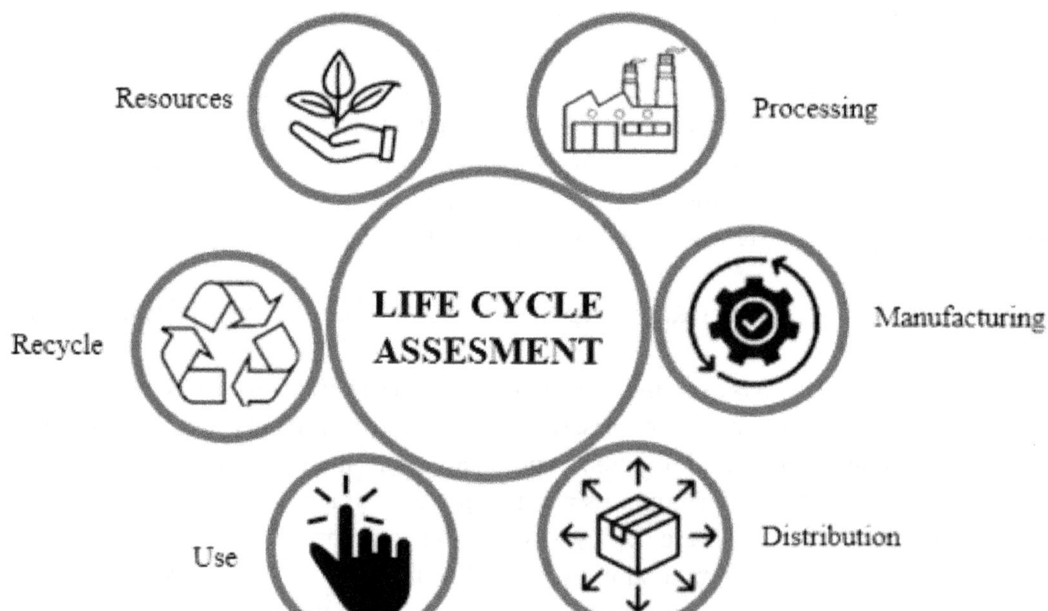

5.3 Identifying Hotspots and Opportunities for Environmental Improvement

Environmental issues have taken centre stage due to their profound impact on our planet. Identifying areas of concern and opportunities for environmental betterment is imperative for securing a sustainable future. One pressing environmental hotspot is air pollution, primarily driven by the combustion of fossil fuels for energy production and transportation (Mumtaz et al., 2023). These activities release pollutants like particulate matter, nitrogen oxides, and sulfur dioxide into the atmosphere, leading to adverse effects on human health, including respiratory diseases and premature deaths. Additionally, they contribute to smog formation and acid rain, causing harm to ecosystems and infrastructure. Deforestation stands out as a critical environmental concern, as it involves the removal of forests, resulting in various adverse consequences (Daiyoub et al., 2023). Forests play a pivotal role in carbon sequestration, and when cleared for purposes such as agriculture, urban development, or logging, carbon dioxide is released into the atmosphere, exacerbating climate change. Deforestation also leads to biodiversity loss and disrupts ecosystems, affecting wildlife and habitats. The transition to renewable energy sources, such as wind, solar, and hydropower, presents a significant opportunity for environmental improvement (X. H. Chen et al., 2023). Unlike fossil fuels, these sources do not emit greenhouse gases during electricity generation, making them essential in the fight against climate change. Governments and businesses can invest in renewable energy infrastructure and technologies to reduce carbon emissions.

The adoption of sustainable agriculture practices can also yield substantial environmental benefits (Dubbert et al., 2021). Techniques such as crop rotation, organic farming, and reduced pesticide use promote soil health, mitigate water pollution, and reduce the environmental impact of agriculture. Sustainable agriculture additionally fosters biodiversity and enhances ecosystem resilience. Effective waste management is another crucial aspect of environmental betterment (Adu-Gyamfi et al., 2023). Increasing recycling rates and reducing single-use plastics can divert waste from landfills and mitigate pollution in oceans and ecosystems. Waste-to-energy technologies provide an avenue for harnessing energy from waste while minimizing its environmental impact. Enhancing energy efficiency in both industries and households can significantly curtail energy consumption and greenhouse gas emissions (Jahanger et al., 2023). This entails the use of energy-efficient appliances, the improvement of building insulation, and the implementation of industrial processes that minimize energy waste. Energy efficiency measures not only benefit the environment but also lead to cost savings for individuals and businesses.

In conclusion, addressing environmental concerns and seizing opportunities for improvement is paramount to securing a sustainable future. By addressing issues such as air pollution and deforestation, while embracing renewable energy, sustainable agriculture, efficient waste management, and energy conservation, we can collaboratively work toward a cleaner and healthier environment for generations to come.

5.4 Integrating LCA With Supply Chain Design and Decision-Making

Life Cycle Assessment (LCA) is a methodology employed to assess the environmental impact of a product or service throughout its complete life cycle, commencing from the extraction of raw materials and concluding with disposal. This integration empowers businesses to make more sustainable and well-informed decisions while effectively managing their supply chains.

LCA furnishes valuable insights into several facets of supply chain management. Firstly, it serves as a means to evaluate the environmental footprint of products and processes (Whitehead et al., 2015). By quantifying elements such as carbon emissions, water usage, and resource consumption, businesses can pinpoint opportunities to curtail their environmental impact. Secondly, LCA can steer decisions pertaining to sourcing and procurement (Jenssen & De Boer, 2019). It equips organizations with the capability to select suppliers and materials characterized by lower environmental footprints, thus contributing to a more environmentally conscious and responsible supply chain. Moreover, LCA proves invaluable in optimizing transportation and logistics ("Hydrogen Economy," 2023). By scrutinizing the emissions and energy consumption associated with various transportation modes and routes, companies can make choices that are not only more sustainable but also cost-effective. Furthermore, LCA can underpin product design and innovation (Suppipat et al., 2022). Designers can utilize LCA data to make environmentally friendly design decisions, leading to the development of products burdened with reduced environmental impacts. To seamlessly integrate LCA into the fabric of supply chain decision-making, businesses must allocate resources to acquire data collection and analysis tools. Additionally, they should foster cross-functional collaboration and communication to ensure that the findings derived from LCA inform strategic decision-making.

In conclusion, the incorporation of LCA into supply chain design and decision-making processes stands as a critical endeavour for businesses seeking to embrace environmental responsibility and sustainability. It offers a comprehensive perspective on environmental impacts throughout the supply chain and facilitates the identification of opportunities for enhancement. By embracing LCA, companies can make well-informed decisions regarding sourcing, transportation, and product design, all while diminishing their carbon footprint and contributing to a more sustainable future.

6. SOCIAL IMPACT MEASUREMENT IN INDUSTRY 4.0 SCM

6.1 Assessing Social Impacts Across the Supply Chain

This section aims to underscore the paramount significance of evaluating social impacts throughout the supply chain within the context of Industry 4.0. Drawing upon a diverse range of scholarly sources, it aims to shed light on the multifaceted nature of these social impacts.

The advent of Industry 4.0 has ushered in increased automation and the deployment of advanced robotics within manufacturing facilities. While these innovations undoubtedly enhance efficiency, they concurrently raise concerns regarding the displacement of human workers (Ajani, 2023). Furthermore, the challenge of re-skilling and upskilling the workforce to adapt to these transformations has been widely acknowledged. The integration of digital technologies into the supply chain facilitates improved monitoring and management of environmental factors, subsequently reducing the carbon footprint (Chandan et al., 2023). This reduction carries direct implications for local communities, as diminished emissions can lead to enhancements in air quality and public health. These favourable environmental consequences can contribute substantively to social sustainability, yielding benefits for both the workforce and the neighbouring communities. Ethical considerations have gained prominence within the realm of Industry 4.0, especially concerning supply chain management. Companies are increasingly expected to guarantee fair labour practices and ethical sourcing of materials (Costa et al., 2023). Neglecting to address these concerns can result in damage to reputation and face social backlash. The fourth industrial revolution simultaneously offers opportunities for heightened gender diversity and inclusion within the workforce. By advocating for gender equality within STEM fields, Industry 4.0 has the potential to foster a more inclusive society. This social impact holds the potential to empower marginalized groups and bolster social cohesion. Community engagement is an imperative aspect of Industry 4.0. Companies must consider the broader societal context when implementing new technologies (Chan, 2022). The failure to engage with communities can incite resistance and impede the successful implementation of Industry 4.0 practices.

In conclusion, Industry 4.0 harbours the potential to engender profound social impacts across the supply chain. These impacts encompass workforce displacement, ethical considerations, environmental responsibility, and community engagement. To ensure a sustainable and inclusive future within the era of Industry 4.0, companies must proactively evaluate and address these social impacts. Figure 6 shows social impacts and operation in IR 4.0.

6.2 Worker Welfare and Fair Labor Practices in Smart Manufacturing

Industry 4.0 has brought about a profound transformation in the manufacturing sector, introducing smart manufacturing technologies that promise heightened efficiency and productivity. However, as we delve deeper into this era characterized by automation and digitization, it becomes imperative to address the implications for worker well-being and ensure the maintenance of fair labour practices.

The transition to smart manufacturing presents a spectrum of opportunities and challenges for the workforce. Automation, artificial intelligence, and the Internet of Things (IoT) have the potential to streamline processes, reduce errors, and elevate product quality (Stadnicka et al., 2022). These enhancements can lead to increased profitability for businesses, thereby promoting economic stability. Nevertheless, it is of paramount importance to remain vigilant to ensure that the workforce does not bear the disproportionate brunt of these transformative changes. Numerous studies underscore the significance of preserving worker well-being during the Industry 4.0 transformation. Scholars such as Sawant et al. (2022) contend that worker training and upskilling are indispensable to ensure that employees remain relevant in the digital age. Additionally, Mao et al. (2023) underscores the need for creating safe and ergonomic working conditions in smart factories to mitigate occupational hazards. To advocate for fair labour practices, it is essential to incorporate ethical dimensions into smart manufacturing. The establishment of ethical guidelines can serve to safeguard workers' rights and promote social responsibility within the industry (Silva et al., 2022). Furthermore, government regulations and labour laws play a pivotal role in safeguarding workers' interests in smart manufacturing environments (Silva et al., 2022). Worker welfare in the context of Industry 4.0 extends to concerns regarding job security and employment stability. As smart manufacturing technologies continue to evolve, apprehensions regarding job displacement arise (Castillo et al., 2022). Ensuring equitable transition policies and providing opportunities for displaced workers is of paramount importance. Collaborative endeavours involving industries, governments, and labour organizations are instrumental in striking a balance between harnessing the benefits of smart manufacturing and safeguarding worker welfare.

In conclusion, as we navigate the era of Industry 4.0 and smart manufacturing, it is crucial to prioritize worker welfare and uphold fair labour practices. Workers should be equipped with the requisite skills, afforded safe working conditions, and protected by ethical guidelines and regulatory frameworks. By doing so, we can fully harness the transformative potential of smart manufacturing while upholding the dignity and rights of the workforce.

Figure 6. Social impacts and operation in IR 4.0

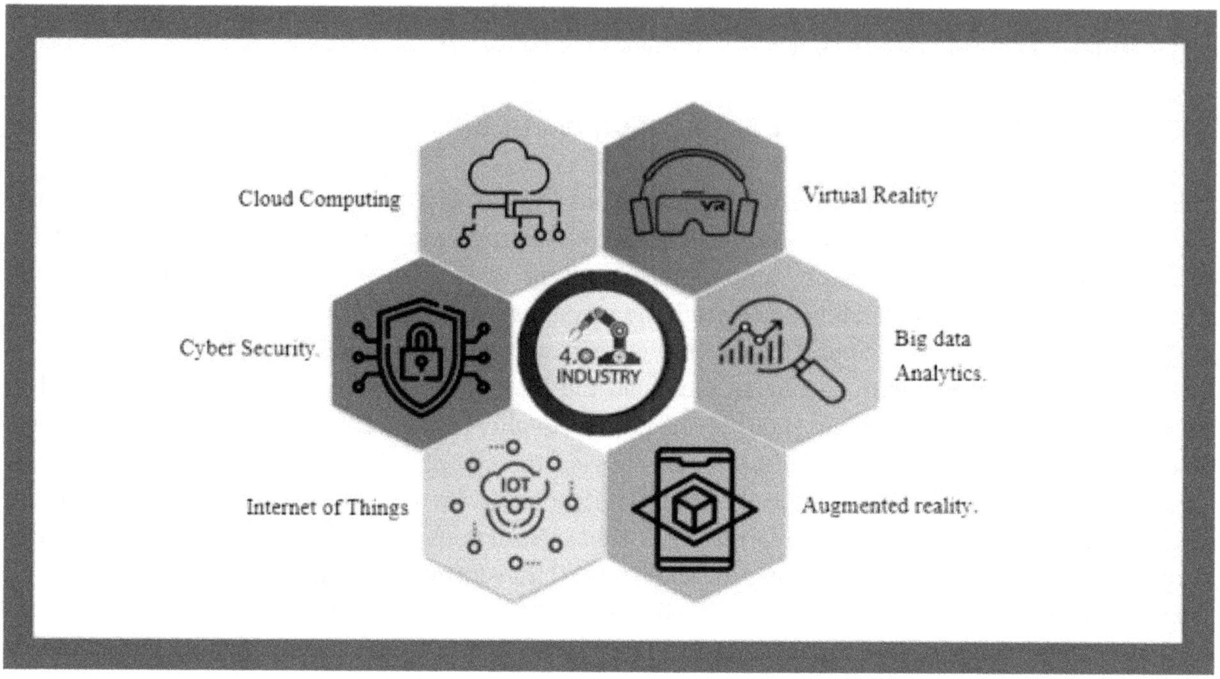

6.3 Supply Chain Diversity and Inclusion Metrics

Diversity and inclusion (D&I) have emerged as critical drivers of success, particularly within the context of Industry 4.0. Industry 4.0 signifies the integration of digital technologies, artificial intelligence, and automation into manufacturing and supply chain operations. As organizations embrace this new industrial era, it becomes paramount to grasp the significance of diversity and inclusion indicators in ensuring sustainable growth and competitiveness. This section delves into the importance of diversity and inclusion metrics in the context of the supply chain within Industry 4.0, offering insights substantiated by relevant research.

Varied teams within the supply chain play a pivotal role in fostering creativity and problem-solving abilities (Gu et al., 2023). Research (Robson & Tsou, 2023) indicates that diverse teams can outperform homogeneous ones. In the context of Industry 4.0, metrics such as gender, race, age, and ethnicity can be employed to assess the workforce's composition, ensuring a broad spectrum of viewpoints. Metrics related to supplier diversity are instrumental in evaluating an organization's inclusivity in its procurement processes (Sordi et al., 2022). They gauge the extent to which businesses engage with suppliers from diverse backgrounds, thereby contributing to economic development across varied communities. Initiatives promoting supplier diversity can enhance innovation and competitiveness (Le et al., 2022). Metrics that assess inclusive leadership gauge the effectiveness of leaders in cultivating an inclusive culture (Baig, 2023). Leaders who prioritize inclusivity are more likely to attract and retain diverse talent. In Industry 4.0, such leaders play a crucial role in nurturing an environment where diverse teams can thrive (Ly, 2023).

Metrics related to the diversity of an organization's customer base hold significance in Industry 4.0 (Palsodkar et al., 2023). A diverse customer base reflects a wide-reaching market presence and the capacity to meet the demands of various demographics, potentially leading to increased sales and customer loyalty. Evaluating employee engagement and satisfaction is pivotal for understanding the impact of inclusive practices on the workforce (Fan et al., 2023). Inclusive workplaces tend to foster higher employee morale and productivity. These metrics serve as valuable indicators of a company's commitment to diversity and inclusion. According to research by Volkov et al. (2022), diverse teams exhibit greater innovation and adaptability, qualities of utmost importance in Industry 4.0. Metrics about innovation, such as the number of patents or new product developments, can be linked to the diversity of the teams responsible for these achievements. Metrics concerning employee retention and turnover shed light on the influence of diversity and inclusion efforts on workforce stability (Volkov et al., 2022). High turnover rates among specific demographic groups may signal underlying inclusion-related issues, making it essential for organizations to monitor these metrics and address retention challenges.

Furthermore, diversity and inclusion metrics can significantly impact an organization's ethical reputation. Companies that champion diversity are more likely to attract socially conscious consumers and investors, ultimately positively affecting their bottom line. Compliance metrics ensure that organizations adhere to legal requirements concerning diversity and inclusion (Zowghi & Da Rimini, 2023). Non-compliance can lead to legal complications and harm an organization's reputation. Metrics within this category help organizations maintain legal compliance. Finally, assessing the return on investment (ROI) of diversity and inclusion initiatives is crucial in Industry 4.0. Organizations must evaluate the financial impact of their D&I efforts, which may encompass increased revenue, cost savings, or improved market share.

In the era of Industry 4.0, supply chain diversity and inclusion metrics are indispensable for organizations aspiring to thrive in a rapidly evolving business landscape. These metrics encompass various aspects, ranging from workforce diversity to customer base diversity, and they play a pivotal role in enhancing innovation, employee satisfaction, and ethical standing. Companies that invest in measuring and enhancing diversity and inclusion metrics are poised to gain a competitive edge and long-term success in this age of digital transformation.

6.4 Community Engagement and Local Economic Development

This section delves into the pivotal role of community engagement in promoting local economic growth within the context of Industry 4.0, drawing insights from various scholarly sources. Initiatives in community engagement that prioritize the development of local workforce skills are instrumental in driving local economic growth. Collaborative endeavours involving local businesses, educational institutions, and government bodies ensure that the workforce possesses the requisite digital skills demanded by Industry 4.0. Sibhensana and Maistry (2023) underscore the significance of community engagement in fostering innovation by providing a platform for knowledge exchange and collaboration. Active participation of local communities in innovative ecosystems enables them to create and adapt new technologies, thereby enhancing competitiveness. Entrepreneurial activities often serve as a driving force behind local economic growth (Ibrahimova & Moog, 2023). Programs such as business incubators and mentorship initiatives, facilitated through community engagement, empower local entrepreneurs to harness Industry 4.0 technologies for business expansion. Community engagement can be leveraged by local governments and industry leaders to attract investment (Broadhead, 2023). By engaging with the community to showcase the advantages of a technologically advanced local economy, they can attract investors seeking opportunities in Industry 4.0 sectors.

Sustainable practices are integral to Industry 4.0. Community engagement plays a vital role in raising awareness about environmental and social responsibility, motivating businesses to adopt sustainable approaches that benefit both the community and the economy. Infrastructure development is crucial to support Industry 4.0 activities (Sarkar et al., 2022). Community engagement can influence decisions related to infrastructure investments, ensuring they align with the needs of local businesses and residents. It's important to note that Industry 4.0 has the potential to exacerbate socio-economic disparities (Ocelik et al., 2023). Community engagement efforts can be directed toward inclusive policies and programs that bridge these gaps, ensuring that the benefits of technological advancement are accessible to all. Local economic development should encompass not only financial aspects but also the overall quality of life (Widianingsih et al., 2023). Community engagement enables a holistic approach, addressing factors like healthcare, education, and cultural development. Engaging with the local community can also enhance the region's global competitiveness. A well-prepared local workforce and a supportive community can position an area as an attractive destination for global companies seeking to establish Industry 4.0 operations. Effective community engagement necessitates ongoing monitoring and evaluation (Amosse et al., 2023). Regular assessments help identify areas that require improvement and adapt strategies to the evolving dynamics of Industry 4.0.

In conclusion, community engagement serves as a fundamental driver of local economic development in the era of Industry 4.0. It acts as a catalyst for enhancing workforce skills, promoting innovation, strengthening entrepreneurship, attracting investment, fostering sustainable practices, developing infrastructure, mitigating inequalities, enhancing the quality of life, ensuring global competitiveness, and facilitating continuous improvement. As we advance further into the digital age, fostering collaboration between businesses, government agencies, educational institutions, and local communities will be crucial for realizing the full potential of Industry 4.0 for local economic growth.

7. ECONOMIC SUSTAINABILITY MEASUREMENT IN SMART SUPPLY CHAINS

7.1 Evaluating Cost Efficiency and Resource Optimization

In the current fiercely competitive business environment, enterprises are increasingly turning to intelligent supply chain solutions to bolster cost-effectiveness and optimize resource utilization. This section delves into the significance of assessing cost efficiency and resource optimization within smart supply chains, shedding light on key strategies and technologies that empower businesses to maintain their competitive edge in a swiftly evolving market.

A cornerstone of a smart supply chain is the incorporation of Internet of Things (IoT) devices. These devices, such as sensors and RFID tags, deliver real-time data on inventory levels, product conditions, and transportation routes (Khadem, 2023). Leveraging IoT data enables companies to trim inventory carrying costs, mitigate product spoilage, and streamline transportation routes, ultimately yielding cost savings. Predictive analytics stands as another pivotal tool for enhancing cost efficiency within smart supply chains. Through the analysis of historical data and current trends, companies can make well-informed decisions regarding inventory management, demand forecasting, and order fulfilment (Bharadiya, 2023). This proactive approach not only reduces surplus inventory but also forestalls stockouts, ensuring efficient resource allocation. Blockchain technology has emerged as a notable player in supply chain management for its capacity to elevate transparency and traceability (Kumari et al., 2023). Through blockchain, companies can track product movement from source to consumer, diminishing the risk of fraud and counterfeiting. This transparency fosters more efficient resource allocation and long-term cost savings. Automation and robotics wield significant influence in optimizing resource utilization within smart supply chains (Despeisse et al., 2023). Automated warehouses and robotic pickers augment the speed and precision of order fulfilment, curbing labour costs and enhancing overall efficiency. These technologies also enable continuous operations, further bolstering cost efficiency.

Machine learning algorithms are advancing in their ability to predict consumer demand with greater accuracy (Yaiprasert & Hidayanto, 2023). By precisely forecasting demand, companies can minimize excess inventory and diminish carrying costs. Additionally, machine learning can fine-tune pricing strategies, ensuring that products are sold at the optimal price point to maximize profits. Sustainability has assumed a central role in supply chain management. Implementation of eco-friendly practices, such as green packaging and transportation, not only mitigates environmental impact but also yields cost savings through energy conservation and waste reduction. Moreover, customers are increasingly favouring companies that prioritize sustainability, imparting a competitive advantage. Given the heavy reliance on data exchange and digital connectivity, data security is paramount within smart supply chains (Nozari & Edalatpanah, 2023). Robust cybersecurity measures are indispensable to safeguard sensitive information against breaches, which could lead to costly disruptions and damage to reputation. Close collaboration with suppliers can result in superior resource optimization. By sharing information and collaborating on inventory management and production scheduling, companies can truncate lead times and inventory levels, ultimately slashing costs (Dadaneh et al., 2023). Continuous improvement methodologies, such as Six Sigma and Lean, hold utmost importance within smart supply chains. These methodologies zero in on waste elimination, process enhancement, and quality improvement, yielding cost reductions and heightened efficiency. Finally, smart supply chains hinge on robust performance metrics for gauging cost efficiency and resource optimization (Zhao et al., 2023). Key performance indicators (KPIs) like inventory turnover, on-time delivery, and order accuracy empower companies to monitor progress and make data-driven decisions for continuous enhancement.

Figure 7. Benefits of efficient administration of smart supply chain

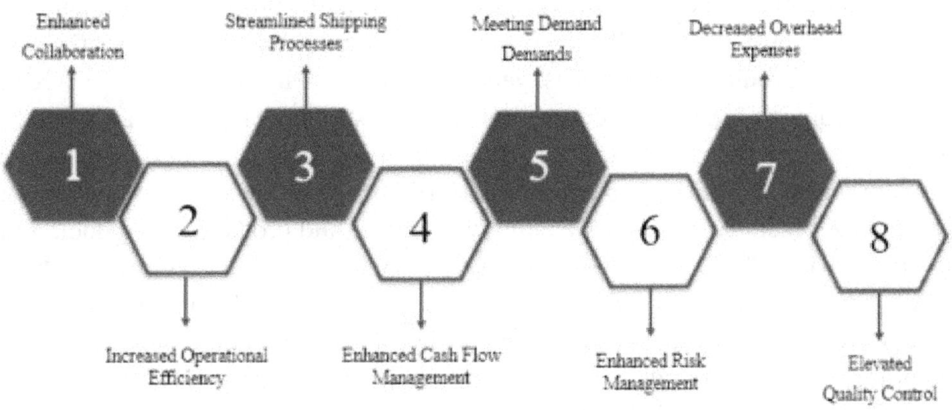

In summation, the evaluation of cost efficiency and resource optimization within smart supply chains is imperative for businesses seeking to thrive in today's competitive landscape. By harnessing technologies such as IoT, predictive analytics, and blockchain, alongside adopting sustainable practices and collaborating with suppliers, companies can curtail costs, optimize resource utilization, and secure a competitive edge. Persistent commitment to improvement and rigorous performance metrics are vital for sustaining these gains and ensuring enduring success in the realm of smart supply chains. Figure 7 shows the benefits of efficient administration of smart supply chain.

7.2 Financial Indicators for Sustainable SCM

Businesses are increasingly incorporating sustainability into their supply chain strategies to mitigate risks, cut costs, and bolster their reputations. Financial indicators play a pivotal role in gauging the effectiveness of these sustainability initiatives, offering quantifiable insights into their influence on a company's financial bottom line.

One of the primary financial metrics linked to Sustainable Supply Chain Management (SSCM) is cost reduction. By implementing sustainable practices within the supply chain, companies can curtail expenses associated with energy consumption, waste disposal, and resource utilization (Hegab et al., 2023b). These cost savings directly contribute to increased profitability and serve as tangible outcomes of sustainable supply chain practices. Sustainable supply chain initiatives can also fuel revenue growth by enhancing customer satisfaction and expanding market opportunities. According to Jenneboer et al. (2022), companies embracing sustainable practices often witness heightened customer loyalty and gain access to new markets, resulting in elevated revenues. Effective risk management represents another financial benefit of SSCM. Companies can diminish their exposure to supply chain disruptions caused by environmental or social factors, which ultimately bolsters financial stability (Eldem et al., 2022). This risk mitigation contributes to the long-term financial well-being of the organization. Compliance with environmental and social regulations is indispensable for avoiding fines and legal entanglements. Adherence to these regulations can also yield financial benefits, as companies that fail to comply may face substantial financial penalties and harm to their reputation. Collaboration with suppliers in the adoption of sustainable practices can lead to cost savings and efficiency improvements (Ying-Jun et al., 2022). Effective collaboration can enhance financial performance through streamlined processes and reduced supply chain disruptions. A positive brand reputation is closely linked to financial success. Sustainable supply chain practices can enhance a company's image and brand value. A strong brand can command higher prices and foster customer loyalty. Innovation driven by sustainability initiatives can result in the development of new products and services, generating additional revenue streams (Oe et al., 2022). Innovation can set a company apart from competitors and boost financial performance. Companies with strong sustainability records often find it easier to access capital at favourable terms. Financial institutions and investors increasingly consider sustainability performance as a key factor in investment decisions. Moreover, sustainable practices can improve employee morale and productivity, reducing turnover and training costs (Bilderback, 2023). Employee satisfaction can have a positive impact on the bottom line.

In conclusion, financial indicators serve as indispensable tools for evaluating the influence of sustainable supply chain management on a company's financial performance. These indicators encompass cost reduction, revenue growth, risk mitigation, compliance, collaboration, reputation, innovation, access to capital, and employee productivity. Companies that strategically integrate sustainability into their supply chain practices stand to gain not only in terms of financial benefits but also in reinforcing their commitment to environmental and social responsibility.

7.3 Quantifying the Business Case for Sustainable Practices

Implementing sustainable practices in supply chains can lead to significant cost reductions (Huma et al., 2022). For instance, companies can adopt energy-efficient transportation methods, which not only reduce carbon emissions but also lower fuel and operational costs. Additionally, by minimizing waste and optimizing resource use, businesses can save money on raw materials and disposal expenses (Pranata & Adhariani, 2023). Sustainable practices directly contribute to improved cost-efficiency, enhancing a company's profitability. Consumer preferences are increasingly favouring environmentally conscious products and businesses (Nicolosi et al., 2023). Companies that integrate sustainability into their supply chains can tap into a growing market segment of eco-conscious consumers. Meeting this demand not only increases sales but also enhances brand loyalty. Businesses that effectively communicate their sustainable practices to customers often enjoy a competitive advantage and stronger customer relationships. Sustainability measures help mitigate various risks, including those related to climate change and resource scarcity (T. T. Nguyen et al., 2023). By diversifying suppliers, reducing dependence on single resources, and ensuring environmental resilience, companies can better withstand disruptions. For example, a business with a sustainable sourcing strategy is less vulnerable to supply chain interruptions caused by climate-related events like hurricanes or droughts. Such resilience safeguards against financial losses and reputation damage. Embracing sustainability often drives innovation within a company. Sustainable supply chain practices can lead to the development of new, environmentally friendly products and processes (Martínez-Falcó et al., 2023). Innovations like these can give companies a competitive edge by differentiating them in the market. Moreover, sustainability-driven innovations may open up new revenue streams and business opportunities. Being at the forefront of sustainable practices can position a company as an industry leader.

Sustainable supply chain practices contribute to the long-term viability and resilience of a business (Zahari et al., 2023). By responsibly managing resources, companies can ensure the availability of essential inputs even in the face of resource depletion or market fluctuations. This long-term view is crucial for strategic planning, ensuring that a business remains sustainable and profitable in the years to come. In summary, these five points highlight the tangible benefits of integrating sustainability into smart supply chains. From cost reductions and customer demand to risk mitigation, innovation, and long-term viability, adopting sustainable practices is not only good for the environment but also essential for achieving financial success and maintaining a competitive edge in today's business landscape.

8. SUSTAINABLE INNOVATION AND INDUSTRY 4.0 SCM

8.1 Integrating Sustainability Into Innovation and R&D Processes

Industry 4.0 has ushered in a transformative era in manufacturing, promising heightened efficiency, automation, and connectivity. Yet, it has also raised concerns about its potential environmental and social impacts. To confront these challenges, businesses are increasingly recognizing the significance of integrating sustainability into their innovation and research & development (R&D) processes, particularly within the realm of Sustainable Supply Chain Management (SSCM).

Industry 4.0, characterized by the deployment of technologies like the Internet of Things (IoT), artificial intelligence (AI), and data analytics, offers a wealth of opportunities to advance sustainability across the supply chain. This section delves into how businesses are harnessing these technologies to promote sustainability, drawing insights from various sources. One critical area where sustainability is being integrated is in optimizing resource utilization. Using IoT sensors and real-time data analytics, companies can monitor resource consumption more effectively, leading to reduced waste and enhanced efficiency. Additionally, AI-driven demand forecasting and inventory management systems assist in minimizing overproduction, thereby curbing resource depletion and carbon emissions (Onyeaka et al., 2023). Sustainability is also becoming increasingly ingrained in the product design phase. Innovations like eco-design software empower companies to create products with a smaller environmental footprint (García-Alonso et al., 2023). Furthermore, collaborative platforms and digital twins facilitate efficient cross-functional communication, ensuring that sustainability objectives are seamlessly integrated into product development (Das, 2023). Concerning supplier relationships, Industry 4.0 technologies enable businesses to engage in sustainable sourcing and procurement. For instance, blockchain technology helps verify the authenticity of eco-friendly claims, guaranteeing that suppliers adhere to sustainability standards (Guo, 2023). AI-powered supplier risk assessment tools assist in identifying potential environmental and ethical risks within the supply chain (Ahmed, 2023). Moreover, Industry 4.0 makes circular economy principles more attainable. Reverse logistics systems, enabled by IoT, enable companies to recover, recycle, and refurbish products, thereby reducing waste and conserving resources (Butt et al., 2023).

In conclusion, Industry 4.0 provides fertile ground for integrating sustainability into innovation and R&D processes, particularly within SSCM. By leveraging technologies such as IoT, AI, and blockchain, businesses can minimize resource usage, enhance product design, bolster supplier relationships, and move closer to achieving circular economy objectives. These advancements are not only essential for addressing environmental and social challenges but also for ensuring long-term competitiveness and resilience in the ever-evolving industrial landscape.

8.2 Responsible Design and Sustainable Product Development

Responsible design and sustainable product development stand as foundational principles that contribute significantly to the creation of environmentally conscious and socially accountable products. According to Jain and Kukreja (2023), responsible design encompasses the product design processes aimed at minimizing adverse environmental effects, such as resource depletion and pollution, while maximizing favourable social and economic outcomes. This approach aligns harmoniously with the tenets of sustainable supply chain management, emphasizing responsible sourcing and ethical production practices. Sustainable product development extends well beyond the mere design phase, encompassing the entire product lifecycle, from concept inception to eventual disposal. As highlighted by Zong et al. (2023), sustainable product development entails a continuous enhancement process, considering factors like recyclability, longevity, and energy efficiency throughout the product's existence. In this context, fostering collaboration among supply chain partners becomes pivotal to ensure the pervasive adoption of sustainable practices at every juncture. The implementation of responsible design and sustainable product development is supported by an array of tools and frameworks, such as Life Cycle Assessment (LCA) and eco-design guidelines. LCA empowers businesses to assess their products' environmental impact, aiding in the identification of opportunities for refinement. Conversely, eco-design guidelines provide a structured approach to the incorporation of sustainability principles into the product development process. Furthermore, it remains imperative to engage with consumers who are increasingly prioritizing sustainability. As emphasized by Vizcaino (2023), transparent communication regarding a product's sustainable attributes can have a positive influence on consumer choices. Therefore, coupling responsible design and sustainable product development with effective marketing strategies that accentuate these features becomes essential.

In summary, responsible design and sustainable product development represent integral facets of sustainable supply chain management. Embracing these principles not only reduces the ecological footprint but also elevates brand reputation and fosters enduring profitability. To excel in the evolving business landscape, companies must place sustainability at the forefront of their supply chain operations, encompassing every aspect from initial product design to end-of-life considerations. Figure 8 shows 5 ways to improve supply chain sustainability.

Figure 8. 5 ways to improve supply chain sustainability

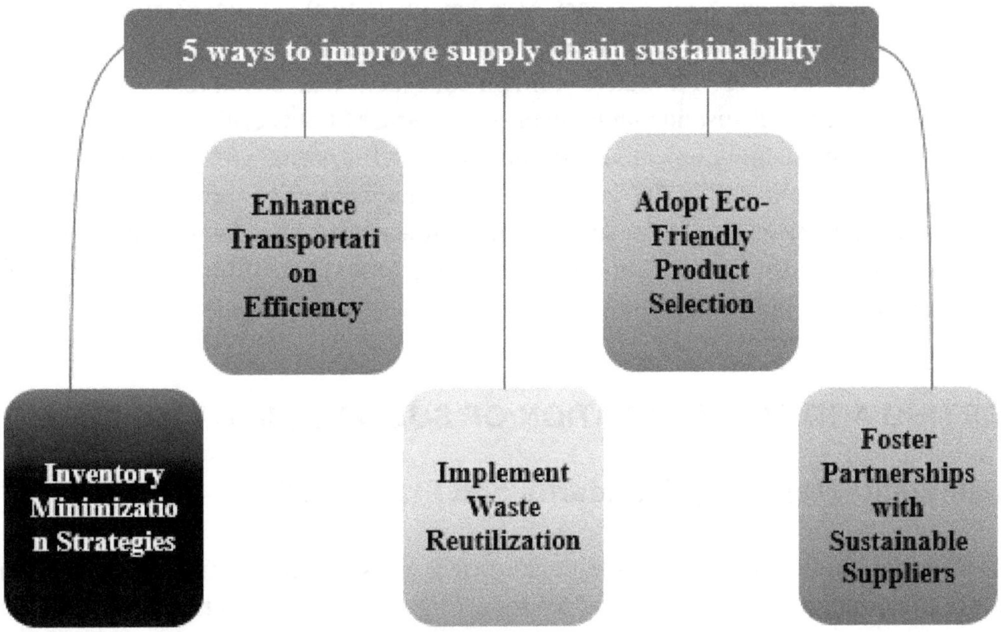

8.3 Measuring the Impact of Sustainable Innovations on SCM

In the pursuit of Sustainable Supply Chain Management (SSCM) goals, sustainable innovations play a pivotal role, encompassing novel technologies, processes, and strategies aimed at diminishing environmental impact and fostering societal well-being. This section delves into the significance of gauging the influence of sustainable innovations on SSCM and underscores essential methods for such assessment.

To effectively measure the impact of sustainable innovations on SSCM, organizations must establish and monitor specific Key Performance Indicators (KPIs), as emphasized by Wu and Xie (2023). These performance metrics provide a quantifiable foundation for evaluating progress. For example, metrics like the reduction in carbon emissions and waste can serve as valuable yardsticks for assessing the environmental ramifications of sustainability endeavours. Moreover, organizations should embrace sustainability metrics and reporting frameworks to appraise their SSCM endeavours. Recognized frameworks such as the Global Reporting Initiative (GRI) and the Sustainability Accounting Standards Board (SASB) furnish guidelines for quantifying and disclosing sustainability-related data, as articulated by Ali et al. (2023). The Lifecycle Assessment (LCA) proves to be another indispensable instrument for evaluating the influence of sustainable innovations on SSCM, as expounded by Okogwu et al. (2023). LCA scrutinizes the ecological footprint of products and processes across their entire lifecycle, encompassing aspects like raw material extraction, production, transportation, and eventual disposal. By conducting LCAs, organizations can pinpoint areas necessitating enhancement and make well-informed choices regarding innovation implementation. Transparency within the supply chain emerges as an essential element for evaluating the impact of sustainable innovations. As proposed by Lee and Zhang (2023), the adoption of blockchain technology can enhance transparency by furnishing a secure and immutable ledger of supply chain data. This empowers organizations to trace product origins and validate sustainability claims. In addition to environmental considerations, evaluating the social impact of sustainable innovations assumes paramount importance. Social Impact Assessments (SIAs) aid organizations in comprehending the consequences of their initiatives on communities and labour conditions, as underscored by Efe (2023). This guarantees that SSCM initiatives remain congruent with social responsibility objectives.

Measuring the influence of sustainable innovations on SSCM holds critical significance for organizations dedicated to sustainability objectives. By deploying KPIs, sustainability metrics, LCAs, supply chain transparency measures, and social impact assessments, enterprises can garner a comprehensive understanding of the effectiveness of their sustainability endeavours. This data-driven approach not only fosters accountability but also fosters a continuous improvement ethos, ultimately contributing to more ethical and sustainable supply chains.

9. REPORTING AND COMMUNICATION OF SUSTAINABILITY METRICS

9.1 Sustainability Reporting Standards and Frameworks

The Global Reporting Initiative (GRI) is widely acknowledged as a framework for sustainability reporting (Moggi, 2023). It offers a structured method for reporting on different facets of supply chain sustainability, encompassing environmental, social, and economic aspects. By employing GRI, organizations can effectively convey their sustainability performance to stakeholders, thereby enhancing transparency and accountability.

For supply chain sustainability, ISO standards 14001 and 45001 are of paramount importance. ISO 14001 guides environmental management systems, assisting organizations in reducing their environmental footprint and complying with regulations (Waxin, 2023). On the other hand, ISO 45001 centres on occupational health and safety, prioritizing the well-being of workers within supply chain operations. Adherence to these standards signifies a dedication to sustainable practices and risk mitigation. The Carbon Disclosure Project (CDP) framework encourages businesses to disclose environmental impact data, such as carbon emissions and water consumption (Tavanti, 2023). This disclosure fosters transparency in supply chains, facilitates benchmarking, and aids organizations in pinpointing areas for enhancement, especially within the realm of sustainability reporting. The United Nations' Sustainable

Development Goals (SDGs) offer a global framework for sustainable development (Sugiawan et al., 2023). Many organizations align their efforts in supply chain sustainability with specific SDGs, such as responsible consumption and production (Goal 12) or clean water and sanitation (Goal 6). This alignment allows organizations to contribute to broader global sustainability objectives while enriching their reporting practices. The Dow Jones Sustainability Indices (DJSI) assess, and rank companies based on their sustainability performance, including supply chain practices (L. Li et al., 2023). Being featured in these indices is a prestigious recognition that can attract socially responsible investors and customers. It serves as an external validation of a company's commitment to sustainability and ethical conduct. The Sustainability Accounting Standards Board (SASB) offers industry-specific sustainability standards, enabling organizations to focus their reporting efforts on the most pertinent sustainability issues within their sector (Goswami et al., 2023). This specificity ensures that sustainability reporting is tailored to the unique challenges and opportunities faced by each industry, enhancing the relevance and accuracy of the information disclosed.

In summary, these six points encompass fundamental aspects of sustainability reporting standards and frameworks in the context of sustainable supply chain management. They encompass a wide array of dimensions, spanning from environmental and social responsibility to industry-specific reporting, assisting organizations in navigating the intricate landscape of sustainability reporting while promoting transparency and accountability.

9.2 Integrated Reporting for Sustainable SCM

Integrated reporting, as elucidated by the International Integrated Reporting Council, represents a comprehensive approach that amalgamates financial, environmental, social, and governance (ESG) data into a unified report (Rendtorff, 2023). This methodology empowers organizations to convey their process of value creation, performance, and influence on diverse stakeholders in a more transparent manner.

For businesses aiming to reduce their ecological footprint, augment social responsibility, and secure enduring profitability, sustainable supply chain management stands as an imperative (Khan et al., 2023). Integrated reporting assumes a central role in propelling these sustainability objectives forward. It empowers companies to furnish a holistic portrayal of their sustainability practices and their integration within supply chain operations. Through the utilization of integrated reporting, businesses can elevate levels of accountability and transparency (Galeone et al., 2023). They can spotlight their unwavering dedication to environmental preservation, social responsibility, and ethical governance. Additionally, integrated reporting aids companies in pinpointing potential sustainability-related risks and opportunities within their supply chains. Furthermore, it amplifies stakeholder engagement (Hamad et al., 2022), facilitating effective communication of sustainability performance to investors, customers, and regulatory entities. This forthright communication fosters trustworthiness and credibility and contributes to the cultivation of robust relationships with an array of stakeholders. The adoption of integrated reporting for sustainable supply chain management aligns seamlessly with globally recognized sustainability frameworks, including the United Nations Sustainable Development Goals and the Global Reporting Initiative (Subramaniam et al., 2023). These frameworks underscore the significance of transparency, accountability, and sustainable practices in the realm of business operations.

In summation, integrated reporting emerges as a potent tool for organizations dedicated to achieving sustainability in supply chain management. By amalgamating financial, environmental, social, and governance information into a unified report, businesses can enhance transparency, accountability, stakeholder engagement, and sustainability performance. The embrace of integrated reporting not only harmonizes with worldwide sustainability frameworks but also contributes to the enduring success and resilience of businesses in an increasingly sustainability-conscious world.

9.3 Communicating Sustainability Performance to Stakeholders

Effective communication of sustainability performance within Supply Chain Management (SCM) starts with the identification and engagement of stakeholders (Siems et al., 2022). These stakeholders encompass employees, customers, investors, and the communities affected by the supply chain. Their active involvement is indispensable for assessing and enhancing sustainability initiatives. Stakeholder engagement revolves around the active inclusion of individuals with an interest in or influence on a company's sustainability endeavours. This engagement can manifest in various ways, such as surveys, meetings, and feedback mechanisms. By engaging stakeholders, companies gain invaluable insights, foster trust, and ensure that their sustainability initiatives align with the expectations of these critical groups. Transparency serves as a foundational principle in communication within SCM (Sunmola & Burgess, 2023). It entails the provision of clear, honest, and comprehensive information to stakeholders regarding a company's sustainability endeavours. This practice nurtures trust and accountability. Transparency involves a commitment to openly and candidly discuss both successes and challenges in sustainability performance. It encompasses the disclosure of data related to environmental impact, social responsibility, and ethical practices. Transparent communication establishes credibility and underscores a dedication to addressing sustainability issues. Figure 9 shows reporting and communication of sustainability metric.

Figure 9. Reporting and communication of sustainability metric

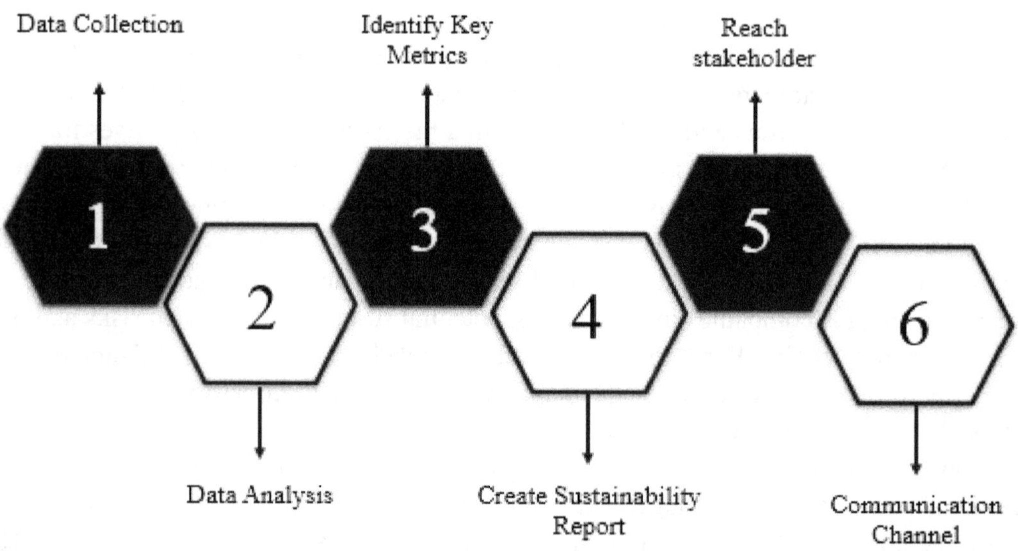

Companies must engage in sustainability reporting, adhering to established standards like the Global Reporting Initiative (GRI) guidelines (Khatri & Kjærland, 2023). This structured approach aids in presenting sustainability performance consistently and comprehensibly. Sustainability reporting entails the collection, analysis, and disclosure of data about a company's environmental, social, and governance (ESG) performance. Adherence to recognized standards like GRI ensures that the information is conveyed in a standardized format, simplifying the task of stakeholders who seek to compare and assess performance across different companies. Effective communication extends to suppliers and partners within the supply chain (Grimm et al., 2022). Collaborative efforts to share sustainability objectives and achievements contribute to overall performance improvement. Collaboration with supply chain partners and suppliers stands as a critical element in achieving sustainability objectives. Through open dialogue about sustainability goals and the sharing of best practices, companies can catalyze positive changes throughout the entire supply chain, minimizing environmental impact and promoting responsible practices. The integration of technology facilitates real-time tracking and sharing of sustainability data, rendering communication more dynamic (A. A. Khan et al., 2023). Technologies like data analytics, Internet of Things (IoT) sensors, and supply chain management software empower companies to gather and disseminate sustainability data in real time. This not only enhances reporting accuracy but also enables immediate responses to issues and opportunities, elevating overall sustainability performance. Consumers exert substantial influence in sustainability-focused communication (Lu & Tian, 2023). Companies should emphasize how their products or services align with consumers' sustainability expectations. In today's marketplace, consumers exhibit a growing awareness of sustainability issues. To resonate with environmentally and socially conscious consumers, companies should communicate how their offerings contribute to sustainability objectives. This may encompass information about eco-friendly materials, responsible sourcing, and ethical production practices, all of which can attract and retain environmentally conscious customers.

Incorporating these six points into a sustainable supply chain management strategy not only enhances a company's environmental and social performance but also forges trust and credibility with stakeholders, nurturing long-term sustainability and success. In conclusion, the communication of sustainability performance in Sustainable Supply Chain Management is essential for achieving environmental and social objectives. Transparency, stakeholder engagement, adherence to standards, and the utilization of technology are pivotal facets of effective communication. Through these endeavours, companies can build trust, bolster their reputation, and contribute to a more sustainable future.

10. FUTURE TRENDS AND RESEARCH DIRECTIONS IN SUSTAINABILITY METRICS FOR INDUSTRY 4.0 SCM

10.1 Evolving Industry 4.0 Technologies and Their Impact on Sustainability Measurement

Automation, a central element of Industry 4.0, utilizes smart sensors and actuators to optimize machinery performance (Czeczot et al., 2023). This technology plays a pivotal role in significantly curbing energy consumption and resource wastage. Through process automation and real-time adjustments, businesses can substantially reduce their carbon footprint. For instance, in manufacturing facilities, smart thermostats can precisely regulate heating and cooling systems, conserving energy and reducing operational expenses. Advanced data analytics tools empower businesses to monitor resource usage in real time (Wolniak, 2023). This data-driven approach entails the collection and analysis of extensive data sets to pinpoint inefficiencies and opportunities for sustainable practices. For example, data analytics can unveil instances of energy waste within a factory, allowing for targeted enhancements that result in resource preservation and cost reduction. Industry 4.0 technologies assume a pivotal role in advancing the concept of the circular economy. IoT sensors and interconnected devices facilitate the tracking and recycling of materials throughout their lifecycle (Rane et al., 2023). This approach allows for the reuse or repurposing of products and materials, thereby reducing waste and fostering a more sustainable and environmentally friendly approach to manufacturing. For instance, sensors can monitor the condition of machine components and determine when refurbishment is preferable to disposal. IoT-connected devices also play a vital role in monitoring and mitigating carbon emissions (Mohanasundaram et al., 2023). By continuously collecting emissions data, companies can establish emission reduction targets and ensure compliance with environmental regulations. Real-time monitoring enables swift responses to deviations, resulting in minimized emissions. This not only benefits the environment but also enhances a company's reputation as an environmentally responsible entity.

Industry 4.0 technologies enhance transparency and sustainability within the supply chain (Su et al., 2023). For instance, blockchain technology offers an immutable ledger for tracing the origins and carbon footprint of products across the supply chain. This transparency empowers consumers and businesses to make informed choices, favouring products with environmentally responsible supply chains. Furthermore, it aids in identifying and rectifying inefficiencies within the supply chain, thus reducing waste and resource consumption.

These five points underscore how Industry 4.0 technologies are driving substantial changes in sustainability measurement, leading to more efficient and environmentally conscious industrial processes. By embracing these technologies, businesses can not only enhance their profitability but also make positive contributions to global sustainability objectives. In conclusion, Industry 4.0 technologies wield a transformative influence on sustainability measurement, empowering businesses to optimize resource utilization, diminish emissions, and bolster supply chain transparency. As these technologies continue to evolve, their role in sustainability measurement will become increasingly critical. Organizations that embrace Industry 4.0 not only reap the benefits of heightened operational efficiency but also actively contribute to environmental and social sustainability.

10.1 Advances in Data Analytics and Artificial Intelligence for Sustainable SCM

In recent years, there has been significant progress in incorporating data analytics and artificial intelligence (AI) into the field of supply chain management. This integration often denoted as Advances in Data Analytics and Artificial Intelligence for Sustainable Supply Chain Management, has brought about a profound transformation in how businesses handle their supply chain operations.

One of the most noteworthy developments in sustainable supply chain management, facilitated by data analytics and AI, is the enhancement of forecasting (Kashem et al., 2023). Firms can now scrutinize extensive historical data to predict future demand patterns with greater precision. Consequently, they can foresee fluctuations in customer demand and adapt their production and inventory management strategies accordingly. This not only results in reduced surplus inventory but also mitigates the risk of stockouts, ultimately leading to cost savings and heightened customer satisfaction. AI-powered algorithms take inventory management to the next level by considering various factors such as seasonality, market trends, and supplier performance (Ahmed, 2023). These algorithms continuously fine-tune inventory levels, ensuring that businesses maintain optimal stock quantities to meet demand without overstocking. This not only diminishes carrying costs but also curbs wastage since products are less likely to become obsolete or expire. The amalgamation of IoT sensors and AI algorithms furnishes real-time visibility into every facet of the supply chain (Kumari & Lele, 2023). This empowers companies to monitor product movement, assess their condition, evaluate equipment performance, and even gauge the environmental impact of transportation in real time. Armed with this timely insight, companies can make informed decisions on the fly, swiftly responding to disruptions such as delays or quality issues, thereby enhancing supply chain resilience.

Sustainable supply chain management also reaps the benefits of AI-driven routing algorithms (Ayoubi et al., 2023). These algorithms factor in environmental considerations like emissions and fuel consumption when determining the most efficient transportation routes. By opting for eco-friendly routes, companies can reduce their carbon footprint, and align their operations with sustainability objectives, all while potentially trimming transportation costs. Data analytics plays a pivotal role in pinpointing sustainable sourcing alternatives (Benzidia et al., 2023). Firms can scrutinize the environmental and ethical impact of their suppliers, ensuring compliance with sustainability standards. This not only burns a company's reputation but also diminishes the risk of supply chain disruptions related to ethical lapses or regulatory non-compliance. AI-powered predictive maintenance transcends mere efficiency gains in the supply chain; it can substantially curtail downtime and maintenance expenditures (Balasubramanian et al., 2023). By analyzing equipment data, AI can forecast when machinery is likely to fail and schedule maintenance proactively. This not only augments equipment reliability but also prolongs its lifespan, reducing the need for frequent replacements and minimizing the environmental footprint.

This signifies a paradigm shift in supply chain management, ushering in opportunities for cost reduction, heightened efficiency, and environmental responsibility. As these technologies continue to evolve, companies that embrace them are poised to secure a competitive edge in today's global marketplace. Nonetheless, it is imperative to address ethical concerns and data security issues associated with the utilization of AI and data analytics in supply chain management. In conclusion, the fusion of data analytics and AI in supply chain management, as exemplified in E10.2, is reshaping how companies conduct their supply chain operations. These advancements offer a comprehensive approach to sustainability by cutting waste, emissions, and operational expenses, all while elevating customer satisfaction and risk management.

Figure 10. Future treads of industry 5.0

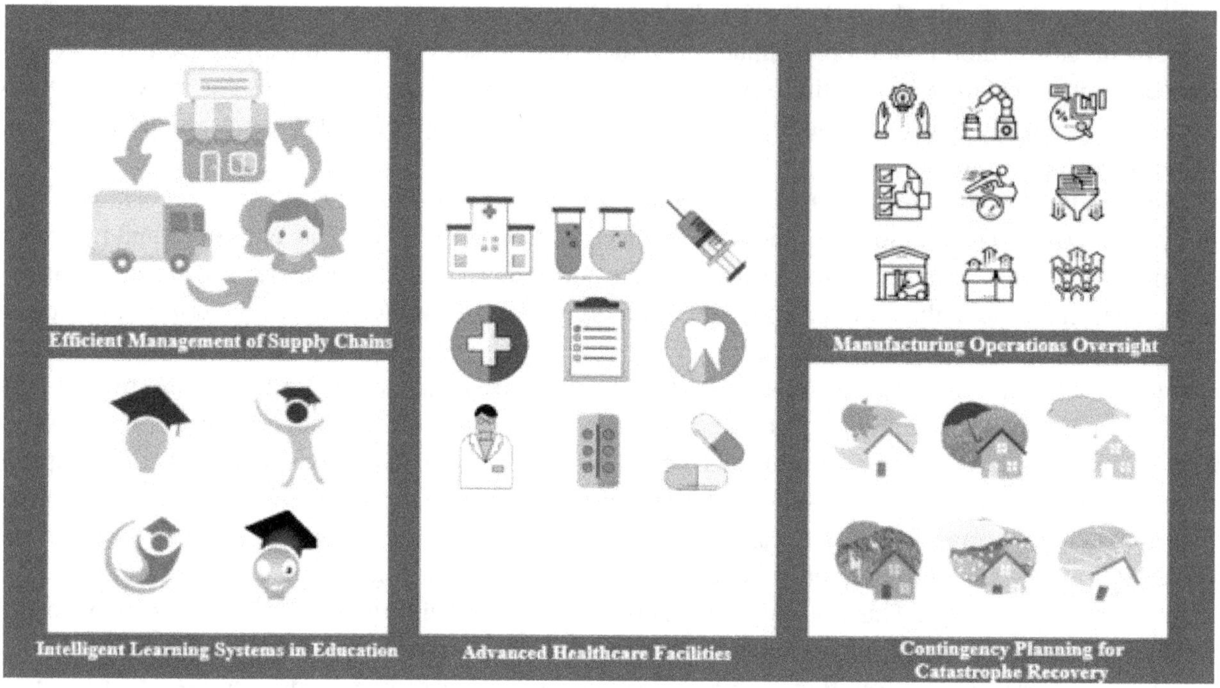

10.3 Addressing Challenges and Gaps in Sustainability Metrics

Sustainability metrics need to account for the unique priorities of specific industries while still maintaining universal indicators. For instance, when assessing environmental metrics, an automotive manufacturer may prioritize reducing emissions, whereas a food producer may focus on minimizing food waste. Companies need to tailor their metrics to align with the sustainability objectives of their respective sectors. The reliability of sustainability data holds paramount importance for making well-informed decisions (Y. Chen et al., 2023). Collaborative efforts between the public and private sectors can play a pivotal role in ensuring the accuracy and accessibility of data. Technologies like blockchain and IoT can streamline the processes of collecting and verifying data, enhancing data integrity. Sustainability metrics should also strike a balance between short-term gains and long-term sustainability (Salim, 2023). Companies can achieve this equilibrium by incorporating lifecycle assessments (LCAs) into their metrics. LCAs take into account the entire lifespan of a product, from production to disposal, promoting sustainable practices that endure over time. Engaging with stakeholders is another critical aspect of obtaining a holistic view of sustainability (Dessart & Standaert, 2023). Initiatives focused on transparency and the utilization of collaborative platforms facilitate communication with suppliers, customers, and other stakeholders. This fosters a shared sense of responsibility for sustainability across the supply chain. Small and medium-sized enterprises (SMEs) often grapple with the financial burden of measuring sustainability. Governments can incentivize the adoption of sustainable practices among SMEs by offering tax breaks or subsidies, making it economically feasible for them to integrate sustainability measures into their operations (Wasiq et al., 2023). Furthermore, sustainability metrics should encourage a continuous commitment to improvement and innovation. Companies can drive innovation by incorporating sustainability goals into performance evaluations and reward systems. This approach motivates employees to seek out innovative and sustainable solutions in their daily work (Albloushi et al., 2022).

In conclusion, addressing the challenges and gaps in sustainability metrics within supply chain management is pivotal for organizations striving to make meaningful contributions to a more sustainable future. By considering sector-specific requirements, improving data collection methods, engaging stakeholders, and fostering innovation, companies can develop effective sustainability metrics that align with their supply chain operations.

11. CONCLUSION

11.1 Summary of Sustainability Metrics and Measurement in Industry 4.0-Enabled SCM

Businesses in the world are not only focusing on profits but also on being environmentally and socially responsible. This shift towards sustainability has become even more critical in the context of Industry 4.0-enabled supply chain management. Industry 4.0, characterized by the integration of digital technologies into manufacturing and supply chain processes, offers new opportunities for measuring and improving sustainability. One of the key aspects of sustainability in Industry 4.0-enabled supply chains is the measurement of environmental impact. This includes tracking energy consumption, greenhouse gas emissions, and resource usage. With the help of advanced sensors and data analytics, companies can monitor these metrics in real time. By doing so, they can identify areas where they can reduce their environmental footprint, such as optimizing transportation routes to minimize fuel consumption. Social sustainability is another crucial dimension. This involves assessing labour conditions, worker safety, and the impact on local communities. In Industry 4.0, monitoring and ensuring fair labour practices are facilitated through data-driven systems. Companies can use metrics like employee turnover rates and workplace safety incidents to gauge their social responsibility performance. Moreover, economic sustainability is a core concern. It involves evaluating the financial viability of supply chain operations while considering long-term profitability. Industry 4.0 technologies enable better cost control, forecasting, and risk management. By measuring financial metrics like return on investment and total cost of ownership, businesses can make informed decisions that balance short-term gains with long-term sustainability. The integration of sustainability metrics into Industry 4.0 systems allows for continuous improvement. Companies can set targets, track progress, and adjust strategies accordingly. This data-driven approach empowers businesses to make informed decisions that align with their sustainability goals.

In conclusion, Industry 4.0-enabled supply chain management offers new avenues for measuring and improving sustainability. By monitoring environmental, social, and economic metrics, companies can enhance their environmental responsibility, promote fair labour practices, and ensure long-term profitability. Embracing sustainability in Industry 4.0 is not only good for the planet and people but also for the bottom line. This chapter highlights the importance of sustainability metrics in Industry 4.0-enabled supply chain management, emphasizing their role in achieving a more responsible and prosperous future for businesses and society.

11.2 Recommendations for Effective Sustainable SCM in Industry 4.0

To ensure sustainability in this new era, companies need to adopt effective practices. Here are some straightforward recommendations for achieving sustainable supply chain management in Industry 4.0. In Industry 4.0, technology is a game-changer. By adopting advanced technologies like IoT and AI, companies can gain real-time insights into their supply chains. For instance, IoT sensors on products can track their location, temperature, and condition throughout the journey. AI can analyze this data to predict maintenance needs, reducing downtime and enhancing efficiency. Blockchain technology ensures the transparency and security of transactions across the supply chain. Embracing these technologies not only streamlines operations but also supports sustainability by reducing waste, energy consumption, and emissions. Collaboration and data sharing are vital in the modern supply chain. When companies collaborate with suppliers, partners, and customers, they can share crucial information, such as demand forecasts and inventory levels. This collaborative approach allows for better demand planning, which, in turn, reduces the overproduction of goods and unnecessary transportation, minimizing the carbon footprint. By working together and sharing data, businesses can collectively optimize their supply chains and reduce environmental impact.

Energy efficiency is not only about saving costs but also about reducing the carbon footprint. Companies can prioritize energy-efficient practices by optimizing their manufacturing processes and transportation routes. For example, upgrading machinery to more energy-efficient models, implementing energy management systems, and using renewable energy sources can significantly reduce energy consumption. This not only lowers greenhouse gas emissions but also positions the company as environmentally responsible. Sustainable sourcing involves selecting suppliers that adhere to ethical and environmentally friendly practices. This means evaluating suppliers not only based on cost but also their commitment to fair labour conditions, responsible resource extraction, and reduced environmental impact. Sustainable sourcing supports the reduction of deforestation, habitat destruction, and human rights violations associated with some supply chains. By sourcing responsibly, companies can contribute to global sustainability efforts. A circular economy approach emphasizes product longevity and recyclability. Companies can design products with durability in mind, making them easier to repair and refurbish. Additionally, they can establish take-back programs to recover and recycle materials from end-of-life products. By adopting a circular economy model, companies minimize waste and reduce the demand for new resources, ultimately lessening their environmental footprint. In today's world, supply chains are vulnerable to various risks, including climate-related events, geopolitical issues, and global health crises. Effective risk management involves identifying potential disruptions and developing contingency plans. By proactively addressing these risks, companies can ensure the resilience of their supply chains and minimize the negative environmental impacts that disruptions can cause. To successfully implement sustainability initiatives and leverage new technologies, employees need the right skills and knowledge. Providing training and education programs can empower the workforce to adapt to Industry 4.0 changes and contribute to sustainability efforts. Skilled employees can identify opportunities for innovation, energy savings, and process improvements, driving positive environmental outcomes.

Communicating sustainability efforts to consumers is essential. When consumers are aware of a company's commitment to sustainability, they can make informed choices. Transparent communication about sustainable sourcing, product recyclability, and environmental initiatives can attract eco-conscious customers and enhance the company's reputation. Moreover, consumer demand for sustainable products can drive positive changes throughout the supply chain as companies respond to market preferences.

In Industry 4.0, sustainable supply chain management is crucial for long-term success. By embracing technology, fostering collaboration, prioritizing sustainability, and continuously improving processes, businesses can reduce their environmental footprint and thrive in a rapidly changing landscape. These recommendations offer a practical guide for achieving effective sustainable supply chain management in the digital age.

REFERENCES

Aadil, F., Mehmood, B., Hasan, N. U., Lim, S., Ejaz, S., & Jhanjhi, N. Z. (2021). Remote health monitoring using IoT-Based Smart Wireless Body Area Network. *Computers, Materials & Continua*, *68*(2), 2499–2513. doi:10.32604/cmc.2021.014647

Achibane, M., & Errahoui, A. (2023). Predicting the future value of gold: A time series approach. Zenodo *(CERN European Organization for Nuclear Research)*. doi:10.5281/zenodo.8023613

Adu-Gyamfi, G., Asamoah, A. N., Nketiah, E., Obuobi, B., Adjei, M., Cudjoe, D., & Zhu, B. (2023). Reducing waste management challenges: Empirical assessment of waste sorting intention among corporate employees in Ghana. *Journal of Retailing and Consumer Services*, *72*, 103261. doi:10.1016/j.jretconser.2023.103261

Adwiyah, R., Syaukat, Y., Indrawan, D., & Mulyati, H. (2023). Examining Sustainable Supply Chain Management (SSCM) Performance in the Palm Oil Industry with the Triple Bottom Line Approach. *Sustainability (Basel)*, *15*(18), 13362. doi:10.3390/su151813362

Ahmed, A. (2023). Artificial Intelligence's Integration in Supply Chain Management: A Comprehensive Review. *ResearchGate*. https://www.researchgate.net/publication/372965863_Artificial_Intelligence%27s_Integration_in_Supply_Chain_Management_A_Comprehensive_Review

Ajani, Y. A. (2023). Adoption of robots in open and distance learning university libraries: A Global Overview based on review of literature. *Journal of Library & Information Services in Distance Learning*, *17*(3-4), 1–22. doi:10.1080/1533290X.2023.2234359

AlAdwani, H. (2023). A Systematic Review of IoT integration on health monitoring System. *International Journal of Engineering and Management Research*, *13*(1), 50–59. doi:10.31033/ijemr.13.1.6

Albloushi, B., Alharmoodi, A., Jabeen, F., Mehmood, K., & Farouk, S. (2022). Total quality management practices and corporate sustainable development in manufacturing companies: The mediating role of green innovation. *Management Research Review*, *46*(1), 20–45. doi:10.1108/MRR-03-2021-0194

Ali, I., Fukofuka, P. T., & Narayan, A. K. (2023). Critical reflections on sustainability reporting standard setting. *Sustainability Accounting. Management and Policy Journal*, *14*(4), 776–791. doi:10.1108/SAMPJ-01-2022-0054

Ali, I., Jhanjhi, N. Z., Amsaad, F., & Razaque, A. (2022). The role of Cutting-Edge Technologies in Industry 4.0. In Chapman and Hall/CRC eBooks (pp. 97–109). doi:10.1201/9781003203087-4

Almusaylim, Z. A., & Jhanjhi, N. Z. (2018). A review on smart home present state and challenges: Linked to context-awareness internet of things (IoT). *Wireless Networks*, *25*(6), 3193–3204. doi:10.1007/s11276-018-1712-5

Alshammari, M. O., Almulhem, A. A., & Jhanjhi, N. Z. (2017). Internet of Things (IoT) : Charity automation. *International Journal of Advanced Computer Science and Applications*, *8*(2). Advance online publication. doi:10.14569/IJACSA.2017.080222

Amosse, F., Kinshella, M. W., Boene, H., Sharma, S., Nhamirre, Z., Tchavana, C., Magee, L. A., Von Dadelszen, P., Sevene, E., Vidler, M., & Munguambe, K. (2023). The development and implementation of a community engagement strategy to improve maternal health in southern Mozambique. *PLOS Global Public Health*, *3*(1), e0001106. doi:10.1371/journal.pgph.0001106 PMID:36962956

Ananna, F. F., Nowreen, R., Jahwari, S. S. R. A., Costa, E., Angeline, L., & Sindiramutty, S. R. (2023). Analysing Influential factors in student academic achievement: Prediction modelling and insight. *International Journal of Emerging Multidisciplinaries Computer Science & Artificial Intelligence*, *2*(1). Advance online publication. doi:10.54938/ijemdcsai.2023.02.1.254

Atta, K. K., Aeri, M., Grover, A., Agarwal, J., Kumar, P., & Raghu, T. (2023). Secured supply chain management system for fisheries through IoT. *Measurement. Sensors*, *25*, 100632. doi:10.1016/j.measen.2022.100632

Attaoui, Z. E. (2023). Impact of the implementation of the Lean Six Sigma process within Moroccan environmental SMEs. *E3S Web of Conferences, 412*, 01051. doi:10.1051/e3sconf/202341201051

Ayoubi, H., Tabaa, Y., & Kharrim, M. E. (2023). Artificial intelligence in green management and the rise of digital lean for sustainable efficiency. *E3S Web of Conferences, 412*, 01053. doi:10.1051/e3sconf/202341201053

Azam, H., Dulloo, M. I., Majeed, M. H., Wan, J. P. H., Xin, L. T., & Sindiramutty, S. R. (2023). Cybercrime Unmasked: Investigating cases and digital evidence. *International Journal of Emerging Multidisciplinaries Computer Science & Artificial Intelligence*, *2*(1). Advance online publication. doi:10.54938/ijemdcsai.2023.02.1.255

Azam, H., Dulloo, M. I., Majeed, M. H., Wan, J. P. H., Xin, L. T., Tajwar, M. A., & Sindiramutty, S. R. (2023). Defending the Digital Frontier: IDPS and the Battle Against Cyber Threat. *International Journal of Emerging Multidisciplinaries: Computer Science*, *2*(1). Advance online publication. doi:10.54938/ijemdcsai.2023.02.1.253

Azam, H., Tajwar, M. A., Mayhialagan, S., Davis, A. J., Yik, C. J., Ali, D., & Sindiramutty, S. R. (2023). Innovations in Security: A study of cloud Computing and IoT. *International Journal of Emerging Multidisciplinaries Computer Science & Artificial Intelligence*, *2*(1). Advance online publication. doi:10.54938/ijemdcsai.2023.02.1.252

AzamH.TanM.PinL. T.SyahmiM. A.QianA. L. W.JingyanH.UddinH.SindiramuttyS. R. (2023). Wireless Technology Security and Privacy: A Comprehensive Study. Preprints. doi:10.20944/preprints202311.0664.v1

Bach, M. P., Topalović, A., Krstić, Ž., & Ivec, A. (2023). Predictive Maintenance in Industry 4.0 for the SMEs: A Decision Support System case Study using Open-Source Software. *Designs*, *7*(4), 98. doi:10.3390/designs7040098

Baig, S. A. (2023, May 16). *Examining the role of diversity and inclusion in modern human resource Management: Best practices and challenges*. http://asmarapublications.com/journals/index.php/PMS/article/view/9

Balasubramanian, S., Shukla, V., & Kavanancheeri, L. (2023). Improving Supply Chain Sustainability Using Artificial Intelligence: Evidence from the Manufacturing Sector. In Environmental footprints and eco-design of products and processes (pp. 43–59). doi:10.1007/978-981-99-4894-9_4

Barbhuiya, S., & Das, B. (2023). Life Cycle Assessment of construction materials: Methodologies, applications and future directions for sustainable decision-making. *Case Studies in Construction Materials*, *19*, e02326. doi:10.1016/j.cscm.2023.e02326

Begum, K. (2023, August 30). *Health care data privacy and Compliance: Navigating Regulatory landscape*. Central Asian Journal of Medical and Natural Science - Central Asian Studies. https://cajmns.centralasianstudies.org/index.php/CAJMNS/article/view/1758

Bharadiya, J. (2023). Machine learning and AI in Business intelligence: Trends and opportunities. *ResearchGate*. https://www.researchgate.net/publication/371902170_Machine_Learning_and_AI_in_Business_Intelligence_Trends_and_Opportunities

Bilderback, S. (2023). Integrating training for organizational sustainability: The application of Sustainable Development Goals globally. *European Journal of Training and Development*. Advance online publication. doi:10.1108/EJTD-01-2023-0005

Broadhead, J. (2023). *The role of nonprofit housing developers in addressing the affordable housing crisis: A case study of LInC Housing*. DigitalCommons@CalPoly. https://digitalcommons.calpoly.edu/cmsp/704/

Buonomano, A., Del Papa, G., Giuzio, G. F., Palombo, A., & Russo, G. (2023). Future pathways for decarbonization and energy efficiency of ports: Modelling and optimization as sustainable energy hubs. *Journal of Cleaner Production*, *138389*. Advance online publication. doi:10.1016/j.jclepro.2023.138389

Butt, A. S., Ali, I., & Govindan, K. (2023). The role of reverse logistics in a circular economy for achieving sustainable development goals: A multiple case study of retail firms. *Production Planning and Control*, 1–13. doi:10.1080/09537287.2023.2197851

Castillo, M., Monroy, R., & Ahmad, R. (2022). Scientometric analysis and systematic review of smart manufacturing technologies applied to the 3D printing polymer material extrusion system. *Journal of Intelligent Manufacturing*. Advance online publication. doi:10.1007/s10845-022-02049-1

Chan, A. (2022). GPT-3 and InstructGPT: Technological dystopianism, utopianism, and "Contextual" perspectives in AI ethics and industry. *AI and Ethics*, *3*(1), 53–64. doi:10.1007/s43681-022-00148-6

Chandan, A., John, M., & Potdar, V. (2023). Achieving UN SDGs in food supply chain using blockchain technology. *Sustainability (Basel)*, *15*(3), 2109. doi:10.3390/su15032109

Charfeddine, L., & Umlai, M. I. (2023). ICT sector, digitization and environmental sustainability: A systematic review of the literature from 2000 to 2022. *Renewable & Sustainable Energy Reviews*, *184*, 113482. doi:10.1016/j.rser.2023.113482

Chen, X., He, C., Chen, Y., & Xie, Z. (2022). Internet of Things (IoT)—Blockchain-enabled pharmaceutical supply chain resilience in the post-pandemic era. *Frontiers of Engineering Management*, *10*(1), 82–95. doi:10.1007/s42524-022-0233-1

Chen, X. H., Tee, K., Elnahass, M., & Ahmed, R. R. (2023). Assessing the environmental impacts of renewable energy sources: A case study on air pollution and carbon emissions in China. *Journal of Environmental Management*, *345*, 118525. doi:10.1016/j.jenvman.2023.118525 PMID:37421726

Chen, Y., Zhao, K., Liu, G. G., & Chen, W. (2023). Health technology assessment to inform decision making in China: Progress, challenges, and sustainability. *BMJ (Clinical Research Ed.)*, *068910*. Advance online publication. doi:10.1136/bmj-2021-068910 PMID:37321607

Chohan, I. M., Ahmad, A., Sallih, N., Bheel, N., Ali, M., & Deifalla, A. F. (2023). A review on life cycle assessment of different pipeline materials. *Results in Engineering*, *19*, 101325. doi:10.1016/j.rineng.2023.101325

Chu, L. K., Doğan, B., Abakah, E. J. A., Ghosh, S., & Albeni, M. (2022). Impact of economic policy uncertainty, geopolitical risk, and economic complexity on carbon emissions and ecological footprint: An investigation of the E7 countries. *Environmental Science and Pollution Research International*, *30*(12), 34406–34427. doi:10.1007/s11356-022-24682-2 PMID:36512279

Costa, F., Frecassetti, S., Rossini, M., & Staudacher, A. P. (2023). Industry 4.0 digital technologies enhancing sustainability: Applications and barriers from the agricultural industry in an emerging economy. *Journal of Cleaner Production*, *408*, 137208. doi:10.1016/j.jclepro.2023.137208

CronaB.ParlatoG.LadeS. J.FetzerI.MausV. (2023). Going beyond carbon: An "Earth System Impact" score to better capture corporate and investment impacts on the Earth system. *Social Science Research Network*. doi:10.2139/ssrn.4495331

Czeczot, G., Rojek, I., Mikołajewski, D., & Sangho, B. (2023). AI in IIoT Management of Cybersecurity for Industry 4.0 and Industry 5.0 Purposes. *Electronics (Basel)*, *12*(18), 3800. doi:10.3390/electronics12183800

Dadaneh, D. Z., Moradi, S., & Alizadeh, B. (2023). Simultaneous planning of purchase orders, production, and inventory management under demand uncertainty. *International Journal of Production Economics*, *109012*, 109012. Advance online publication. doi:10.1016/j.ijpe.2023.109012

Daiyoub, A., Gelabert, P., Saura-Mas, S., & Vega-García, C. (2023). War and Deforestation: Using Remote Sensing and Machine Learning to Identify the War-Induced Deforestation in Syria 2010–2019. *Land (Basel)*, *12*(8), 1509. doi:10.3390/land12081509

DasS. (2023). Digital Twin Technology: Enhancing efficiency and Decision-Making in Industry 4.0. *Social Science Research Network*. doi:10.2139/ssrn.4459204

De Lima, F. A., & Seuring, S. (2023). A Delphi study examining risk and uncertainty management in circular supply chains. *International Journal of Production Economics, 258,* 108810. doi:10.1016/j.ijpe.2023.108810

De Souza Miguel, P. L., & Tonelli, M. J. (2022). Supplier diversity for socially responsible purchasing: An empirical investigation in Brazil. *International Journal of Physical Distribution & Logistics Management, 53*(1), 93–114. doi:10.1108/IJPDLM-09-2021-0407

Debnath, B., Shakur, M. S., Bari, A. M., Saha, J. K., Porna, W. A., Mishu, M. J., Islam, A. R. M. T., & Rahman, M. (2023). Assessing the critical success factors for implementing industry 4.0 in the pharmaceutical industry: Implications for supply chain sustainability in emerging economies. *PLoS One, 18*(6), e0287149. doi:10.1371/journal.pone.0287149 PMID:37319165

Despeisse, M., Johansson, B., Bokrantz, J., Braun, G., Chari, A., Chen, X., Fang, Q., Chávez, C. G., Skoogh, A., Stahre, J., Mathew, N. T., Bekar, E. T., Wang, H., & Örtengren, R. (2023). Battery production Systems: state of the art and future developments. In IFIP advances in information and communication technology (pp. 521–535). doi:10.1007/978-3-031-43688-8_36

Dessart, L., & Standaert, W. (2023). Strategic storytelling in the age of sustainability. *Business Horizons, 66*(3), 371–385. doi:10.1016/j.bushor.2023.01.005

Dharmayanti, N., Ismail, T., Hanifah, I. A., & Taqi, M. (2023). Exploring Sustainability Management Control System and Eco-Innovation Matter Sustainable Financial Performance: The role of Supply Chain Management and Digital Adaptability in Indonesian context. *Journal of Open Innovation, 100119*(3), 100119. Advance online publication. doi:10.1016/j.joitmc.2023.100119

Duarte, S., Cabrita, M. D. R., & Cruz-Machado, V. (2023). Green Supply Chain Practices: Toward A Sustainable Industry Development. *E3S Web of Conferences, 409,* 01004. doi:10.1051/e3sconf/202340901004

Dubbert, C., Abdulai, A., & Mohammed, S. (2021). Contract farming and the adoption of sustainable farm practices: Empirical evidence from cashew farmers in Ghana. *Applied Economic Perspectives and Policy, 45*(1), 487–509. doi:10.1002/aepp.13212

Efe, A. (2023). *An assessment on the problems and possible solutions of artificial intelligence tools and techniques on execution, monitoring and reporting of impact investments.* Girişimcilik İnovasyon Ve Pazarlama Araştırmaları Dergisi., doi:10.31006/gipad.1263598

Eldem, B., Kluczek, A., & Baginski, J. P. (2022). The COVID-19 Impact on Supply Chain Operations of Automotive Industry: A Case study of Sustainability 4.0 based on Sense–ADApt–Transform Framework. *Sustainability (Basel), 14*(10), 5855. doi:10.3390/su14105855

EpendiU.RochimA. F.WibowoA. (2023). An Assessment Model for Sustainability City Using Crowdsourced Data Based on General System Theory: A Design Science Methodology Approach. *Preprintprints.org*. doi:10.20944/preprints202309.0349.v1

Fan, P., Song, Y., Fang, M., & Chen, X. (2023). Creating an age-inclusive workplace: The impact of HR practices on employee work engagement. *Journal of Management & Organization, 29*(6), 1–19. doi:10.1017/jmo.2023.18

Fang, B., Yu, J., Chen, Z., Osman, A. I., Farghali, M., Ihara, I., Hamza, E., Rooney, D., & Yap, P. (2023). Artificial intelligence for waste management in smart cities: A review. *Environmental Chemistry Letters*, *21*(4), 1959–1989. doi:10.1007/s10311-023-01604-3 PMID:37362015

Galeone, G., Onorato, G., Shini, M., & Dell'Atti, V. (2023). Climate-related financial disclosure in integrated reporting: What is the impact on the business model? The case of Poste Italiane. *Accounting Research Journal*, *36*(1), 21–36. doi:10.1108/ARJ-04-2022-0107

García-Alonso, R., Landeta-Manzano, B., Landín, G. A., & Laskurain-Iturbe, I. (2023). Analysing Barriers to achieving SDG 7. Managing green product development in the wind energy sector. In IFIP advances in information and communication technology (pp. 666–682). doi:10.1007/978-3-031-43688-8_46

Gavai, A., Bouzembrak, Y., Mu, W., Martin, F., Kaliyaperumal, R., Van Soest, J., Choudhury, A., Huang, Z., Dekker, A., & Marvin, H. (2023). Applying federated learning to combat food fraud in food supply chains. *NPJ Science of Food*, *7*(1), 46. Advance online publication. doi:10.1038/s41538-023-00220-3 PMID:37658060

Geiberger, P., Liu, Z., Berg, M., & Domay, C. (2023). *Monitoring energy usage of heavy-haul iron ore trains with on-board energy meter for improving energy efficiency*. Emerald Logo. doi:10.1108/RS-04-2023-0020

Goswami, K., Islam, M., & Evers, W. (2023). A case study on the blended reporting phenomenon: A Comparative analysis of Voluntary Reporting Frameworks and Standards—GRI, IR, SASB, and CDP. *The International Journal of Sustainability Policy and Practice*, *19*(2), 35–64. doi:10.18848/2325-1166/CGP/v19i02/35-64

Grimm, J. H., Hofstetter, J. S., & Sarkis, J. (2022). Corporate sustainability standards in multi-tier supply chains – an institutional entrepreneurship perspective. *International Journal of Production Research*, *61*(14), 4702–4724. doi:10.1080/00207543.2021.2017053

Gu, M. H., Zhang, Y., Li, D., & Huo, B. (2023). The effect of high-involvement human resource management practices on supply chain resilience and operational performance. *Journal of Management Science and Engineering*, *8*(2), 176–190. doi:10.1016/j.jmse.2022.12.001

Guo, W. (2023). Exploring the Role of Information Technology in Implementing Integrated Green Supply Chain Management in China. *DREAM*, *2*(01), 42–48. doi:10.56982/dream.v2i01.111

Hamad, S., Lai, F. W., Shad, M. K., Khatib, S. F. A., & Ali, S. E. A. (2022). Assessing the implementation of sustainable development goals: Does integrated reporting matter? *Sustainability Accounting. Management and Policy Journal*, *14*(1), 49–74. doi:10.1108/SAMPJ-01-2022-0029

Hayat, A., Shahare, V., Sharma, A. K., & Arora, N. (2023). Introduction to industry 4.0. In Studies in big data (pp. 29–59). doi:10.1007/978-981-19-8730-4_2

He, B., & Mao, H. (2023). Digital Twin-Driven Product Sustainable design for low carbon footprint. *Journal of Computing and Information Science in Engineering*, *23*(6), 060805. Advance online publication. doi:10.1115/1.4062427

Hegab, H., Shaban, I. S., Jamil, M., & Khanna, N. (2023). Toward sustainable future: Strategies, indicators, and challenges for implementing sustainable production systems. *Sustainable Materials and Technologies*, *36*, e00617. doi:10.1016/j.susmat.2023.e00617

Ilegab, II., Shaban, I. S., Jamil, M., & Khanna, N. (2023b). Toward sustainable future: Strategies, indicators, and challenges for implementing sustainable production systems. *Sustainable Materials and Technologies*, *36*, e00617. doi:10.1016/j.susmat.2023.e00617

Huang, J., & Yu, S. (2023). A study on global national green GDP accounting based on the System of Integrated Environmental-Economic Accounting. *Highlights in Business. Economics and Management*, *12*, 272–278. doi:10.54097/hbem.v12i.8362

Huffman, M., Wang, Q., & Khan, F. (2023). Analysis of Sustainability Metrics from a Process Design and Operation Perspective. *Process Safety and Environmental Protection*, *177*, 1351–1365. doi:10.1016/j.psep.2023.08.001

Huma, S., Siddiqui, D. A., & Ahmed, W. (2022). Understanding the impact of Green supply chain management practices on operational competitive capabilities. *The TQM Journal*. Advance online publication. doi:10.1108/TQM-08-2021-0246

Humayun, M., Alsaqer, M., & Jhanjhi, N. Z. (2022). Energy optimization for smart cities using IoT. *Applied Artificial Intelligence*, *36*(1), 2037255. Advance online publication. doi:10.1080/08839514.2022.2037255

Humayun, M., Jhanjhi, N., & Alamri, M. Z. (2020). IoT-based Secure and Energy Efficient scheme for E-health applications. *Indian Journal of Science and Technology*, *13*(28), 2833–2848. doi:10.17485/IJST/v13i28.861

Humayun, M., Jhanjhi, N. Z., Alruwaili, M., Amalathas, S. S., Balasubramanian, V., & Selvaraj, B. (2020c). Privacy protection and energy optimization for 5G-Aided industrial internet of things. *IEEE Access : Practical Innovations, Open Solutions*, *8*, 183665–183677. doi:10.1109/ACCESS.2020.3028764

Humayun, M., Jhanjhi, N. Z., Hamid, B., & Ahmed, G. (2020b). Emerging smart logistics and transportation using IoT and blockchain. *IEEE Internet of Things Magazine*, *3*(2), 58–62. doi:10.1109/IOTM.0001.1900097

Hydrogen economy. (2023). In *Elsevier eBooks*. doi:10.1016/C2021-0-01531-5

Ibrahimova, G., & Moog, P. (2023). Colonialism versus independence—The role of entrepreneurial ecosystems in Azerbaijan over time. *Small Business Economics*, *61*(3), 1289–1336. Advance online publication. doi:10.1007/s11187-022-00725-3

Ishak, S. Z., Shaharudin, M. R., Salim, N. A., Zainoddin, A. I., & Deng, Z. (2023). The effect of supply chain adaptive strategies during the COVID-19 pandemic on firm performance in Malaysia's semiconductor industries. *Global Journal of Flexible Systems Managment*, *24*(3), 439–458. doi:10.1007/s40171-023-00347-y

Ismail, S., Reza, H., Salameh, K., Zadeh, H. K., & Vasefi, F. (2023). Toward an Intelligent Blockchain IoT-Enabled fish Supply Chain: A Review and Conceptual framework. *Sensors (Basel)*, *23*(11), 5136. doi:10.3390/s23115136 PMID:37299864

Jabeen, T., Jabeen, I., Ashraf, H., Jhanjhi, N. Z., Yassine, A., & Hossain, M. S. (2023). An intelligent healthcare system using IoT in wireless sensor network. *Sensors (Basel)*, *23*(11), 5055. doi:10.3390/s23115055 PMID:37299782

Jahanger, A., Ozturk, I., Onwe, J. C., Joseph, T. E., & Hossain, M. R. (2023). Do technology and renewable energy contribute to energy efficiency and carbon neutrality? Evidence from top ten manufacturing countries. *Sustainable Energy Technologies and Assessments*, *56*, 103084. doi:10.1016/j.seta.2023.103084

Jain, V., & Kukreja, V. (2023). *Multidisciplinary approaches to sustainable human development*. IGI Global. doi:10.4018/978-1-6684-8223-0

Jenneboer, L., Herrando, C., & Constantinides, E. (2022). The Impact of chatbots on Customer Loyalty: A Systematic literature review. *Journal of Theoretical and Applied Electronic Commerce Research*, *17*(1), 212–229. doi:10.3390/jtaer17010011

Jenssen, M. M., & De Boer, L. (2019). Implementing life cycle assessment in green supplier selection: A systematic review and conceptual model. *Journal of Cleaner Production*, *229*, 1198–1210. doi:10.1016/j.jclepro.2019.04.335

Jhanjhi, N. Z., Humayun, M., & Almuayqil, S. N. (2021). Cyber security and privacy issues in industrial internet of things. *Computer Systems Science and Engineering*, *37*(3), 361–380. doi:10.32604/csse.2021.015206

Jhanjhi, N. Z., Low, T. J., & Alghamdi, T. A. (2015). Enhancing routing energy efficiency of Wireless Sensor Networks. *2015 17th International Conference on Advanced Communication Technology (ICACT)*. 10.1109/ICACT.2015.7224928

Joseph, C., Rahmat, M., Yusuf, S. N. S., Janang, J. T., & Madi, N. (2022). The ethical value disclosure index from the lens of SDG 16 and institutional theory. *International Journal of Ethics and Systems*, *39*(3), 612–628. doi:10.1108/IJOES-05-2021-0109

Kagermann, H. (2014). Change through Digitization—Value Creation in the age of industry 4.0. In Springer eBooks (pp. 23–45). doi:10.1007/978-3-658-05014-6_2

KanhaiyaK. (2023). Leveraging professional roles to foster sustainable development: Contributions to the sustainable development goals in the workplace. *Social Science Research Network*. doi:10.2139/ssrn.4479782

Kanwal, N., Janssen, E. M., & Engan, K. (2023). Balancing privacy and progress in artificial intelligence: Anonymization in histopathology for biomedical research and education. *arXiv (Cornell University)*. https://doi.org//arxiv.2307.09426 doi:10.48550

Kashem, M. A., Shamsuddoha, M., Nasir, T., & Chowdhury, A. A. (2023). Supply Chain Disruption versus Optimization: A Review on Artificial Intelligence and Blockchain. *Knowledge (Beverly Hills, Calif.)*, *3*(1), 80–96. doi:10.3390/knowledge3010007

Kelling, I., & Lawan, I. (2023). Equality, diversity and inclusion: A way forward for aquaculture in Scotland. *Frontiers*, *2*, 1151853. Advance online publication. doi:10.3389/faquc.2023.1151853

Khadem, M. (2023, August 25). *Application of artificial intelligence in supply chain revolutionizing efficiency and optimization*. http://bgsiran.ir/journal/ojs-3.1.1-4/index.php/IJIEOR/article/view/34

Khan, A., Jhanjhi, N. Z., & Humayun, M. (2022). The role of cybersecurity in smart cities. In Chapman and Hall/CRC eBooks (pp. 195–208). doi:10.1201/9781003203087-9

Khan, A. A., Laghari, A. A., Rashid, M., Li, H., Javed, A. R., & Gadekallu, T. R. (2023). Artificial intelligence and blockchain technology for secure smart grid and power distribution Automation: A State-of-the-Art Review. *Sustainable Energy Technologies and Assessments*, *57*, 103282. doi:10.1016/j.seta.2023.103282

Khan, S. R., Tabish, M., & Zhang, Y. (2023). Embracement of industry 4.0 and sustainable supply chain practices under the shadow of practice-based view theory: Ensuring environmental sustainability in corporate sector. *Journal of Cleaner Production*, *398*, 136609. doi:10.1016/j.jclepro.2023.136609

Khan, S. R., Yu, Z., & Farooq, K. (2022). Green capabilities, green purchasing, and triple bottom line performance: Leading toward environmental sustainability. *Business Strategy and the Environment*. Advance online publication. doi:10.1002/bse.3234

Khang, A., Jadhav, B., & Birajdar, S. (2023). Industry Revolution 4.0. In CRC Press eBooks (pp. 11–34). doi:10.1201/9781003357070-2

Khatri, I., & Kjærland, F. (2023). Sustainability reporting practices and environmental performance amongst nordic listed firms. *Journal of Cleaner Production*, *418*, 138172. doi:10.1016/j.jclepro.2023.138172

Kiehle, J., Kopsakangas-Savolainen, M., Hilli, M., & Pongrácz, E. (2023). Carbon footprint at institutions of higher education: The case of the University of Oulu. *Journal of Environmental Management*, *329*, 117056. doi:10.1016/j.jenvman.2022.117056 PMID:36549059

Korucuk, S., Tirkolaee, E. B., Aytekin, A., Karabašević, D., & Karamaşa, Ç. (2023). Agile supply chain management based on critical success factors and most ideal risk reduction strategy in the era of industry 4.0: application to plastic industry. *Operations Management Research*. doi:10.1007/s12063-023-00360-5

Krishnan, S., Thangaveloo, R., Rahman, S. B. A., & Sindiramutty, S. R. (2021). Smart Ambulance Traffic Control system. *Trends in Undergraduate Research*, *4*(1), c28–c34. doi:10.33736/tur.2831.2021

Kumar, A., & Basu, R. (2023). Do eco-labels trigger green product purchase intention among emerging market consumers? *Journal of Indian Business Research*, *15*(3), 466–492. doi:10.1108/JIBR-09-2022-0248

Kumar, A. A., Zaman, U. K. U., & Plapper, P. (2023). Collaborative robots. In CRC Press eBooks (pp. 90–106). doi:10.1201/9781003327523-8

Kumari, S., & Lele, V. (2023). Synergy of CRM and Industry 4.0: Advancing supply chain management and customer experience via digital innovations. *SSRG International Journal of Industrial Engineering*, *10*(1), 20–25. doi:10.14445/23499362/IJIE-V10I1P104

Kumari, S., Sarkar, B., & Singh, G. (2023). Blockchain-based CRM solutions: Securing customer data in the digital transformation era. *International Journal of Computer Trends and Technology*, *71*(4), 27–36. doi:10.14445/22312803/IJCTT-V71I4P105

Le, T. T., Vo, X. V., & Venkatesh, V. (2022). Role of green innovation and supply chain management in driving sustainable corporate performance. *Journal of Cleaner Production*, *374*, 133875. doi:10.1016/j.jclepro.2022.133875

Lee, K. L., & Zhang, T. (2023). Revolutionizing Supply Chains: Unveiling the power of blockchain technology for enhanced transparency and performance. *International Journal of Technology, Innovation and Management*, *3*(1), 19–27. doi:10.54489/ijtim.v3i1.216

Lee, S., Abdullah, A., Jhanjhi, N. Z., & Kok, S. (2021). Classification of botnet attacks in IoT smart factory using honeypot combined with machine learning. *PeerJ*, *7*, e350. doi:10.7717/peerj-cs.350 PMID:33817000

Lenzen, M., Tzeng, M. W., Floerl, O., & Zaiko, A. (2023). Application of multi-region input-output analysis to examine biosecurity risks associated with the global shipping network. *The Science of the Total Environment*, *854*, 158758. doi:10.1016/j.scitotenv.2022.158758 PMID:36113796

Li, L., Zheng, X., & Wang, S. (2023). The Effect of sustainability information disclosure on the cost of equity capital: An empirical analysis based on Gartner Top 50 supply chain rankings. *Journal of Risk and Financial Management*, *16*(8), 358. doi:10.3390/jrfm16080358

Li, M., Li, M., Guo, D., Qu, T., & Guo, D. (2023). Real-Time Data-Driven Out-of-Order synchronization for production and intralogistics in Multiresource-Constrained assembly systems. *IEEE Transactions on Systems, Man, and Cybernetics. Systems*, *53*(12), 1–13. doi:10.1109/TSMC.2023.3298927

Liu, L., Song, W., & Liu, Y. (2023). Leveraging digital capabilities toward a circular economy: Reinforcing sustainable supply chain management with Industry 4.0 technologies. *Computers & Industrial Engineering*, *178*, 109113. doi:10.1016/j.cie.2023.109113

Lu, Y., & Tian, Y. (2023). *Sustainability-Driven consumer experience design of an online retail system for household appliances*. ICST Transactions on Scalable Information Systems. doi:10.4108/eetsis.3331

Lubag, M., Bonifácio, J., Tan, J. M., Concepcion, R. II, Mababangloob, G. R., Galang, J. G., & Maniquiz-Redillas, M. C. (2023). Diversified impacts of enabling a Technology-Intensified agricultural supply chain on the quality of life in hinterland communities. *Sustainability (Basel)*, *15*(17), 12809. doi:10.3390/su151712809

Ly, B. (2023). *Inclusion leadership and employee work engagement: The role of organizational commitment in Cambodian public organization*. Asia-Pacific Management Review. doi:10.1016/j.apmrv.2023.06.003

Manchuri, A. R., Akhila, K., Abu Saleh, A., & Sindiramutty, S. R. (2024). Application of Supervised Machine Learning Models in Biodiesel Production Research - A Short Review. *Borneo Journal of Sciences and Technology*, *6*(1), 96–104. doi:10.35370/bjost.2024.6.1-10

Mao, W., Hu, Y., Yang, X., Ren, W., & Fang, H. (2023). ARE-Platform: An augmented Reality-Based ergonomic evaluation solution for smart manufacturing. *International Journal of Human-Computer Interaction*, 1–16. doi:10.1080/10447318.2023.2173894

Martínez-Falcó, J., Sánchez-García, E., Millan-Tudela, L. A., & Marco-Lajara, B. (2023). The role of green agriculture and green supply chain Management in the Green Intellectual Capital–Sustainable Performance Relationship: A structural equation modeling analysis applied to the Spanish wine industry. *Agriculture*, *13*(2), 425. doi:10.3390/agriculture13020425

Matin, A., Islam, R., Wang, X., Huo, H., & Xu, G. (2023). AIoT for sustainable manufacturing: Overview, challenges, and opportunities. *Internet of Things : Engineering Cyber Physical Human Systems*, *100901*, 100901. Advance online publication. doi:10.1016/j.iot.2023.100901

Meier, S., Klarmann, S., Thielen, N., Pfefferer, C., Kuhn, M., & Franke, J. (2023). A process model for systematically setting up the data basis for data-driven projects in manufacturing. *Journal of Manufacturing Systems*, *71*, 1–19. doi:10.1016/j.jmsy.2023.08.024

Minoofar, A., Gholami, A., Eslami, S., Haji-Zadeh, A., Gholami, A., Zandi, M., Ameri, M., & Kazem, H. A. (2023). Renewable energy system opportunities: A sustainable solution toward cleaner production and reducing carbon footprint of large-scale dairy farms. *Energy Conversion and Management*, *293*, 117554. doi:10.1016/j.enconman.2023.117554

Moggi, S. (2023). Sustainability reporting, universities and global reporting initiative applicability: A still open issue. *Sustainability Accounting. Management and Policy Journal*, *14*(4), 699–742. doi:10.1108/SAMPJ-05-2022-0257

Mohanasundaram, T., Vetrivel, S., & Krishnamoorthy, V. (2023). *Applications of IoTSG in Smart Industrial Monitoring Environments*. Wiley. doi:10.1002/9781119812524.ch12

Mumtaz, R., Amin, A., Khan, M. A., Asif, M., Anwar, Z., & Bashir, M. J. (2023). Impact of green energy transportation systems on urban air quality: A predictive analysis using spatiotemporal deep learning techniques. *Energies*, *16*(16), 6087. doi:10.3390/en16166087

Muzammal, S. M., Murugesan, R. K., & Jhanjhi, N. Z. (2021). A Comprehensive Review on Secure Routing in Internet of Things: Mitigation Methods and Trust-Based Approaches. *IEEE Internet of Things Journal*, *8*(6), 4186–4210. doi:10.1109/JIOT.2020.3031162

Nguyen, A. T., Ha, V. D., Ngo, H. K., Le, N., Khong, P. M., Thi, N. T., Trinh, M. T., Nguyen, T. D., Ngo, T. Q. K., Vu, L. C., Thi, M. L., Le, A. H. T., Tran, B. M., & Nguyen, V. T. (2023). Understanding the importance of Eco-Labeling for organic foods at UNESCO Biosphere Reserves: A case study of the cocoa powder at the Dong Nai, Vietnam. *Sustainability (Basel)*, *15*(12), 9603. doi:10.3390/su15129603

Nguyen, T. T., Grote, U., Neubacher, F., Rahut, D. B., Hung, M. D. O., & Paudel, G. P. (2023). Security risks from climate change and environmental degradation: Implications for sustainable land use transformation in the Global South. *Current Opinion in Environmental Sustainability*, *63*, 101322. doi:10.1016/j.cosust.2023.101322

Nicolosi, A., Laganà, V. R., & Di Gregorio, D. (2023). Habits, Health and Environment in the Purchase of Bakery Products: Consumption Preferences and Sustainable Inclinations before and during COVID-19. *Foods*, *12*(8), 1661. doi:10.3390/foods12081661 PMID:37107456

Niyommaneerat, W., Suwanteep, K., & Chavalparit, O. (2023). Sustainability indicators to achieve a circular economy: A case study of renewable energy and plastic waste recycling corporate social responsibility (CSR) projects in Thailand. *Journal of Cleaner Production*, *391*, 136203. doi:10.1016/j.jclepro.2023.136203

Nova, K. (2023, June 9). *AI-Enabled Water Management Systems: An analysis of system components and interdependencies for water conservation.* https://studies.eigenpub.com/index.php/erst/article/view/12

Nozari, H., & Edalatpanah, S. A. (2023). Smart Systems Risk management in IoT-Based supply chain. In Industrial and applied mathematics (pp. 251–268). doi:10.1007/978-981-19-9909-3_11

Nugroho, A. (2023). *The effect of household income and consumption on family welfare with lifestyle as a moderating variable.* https://doi.org/ doi:10.35335/ijafibs.v11i2.96

Nydrioti, I., & Grigoropoulou, H. (2022). Using the water footprint concept for water use efficiency labelling of consumer products: The Greek experience. *Environmental Science and Pollution Research International*, *30*(8), 19918–19930. doi:10.1007/s11356-022-23573-w PMID:36242669

Ocelik, V., Kolk, A., & Ciulli, F. (2023). Multinational enterprises, Industry 4.0 and sustainability: A multidisciplinary review and research agenda. *Journal of Cleaner Production*, *413*, 137434. doi:10.1016/j.jclepro.2023.137434

Oe, H., Yamaoka, Y., & Duda, K. (2022). How to Sustain Businesses in the Post-COVID-19 Era: A focus on innovation, sustainability and leadership. *Business Ethics and Leadership*, *6*(4), 1–9. doi:10.21272/bel.6(4).1-9.2022

Okogwu, N. C., Agho, N. M. O., Adeyinka, N. M. A., Odulaja, N. B. A., Eyo-Udo, N. N. L., Daraojimba, N. C., & Banso, N. A. (2023). Exploring the integration of sustainable materials in supply chain management for environmental impact. *Engineering Science & Tecnology Journal*, *4*(3), 49–65. doi:10.51594/estj.v4i3.546

Onyeaka, H., Tamasiga, P., Nwauzoma, U. M., Miri, T., Juliet, U. C., Nwaiwu, O., & Akinsemolu, A. A. (2023). Using artificial intelligence to tackle food waste and enhance the circular economy: Maximising resource Efficiency and Minimising Environmental Impact: A review. *Sustainability (Basel)*, *15*(13), 10482. doi:10.3390/su151310482

Palsodkar, M., Yadav, G., & Nagare, M. (2023). Integrating Industry 4.0 and agile new product development practices to evaluate the penetration of sustainable development goals in manufacturing industries. *Journal of Engineering, Design and Technology*. doi:10.1108/JEDT-02-2022-0101

Pata, U. K., Caglar, A. E., Kartal, M. T., & Depren, S. K. (2023). Evaluation of the role of clean energy technologies, human capital, urbanization, and income on the environmental quality in the United States. *Journal of Cleaner Production*, *402*, 136802. doi:10.1016/j.jclepro.2023.136802

Pfaff, Y. M. (2023). Agility and digitalization: Why strategic agility is a success factor for mastering digitalization – evidence from Industry 4.0 implementations across a supply chain. *International Journal of Physical Distribution & Logistics Management, 53*(5/6), 660–684. doi:10.1108/IJPDLM-06-2022-0200

Pivoto, D. G. S., De Almeida, L. F. F., Da Rosa Righi, R., Rodrigues, J. J. P. C., Lugli, A. B., & Alberti, A. M. (2021). Cyber-physical systems architectures for industrial internet of things applications in Industry 4.0: A literature review. *Journal of Manufacturing Systems, 58*, 176–192. doi:10.1016/j.jmsy.2020.11.017

Ponnusamy, V., Aun, Y., Jhanjhi, N. Z., Humayun, M., & Almufareh, M. F. (2022). IoT wireless intrusion detection and network Traffic Analysis. *Computer Systems Science and Engineering, 40*(3), 865–879. doi:10.32604/csse.2022.018801

Pranata, M., & Adhariani, D. (2023). Analysis of the potential implementation of Material Flow Cost Accounting (MFCA) in muslim fashion SMEs Y. *International Journal of Financial, Accounting, and Management, 5*(1), 97–111. doi:10.35912/ijfam.v5i1.1512

Ramdurai, B. (2020). *Detailed Review of Cloud based Mobile application for the stroke patient. arXiv*. Cornell University. doi:10.14445/22312803

Rane, S. B., Potdar, P. R., & Aware, S. (2023). *Strategies for development of smart and green products using Blockchain-IoT integrated architecture*. Operations Management Research. doi:10.1007/s12063-023-00398-5

Rani, S., Bhambri, P., Kataria, A., Khang, A., & Sivaraman, A. K. (2023). *Big data, cloud computing and IoT: Tools and Applications*. CRC Press. doi:10.1201/9781003298335

Rathod, S. (2023, July 16). *Ensuring Optimized Storage with Data Confidentiality and Privacy-Preserving for Secure Data Sharing Model Over Cloud*. https://www.ijisae.org/index.php/IJISAE/article/view/3140

Rayar, P., & Kumar, K. N. V. (2023). Triple bottom line Sustainability and Industry 4.0 implementation in Indian MSMEs: a Conceptual model. In Smart innovation, systems and technologies (pp. 425–432). doi:10.1007/978-981-19-8497-6_39

RayhanA.GrossD. (2023). Sustainable Business Ideas: The Ultimate guide to starting and running a profitable and Eco-Friendly business. *ResearchGate*. doi:10.13140/RG.2.2.35344.99847

Reddy, T. T., Devi, Y. R., & Kavita, G. (2023). Logistics, traceability in food supply chain management. *E3S Web of Conferences, 391*, 01075. doi:10.1051/e3sconf/202339101075

Rendtorff, J. D. (2023). Responsible Business and Integrated Stakeholder Reporting: towards a stakeholder model for integrated reporting of ESG and SDG. In Ethical economy (pp. 49–59). doi:10.1007/978-3-031-26959-2_6

Rivera, L., Ortíz, N. R., Moreno, G., & Páez-Gabriunas, I. (2023). The effect of company ownership on the environmental practices in the supply chain: An Empirical approach. *Sustainability (Basel), 15*(16), 12450. doi:10.3390/su151612450

Robson, G. J., & Tsou, J. Y. (2023). *Technology Ethics: A Philosophical Introduction and Readings*. Taylor & Francis. doi:10.4324/9781003189466

Saccani, N., Bressanelli, G., & Visintin, F. (2023). Circular supply chain orchestration to overcome Circular Economy challenges: An empirical investigation in the textile and fashion industries. *Sustainable Production and Consumption*, *35*, 469–482. doi:10.1016/j.spc.2022.11.020

Saidani, M., Bayless, J. R., Huey, D., Kim, H. M., & Anderson, K. L. (2023). Life cycle assessment and circular economy indicators to design sustainable electric outboards: results from workshops with industrial experts. *Proceedings of the Design Society*, *3*, 2445–2454. doi:10.1017/pds.2023.245

Saleem, J., Tahir, F., Baig, M. Z. K., Al-Ansari, T., & McKay, G. (2023). Assessing the environmental footprint of recycled plastic pellets: A life-cycle assessment perspective. *Environmental Technology & Innovation*, *32*, 103289. doi:10.1016/j.eti.2023.103289

Saleem, J., Tahir, F., Baig, M. Z. K., Al-Ansari, T., & McKay, G. (2023b). Assessing the environmental footprint of recycled plastic pellets: A life-cycle assessment perspective. *Environmental Technology & Innovation*, *32*, 103289. doi:10.1016/j.eti.2023.103289

Salim, S. (2023). Promoting firm performance via board of directors effectiveness: A study of financial services companies... *ResearchGate*. https://www.researchgate.net/publication/373777145_PROMOTING_FIRM_PERFORMANCE_VIA_BOARD_OF_DIRECTORS_EFFECTIVENESS_A_STUDY_OF_FINANCIAL_SERVICES_COMPANIES_IN_NEW_ORLEANS

Sankar, S., Ramasubbareddy, S., Luhach, A. K., Deverajan, G. G., Alnumay, W. S., Jhanjhi, N. Z., Ghosh, U., & Sharma, P. K. (2020). Energy efficient optimal parent selection based routing protocol for Internet of Things using firefly optimization algorithm. *Transactions on Emerging Telecommunications Technologies*, *32*(8), e4171. Advance online publication. doi:10.1002/ett.4171

Saqib, N., Durán, I. A., & Ozturk, I. (2023). Unraveling the Interrelationship of Digitalization, Renewable Energy, and Ecological Footprints within the EKC Framework: Empirical Insights from the United States. *Sustainability (Basel)*, *15*(13), 10663. doi:10.3390/su151310663

Sarkar, B. D., Shankar, R., & Kar, A. K. (2022). Port logistic issues and challenges in the Industry 4.0 era for emerging economies: An India perspective. *Benchmarking*, *30*(1), 50–74. doi:10.1108/BIJ-08-2021-0499

Sarpong, F. A., Sappor, P., Nyantakyi, G., Ahakwa, I., Agyeiwaa, O. E., & Cobbinah, B. B. (2023). From traditional roots to digital bytes: Can digitalizing ESG improves Ghanaian rural banks' brand equity through stakeholder engagement, and customer loyalty? *Cogent Business & Management*, *10*(2), 2232159. Advance online publication. doi:10.1080/23311975.2023.2232159

Sawant, R., Thomas, B., & Kadlag, S. (2022). Reskilling and upskilling: To stay relevant in today's industry. *International Review of Business and Economics*, *7*(1). Advance online publication. doi:10.56902/IRBE.2022.7.1.4

Schneider, J., Abraham, R., Meske, C., & Brocke, J. V. (2022). Artificial Intelligence Governance For Businesses. *Information Systems Management*, 1–21. doi:10.1080/10580530.2022.2085825

Seong, T. B., Ponnusamy, V., Jhanjhi, N. Z., Annur, R., & Talib, M. (2021). A comparative analysis on traditional wired datasets and the need for wireless datasets for IoT wireless intrusion detection. *Indonesian Journal of Electrical Engineering and Computer Science*, *22*(2), 1165. doi:10.11591/ijeecs.v22.i2.pp1165-1176

Shabir, I., Dash, K. K., Dar, A. H., Pandey, V. K., Fayaz, U., Srivastava, S., & Nisha, R. (2023). Carbon footprints evaluation for sustainable food processing system development: A comprehensive review. *Future Foods : a Dedicated Journal for Sustainability in Food Science*, *7*, 100215. doi:10.1016/j.fufo.2023.100215

Sibhensana, B., & Maistry, S. (2023). Conceptualising public-private partnerships for social innovation through community engagement in higher education institutions. *South African Journal of Higher Education*, 1–21. doi:10.20853/37-1-5669

Siems, E., Seuring, S., & Schilling, L. (2022). Stakeholder roles in sustainable supply chain management: A literature review. *Journal of Business Economics*, *93*(4), 747–775. doi:10.1007/s11573-022-01117-5

Silva, P. M., Moreira, A. C., & Mota, J. (2022). Employees' perception of corporate social responsibility and performance: The mediating roles of job satisfaction, organizational commitment and organizational trust. *Journal of Strategy and Management*, *16*(1), 92–111. doi:10.1108/JSMA-10-2021-0213

Sindiramutty, S. R. (2023). Autonomous Threat Hunting: a future paradigm for AI-Driven Threat intelligence. *arXiv (Cornell University)*. https://doi.org//arxiv.2401.00286 doi:10.48550

Sindiramutty, S. R., Jhanjhi, N. Z., Ray, S. K., Jazri, H., Khan, N. A., & Gaur, L. (2024). Metaverse: Virtual Meditation. In Metaverse Applications for Intelligent Healthcare (pp. 93–158). doi:10.4018/978-1-6684-9823-1.ch003

Sindiramutty, S. R., Jhanjhi, N. Z., Ray, S. K., Jazri, H., Khan, N. A., Gaur, L., Gharib, A. H., & Manchuri, A. R. (2024). Metaverse: Virtual Gyms and Sport. In Metaverse Applications for Intelligent Healthcare (pp. 24–92). doi:10.4018/978-1-6684-9823-1.ch002

Sindiramutty, S. R., Jhanjhi, N. Z., Tan, C. E., Khan, N. A., Gharib, A. H., & Yun, K. J. (2024). Applications of blockchain technology in supply chain management. In Advances in logistics, operations, and management science book series (pp. 248–304). doi:10.4018/978-1-6684-7625-3.ch009

Sindiramutty, S. R., Jhanjhi, N. Z., Tan, C. E., Khan, N. A., Shah, B., & Gaur, L. (2024). Securing the digital supply chain cyber threats and vulnerabilities. In Advances in logistics, operations, and management science book series (pp. 156–223). doi:10.4018/978-1-6684-7625-3.ch007

Sindiramutty, S. R., Jhanjhi, N. Z., Tan, C. E., Tee, W. J., Lau, S. P., Jazri, H., Ray, S. K., & Zaheer, M. A. (2024). IoT and AI-Based Smart Solutions for the Agriculture Industry. In Advances in Explainable AI Applications for Smart Cities (pp. 317–351). doi:10.4018/978-1-6684-6361-1.ch012

Sindiramutty, S. R., Tan, C., Lau, S. P., Thangaveloo, R., Gharib, A. H., Manchuri, A. R., Khan, N. A., Tee, W. J., & Muniandy, L. (2024). Explainable AI for Cybersecurity. In Advances in Explainable AI Applications for Smart Cities (pp. 31–97). doi:10.4018/978-1-6684-6361-1.ch002

Sindiramutty, S. R., Tan, C., Tee, W. J., Lau, S. P., Balakrishnan, S., Kaur, S. D. A., Jazri, H., & Aslam, M. (2024). Modern Smart Cities and Open Research Challenges and Issues of Explainable Artificial Intelligence. In Advances in Explainable AI Applications for Smart Cities, (pp. 389–424). doi:10.4018/978-1-6684-6361-1.ch015

Sindiramutty, S. R., Tee, W. J., Balakrishnan, S., Kaur, S., Thangaveloo, R., Jazri, H., Khan, N. A., Gharib, A. H., & Manchuri, A. R. (2024). Explainable AI in Healthcare Application. In Advances in Explainable AI Applications for Smart Cities (pp. 123–176). doi:10.4018/978-1-6684-6361-1.ch005

Singh, A., Kumar, V., Verma, P., & Ramtiyal, B. (2022). Can suppliers be sustainable in construction supply chains? Evidence from a construction company using best worst approach. *Management of Environmental Quality*. Advance online publication. doi:10.1108/MEQ-03-2022-0057

Singh, A., Madaan, G., Hr, S., & Kumar, A. (2022). Smart manufacturing systems: A futuristics roadmap towards application of industry 4.0 technologies. *International Journal of Computer Integrated Manufacturing*, *36*(3), 411–428. doi:10.1080/0951192X.2022.2090607

Singh, U. P. (2023, July 22). *Development of sustainable and biodegradable materials for packaging*. http://jsrt.innovascience.uz/index.php/jsrt/article/view/246

Sivaraman, P., Ilakiya, P., Prabhu, M., & Ajayan, A. (2023). Real-Time gearbox defect detection using IIOT-Based Condition Monitoring System. *SAE Technical Paper Series*. doi:10.4271/2023-01-5057

Soori, M., Arezoo, B., & Dastres, R. (2023). Internet of things for smart factories in industry 4.0, a review. *Internet of Things and Cyber-physical Systems*, *3*, 192–204. doi:10.1016/j.iotcps.2023.04.006

Sordi, A., Tate, W. L., & Huang, F. (2022). Going beyond supplier diversity to economic Inclusion: Where are we now and where do we go from here? *Journal of Purchasing and Supply Management*, *28*(2), 100751. doi:10.1016/j.pursup.2022.100751

Stadnicka, D., Sęp, J., Amadio, R., Mazzei, D., Tyrovolas, M., Stylios, C., Carreras-Coch, A., Merino, J. A., Żabiński, T., & Navarro, J. (2022). Industrial needs in the fields of artificial intelligence, internet of things and edge computing. *Sensors (Basel)*, *22*(12), 4501. doi:10.3390/s22124501 PMID:35746287

Su, D., Zhang, L., Hua, P., Saeidi, P., & Tirkolaee, E. B. (2023). Technical challenges of blockchain technology for sustainable manufacturing paradigm in Industry 4.0 era using a fuzzy decision support system. *Technological Forecasting and Social Change*, *188*, 122275. doi:10.1016/j.techfore.2022.122275

Subramaniam, N., Akbar, S., Situ, H., Ji, S., & Parikh, N. (2023). Sustainable development goal reporting: Contrasting effects of institutional and organisational factors. *Journal of Cleaner Production*, *411*, 137339. doi:10.1016/j.jclepro.2023.137339

Sugiawan, Y., Kurniawan, R., & Managi, S. (2023). Assessing the United Nations sustainable development goals from the inclusive wealth perspective. *Scientific Reports*, *13*(1), 1601. Advance online publication. doi:10.1038/s41598-023-28540-0 PMID:36709239

Sunmola, F., & Burgess, P. (2023). Transparency by design for Blockchain-Based supply chains. *Procedia Computer Science*, *217*, 1256–1265. doi:10.1016/j.procs.2022.12.324

Suppipat, S., Chotiratanapinun, T., Teachavorasinskun, K., & Hu, A. H. (2022). Designer's guide for life cycle Assessment. In Springer eBooks (pp. 15–29). doi:10.1007/978-3-031-15060-9_2

Tavanti, M. (2023). Assessing and measuring sustainability impact. In Sustainable development goals series (pp. 453–473). doi:10.1007/978-3-031-36907-0_17

Tschentscher, T., Chege, N., & Remaury, H. (2023). An Integrated Seascape Approach to Revitalise Ecosystems and Livelihoods in Shimoni-Vanga, Kenya. In SpringerLink (pp. 179–202). doi:10.1007/978-981-99-1292-6_10

Ueda, D., Kakinuma, T., Fujita, S., Kamagata, K., Fushimi, Y., Ito, R., Matsui, Y., Nozaki, T., Nakaura, T., Fujima, N., Tatsugami, F., Yanagawa, M., Hirata, K., Yamada, A., Tsuboyama, T., Kawamura, M., Fujioka, T., & Naganawa, S. (2023). Fairness of artificial intelligence in healthcare: Review and recommendations. *Japanese Journal of Radiology*. Advance online publication. doi:10.1007/s11604-023-01474-3 PMID:37540463

Ullah, A., Azeem, M., Ashraf, H., Alaboudi, A. A., Humayun, M., & Jhanjhi, N. Z. (2021). Secure healthcare Data Aggregation and Transmission in IoT—A survey. *IEEE Access : Practical Innovations, Open Solutions*, *9*, 16849–16865. doi:10.1109/ACCESS.2021.3052850

Ullah, A., Ishaq, N., Azeem, M., Ashraf, H., Jhanjhi, N. Z., Humayun, M., Tabbakh, T., & Almusaylim, Z. A. (2021b). A survey on continuous object tracking and boundary detection schemes in IoT assisted wireless sensor networks. *IEEE Access : Practical Innovations, Open Solutions*, *9*, 126324–126336. doi:10.1109/ACCESS.2021.3110203

Unhelkar, B., Joshi, S. K., Sharma, M., Prakash, S., Mani, A. K., & Prasad, M. (2022). Enhancing supply chain performance using RFID technology and decision support systems in the industry 4.0–A systematic literature review. *International Journal of Information Management Data Insights*, *2*(2), 100084. doi:10.1016/j.jjimei.2022.100084

Vazifeh, Z., Bensebaa, F., Shadbahr, J., Gonzales-Calienes, G., Mafakheri, F., Benali, M., Ebadian, M., & Vézina, P. L. (2023). Forestry based products as climate change solution: Integrating life cycle assessment with techno-economic analysis. *Journal of Environmental Management*, *330*, 117197. doi:10.1016/j.jenvman.2022.117197

Verma, S., Kaur, S., Rawat, D. B., Chen, X., Alex, L. T., & Jhanjhi, N. Z. (2021). Intelligent framework using IoT-Based WSNs for wildfire detection. *IEEE Access : Practical Innovations, Open Solutions*, *9*, 48185–48196. doi:10.1109/ACCESS.2021.3060549

Vizcaino, N. (2023). *How do the Female Attitudes Towards Sustainable Branding Influence Purchase Intention in the Sportswear Industry : A qualitative study of women aged 20-50.* DIVA. https://www.diva-portal.org/smash/record.jsf?pid=diva2%3A1763924&dswid=-4010

Volkov, B. B., Ragon, B., Doyle, J. M., & Bredella, M. A. (2022). Adaptive capacity and preparedness of Clinical and Translational Science Award Program hubs: Overview of an environmental scan. *Journal of Clinical and Translational Science*, *7*(1), e31. Advance online publication. doi:10.1017/cts.2022.400 PMID:36845304

Voukkali, I., Papamichael, I., Loizia, P., Lekkas, D., Rodríguez-Espinosa, T., Pedreño, J. N., & Zorpas, A. A. (2023). Waste metrics in the framework of circular economy. *Waste Management & Research*, *41*(12), 1741–1753. Advance online publication. doi:10.1177/0734242X231190794 PMID:37602734

Wang, H., Feil, J., & Yu, X. (2023). Let the data speak about the cut-off values for multidimensional index: Classification of human development index with machine learning. *Socio-Economic Planning Sciences*, *87*, 101523. doi:10.1016/j.seps.2023.101523

Wang, X. E., Su, X., & Bi, K. (2023). Achieving synergies of carbon emission reduction, cost savings, and asset investments in China's industrial sector: Towards sustainable practices. *Sustainability (Basel)*, *15*(14), 10956. doi:10.3390/su151410956

Wasiq, M., Kamal, M., & Ali, N. (2023). Factors influencing green innovation adoption and its impact on the sustainability performance of Small- and Medium-Sized Enterprises in Saudi Arabia. *Sustainability (Basel)*, *15*(3), 2447. doi:10.3390/su15032447

Wasumwa, N. S. A. (2023). Safeguarding the future: A comprehensive analysis of security measures for smart grids. *World Journal of Advanced Research and Reviews*, *19*(1), 847–871. doi:10.30574/wjarr.2023.19.1.1387

Waxin, M. (2023). *Environmental management systems in public sector*. https://dspace.aus.edu/xmlui/handle/11073/25241

Wen, B. O. T., Syahriza, N., Xian, N. C. W., Wei, N., Shen, T. Z., Hin, Y. Z., Sindiramutty, S. R., & Nicole, T. Y. F. (2024). Detecting cyber threats with a Graph-Based NIDPS. In Advances in logistics, operations, and management science book series (pp. 36–74). doi:10.4018/978-1-6684-7625-3.ch002

Whitehead, B., Andrews, D., Shah, A., & Maidment, G. (2015). Assessing the environmental impact of data centres part 2: Building environmental assessment methods and life cycle assessment. *Building and Environment*, *93*, 395–405. doi:10.1016/j.buildenv.2014.08.015

Widianingsih, I., Abdillah, A., Herawati, E., Dewi, A. U., Miftah, A. Z., Adikancana, Q. M., Pratama, M. N., & Sasmono, S. (2023). Sport Tourism, Regional Development, and Urban Resilience: A focus on regional economic development in Lake Toba District, North Sumatra, Indonesia. *Sustainability (Basel)*, *15*(7), 5960. doi:10.3390/su15075960

Widodo, R. E., & Napitupulu, T. A. (2023). Exploring The Impact Of Live Streaming For Ecommerce Business A Systematic Literature Review. *ResearchGate*. https://www.researchgate.net/publication/373572273_Exploring_The_Impact_Of_Live_Streaming_For_Ecommerce_Business_A_Systematic_Literature_Review

Wolniak, N. (2023). Functioning of real-time analytics in business. *Zeszyty Naukowe, 2023*(172). doi:10.29119/1641-3466.2023.172.40

Wu, D., & Xie, L. (2023). From concept to reality: Leveraging green innovation and supply chain management for sustainable corporate performance. *Environmental Science and Pollution Research International*, *30*(46), 102574–102585. Advance online publication. doi:10.1007/s11356-023-29351-6 PMID:37668785

Yaiprasert, C., & Hidayanto, A. N. (2023). AI-driven ensemble three machine learning to enhance digital marketing strategies in the food delivery business. *Intelligent Systems With Applications, 18*, 200235. doi:10.1016/j.iswa.2023.200235

Yenugula, M., Sahoo, S. K., & Goswami, S. S. (2023). Cloud computing in supply chain management: Exploring the relationship. *Management Science Letters, 13*(3), 193–210. doi:10.5267/j.msl.2023.4.003

Ying-Jun, F., Lai, K., & Zhu, Q. (2022). Green supply chain innovation: Emergence, adoption, and challenges. *International Journal of Production Economics, 248*, 108497. doi:10.1016/j.ijpe.2022.108497

Yosef, F. A., Jum'a, L., & Alatoom, M. (2023). Identifying and categorizing sustainable supply chain practices based on triple bottom line dimensions: Evaluation of practice implementation in the cement industry. *Sustainability (Basel), 15*(9), 7323. doi:10.3390/su15097323

Zahari, M. K., Zakuan, N., Yusoff, M. F. M., Saman, M. Z. M., Khan, M. N. A., Muharam, F. M., & Yaacob, T. Z. (2023). Viable Supply Chain Management toward Company Sustainability during COVID-19 Pandemic in Malaysia. *Sustainability (Basel), 15*(5), 3989. doi:10.3390/su15053989

Zhao, N., Hong, J., & Lau, K. H. (2023). Impact of supply chain digitalization on supply chain resilience and performance: A multi-mediation model. *International Journal of Production Economics, 259*, 108817. doi:10.1016/j.ijpe.2023.108817 PMID:36852136

Zhong, Y., & Cheol, M. H. (2023). Investigating the Impact of Industry 4.0 Technology through a TOE-Based Innovation Model. *Systems, 11*(6), 277. doi:10.3390/systems11060277

Zong, J., Zhang, X., Yang, Y., Li, H., & Yuan, H. (2023). Guideline for Green Design of Computer Products. *SHS Web of Conferences, 155*, 03025. 10.1051/shsconf/202315503025

Zowghi, D., & Da Rimini, F. (2023). Diversity and inclusion in artificial intelligence. *arXiv (Cornell University)*. https://doi.org//arxiv.2305.12728 doi:10.48550

Chapter 9
Ethical and Social Implications of Industry 4.0 in SCM

Azeem Khan
https://orcid.org/0000-0003-2742-8034
University Islam Sultan Sharif Ali, Brunei

NZ Jhanjhi
https://orcid.org/0000-0001-8116-4733
Taylor's University, Malaysia

Sayan Kumar Ray
Taylor's University, Malaysia

Fathi Amsaad
Wright State University, USA

R. Sujatha
https://orcid.org/0000-0002-1993-7544
Vellore Institute of Technology, India

ABSTRACT

This chapter critically evaluates the integration of Industry 4.0 technologies within the context of supply chain management (SCM), with a specific focus on examining its ethical and social implications. The research highlights the significant changes in workforce dynamics, the ethical considerations surrounding data-driven operations, and the importance of human-centered designs in the digital age, as they pertain to labor practices, data ethics, governance, and future prospects. This study employs a combination of literature reviews, case studies, and expert opinions to provide a comprehensive understanding of the importance of ethical considerations. These considerations encompass various aspects such as labor fairness, privacy, dilemmas related to artificial intelligence, and the integrity of data. Simultaneously, it brings attention to the societal consequences such as changes in employment patterns, the need for acquiring new skills, and the demand for inclusivity and fairness in the face of technological advancements.

DOI: 10.4018/979-8-3693-1363-3.ch009

1. INTRODUCTION

In the current global context, characterized by the imminent onset of the Fourth Industrial Revolution(IR4.0) (Khan, Jhanjhi, & Sujatha, 2022; Sujatha, Prakash, & Jhanjhi, 2022), there is a notable convergence of digital technology (Shah, Sial, Jhanjhi, & Gaur, 2023) with established industries. This phenomenon presents a multitude of prospects and challenges that are of interest to academics, professionals, and decision-makers alike. The phenomenon commonly referred to as 'Industry 4.0' as depicted in Fig 1.0, encompasses not only technological progress but also necessitates a thorough examination of its ethical and societal implications. The intersection between these two areas is particularly evident within the field of SCM (Ashraf et al., 2023).

Supply Chain Management, which has traditionally been perceived as the essential component facilitating the efficient transfer of goods, services, and information in global commerce, is currently undergoing a significant transformation (Park et al., 2023). The advent of technological advancements such as the Internet of Things (IoT) (I. Hussain et al., 2022), artificial intelligence (AI) (Gaur, Jhanjhi, Bakshi, & Gupta, 2022), and machine learning (Adhikari et al., 2023) have pushed supply chain management in the era of Industry 4.0 to become more intelligent, adaptable, and highly responsive to immediate fluctuations. While these characteristics have positive implications for enhancing organizational efficiencies and improving customer satisfaction, they also introduce a range of ethical and societal implications. For example, how do these automated systems incorporate considerations for the ethical treatment of employees? The ethical sourcing, storage, and deployment of data, often referred to as the "oil of the digital era," necessitates careful consideration to avoid encroaching upon individual privacy rights (Bernal, 2014; Payton & Claypoole, 2023). What are the societal implications that arise from the shifting of job roles, which necessitate the acquisition of new skill sets and potentially render certain roles obsolete?

Figure 1. Stages of industrial revolution (Phuyal, Bista, & Bista, 2020)

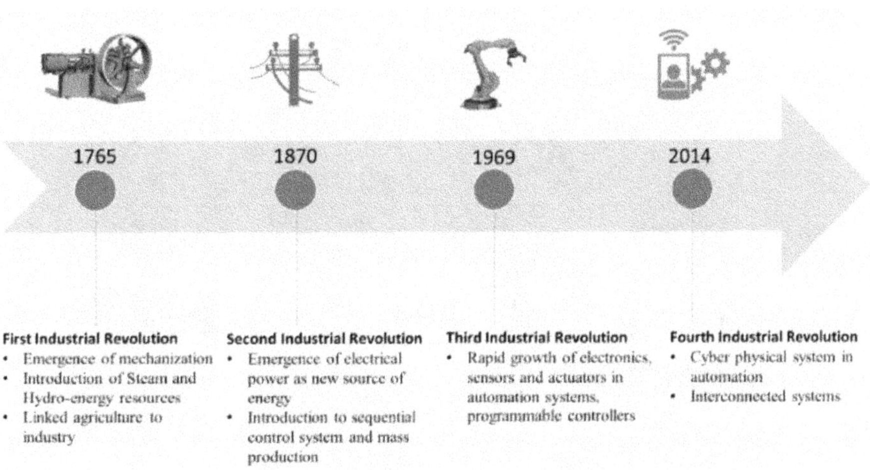

The objective of this chapter, titled "Ethical and Social Implications of Industry 4.0 in Supply Chain Management", is to address these issues. It seeks to provide an account of the existing landscape while also offering guidance to SCM practitioners, scholars, and students in adopting ethically and socially responsible practices within the context of Industry 4.0 (Humayun, 2021). By subjecting the chapter to thorough academic examination, complemented by the inclusion of practical case studies and expert opinions, the aim is to present a comprehensive analysis that accurately represents the current state of knowledge. Additionally, the chapter seeks to provide guidance by offering a direction that is guided by ethical principles and a forward-thinking perspective on societal implications.

As we commence this endeavor, it is imperative to acknowledge that the ethical and social ramifications of Industry 4.0 in supply chain management are not insignificant or secondary considerations. The objects in question hold a prominent position within the ongoing discussion, requiring a significant amount of focus and consideration, potentially even surpassing the attention given to the impressive technological advancements they are associated with. Therefore, this initial section establishes the context by highlighting the obstacles and possibilities that await, while also underscoring the collective duty of all involved parties to guarantee that advancements in supply chain management are based on ethical principles and contribute to societal well-being.

1.1 Overview of Industry 4.0: Redefining the Landscape of the Supply Chain

The term "Industry 4.0," which arose from high-tech strategy discussions in Germany, has now become the globally recognized nomenclature for the Fourth Industrial Revolution. Industry 4.0 differs from its predecessors in that it incorporates cyber-physical systems, real-time data analytics, and advanced interconnected devices into traditional manufacturing and business processes. Its core goal is to build "smart factories" and, by extension, "smart supply chains"—entities as depicted in Figure 3, that are autonomous, self-monitoring, and inherently responsive to change (Patil, Baramati, Dhone, & Chourasiya, 2023).

Figure 2. SCM in the age of Industry 4.0: A comprehensive overview (Barreto, Amaral, & Pereira, 2017)

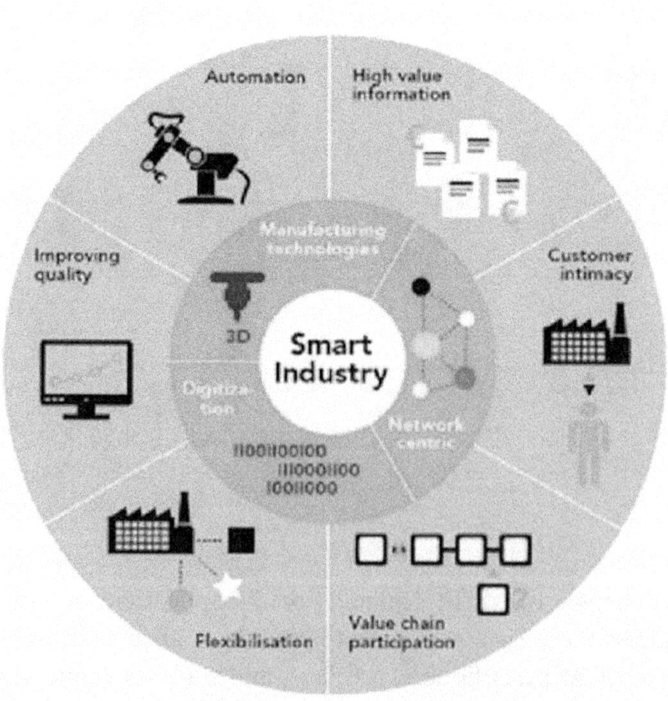

The implications of Industry 4.0 for Supply Chain Management are profound and multifaceted. On the one hand, there is an undeniable benefit. Advanced sensors enable real-time tracking of goods, ensuring on-time delivery and reducing losses. Predictive analytics (Annadurai et al., 2022), powered by machine learning algorithms (Tayyab et al., 2023), can forecast demand with unrivaled accuracy, assisting in inventory management and reducing waste. Blockchain technology (Shah, Jhanjhi, & Laraib, 2023) promises transparency and traceability, which are critical in an age when consumers are increasingly concerned about the origins and journey of the products they buy (Ghobakhloo, Fathi, Iranmanesh, Maroufkhani, & Morales, 2021).

However, digitization brings with it new challenges. Traditional linear supply chains are being transformed into complex supply network systems. While data is beneficial, there are concerns about its security, authenticity, and potential for misuse (Khan, Jhanjhi, & Humayun, 2022). Furthermore, as supply chains become more automated, job displacements loom, necessitating a re-examination of roles, responsibilities, and the very nature of human-machine collaboration within these systems (Shao, Liu, Li, Chaudhry, & Yue, 2021).

1.2 Importance of Ethical and Social Considerations in Industry 4.0-Enabled SCM

While the technological marvels of Industry 4.0 may be the obvious focus for many, the ethical and social dimensions they introduce, particularly in SCM, must not be overlooked. Indeed, these considerations are critical, because technology that lacks an ethical foundation or a social conscience risk causing more harm than good.

Ethically, the world of SCM is confronted with novel challenges. How does one ensure that data, which is critical to these advanced systems, is not only secure but also ethically sourced and used? What are firms' responsibilities when AI-driven decisions unintentionally perpetuate biases or result in unjust outcomes? These aren't just hypothetical scenarios; they're real-world challenges that companies are facing as they integrate Industry 4.0 technologies into their supply chains.

Social considerations are also important. As automation and AI become more integrated into SCM, significant job displacement is possible. While new roles will undoubtedly emerge, the transition can be turbulent, with some industries experiencing more severe disruptions than others. Aside from job roles, there is also the societal impact to consider. For example, how does a hyper-efficient, AI-powered supply chain affect local economies, particularly those that have historically relied on manual, labor-intensive processes?

Understanding and addressing these ethical and social challenges is a business imperative, not an academic exercise. Companies that successfully navigate this complex maze will not only be ethically sound, but will also have a competitive advantage, as consumers, regulators, and society at large demand more responsible, transparent, and socially conscious business practices.

1.3 Scope and Objectives of Research

It is critical to define the scope and objectives of any scholarly endeavor in order to ensure clarity of vision and purposeful direction. This section aims to articulate the research's boundaries, aspirations, and intent regarding the ethical and social implications of Industry 4.0 within the context of Supply Chain Management.

Scope:

The research primarily revolves around the domain of SCM, with a particular emphasis on its transformation as a result of the advent of Industry 4.0 technologies. This entails investigating both the macro and micro dimensions. The research assesses the overarching shifts in the supply chain landscape—how networks are formed, how goods and information flow, and the changing dynamics of global commerce in the age of digital interconnectivity—at the macro level. At a granular level, it evaluates the actual technologies driving change (whether AI, IoT, blockchain, or others), the operational nuances they introduce, and the resulting challenges and opportunities.

Objectives:

1. **Technological Assessment:** To gain a thorough understanding of the suite of technologies labeled Industry 4.0 and their direct implications for SCM. This includes not only identifying them but also explaining their functional characteristics, benefits, and potential drawbacks.
2. **Ethical Evaluation:** To critically assess the ethical issues raised by the incorporation of these technologies. This includes concerns about data privacy, equitable AI deployment, algorithmic bias, and the broader moral responsibilities of organizations operating in this new paradigm.
3. **Social Investigation:** To investigate the societal implications of an Industry 4.0-infused SCM. This includes potential job losses, the emergence of new roles, the effects on local and global economies, and the resulting shifts in societal structures and norms.
4. **Suggestions and Frameworks:** To develop actionable strategies and frameworks for businesses, policymakers, and educators to use. These recommendations aim to make the transition to an Industry 4.0-aligned SCM not only smooth, but also ethical and socially responsible.
5. **Prospects for the Future:** Given the dynamic nature of technology and its rapid evolution, anticipating future trends and challenges is critical. Thus, one goal is to forecast where SCM will go in the next decade and what new ethical and societal challenges will emerge.

In essence, this study intends to serve as both a beacon and a guide. It aims to shed light on the intricate interaction between SCM and Industry 4.0, illuminating the associated challenges and opportunities. It aspires to guide stakeholders—whether business leaders, technocrats, scholars, or students—on a path that acknowledges the critical importance of ethical integrity and societal well-being in this transformative era.

1.4 Key Concepts and Definitions

In order to comprehensively explore the complex relationship between Industry 4.0 and supply chain management (SCM), it is imperative that we establish a solid understanding of the fundamental concepts involved. It is crucial to possess a thorough comprehension of these concepts, as they will function as foundational elements for our ongoing discourse. In this analysis, we will delve into the intricacies of each term and examine the significant ramifications they possess within the intricate fabric of contemporary supply chains.

Industry 4.0:

Industry 4.0, commonly referred to as the Fourth Industrial Revolution, represents a significant paradigm shift in the domain of manufacturing and production, characterized by its potential to bring about profound transformative effects. The preceding revolutions have been characterized by the introduction of steam engines, electricity, and computer technology. In contrast, Industry 4.0 as depicted in Figure 3, represents a significant development that integrates the physical and digital realms, marking the advent of intelligent systems and automation. The current era encompasses more than just the incorporation of digital technology. It represents the emergence of adaptive environments, wherein machines are interconnected, exchanging data and knowledge, and frequently making decisions with limited human involvement.

Figure 3. IR4.0 technologies revisited (electronics)

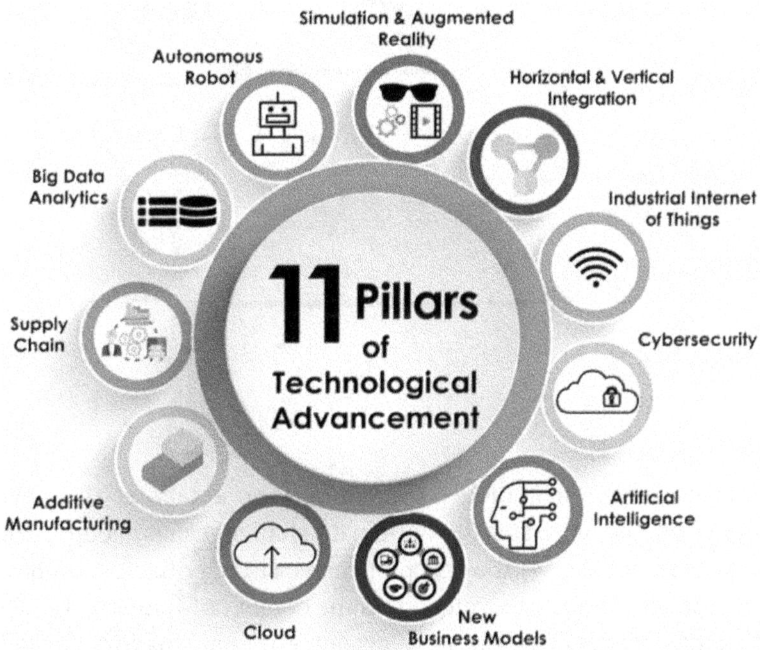

In a more expansive context, Industry 4.0 has the capacity to fundamentally transform entire ecosystems. The process from product inception to final delivery involves a cohesive integration of human ingenuity and machine accuracy. The incorporation of the Internet of Things (IoT), Artificial Intelligence (AI), robotics, and advanced analytics into various sectors holds the potential to bring about significant advancements, not only in terms of operational effectiveness, but also in revolutionizing the way industries perceive and achieve value (Alkinani, Almazroi, & Khan, 2021; Anandan, Deepak, Suseendran, & Jhanjhi, 2021; Gaur, Solanki, Wamba, & Jhanjhi, 2021).

Supply Chain Management (SCM):

Supply Chain Management (SCM) refers to the systematic management of the movement and coordination of goods and services within a business or organization as shown in Figure 4. The concept involves the transportation and retention of primary resources, intermediate inventory, and final products. However, with the advent of Industry 4.0, supply chain management is experiencing a significant transformation. The integration of real-time data, predictive analytics, and interconnected networks has revolutionized supply chains, shifting them from linear sequences to dynamic and responsive systems (Acharjya, Mitra, & Zaman, 2022).

Figure 4. Elements of SCM (procureport)

Decisions are no longer solely reliant on historical data, as contemporary advancements in real-time information and analytics enable companies to anticipate challenges and adapt their strategies accordingly. Supply chain management (SCM) is a comprehensive strategy that encompasses the supervision and enhancement of a product's entire lifecycle within the context of Industry 4.0. Its primary objective is to ensure the appropriate placement and timing of products, thereby maximizing value and minimizing inefficiencies (Schoenherr, Mena, Vakil, & Choi, 2023).

Cyber-Physical Systems:

Cyber-Physical Systems (CPS) form the core of Industry 4.0. These systems combine computer-based algorithms with tangible processes, as shown in Figure 5. Sensors are responsible for gathering data from the physical environment, which is subsequently processed by algorithms to generate decisions. These decisions are then implemented within the physical realm. The revolutionary aspect of CPS lies in its inherent ability to engage in a continuous cycle of adaptability, wherein it possesses the capacity to self-correct, acquire knowledge, and optimize its performance (Singh & Kumar, 2023).

Figure 5. A conceptual map: A guide to understanding cyber-physical systems (L. Wang, Törngren, & Onori, 2015)

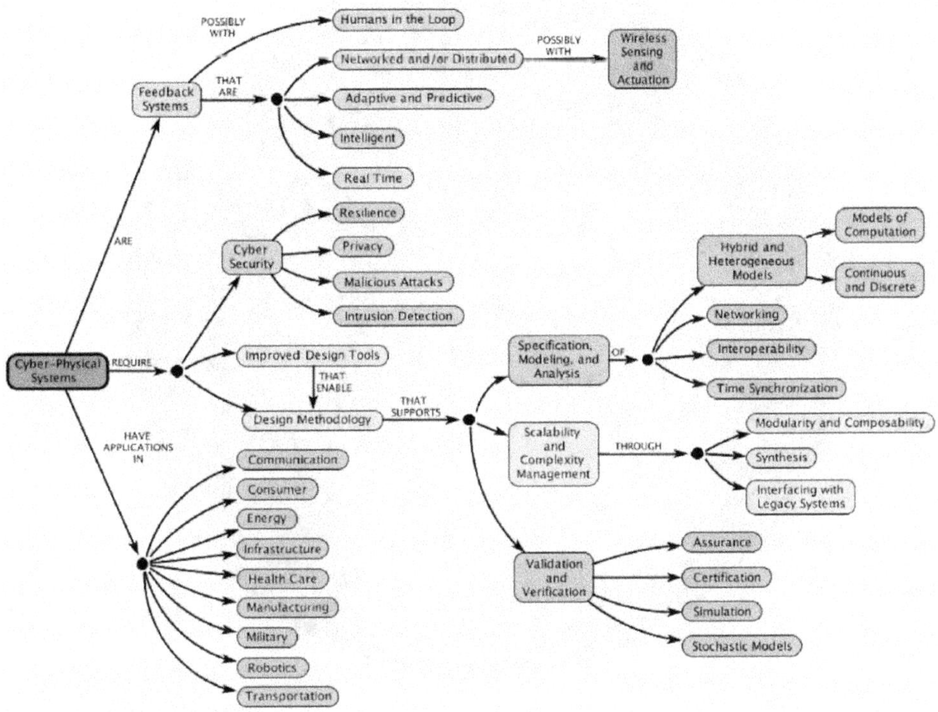

The implications for industries are significant and transformative. These systems enable the development of intelligent factories and infrastructures, improved health systems, and enhanced network efficiency. Within the realm of supply chain management (SCM), real-time monitoring and adjustments are facilitated, thereby guaranteeing optimal operational efficiency and significantly enhanced responsiveness to unanticipated challenges (Rosado et al., 2022).

Artificial Intelligence (AI):

Artificial Intelligence (AI) refers to the development of machines capable of cognitive processes, such as analyzing extensive datasets, identifying patterns, and making well-informed judgments. However, in the realm of supply chain management, artificial intelligence (AI) emerges as a tool with exceptional potential. The utilization of artificial intelligence (AI) presents a range of capabilities that were previously considered unachievable, such as the ability to forecast fluctuations in demand and optimize inventory in real-time (Chaudhary, Gaur, Chakrabarti, & Jhanjhi, 2023; Naqvi, Sheraz, Mehmood, & Yasin, 2023).

Figure 6. Artificial intelligence (towardsdatascience)

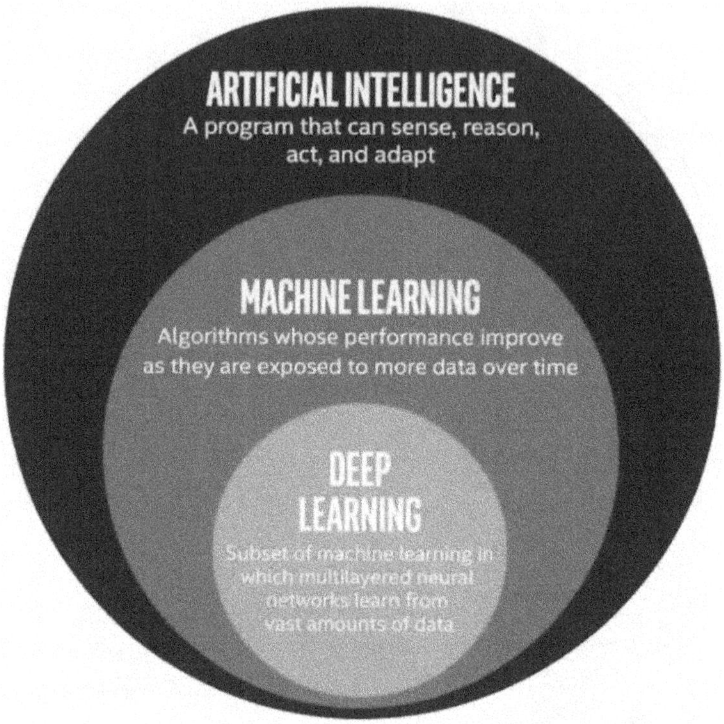

The profound integration of this technology into supply chain management signifies the advent of a novel era in which decision-making is no longer solely reliant on historical data, but rather guided by predictive insights. Artificial intelligence (AI)-enabled supply chain management systems possess the ability to anticipate potential difficulties, develop appropriate remedies, and continuously enhance operational procedures. This implies the existence of supply chains that exhibit not only high levels of efficiency but also possess the ability to continuously adapt and acquire knowledge, thereby enabling organizations to maintain a competitive edge in their operational approaches (C. Sharma, 2023).

Ethics in Supply Chain Management:

The field of Supply Chain Management extends beyond operational processes and encompasses the ethical obligations of businesses. In the current era characterized by heightened transparency, consumers are displaying a growing awareness regarding the origins and supply chains of the products they purchase. Consequently, ethical considerations have gained significant prominence and attention. The incorporation of Industry 4.0 technologies presents a range of intricate ethical quandaries, encompassing aspects such as sourcing, transparency, automation, and data management, despite the multitude of advantages it offers (Simon, Jhanjhi, Goh, & Sukumaran, 2022).

Moreover, with the increasing integration of automation and artificial intelligence (AI) in supply chain management, concerns regarding the impartiality of decision-making, the equitable implementation of automation, and the potential biases inherent in algorithms become apparent. It is imperative to comprehend that with the growing integration of technology in supply chain management, organizations bear a heightened obligation to guarantee the ethical utilization of these tools. The values of an organization are reflected in every decision made by an automated system, thereby highlighting the essential nature of ethical considerations in the field of supply chain management during the industry 4.0 era (Sobb, Turnbull, & Moustafa, 2020).

Societal Implications:

The integration of Industry 4.0 with supply chain management not only impacts industries, but also carries significant ramifications for society as a whole. The implementation of automation and digitization in various processes has resulted in consequential impacts on employment, skill demands, and societal structures. On the one hand, it is observed that certain job positions become obsolete or undergo transformations, thereby requiring individuals to acquire new skill sets. Consequently, this phenomenon gives rise to discussions and deliberations regarding the displacement of employment opportunities.

Simultaneously, with the increasing transparency of supply chains, consumers are becoming more cognizant, resulting in changes in their purchasing behaviors and a heightened desire for ethical sourcing and production. The fundamental characteristics of work undergo transformation, placing significant importance on digital literacy and adaptability. The redefinition of work, in conjunction with the societal changes brought about by highly efficient and digitized supply chains, necessitates a comprehensive comprehension to ensure that progress results in inclusive economic development rather than exacerbating social disparities.

Blockchain:

The concept of blockchain as shown in Figure 7, which first gained attention as the underlying technology for cryptocurrencies, has since been recognized for its significant potential in the field of supply chain management. Fundamentally, blockchain technology provides a decentralized ledger that is characterized by transparency, immutability, and resistance to tampering. Within the realm of supply chain management, this concept pertains to a continuous and uninterrupted flow of validated information, encompassing the entire journey of a product from its point of origin to its ultimate destination (Tiwari, Sharma, Choi, & Lim, 2023).

Figure 7. Principal traits of blockchain technology (Hazra, Alkhayyat, & Adhikari, 2022)

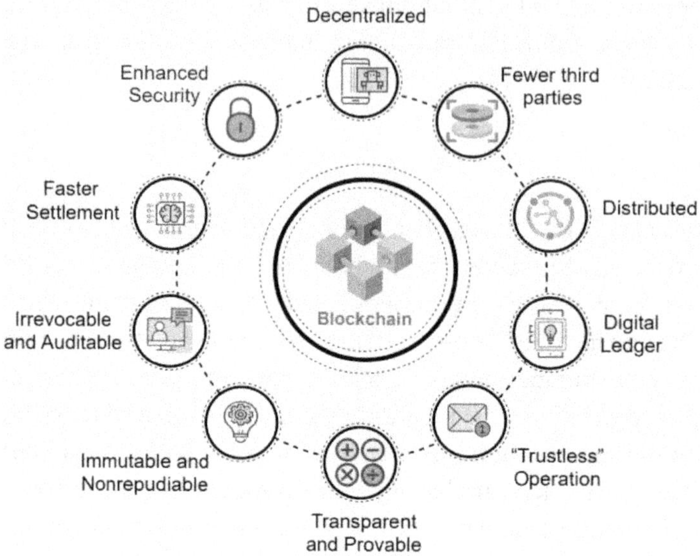

The implementation of blockchain technology enables all participants involved in the supply chain to authenticate products, monitor their trajectory, and guarantee adherence to established standards and regulations. The degree of transparency and traceability exhibited not only fosters trust but also assists in addressing ethical considerations pertaining to the sourcing, authenticity, and quality of products. In the realm of industries, the potential of blockchain extends beyond mere operational efficiency, as it represents a significant shift towards a novel epoch characterized by enhanced trust and accountability within the supply chain management domain(Rajmohan, Kumar, Pavithra, & Sandhya).

Data Privacy and Security:

The incorporation of Industry 4.0 technologies into supply chain management inevitably results in the production and retention of extensive quantities of data. Each device, sensor, and transaction can be considered as a data point. The aforementioned dataset possesses significant potential for optimization and predictive analytics; however, it also introduces considerable obstacles in relation to data privacy and security (Humayun, Hamid, Jhanjhi, Suseendran, & Talib, 2021).

The objective extends beyond the protection of data against breaches or cyberattacks; it encompasses the ethical handling of data, frequently of a personal and sensitive nature. The responsible management of this data, including its ethical utilization, storage, and dissemination, assumes utmost importance. Organizations must navigate the delicate balance of utilizing data to enhance supply chain management efficiency, while simultaneously upholding privacy regulations and adhering to ethical principles (Hazra et al., 2022).

Job Displacement and Reskilling:

The phenomenon of job displacement and the subsequent need for reskilling has become a topic of concern due to the rapid advancement of technology, which, although promising increased efficiency, raises questions about its effects on the labor market. With the integration of Industry 4.0 technologies into supply chain management, it is anticipated that certain job roles may become obsolete, resulting in potential job displacements. Nevertheless, it is imperative to acknowledge that this narrative is not unilaterally biased. In conjunction with the gradual elimination of specific occupations, novel positions arise that focus on the supervision, examination, and enhancement of these emerging systems (Hangl, Krause, & Behrens, 2023).

The dual nature of Industry 4.0 underscores the significance of reskilling and upskilling endeavors. The objective extends beyond mere workforce preparation for future employment opportunities, encompassing the imperative of enabling individuals to effectively leverage the capabilities presented by technological progress. This entails fostering a symbiotic integration of human expertise and machine efficiency (Hoberg, Thornton, & Wieland, 2020).

Stakeholder Collaboration:

The significance of stakeholder collaboration in supply chain management is heightened by the interconnectedness emphasized by Industry 4.0. Supply chains are no longer isolated sequences, but rather interconnected ecosystems in which actions in one segment can have ripple effects throughout. The significance of cohesive strategies, shared visions, and collaborative efforts is emphasized by this interconnectedness (Ghobakhloo et al., 2021).

Each stakeholder, including suppliers, manufacturers, logistics providers, and consumers, plays a crucial role in the overall functioning of the system. The efficacy of supply chain management in the era of Industry 4.0 relies on the establishment of synergistic collaborations, wherein common objectives are pursued through the utilization of shared resources. This approach guarantees the cohesive development of the entire supply chain, thereby optimizing value generation at each stage (Roman, Alcaraz, Lopez, & Sakurai, 2023).

1.5 Chapter Organization

The chapter titled "Ethical and Social Implications of Industry 4.0 in Supply Chain Management" is structured into ten distinct sections. Section 1 begins the introduction by illustrating the transformative impact of Industry 4.0 on supply chain management, while concurrently emphasizing the primary objectives and essential terminology of the study. Section 2 discusses Ethical Considerations in the Context of Industry 4.0 Supply chain management encompasses a range of topics including equitable labor practices, safeguarding data privacy, enhancing operational transparency, and assessing the broader societal implications associated with increased automation. Section 3 emphasis is on societal Implications of Industrialization exploring the transformation of employment, the imperative of a heterogeneous labor force, and the significant societal transformations resulting from emerging technologies.

Section 4 focusses on the ethical considerations and accountability in Data Analysis which is the field of Data Management and places significant emphasis on the prudent utilization of customer data, particularly in the context of employing artificial intelligence (AI) tools. Section 5 discussion pertains to Human-Centered Design, which underscores the significance of incorporating the needs of individuals during the development and implementation of Industry 4.0 tools. Additionally, it delves into the effective collaboration between humans and machines. Section 6 of the chapter delves into the governance and regulatory aspects pertaining to Industry 4.0, encompassing the established guidelines and protocols that govern its operations. Additionally, it highlights the imperative of adhering to emerging ethical standards in order to ensure responsible and sustainable implementation of Industry 4.0 technologies.

Section 7 highlights the significance of stakeholder engagement, emphasizing the need for collaborative efforts, establishment of ethical supply chain partnerships, and prioritization of stakeholder preferences. Section 8 elaborates the significance of impact assessment and responsible innovation endeavors to comprehensively evaluate the favorable and unfavorable consequences associated with Industry 4.0 initiatives, while advocating for the promotion of constructive technological advancements. Section 9 delves into the forthcoming trends that are anticipated to pose challenges in the future. Additionally, it explores the potential of novel tools in enhancing the ethical aspects of supply chains. The Last Section 10 is the conclusion which serves to succinctly recapitulate the primary arguments and propose a path for future action, all within the framework of upholding ethical principles.

2. ETHICAL ISSUES IN INDUSTRY 4.0-DRIVEN SCM

The ethical concerns arising from the implementation of Industry 4.0-driven supply chain management are a topic of significant academic interest. As we delve into the realm of Industry 4.0's impact on Supply Chain Management, the ethical dilemmas become more prominent. The integration of digital innovations into conventional supply chain practices raises a multitude of ethical considerations, necessitating organizations to reevaluate and realign their ethical frameworks in response to this technological transformation.

2.1 Fair Labor Practices and Workers' Rights in Smart Manufacturing

The emergence of smart manufacturing, which is distinguished by the integration of cyber-physical systems and interconnected devices, undeniably contributes to the optimization of operational efficiencies. Nevertheless, it concurrently undermines conventional labor practices. The rise of automated systems has sparked concerns regarding potential job displacements. The ethical obligation subsequently transitions to the imperative of safeguarding workers from being reduced to mere statistical redundancies. In the context of automation, it is imperative for companies to ensure the provision of equitable remuneration, reasonable working hours, and secure working environments. Furthermore, it is crucial from an ethical standpoint to allocate resources towards reskilling initiatives, which enable employees to adjust to the evolving paradigm and maintain the significance and appreciation of their knowledge and skills (Deepak Kumar et al., 2023; Sadiku, Ajayi-Majebi, & Adebo, 2023).

In addition to its immediate implications, smart manufacturing also has the potential to reshape the dynamic between workers and employers. The delicate equilibrium between supervision and intrusion must be carefully maintained when utilizing real-time monitoring capabilities. In order to uphold ethical standards, it is imperative that surveillance practices do not encroach upon the privacy rights of workers, thereby promoting an environment characterized by trust rather than perpetual monitoring (Rahanu, Georgiadou, Siakas, Ross, & Berki, 2021).

2.2 Privacy Concerns in the Era of Data-Driven Supply Chains

The exploitation of data-driven supply chains, which are powered by sensors, Internet of Things (IoT) devices, and analytics, has the potential to give unrivaled forecasting capabilities as well as real-time operational insights. Despite this, there is a heightened duty to protect sensitive and confidential information in the face of the vast amount of data that is being generated. A major cause for concern is the likelihood that personal information, whether it pertains to workers or consumers, would be utilized inappropriately or that unauthorized parties will gain access to it. In this specific context, ethical supply chain management covers not only the installation of robust cybersecurity (Jhanjhi, Khan, Ahmad, & Hussain, 2022) rules, but also the development of transparency in the collecting and exploitation of data. In other words, it goes beyond just having strong cybersecurity policies in place.

Table 1. Data-centric supply chains: Privacy issues

Concern Area	Privacy Risks	Potential Consequences	Mitigation Strategies
Data Collection	Excessive collection of sensitive vendor and customer information	Identity theft, corporate espionage	Limit data collection to essential info only
Data Storage	Inadequate encryption and protection measures	Unauthorized data access	Implement robust encryption and access control
Data Sharing	Sharing data with third parties without adequate safeguards	Data leaks, misuse	Vet third parties; establish stringent data sharing agreements
Vendor Management	Vendors may not adhere to privacy best practices	Supply chain vulnerabilities	Conduct regular audits; require compliance certification
User Consent	Lack of transparency in how data is used	Legal consequences, loss of trust	Clearly explain data usage and obtain explicit consent
Data Integration	Integration of various data sets could lead to more comprehensive profiles	Increased risk of identity theft	Use anonymization techniques
Location Tracking	Real-time tracking of goods can reveal sensitive location information	Competitive disadvantages	Limit real-time tracking to essential use cases only
Employee Monitoring	Extensive surveillance of employee productivity and behavior	Workplace privacy invasion	Limit monitoring to business-essential activities
IoT Devices	IoT devices in the supply chain can be hacked to obtain sensitive data	Security breaches	Ensure IoT security measures are in place
Regulatory Compliance	Failure to adhere to General Data Protection Regulation (GDPR) and California Consumer Privacy Act (CCPA)	Legal penalties, reputation damage	Maintain updated knowledge of and compliance with regulations

Moreover, it is imperative to establish precise delineations for determining the parameters of "essential data." Given its ability to monitor and evaluate various aspects such as consumer purchasing behaviors and employee performance indicators, there exists an ethical imperative to distinguish between valuable insights and intrusive surveillance. It is imperative for organizations to consistently evaluate the ethical implications of their data strategies, ensuring that they are in accordance with both regulatory frameworks and societal norms (Shayganmehr, Kumar, Garza-Reyes, & Moktadir, 2021).

2.3 Ensuring Transparency and Accountability in Supply Chain Operations

In order to promote a culture of transparency and accountability within supply chain operations, it is imperative to implement effective measures. These measures should aim to enhance visibility and traceability throughout the entire supply chain, from the sourcing of raw materials to the delivery of finished products. One key approach to achieving transparency and accountability is through the implementation of robust tracking systems.

The emergence of technologies such as blockchain offers a potentially advantageous pathway for attaining transparency within supply chains. From the procurement of raw materials to the final delivery of the end product, each transaction has the potential to be documented, authenticated, and disseminated. Nevertheless, the mere existence of these technologies does not ensure ethical practices. It is imperative for businesses to proactively engage in utilizing these tools to achieve authentic transparency, rather than merely engaging in superficial and symbolic actions. This entails transparently disclosing details pertaining to sourcing practices, environmental impacts, and labor conditions.

Additionally, transparency and accountability are intricately interconnected. Transparency in information dissemination constitutes a fundamental aspect, albeit not the sole component, of the overall framework. In addition, businesses are required to assume responsibility for their conduct. This involves the establishment of effective mechanisms for addressing grievances, conducting regular audits to ensure ethical compliance, and actively addressing the concerns of various stakeholders, including employees, consumers, and environmental advocates (Quarshie, Salmi, & Leuschner, 2016; Svensson, 2009).

2.4 Addressing Ethical Dilemmas in AI and Automation in SCM

Artificial Intelligence has the capacity to bring about significant transformations in Supply Chain Management, providing a range of solutions that encompass predictive analytics and intelligent automation. However, the process of this transformation is accompanied by a multitude of ethical quandaries. One of the foremost concerns pertains to the inherent opaqueness of certain AI models, commonly referred to as the 'black box' nature, which hinders the understanding of their decision-making processes (Ma, Zhang, & Zhang, 2018). Ambiguity within the supply chain domain can result in the emergence of unexplained biases, inaccuracies, or potentially unethical autonomous decision-making. There exists a significant demand for the development of interpretable Artificial intelligence models that facilitate the inclusion of human oversight and intervention (Ha & Nam, 2016).

Moreover, the allocation of decision-making authority to automated systems gives rise to inquiries regarding accountability. In situations where decisions driven by artificial intelligence result in unfavorable consequences, the task of identifying responsibility becomes complex. Who should be held responsible for the outcome: the software developers, the SCM executives who implemented the AI, or the AI itself? It is imperative to establish ethical guidelines in order to effectively navigate the complex and ambiguous realm of automation. These guidelines are necessary to ensure that automation not only improves decision-making processes, but also upholds moral responsibility, rather than diminishing it (Soni & Soni, 2019).

2.5 Impact of Industry 4.0 on Local Communities and Societies

The ramifications of Industry 4.0 in supply chain management extend beyond the confines of manufacturing facilities and storage spaces, impacting nearby communities and wider societies. The potential consequences of technological advancements include the possibility of localized job displacement, wherein specific regions may experience economic downturns as industries transition towards automation-focused centers. Corporations bear an ethical responsibility to prevent the negative consequences of technological advancement from leading to societal decline. Initiatives aimed at bolstering local economies, encompassing community development projects as well as educational programs, assume a paramount significance (Kumar & Mallipeddi, 2022; Xu, Lu, Vogel-Heuser, & Wang, 2021).

Moreover, with the increasing globalization and interconnectivity of supply chains, it is crucial to take into account the wider societal implications. The decisions formulated within corporate boardrooms possess the potential to impact environmental sustainability in geographically distant areas or exert influence on labor markets in remote regions. Acknowledging the extensive impact on a global scale and actively striving towards a growth model that is fair, environmentally responsible, and promotes inclusivity becomes a moral obligation for businesses operating within the context of the industry 4.0 driven landscape (M. N. Hussain, 2023; Maharana & Lathabhavan, 2023).

3. SOCIAL IMPLICATIONS OF INDUSTRY 4.0 IN SCM

The convergence of Industry 4.0 and Supply Chain Management gives rise to both ethical considerations and significant social implications. The transformative impact of digital technologies on supply chain management extends beyond its operational aspects, as it also has unintended consequences on various social dimensions. These technologies have the potential to shape workforce dynamics, promote sustainability, and contribute to equitable growth. The comprehensive comprehension of Industry 4.0's wider societal consequences necessitates a meticulous examination of these intricate social dynamics (Hoffmann & Prause, 2018). The term "Industry 4.0" is used to describe the current manufacturing and production paradigm shift brought about by the widespread use of digital technologies like the Internet of Things (IoT)(Jabeen et al., 2023), artificial intelligence (AI) (Jayakumar, Brohi, & Jhanjhi, 2021), big data analytics (Alferidah & Jhanjhi, 2020), and sophisticated robots. In particular, Supply Chain Management has been profoundly impacted by this transformation. The following table provides a more in-depth look at these societal effects:

Table 2. Societal shifts in supply chain dynamics and IR4.0

Aspect	Social Implication	Detailed Discussion	Mitigation or Enhancement Strategies
Employment	Job displacement due to automation	The adoption of AI, robotics, and other automation tools may reduce the need for certain manual tasks, leading to job losses, especially for low-skilled workers. However, new roles may emerge that require different skill sets.	Retraining programs, continuous learning opportunities, education in STEM fields.
Work Quality	Improved safety and efficiency	Digital technologies can monitor and regulate operations in real-time, reducing workplace accidents and increasing efficiency. But this could also lead to intense monitoring and reduced autonomy for workers.	Ensure ethical use of surveillance, provide workers with a say in their operational environment.
Skill Requirements	Need for upskilled and reskilled workforce	Workers need to be familiar with digital tools, data analytics, and other modern techniques, raising the bar for required skills in SCM.	Invest in training programs, partner with educational institutions for skill development.
Work-life Balance	Flexible working conditions	Remote monitoring and management tools can allow employees to work from varied locations, potentially improving work-life balance. But it could also blur the boundaries between work and personal time.	Implement clear guidelines for work hours, encourage breaks, and disconnect times.
Globalization	Easier collaboration across borders	Digital platforms allow for real-time communication and collaboration regardless of geography, fostering a more globalized workforce in SCM.	Cross-cultural training, understanding time zones and local customs for effective collaboration.
Economic Disparities	Widening gap between tech-savvy and non-tech companies	Companies that can afford and adapt to Industry 4.0 technologies may have a competitive edge over smaller, less technologically advanced firms, potentially increasing economic disparities.	Government incentives for smaller firms, consortiums to share resources and knowledge.
Transparency and Trust	Increased demand for supply chain transparency	With digital traceability, consumers demand more transparency about product origins, materials, and labor conditions. This can build trust but also opens up companies to greater scrutiny.	Adopt ethical practices, use technology to provide real-time data to consumers.
Data Privacy	Concerns about personal and sensitive data breaches	As SCM integrates more digital solutions, the amount of data being collected and stored increases, raising concerns about data security and privacy.	Implement robust cybersecurity measures, regular audits, and adhere to global data protection regulations.
Environmental Concerns	Enhanced sustainability monitoring	Digital tools can track and optimize energy use, emissions, and waste in real-time. This can lead to greener supply chains but also demands responsibility in e-waste management.	Adopt eco-friendly practices, e-waste management programs, and promote circular economy principles.
Social Responsibility	Increased corporate social responsibility (CSR) due to visibility	With greater visibility into the supply chain, there's a higher expectation for companies to ensure ethical labor practices, fair wages, and positive community relations.	Regular audits, partnering with ethical suppliers, community engagement programs.

Industry 4.0 offers SCM many benefits but also many socially significant concerns. Socially responsible businesses must recognize and handle these concerns.

3.1 Job Displacement and Workforce Transition in Smart Factories

Smart factories, which are representative of the fourth industrial revolution (Industry 4.0), offer the potential for unparalleled levels of efficiency, precision, and productivity. However, these challenges present notable obstacles to the conventional framework of the workforce. The performance of tasks once exclusively carried out by humans is progressively being assumed by automated processes and intelligent machines. As a result, there is a potential for significant job displacement due to the risk of job roles becoming obsolete. The immediate aftermath gives rise to concerns regarding economic stability, as individuals who have been affected must confront the challenges of unemployment and the subsequent socio-economic consequences (Awodele, Ngige, & Balogun, 2021).

Nevertheless, the issue at hand extends beyond the mere disappearance of conventional societal positions. Smart factories also represent the emergence of novel, specialized job roles that are focused on supervising, maintaining, and enhancing these automated procedures. The workforce transition involves the gradual elimination of certain job roles and the simultaneous introduction of new positions that are centered around technology. The dynamic nature of this changing environment necessitates careful consideration in order to facilitate a seamless transition and minimize the negative societal consequences associated with unemployment (Anshari, Syafrudin, & Fitriyani, 2022).

3.2 Reskilling and Upskilling for Industry 4.0 Employment

In light of the unavoidable shift in the workforce, initiatives aimed at reskilling and upskilling individuals have emerged as imperative endeavors with significant societal implications. The rapid pace of technological advancement surpasses the conventional paths of education, resulting in a discernible disparity in skills. Addressing this disparity necessitates a collaborative endeavor, wherein businesses, educational institutions, and governments join forces to redefine curricula and training initiatives. These initiatives have the objective of providing the current workforce with the necessary skills to succeed in an Industry 4.0 setting (L. Li, 2022).

In addition to the imperative of acquiring new skills, there exists a more encompassing societal obligation to cultivate a milieu that promotes continuous learning throughout one's lifetime. The industry 4.0 paradigm is characterized by its dynamic nature, as it encompasses a constant evolution of technologies. As a result, it is imperative for the workforce to adjust to this dynamic nature by embracing the concept of continuous learning as an integral component of professional development. This transition not only guarantees the ability to find employment but also fosters a more adaptable, creative, and robust societal structure, prepared to navigate the intricacies of a swiftly evolving industrial environment (Dash, Farooq, Panda, & Sandhyavani, 2019).

3.3 Promoting Diversity and Inclusivity in the Technological Workforce

The advent of Industry 4.0 presents a favorable occasion to rectify longstanding disparities within the technological labor force. Historically, there has been a lack of representation of specific demographic groups in technology-focused positions, which can be attributed to factors such as gender, ethnicity, and socio-economic backgrounds. With the emergence of novel job profiles within the supply chain management sector, it is imperative to uphold a social responsibility to ensure equal accessibility to these opportunities, regardless of individuals' backgrounds (Ustundag, Cevikcan, & Karacay, 2018).

Advocating for the enhancement of diversity and inclusivity within the workforce of Industry 4.0 is not solely a matter of ethics, but also holds strategic significance. Diverse teams possess a range of perspectives, thereby promoting innovation and comprehensive approaches to problem-solving. Through the deliberate implementation of inclusive hiring practices, the establishment of mentorship programs, and the creation of work environments that foster productivity, businesses have the opportunity to leverage the numerous benefits associated with a diverse workforce. This not only promotes social equity but also enhances operational excellence (Dhanpat, Buthelezi, Joe, Maphela, & Shongwe, 2020).

3.4 Social Responsibility and Sustainable Supply Chain Management

The advent of Industry 4.0 has bestowed SCM operations with significant capabilities, enabling them to exert profound and enduring effects on societies. These effects can manifest in both beneficial and detrimental ways. The concept of environmental sustainability has emerged as a critical area of focus, wherein supply chains play a significant role in shaping carbon footprints, waste management practices, and resource utilization. It is incumbent upon businesses to embrace sustainable practices, not solely as a means of meeting regulatory requirements, but rather as fundamental elements of their operational philosophy (Chen, Wang, & Li, 2023).

However, sustainability extends beyond the realm of environmental considerations. Social sustainability is a critical aspect that encompasses various elements such as fair labor practices, community engagement, and ethical sourcing. Business enterprises, by virtue of their supply chain management activities, establish a social compact with the local communities in which they conduct their operations. Honoring this contractual agreement encompasses not only the act of extracting value, but also engaging in reciprocal actions, making positive contributions to societal welfare, and promoting sustainable growth (Novitasari, Wijaya, Agustin, Gunardi, & Dana, 2023).

3.5 Influence of Industry 4.0 on Social Equity and Access to Technology

The advent of Industry 4.0 has the capacity to facilitate the equalization of technological access, thereby mitigating socio-economic disparities. Nevertheless, in the absence of deliberate endeavors, it has the potential to further intensify pre-existing disparities. The increasing integration of advanced technologies within supply chain management raises concerns regarding the potential creation of a dichotomy. This dichotomy would manifest as a division between individuals or organizations who possess access to these technologies and the subsequent opportunities they afford, and those who lack such access. The occurrence of this bifurcation has the potential to result in social stratification, whereby one's societal status is influenced by their level of technological expertise (Nguyen, Mani, Kha M, & Papadopoulos, 2023).

In order to address this issue, it is imperative to give precedence to ensuring fair and equal access to Industry 4.0 technologies. Efforts should be directed towards ensuring that the benefits of these advancements are accessible to all segments of society. This encompasses the objectives of ensuring the affordability of technology, promoting digital literacy, and facilitating the development of infrastructure to facilitate widespread adoption of technology. Through proactive advocacy for social equity within the framework of Industry 4.0, enterprises have the capacity to mold a forthcoming era in which technological advancements lead to comprehensive societal progress (Picasso, Biazzin, Paiva, & Beal Partyka, 2023).

4. DATA ETHICS AND RESPONSIBLE DATA MANAGEMENT IN SCM

In the era of Industry 4.0, data plays a fundamental role in the foundation of contemporary Supply Chain Management practices. The utilization of data in various contexts gives rise to a multitude of ethical considerations, thereby requiring the establishment of robust frameworks to ensure responsible management of data. With the growing reliance on data in supply chains, it is crucial for businesses aiming to achieve operational excellence and ethical integrity to possess a comprehensive understanding of and adeptness in managing the ethical complexities associated with this trend (Bag, Rahman, Srivastava, Shore, & Ram, 2023).

4.1 Ethical Use of Customer Data in Supply Chains

The utilization of customer data, encompassing purchasing patterns and personal information, presents significant opportunities for enhancing supply chain optimization. Nevertheless, the acquisition and utilization of [subject] entail significant ethical obligations. It is imperative for firms to guarantee the transparent sourcing of data, accompanied by explicit consent, and to restrict its usage solely to its intended purpose. The improper utilization or commercialization of this data not only violates the confidence placed in an entity, but also gives rise to ethical concerns regarding a company's dedication to its various parties of interest (J. Wang & Feng, 2023).

Furthermore, with the increasing convergence of data-driven personalization and intrusive surveillance, it is imperative for companies to exercise caution. The utilization of customer data has the potential to enhance the user experience; however, excessive utilization can encroach upon the rights to privacy of individuals. Therefore, it is imperative to maintain a delicate balance wherein customer insights serve as the driving force behind supply chain management processes, without jeopardizing ethical principles or eroding customer trust (Dhirani, Mukhtiar, Chowdhry, & Newe, 2023).

4.2 Data Privacy and Security in Connected Manufacturing

Connected manufacturing ecosystems, which are considered key features of Industry 4.0, facilitate the smooth transmission of data among different components of the supply chain management system. However, the interconnectivity of systems also magnifies vulnerabilities, thereby elevating the significance of data security as a primary concern. The consequences of breaches, encompassing both financial losses and reputational harm, can have a profoundly destructive impact. Moreover, the occurrence of breaches has the potential to compromise confidential data, thereby posing a significant threat to both individuals and businesses (Benyahya, Collen, Kechagia, & Nijdam, 2022).

Hence, the implementation of robust data security protocols is imperative. This encompasses a range of measures, including technical safeguards like encryption and intrusion detection systems, as well as organizational approaches such as employee training and third-party vetting. In the domain of interconnected manufacturing, characterized by a vast and intricate data landscape, it is imperative to adopt proactive measures to guarantee the privacy and security of data, as they are not merely suggested but indispensable (Tsao, Yang, Zoepf, & Pavone, 2022).

4.3 Balancing Data-Driven Decision Making and Ethical Considerations

The utilization of data-driven decision-making in supply chain management provides a means of achieving optimization that is characterized by objectivity, efficiency, and frequently enhanced accuracy. Nevertheless, an excessive dependence on data may occasionally conflict with ethical considerations. For example, specific strategies based on data analysis may prioritize financial gain over ethical considerations, such as the exploitation of labor in regions characterized by low costs but inadequate working conditions (Jahani, Jain, & Ivanov, 2023).

Therefore, it is important to exercise ethical discernment when interpreting and applying data, despite its potential to offer valuable tools for decision-making. It is imperative for organizations to incorporate ethical safeguards and mechanisms within their data analytics procedures, thereby guaranteeing that the derived insights are in accordance with the company's ethical framework and societal obligations (Rawindaran, 2023).

4.4 The Role of Blockchain in Enhancing Data Transparency and Integrity

The utilization of blockchain technology has emerged as a powerful mechanism for enhancing data ethics within the realm of supply chain management. Blockchain technology offers unparalleled transparency due to its decentralized and immutable nature, enabling stakeholders at every stage of the supply chain management process to verify the authenticity of data. Blockchain technology provides a transparent and tamper-resistant ledger that can be utilized for various purposes, ranging from monitoring the sourcing of raw materials to verifying the authenticity of products for end-users (Ar et al., 2020).

Furthermore, the potential of blockchain technology encompasses the ability to address the issue of counterfeit goods, ensure the ethical sourcing of products, and streamline audits through the provision of transparent and immutable transaction records. The incorporation of blockchain technology into supply chain management procedures has the potential to greatly augment the integrity and transparency of data, thereby strengthening trust among various stakeholders and bolstering the implementation of ethical practices (Laboso, Martin, & Thiyagarajan, 2023).

4.5 Ethical Considerations in Supply Chain Analytics and AI Applications

The integration of AI-driven analytics into supply chain management presents a range of ethical challenges. Although these tools possess the capability to accurately predict, analyze, and optimize supply chain operations, their functionality is contingent upon the data they receive. The presence of biased or skewed data has the potential to result in AI systems making decisions that unintentionally perpetuate pre-existing prejudices or fail to consider certain stakeholders (Lele & Lele, 2019).

Moreover, the opaqueness of certain AI algorithms, commonly referred to as "black-box" algorithms, can obfuscate the underlying decision-making processes, resulting in a dearth of transparency and accountability. Therefore, it is imperative for businesses to ensure the ethical alignment of artificial intelligence (AI) when implementing it in supply chain management. This entails the utilization of impartial training data, consistent evaluation of AI decisions to ensure fairness and precision, and a commitment to transparency in the process of making AI-driven decisions. The realization of the full potential of artificial intelligence (AI) in supply chain management can only be achieved when ethical standards are upheld (Saidakhrarovich & Tursunovich, 2022).

5. HUMAN-CENTERED DESIGN AND USER EXPERIENCE IN SMART MANUFACTURING

The prominence of user experience and human-centered design in smart manufacturing is often emphasized within the context of the Fourth Industrial Revolution, which is characterized by a range of technological advancements. As the integration of machines with human processes becomes more prevalent, it becomes crucial to prioritize the user's needs and ensure that the technology serves them, rather than the other way around. This paradigm shift, characterized by a deep regard for the needs and limitations of human beings, presents a manufacturing environment that is more encompassing, streamlined, and morally upright (Abikoye et al., 2021).

The integration of human-centered designs extends beyond mere considerations of aesthetics or interface usability. This represents a significant paradigm shift, wherein there is a prioritization of the needs, capabilities, and overall well-being of the end user. When smart manufacturing solutions are developed with a human-centric approach, they are more likely to be well-received by users, leading to easier adoption and operation (Masum, 2023).

5.1 Considering Human Factors in the Development of Industry 4.0 Technologies

In the context of developing advancements for Industry 4.0, the comprehensive comprehension and seamless incorporation of human factors can significantly impact the adoption and utilization of such innovations. This methodology necessitates the integration of ergonomics, cognitive psychology, and user experience design. By prioritizing the alignment of technologies with human capabilities and limitations, we enhance their effectiveness and mitigate potential safety risks (Melnyk, Kubatko, Matsenko, Balatskyi, & Serdyukov, 2023).

The concept of human factors encompasses a wide range of elements, including physical interaction, cognitive loads, emotional impacts, and social considerations. The recognition of these layers guarantees that the technologies developed are not only efficient but also intuitive, thereby minimizing the obstacles to their adoption and ensuring a smoother integration into current workflows (Tortorella, Fogliatto, Kumar, Gonzalez, & Pepper, 2023).

5.2 Usability and Accessibility of Industry 4.0 Systems in SCM

The integration of Industry 4.0 into supply chain management highlights the significance of system usability and accessibility. Merely possessing power or efficiency is inadequate for a system; if its complexity surpasses its usefulness, its adoption may be hindered. By placing a strong emphasis on usability, we prioritize the design and functionality of technology to effectively cater to the needs and preferences of its users, rather than requiring users to conform to the technology's limitations.

Beyond the concept of usability lies the domain of accessibility. In order to foster inclusivity, it is imperative that Industry 4.0 technologies are developed with the intention of accommodating not only the typical user, but also individuals with diverse abilities, cultural backgrounds, and varying access to resources. The implementation of this all-encompassing strategy guarantees that the benefits of technological progress are accessible to a wider range of individuals, thereby promoting fairness and inclusiveness (Tashtoush et al., 2022).

5.3 Human-Robot Collaboration and Trust in Smart Factories

The depiction of industrious smart factories frequently encompasses the collaboration between human workers and robotic counterparts. The realization of a collaborative future is contingent upon the establishment and maintenance of mutual trust. In this envisioned future, robots transcend their conventional role as mere tools and instead become collaborators, thereby necessitating the development of designs that facilitate symbiotic interactions. The design challenges involve the imperative of guaranteeing safety, predictability, and mutual adaptability (Othman & Yang, 2023).

Furthermore, the cultivation of trust is a complex undertaking. There is a requirement for both dependable and consistent robot behavior, as well as a need for transparency in their decision-making processes. It is imperative for workers to possess a comprehensive understanding of the underlying rationale behind the behavioral patterns exhibited by a robotic collaborator. This knowledge fosters an environment characterized by predictability and a sense of ease. The complete realization of human-robot collaboration's maximum capabilities can only occur within such a specific context (S. Li et al., 2023).

5.4 The Role of Design Thinking in Addressing Ethical and Social Implications

The iterative and human-centric approach of design thinking makes it particularly well-suited to address the ethical and societal challenges associated with Industry 4.0. By incorporating empathy and a comprehensive understanding as fundamental aspects of the innovation process, it becomes possible to proactively recognize and tackle potential obstacles, such as unforeseen user difficulties or wider societal consequences (Villegas-Galaviz & Martin, 2023).

The iterative nature of design thinking, with a focus on prototyping and feedback, guarantees a perpetual synchronization with the requirements and desires of individuals. The adaptive process, particularly within the domain of smart manufacturing, has the potential to act as a safeguard against unintended ethical lapses, guaranteeing that technological advancements are firmly rooted in the well-being of humanity and ethical principles (Widder & Wong, 2023).

6. GOVERNANCE AND REGULATIONS FOR ETHICAL INDUSTRY 4.0 SCM

The establishment and enforcement of governance and regulations play a crucial role in upholding ethical standards and ensuring accountability in the context of integrating Industry 4.0 into supply chain management. As companies globally embrace and adjust to the technologies associated with the Fourth Industrial Revolution, the implementation of standardized governance measures guarantees that ethical and societal considerations are given top priority. The successful navigation of the digital era by SCM, while maintaining stakeholder trust and societal welfare, is contingent upon the implementation of appropriate checks and balances (H. Sharma, Garg, Sewani, & Kashef, 2023).

Achieving a harmonious equilibrium between fostering innovation and safeguarding diverse interests poses a formidable challenge. The complex interplay between international and regional laws, coupled with the rapid pace of technological progress, calls for a flexible yet strong regulatory structure that serves as a guiding principle for ethical practices and advancements in innovation (Dathe, Dathe, Dathe, & Helmold, 2022).

6.1 International and Regional Regulations Impacting Industry 4.0

To effectively navigate the global impact of supply chains, it is imperative to possess comprehensive knowledge of the regulations pertaining to Industry 4.0 at both international and regional levels. The regulations, frequently established by international organizations and individual countries, strive to establish fundamental standards for security, transparency, data protection, and other related aspects. Nevertheless, these constraints should not be regarded as mere limitations, but rather as a valuable tool for effectively navigating the complex global landscape (Bag & Pretorius, 2022).

It is imperative for organizations to possess a comprehensive understanding of and adapt to these diverse legislations, thereby ensuring compliance while also capitalizing on the opportunities they present. The existence of varying regulations across different regions presents certain difficulties, but it also provides opportunities to align operations in a manner that adheres to ethical standards and optimizes effectiveness (Raj, Dwivedi, Sharma, de Sousa Jabbour, & Rajak, 2020).

6.2 Responsible Innovation and Ethical Guidelines for Technological Development

The responsible guidance of innovation is of utmost importance in the era of Industry 4.0. The advent of digital transformation presents significant opportunities, yet simultaneously raises ethical dilemmas. Organizations must rely on comprehensive ethical guidelines when formulating their technological strategies (Jobin, Ienca, & Vayena, 2019).

By incorporating ethical considerations into the process of innovation, businesses are able to proactively identify and mitigate potential challenges and drawbacks. The implementation of a proactive strategy, based on principles that prioritize human well-being and sustainable practices, guarantees that technological progress enhances societal environments rather than diminishing them (Hagendorff, 2020).

6.3 Establishing Ethical Supply Chain Standards and Certifications

Within the intricate domain of supply chain management, certifications and standards serve as indicators of trustworthiness and dependability. Ethical supply chain standards serve as a fundamental framework for conducting responsible operations, while also providing organizations with a chance to distinguish themselves within a highly competitive market (Narula, 2019).

These certifications, frequently supported by international entities, serve as more than mere symbols. They indicate an organization's dedication to maintaining ethical, sustainable, and socially responsible behaviors. Over time, the adherence to these standards has the potential to facilitate enhanced stakeholder relations, bolster brand reputation, and generate a significant positive influence on global supply chain ecosystems (Chkanikova & Sroufe, 2021).

6.4 Ensuring Compliance With Ethical Practices and Industry Standards

The implementation of standards and regulations presents a significant hurdle in terms of ensuring adherence. It is imperative for organizations to not only possess knowledge of these ethical standards but also to actively integrate them into their operational framework. Compliance encompasses more than simply evading penalties; it involves advocating for a comprehensive ethical supply chain management framework (Shneiderman, 2020).

By implementing robust internal audit mechanisms, continuous training programs, and feedback loops, organizations can effectively uphold ethical practices and surpass industry standards on a consistent basis. This commitment not only serves to protect against potential damage to one's reputation, but also strengthens an organization's standing as a moral authority within the context of Industry 4.0 (Shojaeshafiei, Etzkorn, & Anderson, 2020).

7. STAKEHOLDER ENGAGEMENT AND ETHICAL SUPPLY CHAIN PARTNERSHIPS

The core of a supply chain is comprised of stakeholders, which are entities that possess a vested interest in the functioning of the supply chain. In the era of Industry 4.0, the transformation and growing complexity of supply chains have led to an amplified significance of stakeholders. By adopting ethical, transparent, and collaborative approaches, organizations can ensure the resilience and responsibility of their supply chain management strategies (Blok, 2019).

The fundamental basis of ethical supply chain partnerships lies in the establishment of mutual trust and the alignment of shared values. Within the context of a highly interconnected global ecosystem, the pursuit of organizational growth extends beyond individual entities and encompasses the promotion of collective welfare. By actively participating and working together, supply chains have the ability to effectively tackle common obstacles and jointly develop solutions that prioritize ethical considerations (Brun, Karaosman, & Barresi, 2020).

7.1 Collaboration With Suppliers and Partners to Address Ethical Concerns

Suppliers and partners hold a crucial role within the expansive framework of supply chain operations. Engaging in collaborative efforts with relevant stakeholders to collectively address mutual ethical concerns contributes to the establishment of a harmonious and resilient supply chain management ecosystem. This collaborative effort extends beyond mere transactional relationships, delving into the realms of shared problem-solving and co-creation.

Organizations can proactively address potential challenges and develop solutions through the cultivation of open dialogues, collaborative workshops, and the establishment of shared ethical frameworks. The implementation of an integrated approach serves to strengthen the supply chain and maintain a consistent emphasis on ethical considerations throughout all stages (Dahlmann & Roehrich, 2019).

7.2 Stakeholder Engagement for Ethical Decision Making in SCM

Every decision made within the realm of supply chain management has consequential impacts that extend beyond the immediate context, affecting a multitude of stakeholders involved in the process. The involvement of these stakeholders in the decision-making process guarantees the inclusion of a wide range of viewpoints, resulting in more comprehensive and morally sound results. This endeavor encompasses more than mere consultation; it entails collaborative efforts to shape the future of supply chain management.

Stakeholder engagement forums, feedback mechanisms, and collaborative platforms provide opportunities for the inclusion of a wide range of perspectives. By placing importance on these perspectives, organizations can develop supply chain management strategies that are not only effective but also ethically sound and mindful of wider societal consequences (Attanasio, Preghenella, De Toni, & Battistella, 2022).

7.3 Supplier Diversity and Inclusive Procurement Practices

In the context of ethical supply chain management, the principle of inclusivity holds utmost significance. The promotion of supplier diversity aims to incorporate a wider range of partners with diverse backgrounds and perspectives into the supply chain. Inclusive procurement transcends mere compliance and entails enhancing the supply chain through the integration of diverse perspectives, fostering equity, and catalyzing socio-economic advancement.

By placing supplier diversity as a priority, organizations not only bolster their ability to withstand challenges but also make a positive impact on wider societal advancement. This approach demonstrates an organization's dedication to ethical principles, promotes the development of new ideas, and facilitates the establishment of a more comprehensive global economy (Seyedghorban, Samson, & Tahernejad, 2020).

7.4 Building Trust and Long-Term Relationships Through Ethical Supply Chains

Trust is a fundamental cornerstone in establishing and maintaining a successful and mutually beneficial supply chain partnership. In the ever-evolving realm of Industry 4.0, the imperative of cultivating trust becomes increasingly paramount as supply chains undergo transformation and adaptation. The establishment of trust is predicated upon ethical operations, the practice of transparency, and the ongoing engagement of stakeholders.

Organizations can foster enduring and mutually beneficial relationships with their stakeholders by placing a high emphasis on ethical considerations. Partnerships of this nature, characterized by mutual respect and shared values, contribute to the sustainability and robustness of the supply chain. In an epoch characterized by swift transformations and unpredictability, trust assumes a pivotal role in steering supply chain management (SCM) towards enduring achievements (Razak, Hendry, & Stevenson, 2023).

8. IMPACT ASSESSMENT AND RESPONSIBLE INNOVATION

The imperative of evaluating the effects and promoting ethical advancement is inherent in the revolutionary capabilities of Industry 4.0 technologies. This approach guarantees that the implementation of technology enhances the global socio-economic structure rather than jeopardizing it. Through the integration of proactive impact assessment and responsible innovation, organizations have the ability to anticipate potential challenges, develop comprehensive solutions, and advocate for a sustainable vision in the context of supply chain management.

8.1 Ethical Impact Assessment of Industry 4.0 Technologies

Prior to implementing any Industry 4.0 technology, it is imperative to conduct a comprehensive evaluation of its ethical implications. An ethical impact assessment offers a comprehensive framework for evaluating the potential positive and negative outcomes of technology on society, the environment, and the economy. Through proactive consideration of these effects, organizations can make well-informed choices, thereby ensuring that their innovations have a positive impact on the wider ecosystem.

These assessments not only identify potential challenges but also highlight strategies for maximizing societal benefit. By means of these assessments, adjustments can be made to technologies, standards can be established, and implementations can be harmonized with ethical principles, guaranteeing their alignment with the values of stakeholders and societal norms (Bai, Dallasega, Orzes, & Sarkis, 2020).

8.2 Responsible Research and Innovation in Smart Manufacturing

The advancement of smart manufacturing is propelled by research and innovation. Nevertheless, it is imperative to acknowledge that this motivation must be accompanied by a sense of duty in order to guarantee the ethical soundness of these progressions. The concept of responsible research and innovation (RRI) entails the integration of technological progress with the requirements and principles of society.

Responsible Research and Innovation (RRI) encompasses methodologies that are inclusive, anticipatory, and reflexive, taking into account the wider ramifications of innovations. Through the promotion of collaboration among researchers, innovators, stakeholders, and end-users, Responsible Research, and Innovation (RRI) guarantees that smart manufacturing technologies not only improve efficiency but also prioritize societal well-being and sustainability (Pacaux-Lemoine & Trentesaux, 2019).

8.3 Measuring and Evaluating Ethical Performance in SCM

Merely advocating for ethical principles is insufficient; it is imperative to consistently assess and appraise their observance and effectiveness. In the field of supply chain management, the convergence of multiple nodes and stakeholders necessitates the establishment of standardized ethical performance metrics. Once established, these metrics serve as a reliable measure to assess the ethical state of the supply chain.

Regular evaluations, audits, and feedback loops serve to ensure that these metrics are not merely static indicators, but rather dynamic tools that adapt and develop in response to the evolving landscape. This proactive approach guarantees the prompt identification, resolution, and correction of ethical deviations, thereby maintaining a consistent alignment of supply chain management operations with ethical principles (Ogbuke, Yusuf, Dharma, & Mercangoz, 2022).

8.4 The Role of Sustainability Reporting in Addressing Ethical Concerns

Sustainability reporting functions as a means of facilitating communication and fostering engagement between organizations and their various stakeholders. Organizations can effectively convey their dedication to ethical supply chain management by means of comprehensive reports that provide detailed information on sustainability initiatives, accomplishments, and obstacles. This transparent communication enables stakeholders to gain a clear understanding of the organization's commitment to ethical practices in SCM. The implementation of transparency measures serves to strengthen the trust of stakeholders and facilitates the development of collaborative solutions.

However, these reports serve a purpose beyond mere communication. Organizational ethics are effectively mirrored by these entities, which serve to reflect the ethical standing of an organization while also drawing attention to areas that require enhancement. Organizations can maintain accountability, promote stakeholder engagement, and continuously enhance their ethical supply chain management (SCM) strategies through the consistent dissemination of sustainability reports (Fritz, 2019).

9. FUTURE TRENDS AND RESEARCH DIRECTIONS IN ETHICAL INDUSTRY 4.0 SCM

The convergence of Industry 4.0 and supply chain management presents a promising and dynamic landscape, characterized by a multitude of potential opportunities and accompanying challenges. In light of ongoing technological advancements, it is crucial to comprehend the ever-changing ethical dilemmas and incorporate multidisciplinary research in order to navigate this evolving landscape effectively. Successfully navigating the challenges of the future necessitates the possession of a vision that encompasses not only a deep understanding of technology, but also a strong ethical foundation (Ali, 2022).

Supply Chain Management has been transformed by the use of Industry 4.0 (IR4.0) technologies including artificial intelligence (AI), the internet of things (IoT), and blockchain. However, there are social and ethical questions raised by this integration. Due to rising consumer expectations for complete product traceability, technologies like blockchain and the Internet of Things (IoT) are being explored as viable solutions. While automation improves productivity, it also raises concerns like the displacement of workers. Here, the focus should be on augmenting human functions rather than replacing them, with a focus on reskilling and human-AI collaboration. Also under review is data management, with proponents calling for more effective procedures that protect users' privacy without sacrificing productivity. Finally, as global concerns about sustainability grow, SCM is under increasing pressure to include environmentally friendly and ethical methods while also being sensitive to cultural differences.

9.1 Evolving Ethical Challenges in the Continuous Advancement of Industry 4.0

The rapid and continuous progress of Industry 4.0 necessitates the ongoing evolution of ethical challenges. The evaluation of societal, environmental, and economic implications becomes necessary as technologies progress and novel innovations arise. Staying informed about these evolving challenges necessitates a combination of technological expertise and ethical discernment.

Organizations can maintain a competitive edge in the face of dynamic challenges by cultivating a culture that promotes ongoing learning, attentiveness, and active engagement with stakeholders. The implementation of proactive anticipation measures guarantees the maintenance of innovative and ethically sound supply chain management strategies (V. Sharma et al., 2022).

9.2 The Role of Emerging Technologies in Shaping Ethical SCM

The potential of emerging technologies, such as quantum computing and advanced biotechnologies, holds the promise of bringing about a further revolution in supply chain management (SCM).

Table 3. Emerging technologies role in shaping ethical SCM

Emerging Technology	Role in Ethical SCM	Detailed Discussion	Mitigation or Enhancement Strategies
Blockchain	Ensuring transparency and traceability	Blockchain can provide a secure and immutable ledger of transactions. This makes it easier to track products from source to consumer, ensuring the authenticity and ethical sourcing of products.	Promote adoption of blockchain standards across the supply chain. Foster industry collaboration for uniform practices.
Artificial Intelligence (AI)	Enhancing decision-making	AI can analyze vast amounts of data to identify patterns, predict supply chain disruptions, and ensure that decisions align with ethical standards.	Develop AI models with transparency, ensuring they're free from biases and prioritize ethical considerations.
Internet of Things (IoT)	Real-time monitoring and feedback	IoT devices can provide real-time data about product conditions, transportation, and more. This can ensure products are stored and transported under ethical and sustainable conditions.	Implement robust security measures to protect IoT data. Ensure ethical sourcing of IoT components.
Augmented Reality (AR)	Training and immersive understanding	AR can offer immersive training experiences for supply chain workers, promoting understanding and adherence to ethical practices without real-world consequences.	Use AR to promote transparent communication about supply chain practices to stakeholders.
Drones	Efficient and eco-friendly deliveries	Drones can reduce the carbon footprint of deliveries and access remote areas, ensuring products are delivered in an environmentally friendly and inclusive manner.	Adhere to regulations and safety protocols. Ensure drones are used in a non-invasive manner respecting privacy norms.
Big Data Analytics	Identifying trends and improving transparency	Analyzing large datasets can reveal insights about the supply chain, ensuring that unethical practices are identified and addressed swiftly. It also aids in demand forecasting to reduce wastage.	Ensure data privacy, and only collect necessary data. Use insights responsibly to drive ethical actions.
Robotics	Automating repetitive tasks and ensuring standardization	Robots can ensure tasks are performed uniformly without human error, maintaining product quality, and ensuring that ethical standards are consistently met during manufacturing.	Ensure robots are sourced and used ethically, provide retraining for displaced workers, and maintain human oversight to ensure ethical operations.
3D Printing	On-demand production reducing wastage	3D printing can reduce overproduction and wastage by producing items on demand. It ensures resources are used more ethically and sustainably.	Ensure materials used in 3D printing are sustainably sourced and that waste is minimized or recycled.

Nevertheless, it is imperative to ensure that their integration is aligned with ethical considerations. Each emerging technology presents unique ethical dilemmas that necessitate resolution in order to uphold the ethical foundations of Supply Chain Management (Norgren & Janzon Hägglund, 2023).

As discussed in Table 3.0, By comprehending the intricacies of these emerging technologies and their potential ramifications, organizations can shape supply chain management strategies that are prepared for the future while also being ethically sound. The harmonization process will be significantly influenced by collaborative research, stakeholder engagement, and ethical impact assessments.

These technologies help firms increase efficiency ethically by increasing transparency, product traceability, and operations optimization. As these tools are incorporated, ethical issues like data privacy and employment displacement must be addressed. Forward-thinking SCM welcomes these advancements while actively minimizing their drawbacks, providing transparent, responsible, and societally beneficial supply chains.

9.3 Integrating Ethics and Sustainability Into SCM Strategies

The future trajectory of supply chain management extends beyond mere operational efficiency, encompassing the generation of value that aligns with the pillars of society, environment, and economy. The incorporation of ethical and sustainable principles into supply chain management strategies guarantees the comprehensive advantage of operations. The integration in question should not be regarded as a mere afterthought, but rather as a fundamental principle that ought to inform and shape all strategic decision-making processes (Dharmayanti, Ismail, Hanifah, & Taqi, 2023).

By prioritizing ethics and sustainability within the context of supply chain management, organizations have the ability to establish value chains that generate benefits for all stakeholders, rather than solely focusing on shareholders. The implementation of this integrated approach holds the potential to create a future in which supply chains serve as channels for comprehensive and interconnected development (Tariq, Nisar, Mahmood, & Moeen, 2023).

9.4 Multidisciplinary Research Approaches to Address Complex Ethical Issues

The ethical dilemmas posed by the supply chain management of Industry 4.0 are complex and varied. The task of addressing these issues necessitates the adoption of a multidisciplinary research approach, wherein professionals from various fields such as technology, ethics, sociology, environmental studies, and economics come together to develop comprehensive and integrated solutions. Through the promotion of collaborative research, intricate ethical dilemmas can be thoroughly examined, comprehended, and effectively resolved.

The utilization of a multidisciplinary approach guarantees that solutions are not solely focused on technological efficacy, but also encompass considerations of social justice, environmental sustainability, and economic feasibility. By advocating for these research paradigms, it is possible to envision a future for Supply Chain Management that is characterized by innovation and ethical enrichment (West & Schill, 2022).

10. CONCLUSION

In conclusion, it can be inferred that the aforementioned points collectively support the notion that the examination of the complex relationship between Industry 4.0 and Supply Chain Management reveals that we are currently on the verge of a significant period of transformation. The numerous opportunities brought about by this convergence are as immense as the challenges they pose. However, as the progression of technological advancements continues, it becomes increasingly apparent that the trajectory of this development will be guided by ethical principles and societal concerns. In an era characterized by rapid digital advancements, there exists a temptation to eagerly adopt every innovation. However, it is crucial for both organizations and individuals to take a moment to contemplate, evaluate, and ascertain that the chosen trajectory is not only technologically progressive, but also ethically robust and socially inclusive.

10.1 Recapitulation of Key Findings

1. The integration of Industry 4.0 technologies with supply chain management is not only a transformative process but also a significant reconfiguration of the fundamental principles that underpin conventional supply chain operations. This amalgamation enhances the agility, transparency, and responsiveness of supply chain systems.
2. The complexity of ethical dilemmas is increasing as a result of technological advancements, encompassing areas such as data ethics, labor rights, and transparent governance.
3. The revolution in question has far-reaching societal implications, which have substantial consequences for job markets, educational models, and community cohesion.
4. The ethical management and privacy of data have become imperative rather than optional due to its pivotal role in this new era.
5. The implementation of a human-centric approach in the context of smart manufacturing guarantees that technology functions as a facilitator rather than a destabilizing force.
6. The increasing prevalence of globalized supply chains necessitates the prominent involvement of international regulations and ethical standards in order to foster coherence and establish trust across national boundaries.
7. The process of engaging with stakeholders encompasses more than mere collaboration, as it involves the joint creation of ethical trajectories and the cultivation of long-lasting relationships founded on mutual respect and shared principles.
8. When impact assessments and sustainability reporting are conducted with thoroughness and rigor, they serve as beacons of transparency, providing guidance for responsible innovation and cultivating trust.
9. The scope of ethical Industry 4.0 supply chain management (SCM) is extensive and continually developing, offering promising opportunities for interdisciplinary research and comprehensive strategies.

10.2 Summary of Ethical and Social Implications of Industry 4.0 in SCM

This section provides a concise overview of the ethical and social implications associated with the implementation of Industry 4.0 in supply chain management.

1. The complexities associated with artificial intelligence (AI) and automation are giving rise to a host of ethical dilemmas, encompassing issues such as fair decision-making processes and the impact on societal employment patterns.
2. Robust mechanisms are imperative in order to uphold the sanctity of data within interconnected supply chain management, with a particular focus on ensuring privacy, ethical utilization, and transparent access.
3. The social implications of technological advancements are complex and require effective strategies to address challenges related to workforce transitions, efforts to acquire new skills, and the integration of these changes into society.
4. In the context of supply chain management, the erosion of geographical boundaries necessitates the prioritization of ethical practices, the promotion of inclusivity, and the preservation of diversity. These actions are no longer optional initiatives, but rather essential requirements.

5. The forthcoming expedition is replete with intricacies; however, by employing strategic foresight, ongoing adaptation, and a steadfast dedication to ethical principles, the obstacles can be converted into advantageous circumstances.

10.3 Recommendations for Ethical Decision-Making in Smart Supply Chains

When operating within the extensive realm of Industry 4.0-integrated supply chain management, it is imperative for organizations to establish their strategies on a strong ethical foundation. The importance of stakeholder involvement is crucial. Organizations can cultivate a culture of shared ethical values and mutual growth by facilitating an ecosystem that encourages stakeholders from diverse backgrounds to express their perspectives.

Moreover, with the rapid advancement of technology pushing us into unfamiliar domains, the importance of ongoing education becomes indisputable. Investment in training and development endeavors guarantees the cultivation of teams that possess not only technical proficiency but also a heightened sense of ethical awareness. By incorporating human-centric principles into the core of supply chain management strategy, organizations can guarantee that technological advancements enhance human capabilities instead of overshadowing them.

Finally, it is of utmost importance to adopt an anticipatory approach rather than a solely reactionary one when addressing ethical dilemmas. Organizations can proactively anticipate and tackle ethical challenges by incorporating routine ethical audits, impact assessments, and transparent reporting mechanisms. As we progress, it is imperative to emphasize the following guiding principle: foster collaboration, promote education, drive innovation, while consistently upholding ethical considerations as fundamental.

REFERENCES

Abikoye, O. C., Bajeh, A. O., Awotunde, J. B., Ameen, A. O., Mojeed, H. A., Abdulraheem, M., . . . Salihu, S. A. (2021). Application of internet of thing and cyber physical system in Industry 4.0 smart manufacturing. In Emergence of Cyber Physical System and IoT in Smart Automation and Robotics: Computer Engineering in Automation (pp. 203-217). Springer.

Acharjya, D. P., Mitra, A., & Zaman, N. (2022). *Deep learning in data analytics*. Springer. doi:10.1007/978-3-030-75855-4

Adhikari, S., Gangopadhayay, T. K., Pal, S., Akila, D., Humayun, M., Alfayad, M., & Jhanjhi, N. (2023). A Novel Machine Learning-Based Hand Gesture Recognition Using HCI on IoT Assisted Cloud Platform. *Computer Systems Science and Engineering*, *46*(2). Advance online publication. doi:10.32604/csse.2023.034431

Alferidah, D. K., & Jhanjhi, N. (2020). *Cybersecurity impact over bigdata and iot growth.* Paper presented at the 2020 International Conference on Computational Intelligence (ICCI). 10.1109/ICCI51257.2020.9247722

Ali, S. B. (2022). Industrial revolution 4.0 and supply chain digitization: future of supply chain management. *South Asian Journal of Social Review, 1*(1), 21-41.

Alkinani, M. H., Almazroi, A. A., & Khan, N. A. (2021). 5G and IoT based reporting and accident detection (RAD) system to deliver first aid box using unmanned aerial vehicle. *Sensors (Basel)*, *21*(20), 6905. doi:10.3390/s21206905

Anandan, R., Deepak, B., Suseendran, G., & Jhanjhi, N. Z. (2021). Internet of Things Platform for Smart Farming. *Human Communication Technology: Internet of Robotic Things and Ubiquitous Computing*, 337-369.

Annadurai, C., Nelson, I., Devi, K. N., Manikandan, R., Jhanjhi, N., Masud, M., & Sheikh, A. (2022). Biometric Authentication-Based Intrusion Detection Using Artificial Intelligence Internet of Things in Smart City. *Energies*, *15*(19), 7430. doi:10.3390/en15197430

Anshari, M., Syafrudin, M., & Fitriyani, N. L. (2022). Fourth industrial revolution between knowledge management and digital humanities. *Information (Basel)*, *13*(6), 292. doi:10.3390/info13060292

Ar, I. M., Erol, I., Peker, I., Ozdemir, A. I., Medeni, T. D., & Medeni, I. T. (2020). Evaluating the feasibility of blockchain in logistics operations: A decision framework. *Expert Systems with Applications*, *158*, 113543. doi:10.1016/j.eswa.2020.113543

Ashraf, H., Hanif, M., Ihsan, U., Al-Quayed, F., Humayun, M., & Jhanjhi, N. (2023). *A Secure and Reliable Supply chain management approach integrated with IoT and Blockchain.* Paper presented at the 2023 International Conference on Business Analytics for Technology and Security (ICBATS). 10.1109/ICBATS57792.2023.10111371

Attanasio, G., Preghenella, N., De Toni, A. F., & Battistella, C. (2022). Stakeholder engagement in business models for sustainability: The stakeholder value flow model for sustainable development. *Business Strategy and the Environment*, *31*(3), 860–874. doi:10.1002/bse.2922

Awodele, O., Ngige, O., & Balogun, T. (2021). *Industry 4.0: The Impact of Technology on the Output Potentials of Skilled and Unskilled Workforce in Developing Countries.* Paper presented at the ECIAIR 2021 3rd European Conference on the Impact of Artificial Intelligence and Robotics.

Bag, S., & Pretorius, J. H. C. (2022). Relationships between industry 4.0, sustainable manufacturing and circular economy: Proposal of a research framework. *The International Journal of Organizational Analysis*, *30*(4), 864–898. doi:10.1108/IJOA-04-2020-2120

Bag, S., Rahman, M. S., Srivastava, G., Shore, A., & Ram, P. (2023). Examining the role of virtue ethics and big data in enhancing viable, sustainable, and digital supply chain performance. *Technological Forecasting and Social Change*, *186*, 122154. doi:10.1016/j.techfore.2022.122154

Bai, C., Dallasega, P., Orzes, G., & Sarkis, J. (2020). Industry 4.0 technologies assessment: A sustainability perspective. *International Journal of Production Economics*, *229*, 107776. doi:10.1016/j.ijpe.2020.107776

Barreto, L., Amaral, A., & Pereira, T. (2017). Industry 4.0 implications in logistics: An overview. *Procedia Manufacturing*, *13*, 1245–1252. doi:10.1016/j.promfg.2017.09.045

Benyahya, M., Collen, A., Kechagia, S., & Nijdam, N. A. (2022). Automated city shuttles: Mapping the key challenges in cybersecurity, privacy and standards to future developments. *Computers & Security*, *122*, 102904. Advance online publication. doi:10.1016/j.cose.2022.102904

Bernal, P. (2014). *Internet privacy rights: rights to protect autonomy*. Cambridge University Press. doi:10.1017/CBO9781107337428

Blok, V. (2019). From participation to interruption: toward an ethics of stakeholder engagement, participation and partnership in corporate social responsibility and responsible innovation. *International Handbook on Responsible Innovation: A Global Resource*, 243.

Brun, A., Karaosman, H., & Barresi, T. (2020). Supply chain collaboration for transparency. *Sustainability (Basel)*, *12*(11), 4429. doi:10.3390/su12114429

Chaudhary, M., Gaur, L., Chakrabarti, A., & Jhanjhi, N. (2023). Unravelling the Barriers of Human Resource Analytics: Multi-Criteria Decision-Making Approach. *Journal of Survey in Fisheries Sciences*, 306-321.

Chen, X., Wang, C., & Li, S. (2023). The impact of supply chain finance on corporate social responsibility and creating shared value: A case from the emerging economy. *Supply Chain Management*, *28*(2), 324–346. doi:10.1108/SCM-10-2021-0478

Chkanikova, O., & Sroufe, R. (2021). Third-party sustainability certifications in food retailing: Certification design from a sustainable supply chain management perspective. *Journal of Cleaner Production*, *282*, 124344. doi:10.1016/j.jclepro.2020.124344

Dahlmann, F., & Roehrich, J. K. (2019). Sustainable supply chain management and partner engagement to manage climate change information. *Business Strategy and the Environment*, *28*(8), 1632–1647. doi:10.1002/bse.2392

Dash, D., Farooq, R., Panda, J. S., & Sandhyavani, K. (2019). Internet of Things (IoT): The New Paradigm of HRM and Skill Development in the Fourth Industrial Revolution (Industry 4.0). *IUP Journal of Information Technology, 15*(4).

Dathe, T., Dathe, R., Dathe, I., & Helmold, M. (2022). *Corporate social responsibility (CSR), sustainability and environmental social governance (ESG): Approaches to ethical management*. Springer Nature. doi:10.1007/978-3-030-92357-0

Deepak Kumar, S., Arun Manohar, G., Surya Teja, R., Ramana Rao, P., Mandal, A., Behera, A., & Srinivasa Rao, P. (2023). Smart Manufacturing Technologies in Industry 4.0: Challenges and Opportunities. *Intelligent Manufacturing Management Systems: Operational Applications of Evolutionary Digital Technologies in Mechanical and Industrial Engineering*, 23-57.

Dhanpat, N., Buthelezi, Z. P., Joe, M. R., Maphela, T. V., & Shongwe, N. (2020). Industry 4.0: The role of human resource professionals. *SA Journal of Human Resource Management*, *18*(1), 1–11. doi:10.4102/sajhrm.v18i0.1302

Dharmayanti, N., Ismail, T., Hanifah, I. A., & Taqi, M. (2023). Exploring Sustainability Management Control System and Eco-Innovation Matter Sustainable Financial Performance: The Role of Supply Chain Management and Digital Adaptability in Indonesian Context. *Journal of Open Innovation*, *9*(3), 100119. doi:10.1016/j.joitmc.2023.100119

Dhirani, L. L., Mukhtiar, N., Chowdhry, B. S., & Newe, T. (2023). Ethical dilemmas and privacy issues in emerging technologies: A review. *Sensors (Basel)*, *23*(3), 1151. doi:10.3390/s23031151

Fritz, M. M. (2019). *Sustainable supply chain management. In Responsible Consumption and Production. Encyclopedia of the UN Sustainable Development Goals*. Springer.

Gaur, L., Jhanjhi, N. Z., Bakshi, S., & Gupta, P. (2022). *Analyzing Consequences of Artificial Intelligence on Jobs using Topic Modeling and Keyword Extraction.* Paper presented at the 2022 2nd International Conference on Innovative Practices in Technology and Management (ICIPTM). 10.1109/ICIPTM54933.2022.9754064

Gaur, L., Solanki, A., Wamba, S. F., & Jhanjhi, N. Z. (2021). *Advanced AI techniques and applications in bioinformatics*. CRC Press. doi:10.1201/9781003126164

Ghobakhloo, M., Fathi, M., Iranmanesh, M., Maroufkhani, P., & Morales, M. E. (2021). Industry 4.0 ten years on: A bibliometric and systematic review of concepts, sustainability value drivers, and success determinants. *Journal of Cleaner Production*, *302*, 127052. doi:10.1016/j.jclepro.2021.127052

Ha, B.-C., & Nam, H. (2016). Ethical judgments in supply chain management: A scenario analysis. *Journal of Business and Industrial Marketing*, *31*(1), 59–69. doi:10.1108/JBIM-07-2014-0148

Hagendorff, T. (2020). The ethics of AI ethics: An evaluation of guidelines. *Minds and Machines*, *30*(1), 99–120. doi:10.1007/s11023-020-09517-8

Hangl, J., Krause, S., & Behrens, V. J. (2023). Expert interviews of drivers, barriers and social considerations for AI adoption in SCM. *Technology in Society*, *74*, 102299. doi:10.1016/j.techsoc.2023.102299

Hazra, A., Alkhayyat, A., & Adhikari, M. (2022). Blockchain-aided integrated edge framework of cybersecurity for Internet of Things. *IEEE Consumer Electronics Magazine*.

Hoberg, K., Thornton, L., & Wieland, A. (2020). *How to deal with the human factor in supply chain management?* Emerald Publishing Limited.

Hoffmann, T., & Prause, G. (2018). On the regulatory framework for last-mile delivery robots. *Machines*, *6*(3), 33. doi:10.3390/machines6030033

Hofmann, E., Sternberg, H., Chen, H., Pflaum, A., & Prockl, G. (2019). Supply chain management and Industry 4.0: Conducting research in the digital age. *International Journal of Physical Distribution & Logistics Management*, *49*(10), 945–955. doi:10.1108/IJPDLM-11-2019-399

Humayun, M. (2021). Industry 4.0 and cyber security issues and challenges. *Turkish Journal of Computer and Mathematics Education*, *12*(10), 2957–2971.

Humayun, M., Hamid, B., Jhanjhi, N., Suseendran, G., & Talib, M. (2021). *5G network security issues, challenges, opportunities and future directions: A survey.* Paper presented at the Journal of Physics: Conference Series. 10.1088/1742-6596/1979/1/012037

Hussain, I., Tahir, S., Humayun, M., Almufareh, M. F., Jhanjhi, N., & Qamar, F. (2022). *Health Monitoring System Using Internet of Things (IoT)*. Sensing for Elderly People.

Hussain, M. N. (2023). Evaluating the impact of air transportation, railway transportation, and trade openness on inbound and outbound tourism in BRI countries. *Journal of Air Transport Management, 106*, 102307. doi:10.1016/j.jairtraman.2022.102307

Jabeen, T., Jabeen, I., Ashraf, H., Jhanjhi, N., Yassine, A., & Hossain, M. S. (2023). An Intelligent Healthcare System Using IoT in Wireless Sensor Network. *Sensors (Basel), 23*(11), 5055. doi:10.3390/s23115055

Jahani, H., Jain, R., & Ivanov, D. (2023). Data science and big data analytics: A systematic review of methodologies used in the supply chain and logistics research. *Annals of Operations Research*, 1–58. doi:10.1007/s10479-023-05390-7

Jayakumar, P., Brohi, S. N., & Jhanjhi, N. Z. (2021). *Artificial intelligence and military applications: Innovations, cybersecurity challenges & open research areas*. Academic Press.

Jhanjhi, N., Khan, M. A., Ahmad, M., & Hussain, M. (2022). The Impact of Cyber Attacks on E-Governance During the COVID-19 Pandemic. *Cybersecurity Measures for E-Government Frameworks*, 123.

Jobin, A., Ienca, M., & Vayena, E. (2019). The global landscape of AI ethics guidelines. *Nature Machine Intelligence, 1*(9), 389–399. doi:10.1038/s42256-019-0088-2

Khan, A., Jhanjhi, N. Z., & Humayun, M. (2022). The Role of Cybersecurity in Smart Cities. In *Cyber Security Applications for Industry 4.0* (pp. 195–208). Chapman and Hall/CRC. doi:10.1201/9781003203087-9

Khan, A., Jhanjhi, N. Z., & Sujatha, R. (2022). Emerging Industry Revolution IR 4.0 Issues and Challenges. In Cyber Security Applications for Industry 4.0 (pp. 151-169): Chapman and Hall/CRC.

Kumar, S., & Mallipeddi, R. R. (2022). Impact of cybersecurity on operations and supply chain management: Emerging trends and future research directions. *Production and Operations Management, 31*(12), 4488–4500. doi:10.1111/poms.13859

Laboso, P. K., Martin, A., & Thiyagarajan, P. (2023). *Blockchain Technologies in Data Science: Challenges and Benefits.* Paper presented at the 2023 International Conference on Sustainable Computing and Data Communication Systems (ICSCDS). 10.1109/ICSCDS56580.2023.10104674

Lele, A., & Lele, A. (2019). Artificial intelligence (AI). *Disruptive technologies for the militaries and security*, 139-154.

Li, L. (2022). Reskilling and upskilling the future-ready workforce for industry 4.0 and beyond. *Information Systems Frontiers*, 1–16.

Li, S., Zheng, P., Liu, S., Wang, Z., Wang, X. V., Zheng, L., & Wang, L. (2023). Proactive human–robot collaboration: Mutual-cognitive, predictable, and self-organising perspectives. *Robotics and Computer-integrated Manufacturing, 81*, 102510. doi:10.1016/j.rcim.2022.102510

Ma, L., Zhang, Z., & Zhang, N. (2018). *Ethical dilemma of artificial intelligence and its research progress.* Paper presented at the IOP conference series: materials science and engineering. 10.1088/1757-899X/392/6/062188

Maharana, M., & Lathabhavan, R. (2023). Industry 4.0 and its impact on supply chain management: An overview. *International Journal of Services. Economics and Management, 14*(2), 224–248.

Masum, R. (2023). Cyber Security in Smart Manufacturing (Threats, Landscapes Challenges). *arXiv preprint arXiv:2304.10180.*

Melnyk, L., Kubatko, O., Matsenko, O., Balatskyi, Y., & Serdyukov, K. (2023). *Transformation of the human capital reproduction in line with Industries 4.0 and 5.0.* Academic Press.

Naqvi, S. G., Sheraz, S., Mehmood, I., & Yasin, M. (2023). Cyber-physical Systems and Artificial Intelligence: The Role of Cyber Security, Machine Learning, Threats and benefits to Modern Economies and Industries. *Pakistan Journal of Humanities and Social Sciences, 11*(2), 1513–1522.

Narula, R. (2019). Enforcing higher labor standards within developing country value chains: Consequences for MNEs and informal actors in a dual economy. *Journal of International Business Studies, 50*(9), 1622–1635. doi:10.1057/s41267-019-00265-1

Nguyen, G. N., Mani, V., Kha, M. K., & Papadopoulos, T. (2023). Supply chain social responsibility in labour-intensive industries: A practitioner's perspective. *Production Planning and Control, 34*(4), 371–390. doi:10.1080/09537287.2021.1925172

Norgren, A., & Janzon Hägglund, W. (2023). Implementing Artificial Intelligence in Supply Chain Management: A Qualitative Study of How Manufacturing Companies Can Implement AI to Improve Supply Chain Management. Academic Press.

Novitasari, M., Wijaya, A. L., Agustin, N. M., Gunardi, A., & Dana, L. P. (2023). Corporate social responsibility and firm performance: Green supply chain management as a mediating variable. *Corporate Social Responsibility and Environmental Management, 30*(1), 267–276. doi:10.1002/csr.2353

Ogbuke, N. J., Yusuf, Y. Y., Dharma, K., & Mercangoz, B. A. (2022). Big data supply chain analytics: Ethical, privacy and security challenges posed to business, industries and society. *Production Planning and Control, 33*(2-3), 123–137. doi:10.1080/09537287.2020.1810764

Othman, U., & Yang, E. (2023). Human–robot collaborations in smart manufacturing environments: Review and outlook. *Sensors (Basel), 23*(12), 5663. doi:10.3390/s23125663

Pacaux-Lemoine, M.-P., & Trentesaux, D. (2019). Ethical risks of human-machine symbiosis in industry 4.0: Insights from the human-machine cooperation approach. *IFAC-PapersOnLine, 52*(19), 19–24. doi:10.1016/j.ifacol.2019.12.077

Park, B. I., Xiao, S. S., Shi, Y. P., Wang, M., Wang, B., & Luo, C. (2023). *Future opportunities in supply chain management 4.0.* SAGE.

Patil, S. M., Baramati, P., Dhone, N. C., & Chourasiya, R. H. (2023). Industry 4.0 technologies in the context of Supply Chain Management 4.0. *The Online Journal of Distance Education and e-Learning : TOJDEL, 11*(2).

Payton, T., & Claypoole, T. (2023). *Privacy in the age of Big data: Recognizing threats, defending your rights, and protecting your family.* Rowman & Littlefield. doi:10.5771/9781538167830

Phuyal, S., Bista, D., & Bista, R. (2020). Challenges, opportunities and future directions of smart manufacturing: A state of art review. *Sustainable Futures : An Applied Journal of Technology, Environment and Society*, *2*, 100023. doi:10.1016/j.sftr.2020.100023

Picasso, F. G., Biazzin, C., Paiva, E. L., & Beal Partyka, R. (2023). Socially responsible supply chain initiatives and their outcomes: A taxonomy of manufacturing companies. *Supply Chain Management*, *28*(1), 90–106. doi:10.1108/SCM-11-2020-0578

procureport. (n.d.). *Components of SCM*. Retrieved from https://blog.procureport.com/components-of-supply-chain-management/

Quarshie, A. M., Salmi, A., & Leuschner, R. (2016). Sustainability and corporate social responsibility in supply chains: The state of research in supply chain management and business ethics journals. *Journal of Purchasing and Supply Management*, *22*(2), 82–97. doi:10.1016/j.pursup.2015.11.001

Rahanu, H., Georgiadou, E., Siakas, K., Ross, M., & Berki, E. (2021). *Ethical issues invoked by industry 4.0.* Paper presented at the Systems, Software and Services Process Improvement: 28th European Conference, EuroSPI 2021, Krems, Austria. 10.1007/978-3-030-85521-5_39

Raj, A., Dwivedi, G., Sharma, A., de Sousa Jabbour, A. B. L., & Rajak, S. (2020). Barriers to the adoption of industry 4.0 technologies in the manufacturing sector: An inter-country comparative perspective. *International Journal of Production Economics*, *224*, 107546. doi:10.1016/j.ijpe.2019.107546

Rajmohan, R., Kumar, T. A., Pavithra, M., & Sandhya, S. (n.d.). *Blockchain: Next-generation technology for industry 4.0*. Academic Press.

Rawindaran, N. (2023). Legal Considerations and Ethical Challenges of Artificial Intelligence on Internet of Things and Smart Cities. In Data Protection in a Post-Pandemic Society: Laws, Regulations, Best Practices and Recent Solutions (pp. 217-239): Springer. doi:10.1007/978-3-031-34006-2_8

Razak, G. M., Hendry, L. C., & Stevenson, M. (2023). Supply chain traceability: A review of the benefits and its relationship with supply chain resilience. *Production Planning and Control*, *34*(11), 1114–1134. doi:10.1080/09537287.2021.1983661

Roman, R., Alcaraz, C., Lopez, J., & Sakurai, K. (2023). Current Perspectives on Securing Critical Infrastructures' Supply Chains. *IEEE Security and Privacy*, *21*(4), 29–38. doi:10.1109/MSEC.2023.3247946

Rosado, D. G., Santos-Olmo, A., Sánchez, L. E., Serrano, M. A., Blanco, C., Mouratidis, H., & Fernández-Medina, E. (2022). Managing cybersecurity risks of cyber-physical systems: The MARISMA-CPS pattern. *Computers in Industry*, *142*, 103715. Advance online publication. doi:10.1016/j.compind.2022.103715

Sadiku, M. N., Ajayi-Majebi, A. J., & Adebo, P. O. (2023). Smart Manufacturing. In *Emerging Technologies in Manufacturing* (pp. 49–66). Springer. doi:10.1007/978-3-031-23156-8_4

Saidakhrarovich, G. S., & Tursunovich, K. O. (2022). Digital Future & Cyber Security Necessity. *World Bulletin of Management and Law*, *10*, 31–45.

Schoenherr, T., Mena, C., Vakil, B., & Choi, T. Y. (2023). Creating resilient supply chains through a culture of measuring. *Journal of Purchasing and Supply Management*, *29*(4), 100824. doi:10.1016/j.pursup.2023.100824

Seyedghorban, Z., Samson, D., & Tahernejad, H. (2020). Digitalization opportunities for the procurement function: Pathways to maturity. *International Journal of Operations & Production Management*, *40*(11), 1685–1693. doi:10.1108/IJOPM-04-2020-0214

Shah, I. A., Jhanjhi, N., & Laraib, A. (2023). Cybersecurity and Blockchain Usage in Contemporary Business. In *Handbook of Research on Cybersecurity Issues and Challenges for Business and FinTech Applications* (pp. 49–64). IGI Global.

Shah, I. A., Sial, Q., Jhanjhi, N. Z., & Gaur, L. (2023). The role of the iot and digital twin in the healthcare digitalization process: Iot and digital twin in the healthcare digitalization process. In Digital Twins and Healthcare: Trends, Techniques, and Challenges (pp. 20-34). IGI Global.

Shao, X.-F., Liu, W., Li, Y., Chaudhry, H. R., & Yue, X.-G. (2021). Multistage implementation framework for smart supply chain management under industry 4.0. *Technological Forecasting and Social Change*, *162*, 120354. doi:10.1016/j.techfore.2020.120354

Sharma, C. (2023). Security and Privacy Aspects of Cyber Physical Systems. In *Cyber Physical Systems* (pp. 53–66). Chapman and Hall/CRC.

Sharma, H., Garg, R., Sewani, H., & Kashef, R. (2023). Towards A Sustainable and Ethical Supply Chain Management: The Potential of IoT Solutions. *arXiv preprint arXiv:2303.18135.*

Sharma, V., Raut, R. D., Hajiaghaei-Keshteli, M., Narkhede, B. E., Gokhale, R., & Priyadarshinee, P. (2022). Mediating effect of industry 4.0 technologies on the supply chain management practices and supply chain performance. *Journal of Environmental Management*, *322*, 115945. doi:10.1016/j.jenvman.2022.115945

Shayganmehr, M., Kumar, A., Garza-Reyes, J. A., & Moktadir, M. A. (2021). Industry 4.0 enablers for a cleaner production and circular economy within the context of business ethics: A study in a developing country. *Journal of Cleaner Production*, *281*, 125280. doi:10.1016/j.jclepro.2020.125280

Shneiderman, B. (2020). Bridging the gap between ethics and practice: Guidelines for reliable, safe, and trustworthy human-centered AI systems. *ACM Transactions on Interactive Intelligent Systems*, *10*(4), 1–31. doi:10.1145/3419764

Shojaeshafiei, M., Etzkorn, L., & Anderson, M. (2020). Analytic hierarchy process-based fuzzy measurement to quantify vulnerabilities of web applications. *International Journal of Computer Networks and Communications*, *12*(4), 105–123. doi:10.5121/ijcnc.2020.12407

Simon, C. G. K., Jhanjhi, N. Z., Goh, W. W., & Sukumaran, S. (2022). Applications of machine learning in knowledge management system: A comprehensive review. *Journal of Information & Knowledge Management*, *21*(02), 2250017. doi:10.1142/S0219649222500174

Singh, P. K., & Kumar, A. (2023). Cyber Physical Systems in Supply Chain Management. In *Cyber Physical Systems* (pp. 85–110). Chapman and Hall/CRC.

Sobb, T., Turnbull, B., & Moustafa, N. (2020). Supply chain 4.0: A survey of cyber security challenges, solutions and future directions. *Electronics (Basel)*, *9*(11), 1864. doi:10.3390/electronics9111864

Soni, R. G., & Soni, B. (2019). *Evolution of supply chain management: Ethical issues for leaders.* Paper presented at the Competition Forum.

Sujatha, R., Prakash, G., & Jhanjhi, N. Z. (2022). *Cyber Security Applications for Industry 4.0.* CRC Press. doi:10.1201/9781003203087

Svensson, G. (2009). The transparency of SCM ethics: Conceptual framework and empirical illustrations. *Supply Chain Management, 14*(4), 259–269. doi:10.1108/13598540910970090

Tariq, S., Nisar, Q. A., Mahmood, K., & Moeen, R. (2023). *Supply Chain Strategies and Competitive Advantage: A Roadmap to Achieving Sustainable Performance.* Academic Press.

Tashtoush, Y. M., Darweesh, D. A., Husari, G., Darwish, O. A., Darwish, Y., Issa, L. B., & Ashqar, H. I. (2022). Agile Approaches for Cybersecurity Systems, IoT and Intelligent Transportation. *IEEE Access : Practical Innovations, Open Solutions, 10*, 1360–1375. doi:10.1109/ACCESS.2021.3136861

Tayyab, M., Marjani, M., Jhanjhi, N., Hashem, I. A. T., Usmani, R. S. A., & Qamar, F. (2023). A Comprehensive Review on Deep Learning Algorithms: Security and Privacy Issues. *Computers & Security, 131*, 103297. doi:10.1016/j.cose.2023.103297

Tiwari, S., Sharma, P., Choi, T.-M., & Lim, A. (2023). Blockchain and third-party logistics for global supply chain operations: Stakeholders' perspectives and decision roadmap. *Transportation Research Part E, Logistics and Transportation Review, 170*, 103012. doi:10.1016/j.tre.2022.103012

Tortorella, G., Fogliatto, F. S., Kumar, M., Gonzalez, V., & Pepper, M. (2023). Effect of Industry 4.0 on the relationship between socio-technical practices and workers' performance. *Journal of Manufacturing Technology Management, 34*(1), 44–66. doi:10.1108/JMTM-04-2022-0173

towardsdatascience. (n.d.). *Cousins for Artificial Intelligence.* Retrieved from https://towardsdatascience.com/cousins-of-artificial-intelligence-dda4edc27b55

Tsao, M., Yang, K., Zoepf, S., & Pavone, M. (2022). Trust but Verify: Cryptographic Data Privacy for Mobility Management. *IEEE Transactions on Control of Network Systems, 9*(1), 50–61. doi:10.1109/TCNS.2022.3141027

Ustundag, A., Cevikcan, E., & Karacay, G. (2018). Talent development for Industry 4.0. *Industry 4.0: Managing the digital transformation*, 123-136.

Villegas-Galaviz, C., & Martin, K. (2023). Moral distance, AI, and the ethics of care. *AI & Society*, 1–12. doi:10.1007/s00146-023-01642-z

Wang, J., & Feng, T. (2023). Supply chain ethical leadership and green supply chain integration: A moderated mediation analysis. *International Journal of Logistics, 26*(9), 1145–1171. doi:10.1080/13675567.2021.2022640

Wang, L., Törngren, M., & Onori, M. (2015). Current status and advancement of cyber-physical systems in manufacturing. *Journal of Manufacturing Systems, 37*, 517–527. doi:10.1016/j.jmsy.2015.04.008

West, S., & Schill, C. (2022). Negotiating the ethical-political dimensions of research methods: A key competency in mixed methods, inter-and transdisciplinary, and co-production research. *Humanities & Social Sciences Communications*, *9*(1), 1–13. doi:10.1057/s41599-022-01297-z

Widder, D. G., & Wong, R. (2023). Thinking Upstream: Ethics and Policy Opportunities in AI Supply Chains. *arXiv preprint arXiv:2303.07529*.

Xu, X., Lu, Y., Vogel-Heuser, B., & Wang, L. (2021). Industry 4.0 and Industry 5.0—Inception, conception and perception. *Journal of Manufacturing Systems*, *61*, 530–535. doi:10.1016/j.jmsy.2021.10.006

Chapter 10
Blockchain Technology in Supply Chain Management: Opportunities and Challenges

Mustafa Rehman Khan
https://orcid.org/0000-0002-0250-9092
UCSI University, Kuala Lumpur, Malaysia

Fazeelat Masood
https://orcid.org/0000-0003-1487-6882
Bahria Business School, Karachi, Pakistan

Irum Gul
Balochistan University of Information Technology, Quetta, Pakistan

Muhammad Rahies Khan
Bahria University, Karachi, Pakistan

ABSTRACT

The integration of blockchain technology in supply chains has the potential to transform the industry by improving transparency, traceability, and security. This study provides insight into important aspects for data management in blockchains, such as data kinds, collection tactics, integration methodologies, and data input and delivery accountability. Furthermore, it emphasizes the financial ramifications of blockchain adoption, emphasizing the difficulties that small supply chain enterprises confront due to limited resources. Cultural resistance and deeply embedded corporate procedures are investigated as important operational barriers that could stymie blockchain technology adoption. This study emphasizes the significance of building robust governance models and protocols that promote collaboration and compliance among supply chain actors to manage these difficulties. Moreover, the importance of tackling interoperability issues across different blockchain systems to provide seamless information flow within complicated supply chain networks is emphasized.

DOI: 10.4018/979-8-3693-1363-3.ch010

INTRODUCTION

The supply chain can be defined as a complex network of interconnected organizations engaged in various processes and activities that result in the creation of value through the delivery of products and services to end consumers (Christopher, 1998). In the vast domain of global supply chains, products across international borders, contributing to formations comprised of intricate production processes, transactions, and knowledge exchanges. Notably, global exports of goods reached an astounding $19.48 trillion in 2018 (World Trade Organization, 2019). According to World Bank data, the annual movement of products across international borders exceeds $16 trillion, and the estimated annual cost of global commerce is $1.8 trillion (Maersk Strategy Group, May 2016). The elimination of barriers in the international supply chain has the potential to boost economies by nearly 15 percent and create new employment opportunities (Moavenzadeh, 2013).

Before ultimately reaching consumers, products encounter multiple ownership transitions within the framework of a dynamic supply chain. Supply chains aggregate products from numerous small-scale producers to larger partners for further processing and eventual transformation into end-products, particularly for low-value-added goods such as agricultural and certain mining commodities.

Typically, current supply chain models begin when manufacturers and importers ship their products to subsequent phases of the supply chain (Khan, Khan & Nallaluthan, 2023). This stratum consists of wholesalers who further process the products received from exporters, processors, and other supply chain participants. The final phase includes retailers and food service establishments that facilitate product sales. The encapsulation of data within various supply chain elements, which hinders information sharing, is a significant drawback of this model. Therefore, consumers are unable to verify the origins of the products they intend to purchase (Vara et al., 2018).

Moreover, supply chain stakeholders face challenges in sustaining seamless operations across complex chains of resources, activities, and organizations, especially when numerous small-scale contributors are involved. Traceability is defined by ISO standard 9000 as the capacity to monitor the history, application, use, and location of an item or its attributes using recorded identification data. Absence of openness and incentives can hinder sustainability efforts.

In present-day supply chain systems, consumer trust in the dependability of data remains dubious. In the context of global supply channels, this difficulty is exacerbated. Establishing a trustworthy system, particularly on a global scale, requires a difficult, if not impossible, foundation of trust. However, the emergence of blockchain technology as a disruptive force in various aspects of our daily lives heralds a paradigm shift in overcoming the numerous challenges inherent to supply chains (Andrei, Kwok & Treiblmaier, 2023; Gul, Khan & Ghouri, 2023). The participation of entities in a blockchain-integrated supply chain are depicted in figure 1. Forecasts indicate that the inflection point for blockchain adoption will occur when approximately 10% of the global gross domestic product (GDP) is stored on blockchain ledgers by 2027 (Li, Fu & Cheng, 2020).

Blockchain technology has emerged as a transformative innovation with far-reaching implications for various industries, including supply chain management. Its decentralized and immutable ledger system offers unprecedented levels of transparency, efficiency, and security, revolutionizing traditional supply chain processes (Michelman, 2017). However, alongside its potential benefits, the adoption of blockchain in supply chains also raises significant security concerns (Patel, Bothra & Patel, 2017; Weber et al., 2016). The decentralization of blockchain, while enhancing data security in many aspects, introduces new vulnerabilities that must be carefully addressed to ensure the integrity and reliability of supply chain operations (Tian, 2016). In this context, it is imperative to examine the drivers, value propositions, and operational challenges of blockchain integration in supply chains while also considering the critical aspect of data security. This chapter examines the opportunities, challenges, and potential research avenues that blockchain-based supply chain solutions present. This chapter will establish the foundation and serve as a direction for future research endeavors.

Figure 1. Blockchain-integrated supply chain (Saberi et al., 2019)

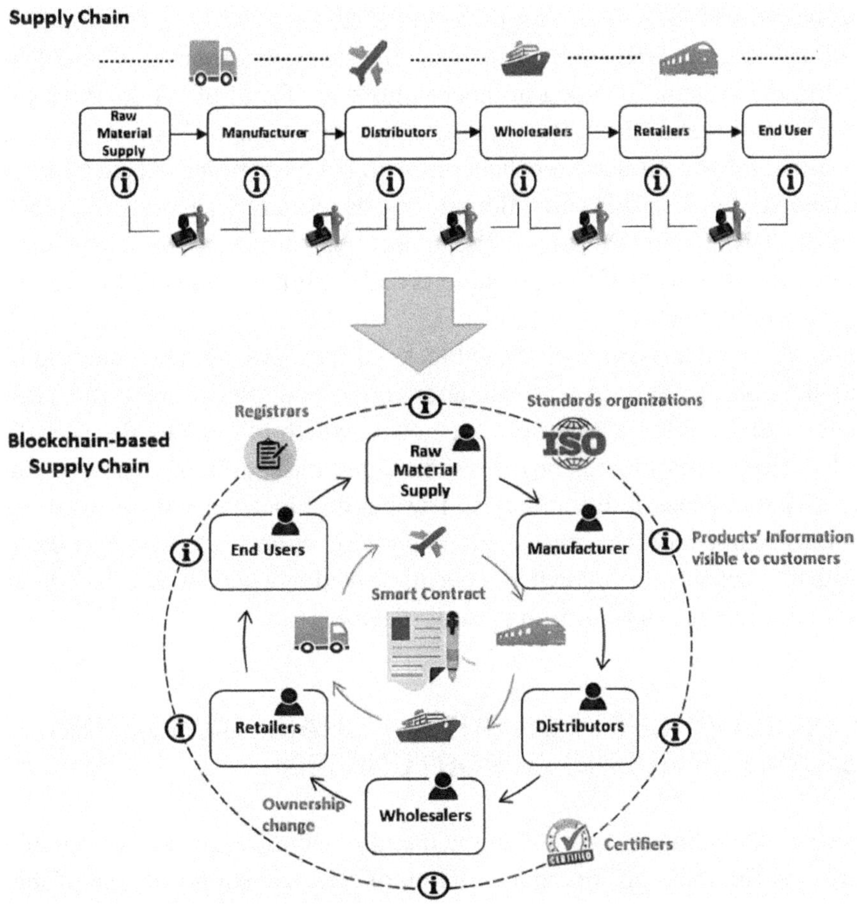

BLOCKCHAIN TECHNOLOGY: THE BEGINNING OF A NEW ERA

The foundational pillars and inception of blockchain technology can be traced to the world of cryptocurrencies, which dates to the 1980s. In December 2008, under the pseudonym Satoshi Nakamoto, an enigmatic author published the seminal paper "Bitcoin: A Peer-to-Peer Electronic Cash System," bringing blockchain technology to the forefront. This transformative concept fuses disciplines including mathematics, cryptology, computer science, and monetary frameworks.

Blockchain technology represents a novel paradigm within the domain of parallel and distributed computing architecture (Yaga et al., 2018). In digital interactions between collaborators, it permits the ability to transcend central servers and trusted authorities. This disruptive force has the potential to herald a profound transformation across a variety of domains in our everyday lives. The foundation of this innovation is the decentralized nature of data storage, where copies of a ledger are distributed across a large network of computers. Each modification is scrupulously timestamped to maintain the data's integrity and transparency. The absence of a requirement for unquestioning faith between stakeholders distinguishes this ecosystem. Rather, trust is founded on the strict adherence to predefined rules regulating data modifications. The entire history of modifications is scrupulously recorded in a transparent, auditable, cryptographically secure, and participant-accessible ledger. In this context, the digital domain resembles the physical world's tangible asset proprietorship.

The core of the blockchain architecture is propelled by a variety of consensus protocols and mechanisms that establish trust in the system. Included in this category are Proof of Work (PoW), Byzantine Fault Tolerance (BFT), Proof of Stake (PoS), Proof of Authority (PoA), and Proof of Elapsed Time (PoET). The primary purpose of these consensus mechanisms is to compare proposed changes to the extant data status and predefined guidelines. This validation process is diligently carried out by blockchain nodes, which are frequently referred to as the computational backbone of the system. Cryptography emerges as a fulcrum, assuring the authenticity of change requests and the immutability of the data by cryptographically connecting sequential blocks.

Privacy emerges as a central issue within the blockchain ecosystem, necessitating the implementation of cryptographic tools to protect participant anonymity. The robustness of the ledger's availability relies on its extensive distribution across network nodes, which eliminates the need for a centralized repository. The blockchain ecosystem is broadly subdivided into public and private platforms, each of which adheres to different accessibility policies. The public blockchain is an open arena that invites participation from any member of the network, allowing both request submission and node operation. In contrast, the private blockchain, also known as a permissioned blockchain, restricts the ability to submit requests and host nodes to a restricted group of authorized parties.

THE IMPACT OF BLOCKCHAIN ON SUPPLY CHAIN: NAVIGATING CHALLENGES AND UNVEILING OPPORTUNITIES

A variety of objectives, including cost optimization, quality assurance, speed, dependability, risk mitigation, sustainability, and flexibility, form the foundation of effective supply chains (Kshetri et al., 2018). In an era when industry has expanded its boundaries into the global arena, simplified supply chain management has become increasingly important. However, modern supply chain systems suffer from a noticeable lack of transparency, making it difficult for customers to determine the genuine worth of items. Forevermore, the complexities of analyzing supply networks in cases of suspected unlawful or immoral behavior provide considerable challenges. The complexity of paperwork, along with onerous processes and slow workflows, exacerbates the existing supply chain difficulties.

A thorough review of current literature on blockchain's implementation in the supply chain area (Agarwal et al., 2022; Gul, Raziq & Khan, 2024; Masood, Khan & Khan, 2024) highlights the inherent benefits of blockchain technology. These benefits arise from its key characteristics such as trust, traceability, authenticity, safety, and security, which cater to the unique requirements of supply chain dynamics. Litke et al. (2019) proposed that incorporating blockchain technology into supply chain procedures yields a slew of advantages, reflecting its usefulness in a variety of application fields. The use of blockchain creates an environment characterized by transparency, decentralization, security, faster transactions, and lower costs. Blockchain simplifies workflows and reduces paperwork by eliminating the need for unnecessary intermediaries and enclosing many daily procedures in digital frameworks. Blockchain, at its heart, builds confidence among trading partners by virtue of its inherent properties. The enhancement of data granularity within the blockchain improves supply chain monitoring capabilities, amplifying safety measures and, as a result, lowering insurance risks. Smart contracts and automated payments are disrupting established paradigms, bringing in efficiency improvements while reducing bureaucratic bottlenecks, notably in the insurance and traceability sectors. These techniques also enable escrowed payments, in which monies are kept until the preset parameters of an agreement are completed, allowing for automated release. In essence, blockchain bridges the infrastructural gap required by pioneering technologies. As a result, the push for integration and cooperation with revolutionary technologies such as AI, Big Data, Cloud Computing, and IoT gathers traction, promising to realize enhanced supply chain systems (Yaga et al., 2018).

Notably, the confluence of IoT and blockchain has enormous promise in the supply chain arena. IoT is already being used to collect data on environmental conditions, cargo management, and compliance with shipping regulations. The combination of IoT with blockchain creates an ecosystem with increased trust, maintaining data consistency and authenticating information from both the digital and physical domains. The convergence of these technologies enables customers to track a product's complete lifespan across the supply chain, increasing transparency and accountability.

The COVID-19 pandemic has highlighted the importance of resilient supply chain infrastructures capable of interacting with varied ecosystems. Given the considerable disruptions suffered by traditional supply chain networks, interoperability and compatibility are more important than ever. Blockchain technology emerges as a means of enabling safe and cost-effective interoperation across disparate supply chain systems, and it is positioned to play a critical role in post-pandemic global supply chain dynamics (Liao, 2020).

While the benefits of blockchain are undeniable, it is critical to remember that it is not a universal solution. Organizations must overcome several hurdles when they implement blockchain-based supply chain solutions. To accord with these creative frameworks, the legislative environment must be reevaluated. The current blockchain systems may not be able to meet the increased transaction throughput demands of supply chains. Given the wide range of actors in supply chains, incentivization becomes critical, demanding compelling motives such as increased efficiency, liquidity, and data security. Further, security and privacy concerns loom big, especially in conjunction with the Internet of Things (IoT). To address these difficulties, the ecosystem must be transformed to support blockchain adaptation.

APPLICABILITY OF BLOCKCHAIN TECHNOLOGY

In the domain of logistics, blockchain technology has initiated transformational projects that are poised to alter the dynamics of the supply chain. A plethora of innovative initiatives have emerged, commanded by supply chain stakeholders and entrepreneurs seeking to boost efficiency and reduce operational expenses. Among these, several noteworthy initiatives stand out, each highlighting the profound impact that blockchain is poised to bring about.

The Global Shipping Business Network (GSBN), a consortium of nine ocean carriers and terminal operators, serves as an illustration. The joint venture between IBM and Maersk, which facilitates seamless global cross-border supply chains for the ocean shipping and logistics industries, is another significant collaboration. United Parcel Service has utilized blockchain technology to optimize cargo pricing futures markets. United Parcel Service expedites the matching of available cargoes with vehicles by combining real-time load matching with data analytics and artificial intelligence.

Similarly, Waltonchain implemented digital and physical elements in a single system. It integrates IoT devices and RFID sensors to assure business process security, traceability, and authenticity (Khan et al., 2016). In industries such as mining and jewelry, where monitoring assets from their origins to the final consumer is of utmost importance, its applicability is particularly noteworthy. The diamond industry, for instance, faces significant obstacles, as burglaries and fraudulent claims cost an estimated $45 billion annually, with a significant portion evading detection. Using blockchain technology, companies such as EverLedger and De Beers, a renowned jewelry manufacturer, facilitate the monitoring of assets throughout their lifecycle, ensuring that consumers receive only authentic, unaltered products.

BHP Billiton, the largest mining company in the world, intends to utilize blockchain technology to improve data monitoring and documenting throughout the mining process. The application of blockchain technology is not limited to a single industry; rather, it promotes transparency, security, and efficacy across multiple sectors. The convergence of blockchain with the Internet of Things (IoT), cloud computing, and data analytics is expected to be heralded in the era of advanced supply chain systems. For instance, Internet of Things sensors are utilized to collect data regarding environmental conditions, thereby optimizing cargo handling and shipment protocols. The McKinsey Global Institute estimates that IoT applications will be worth between $4 and $11 trillion by 2025, highlighting the staggering potential of this convergence. In addition, COVID-19 pandemic highlights the importance of interoperability and compatibility in global supply chain networks. In this regard, blockchain technology is the pivot, enabling dissimilar supply chain systems to interoperate seamlessly and assuring low-cost and highly effective cross-system collaboration.

Despite its transformative potential, however, blockchain technology is not without obstacles. To realize its utmost potential within the supply chain domain, numerous factors must be addressed. To accommodate these novel frameworks, the landscape necessitates legislative reform. Current blockchain platforms must be modified to support the high transaction volume required by supply chains. Motivating stakeholders with efficiency gains, liquidity enhancements, and data security, incentive structures are crucial. Hence, the convergence of blockchain technology in industries catalyzes a profound revolution. From protecting authenticity and provenance in the jewelry industry to optimizing global transportation networks, blockchain emerges as a transformative force with the potential to profoundly alter the supply chain model.

The automobile sector, which is frequently viewed as the driving force behind global supply chains, is on the verge of revolution as a result of the incorporation of blockchain technology. This technology provides a plethora of supply chain use cases that are suited to the specific demands of the automobile industry. Figure 2 depicts a complete overview of prospective application areas where blockchain influences the operations of the automobile sector.

The concept of smart factories has cleared the path for quick retooling and adaptation, providing a significant competitive advantage to smaller-scale production plants. This competitive advantage stems from their capacity to make tailor-made items on a regional basis that suit unique local preferences. In this context, the notion of micro factories emerges as a game-changing production framework, particularly pertinent to the manufacture of next-generation electric automobiles.

Motors manufacturers, for example, have pioneered the construction of vehicle manufacturing micro-factories in cities such as Phoenix, Las Vegas, and Knoxville. These micro-factories house a vast collection of car concepts, encouraging participation from a global community of designers, engineers, manufacturers, and automobile enthusiasts. This breakthrough signals the possibility of decentralized production, democratizing industry as the internet age makes knowledge more widely available. As entrance barriers fall, the possibilities for design and manufacture within the context of distributed production grow more inclusive. However, the effectiveness of these micro factories is dependent on the resilience of the supply chain infrastructure, as weak links in the chain might result in increased distribution costs.

Subsequently, supply chain security appears as a critical success element for micro factory networks. It is critical to have a well-structured supply chain for components such as motors, inverters, electrical boards, lighting, seats, and battery cells. In this sense, the incorporation of blockchain technology into the supply chain provides a possible option for future improvement. The micro factory approach allows each country to build its own personal brand identity via customization that corresponds to market demands. Collaboration acquires popularity as local businesses solidify their presence inside the established automobile sector, spreading the notion of a networked micro factory. The suggested framework proposes the establishment of a globally distributed network via the proliferation of micro factories. While a central authority may benefit such a network, the sharing economy ethos inherent in micro factories does not require its existence. Addressing this difficulty is the smooth dissemination of data across the network without the use of middlemen, which blockchain technology is capable of. Blockchain eliminates the need for a third party by permitting peer-to-peer transactions through cooperation and cryptography. Transactions between micro manufacturers and suppliers take place transparently inside this decentralized system, eliminating the need for central control.

The security features of blockchain are significant, with its architecture requiring an attacker to compromise all nodes in the network, making such efforts very unfeasible. As a result, blockchain appears as a priceless option for bolstering the security and integrity of the micro factory network. This network is supported by smart contracts, which execute defined rules and procedures autonomously in response to certain blockchain-recorded occurrences. In essence, blockchain presents a simplified, safe, and automated method of sending information that does away with the need for middlemen or central authority. It provides unrivaled transparency, speed, accessibility, and coherence, all of which are in sync with the operating paradigm of company networks.

Figure 2. Automotive supply chain (Reddy et al., 2021)

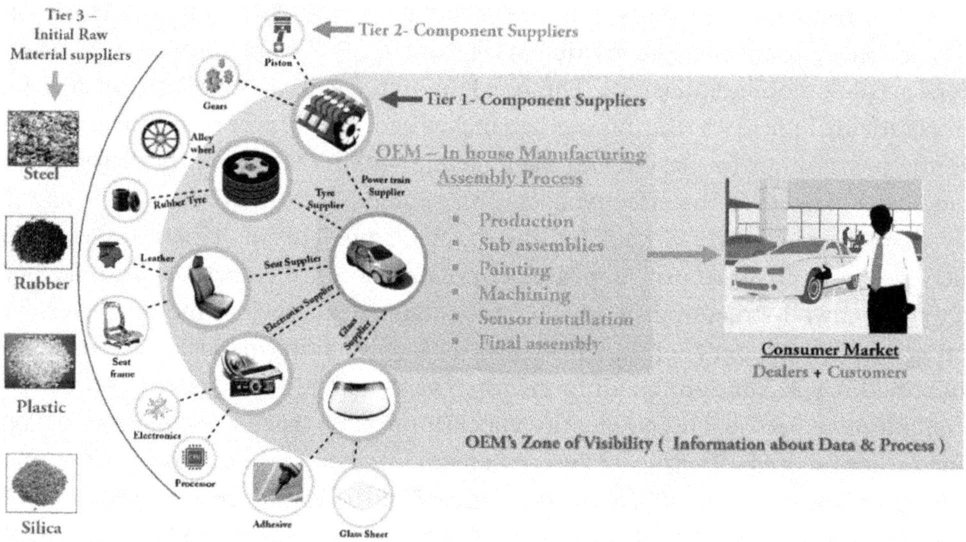

DRIVERS OF BLOCKCHAIN IMPLEMENTATION IN SUPPLY CHAINS

The use of blockchain technology in supply chain management is motivated by three key aspects. Among these criteria, trust is the most prevalent. In the context of supply chains, trust refers to the confidence that information transferred among trade partners is accurate and legitimate, as well as the security of data handled by central authorities. Trust is frequently described as a "shared source of truth" (Michelman, 2017, p. 18), "one data" (Nakasumi, 2017, p. 144), or "one trusted source of data" (Hull et al., 2017, p. 2). Moreover, data security issues have been included into discussion on trust (Collomb and Sok, 2016).

The complexity and geographical dispersion inherent in supply chain operations highlight the importance of obtaining and maintaining reliable data. Blockchain technology plays a critical role in addressing these issues by supporting seamless networks (Bonino and Vergori, 2017; Wang et al., 2017), assuring comprehensive visibility (Li et al., 2017), and sharing information fairly (Nakasumi, 2017). Aside from operational efficiency, such data continuity and reliability foster ethical and socially acceptable company activities.

Clearly, increased consumer awareness of health concerns (e.g., the UK horsemeat scandal, toxic milk powder incidents in China) (Tian, 2016; 2017) and sustainability issues (e.g., child labor, fair trade, organic products) (Abeyratne & Monfared, 2016; Ali, Khan, & Ghouri, 2023) has heightened consumer demand for product authenticity and legitimacy. Consumers want to know about the origins, processing, and sourcing information of the items they buy, emphasizing the need of traceability.

Aside from concerns of traceability and authenticity, another driver for blockchain adoption is public safety and security. Engelenburg et al. (2017) argue adopting blockchain-enabled customs systems in response to possible dangers such as terrorist assaults on marine vessels and cargo. Furthermore, Mackey and Nayyar (2017) argue that the prevalence of counterfeit items in the gray market demands the use of blockchain technology. Scholars such as Guo and Liang (2016) and Kshetri (2017) argue that blockchain's transparency can serve as a powerful cure for legal difficulties in economically weak situations where corruption and fraudulent acts are rampant. Therefore, the adoption of blockchain throughout supply chains is supported by a variety of factors. The primacy of trust, bolstered by concerns of data security, operational efficacy, consumer expectations for traceability, and imperatives for public safety and security, drives the use of blockchain technology in modern supply chain management.

KEY ELEMENTS OF BLOCKCHAIN'S SUPPLY CHAIN MANAGEMENT VALUE PROPOSITION

Visibility and Traceability

The incorporation of blockchain technology into supply chains has the potential to provide significant value, notably in the areas of enhanced visibility and product traceability. Notably, product traceability is expected to emerge as a critical aspect of blockchain implementation in supply chains. The current paradigm of centralized IT platforms and systems responsible for obtaining and approving supply chain data might be inefficient at times. In this context, the use of blockchain-enabled transactions brings a degree of openness that resonates with supply chain participants (Patel et al., 2017). This is demonstrated by the construction of distinct blocks for each transaction, capturing a product's whole digital lifecycle, from conception to manufacture, distribution, and final sale. This increased openness and visibility not only validates product traceability but also ensures its validity and legitimacy (Casey and Wong, 2017; Mansfield, 2017).

The integration of blockchain with field sensor agents enables real-time tracking and the thorough monitoring of product temporal trajectory (Li et al., 2017). Moreover, the inclusion of time-stamping systems results in a higher level of information completeness. Time-stamping, or the temporal sequencing of events, is useful in determining historical events (Abeyratne & Monfared, 2016). This chronologically organized event log, kept within the blockchain, elucidates the existence of relevant data at various temporal junctures, consequently improving the efficacy of time-sensitive activities (Yuan and Wang, 2016; Lee and Pilkington, 2017).

Furthermore, the vast amount of data stored within a blockchain system promotes increased information completeness. The data repository contains a wide range of information, such as ownership history, product-specific features, location history, and environmental effect measurements (Abeyratne and Monfared, 2016). This extensive data coverage includes factors such as price, quality, date, and product condition, enhancing the quality of the information repository (Lee and Pilkington, 2017).

The intrinsic auditability of the blockchain network is a fundamental feature, providing each transaction along the supply chain with an indisputable audit trail. The manifestation of this increased traceability has ramifications that are particularly relevant to industries that rely on product and material origins. The application of blockchain technology to trace the origin and manufacturing trajectory of consumables, such as food components (Foerstl et al., 2017; Tian, 2016), or the provenance of luxury textile goods (Toyoda et al., 2017), clearly takes precedence. Similarly, with the ability to trace pharmaceutical raw materials and finished items, blockchain appears as an efficient weapon in the fight against counterfeit medications (Mackey and Nayyar, 2017).

In practice, crucial supply chains encompassing commodities such as food, diamonds, and medicines have emerged as focus points for blockchain projects. These categories highlight the importance of traceability and product provenance. Knowledge of a product's origin, journey, and footprint within the supply chain not only yields commercial benefits, fostering consumer trust in brands, but also has profound safety implications. For example, Walmart's latest study demonstrates the effectiveness of blockchain-driven tracking by cutting the time it takes to trace a box of sliced mangoes from its US shops to its origin in Mexico from seven days to 2.2 seconds (McKenzie, 2018). This quick and precise tracking technique allows for faster reactions to recalls and food safety problems, reducing the spread of foodborne diseases.

Digitalization and Disintermediation of Supply Chain

The underlying blockchain idea of disintermediation denotes that the security of data integrity relies on the whole network rather than middlemen (Michelman, 2017). It comprises peer-to-peer (P2P) asset transfers and inter-firm trade without the necessity for third-party verification in financial environments (Yuan and Wang, 2016). According to Michelman (2017), blockchain decreases verification and transaction costs by removing middlemen. Wang et al. (2017) underline blockchain's applicability for short-term commercial partnerships, which reduces the cost of creating trust. Polim et al. (2017) provide a blockchain system that allows merchants to send shipments directly to third-party logistics (3PLs) rather than fourth-party logistics (4PLs).

The blockchain's properties line best with vast networks of various organizations, establishing it as a viable solution to the complexities of global supply chains (Abeyratne and Monfared, 2016; Nakasumi, 2017). International commerce, a complicated supply chain practice, requires many players and paper-based processes, which cause delays and impede efficient flow (Harris et al., 2015). Centralized systems are popular; however they have constraints in high-volume, high-speed transactions (Casey and Wong, 2017). A blockchain-based platform may digitize paperwork, creating an immutable, shared record of real-time network transactions.

Guo and Liang (2016) show that substituting trade financing with blockchain dramatically decreases processing time. Engelenburg et al. (2017) suggest using blockchain to provide real-time cargo visibility to customs authorities, improving risk analysis, safety, and security control (Kshetri, 2017). The complexities of international trade frequently contribute to opacity, making it prone to unethical exploitation (Abeyratne and Monfared, 2016; Nakasumi, 2017). Because of its transparency, blockchain, according to Collomb and Sok (2016), can prevent corruption in international trade.

Marine shipping organizations are actively investigating blockchain technologies to overcome inefficiencies in digitalization in complicated cross-border activities. In 2014, for example, Maersk's refrigerated transport from East Africa to Europe involved roughly 30 organizations and more than 200 contacts (IBM, 2017). Documentation expenses in cross-border commerce might be one-fifth of shipping costs (Maersk Press Release, 2018).

IBM and Maersk launched a blockchain experiment in 2016 to improve workflow and visibility, engaging commercial partners, government agencies, and logistics companies. Participants in the network monitor shipment movement, customs paperwork, and bills of lading. Container tracking incorporates real-time access to original supply chain events and records. There is no record alteration without consensus (IBM, 2017). Following a successful trial, IBM and Maersk embarked on a commercialization effort (Zarzuelo, Soeane & Bermúdez, 2020), indicating blockchain's greater use in supply chains beyond the POC and pilot stages.

Data Security Enhancements for Collaborative Information Exchange

The decentralization of blockchain is a data security strategy. Collomb and Sok (2016) and Tian (2016) emphasize the weaknesses of central databases—corruption, fabrication, and asymmetric data generation—which frequently result in data loss or retrieval difficulties.

The immutable data in blockchain is created by transactions kept in chronological blocks of nodes that are universally disseminated (Tian, 2016). Because consensus procedures restrict transaction updates and deletions, immutability is ensured (Patel et al., 2017; Weber et al., 2016). Falsifying information necessitates real-time modification, which is more difficult than just replacing data (Shireesh and Petrovsky, 2016). Patel et al. (2017) highlights its fault-tolerance as a result of many original data sources. Increased data security fosters confidence and trust among supply chain partners and customers.

Data security is important to supply chain participants because it allows them to share secret commercial information. Permissioned blockchains provide increased privacy, auditability, and operational efficiencies (Gupta, 2017; Weber et al., 2016). Participants in a blockchain supply chain encrypt item descriptions and sensitive data, with access controlled by business rules (Engelenburg et al., 2017; Kshetri, 2017). Blockchain protects against fraud and cybercrime, which result in data breaches, financial crimes, and threats to public safety. The hack on Moller-Maersk highlighted supply chain flaws, resulting in a $300 million revenue loss (Milne, 2017). Decentralized systems, as opposed to centralized systems, are less vulnerable to system-wide halts caused by hacking or technological failures. The resiliency of blockchain provides an alternative way to data management.

Access to supply chain data is very secure and unalterable with blockchain. Google works with the NHS to develop a private blockchain for patient data and integrated health record administration. After a severe hack, FedEx explored a blockchain concept. The lack of a single point of failure in blockchain increases its resistance to assaults and decreases participant disputes. Smart contracts incorporated in blockchains reinforce contractual agreements and eliminate the possibility of conflicts. Hence, blockchain technology strengthens supply chain data security and integrity while also providing answers to current data vulnerabilities and difficulties (Weber et al., 2016).

Therefore, in terms of data security and privacy, it's worth mentioning that blockchain implementation frequently incorporates public, private, and hybrid models, each with their own set of security characteristics. Although public blockchains are more visible, sensitive data may face privacy risks. Private blockchains allow for regulated access and data exchange, which helps to solve certain confidentiality concerns (Sabu et al., 2021). By incorporating characteristics of both public and private blockchains, hybrid models try to strike a compromise between openness and privacy (Kshetri, 2017). In addition, cryptographic breakthroughs like zero-knowledge proofs and homomorphic encryption are being investigated to improve privacy in blockchain networks. These strategies enable safe data sharing without disclosing the actual data, which is particularly useful in supply chain scenarios where sensitive information must be transmitted without jeopardizing privacy (Ali et al.,2023).

Smart Contracts Transforming Supply Chains

Smart contracts stand out as a potentially transformational blockchain use within supply chains. A smart contract is a blockchain-based automated transaction system that attempts to satisfy contractual terms while reducing the costs and delays associated with traditional contracts (Gupta, 2017). This paradigm is extremely important for supply chain automation and self-execution.

Smart contracts provide a variety of functions, such as partial or complete self-execution, self-enforcement, and network-based monitoring (Weber et al., 2016). A smart contract, for example, may make a payment to a supplier as soon as the buyer receives a package. In the event of GPS-tracked product returns, real-time position updates can activate blockchain signaling for fast payouts. As a result, smart contracts reduce payment withholding difficulties and improve efficiency by eliminating the requirement for contract registration, monitoring, and updates, resulting in lower operating expenses (Collomb and Sok, 2016; Wang et al., 2017). According to Bocek et al. (2017), smart contracts reduce the need for intermediaries and human interventions, lowering operating costs.

Smart contract adoption might have a substantial impact on industries with transitory and fragmented supply chains, particularly those with numerous layers of suppliers and subcontractors. Because of the multiple stakeholders, complex supply chains in building projects, for example, struggle with tracking job progress and precise cash payment. Smart contracts enable the digital execution of negotiated contracts for relevant parties, the adjustment of programs based on variations, and the release of copyright materials (Leng et al.,2023).

Smart contracts are mostly being tested in financial transactions and settlements. Notably, Slock.it, a German start-up, is running a blockchain-based digital wallet trial, automating payment when passenger cars are charged at stations. When used to commercial trucks, this might completely transform logistical operations. Barclays uses a smart contract to enable automated payment at the time of cargo ownership transfer.

Smart contract capabilities are not available on all blockchains, but they are becoming increasingly popular owing to their versatility and ability to add business logic under certain situations. However, disturbances are more noticeable in this arena. Smart contracts have significant technological (e.g., security), legal (forcing mechanisms for dispute settlement), and societal ramifications (e.g., removal of middlemen and possible employment displacement). Their implementation profoundly transforms organizational and supply chain structures and governance, and it may take decades for them to become the standard in supply chain management (Hull et al., 2017; Wang et al., 2017).

Moreover, the implementation of smart contracts does provide obstacles, notably in terms of legal frameworks and dispute resolution processes. Because smart contracts are self-executing, well-defined legal frameworks are required to manage possible breaches or disputes that may result from code execution. In addition, the creation of "oracle" systems that retrieve external data to trigger smart contract execution is critical to ensuring the quality and dependability of data utilized in contract terms (Marbouh et al., 2020). Additionally, the combination of Internet of Things (IoT) technology with smart contracts shows potential for improving supply chain functionality. IoT devices can give real-time data on the physical status of commodities, allowing smart contracts to automate activities based on predetermined circumstances (Chang, Chen & Lu, 2019).

Technical Difficulties With Blockchain Integration

The use of blockchain technology into supply chains poses significant technological obstacles that must be carefully considered. While blockchain is widely acknowledged for its resilient and decentralized data architecture, it is critical to note that the danger of hacking remains. Vulnerabilities develop when a coalition of miners momentarily controls 50% of the network's mining hash-rate, endangering blockchain security (Yuan and Wang, 2016; Zhao et al., 2016). While conducting a cyber-attack on public (permissionless) blockchains necessitates significant financial and computing resources, permissioned blockchains may be more vulnerable to such breaches (Patel et al., 2017).

Furthermore, latency appears to be a substantial impediment to blockchain adoption. Delays can occur because of the time it takes for each confirmed block of transactions to be added to the ledger (Wang et al., 2017). For example, Ethereum, a popular platform for smart contracts, needs around 17 seconds to add each block, in contrast to the milliseconds typical of non-blockchain databases (Ream et al., 2016). To improve system performance, efficient incentive structures for miners inside the blockchain ecosystem are required (Nakasumi, 2017). Private customizable blockchains emerge as an optimum option for situations defined by quick and dynamic interactions (Weber et al., 2016).

Surprisingly, the protective character of blockchain, which protects against manipulation by vested parties, can also create difficulties. Mistakes on the blockchain have an irreversible characteristic, making rectifications unfeasible (Patel et al., 2017). In this situation, the notion of completing equal and opposing transactions to correct mistakes takes center stage. Additionally, the issue of interoperability among various blockchains and their smooth integration with current IT systems arises as a major challenge that must be addressed. Addressing the various dynamics of interoperability is required for a coherent strategy to data transmission (Collomb and Sok, 2016; Patel et al., 2017; Wang et al., 2017).

Additionally, exploration of consensus mechanisms that underpin blockchain operations is an important component of tackling technological issues. Different consensus methods, such as Proof of Work (PoW) and Proof of Stake (PoS), provide varied levels of security and efficiency, which must be considered considering the supply chain context's unique requirements (Fernandez-Carames & Fraga-Lamas, 2019). Furthermore, developments in blockchain scalability are crucial, especially when contemplating use in large-volume supply chains. Efforts to improve blockchain scalability can result in increased throughput and more efficient transaction processing, better fitting with the needs of complex supply chain networks (Singh, Rathore & Park, 2020).

Operational Difficulties in Blockchain Integration

The incorporation of blockchain into supply chains presents operational complications that require careful consideration. To achieve blockchain functionality in a supply chain setting, all important supply chain partners must collaborate (Kshetri, 2018). Working in the complex world of blockchain-enabled global supply chains necessitates a comprehensive alignment with a variety of legal frameworks, laws, and institutional structures. Successful blockchain adoption in such sophisticated ecosystems is inherently complicated and necessitates thorough execution (Casey and Wong, 2017).

Although blockchain assures that digital transaction properties are tamper-proof, it may not reliably represent the detailed physical flow of commodities across the supply chain (Shireesh and Petrovsky, 2016). The reality highlights the likelihood of unintended errors, conflicts of interest, corruption, and even hostile assaults undermining the integrity of blockchain-enabled activities (Kshetri, 2018). Chen et al. (2017) highlights critical considerations about the kind of data to be kept in blockchains, data gathering strategies, data integration into the system, and responsibility for data input and delivery. Notably, because of the required technical competence and specialized knowledge, the financial ramifications of adopting or participating in a blockchain ecosystem may present issues. The costs of involvement may offer challenges, particularly for small-to-medium-sized supply chain firms with limited expertise and financial resources (Patel et al., 2017; Wang et al., 2017).

The decentralization of blockchain technology, which delegates trust and authority to a dispersed network, is a game changer. This departure from traditional forms of supply chain structure and management may cause supply chain participants to be concerned. Because of the paradigm change that blockchain requires, cultural opposition and ingrained business procedures emerge as severe impediments to adoption (Patel et al., 2017; Wang et al., 2017). To address the operational challenges associated with blockchain integration, it is important to highlight the significance of developing robust governance models and protocols to promote smooth collaboration and compliance across supply chain actors (Fernandez-Carames & Fraga-Lamas, 2019). Furthermore, addressing interoperability challenges across different blockchain systems is critical to ensuring seamless information flow across supply chain stakeholders. Standardized data formats and protocols can help to improve communication within complicated supply chain networks (Kayıkcı & Subramanian, 2022).

RECOMMENDATIONS

Based on the comprehensive analysis presented in the chapter, several recommendations can be made to guide organizations in effectively leveraging blockchain technology within their supply chain management practices. Firstly, organizations must prioritize the establishment of trust and data security measures to ensure the accuracy, legitimacy, and confidentiality of information exchanged among supply chain partners (Collomb and Sok, 2016; Patel et al., 2017; Weber et al., 2016). Implementing robust data security protocols, such as those facilitated by blockchain's decentralized architecture, can bolster confidence and foster transparent relationships within the supply chain ecosystem. Secondly, organizations should focus on enhancing visibility and traceability throughout the supply chain by leveraging blockchain-enabled systems to capture and record critical information, such as product provenance and ownership history (Casey and Wong, 2017; Toyoda et al., 2017). This will not only enhance transparency and authenticity but also enable more efficient recall processes and proactive risk management strategies. Additionally, the adoption of smart contracts stands out as a transformative approach to automate various supply chain processes, thereby reducing manual intervention, minimizing transaction costs, and improving operational efficiency (Gupta, 2017; Wang et al., 2017). By developing smart contract-based systems for payment settlements, contract enforcement, and logistics management, organizations can streamline operations and mitigate potential risks associated with human error or delays. Moreover, it is crucial for organizations to address technological challenges associated with blockchain integration, such as scalability, latency, and interoperability, through targeted research and development initiatives (Nakasumi, 2017; Patel et al., 2017; Singh, Rathore & Park, 2020). Investing in alternative consensus mechanisms and incentive structures can enhance blockchain performance and optimize transaction processing speed within supply chain networks. Furthermore, organizations should prioritize the establishment of robust governance structures and standardized protocols to govern blockchain-enabled supply chain networks, ensuring compliance, transparency, and accountability among participating entities (Fernandez-Carames & Fraga-Lamas, 2019; Kayıkcı & Subramanian, 2022). By fostering collaboration and information sharing through clear communication channels and shared objectives, organizations can enhance trust and facilitate seamless interactions within the supply chain ecosystem. Lastly, organizations must take a strategic approach to deployment by conducting comprehensive feasibility studies, pilot projects, and strategic deployment plans that align with organizational goals and objectives (Casey and Wong, 2017; Patel et al., 2017; Wang et al., 2017). By staying updated on the latest developments and trends in blockchain technology, organizations can capitalize on emerging opportunities and innovations in supply chain management, fostering a culture of continuous learning and adaptation within the organization (Patel et al., 2017; Wang et al., 2017; Ali et al., 2023). Therefore, organizations can effectively harness the transformative potential of blockchain technology to enhance transparency, efficiency, and security within their supply chain operations by implementing these recommendations.

FUTURE RESEARCH DIRECTION

Based on the insights gleaned from the chapter, several promising avenues for future research in the field of blockchain-enabled supply chain management can be identified. Firstly, there is a need for further investigation into the development of advanced data security mechanisms tailored to the unique requirements of blockchain-based supply chain networks (Collomb and Sok, 2016; Patel et al., 2017; Weber et al., 2016). Research efforts could focus on exploring innovative cryptographic techniques, such as zero-knowledge proofs and homomorphic encryption, to enhance privacy and confidentiality while facilitating secure data sharing among supply chain participants (Ali et al., 2023). Additionally, studies examining the effectiveness of different consensus mechanisms, such as Proof of Work (PoW) and Proof of Stake (PoS), in ensuring the integrity and reliability of blockchain operations within large-scale supply chain networks are warranted (Fernandez-Carames & Fraga-Lamas, 2019). Secondly, future research endeavors could delve into the development of interoperability solutions aimed at facilitating seamless integration and communication between disparate blockchain systems and traditional IT infrastructures (Collomb and Sok, 2016; Patel et al., 2017; Wang et al., 2017). Investigating standardized data formats, protocols, and middleware solutions can help overcome interoperability challenges and promote interoperability across supply chain networks (Kayıkcı & Subramanian, 2022). Moreover, studies exploring the integration of Internet of Things (IoT) technology with blockchain-enabled supply chain networks could offer valuable insights into enhancing real-time data visibility and automation capabilities (Chang, Chen & Lu, 2019). Thirdly, there is a need for research focusing on the development of robust governance models and regulatory frameworks to govern blockchain-enabled supply chain networks (Fernandez-Carames & Fraga-Lamas, 2019; Kayıkcı & Subramanian, 2022). Examining the legal implications of smart contracts and decentralized autonomous organizations (DAOs) within supply chain operations can help identify potential legal challenges and inform the development of relevant regulatory frameworks (Marbouh et al., 2020). Additionally, studies exploring the socio-economic impacts of blockchain adoption on supply chain participants and broader society can provide valuable insights into the implications of blockchain technology on employment, economic inequality, and social inclusion (Hull et al., 2017; Wang et al., 2017). Lastly, future research endeavors could focus on exploring the application of blockchain technology in specific industry sectors and supply chain domains, such as healthcare, food safety, and sustainability (Casey and Wong, 2017; Toyoda et al., 2017). Investigating the benefits and challenges of blockchain adoption in these contexts can provide valuable guidance for organizations seeking to leverage blockchain technology to address industry-specific challenges and opportunities (Gul et al., 2024; Masood et al., 2024).

CONCLUSION

The incorporation of blockchain technology into supply chain management signifies a historic shift in how modern businesses and industries operate. this chapter examined the broad impact of blockchain adoption in supply chains, emphasizing both its revolutionary potential and the challenges that it presents. The capacity of blockchain to provide visibility and traceability underscores its value proposition in supply chains. It provides a visible, tamper-proof ledger that records the complete lifecycle of products, boosting confidence and authenticity. Food, jewelry, and pharmaceutical companies have recognized the value of blockchain in verifying product authenticity and safety. Smart contracts, a pillar of blockchain technology, are changing supply chain automation. These self-executing contracts streamline processes, save costs, and improve efficiency, especially in complicated and fragmented supply chains. However, its application necessitates careful consideration of legal frameworks and dispute settlement processes. While blockchain provides improved data security through decentralization, it is not without technological limitations. To reach its full potential, issues such as latency, scalability, and compatibility must be solved. Furthermore, operational complexities develop due to the requirement for collaboration among supply chain partners and the cultural shift required by blockchain. Considering these hurdles, organizations must design robust governance structures, establish standardized protocols, and invest in the necessary technical knowledge to properly integrate blockchain into their supply chains. The path toward blockchain-enabled supply chains may be complicated, but the benefits in terms of transparency, efficiency, and security are certainly valuable. As blockchain technology evolves and finds new uses, its position in supply chain management is expected to rise. Businesses can leverage the full potential of blockchain to transform the future of supply chains by committing to overcoming difficulties and taking a strategic approach to deployment.

REFERENCES

Abeyratne, S. A., & Monfared, R. P. (2016). Blockchain ready manufacturing supply chain using distributed ledger. *International Journal of Research in Engineering and Technology*, *5*(9), 1–10. doi:10.15623/ijret.2016.0509001

Agarwal, U., Rishiwal, V., Tanwar, S., Chaudhary, R., Sharma, G., Bokoro, P. N., & Sharma, R. (2022). Blockchain technology for secure supply chain management: A comprehensive review. *IEEE Access : Practical Innovations, Open Solutions*, *10*, 85493–85517. doi:10.1109/ACCESS.2022.3194319

Ali, A., Al-Rimy, B. A. S., Alsubaei, F. S., Almazroi, A. A., & Almazroi, A. A. (2023). HealthLock: Blockchain-Based Privacy Preservation Using Homomorphic Encryption in Internet of Things Healthcare Applications. *Sensors (Basel)*, *23*(15), 6762. doi:10.3390/s23156762 PMID:37571545

Ali, A., Khan, M. R., & Ghouri, A. M. (2023). Carbon neutrality concept and progress. In Recent Developments in Green Finance, Green Growth and Carbon Neutrality (pp. 85-108). Elsevier. doi:10.1016/B978-0-443-15936-7.00003-7

Andrei, O. J. (2023, May 17). Blockchain technology as a driver of economic development in small economies: A dynamic capabilities framework. *Journal of Decision Systems*, 1–26. Advance online publication. doi:10.1080/12460125.2023.2214304

Apte, S., & Petrovsky, N. (2016). Will blockchain technology revolutionize excipient supply chain management? *Journal of Excipients and Food Chemicals*, *7*(3), 76–78.

Bocek, T., Rodrigues, B. B., Strasser, T., & Stiller, B. (2017, May). Blockchains everywhere-a use-case of blockchains in the pharma supply-chain. In *2017 IFIP/IEEE symposium on integrated network and service management (IM)* (pp. 772-777). IEEE.

Bonino, D., & Vergori, P. (2017). Agent marketplaces and deep learning in enterprises: the composition project. *IEEE 41st Annual Computer Software and Applications Conference (COMPSAC)*, 749-754. 10.1109/COMPSAC.2017.46

Casey, M. J., & Wong, P. (2017). Global supply chains are about to get better, thanks to blockchain. *Harvard Business Review*, *13*, 1–6.

Chang, S. E., Chen, Y. C., & Lu, M. F. (2019). Supply chain re-engineering using blockchain technology: A case of smart contract based tracking process. *Technological Forecasting and Social Change*, *144*, 1–11. doi:10.1016/j.techfore.2019.03.015

Chen, S., Shi, R., Ren, Z., Yan, J., Shi, Y., & Zhang, J. (2017). A blockchain-based supply chain quality management framework. In *2017 IEEE 14th International Conference on E-Business Engineering (ICEBE)* (pp. 172-176). IEEE. 10.1109/ICEBE.2017.34

Christopher, M. (1998). *Logistics and supply chain management: Strategies for reducing cost and improving service*. Financial Times Professional Limited.

Collomb, A., & Sok, K. (2016). Blockchain/Distributed ledger technology (DLT): What impact on the financial sector? *Communications & Stratégies*, *103*, 93–111.

De la Peña Zarzuelo, I., Soeane, M. J. F., & Bermúdez, B. L. (2020). Industry 4.0 in the port and maritime industry: A literature review. *Journal of Industrial Information Integration*, *20*, 100173. doi:10.1016/j.jii.2020.100173

Engelenburg, S. V., Janssen, M., & Klievink, B. (2019). Design of a software architecture supporting business-to-government information sharing to improve public safety and security: Combining business rules, Events and blockchain technology. *Journal of Intelligent Information Systems*, *52*(3), 595–618. doi:10.1007/s10844-017-0478-z

Fernandez-Carames, T. M., & Fraga-Lamas, P. (2019). A review on the application of blockchain to the next generation of cybersecure industry 4.0 smart factories. *IEEE Access : Practical Innovations, Open Solutions*, *7*, 45201–45218. doi:10.1109/ACCESS.2019.2908780

Foerstl, K., Schleper, M. C., & Henke, M. (2017). Purchasing and supply management: From efficiency to effectiveness in an integrated supply chain. *Journal of Purchasing and Supply Management*, *23*(4), 223–228. doi:10.1016/j.pursup.2017.08.004

Gul, I., Khan, N. R., & Ghouri, A. M. (2023). Blockchain-driven supply chain management and open innovation. In *Blockchain Driven Supply Chain Management: A Multi-dimensional Perspective* (pp. 135–154). Springer Nature Singapore. doi:10.1007/978-981-99-0699-4_9

Gul, I., Raziq, A., & Khan, M. R. (2024). Towards sustainable supply chains with blockchain. In achieving secure and transparent supply chains with blockchain technology. In *Achieving Secure and Transparent Supply Chains with Blockchain Technology* (pp. 18–37). IGI Global. doi:10.4018/979-8-3693-0482-2.ch002

Guo, Y., & Liang, C. (2016). Blockchain application and outlook in the banking industry. *Financial Innovation*, *24*(1), 1–12. doi:10.1186/s40854-016-0034-9

Gupta, M. (2017). *E-Book: blockchain for dummies*. IBM. Available at: https://www.ibm.com/downloads/cas/36KBMBOG

Harris, I., Wang, Y., & Wang, H. (2015). ICT in multimodal transport and technological trends: Unleashing potential for the future. *International Journal of Production Economics*, *159*, 88–103. doi:10.1016/j.ijpe.2014.09.005

Hull, R., Batra, V., Chee, Y.-M., Chen, Y., Coblenz, M., Deshpande, P., & Deutsch, A. (2017). Blockchain: distributed event-based processing in a Data-Centric world. *Proceedings of the 11th ACM International Conference on Distributed and Event-Based Systems*, 2-4.

IBM. (2017a). *Maersk and IBM unveil first Industry-Wide Cross-Border supply chain solution on blockchain*. Available at: https://www-03.ibm.com/press/us/en/pressrelease/51712.wss

Kayıkcı, Y., & Subramanian, N. (2022). Blockchain interoperability issues in Supply chain: exploration of mass adoption procedures. In *Big Data and Blockchain for Service Operations Management* (pp. 309–328). Springer International Publishing. doi:10.1007/978-3-030-87304-2_13

Khan, M. R., Khan, M. R., & Nallaluthan, K. (2023). Blockchain Supply Chain Management and Supply Chain Sustainability. In *Blockchain Driven Supply Chain Management: A Multi-dimensional Perspective* (pp. 155–180). Springer Nature Singapore. doi:10.1007/978-981-99-0699-4_10

Khan, N. R., Haq, M. A., Ghouri, A. M., Raziq, A., & Moiz, S. M. (2017). Adaptation of RFID technology in business supply chain success: Empirical findings from a developing country logistic industry. *Calitatea*, *18*(160), 93–99.

Kshetri, N. (2017). Will blockchain emerge as a tool to break the poverty chain in the Global South? *Third World Quarterly*, *38*(8), 1710–1732. doi:10.1080/01436597.2017.1298438

Kshetri, N. (2018). Blockchain's roles in meeting key supply chain management objectives. *International Journal of Information Management*, *39*, 80–89. doi:10.1016/j.ijinfomgt.2017.12.005

Lee, J. H., & Pilkington, M. (2017). How the blockchain revolution will reshape the consumer electronics industry future directions. *IEEE Consumer Electronics Magazine*, *6*(3), 19–23. doi:10.1109/MCE.2017.2684916

Leng, J., Sha, W., Lin, Z., Jing, J., Liu, Q., & Chen, X. (2023). Blockchained smart contract pyramid-driven multi-agent autonomous process control for resilient individualised manufacturing towards Industry 5.0. *International Journal of Production Research*, *61*(13), 4302–4321. doi:10.1080/00207543.2022.2089929

Li, W., Fu, C., & Cheng, D. (2020). Comments on the development of blockchain technology from the perspective of patent analysis. *Frontiers of Engineering Management*, *7*(4), 615–617. doi:10.1007/s42524-020-0101-9

Li, Z., Wu, H., King, B., Miled, Z. B., Wassick, J., & Tazelaar, J. (2017, June). On the integration of event-based and transaction-based architectures for supply chains. In *2017 IEEE 37th International Conference on Distributed Computing Systems Workshops (ICDCSW)* (pp. 376-382). IEEE.

Liao, R. (2020). *How interoperability establishes blockchain's utility and effectiveness for trade finance May 2020*. WEF. https://www.weforum.org/agenda/2020/05/blockchain-interoperability-utility-effectiveness/

Litke, A., Anagnostopoulos, D., & Varvarigou, T. (2019). Blockchains for supply chain management: Architectural elements and challenges towards a global scale deployment. *Logistics*, *3*(1), 5. doi:10.3390/logistics3010005

Mackey, T. K., & Nayyar, G. (2017). A review of existing and emerging digital technologies to combat the global trade in fake medicines. *Expert Opinion on Drug Safety*, *16*(5), 587–602. doi:10.1080/14740338.2017.1313227 PMID:28349715

Maersk Press Release. (2018). *Maersk and IBM to form joint venture applying blockchain to improve global trade and digitise supply chains*. Available at: www.maersk.com/press/press-release-archive/maersk-and-ibm-to-form-joint-venture

Mansfield-Devine, S. (2017). Beyond Bitcoin: Using blockchain technology to provide assurance in the commercial world. *Computer Fraud & Security*, *2017*(5), 14–18. doi:10.1016/S1361-3723(17)30042-8

Marbouh, D., Abbasi, T., Maasmi, F., Omar, I. A., Debe, M. S., Salah, K., Jayaraman, R., & Ellahham, S. (2020). Blockchain for COVID-19: Review, opportunities, and a trusted tracking system. *Arabian Journal for Science and Engineering*, *45*(12), 9895–9911. doi:10.1007/s13369-020-04950-4 PMID:33072472

Masood, F., Khan, N. R., & Khan, M. R. (2024). Blockchain-based supply chain management: A challenge yet an opportunity to gauge. In *Achieving Secure and Transparent Supply Chains with Blockchain Technology* (pp. 267–285). IGI Global. doi:10.4018/979-8-3693-0482-2.ch015

McKenzie, J. (2018). *Why blockchain won't fix food safety – yet*. Available at https://thecounter.org/blockchain-food-traceability-walmart-ibm/

Michelman, P. (2017). Seeing beyond the blockchain hype. *MIT Sloan Management Review*, *58*(4), 17–19.

Milne, R. (2017). Moller-Maersk puts cost of cyber attack at up to $300m. *Financial Times*. Available at: https://www.ft.com/content/a44ede7c-825f-11e7-a4ce-15b2513cb3ff

Moavenzadeh, J., Doherty, S., Philip, R., Geiger, T., Gottfredson, M., Mattios, G., Willink, B. T., Correa, A., Hoekman, B., Jackson, S., Ferrantino, M., & Tsigas, M. (2013). *Enabling trade. Valuing growth opportunities*. World Economic Forum.

Nakasumi, M. (2017). Information sharing for supply chain management based on block chain technology. *IEEE 19th Conference on Business Informatics*, 140-149. 10.1109/CBI.2017.56

Nir, K. (2017). Can blockchain strengthen the internet of things? *IT Professional, 19*(4), 68–72. doi:10.1109/MITP.2017.3051335

Patel, D., Bothra, J., & Patel, V. (2017, January). Blockchain exhumed. In *2017 ISEA Asia Security and Privacy (ISEASP)* (pp. 1-12). IEEE.

Polim, R., Hu, Q., & Kumara, S. (2017). Blockchain in megacity logistics. In *IIE Annual Conference. Proceedings* (pp. 1589-1594). Institute of Industrial and Systems Engineers (IISE).

Ream, J., Chu, Y., & Schatsky, D. (2016). Upgrading blockchains: smart contract use cases in industry. *Deloitte insights*. Available at: https://www2.deloitte.com/us/en/insights/focus/signals-for-strategists/using-blockchain-for-smart-contracts.html

Reddy, K. R. K., Gunasekaran, A., Kalpana, P., Sreedharan, V. R., & Kumar, S. A. (2021). Developing a blockchain framework for the automotive supply chain: A systematic review. *Computers & Industrial Engineering, 157*, 107334. doi:10.1016/j.cie.2021.107334

Saberi, S., Kouhizadeh, M., Sarkis, J., & Shen, L. (2019). Blockchain technology and its relationships to sustainable supply chain management. *International Journal of Production Research, 57*(7), 2117–2135. doi:10.1080/00207543.2018.1533261

Sabu, S., Ramalingam, H. M., Vishaka, M., Swapna, H. R., & Hegde, S. (2021). Implementation of a Secure and privacy-aware E-Health record and IoT data Sharing using Blockchain. *Global Transitions Proceedings, 2*(2), 429–433. doi:10.1016/j.gltp.2021.08.033

Singh, S. K., Rathore, S., & Park, J. H. (2020). Blockiotintelligence: A blockchain-enabled intelligent IoT architecture with artificial intelligence. *Future Generation Computer Systems, 110*, 721–743. doi:10.1016/j.future.2019.09.002

Tian, F. (2016). An agri-food supply chain traceability system for China based on RFID & blockchain technology. In *2016 13th international conference on service systems and service management (ICSSSM)* (pp. 1-6). IEEE.

Tian, F. (2017). A supply chain traceability system for food safety based on HACCP, blockchain & Internet of things. In *2017 International conference on service systems and service management* (pp. 1-6). IEEE.

Toyoda, K., Mathiopoulos, P. T., Sasase, I., & Ohtsuki, T. (2017). A novel blockchain-based product ownership management system (POMS) for anti-counterfeits in the post supply chain. *IEEE Access : Practical Innovations, Open Solutions, 5*, 17465–17477. doi:10.1109/ACCESS.2017.2720760

Vara, R. C., Prieto, J., Prieta, F., & Corchado, J. M. (2018). How blockchain improves supply chain: The case study alimentary supply chain. *Procedia Computer Science, 134*, 393–398. doi:10.1016/j.procs.2018.07.193

Wang, J., Wu, P., Wang, X., & Shou, W. (2017). The outlook of blockchain technology for construction engineering management. *Frontiers of Engineering Management, 4*(1), 67–75. doi:10.15302/J-FEM-2017006

Weber, I., Xu, X., Riveret, R., Governatori, G., Ponomarev, A., & Mendling, J. (2016). Untrusted business process monitoring and execution using blockchain. *Business Process Management: 14th International Conference, BPM 2016, Rio de Janeiro, Brazil, September 18-22, 2016 Proceedings, 14*, 329–347.

World Trade Organization. (2019). *World trade statistical review 2019, 31 May 2019*. Author.

Yuan, Y., & Wang, F. Y. (2016). Towards blockchain-based intelligent transportation systems. In *2016 IEEE 19th international conference on intelligent transportation systems (ITSC)* (pp. 2663-2668). 10.1109/ITSC.2016.7795984

Zhao, J. L., Fan, S., & Yan, J. (2016). Overview of business innovations and research opportunities in blockchain and introduction to the special issue. *Financial Innovation, 2*(1), 1–7. doi:10.1186/s40854-016-0049-2

Chapter 11
Supply Chain Management Using Fermatean Fuzzy-Based Decision Making With ISSOA

Arunadevi Thirumalraj
https://orcid.org/0009-0003-5396-6810
K. Ramakrishnan College of Technology, India

R. J. Anandhi
New Horizon College of Engineering, India

V. Revathi
https://orcid.org/0000-0002-8583-1916
New Horizon College of Engineering, India

S. Stephe
K. Ramakrishnan College of Engineering, India

ABSTRACT

The goal of this research is to create a decision-making process for sustainable supplier selection and order allocation that is known as Fermatean Fuzzy Sets-Based Decision Making (FFS-DMS). The Improved Salp Swarm Optimization (ISSO) approach is used to pick suppliers and allocate the best order quantities. The suggested FFS-ISSA-DMS technique's viability and efficacy are proven through empirical experiments. With an astounding 99.81% accuracy rate, this method outperforms other models that are already in use in this situation.

DOI: 10.4018/979-8-3693-1363-3.ch011

1. INTRODUCTION

The way the healthcare sector approaches SC management has undergone a significant shift in recent years (Habib et al., 2023). Innovative strategies are becoming more and more necessary as hospitals work to deliver high-quality care while cutting costs and increasing overall efficiency. The adoption of Circular SCs (CSC), which prioritize sustainability and the responsible use of resources, is one notable change in this environment. The intensive care unit is a vital component of the hospital ecosystem that requires particular consideration (ICU). The ICU is critical to the patient care continuum, so a smooth and responsive healthcare SC is essential (Rehman, O. U., & Ali 2022). The principles of sustainability and conscientious resource management form the foundation of the Circular SC (CSC) concept. It motivates businesses to cut back on waste, recycle goods, and repurpose materials in order to save money and lessen their environmental impact (Rahman et al 2023). Adopting a circular approach is particularly important in the healthcare industry because of the significant amounts of medical waste generated, the need for quick response in emergency situations, and the requirement for efficient resource allocation (Naseem et al., 2023). The intensive care unit (ICU) occupies a special place in hospitals as the front line of critical patient care, where patient outcomes can be directly impacted by SC efficiency (Mahjoob et al., 2023).

Effective management of the SC is crucial in the intensive care unit to guarantee the timely availability of necessary medical supplies, equipment, and pharmaceuticals. Patients may suffer grave consequences as a result of ICU SC mishandling, shortages, or delays. As a result, for continuous improvement in the intensive care unit SC, Key Performance Indicators (KPIs) must be measured and analyzed (Chen et al., 2023). KPIs give SC managers and healthcare administrators the ability to evaluate the chain's performance, pinpoint areas for development, and make data-driven choices that will improve patient care and efficiency. In order to effectively accomplish these goals, healthcare organizations need to make use of the best tools and techniques. Given its capacity to manage the uncertainty, complexity, and variability inherent in healthcare SC processes, fuzzy-based SC management appears to be the best option (Mostepaniuk et al., 2023 and Xu et al., 2023). There are a number of strong arguments in favor of fuzzy-based SC management in the healthcare industry, especially in intensive care units.

Uncertainties in supply and demand frequently afflict healthcare SC management. Rapid changes in patient needs necessitate SCs to adjust as well. Because Fuzzy logic (FL) performs effectively when handling imprecise and unclear data, it can be applied to modeling the demand and supply patterns that fluctuate in the intensive care unit (Pamucar et al., 2023). ICU patients show different levels of illness, and things can change quickly for them. The SC must adapt to these changes and be flexible. FL ensures that supplies are distributed appropriately to meet changing needs by adapting to the dynamic changes in patient care (Ahmad, F., & John, B. 2023). ICU patients show different levels of illness, and things can change quickly for them. The SC must adapt to these changes and be flexible (Chandra et al., 2023). When patient care needs change, FL can adjust to the new circumstances and make sure that supplies are distributed in a way that best suits the new requirements. Decisions about the healthcare SC frequently take into account a number of factors. Cost, quality, availability, and patient safety are a few examples of these (Deliktaş et al., 2023). FL offers a thorough framework for making decisions in accordance with the standard procedure intricate structure of healthcare SCs and permits the integration of numerous factors. Healthcare organizations can enhance patient care, optimize resource allocation, and add to the healthcare SC's effectiveness and durabilityby implementing a fuzzy-based approach (Luo et al., 2023).

1.1. Motivation

The goal of this study is to solve the difficult issues that contemporary SCs confront, which are typified by their complexity, worldwide dispersion, and variety of elements including laws and cultural norms. Trust and overall performance are hampered by inefficiencies, fraud, and a lack of transparency within supply networks. Using a multi-layer fuzzy-based approach to decision-making, this study aims to enhance hospital Circular SC efficiency,particularly in critical care units. Enhancing the SC's dependability, traceability, and transparency is the aim in order to reduce risks and boost competitiveness. The goal of the study is to maximise supplier selection and order allocation by using cutting-edge methods like Salp Swarm Optimisation and FFS.

1.2. Main Contributions

- Tanh Based Normalization (TN) preprocessing is used to remove nosie from datas.
- In order to meet important decision-making criteria, the FFS based Decision Making (FFS-DMS) technique is introduced for the purpose of allocating orders and choosing sustainable suppliers.
- Utilizing an improved approach for Salp Swarm Optimization (ISSO)to maximise order volumes and supplier selections, with actual investigations proving the usefulness and applicability of the suggested strategy.

1.3 Organization of the Work

The relevant works are summarized in Section 2, the recommended model is briefly explained in Section 3, the findings and validation investigation are shown in Section 4, and the summary as well as the conclusion are given in Section 5.

2. RELATED WORKS

Five management components that were integrated with the use of artificial intelligence (AI) were examined in a research by (Bokhari et al., 2023) risk, disposal, demand, procurement, and logistics. Enhancing SC management's public domain performance was the major goal. The research found that in Pakistan's public distribution networks, bureaucracy posed a substantial adoption barrier, even though artificial intelligence was the most extensively employed technology.

An analysis and evaluation of a computer model for sugarcane production in the Thai sugarcane sector was conducted by (Chansamut, A. 2023). The means and standard deviations were used to examine the data, which were collected from a sample of 10 specialists with knowledge of SC management and information. Raw materials, suppliers, manufacturing locations, distribution networks, wholesalers, customers, and customer satisfaction were the eight main elements of the digital sugarcane production model that were looked at in the research for the Thai SC facility.A Black-Box examination of the digital sugarcane production model of the Thai SC organisation was carried out. The study's findings shown how the digital model's high relevance and usefulness may assist a range of operational tasks and raise sugarcane yield in the Thai SC plant.

In order to meet the issue of choosing suppliers during the COVID-19 pandemic, Pamucar, (Pamucar et al., 2023) combined a state-of-the-art hybrid distance-based evaluation approach with the Measurement Attractiveness via a Categorical-Based assessment approach (MACBETH). Because of the increased degrees of uncertainty, resistance, and ignorance brought on by the COVID-19 pandemic, fuzzy approximation figures were used in this decision-making process. Fuzzy rough numbers, as opposed to conventional fuzzy statistical sampling (FS) and rough numbers, provide benefits for more complex uncertainty frameworks.A thorough sensitivity analysis was carried out, including the features of the decision-making process, the influence of weight coefficients, and the extent to which the results matched those of multiple criteria decision-making (MCDM) approaches that were already in use. To show how applicable the recommended strategy is, a real-world case study involving a hospital in Istanbul, Turkey, was carried out.The most important criteria were those connected to the work and the development of occupational health and safety initiatives, according to the findings of the MACBETH method. Out of all the five providers that were assessed for the case study, A1 had the highest distance score (3.308).

A ground-breaking plan-do-check-act (PDCA) core paradigm for group decision-making is offered by (Ghosh et al., 2023) in their work. To assess the efficiency with which industrial organisations use GSCM. The fuzzy method for order preference by similarity to the ideal solution (FTOPSIS) was used to determine the weights allocated to the different criteria, and the fuzzy analytical hierarchy process (FAHP) was used to rank the organisations. This study used a variety of fuzzy multi-criteria decision-making (MCDM) techniques. A selection was selected for each of the five qualitative categories—environmental, operational, economic, and sustainability—from the corpus of previous research. Three approaches were utilised to collect the data: creating a committee of decision-makers, conducting a survey, and creating a questionnaire. The real-world case study for this research focused on three distinct Indian industrial companies: Organisation A, Organisation B, and Organisation C. These associations represented three distinct industries: the steel, leather, and pharmaceutical sectors. The major objective was to demonstrate a possible practical use of the suggested paradigm in a corporate context. The study of the data showed that the most significant factor was the impact that production-related emissions of hazardous compounds had on the environment. The results, which further establish Organisation C as the industry standard, provide insightful guidance to other businesses aiming to enhance the efficacy of their Green SC Management (GSCM). The issues of ambiguity and vagueness in decision-making were also effectively resolved by the suggested method.

In the work of (Riaz et al., 2023) several dynamic spherical fuzzy aggregation operators (AOs) for "multi-period decision-making" (MPDM) issues were introduced. Decision-makers (DMs) have access to all pertinent data in these situations thanks to the spherical fuzzy numbers (SpFNs) that cover various time periods. When there were competing interests to take into account, AOs were especially important in the decision-making process. The biggest challenge with combining data from many sources was figuring out which aggregating techniques to use. Two novel Einstein AOs were referred to as "spherical fuzzy dynamic Einstein weighted geometric (SpFDEWG) and spherical fuzzy dynamic Einstein weighted averaging (SpFDEWA)]." Several attractive properties of these AOs were investigated in detail. There was also a way given for resolving MPDM problems using the best accessible solutions. The recommended technique was described and a numerical example of municipal SC management was provided. To assess the effectiveness of the suggested method, a comparison of the planned and current studies was made. An authenticity evaluation was carried out to demonstrate the effectiveness of the suggested technique. Dynamic, multi-stage decision analysis is often advantageous for recommended courses of action as well as real decision-making procedures.

In (Hossain et al., 2023) research industry experts were interviewed and the literature was reviewed in order to determine the variables impacting the application of green lean SC management in Bangladesh's ready-made garment sectors. To properly apply GLSCM, these qualities were examined using the fuzzy decision-making trial technique. The components of GLSCM that were determined to be most crucial were capacity utilisation, green buying, and demand volatility, whereas quality improvement and the Kanban system were deemed to be the least important. This research examined the degree of interaction as well as the relationships between the factors under discussion and the methods used to divide them into cause-and-effect categories. If managers use the study's results to create a successful GLSCM system, the organization's overall profitability might rise.

The research by (Mistarihi et al., 2023) proposed a tactical structure that incorporated essential elements of SC anxiety regulation and gave precedence to these portions in a powerful framework. The fuzzy-ELECTRE approach was used into the study of the proposed paradigm to solve the inherent ambiguities and imprecisions that are characteristic of SC interruptions. It provided a thorough and methodical method for assessing and managing SCN variables, using both qualitative and quantitative analyses. An real SC case study was conducted in order to confirm the viability of the proposed framework. The data clearly shows that demand volatility has the most effect on SCN. By providing practitioners and researchers with useful guidance on how to identify the root causes of SC anxiety (SCN) and mitigate its consequences, the findings further demonstrated how successfully the framework addressed SCN. One of this study's primary contributions is the strategic framework it provides for handling interruptions in uncertain situations. The proposed approach facilitated proactive decision-making to mitigate the negative impacts of SCN and enhanced understanding of it.

With a focus on the circular economy, Kaya SK (2023) intends to present a new two-stage group decision-making method for choosing railway material suppliers. This method integrates method to group decision-making reduces computational complexity while increasing performance by aggregating the views of individual decision makers (DMs). We utilised the PF-AHP to generate criterion weights, and the MARCOS-G method to evaluate and select the best provider. A thorough verify the results and the unique approach. Fifty different scenarios were created with different criterion weight values for this aim. Various grey COPRAS, TOPSIS, ARAS, and WASPAS approaches were compared in the validation analysis. Ranking correlation analysis show that the A4 is still the top provider in all 50 situations, and the MARCOS-G is virtually constant as well.

In order to solve the supplier selection challenge during the COVID-19 pandemic, Pamucar D et al. (2023) create a new decision-making procedure that uses MACBETH and a new combinative distance-based assessment process. The COVID-19 epidemic presented decision-makers with a variety of challenges, including a lack of clarity, specificity, and data, so they turned to fuzzy rough numbers—an improvement over the usual fuzzy set—to guide their decisions. When comparing the outcomes to other MCDM approaches, as well as the decision-making approach parameters and the effects of the weight coefficients, we do extensive sensitivity analyses. The suggested technique is demonstrated by an investigation of a real-life case study involving a hospital in Istanbul, Turkey. One of the most important outcomes of the MACBETH technique is the establishment of procedures to ensure the health and safety of workers on the job. With a distance score of 3.308, provider (A1) emerged as the top performer among the five vendors included in the case study.

Utilising two categories of information to produce two sorts of flows, namely superiority and inferiority flows, is what Luqman A and Shahzadi G (2023) call the SIR technique. After that, these flows are used to sort the options either partially or entirely. Novel STOLs have been constructed by utilising sine-trigonometric functions in conjunction with the adaptability of IVq-ROFSs. In addition, we show that the method may be applied and is feasible by doing a case study of GSS. The following are the article's primary contributions: A study has been conducted on the properties and aggregation operators of interval-valued q-rung orthopair fuzzy numbers using sine-trigonometric functions. (2) The SIR method was created using IVq-ROFSs. An algorithm and a flowchart illustrate the suggested method. (3) After that, the method is thought of for use in a GSS case study. (4) We compared our results to the rankings achieved by other methods, such as the IVq-ROF TOPSIS algorithm, to see how they stack up.

By reviewing the literature and consulting with experts in the industry, Hossain MI et al. (2023) investigated what variables impact the adoption of green lean supply chain management in Bangladesh's readymade garment industries. The criteria mentioned above may be examined in order to successfully apply GLSCM using the fuzzy decision-making trial method. The most essential aspects in GLSCM, according to this research, are capacity utilisation, green purchasing, and demand fluctuation; the least important factors, according to this research, are quality improvement and the Kanban system. The degree of contact, the variables' interrelationships, and the factors' classification into the cause-and-effect group were all investigated in this study. Managers may be able to increase their company's overall profitability by using the study's findings to create a more efficient GLSCM system.

By analysing the ideal discount and container leakage costs, Debnath and Sarkar (2023) have proven that a circular economy may successfully reduce and restore waste in a step-by-step fashion. The two-supply chain's joint cost function is optimised using a conventional technique in mixed-integer nonlinear programming. The combined expenses can be decreased by adopting a strategy of delivery for the transportation of the main, trash, and secondary goods. In order to optimise costs, we compare the single-setup-single-delivery policy with the single-setup-multiple-delivery policy. The idea is supported by a substantial numerical result: the total cost of the supply chain drops by almost 90% as soon as the leakage cost goes increased from $5/container to $10/container. Nevertheless, if we go beyond this range, the situation becomes unfeasible; this proves once again how sensitive waste restoration is to optimisation for recycling, which optimises supply chain costs overall. The price discount strategy is another major component of the main chain that aids in reducing waste formation. To optimise the whole supply chain, it is also a very sensitive parameter, as shown in the sensitivity analysis graph.

In a smart three-tiered sustainable supply chain management system, Mridha B et al. (2023) aim to demonstrate the joint impact of limiting carbon emissions and improving the quality of biofuel. The model takes into account scenarios with one supplier, and several retailers. The supplier sends its impure biofuel to the producer so that it can be refined. Even with a smart production system that applies a random production rate, impure biofuel is still created. In order to limit the quantity of impure biofuel and treat it as trash, a two-stage inspection policy with a variable manufacturing rate is being studied. This will make the production process more flexible. The producer then distributes the finished biofuel to various merchants. The goal of introducing a variable selling is to maximise profit. Various inventory-related operational activities, including supplier and manufacturer setup, product transit, and inventory storage, are taken into account in terms of carbon emissions. For the purpose of avoiding unnecessary holding expenses, merchants maintain a true order status as requested by the manufacturer. A particular algebraic approach was used to solve the problem and find the global optimal solution. To guarantee the model's efficacy and maximise profits, four numerical experiments are carried out. The results show that the three tiers' smart production greatly reduced emissions of carbon and impure biofuel, which had a good effect on both the environment and the associated finances. Visualisations, numerical examples, and sensitivity analyses all contribute to proving the integrated system's worth. Furthermore, the study offers several valuable insights for managers.

In order to determine whether fashion-apparel manufacturing organisations in emerging economies drive competitive advantage (CA) through the pursuit of environmental practices, Razzak MR (2023) drew on the combined theoretical perspectives of the resource-based view (RBV) and the sustainable supply chain view. Whether productivity mediates the aforementioned associations is also explored in the study. Sustainable supply chain strategies may impact both output and CA, with productivity serving as a relevant mediator, according to the study, which adds to the literature on strategic management.

2.1. Research Gaps

As the above-mentioned studies show, the study on SC management for hospital care ICUs provides insightful information but still has a number of important gaps. The adoption of AI, supplier selection, GSCM performance, and decision-making techniques are some of the topics covered in these researches; however, the unique difficulties and subtleties present in the ICU context are not as well covered. The need for customised SC solutions meeting the particular requirements of ICU patient care, such as quick response to urgent medical supply needs, is one area of research that still has to be addressed. Furthermore, there is still a dearth of research on the incorporation of cutting-edge technologies like blockchain and the Internet of Things into intensive care unit SCs. To create complete SC strategies tailored to intensive care units and handle the complexities of healthcare delivery in these settings, further research is necessary.

3. PROPOSED METHODOLOGY

The proposed work flow is represented in figure 1 with the connection between each techniques used in this paper.

Figure 1. Proposed framework

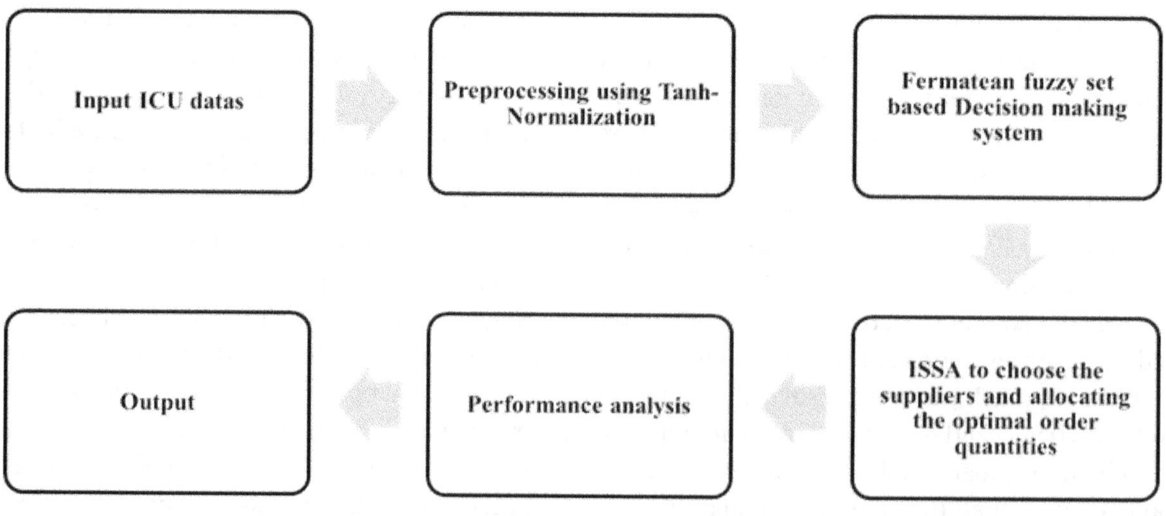

3.1. Preprocessing Using Tanh Based Normalization (TN)

To lessen noise in the data, the study uses a Tanh-based normalisation technique. This technique, This has the concept of Hampel estimators as its basis, entails changing each instance of data, represented by the symbol $x_{i,n}$, as follows:

$$x_{i,n}^{'} = \frac{1}{2}\left\{tanh\left(0.01\left(\frac{x_{i,n} - \mu_i^H}{\sigma_i^H}\right)\right) + 1\right\} \quad (1)$$

Here, σ^H indicates the Hampel estimators' standard deviation and μ^H is the mean. The impact how things work (ψ), It is described in this way, 8is the foundation for these estimators:

$$\psi(z) = \{z0 \le |z| \le u_1, u_1 \times sign(z)u_1 < |z| \le u_2, u_1 \times sign(z) \times \left(\frac{u_3 - |z|}{pu_3 - u_2}\right)u_2 \langle |z| \le u_3, 0|z|\rangle u_3 \quad (2)$$

The sign of z can be found using the eq $z_{i,n} = x_{i,n}$ - med $x_{i,n}$, where sign$(z) = 1$ when $z \ge 0$ and equals 1 when z is higher than or equal to 0. As a function of the parameters u_1, u_2, and u 3, this function is essential in mitigating the effect of values located at the extremes of the distribution when estimating the location and scale parameters. As a result, this method shows resilience to anomalies.It's crucial to carefully select these parameters, taking into account the required level of resilience in addition to the quantity of noise present in the training set. The parameters u 1, u 2, and u 3 in this study are fixed at specified values, as used in (Singh, D., & Singh, B. 2020), namely u_1 = quantile $_{0.7}(|z|)$, u_2 = $_{0.85}(|z|)$, and u 3 = quantile $_0.95(|z|)$. The mean and standard deviation of each feature are used by the authors in lieu of Hampel estimators in a Tanh normalisation (VTN) variant. This is how the normalisation is expressed:

$$x_{i,n}^{'} = \frac{1}{2}\left\{tanh\left(0.01\left(\frac{x_{i,n} - \mu_i}{\sigma_i}\right)\right) + 1\right\} \quad (3)$$

3.2. Fermatean Fuzzy Based DMS

Although FFSs are more adaptable in capturing ambiguous material than IFSs and PFSs, they are nevertheless influenced by intuitionistic FS and Pythagorean fuzzy sets (PFS). Similar to IFSs and PFSs, Fermian fuzzy sets are characterised by three fundamental components: the degree of indeterminacy (π), the degree of non-membership (β), and the degree of participation (α). The section that follows provides an explanation of some of the functions and functions of the FFSs utilised in this study.

Definition 1: Assume that the universe of discourse is X. Consequently, the following definition of a Fermatean fuzzy set, $\tilde{R}$, can be given:

$$\tilde{R} = \left\{ \left\langle x, \alpha_R(x), \beta_R(x) \right\rangle : x \in X \right\} \tag{4}$$

where $\alpha_R(x) : X \to [0.1], \beta_R(x) : X \to [0.1]$, and $0 \leq (\alpha_R(x))^3 + (\beta_R(x))^3 \leq 1$. Furthermore, the level of uncertainty is $\pi_R(x) = \sqrt[3]{1 - (\alpha_R(x))^3 - (\beta_R(x))^3}$. For ease of use, We employ. $\tilde{R} = (\alpha_R, \beta_R)$ to represent this FFS (Senapati et al., 2020).

The differences in the spaces between them corresponding PMGs, FMGs, and IMGs are visually represented in Figure 2.

Figure 2. Areas associated with FMGs, PMGs, and IMGs

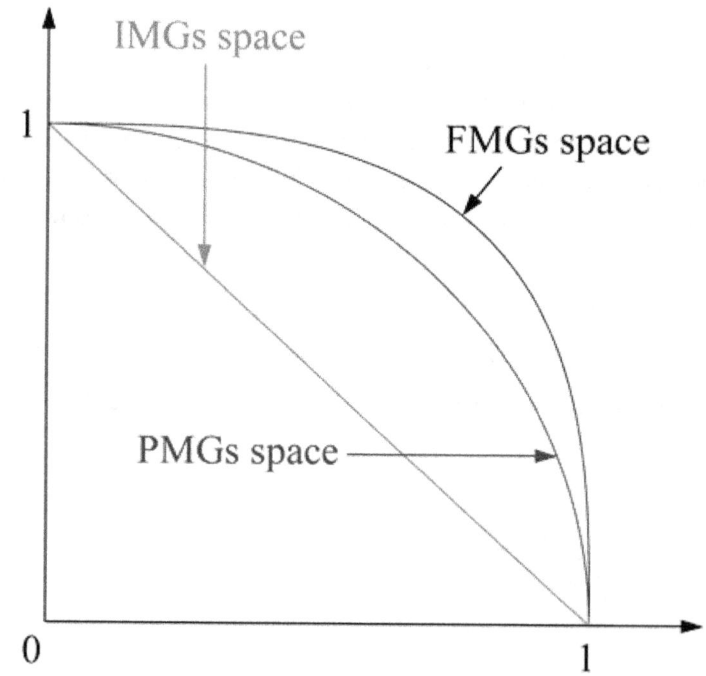

Spaces connected to PMGs, FMGs, and IMGs are where the differences are found.

Definition 2: Let $\tilde{R} = (\alpha_R, \beta_R)$ and $\tilde{S} = (\alpha_S, \beta_S)$ be two FFS, and λ be a positive real number $(\lambda > 0)$. In that case, the FFSs can specify the following operators (Li et al., 2020).

$$\tilde{R} \oplus \tilde{S} = \left(\sqrt[3]{\alpha_R^3 + \alpha_S^3 - \alpha_R^3 \alpha_S^3}, \beta_R \beta_S \right) \tag{5}$$

$$\tilde{R} \otimes \tilde{S} = \left(\alpha_R \alpha_S, \sqrt[3]{\beta_R^3 + \beta_S^3 - \beta_R^3 \beta_S^3} \right) \tag{6}$$

$$\lambda.\tilde{R} = \left(\sqrt[3]{1 - \left(1 - \alpha_R^3\right)^{\lambda}}, \beta_R^{\lambda} \right) \tag{7}$$

$$\tilde{R}^{\lambda} = \left(\alpha_{R'}^{\lambda} \sqrt[3]{1 - \left(1 - \beta_R^3\right)^{\lambda}} \right) \tag{8}$$

Definition 3: Suppose that $\tilde{R} = \left(\alpha_R, \beta_R\right)$ is an FFS. The following is the meaning behind theaccuracy function (A) and score function T for this FFS:

$$T\left(R^{\sim}\right) = \alpha_R^3 - \beta_R^3 \tag{9}$$

$$H\left(R^{\sim}\right) = \alpha_R^3 + \beta_R^3 \tag{10}$$

The two FFSs, $\tilde{R} = \left(\alpha_R, \beta_R\right)$ and $\tilde{S} = \left(\alpha_S, \beta_S\right)$, can be compared using these procedures. When comparing them, there are several conditions.

1. If $T\left(\tilde{R}\right) < T\left(\tilde{S}\right)$, then $\tilde{R} < \tilde{S}$;
2. If $T\left(\tilde{R}\right) > T\left(\tilde{S}\right)$, then $\tilde{R} > \tilde{S}$;
3. If $T\left(\tilde{R}\right) = T\left(\tilde{S}\right)$, then
    i. If $A\left(R^{\sim}\right) < A\left(S^{\sim}\right)$, then $\tilde{R} < S^{\sim}$;
    ii. If $H\left(\tilde{R}\right) > A\left(\tilde{S}\right)$, then $\tilde{R} > \tilde{S}$;
    iii. If $A\left(\tilde{R}\right) = A\left(\tilde{S}\right)$, then $\tilde{R} = \tilde{S}$.
    3. iii. Definition 4: In agreement of an FFS $\tilde{R} = \left(\alpha_R, \beta_R\right)$ is defined as follows:

$$Com\left(\tilde{R}\right) = \left(\beta_R, \alpha_R\right) \tag{11}$$

3. iii. Definition 5: Let $\tilde{R}_i = \left(\alpha_{R_i}, \beta_{R_i}\right)(i = 1,2,\ldots,n)$ be a set of n FFSs, and $w = \left(w_1, w_2, \ldots, w_n\right)^T$ be the weight vector that corresponds to $R_i\left(\Sigma_i w_i = 1\right)$. Next, using the following eq [31], Here is the definition of the Fermatean fuzzy weighted average (FFWA) aggregation operator:

$$FFWA\left(\tilde{R}_1, \tilde{R}_2, \ldots, \tilde{R}_n\right) = \left(\sum_{i=1}^{n} w_i \alpha_{R_{i'}} \sum_{i=1}^{n} w_i \beta_{R_i}\right) \tag{12}$$

3. iii. Definition 6: Definition 3 provided a definition of an FFS's score function. Let $\tilde{R} = \left(\alpha_R, \beta_R\right)$ be an FFS. One can change the value of $T\left(\tilde{R}\right)$ between -1 and 1.A positive scoring function is developed for an FFS based on this range, guaranteeing that it constantly produces a positive defuzzified value.

$$T^P\left(\tilde{X}_{ij}\right) = 1 + T\left(\tilde{X}_{ij}\right) \tag{13}$$

3.3. ISSA

ISSA was utilised as an optimization approach in this paper to decide which suppliers to use and assign the best order numbers.

3.3.1. Principle of Bionics

Salps are marine animals distinguished by their transparent, barrel-shaped bodies, which structurally resemble jellyfish quite a bit. Salps use a special kind of locomotion where they take in water from their environment and use it to propel themselves backward. Because of their delicate bodily tissues, these critters are difficult to keep alive in a lab setting. As a result, study on this species has just made major strides in the last few years, with one particularly fascinating finding being their communal behaviour.

Salps have a unique kind of group behaviour where they are joined end to end to create a "chain" that sways in a sequential fashion rather than being dispersed like in a conventional "group" structure. There is always a leader in a salp chain; these leaders usually have better environmental awareness and are at the top of the chain. Nevertheless, the leader's effect is restricted to the second salp that follows them, as opposed to being felt by the entire group, which is in contradiction to traditional group dynamics. Consequently, every link in the chain is impacted immediately by its immediate boss, resulting in a hierarchical structure that is precisely controlled. This approach is comparable to a stricter and more focused kind of hierarchy where everyone is solely influenced by their "direct leader" and is not subject to higher authority. Thus, layer by layer, the leader's influence over lower-ranking salps decreases. Because of this hierarchy, the lower salps are able to preserve their uniqueness and refrain from mindlessly following the boss. In this study, all salps—aside from the leader—are referred to as "followers" due to their sequential movement pattern.

3.3.2. The Flow of SSA

The following is the optimised SSA (Zhang et al., 2020 and Ma et al., 2019):

Initializing the population comes first. Where d is the salp's geographic dimension and y is its population size. In space, food is present, $F\ F = \left[F_1, F_2, \ldots, F_D\right]^T$. The search space has the following upper and lower bounds: $ub = \left[ub_1, ub_2, \ldots, ub_D\right]$. and $lb = \left[lb_1, lb_2, \ldots, lb_D\right]$. Next, randomise the position of the salp, x_j^i so that $i = 1, 2, \ldots, N, j = 1, 2, \ldots, D$:

$$x_j^i = rand\left(N, D\right) * \left(ub\left(j\right) - lb\left(j\right)\right) + lb\left(j\right) \tag{14}$$

Updating the leader's position is the second part. When it comes to locating food sources and directing the team's activities, the leader is essential. As a result, the following formula is used to update the leader's position:

$$x_j^1 = \{F_j + c_1\left(\left(ub_j - lb_j\right)c_2 + lb_j\right), c_3 \geq 0.5 F_j - c_1\left(\left(ub_j - lb_j\right)c_2 + lb_j\right), c_3 < 0.5 \tag{15}$$

where the symbols x_j^1, ub_j and lb_j represent the locations of the food, leader, and bound. There are three variables for control, c_1, c_2 and c_3.Within [0,1], $c_1\ and\ c_2$ are erratic numbers; c_2 regulates the step size; and c_3 controls the direction. During each iteration, the main controlling variable, c_1 , optimises the algorithm's capacity for exploration and development. To make the method do a worldwide search in the first half of the process and accurate development in the second phase, the amount of the di should be calculated using the equation that follows:

$$c_1 = 2e^{-(Al/Max\_Iteration\ )^2} \tag{16}$$

where the maximum iteration is called Max Iteration and l is the current iteration.

The follower's position was last updated. Only the follower's starting position, speed of travel, and acceleration during motion are related to its position. Newton's law of motion is followed by the motion pattern. As a result, the follower's movement distance R can be written as follows:

$$R = \frac{1}{2}at^2 + v_0 t \tag{17}$$

Time t is the difference in repetition periods, thus t=1; v_0 is the follower's beginning speed of zero; *a* is its rate of acceleration for that repetition; and $a = \left(v_{final} - v_0\right) / t$ is the calculating formula. Since the follower only follows the salp's motion in close vicinity to itself, its motion speed v final $= \left(x_j^{i-1} - x_j^i\right) / t$, where t=1 and $v_0 = 0$, are known, follows.

$$R = \frac{1}{2}\left(x_j^{i-1} - x_j^i\right) \tag{18}$$

As a result, the formula below is employed to update followers' positions:

$$x_i^{i'} = x_j^i + R = \frac{1}{2}\left(x_j^i + x_j^{i-1}\right) \tag{19}$$

Thus, prior to the update, the location of the i -th follower in the j -th dimensional space is represented by the symbol, x_j^f and the position of the follower following the update is denoted by, x_j^1.

3.3.3. Improvement of SSA

1. Initialization of the Population Using Logistic Mapping (LM)

The constant iteration of the population is the core of a swarm intelligence algorithm, therefore initialising this population is crucial and directly affects the final solution and optimization potential. Finding the global optimal solution inside a population requires a rich and diversified starting population, which is extremely desirable. In the absence of past understanding, many algos for swarm intelligence primarily rely on initialization of a random population, and this significantly impacts their performance.

Ergodicity and unpredictability are characteristics of chaotic sequences, therefore starting the population with a chaotic sequence might increase its diversity. These days, tent mapping, LM, and iterative mapping are three frequently used chaotic sequences. This research chooses to employ LM for population initialization through a comparative analysis.

The LM mathematical formula is as follows (Ma et al., 2019):

$$y_{j+1}^i = py_j^i\left(1 - y_j^i\right) \tag{20}$$

$j = 1, 2, \ldots, D$ represents the ordinal number of chaotic variables. whereas $i = 1, 2, \ldots, N$ indicates the size of the population Following LM, the population's initialization formula is as follows:

$$x_j^i = y_j^i * \left(ub\left(j\right) - lb\left(j\right)\right) + lb\left(j\right) \tag{21}$$

2. Symmetric Adaptive Population Division

Because there are half as many followers and leaders as there are salps in the basic SSA, the algorithm searches asymmetrically. In the first iteration, there are few leaders and the ratio is low, which facilitates falling into a local extremum and insufficiently search globally. Nevertheless, the limited number of followers in the late iteration results in poor local search and low optimization accuracy. The literature suggested a leader-follower adaptive adjustment technique as a solution to this issue. Using this method, the study proposes a symmetric adaptive division population where the quantity of salp leaders shows the number of iterations has an adjustable falling tendency in contrast to the number of followers, which displays a growing trend. Because of this, the algorithm will get more accurate throughout the optimisation process by focusing more on global width exploration in the early stages and more in-depth mining around the ideal value in the latter stages. This is the revised formula for symmetric adaptive population division:

Describe the control variable ω.

$$\omega = b \cdot \left(-k \cdot rand() + tan\left(\frac{\pi}{4} - \frac{\pi l}{4 \cdot Max\_Iteration} \right) \right) \quad (22)$$

Here, l is the iteration number that is currently in use, 'Max Iteration' denotes the ultimate quantity of iterations, and b is the percentage coefficient that is intended to balance out proportion imbalances. The ω value steadily drops as it is agitated in tandem with the 'rand' function, while the 'k' variable represents the disturbance deviation factor.

The adjusted quantity of leaders for each iteration is $\omega \cdot N$, and where $1 - \omega \cdot N$ is the number of followers.

3. Analogous Annealing Process Utilising Symmetric Disturbances

Solid annealing principles serve as the basis for the algorithm for simulating annealing. Fundamentally, the goal of this method is to take the existing answer and use it to generate a new one, which it will then accept with a specific probability. This method improves the algorithm's capacity to break out of local optima while preserving a strong degree of variation in the following iterations. In the framework of the simulated annealing, the development of new solutions is very crucial. In this paper, a novel method for generating solutions—symmetric perturbation—is presented. Symmetric perturbation is the process of mapping inside a symmetrical interval, the new solution's location to the existing optimal position. By multiplying the current temperature by a random integer projected into the dimensional space, the dimensions of this symmetrical interval are obtained.

The following is the flow of the symmetric perturbation-based simulated annealing mechanism:

(1) Set the starting temperature T, starting solution S, and the highest quantity of repetitions (Max Iteration) during initialization.
(2) for $l = 1, 2, \ldots,$ Max_Iteration steps (3) to (6).
(3) (3) Change the existing solution, S, in order to get the new one, S'. The following formula is used:

$$S' = T \times rnd(1, d) / normrnd(1, d) + S \quad (23)$$

(4) Determine the incremental value of $df = f(S') - f(S)$, where df represents the evaluation function.
(5) (5) The following is the sampling formula based on the Metropolis criterion:

$$P = \{1, df < 0 e^{-\frac{df}{t}}, df \geq 0 \tag{24}$$

Take the new response with a grain of salt, $e^{-\frac{df}{T}}$ if $df < 0$. (6) The algorithm is terminated if the terms of termination is met, the present solution is the best solution, and the output is produced; if not, the temperature is lowered and step (2) is repeated. Typically, an ongoing stream of fresh ideas that have either achieved the termination temperature or have not been approved serve as the termination condition.

4. ISSA

The SSA has issues with low optimization accuracy and sluggish convergence, as was previously described. In order to tackle these problems, ISSA has implemented multiple improvements. To increase population diversity, a logistic chaotic map is first used for population initialization. Secondly, in order to preserve equilibrium between algorithm creation and exploration capabilities, a symmetric adaptive population division technique is applied. Furthermore, a symmetric perturbation-based simulated annealing process is presented to probabilistically accept poor solutions. The algorithm also gains from a hybrid operation that is derived from genetic algorithms. To create the final new solution, hybridization entails proportionally combining the quantity of fresh approaches that have either reached or failed to reach the termination temperature. This method lessens the effect of perturbation errors while maintaining the advantages of the previous solution. The following is the hybridization formula:

$$S' = \left(1 - \sqrt{c}\right) \times S + \sqrt{c} \times S' \tag{25}$$

where c is a any number at random between 0 and 1. Algorithm 1 of ISSA is given in algorithm 1.

Algorithm 1. ISSA

begin **Decide on the following algorithmic parameters: The amount of people is N, the problem dimension is D, the starting temperature is T, the cooling rate is P, the maximum amount of repetitions is Max Iteration, and so on.**
According to Eq (20), Logistic chaotic map is used to initialize the population.
Each salp person's fitness value is determined, and the best individual is chosen to be the site of the food source.
while ($t <=$ Mrx_Iteration) do
ω is calculated by formula (21)
for $i = 1$ to **N** do
if $(i <= \acute{E} \cdot N)$ do
Revise the leader's role based on Eq (15).
else Adjust the follower's position based on Eq (19).
end if
end for
causing the present optimal salp's location to change S
$S' =$ Mutate (S) Calculate increment $df = f(S) - f(S)$
if $(df < 0)$ do

$S \leftarrow S$:
else
$P = exp(-df / T)$
if (rand $<= P$)

$S' =$ Crossover (S, S')
$S \leftarrow S'T = T^* q$ end if
end if
Updates are made to the location of the food source and the fitness value of each population.
$l = l + 1$. end while
end

4. RESULTS AND DISCUSSIONS

4.1. Experimental Setup

On a typical PC with two Nvidia GeForce GTX 2070 graphics processing units (GPUs), testing were carried out. The experiment was carried out using The Math Works Inc.'s MATLAB (Version 2021a), Natick, Massachusetts, USA. It has a strong hardware configuration with 32.0 GB of RAM and an Intel Core i9-9900K CPU operating at 3.60 GHz. The 16 logical threads and 16 MB of cache memory on this CPU can handle the processing demands of the research.

4.2. Performance Metrics Analysis of FFS Model

The performance metrics used in this paper are as follows:

- ACC: "ratio of the observation of exactly predicted to the whole observations".

$$T^{accuracy} = \frac{\left(Tr^{p} + Tr^{n}\right)}{Tr^{p} + Tr^{n} + Fa^{p} + Fa^{n}} \tag{26}$$

- SEN: "the number of true positives, which are recognized exactly".

$$Se = \frac{Tr^{p}}{Tr^{p} + Fa^{n}} \tag{27}$$

- SPEC: "the number of true negatives, which are determined precisely".

$$Sp = \frac{Tr^{n}}{Fa^{n}} \tag{28}$$

- PR: "the ratio of positive observations that are predicted exactly to the total number of observations that are positively predicted".

$$Pr = \frac{Tr^{p}}{Tr^{p} + Tr^{p}} \tag{29}$$

- F1 score: It is defined as the "harmonic mean between PR and recall. It is used as a statistical measure to rate performance".

$$F1score = \frac{Se.Pr}{Pr + Se} \tag{30}$$

Table 1 compare the performance metrics of various fuzzy methods such as Fuzzy Analytic Hierarchy Process (F-AHP), Fuzzy Multi-Criteria Decision Analysis (F-MCDA), Fuzzy Cognitive Maps (FCM), Fuzzy Technique for Order of Preference by Similarity to Ideal Solution (F-TOPSIS) and proposed Fermatean Fuzzy Sets (FFS).

Table 1. DMS results analysis of various models

Models	ACC	PR	SEN	SPEC	F1
F-AHP	89.46	90.21	89.31	88.21	89.62
F-MCDA	85.50	84.50	85.30	83.40	84.21
FCM	89.57	89.66	89.65	90.70	89.34
FTOPSIS	93.00	92.45	92.65	92.91	91.91
Proposed FFS model	**99.81**	**99.77**	**99.80**	**99.75**	**99.69**

From Table 1 and Figure 3, F-AHP had an ACC of 89.46%, PR of 90.21%, SEN of 89.31%, SPEC of 88.21%, F1 of 89.62%. F-MCDA had an ACC of 85.50%, PR of 84.50%, SEN of 85.30%, SPEC of 83.40%, F1 of 84.21%. FCM had an ACC of 89.57%, PR of 89.66%, SEN of 89.65%, SPEC of 90.70%, F1 of 89.34%. FTOPSIS had an ACC of 93.00%, PR of 92.45%, SEN of 92.65%, SPEC of 92.91%, F1 of 91.91%. Proposed FFS method achieved an ACC of 99.81%, PR of 99.77%, SEN of 99.80%, SPEC of 99.75%, F1 of 99.69%.

Figure 3. Validation analysis of FFS model

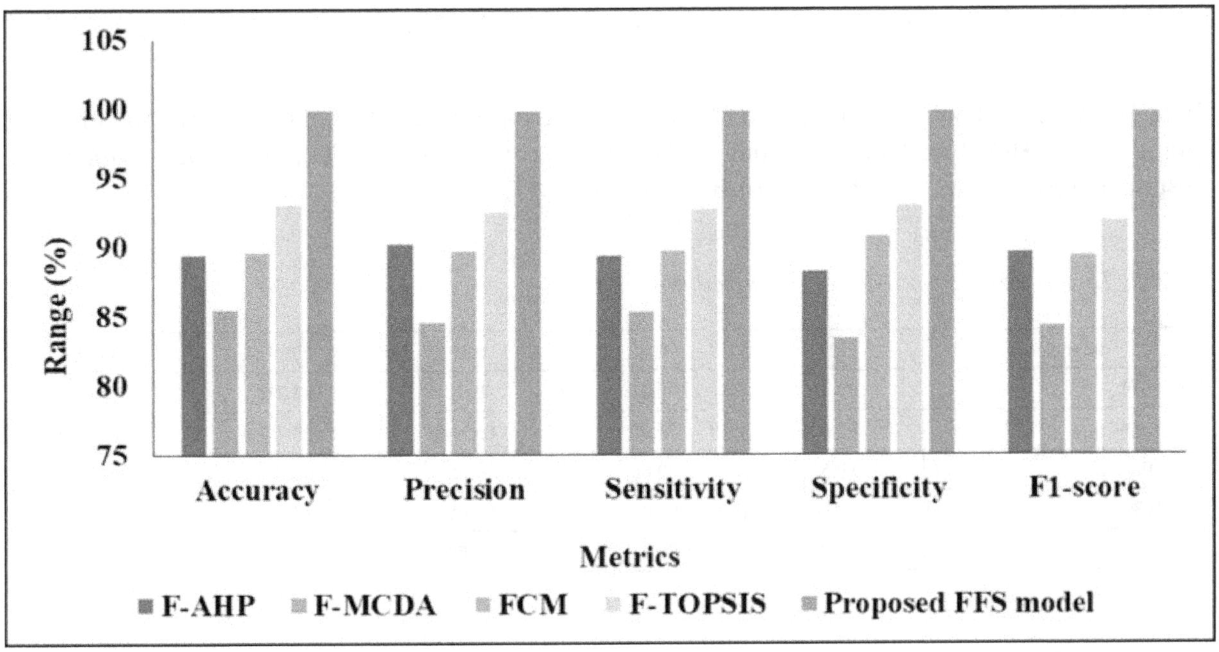

4.3. Analysis of Proposed Model

Fill Rate: Calculates the proportion of orders that arrive on schedule. Greater values are preferred:

$$Fill\,Rate = \left(Total\,Orders\,Filled\,on\,Time\ /Total\,Orders\right)\ {*}100 \tag{31}$$

Order Accuracy: Assesses the proportion of correctly filled orders.

$$Order\,Accuracy = \left(Number\,of\,Accurate\,Orders\ /Total\,Orders\right)\ {*}100 \tag{32}$$

Stockout Rate: Shows the proportion of times that the requested item is out of stock.

$$SR = \left(Number\,of\,Stockouts\ /Total\,Orders\right)\ {*}100 \tag{33}$$

Emergency Order Rate: Shows how frequently orders are placed at the last minute or with urgency, which may indicate problems with the SC.

$$EOR = \left(Number\,of\,Emergency\,Orders\ /Total\,Orders\right)\ {*}100 \tag{34}$$

Waste Reduction Rate: Evaluates the success of initiatives to reduce waste in the SC.

$$Waste\,Reduction\,Rate = \left(Value\,of\,Waste\,Reduction\ /Total\,Supply\,Chain\,Costs\right)\ {*}100 \tag{35}$$

Table 2 show the comparison of proposed FFS with various optimization techniques such as Grasshopper optimization (GHO), Fruitfly optimization (FFO), Jellyfish optimization (JFO), Honey Bee optimization (HBO) and proposed improved salp swarm optimization (ISSA).

Table 2. Testing results analysis of proposed model

Models	FR	OA	SR	EOR	WRR
FFS-GHO	89.46	90.21	89.31	88.21	88.42
FFS-FFO	85.50	84.50	85.30	83.40	85.50
FFS-JFO	89.57	89.66	89.65	90.70	90.94
FFS-HBO	93.00	92.45	92.65	92.91	92.24
FFS-ISSA	**99.81**	**99.81**	**99.80**	**99.75**	**99.42**

From Table 2 and Figure 4, FFS-GHO model had an FR of 89.46%, OA of 90.21%, SR of 89.31%, EOR of 88.21%, WRR of 88.42%. FFS-FFO model had an FR of 85.50%, OA of 84.50%, SR of

85.30%, EOR of 83.40%, WRR of 85.50%. FFS-JFO model had an FR of 89.57%, OA of 89.66%, SR of 89.65%, EOR of 90.70%, WRR of 90.94%. FFS-HBO model had an FR of 93.00%, OA of 92.45%, SR of 92.65%, EOR of 92.91%, WRR of 92.24%. FFS-ISSA model had an FR of 99.81%, OA of 99.81%, SR of 99.80%, EOR of 99.75%, WRR of 99.42%. For a number of reasons, the suggested model which combines ISSA with FFS performs better than other SC management models. First off, in complex and dynamic SC systems, FFS provide more flexible and nuanced representations of uncertainty, which improves decision-making. Second, by mimicking the cooperative behaviour of salps, ISSA improves the model's capacity to identify optimum solutions. When fuzzy logic and optimisation approaches are used, a potent synergy is created that enhances decision-making systems' accuracy and efficiency. The model is a great option for handling the complexities and difficulties of contemporary SC management because of its versatility and resilience in real-world SC situations.

Figure 4. Result analysis using performance metrics of DMS

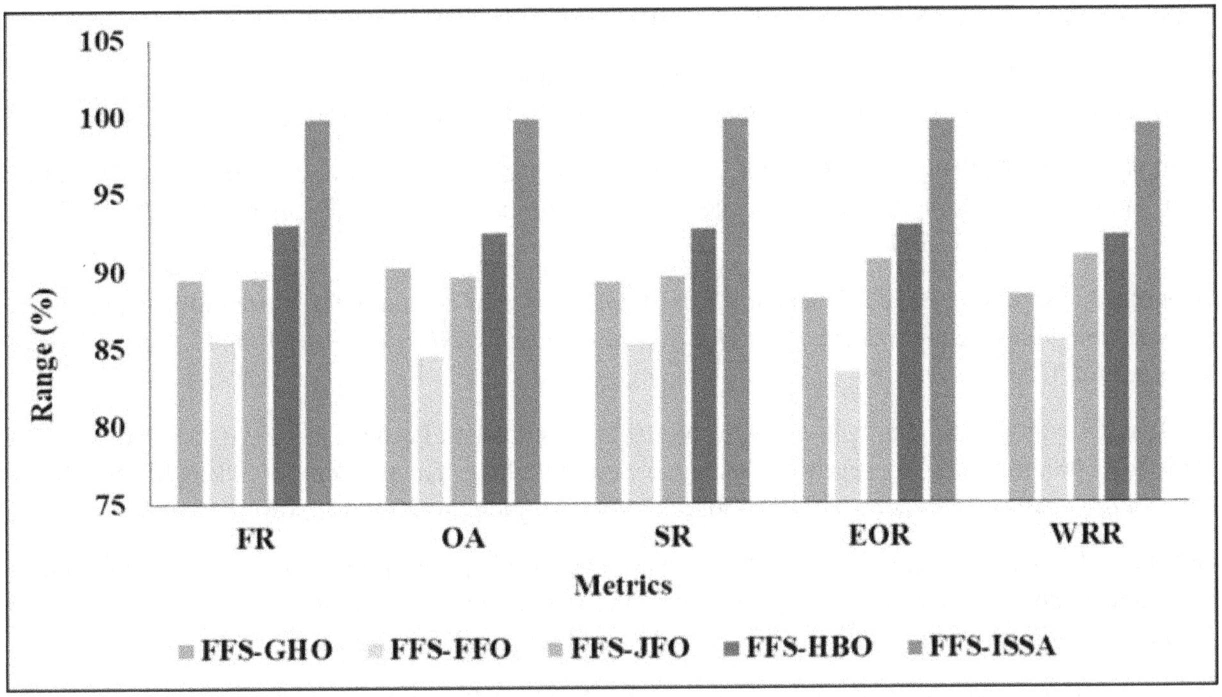

5. CONCLUSION

The research concludes by introducing a Fermatean fuzzy-based decision-making strategy that uses key performance indicator (KPI) analysis to improve hospital Circular SC (CSC) performance, with an emphasis on critical care units (ICUs). The study tackles the crucial problems of SC transparency and traceability, which are necessary to increase productivity and reduce the dangers of fraud, inefficiencies, and a lack of confidence. This study first done preprocessing using Tanh-normalization in data. Then the paper provides a possible solution to these problems by creating the FFS based Decision Making (FFS-DMS) technique and using improved Salp Swarm Optimisation (ISSO) for supplier selection and order allocation. The proposed FFS-ISSA-DMS outperform other existing model by achieving 99.81% accuracy rate Future studies might examine how to improve SC transparency and traceability by integrating cutting-edge technology like blockchain and IoT.

REFERENCES

Ahmad, F., & John, B. (2023). A fuzzy quantitative model for assessing the performance of pharmaceutical supply chain under uncertainty. *Kybernetes*, *52*(3), 828–873. doi:10.1108/K-08-2021-0750

Bokhari, S. A. A., Duggal, K., & Myeong, S. (2023). Artificial Intelligence Application in Supply Chain Management in Government Sector of Pakistan. *Engineering Proceedings*, 37.

Chandra, D., Vipin, B., & Kumar, D. (2023). A fuzzy multi-criteria framework to identify barriers and enablers of the next-generation vaccine supply chain. *International Journal of Productivity and Performance Management*, *72*(3), 827–847. doi:10.1108/IJPPM-08-2020-0419

Chansamut, A. (2023). Digital model for Sugarcane Production for the Factory in Thai Supply Chain. *International Journal of Supply Chain Management*, *12*(3), 90–94. doi:10.59160/ijscm.v12i3.6133

Chen, L., Dong, T., Peng, J., & Ralescu, D. (2023). Uncertainty Analysis and Optimization Modeling with Application to Supply Chain Management: A Systematic Review. *Mathematics*, *11*(11), 2530. doi:10.3390/math11112530

Debnath, A., & Sarkar, B. (2023, January 20). Effect of circular economy for waste nullification under a sustainable supply chain management. *Journal of Cleaner Production*, *385*, 135477. doi:10.1016/j.jclepro.2022.135477

Deliktaş, D., Karagoz, S., Simić, V., & Aydin, N. (2023). A stochastic Fermatean fuzzy-based multi-choice conic goal programming approach for sustainable supply chain management in end-of-life buildings. *Journal of Cleaner Production*, *382*, 135305. doi:10.1016/j.jclepro.2022.135305

Ghosh, S., Mandal, M. C., & Ray, A. (2023). A PDCA based approach to evaluate green supply chain management performance under fuzzy environment. *International Journal of Management Science and Engineering Management*, *18*(1), 1–15. doi:10.1080/17509653.2022.2027292

Habib, A., Khan, Z. A., Riaz, M., & Marinkovic, D. (2023). Performance Evaluation of Healthcare Supply Chain in Industry 4.0 with Linear Diophantine Fuzzy Sine-Trigonometric Aggregation Operations. *Mathematics*, *11*(12), 2611. doi:10.3390/math11122611

Hossain, M. I., Al Amin, M., Baldacci, R., & Rahman, M. H. (2023). Identification and Prioritization of Green Lean Supply Chain Management Factors Using Fuzzy DEMATEL. *Sustainability (Basel)*, *15*(13), 10523. doi:10.3390/su151310523

Hossain, M. I., Al Amin, M., Baldacci, R., & Rahman, M. H. (2023, July 4). Identification and prioritization of green lean supply chain management factors using fuzzy DEMATEL. *Sustainability (Basel)*, *15*(13), 10523. doi:10.3390/su151310523

Kaya, S. K. (2023, March). A novel two-phase group decision-making model for circular supplier selection under picture fuzzy environment. *Environmental Science and Pollution Research International, 30*(12), 34135–34157. doi:10.1007/s11356-022-24486-4 PMID:36508096

Li, J., Wang, L., & Tan, X. (2020). Sustainable design and optimization of coal supply chain network under different carbon emission policies. *Journal of Cleaner Production, 250*, 119548. doi:10.1016/j.jclepro.2019.119548

Luo, J., Huang, M., Bai, Y., & Li, J. (2023). Supply Chain Management during a Public Health Emergency of International Concern: A Bibliometric and Content Analysis. *Processes (Basel, Switzerland), 11*(3), 713. doi:10.3390/pr11030713

Luqman, A., & Shahzadi, G. (2023, November). Multi-criteria group decision-making based on the interval-valued q-rung orthopair fuzzy SIR approach for green supply chain evaluation and selection. *Granular Computing., 8*(6), 1937–1954. doi:10.1007/s41066-023-00411-z

Ma, B., Ni, H., Zhu, X., & Zhao, R. (2019). A Comprehensive Improved Salp Swarm Algorithm on Redundant Container Deployment Problem. *IEEE Access : Practical Innovations, Open Solutions, 7*, 136452–136470. doi:10.1109/ACCESS.2019.2933265

Mahjoob, A., Alfadhli, Y., & Omachonu, V. (2023). Healthcare Waste and Sustainability: Implications for a Circular Economy. *Sustainability (Basel), 15*(10), 7788. doi:10.3390/su15107788

Mistarihi, M. Z., & Magableh, G. M. (2023). Unveiling Supply Chain Nervousness: A Strategic Framework for Disruption Management under Fuzzy Environment. *Sustainability (Basel), 15*(14), 11179. doi:10.3390/su151411179

Mostepaniuk, A., Akalin, T., & Parish, M. R. (2023). Practices Pursuing the Sustainability of A Healthcare Organization: A Systematic Review. *Sustainability (Basel), 15*(3), 2353. doi:10.3390/su15032353

Mridha, B., Pareek, S., Goswami, A., & Sarkar, B. (2023, February 1). Joint effects of production quality improvement of biofuel and carbon emissions towards a smart sustainable supply chain management. *Journal of Cleaner Production, 386*, 135629. doi:10.1016/j.jclepro.2022.135629

Naseem, M. H., Yang, J., Zhang, T., & Alam, W. (2023). Utilizing Fuzzy AHP in the Evaluation of Barriers to Blockchain Implementation in Reverse Logistics. *Sustainability (Basel), 15*(10), 7961. doi:10.3390/su15107961

Pamucar, D., Torkayesh, A. E., & Biswas, S. (2023). Supplier selection in healthcare supply chain management during the COVID-19 pandemic: A novel fuzzy rough decision-making approach. *Annals of Operations Research, 328*(1), 977–1019. doi:10.1007/s10479-022-04529-2 PMID:35039705

Pamucar, D., Torkayesh, A. E., & Biswas, S. (2023, September). Supplier selection in healthcare supply chain management during the COVID-19 pandemic: A novel fuzzy rough decision-making approach. *Annals of Operations Research, 328*(1), 977–1019. doi:10.1007/s10479-022-04529-2 PMID:35039705

Rahman, A. U., Alballa, T., Alqahtani, H., & Khalifa, H. A. E. W. (2023). A Fuzzy Parameterized Multiattribute Decision-Making Framework for Supplier Chain Management Based on Picture Fuzzy Soft Information. *Symmetry, 15*(10), 1872. doi:10.3390/sym15101872

Razzak, M. R. (2023, March 7). Mediating effect of productivity between sustainable supply chain management practices and competitive advantage: Evidence from apparel manufacturing in Bangladesh. *Management of Environmental Quality*, *34*(2), 428–445. doi:10.1108/MEQ-01-2022-0022

Rehman, O. U., & Ali, Y. (2022). Enhancing healthcare supply chain resilience: Decision-making in a fuzzy environment. *International Journal of Logistics Management*, *33*(2), 520–546. doi:10.1108/IJLM-01-2021-0004

Riaz, M., Farid, H. M. A., Jana, C., Pal, M., & Sarkar, B. (2023). Efficient city supply chain management through spherical fuzzy dynamic multistage decision analysis. *Engineering Applications of Artificial Intelligence*, *126*, 106712. doi:10.1016/j.engappai.2023.106712

Senapati, T., & Yager, R. R. (2020). Fermatean fuzzy sets. *Journal of Ambient Intelligence and Humanized Computing*, *11*(2), 663–674. doi:10.1007/s12652-019-01377-0

Singh, D., & Singh, B. (2020). Investigating the impact of data normalization on classification performance. *Applied Soft Computing*, *97*, 105524. doi:10.1016/j.asoc.2019.105524

Xu, B., Liu, W., & Li, J. (2023). Resilience Regulation Strategy for Container Port Supply Chain under Disruptive Events. *Journal of Marine Science and Engineering*, *11*(4), 732. doi:10.3390/jmse11040732

Zhang, J., & Wang, J. S. (2020). Improved Salp Swarm Algorithm Based on Levy Flight and Sine Cosine Operator. *IEEE Access : Practical Innovations, Open Solutions*, *8*, 99740–99771. doi:10.1109/ACCESS.2020.2997783

Chapter 12
Industry 4.0 or Pharma 4.0?
Assessing Suitability, Benefits, Challenges, and Opportunities for Healthcare Supply Chains

Muhammad Ibrahim Khan
Iqra University, Pakistan

Mirza Amin Ul Haq
Iqra University, Pakistan

Mustafa Rehman Khan
https://orcid.org/0000-0002-0250-9092
UCSI University, Kuala Lumpur, Malaysia

Arsalan Mujahid Ghouri
https://orcid.org/0000-0001-5419-8946
London South Bank University, UK

Raheel Farooqui
Bahria University, Karachi, Pakistan

ABSTRACT

This chapter examines the convergence of Industry 4.0 and Pharma 4.0 in the context of healthcare supply chains. It investigates the potential applications of these industrial revolutions to enhance the flexibility, benefits, challenges, and opportunities of healthcare supply chains. This chapter highlights the application of state-of-the-art technology to create intelligent, adaptable, and personalized supply chain systems for the healthcare and pharmaceutical sectors. The literature on "Pharma Industry 4.0" is reviewed, with a focus on the opportunities for sustainable value creation and pharmaceutical supply chain research. Healthcare supply chain has some serious issues like counterfeit drugs, non-transparent supply chain, unfear track and trace system of medicines and biomedical instruments. The authors identified the potential solutions for these issues with the help of current innovative technologies and practices.

DOI: 10.4018/979-8-3693-1363-3.ch012

1. INTRODUCTION

The convergence of Industry 4.0 and Pharma 4.0 presents a significant opportunity for the pharmaceutical industry to undergo transformation in the context of healthcare supply chains (Sharma et al., 2023). The present book chapter undertakes a thorough analysis, assessing the suitability, benefits, challenges, and prospects that result from the integration of these state-of-the-art technologies into health care supply chains. Munirathinam (2020) says that the term "industry 4.0," often known as the "fourth industrial revolution," describes the blending of digital and conventional production processes. This marks the beginning of an era of intelligent, automated, and networked systems and includes big data, the Internet of Things (IoT), cyber-physical systems, and artificial intelligence (AI).

With a special focus on the pharmaceutical sector, Pharma 4.0 aims to transform medication discovery, production, and distribution. Digital technologies are being used in the pharmaceutical industry in a number of areas, including as production, packaging, diagnostics, and analysis. Primary manufacturers, secondary manufacturers, logistics service providers/wholesalers, and healthcare providers make up the intricate network that is the pharmaceutical supply chain (Arden et al., 2021). With the introduction of Industry 4.0 and Pharma 4.0 technologies, tailored solutions, agility, and sustainable value generation are promised. It is critical to comprehend how these developments fit into healthcare supply chains in order to maximize productivity, guarantee quality, and deal with the constantly changing needs of the healthcare ecosystem (Rad et al., 2022; Shashi 2023).

To sum up, this book chapter provides a thorough overview of the dynamic landscape produced by Industry 4.0 and Pharma 4.0 for those involved in the healthcare supply chain. It aims to clear the path for an educated and strategic adoption of these technologies by methodically evaluating their applicability, advantages, difficulties, and possibilities. This will eventually improve the responsiveness and resilience of health care supply chains. (Khan et al., 2017) suggest that businesses should put more of an emphasis on technology that is explicit and facilitates the adoption of new, cutting-edge technology in the workplace. Companies should encourage their team members by giving them independence, incentives, awards, and recognition for their creative workers.

(Ghouri et al., 2023) developed and evaluated a novel artificial intelligence (AI)-based Omni channel blood supply chain (OBSC) model utilizing feedback from semi structured interviews with health care professionals working in a blood supply chain. In critical scenarios for blood supply networks, the imbalance between supply and demand is addressed by the suggested AI-based OBSC model. Blockchain technology application areas were categorized as safety and security, tracking and tracing, drug delivery, and prevention of counterfeit drugs. Preventing counterfeit drugs was the most often mentioned category, which is in line with the main goal of the pharmaceutical sector (Zakari, et al., 2022).

The objective of this chapter to address the questions is how we see the future of Pharma 4.0 with respect to industry 4.0. By analyzing the existing literature we will be able to find the current status of pharma 4.0 and practical implications in the age of industry 4.0.

RQ 1. How does Industry 4.0, also known as Pharma 4.0, address the unique technology and operational requirements of health care supply chains?

RQ 2. What obstacles can health care supply chains encounter when putting Industry 4.0 or Pharma 4.0 into practice, and how might these obstacles be overcome?

RQ 3. What opportunities and benefits are associated with the adoption of industry 4.0, pharma 4.0 for the healthcare supply chain. And how it can be maximized?

2. LITERATURE REVIEW

2.1 Understanding Industry 4.0 vs. Pharma 4.0

The fourth industrial revolution, known as "industry4.0," is defined by the incorporation of innovative technologies and data-driven solutions into production processes. It places a strong emphasis on utilizing cloud computing, the Internet of Things (IoT), and cyber-physical systems to build intelligent, networked production systems that can boost output, productivity, and decision-making (Sharma et al., 2023). Industry 4.0 seeks to transform conventional manufacturing techniques by facilitating greater automation, improved machine-to-machine communication, and the use of real-time data for production optimization and predictive maintenance. The goal is to build an industrial ecosystem that is more responsive, efficient, and flexible so that it can change to meet shifting consumer and market demands.

Contrarily, Pharma 4.0 is a particular implementation of Industry 4.0 ideas in the pharmaceutical sector. It entails the integration of data analytics and digital technologies to improve supply chain management, production, quality control, research and development, and other aspects of pharmaceutical manufacturing. Pharma 4.0 is centered on utilizing innovative technologies like big data analytics, artificial intelligence, and smart sensors to enhance pharmaceutical processes, guarantee the quality and safety of products, and maximize production efficiency. In order to satisfy the population's changing healthcare needs, it seeks to expedite the development and delivery of novel, high-quality pharmaceuticals while streamlining pharmaceutical operations and cutting costs.

Word "phama 4.0" first coined by the International Society of Pharmaceutical Engineering (ISPE) in 2017. It refers to the adoption of Industry 4.0 technologies in the health care supply chain system. It is an operational model that helps the pharmaceutical sector achieves digital maturity, data integrity, and industry 4.0 capabilities for their sustainable supply chains. Pharmaceutical supply chains are crucial instruments to establish in order to support the operational and managerial goals as well as future demands of pharmaceutical goods throughout their life cycle (Lws 40 years).

2.2 Blockchain Technology

Blockchain is revolutionary technology which is introduced by Satoshi Nakamoto in 2008. The initial use of blockchain technology was in crypto currency (Ravi et al., 2022). Key issues with data transparency, traceability, immutability, audit, provenance, flexible access, privacy, and security confront today's healthcare data management systems (AbuHalimeh & Ali, 2023).Despite block chain's great potential to solve traditional supply chain problems, there is a dearth of research on its application in pharmaceutical supply chains (PSCs) (Ghadge et al., 2022).

Furthermore, many of the healthcare systems now in use for data management are centralized, which increases the possibility of a single point of failure in the event of a natural disaster. The way data is managed in the healthcare industry might be drastically revolutionized, reshaped, and transformed by blockchain, an up-and-coming and disruptive decentralized technology (Yaqoob et al., 2021)."Industry4.0" describes the deployment of "smart" devices along the value chain that are able to autonomously connect with one another. The Fourth Industrial Revolution, which is described as a new degree of association and control over the value chain of the product lifecycle with an emphasis on more customized customer demands, has been referred to in recent years as "industry 4.0."

Innovative technologies like artificial intelligence (AI) and the Internet of Things (IoT) are used in the pharmaceutical sector. The pharmaceutical industry is using artificial intelligence (AI) more and more these days. AI has the potential to improve formulation results while saving time and money. AI makes robots that are just as intelligent as humans. The pharmaceutical industry has reinvented the process of developing new pharmaceuticals with the application of AI in recent years. AI may primarily be used in the study and creation of essential, game-changing drugs. Radiology and radiation have been thought to benefit greatly from artificial intelligence. Almost all aspects of clinical trials, including patient happiness, monitoring medication adherence, exchanging medical records, analysis, and design, may be impacted by AI. Block chain has the potential make transparent the supply chain process of programmatic advertising and prevent the whole ecosystem from ad fraud (Khan M. I., 2024).

The Internet of Things (IoT) is an intelligent network that employs a human-computerization system to reduce human labor. IoT includes both software and hardware architecture. The pharmaceutical industry is one where Internet of Things is revolutionizing. For easy conduction, the pharmaceutical industry's IoT blueprint is essential. Connecting disparate individuals and supply chain operations into a single network with enhanced capacity and reduced expenses while maintaining safety and security is made easier by IoT. In the pharmaceutical industry, IoT offers healthcare services. Advanced technology (e.g., AI and IoT) is used in the creation of pharmaceuticals for small-scale manufacturing in diagnostic-based therapeutics. The internets of things (IoT) paradigm's quick advancements have completely changed the healthcare sector by bringing about significant advancements in prescription medication data, insurance information, and e-health/medical records (EHR/EMR) (Ray et al., 2020; Griggs et al., 2018).

The vast production and consumption of goods that eventually jeopardize human and animal life as well as the interests of future generations is the primary cause of most environmental and climatic problems. One tactical solution to these disasters appears to be sustainable supply chain management, whose application is rather difficult yet flexible. Through Block chain based supply chain we can achieve sustainability (Khan et al, .2023).

2.3 Counterfeit Drugs Entering the Supply Chain

The integrity and sustainability of the entire ecosystem are seriously threatened by the introduction of fake medications into the pharmaceutical supply chain. In addition to the direct health risks to consumers, the widespread use of fake medications erodes patient and pharmaceutical company trust, which lowers market share and brand reputation. Addressing this issue, however, offers sustainable pharmaceutical supply chains the chance to improve their traceability technologies and put in place strong quality control procedures. Pharmacies can be guaranteed to be authentic and safe by using supply chains that are transparent and secure, thanks to the use of innovative tracking and authentication technologies like blockchain and serialization. Furthermore, by promoting moral and responsible business conduct, these initiatives not only protect public health but also help the pharmaceutical industry develop a culture of trust and accountability (Haq & Esuka, 2018).

We are now in the era of Industry 4.0 as a result of the four developmental stages. The fourth industrial revolution, or "Industry 4.0," will affect how goods are produced. The pharmaceutical industry will benefit from Industry 4.0 since it will make it simpler to produce sophisticated medicines. Processes are now more flexible due to Industry 4.0 and its innovative technologies like artificial intelligence (AI), robots, and the Internet of Things (IoT) (Arden et al., 2021). The goal of introducing Industry 4.0 was to eliminate the need for human labor and simplify complex operations. It is utilized in numerous aspects of the pharmaceutical industry, including manufacture, packaging, diagnosis, and analysis. Building a connection between business and sustainability, Industry 4.0 promotes sustainable growth. By implementing advanced Industry 4.0 production practices, sustainability may be observed. Additionally, Industry 4.0 may improve pharmaceutical production in terms of flexibility, costs, standards, and safety. It has been noted that Industry 4.0 encourages sustainable growth by introducing innovative technologies that result in flexible production procedures (Sharma et al., 2023).

Pharmaceutical companies employ "advanced analytics" from Industry 4.0 across the complete value chain, including R&D, safety, production, and regulation. The pharmaceutical business plays a vital role in the healthcare system by producing and selling drugs, biological products, and therapeutic devices that are used to identify and treat illnesses. It also conducts research to develop new products that benefit human welfare.co Therefore, it would be essential to maintain the standard of the pharmaceutical items to prevent health concerns as many of them are lifesaving (Ugvekar et al., 2021).

Therapeutic agents are made available by the pharmaceutical industry to treat illnesses. It improved the population health. Through research and development, the pharmaceutical sector creates innovative medications that enhance patients' quality of life around the globe. The pharmaceutical industry provides a significant benefit to global prosperity (Zozaya et al., 2019). The pharmaceutical business is always looking for new and creative ways to extend people's lives and make them healthier. The manufacturing of pharmaceutical products directly increases the world's gross domestic product and creates jobs for a large number of people. Although pharmaceuticals are utilized in the diagnosis and treatment of illnesses, they can occasionally have negative side effects. One of the primary issues facing mankind, according to reports, is the presence of toxins like medicines in drinkable water systems (Peake, Braund, Tremblay, & Tong, 2016).

In the era of fast growing technological advancements and the convergence of digital innovations, the concept of "Industry 4.0" and "Pharma 4.0" have surfaced as essential agents of change cutting across diverse sectors. Within this evolving landscape, the healthcare industry has become a focal point for in-depth scrutiny, as it navigates the adoption of these transformative paradigms. This introduction chapter serves as the foundation for a holistic investigation into the profound impact of Industry 4.0 and Pharma 4.0 on healthcare supply chains, dissecting their applicability, advantages, barriers, and prospects (Malheiro et al., 2023).

The advancement from Industry 3.0 to Industry 4.0 suggests a significant shift in the way supply chain processes are managed. In the era of Industry 3.0, the primary focusing to transform various supply chains process in digital and computerized process. Such as (ERP) Enterprise Resource Planning and (EDI) Electronic Discharge of Information systems were introduced, the main purpose of that advancement to streamline manufacturing process and systematizing tasks like purchase orders and documentation (Farziyeva & Dhanik, 2022). However, Industry 4.0 emerged as the next phase of technological transformation in the 21st century. Industry 4.0 focuses on to ensure data-driven transparency in supply chain processes while ensuring security and encryption. The main purpose to generalize supply chain processes and encourages stakeholders to work on a more digital approach, finally leading to increased sustainability.

In Industry 3.0, data was mostly used for internal processes and limited stakeholder management. These limitations create some challenges in achieving effective collaboration and sustainability through the supply chain. Using innovative technologies like Artificial Intelligence (AI), Blockchain, Cloud Computing, Internet of Things (IoT), and Cyber Physical Systems (CPS), Industry 4.0 aims to address these issues (Pelaez, et al., 2023). The process of globalization, which has increased connectivity, simultaneously introduces a higher level of complexity. The effectiveness and efficiency of meeting societal requirements are continually evaluated across multiple dimensions (Farziyeva & Dhanik, 2022). Thus, it becomes imperative to examine how industry 4.0 applications, a potentially significant topic across industries, can integrate and redefine the workflow within supply chains networks, fostering enhanced traceability, transparency, and collaboration among supply chain actors. This evolution addresses the collaboration gap that was evident in Industry 3.0 applications and enables trustworthy and flexible stakeholder management.

2.4 Privacy

Individuals have the fundamental right to data privacy and protection (Ventura & Coeli, 2018). Information gathered by healthcare institutions frequently includes medical and personal information about patients. A data breach puts all of that information at danger of being compromised, which would be detrimental to the entire goal of digitizing healthcare. It is possible to identify the necessity for efficient data protection with regard to the healthcare industry by taking this factor into account. Furthermore, this demonstrates the applicability of the research and the design criteria for the study's important factors. "Electronic health records (EHRs)" are a common digital tool that gives individuals access to the medical data they require. Important patient data can also be shared by service providers via "health information exchanges (HIEs)". But there are concerns related to data security with this method. EHR patient records include information on the patient's medical history, social security number, course of treatment, insurance, and payment data (Cowie, et al., 2016).

In order to achieve one, we frequently have to give up the other. Visibility and privacy are generally mutually exclusive. The greatest solution for this trade-off is blockchain, which can guarantee the authenticity of data made publicly available while maintaining the privacy of an entity's private information hidden and without compromising it. The items in a pharmaceutical supply chain system may be verified without revealing any details on the manufacturing process. However, many network users will be able to view the patient's medical record without being aware of the patient's personal information (Haq & Esuka, 2018).

Patients are reluctant to offer useful information for the Blockchain-based solution because they are worried about their privacy being compromised. Past incidents, such as privacy leakage situations like AMCA (American Medical Collection Agency) data breach in 2018, erode the patient's faith in data protection. (Agbo et al., 2019) mentioned that Enhanced privacy and security of data Health data security is ensured by block chain's immutability virtue. The health data cannot be removed, distorted, or changed once it is added to a blockchain system. On a blockchain system, information is time-stamped, encrypted, and kept in chronological order.

3. METHODOLOGY

Rousseau et al. (2008) state that the systematic literature review (SLR) approach, also known as synthesis, "is the critical first step in the effective use of scientific evidence". The rigorous literature review procedure used for this research is described in this section. The procedures described by the methods put out by Transfield et al. (2003) and Okoli (2015), which include (a) Planning, (b) Selection, (c) Extraction, and (d) Execution, served as the foundation for the search and review process.

We used to search many well-known and up-to-date research databases, such as Google Scholar, Semantic Scholar, and IEEE Xplore databases, to find relevant literature. These databases offer selective coverage, superior content, and a wider range of publications. Creating keywords and strings to extract relevant scholarly articles from the database is the first step in the selection process in a systematic literature review (SLR). Typically, the boolean operators "AND", "OR", "NOT", and so forth are used for this. In this systematic literature review, the terms "industry 4.0," "pharma 4.0," "sustainability," "medical 4.0," and "health care" were employed. In order to incorporate only relevant papers and maintain a reasonable quantity of articles for the research, a screening mechanism was implemented. Additionally, any items older than ten years were removed. This facilitates post-auditing and replication of the research as well.

After doing a search on the selective database, 8524 items were found. The number of articles was decreased to 2231 after these first findings were filtered and restricted to search strings in abstracts and keywords. Peer-reviewed studies from the fields of business management & accounting, health care and medical sciences, and economics that had been published during the previous 10 years were also excluded from the screening process. As a result, there were 61 articles and 15 reports are left, which have been included in this SLR for in-depth evaluation and analysis. In Figure 1, a PRISMA flow diagram is shown.

Figure 1. PRISMA flow diagram for literature search

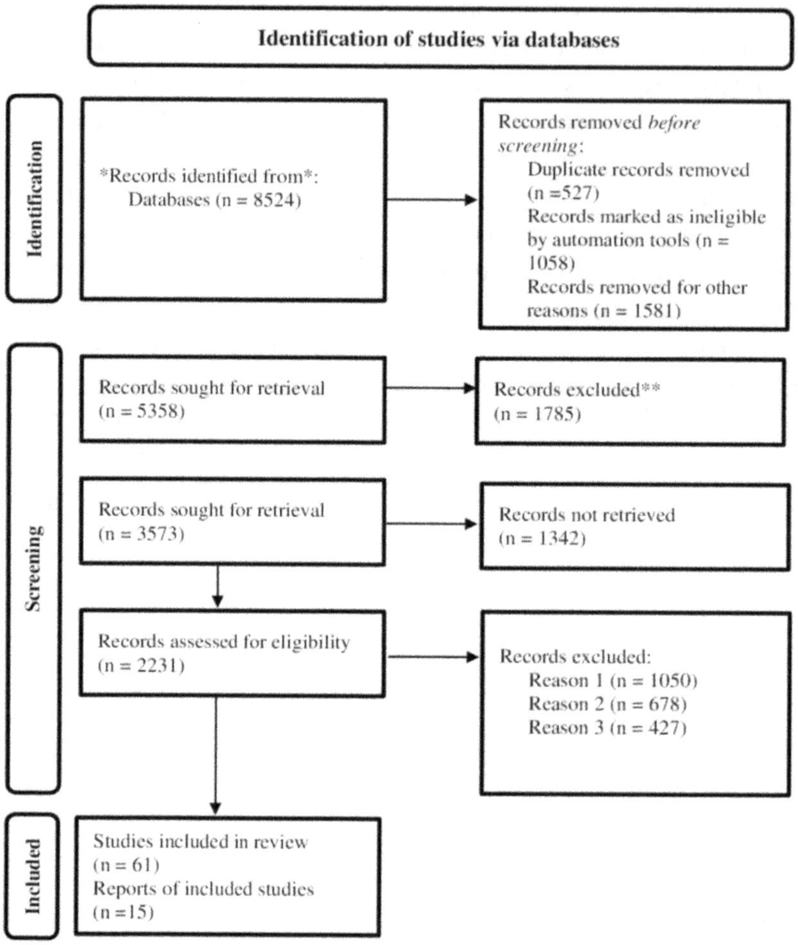

*Records means all related literature work which has been done till today. It includes journal articles, case studies, industry news, organization reports etc.

4. THEMATIC FINDINGS

This chapter focuses on discussing the thematic findings in the research and reporting the main findings relevant to answering the research questions. Relevant research questions have been framed in the introduction, and understanding and deciphering the answers to the research questions will be the ultimate motive of this thematic findings chapter. This chapter will try to focus on the frameworks that have been developed and incorporated into the supply chain systems to ensure transparency measures in sustainability and the ability to measure and report these measures correctly. This chapter also intends to analyze digitalization and the efforts by the industry and the government to ensure that the latest technologies are adopted to ensure sustainability

4.1 Challenges of Implementing Pharma 4.0 in the Pharmaceutical Industry

Healthcare supply chains, which offer essential services for daily living, are complex, worldwide, and comprise several firms. Impurities including a lack of transparency, incorrect information, and a restricted data provenance are introduced by the complexity of the healthcare system. One of the main effects of the current supply chain is counterfeit medication, which not only negatively impacts people's health but also causes significant financial hardship for the healthcare sector. Studies already conducted have underlined how important it is for the healthcare system to have a robust end-to-end tracking and tracing mechanism. The elimination of counterfeit pharmaceuticals and the assurance of product safety are the main goals of this end-to-end drug tracking system. Now a days the track and trace systems used in health care supply chain are centralized and they have some major problems like transparency, privacy and authenticity (Musamih, et al., 2016).

Prior to the advent of Industry 4.0, conventional technologies used a three-step energy conversion procedure. Traditional manufacturing does not adequately address the needs of patient populations, both military and civilian, and healthcare providers because it is not sufficiently capable of monitoring and controlling automated and complex manufacturing processes to produce personalized products expertly and beneficially (Sharma et al., 2023). The advancement of materials using conventional processes has hit a limit, even for uses in medicine. The disadvantages of classic medication delivery systems include their low therapeutic indices and poor solubility in water. New drug development is expensive and routine production processes that include batch processing are frequently inefficient. Pharma 4.0's automation features might help the pharmaceutical industry. Significant challenges encountered by earlier innovations or revolutions include the high price of producing novel treatments, unclear procedures, and inefficient regular manufacturing that results in batch failures (Steinwandter et al.,2019).

Now a day's one of the most challenging things in pharmaceutical industry is counterfeit drugs. What is mean by counterfeit drugs? According to WHO definition "the drugs which is made illegally, mislabeled, produced with low quality raw material, the source detail and identity of source is unknown or hidden and the define standards for production is not followed is known to be fake or counterfeit drugs". According to a World Health Organization (WHO) assessment, every tenth medication used by patients in underdeveloped nations is either fake or of poor quality (WHO, William 2014, White 2022). This report may be not accurate and the ratio of counterfeit drugs are maybe increase or decrease in numbers but alarming situation is " that the pharmaceutical supply chain has the room to add these counterfeit drugs in the supply chain system. Around 0.7 Million deaths are occurred due Malaria and 0.2 Million deaths are due to counterfeit drugs worldwide.

4.2 High Cost and Time Consumption

Healthcare supply chains face many obstacles when implementing Industry 4.0 and Pharma 4.0, most of which are related to high costs and time commitment. The integration of advanced technologies results in high initial costs because it requires significant financial investments in infrastructure upgrades, training, and the adoption of sophisticated equipment (Ding, 2018).The complex nature of these technologies requires thorough employee training, which can further drain time and resources. When old systems and procedures are modified to meet Industry 4.0 and Pharma 4.0 criteria, there are sometimes delays and disruptions in production during this phase of change. Furthermore, it takes more time and money to validate new systems' efficacy and ensure regulatory compliance (Sharma et al., 2023).

These difficulties highlight the necessity of rigorous budgetary planning, efficient change management techniques, and the creation of long-term implementation plans in order to reduce expenses and time constraints throughout the integration process. In order to successfully integrate Industry 4.0 and Pharma 4.0 and enhance patient outcomes and the efficiency of the healthcare supply chain, it is imperative that these obstacles be addressed.

4.3 Little Awareness and Understanding of Sustainability

Adoption of Industry 4.0 and Pharma 4.0 in healthcare supply chains is being limited by a widespread lack of understanding and familiarity with sustainable standards. In the healthcare industry, sustainable practices are often underestimated while playing a critical role in ensuring the resilience and long-term profitability of supply chains (Tortorella et al., 2023). This leads to a broad disregard for environmentally friendly manufacturing and distribution methods as well as an ignorance of how activities affect the environment. When there is a lack of understanding, it usually leads to inaction on waste reduction, energy efficiency, or introduction of environmentally friendly industrial methods (Ferronato & Torretta, 2019). Moreover, a deficiency of knowledge about the potential benefits of sustainability makes it more challenging to adopt environmentally friendly practices, leading to missed opportunities to save costs and improve operational efficiency. To solve this issue and encourage stakeholders to integrate eco-friendly practices into their healthcare supply chain operations, education and awareness campaigns emphasizing the benefits of sustainable practices are required (Maryville 2019).

4.4 Insufficient Investment for Technological Advancement

The lack of proper funding for technical development is still one of the main barriers to the implementation of Industry 4.0 and Pharma 4.0 in the supply chains that handle health care. The high expenses associated with adopting new technologies like digital supply chain systems and the Internet of Things make it difficult to integrate them into existing infrastructures. In addition, financial constraints and a lack of financing prevent healthcare institutions from fully using the potential benefits of these advances (Ding, 2018). Without enough financing, it becomes more difficult to deploy innovative technological tools that might enhance supply chain management and increase operational efficiency. Because of this, the industry finds it difficult to keep up with the rapid evolution of technology, which eventually keeps Industry 4.0 and Pharma 4.0 in the health care supply chain from realizing their full potential (Huang et al., 2023).

4.5 Digitalized Product Monitoring and Traceability

Digitalized product monitoring and traceability are the most significant of the issues that come with implementing Industry 4.0 and Pharma 4.0 in health care supply chains. The use of digital technology enables the real-time monitoring of many characteristics, such as temperature, humidity, and location, which ensures the uniformity and safety of pharmaceutical products throughout the supply chain. By combining IoT sensors with advanced tracking systems, stakeholders may have more insight and control over the whole product path, from manufacture to distribution and delivery (Ma et al., 2022: Arden et al., 2021).

This greater transparency helps to swiftly identify and address any quality concerns, which reduces the likelihood of product recalls and enhances patient safety generally. Additionally, supply chain managers may use digital traceability to cut costs and boost operational performance by identifying bottlenecks, managing inventory more skillfully, and streamlining shipping procedures (Gottipolu, 2020). Despite these benefits, there are still problems that need to be overcome, such the challenge of connecting different digital systems, safeguarding data security and privacy, and the necessity of industry standardization. Overcoming these challenges will need strong stakeholder engagement, investments in secure digital infrastructure, and the development of common protocols and standards to ensure seamless data interchange and interoperability throughout the supply chain.

4.6 Compliance and Coordination of Stakeholders

The adoption of Industry 4.0 and Pharma 4.0 in healthcare supply chains have some challenges with stakeholder coordination and compliance, such as:

1. Regulatory Compliance: Upholding industry-specific rules and regulations in relation to the adoption of innovative technologies is essential to preserving standards for both quality and safety.
2. Interoperability: Ensuring smooth communication and data sharing among diverse systems and platforms is essential for coordinating multiple stakeholders, such as manufacturers, suppliers, and distributors.
3. Data Security and Privacy: To avoid unwanted access and breaches, managing private and sensitive patient data calls for strong cyber security procedures and controls.
4. Collaborative Culture: Industry 4.0 and Pharma 4.0 cannot be successfully adopted and integrated unless a collaborative culture is fostered among stakeholders, including healthcare providers, technology providers, and regulatory bodies.
5. Training and Skill Development: Successful implementation and operation of Industry 4.0 and Pharma 4.0 solutions depend on stakeholders having the skills and knowledge to take advantage of innovative technologies.

5. IMPORTANCE OF ASSESSING THEIR SUITABILITY, BENEFITS, CHALLENGES, AND OPPORTUNITIES FOR HEALTHCARE SUPPLY CHAINS

Evaluating the suitability, advantages, difficulties, and prospects of healthcare supply chains is essential to guaranteeing the efficient and successful provision of medical services. Healthcare organizations can make sure that their supply chains are suited to the unique requirements of the healthcare industry, such as timely and precise delivery of essential medical supplies, by assessing their suitability (Kilpatrick, et al., 2020). Gaining an understanding of the advantages makes it possible to pinpoint possible areas for development, which enables healthcare companies to improve patient care, cut expenses, and streamline operations. Simultaneously, acknowledging the obstacles present in healthcare supply chains, such as possible disturbances or limited resources, enables the creation of preemptive tactics to minimize hazards and guarantee uninterrupted services. Furthermore, identifying opportunities within healthcare supply chains can lead to the implementation of innovative technologies, optimized logistics, and strategic partnerships, thereby fostering advancements in healthcare delivery and patient outcome (Zamiela et al., 2022).

5.1 Increased Efficiency and Productivity

Pharma 4.0 and Industry 4.0 provide a number of advantages to healthcare supply chains that boost production and efficiency. Among these benefits are the following: Enhanced Connectivity: Industry 4.0 encourages linked systems that allow for smooth data exchange and communication across different healthcare supply chain participants. This promotes more effective coordination and decision-making processes (Haleem et al., 2022). Automation and Streamlining: The automation of activities, the streamlining of workflows and the reduction of mistake potential are all encouraged by Industry 4.0 and Pharma 4.0. These actions improve the overall operational efficiency of healthcare supply chains. Data-Driven Insights: These innovative technologies make it possible to gather and analyze enormous volumes of data, which produces insightful information that can be used to improve the procurement, production, and inventory management procedures in healthcare supply chains (Javaid et al., 2022). Enhanced Quality Control Industry 4.0 and Pharma 4.0 provide real-time monitoring and quality control procedures, guaranteeing compliance with legal requirements and the provision of premium medical supplies.

5.2 Customized Medications

From a Pharma 4.0 standpoint, customized drugs are a major breakthrough in the pharmaceutical sector that allow for more precise customization of drug formulations to meet the needs of individual patients. Pharma 4.0 makes it easier to produce personalized medications by utilizing technologies like 3D printing and the Internet of Things. This enables the creation of drug release profiles and dosages that are unique to each patient. This strategy is in line with the main objective of personalized medicine, which stresses giving the appropriate medication to the appropriate patient at the appropriate time (Andreadis et al., 2022). Pharma 4.0 aims to improve patient outcomes and treatment efficacy by incorporating these technological innovations and guaranteeing that medications are precisely tailored to meet individual patient characteristics and medical needs. A new era of individualized and successful pharmaceutical interventions may be brought about by this personalized approach, which has the potential to completely transform patient care and treatment plans.

5.3 Additive Manufacturing

From the points of view of Industry 4.0 and Pharma 4.0, additive manufacturing has revolutionized the pharmaceutical and manufacturing sectors by introducing innovative methods of production and enhanced customizability. Customized drug formulations and medical devices can now be produced by the pharmaceutical industry thanks to additive manufacturing, commonly referred to as 3D printing. This has allowed for the precise customization of drug regimens to meet the needs and preferences of individual patients (Sharma et al., 2023). By simplifying the administration of treatments catered to the specific requirements of each patient and improving overall therapeutic outcomes, this approach has significantly advanced personalized medicine. In the larger framework of Industry 4.0, additive manufacturing has completely transformed conventional manufacturing processes by enabling the rapid and economical production of complex parts and components. Increased production efficiency, decreased waste, and improved product design flexibility have resulted from the incorporation of additive manufacturing into Industry 4.0 initiatives, which has raised operational agility and competitiveness in the manufacturing sector (Mobarak, et al., 2023).

5.4 Improved Patient Data Analysis

Enhancing the analysis of patient data is essential to Industry 4.0 and Pharma 4.0. The use of technology and digital innovations makes it possible to analyze patient data more thoroughly and effectively in the era of Industry 4.0 and Pharma 4.0. Pharmaceutical companies can now collect and analyze data using machines thanks to these advancements, which creates flexible and efficient processes. Industry 4.0 offers the framework for real-time patient data collection and analysis by merging physical and digital systems (Mukhlas et al., 2022). More individualized and accurate treatment plans are made possible by this data-driven approach, which also makes it possible to spot trends and patterns that can guide clinical trials and medication development. Additionally, Pharma 4.0's focus on interconnectivity and Big Data utilization improves the analysis of patient data even more. The amalgamation of artificial intelligence and machine learning algorithms facilitates the more extensive and precise analysis of patient data. This degree of analysis can help identify possible health risks proactively, lead to earlier and more accurate diagnoses, and improve treatment outcomes (Haleem et al., 2022). All things considered, Pharma 4.0 and Industry 4.0 offer the framework and instruments for enhanced patient data analysis, leading to more efficient and customized healthcare outcomes through the integration of technology and data analysis capabilities.

5.5 Resource Optimization

The pharmaceutical industry's "Pharma 4.0" digital operating model combines the ideas of Industry 4.0 to maximize resources and boost productivity (Sharma et al., 2023). Pharma 4.0 integrates digital tools and technologies to enable proactive resource management, process automation, and real-time data analysis. Organizations can improve their resource utilization by employing data-driven decision-making and identifying waste or inefficiencies in their supply chain, marketing, research, and production processes. Digital twins, or digital copies of real assets and operations, are used more easily thanks to Pharma 4.0. Increased connectivity and transparency made possible by these digital twins help organizations track and manage resources in real-time, spot inefficiencies or bottlenecks, and make the necessary corrections to optimize resource allocation (Hariry et al., 2021). There are obstacles unique to implementing Pharma 4.0 and attaining better resource optimization. The need for significant investment in digital infrastructure and technologies, as well as the integration of legacy systems with new digital solutions, are a few of these difficulties.

Ensuring data integrity and compliance with current GMP standards and regulatory guidelines may also present difficulties. However, these difficulties are outweighed by the advantages of Pharma 4.0 and enhanced resource optimization. The COVID-19 pandemic has significantly improved digital technologies' adaptability in the pharmaceutical and healthcare sectors. With its emphasis on automation and digitization, Pharma 4.0 is now even more pertinent in this setting (Khan & Manzoor, 2021). Pharma 4.0 streamlines and boosts productivity throughout the value chain to give pharmaceutical companies a competitive edge. This entails integrating self-organizing and autonomous manufacturing facilities, facilitating quick decision-making, and streamlining drug manufacturing through real-time optimization and control systems.

6. OPPORTUNITIES FOR SUSTAINABLE PHARMACEUTICAL SUPPLY CHAIN

The researchers explore both the positive aspects and potential challenges associated with the integration of Industry 4.0 and Pharma 4.0 in healthcare supply chains:

1. **Better Product Protection and Supply Chain Security**: Industry 4.0 in the pharmaceutical industry provides better tools for supply chain security and product protection, which helps to maintain the general integrity of healthcare supply chains (Sharma et al., 2023).
2. **Empirical Research for Performance Improvement**: Research indicates that the interaction of new technologies with pharmaceutical supply chains often referred to as "Pharma 4.0" improves supply chain performance. This involves applying managerial techniques to boost productivity.
3. **Beneficial Effect on Hospital Performance**: As part of Pharma 4.0, integrating Industry 4.0 into medical treatments is said to have a short-term beneficial effect on hospitals' performance, demonstrating prospective advantages for healthcare delivery (Tortorella 2023).
4. **Implications for Supply Chain Performance:** Both favorable and unfavorable effects on supply chain performance are highlighted by a thorough analysis of Industry 4.0 technology. To optimize the integration process, it is important to comprehend these ramifications (Rad, et al., 2022).
5. **Using Cyber-Physical Technology to Increase System Smartness:** Industry 4.0, the latest industrial revolution, uses cyber-physical technology to increase system smartness, which includes autonomous devices. The progression from Industry 4.0 to Pharma 4.0 reflects this shift (Hariry et al., 2021).
6. **Integration for Sustainable Supply Chains:** Industry 4.0's contribution to supply chains includes sustainability promotion. Supply chain sustainability and Industry 4.0 integration is a novel strategy that highlights the necessity for a fair assessment of the integration's environmental effects (Naseem & Yang, 2021).

6.1 Sustainable Manufacturing and Distribution

In the pharmaceutical industry, supply chains that are socially and environmentally responsible can be established through sustainable manufacturing and distribution. Using sustainable practices encourages resource efficiency and long-term cost savings in addition to guaranteeing a decrease in waste production and carbon footprints. Utilizing renewable energy sources, like solar or wind power, is a key component of sustainable manufacturing initiatives as it helps minimize dependency on fossil fuels and lower greenhouse gas emissions overall (Raman et al., 2023). Furthermore, a more sustainable approach to drug development can be fostered by incorporating green chemistry principles and using bio-based materials in pharmaceutical production to significantly reduce the environmental impact of manufacturing processes. The distribution stage is essential to improving the sustainability of pharmaceutical supply chains, working hand in hand with sustainable manufacturing. Reducing energy consumption and the environmental impact of product delivery can be achieved by putting effective logistics strategies into practice, such as optimizing transportation routes and using eco-friendly packaging materials. Additionally, the integration of innovative tracking technologies and real-time monitoring systems improves visibility across the distribution network, making it easier to spot possible inefficiencies early and take swift corrective action. All of these factors contribute to the overall resilience and sustainability of the supply chain (Puhlmann et al., 2024).

Regulatory agencies, suppliers, pharmaceutical companies, and other stakeholders must work together to promote a sustainable culture throughout the whole pharmaceutical supply chain. In addition to encouraging increased accountability, participating in open dialogue, knowledge exchange, and cooperative efforts for sustainable development guarantees that sustainability goals and objectives are in line with each other across the ecosystem of the supply chain (Chauhan et al., 2022). Through leveraging sustainable manufacturing and distribution practices, the pharmaceutical industry can maintain its environmental stewardship, participate in international efforts to mitigate climate change, and ultimately promote the welfare of both humanity and the environment.

6.2 Decentralized Supply Chain Closer to the Patient

A game-changing possibility for sustainable pharmaceutical supply chains is a decentralized supply chain model that puts the patient's proximity first (Sahoo et al., 2022). This strategy promotes improved health outcomes and patient satisfaction by guaranteeing the timely and effective delivery of medications, thereby facilitating enhanced patient-centricity. Pharmaceutical companies can minimize the environmental impact of long-distance drug delivery and significantly reduce transportation-related carbon emissions by implementing agile logistics strategies and setting up localized distribution centers. Decentralized supply chains also empower local economies and encourage community involvement, which advances social sustainability and strengthens the bond between pharmaceutical companies and the communities they service (Amjad et al., 2023). Adopting this decentralized, patient-focused supply chain paradigm enhances pharmaceutical supply chains' overall responsiveness and resilience and is consistent with the larger sustainability objectives of lessening their negative effects on the environment and enhancing community well-being.

6.3. Exploring the Impact of Industry 4.0 on Healthcare Supply Chains

Pharma 4.0 is the result of the four manufacturing transformational phases. Pharma 4.0 refers to the modernization of the pharmaceutical sector via the integration of innovative technology and digital tactics. The pharmaceutical industry may be able to overcome obstacles if Industry 4.0 concepts are adopted. In the pharmaceutical industry, Industry 4.0's mission is to quickly, cheaply, and effectively create and produce innovative, personalized goods that meet the diverse tastes and needs of customers. The Pharma 4.0 operating model is the result of adding Industry 4.0 and the International Council of Harmonization (ICH). The pharmaceutical industry's use of Industry 4.0 has given the pharmacy sectors a competitive edge (Ding, 2018; Lakner et al., 2019).

Because Industry 4.0 boosts productivity and brings new possibilities for the circular economy, transparency, and product customization, it may benefit sustainability along the whole value chain. The adoption of Industry 4.0 is one of the primary drivers behind the modernization of the pharmaceutical and biopharmaceutical sectors. Industry 4.0 uses freely available footprint information and verifiable research to minimize the ecological effect of a process or product (Filho et al., 2022).

Demands from the market became much more intense and labor-intensive as Industry 4.0 emerged. Digitalization, a key part of pharma 4.0, will connect everything and create new levels of precision and adaptability for a digitalized plant floor. It was suggested that Industry 4.0 would enhance production in order to achieve maximum mass customization at a reasonable cost and short product life cycles. The goals of Industry 4.0 for digitizing labs and applying automation to various procedures used in hospitals and general healthcare are included in Health 4.0. In the pharmaceutical industry, Industry 4.0 offers improved tools for supply chain security and product protection (Sharma, 2023)

Pharma 4.0 is a shift in the pharmaceutical sector that uses "machines" to gather and analyze data so that processes can become more flexible and efficient. Massive data processing, networking, artificial intelligence, cooperative robotics, and distributed cloud service-based architectures are the engines driving Pharma 4.0. In the pharmaceutical industry, Industry 4.0 facilitates increased operational efficiency, such as reduced resource consumption. By speeding up the analysis of patient data and empowering them to maximize resources for better patient outcomes, Health 4.0 is intended to enhance the capacity of medical professionals (Arden et al., 2021).

Industry 4.0 optimizes the entire value chain, or the life cycle of a product, from its conception to its development, manufacturing, use, upkeep, and recycling. It also improves production flows. Industry 4.0 is a smart production networking system that links products and instruments without requiring human intervention. Furthermore, increased data density reduces productivity and encourages the pharmaceutical industry to develop more specialized and tailored pharmaceutical products that are appropriate for tailored medication treatment rather than the current "one-size-fits-all" strategy (Barenji et al., 2019). Biopharmaceuticals can benefit greatly from the application of Industry 4.0 technologies and goals, which could lead to significant advancements in biomedicine production, availability, and advancement. The goal of the Industry 4.0 plan is to link production equipment to goods through hyper-connected technologies and unify the whole manufacturing process (Shi et al., 2020).

"Industry 4.0," or the fourth industrial revolution, is gaining traction, especially in the aftermath of the epidemic and the present unsteady political environment globally. It is seen as a way to channel all stakeholders under the design of a digital supply chain and encourage a more open network. Academics and industry are currently working to address the dynamic demand for organizations to adopt higher flexibilities as a result of business requirements, customer-oriented supply chain solutions, and rapid changes in the market. Numerous research articles discuss various methods to accomplish this, such as blockchain solutions, virtual and augmented reality that imitates negotiations, cloud-based solutions, and cyber-physical systems (Berg, et al., 2021).

Adoption of various technologies can face specific challenges, such as those related to finances, the development of digital infrastructure, resistance to innovation, and so forth. Nonetheless, further investigation into various Industry 4.0 applications may be necessary in order to select the appropriate one. Due to its capacity for secure traceability and decentralization, blockchain technology is an intriguing solution that is currently being applied throughout supply chains. This suggests that it may be a viable option to investigate within the context of Industry 4.0 and digitalization as a solution. Recent research has focused on automating financial systems under blockchain governance, which may pave the way for multi-channel or multi-stakeholder communication channels (Xia et al., 2023).

Expected benefits include a transparent transaction and a decentralized power mechanism that encourage user cooperation and mutual trust amongst all parties. Such a technology may be able to draw more validation transactions in the process of locating the best manufacturers or suppliers when innovators or idea owners are also taken into account. An open channel built on blockchain technology may also impede the growth of investor and financier confidence, which is bolstered by a digital financial regulatory framework (Javaid et al., 2021). Major stakeholders that communicate with manufacturers and suppliers would also facilitate greater data sharing while defending competitive interests that could result in the achievement of sustainable, economic goals and a reduction in costs related to stakeholder interactions and negotiations, as previously mentioned in the literature (Khan et al., 2016).

7. PRACTICAL CASE STUDIES

1. FarmaTrust offers a blockchain-based end-to-end pharmaceutical product provenance system that is suitable for corporate use. With this approach, counterfeit or substandard medications are prevented from entering the pharmaceutical supply chain; protecting customers who may use their free Consumer Confidence App to verify the legitimacy of pharmaceuticals. FarmaTrust has strategically made sure to leverage modern technologies, such as mobile phone technology and different exclusive software that FarmaTrust has developed, to create solutions that can function anywhere in the world, whether it is Mongolia or Germany (FarmaTrust).
2. Merck is implementing Pharma 4.0 in their production process to enhance quality control and traceability. Through the creation of digital twins for primary packaging, the proof of concept (PoC) seeks to revolutionize the pharmaceutical supply chain. They assert that members will get complete transparency and digital trust through a single, linked network, which will save costs, enhance quality, and even open up new business opportunities because of process automation. The innovative solution, which is applied to Gerresheimer items, anchors physical things securely in the digital realm using a blockchain-based platform and multi-patented authentication technology created by Merck (Packaging Europe, 2022).
3. According to LogiPharma (2021) to support the shift in the pharmaceutical supply chain from production to end-user, Novartis is experimenting with different strategies to leverage digital technology, and notably artificial intelligence, to help in the planning, monitoring, and delivery of medicine to patients. Artificial intelligence is one aspect of Industry 4.0 that Novartis is keen to make a pillar of its digital transformation in cell therapy. The Novartis representative continued on, "[Novartis] is still investigating where best to apply AI in the manufacturing process." "Novartis is investigating how artificial intelligence (AI) can assist us in identifying opportunities within our data to make more economical purchases of materials used in the manufacturing process."
4. The Bosch Pharma has a long journey with industry 4.0 revolution and progress. An artificial intelligence (AI) system that can identify and address irregularities and failures in the manufacturing process early on has been created by the Bosch Center for Artificial Intelligence (BCAI). This application of AI guarantees better goods and more environmentally friendly, productive production. Approximately 50 facilities and 800 manufacturing lines are already supported by the AI solution, which will ultimately be implemented in all 240 Bosch factories.

In order to improve quality control and perform predictive maintenance, Bosch implemented Industry 4.0 in its factories. The World Economic Forum has recognized a Bosch facility as an Industry 4.0 lighthouse project for the second time. Bosch provides an example of how digitalized production and logistics can improve both efficiency and quality in equal measure in Suzhou, China. In 2018, Bosch included their facility in Wuxi, China, on the list of outstanding examples. The World Economic Forum emphasized there that linked solutions' capacity for predictive maintenance and troubleshooting sets an example for factories of the future (Bosch, 2021).

5. According to (Tracxn, 2023) report, Blockchain is being widely used in healthcare start-ups in India, including Plenum Data, Shivom, NHCT, Vitraya, UHID, MedBlocks, and Rolyte. These companies offer blockchain- and IoT-based solutions for data security, data integration, and management. A blockchain-based system for managing health insurance claims is offered by Vitraya

Technologies. It provides options for hospitals, healthcare providers, and insurers to process and pay claims together. For claim settlement, rewards, and fraud detection, it makes use of blockchain-based technologies and smart contacts.

Patients may schedule telehealth appointments with GraphMyHealth, an AI-powered tool. Patients may schedule appointments, have online video consultations with medical professionals, schedule preventative health check-ups, tests, prescription drugs, and other medical and home care services using the mobile app. Blockchain technology and AI technologies are integrated into the platform.

8. CONCLUSION

In conclusion, a dynamic view of opportunities and problems is revealed by investigating Industry 4.0 and Pharma 4.0 in the context of health care supply chains. The pharmaceutical industry has enormous potential to improve efficiency, sustainability, and customized solutions as a result of the confluence of digital technology and pharmaceutical processes. The positive effects of Industry 4.0 and Pharma 4.0, which range from improved flexibility and cost-effectiveness to sustained value generation, have been made clear by our assessment. However, there are challenges associated with using these technologies. Because the pharmaceutical industry is highly regulated, considerations like patient safety, product quality, and data integrity are necessary. To mitigate these risks, a thorough understanding of the unique requirements of the pharmaceutical supply chain and strategic planning are essential.

REFERENCES

AbuHalimeh, A., & Ali, O. (2023). Comprehensive review for healthcare data quality challenges in blockchain technology. *Frontiers in Big Data*, 1-12.

Agbo, C., Mahmoud, Q., & Eklund, J. (2019). Blockchain Technology in Healthcare: A Systematic Review. *Health Care*. PMID:30987333

Amjad, A., Kordel, P., & Fernandes, G. (2023). A Review on Innovation in Healthcare Sector (Telehealth) through Artificial Intelligence. *Sustainability (Basel)*, *15*(8), 6655. doi:10.3390/su15086655

Andreadis, I., Gioumouxouzis, C., Eleftheriadis, G., & Fatouros, D. (2022). The Advent of a New Era in Digital Healthcare: A Role for 3D Printing Technologies in Drug Manufacturing? *Pharmaceutics*.

Arden, N., Fisher, A., Tyner, K., Yu, L., Lee, S., & Kopcha, M. (2021). Industry 4.0 for pharmaceutical manufacturing: Preparing for the smart factories of the future. *International Journal of Pharmaceutics*, *602*, 120554. doi:10.1016/j.ijpharm.2021.120554 PMID:33794326

Barenji, R. V., Akdag, Y., Yet, B., & Oner, L. (2019). Cyber-physical-based PAT (CPbPAT) framework for Pharma 4.0. *International Journal of Pharmaceutics*, *567*, 118445. doi:10.1016/j.ijpharm.2019.06.036 PMID:31226474

Berg, H., Bendix, P., Jansen, M., Blevennec, K., Bottermann, P., & Melgar, M. M. (2021). *Unlocking the potential of Industry 4.0 to reduce the environmental impact of production*. Eionet Report.

Bosch. (2021). *Ten years of Industry 4.0.* Bosch.

Chauhan, C., Kaur, P., Arrawatia, R., Ractham, P., & Dhir, A. (2022). Supply chain collaboration and sustainable development goals (SDGs). Teamwork makes achieving SDGs dream work. *Journal of Business Research, 147*, 290–307. doi:10.1016/j.jbusres.2022.03.044

Cowie, M., Blomster, J., Curtis, L., Duclaux, S., Ford, I., & Fritz, F. (2016). Electronic health records to facilitate clinical research. *Clinical Research in Cardiology; Official Journal of the German Cardiac Society*. PMID:27557678

*Digital twin solution from Merck offers increased traceability*2022Packaging Europe.

Ding, B. (2018). Pharma Industry 4.0: Literature review and research opportunities in sustainable pharmaceutical supply chains. *Process Safety and Environmental Protection, 119*, 115–130. doi:10.1016/j.psep.2018.06.031

FarmaTrust. (n.d.). *Pharmaceutical Tracking & Data Services*. FarmaTrust.

Farziyeva, G., & Dhanik, N. (2022). *Digital Transition of Supply Chain with Industry 4.0 Applications*. Academic Press.

Ferronato, N., & Torretta, V. (2019). Waste Mismanagement in Developing Countries: A Review of Global Issues. *International Journal of Environmental Research and Public Health*, 1–28. PMID:30909625

Filho, M. G., Monteiro, L., Mota, R. d., Gonella, J. d., & Campos, L. M. (2022). The Relationship between Circular Economy, Industry 4.0 and Supply Chain Performance: A Combined ISM/Fuzzy MICMAC Approach. *Sustainability*.

Ghadge, A., Bourlakis, M., Kamble, S., & Seuring, S. (2022). Blockchain implementation in pharmaceutical supply chains: A review and conceptual framework. *International Journal of Production Research*, 6633–6651.

Ghouri, A. M., Khan, H., Venkatesh, M., Haq, M. A., & Jabbour, A. L. (2023). *An Artificial-Intelligence-Based Omnichannel Blood Supply Chain: A Pathway for Sustainable Development*. Academic Press.

Gottipolu, R. (2020). *Securing the Pharmaceutical Supply Chain with Full Traceability*. PharmaTech.com.

Griggs, K. N., Ossipova, O., Kohlios, C. P., Baccarini, A. N., Howson, E. A., & Hayajneh, T. (2018). *Healthcare Blockchain System Using Smart Contracts for Secure Automated Remote Patient Monitoring*. Med Syst. doi:10.1007/s10916-018-0982-x

Haleem, A., Javaid, M., Singh, R. P., & Suman, R. (2022). Medical 4.0 technologies for healthcare: Features, capabilities, and applications. *Internet of Things and Cyber-Physical Systems*, 12-30.

Haq, I., & Esuka, O. M. (2018). Blockchain Technology in Pharmaceutical Industry to Prevent Counterfeit Drugs. *International Journal of Computer Applications, 180*(25), 8–12. doi:10.5120/ijca2018916579

Hariry, R. E., Barenji, R. V., & Paradkar, A. (2021). *From Industry 4.0 to Pharma 4.0*. Academic Press.

Huang, K., Wang, K., Lee, P., & Yeung, A. C. (2023). The Impact of Industry 4.0 on Supply Chain Capability and Supply Chain Resilience: A Dynamic Resource-Based View. *International Journal of Production Economics, 262*, 108913. doi:10.1016/j.ijpe.2023.108913

Javaid, M., Haleem, A., Singh, R. P., Khan, S., & Suman, R. (2021). Blockchain technology applications for Industry 4.0: A literature-based review. *Blockchain: Research and Applications.*

Javaid, M., Haleem, A., Singh, R. P., Suman, R., & Gonzalez, E. S. (2022). Understanding the adoption of Industry 4.0 technologies in improving environmental sustainability. *Sustainable Operations and Computers*, 203-217.

Khan, M., Hussain, M., & Saber, H. M. (2016). Information sharing in a sustainable supply chain. *International Journal of Production Economics, 181*, 208–214. doi:10.1016/j.ijpe.2016.04.010

Khan, M. I. (2024). Impact of Blockchain Technology on Transparency and Trust in Programmatic Advertising Supply Chain. In M. R. Khan, N. R. Khan, & A. M. Ghouri (Eds.), Achieving Secure and Transparent Supply Chains With Blockchain Technology (pp. 57-69). IGI Global. doi:10.4018/979-8-3693-0482-2.ch004

Khan, M. R., Ali, A., & Rind, A. A. (2024). Blockchain Technology and Supply Chain Sustainability: A View From UNSDG Perspective. In Achieving Secure and Transparent Supply Chains With Blockchain Technology (pp. 1-17). IGI Global. doi:10.4018/979-8-3693-0482-2.ch001

Khan, M. R., Khan, M. R., & Nallaluthan, K. (2023). Blockchain Supply Chain Management and Supply Chain Sustainability. In *Blockchain Driven Supply Chain Management: A Multi- dimensional Perspective* (pp. 155–180). Springer Nature Singapore. doi:10.1007/978-981-99-0699-4_10

Khan, M. R., Khan, N. R., Tufail, M., & Ali, L. (2023). A Path Towards A Greener Future Fostering Green Supply Chain, Green Marketing, And Environmental Sustainability. *LogForum, 19* (1).

Khan, M. R., & Manzoor, A. (2021). Application and Impact of New Technologies in the Supply Chain Management During COVID-19 Pandemic: A Systematic Literature Review. *International Journal of Economics and Business Administration.*

Khan, N., Haq, M. A., Ghouri, A. M., Raziq, A., & Moiz, S. M. (2017). Adaptation of RFID Technology in Business Supply Chain Success: Empirical Findings from a Developing Country Logistic Industry. *Quality Management.*

Khan, N. R., Khan, M. R., & Ghouri, A. M. (2024). Industry 4.0 on the Way to Companies Performance. In Quality Management, Value Creation, and the Digital Economy (pp. 99- 120). Routledge.

Kilpatrick, J., Barter, L., Alexander, C., Brown, J., Calderon, R., & Carruthers, R. (2020). *Managing supply chain risk and disruption.* Deloitte.

Lakner, Z., Kiss, A., Popp, J., Zeman, Z., Mate, D., & Olah, J. (2019). From Basic Research to Competitiveness: An Econometric Analysis of the Global Pharmaceutical Sector. *Sustainability (Basel), 11*(11), 3125. doi:10.3390/su11113125

Ma, J. Y., Shi, L., & Kang, T. W. (2022). The Effect of Digital Transformation on the Pharmaceutical Sustainable Supply Chain Performance: The Mediating Role of Information Sharing and Traceability Using Structural Equation Modeling. *Sustainability (Basel), 15*(1), 649. doi:10.3390/su15010649

Malheiro, V., Duarte, J., Veiga, F., & Melo, F. M. (2023). Exploiting Pharma 4.0 Technologies in the Non-BiologicalComplex Drugs Manufacturing: Innovations and Implications. *Pharmaceutics, 15*(11), 2545. doi:10.3390/pharmaceutics15112545 PMID:38004525

Mobarak, M. H., Islam, M. A., Hossain, N., Al Mahmud, M. Z., Rayhan, M. T., & Nishi, N. J. (2023). *Recent advances of additive manufacturing in implant fabrication A review*. Applied Surface Science Advances. doi:10.1016/j.apsadv.2023.100462

Mukhlas, A., Talip, B., Mustapha, J. C., & Ismail, S. (2022). Industry 4.0 (IR 4.0) for Pharmaceutical Industry: An Exploratory Review. *International Visualization, Informatics and Technology Conference (IVIT.*

Munirathinam, S. (2020). Industry 4.0: Industrial Internet of Things (IIOT). In The Digital Twin Paradigm for Smarter Systems and Environments: The Industry Use Cases (pp. 129-164). Academic Press.

Musamih, A., Salah, K., Jayaraman, R., Arshad, J., Debe, M., & Al Hammad, Y. (2016). A Blockchain-based Approach for Drug Traceability in Healthcare Supply Chain. *IEEE Access : Practical Innovations, Open Solutions*.

Naseem, M. H., & Yang, J. (2021). Role of Industry 4.0 in Supply Chains Sustainability:A Systematic Literature Review. *Sustainability (Basel), 13*(17), 9544. doi:10.3390/su13179544

News, I. (2021). *Novartis' Industry 4.0 Tech Transforms Cell Therapy Manufacturing*. LogiPharma.

Okoli, C. (2015). A Guide to Conducting a Standalone Systematic Literature Review. *Communications of the Association for Information Systems, 37*. Advance online publication. doi:10.17705/1CAIS.03743

Peake, B., Braund, R., Tremblay, L., & Tong, A. (2016). Impact of pharmaceuticals on the environment. *The Life-Cycle of Pharmaceuticals in the Environment.*

Pelaez, R. M., Brust, A. O., Rivera, S., Felix, V., Ostos, R., & Brito, H. (2023). Role of Digital Transformation for Achieving Sustainability: Mediated Role of Stakeholders, Key Capabilities, and Technology. *Sustainability*, 1–27.

Puhlmann, N., Vidaurre, R., & Kummerer, K. (2024). Designing greener active pharmaceutical ingredients: Insights from pharmaceutical industry into drug discovery and development. *European Journal of Pharmaceutical Sciences, 192*, 106614. doi:10.1016/j.ejps.2023.106614 PMID:37858896

Rad, F. F., Oghazi, P., Palmie, M., Chirumalla, K., Pashkevich, N., Patel, P. C., & Sattari, S. (2022). Industry 4.0 and supply chain performance: A systematic literature review of the benefits, challenges, and critical success factors of 11 core technologies. *Industrial Marketing Management, 105*, 268–293. doi:10.1016/j.indmarman.2022.06.009

Raman, R., Sreenivasan, A., Ma, S., Patwardhan, A., & Nedungadi, P. (2023). Green Supply Chain Management Research Trends and Linkages to UN Sustainable Development Goals. *Sustainability (Basel), 15*(22), 15848. doi:10.3390/su152215848

Ravi, D., Ramachandran, S., Vignesh, R., Falmari, V. R., & Brindha, M. (2022). *Privacy preserving transparent supply chain management through Hyperledger Fabric*. Academic Press.

Ray, P. P., Dash, D., De, D., Salah, K., & Kumar, N. (2020). Blockchain for IoT-Based Healthcare: Background, Consensus, Platforms, and Use Cases. *IEEE Systems Journal*.

Rousseau, D., Manning, J., & Denyer, D. (2008). Evidence in Management and Organizational Science Assembling the Field's Full Weight of Scientific Knowledge Through Syntheses. *The Academy of Management Annals*, *2*(1), 475–515. doi:10.5465/19416520802211651

Sahoo, S., Kumar, S., Sivarajah, U., Lim, W. M., Westland, J., & Kumar, A. (2022). Blockchain for sustainable supply chain management:trends and ways forward. *Electronic Commerce Research*. Advance online publication. doi:10.1007/s10660-022-09569-1

Sharma, D., Pate, P., & Shah, M. (2023). A comprehensive study on Industry 4.0 in the pharmaceutical industry for sustainable development. *Environmental Science and Pollution Research International*, *30*(39), 90088–90098. doi:10.1007/s11356-023-26856-y PMID:37129827

Shi, Z., Xie, Y., Xue, W., Chen, Y., Fu, L., & Xu, X. (2020). Smart factory in Industry 4.0. *Systems Research and Behavioral Science*, *37*(4), 607–617. doi:10.1002/sres.2704

Steinwandter, V., Borchert, D., & Herwing, C. (2019). Data science tools and applications on the way to Pharma 4.0. *Drug Discovery Today*, *24*(9), 1795–1805. doi:10.1016/j.drudis.2019.06.005 PMID:31207205

*The History Of Pharmaceutical Manufacturing: Industry 1.0 To Pharma 4.0*2017LWS 40 Years.

*The Importance of Environmental Awareness When Running a Business*2019Maryville University.

Tortorella, G. L., Prashar, A., Antony, J., Fogliatto, F. S., Gonzalez, V., & Filho, M. G. (2023). Industry 4.0 adoption for healthcare supply chain performance during COVID-19 pandemic in Brazil and India: the mediating role of resilience abilities development. *Operations Management Research*.

Tracxn. (2023). *Blockchain in Healthcare Startups in India*. Author.

Tranfield, D., Denyer, D., & Smart, P. (2003). Towards a Methodology for Developing Evidence-Informed Management Knowledge by Means of Systematic Review. *British Journal of Management*, *14*(3), 207–222. doi:10.1111/1467-8551.00375

Ugvekar, N., Kamath K, K., Subramanyam, E., & Shabaraya, A. (2021). A Review on Change Management System in Pharmaceutical Industry. *International Journal of Drug Regulatory Affairs*.

Ventura, M., & Coeli, C. M. (2018). *Beyond privacy: the right to health information, personal data protection, and governance*. Sci ELO Brazil.

White, C. M. (2022). *Dangerous Counterfeit Drugs are Putting Millions at Risk, a New Study Says*. UConn Today.

Williams, L. (2014). *The Real Impact of Counterfeit Medications*. US Phamacist.

Xia, J., Li, H., & He, Z. (2023). The Effect of Blockchain Technology on Supply Chain Collaboration: A Case Study of Lenovo. *Systems*, *11*(6), 1–25. doi:10.3390/systems11060299

Yaqoob, I., Salah, K., Jayaraman, R., & Al-Hammad, Y. (2021). Blockchain for healthcare data management: Opportunities,challenges, and future recommendations. *Neural Computing & Applications*.

Zakari, N., Al-Razgan, M., Alsaadi, A., Alshareef, H., Al saigh, H., Alashaikh, L., Alharbi, M., Alomar, R., & Alotaibi, S. (2022). Blockchain technology in the pharmaceutical industry: A systematic review. *PeerJ. Computer Science*, *8*, 1–26. doi:10.7717/peerj-cs.840 PMID:35634106

Zamiela, C., Ibne Hossain, N., & Jaradat, R. (2022). Enablers of resilience in the healthcare supply chain: A case study of U.S healthcare industry during COVID-19 pandemic. *Research in Transportation Economics*, *93*, 101174. doi:10.1016/j.retrec.2021.101174

Zozaya, N., Alcala, B., & Galindo, J. (2019). *The offset effect of pharmaceutical innovation: A review study*. Global & Regional Health Technology Assesment.

Chapter 13
Industry 4.0:
Future Trends and Research Directions

Siva Raja Sindiramutty
Taylor's University, Malaysia

NZ Jhanjhi
https://orcid.org/0000-0001-8116-4733
Taylor's University, Malaysia

Chong Eng Tan
https://orcid.org/0000-0002-3990-3501
Universiti Malaysia Sarawak, Malaysia

Sei Ping Lau
Universiti Malaysia Sarawak, Malaysia

Lalitha Muniandy
Tunku Abdul Rahman University of Management and Technology, Malaysia

Abdalla Hassan Gharib
Zanzibar University, Tanzania

Humaira Ashraf
https://orcid.org/0000-0001-5067-3172
Taylor's University, Malaysia

Raja Kumar Murugesan
https://orcid.org/0000-0001-9500-1361
Taylor's University, Malaysia

ABSTRACT

The advent of Industry 4.0, characterized by the integration of digital technologies into industrial processes, has ushered in a transformative era for manufacturing and beyond. This chapter delves into the future trends and research directions that will shape the landscape of Industry 4.0 in the coming years. One prominent trend is the continued proliferation of the internet of things (IoT) and its convergence with artificial intelligence (AI). As IoT devices become more interconnected and intelligent, they will enable real-time data analysis, predictive maintenance, and adaptive manufacturing, fostering increased efficiency and cost-effectiveness across industries. Moreover, the rise of edge computing is set to redefine data processing and analytics. The deployment of powerful computing resources closer to the data source promises reduced latency and enhanced decision-making capabilities, particularly critical in applications like autonomous manufacturing and remote robotics.

DOI: 10.4018/979-8-3693-1363-3.ch013

1. INTRODUCTION TO INDUSTRY 4.0

1.1 Definition and Evolution of Industry 4.0

Industry 4.0, often referred to as the fourth industrial revolution, represents a revolutionary idea signifying the infusion of digital technologies into various facets of manufacturing and production processes. This encompasses a broad spectrum of technological advancements, including the IoT, AI, big data analytics, cloud computing, and cyber-physical systems, among others. The term "Industry 4.0" was initially introduced in 2011 through the German government's High-Tech Strategy initiative to describe the ongoing revolution in manufacturing marked by the convergence of digital, physical, and biological systems. The evolution of Industry 4.0 has been shaped by several pivotal factors. Firstly, the rapid advancement of technology has played a central role in propelling the development of Industry 4.0. The proliferation of interconnected devices and sensors, combined with the exponential growth of computing power, has enabled the real-time collection and analysis of vast amounts of data. This, in turn, has paved the way for predictive maintenance, optimized production processes, and enhanced decision-making within manufacturing environments (Psarommatis et al., 2023).

Secondly, the growing demand for personalized and customized products has led to the emergence of adaptable and agile manufacturing systems. Industry 4.0 facilitates the implementation of smart factories where machines and processes can be swiftly reconfigured to accommodate varying production requirements (Ding et al., 2021). Furthermore, the concept of Industry 4.0 promotes the creation of value networks rather than traditional linear supply chains. This implies that stakeholders within the manufacturing ecosystem collaborate closely through digital platforms, sharing information and resources to enhance efficiency and foster innovation. Additionally, the integration of AI and Machine Learning (ML) algorithms has empowered machines with learning capabilities, augmenting their capacity to adapt to dynamic conditions and make autonomous decisions (Makanda et al., 2023). This is particularly evident in the context of autonomous robots and self-driving vehicles within smart manufacturing environments. The implications of Industry 4.0 are profound. Manufacturers can achieve heightened levels of efficiency, quality, and sustainability through predictive analytics that optimize energy consumption and resource allocation (Sajjad et al., 2023). Furthermore, the concept of "servitization" comes to the forefront as products transform into services, facilitated by continuous monitoring of product performance and condition (Presti et al., 2023).

In conclusion, Industry 4.0 embodies a transformative shift in the manufacturing landscape, characterized by the integration of digital technologies into various facets of production processes. The evolution of Industry 4.0 has been propelled by technological advancements, the demand for customization, the need for flexibility, and the rise of value networks. The integration of AI, big data, and IoT technologies has paved the way for smart factories and autonomous decision-making. The implications of Industry 4.0 are far-reaching, enabling improved efficiency, quality, sustainability, and a reshaping of traditional business models. Figure 1.0 shows evolution of Industry 4.0

Figure 1. Evolution of industry

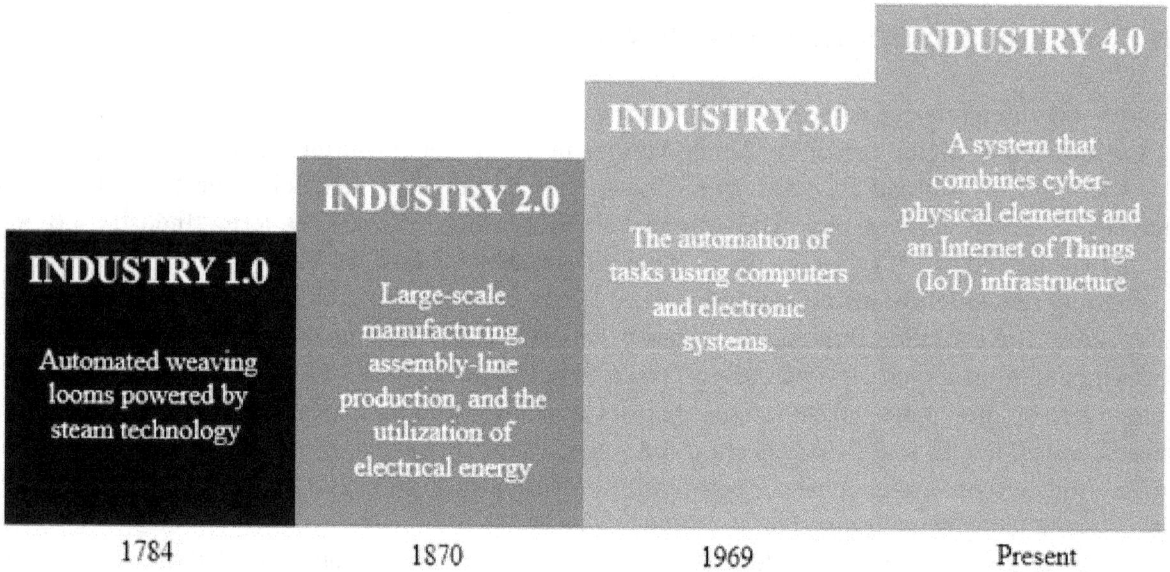

1.2 Key Concepts and Pillars of Industry 4.0

1. **Cyber-Physical Systems (CPS)**: At the heart of Industry 4.0 are Cyber-Physical Systems (CPS). CPS refers to the integration of physical processes with digital technologies. These systems combine sensors, actuators, and communication mechanisms with computational elements to create smart, interconnected entities. CPS enable real-time monitoring, control, and optimization of physical processes, blurring the lines between the physical and digital worlds.
2. **IoT**: IoT is a critical component of Industry 4.0, encompassing the vast network of interconnected devices and sensors. These devices collect and transmit data, enabling seamless communication between machines, products, and systems. IoT facilitates the creation of a "smart" environment where data-driven decision-making and automation become possible.
3. **Big Data and Analytics**: The proliferation of data in Industry 4.0 is immense. Big Data and advanced analytics play a crucial role in making sense of this data. Through sophisticated algorithms and ML, manufacturers can extract valuable insights from vast datasets, leading to improved decision-making, predictive maintenance, and process optimization.
4. **AI and ML**: AI and ML algorithms empower machines and systems to learn from data, adapt to changing conditions, and make autonomous decisions. In Industry 4.0, AI is used for predictive maintenance, quality control, and even autonomous decision-making in manufacturing processes.
5. **Additive Manufacturing (3D Printing)**: Additive Manufacturing, often referred to as 3D printing, is a disruptive technology in Industry 4.0. It allows for the creation of complex, customized products layer by layer, reducing waste and enabling rapid prototyping and production.
6. **Cloud and Edge Computing**: Cloud computing and edge computing are integral to Industry 4.0's IT infrastructure. Cloud resources offer scalable storage and processing capabilities, while edge computing enables real-time data analysis and decision-making at the source, reducing latency and enhancing efficiency.

7. **Robotics and Automation**: Robotics and automation have advanced significantly in Industry 4.0. Collaborative robots (cobots) work alongside humans, performing repetitive tasks with precision and consistency. Automation enhances productivity and quality while reducing the risk of human error.
8. **Connectivity and Interoperability**: Industry 4.0 relies on seamless connectivity between devices, systems, and stakeholders. Interoperability ensures that different machines and technologies can communicate effectively, enabling the flow of information across the entire value chain.

1.3 Importance and Impact of Industry 4.0 on Various Sectors

Industry 4.0 represents a technological revolution that integrates cutting-edge digital technologies into traditional industries. This transformation encompasses a wide array of technologies, including the IoT, AI, big data analytics, robotics, and additive manufacturing. Its impact on various sectors cannot be understated, driving improvements in efficiency, innovation, and competitiveness. This section explores the significance and consequences of Industry 4.0 across diverse industries.

The manufacturing sector has undergone significant changes as a result of Industry 4.0. Smart factories, equipped with IoT-enabled sensors, enable real-time monitoring of equipment and processes, reducing downtime and boosting productivity (Behera et al., 2023). This has resulted in more streamlined production lines and higher-quality products. Furthermore, the integration of AI and ML has enabled predictive maintenance, reducing maintenance costs and optimising resource utilization (Rao et al., 2023). In the healthcare sector, Industry 4.0 has revolutionized patient care. Wearable devices and IoT-enabled medical equipment provide real-time health data, enabling remote patient monitoring and early disease detection (Khan et al., 2023). AI-driven diagnostic tools enhance accuracy in medical imaging and interpretation (Rea et al., 2023), ultimately leading to more timely and precise treatments. The transportation sector has embraced Industry 4.0 to enhance efficiency and safety. Autonomous vehicles, guided by AI algorithms and sensor technologies, are being developed to reduce accidents and optimize traffic flow (Mhlanga, 2023). Additionally, smart logistics systems, powered by IoT devices, improve supply chain visibility, reducing delays and enhancing resource management (Shamsuddoha et al., 2023). Industry 4.0 has transformed agriculture into a realm of “smart farming.” Sensors, drones, and AI-driven data analytics are utilized to monitor soil conditions, crop health, and weather patterns, optimizing irrigation and fertilization processes (Kunhare et al., 2023). This not only increases crop yields but also promotes sustainable farming practices. In the energy sector, Industry 4.0 plays a pivotal role in smart grid management. IoT devices enable real-time monitoring of energy consumption and distribution, facilitating load balancing and reducing energy wastage (Sankarananth et al., 2023). AI algorithms predict energy demand patterns, aiding in efficient energy generation and distribution.

Industry 4.0 has ushered in a transformative wave across various sectors, reshaping operations, processes, and business models. The manufacturing sector benefits from heightened efficiency and improved quality, while healthcare leverages real-time data for enhanced patient care. Transportation experiences increased safety and smarter logistics, and agriculture embraces precision farming practices. The energy sector achieves smarter grid management and optimized energy utilization. As Industry 4.0 continues to evolve, its impact on these sectors will deepen, ushering in an era of increased innovation, sustainability, and competitiveness.

1.4 Overview of Current State and Adoption of Industry 4.0 Technologies

The emergence of Industry 4.0 has brought about substantial progress in automation, data exchange, and intelligent manufacturing. As Industry 4.0 technologies gain widespread acceptance, various sectors are undergoing profound transformations in their processes and productivity. This section offers an overview of the present status of Industry 4.0 technologies and their integration across different industries.

Industry 4.0 is characterized by the fusion of physical and digital systems. Advanced automation tools like robotics and AI are extensively employed to boost efficiency and precision in manufacturing processes. Smart factories equipped with IoT devices gather real-time data, enabling proactive decision-making and predictive maintenance (O'Connell et al., 2023; Almusaylim & Jhanjhi, 2018). The ubiquity of data is a defining feature of Industry 4.0. Big data analytics empowers organizations to draw valuable insights from extensive datasets, resulting in improved production planning, inventory management, and demand forecasting (CİĞERCİ, 2023). The interconnectivity among machines and systems through the Industrial Internet of Things (IIoT) facilitates seamless communication and coordination within the production ecosystem (Ghajar & Reich, 2023). The integration of cyber and physical systems serves as the cornerstone of Industry 4.0. These systems allow real-time monitoring, control, and optimization of manufacturing processes (Lampropoulos & Siakas, 2022). Embedded sensors and actuators collect data from the physical world, which is then analyzed and acted upon in the digital realm. Despite the promising potential, the adoption of Industry 4.0 technologies encounters several challenges. A significant obstacle is the initial investment required for infrastructure and workforce training (Deivanayagampillai et al., 2023; Alshammari et al., 2017). Concerns regarding data security and privacy also hinder widespread implementation. Moreover, the transformation of existing processes to align with Industry 4.0 principles demands meticulous planning and effective change management (Rosário & Dias, 2023).

In conclusion, Industry 4.0 technologies are revolutionizing industries by ushering in a new era of intelligent manufacturing, automation, and data-driven decision-making. The integration of cyber-physical systems, data analytics, and connectivity is reshaping traditional business models and operational paradigms. While challenges like investment costs and security concerns persist, the potential benefits are compelling companies to embrace this transformative wave. The impact of Industry 4.0 extends beyond manufacturing, influencing various sectors and promising enhanced efficiency and innovation.

1.5 Scope and Objectives of the Chapter

The chapter on "Industry 4.0: Future Trends and Research Directions" aims to provide a comprehensive exploration of the transformative landscape that Industry 4.0 presents across various sectors. The scope of this chapter encompasses a multidimensional analysis of Industry 4.0, spanning its foundational concepts, enabling technologies, challenges, opportunities, and prospects. The primary objective of this chapter is to equip readers with an in-depth understanding of Industry 4.0's evolution, significance, and impacts on diverse industries. By delving into the core concepts and pillars of Industry 4.0, readers will gain insights into how the fusion of digital technologies with manufacturing processes is reshaping production, supply chains, and workforce dynamics. The chapter will investigate the current state of Industry 4.0 adoption, shedding light on real-world implementations, while also addressing the hurdles that hinder its full realization. The chapter will further delve into the technological foundations of Industry 4.0, dissecting the pivotal role played by IoT, AI, CPS, data analytics, and more. It will address integration challenges, focusing on connecting legacy systems and ensuring data security in the era of interconnected manufacturing. Additionally, the chapter will explore the implications of Industry 4.0 on supply chain management, workforce dynamics, sustainability, and the circular economy. By highlighting challenges ranging from privacy concerns to regulatory implications, the chapter aims to provide a comprehensive understanding of the hurdles faced in the adoption of Industry 4.0. Lastly, it will delve into futuristic trends, including advancements in quantum computing and ethical considerations, and conclude with a series of illuminating case studies that showcase real-world Industry 4.0 implementations across industries. Overall, the chapter strives to provide readers with a panoramic view of Industry 4.0, equipping them with the knowledge needed to navigate the ever-evolving landscape of smart manufacturing, make informed decisions, and contribute to the ongoing discourse and progress within this transformative domain.

Figure 2. Technology enabling Industry 4.0

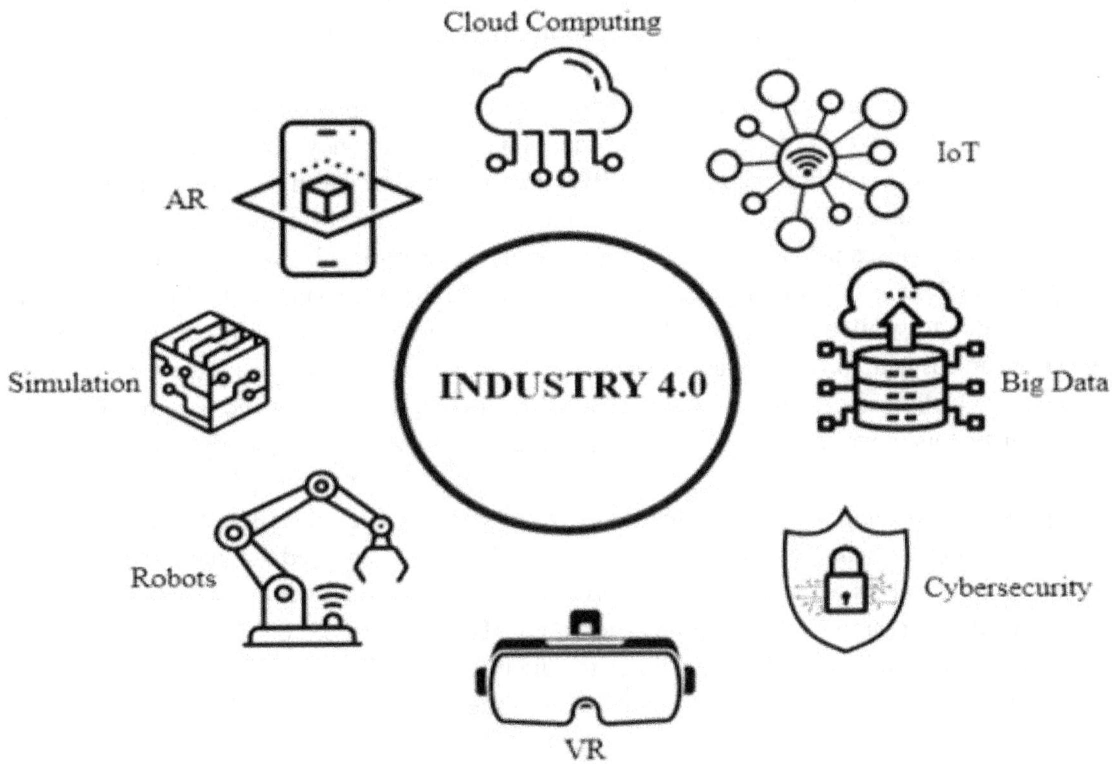

2. ENABLING TECHNOLOGIES IN INDUSTRY 4.0

2.1 IoT and its Role in Industry 4.0

The IoT plays a central role in Industry 4.0, a revolutionary shift that is reshaping the industrial landscape profoundly (Kiradoo, 2023). Essentially, IoT empowers various industries by enabling seamless connectivity and data exchange among numerous devices and systems. This marks the beginning of an era characterized by remarkable efficiency and innovation (Shee, 2023).

One of the most crucial contributions of IoT lies in data acquisition. Sensors and intelligent devices positioned throughout manufacturing facilities, supply chains, and even consumer products now serve as the frontiers of real-time data collection (Shee, 2023; Aadil et al., 2021). These sensors serve as the "eyes and ears" of the modern industrial ecosystem, tirelessly collecting data from every corner of operations. This data, a valuable source of insights, is then efficiently transmitted through networks, forming the lifeblood of real-time monitoring and control systems (Kiradoo, 2023). The ability to access up-to-the-minute information is particularly transformative for industries where even a slight delay could result in substantial losses. Automation, another fundamental aspect of Industry 4.0, reaches its peak through IoT (Attaran, 2021). For instance, smart manufacturing systems have harnessed IoT to coordinate production lines with unprecedented precision, reducing downtime and enhancing overall productivity (Soori et al., 2023). These systems have evolved into self-regulating entities where machines, equipped with IoT sensors, can proactively detect faults and trigger maintenance requests, preventing costly breakdowns and production interruptions. Figure 2 shows technology enabling the Industry 4.0 .

Predictive maintenance, driven by IoT, represents a significant game-changer (Ullah et al., 2023). The combination of historical and real-time data empowers machines to predict their maintenance requirements. This shift minimizes unexpected downtime, enhances efficiency, and extends the operational life of machinery, offering a highly compelling ROI. In the complex realm of supply chains, IoT serves as a guardian of efficiency (Dutta et al., 2022; Ponnusamy et al., 2021). Sensors attached to shipping containers and warehouses provide real-time tracking of inventory levels and conditions, ensuring the safe and punctual delivery of products (Jarašūnienė et al., 2023; Humayun et al., 2022). This not only reduces losses due to spoilage or damage but also improves the overall reliability of the supply chain. IoT also excels in ensuring product quality (Hu et al., 2023). By continuously monitoring and analyzing data at every production stage, sensors can swiftly detect deviations from desired parameters, leading to real-time adjustments, lower defect rates, higher product quality, and consequently, increased customer satisfaction.

In the pursuit of sustainability, the influence of IoT is strongly felt (Ehsanifar et al., 2023; Jabeen et al., 2023). For instance, the integration of IoT in smart buildings has enabled the intelligent management of resources. This involves adjusting lighting and temperature based on occupancy and environmental conditions, resulting in significant energy conservation (Heidary et al., 2023). However, the true potential of IoT goes beyond data collection; it lies in data utilization. The vast amounts of generated data are effectively harnessed through advanced analytics (Abughazala & Muccini, 2023). This data-driven decision-making greatly enhances business intelligence and strategic planning, providing organizations with a competitive advantage in today's data-centric world. Nevertheless, in this age of hyperconnectivity, safeguarding sensitive data is of utmost importance (Al-Sherideh et al., 2023; Anandan et al., 2022). Robust cybersecurity measures are essential to protect against potential breaches and threats. IoT's transformative impact extends not only to machines but also to the workforce. Collaborative robots, known as "cobots," working alongside human operators, have become a reality (Balanzar Almazan, 2023; Humayun et al., 2020). This collaboration enhances productivity by automating repetitive and physically demanding tasks, allowing human workers to concentrate on tasks requiring creativity and problem-solving skills. As the IoT landscape continues to evolve, its role in Industry 4.0 will become increasingly prominent. Technologies such as 5G are poised to offer faster and more reliable connectivity, further amplifying IoT's capabilities (El-Haggar et al., 2023; Seong et al., 2021). Additionally, the synergy between IoT

AI and ML will make IoT systems more intelligent. They will possess the ability to make autonomous decisions, optimize operations, and adapt dynamically to changing conditions.

In summary, the IoT serves as the cornerstone of Industry 4.0, steering digital transformation across various industries. Its prowess in connecting, collecting, and analyzing data is ushering in a new era characterized by efficiency, quality, and sustainability. While challenges like cybersecurity must be addressed proactively, the lasting impact of IoT on the future of the industry is undeniable. Embracing IoT is not just a choice but a necessity for organizations aiming to remain competitive and relevant in today's modern industrial landscape.

2.2 Cyber-Physical Systems (CPS) and Their Integration in Manufacturing

In recent years, there has been a profound transformation in the manufacturing industry, primarily driven by the incorporation of CPS into production processes. This integration has been instrumental in ushering in the era of Industry 4.0, a new industrial revolution marked by the convergence of digital technologies, automation, and data-driven decision-making. In this section, we delve into the concept of CPS and how its integration is reshaping manufacturing within the context of Industry 4.0, with a particular emphasis on its implications for efficiency, productivity, and competitiveness.

CPS represent intelligent systems that seamlessly bridge the physical and virtual realms, facilitating seamless communication among machinery, products, and humans (Hamzah et al., 2023). This integration is made possible through the IoT, wherein physical devices are equipped with sensors, actuators, and connectivity to exchange data in real time. These systems are revolutionizing manufacturing by providing deeper insights into the production process, enabling predictive maintenance, and elevating overall efficiency (Keung et al., 2023). One of the primary advantages of CPS integration in manufacturing is the enhancement of operational efficiency. Smart factories equipped with CPS can continuously monitor and optimize production processes. Real-time data from sensors on machines and products are analyzed to detect bottlenecks and inefficiencies, allowing for swift adjustments (Liu et al., 2023; Ali et al., 2022). This results in reduced downtime and waste, leading to significant cost savings. Furthermore, CPS-enabled manufacturing facilities exhibit high adaptability. They can swiftly respond to shifts in market demands and efficiently customize products (Makanda et al., 2023). For example, in the automotive sector, CPS integration permits the production of various car models on the same assembly line with minimal reconfiguration time. Such flexibility is paramount in today's dynamic market landscape. CPS also revolutionised maintenance practices. Predictive maintenance, made feasible through continuous data monitoring, aids in the early identification of potential equipment failures (Thanigaivelan et al., 2023). This reduces downtime and prevents expensive breakdowns, ultimately enhancing overall equipment effectiveness (OEE) (Jamil et al., 2023). Additionally, remote monitoring and diagnostics become possible, diminishing the need for on-site technicians and further reducing operational expenses. Furthermore, CPS integration elevates product quality through real-time tracking and traceability. Manufacturers can oversee the entire production process, ensuring that products meet rigorous quality standards (Xiao et al., 2023). This not only enhances customer satisfaction but also aids in compliance with industry regulations and standards.

In conclusion, the integration of Cyber-Physical Systems into manufacturing, within the framework of Industry 4.0, represents a transformative shift that offers a multitude of advantages. These systems enhance operational efficiency, adaptability, and product quality, all while enabling predictive maintenance. However, manufacturers must remain vigilant regarding cybersecurity concerns as they embrace this technological revolution. With its potential to reshape manufacturing, CPS integration undeniably stands as a pivotal driver of the success of Industry 4.0.

2.3 Big Data and Analytics for Decision-Making in Industry 4.0

Industry 4.0 heavily relies on the collection of data through an array of sensors and IoT devices (Zaman et al., 2023; Khan et al., 2022). These sensors actively monitor machinery, processes, and even employee activities, generating an extensive volume of data. This real-time data collection empowers proactive maintenance practices, ensuring that machinery receives service only when necessary, thus reducing downtime and associated costs.

Predictive maintenance made possible through the application of big data and analytics, has emerged as a critical facet of Industry 4.0 (Bach et al., 2023). By utilizing historical and real-time data, algorithms predict when equipment is likely to fail. Companies that implement predictive maintenance can avert costly breakdowns and extend the lifespan of their machinery. The imperative of ensuring product quality is paramount in manufacturing. Big data analytics contribute significantly to quality control by scrutinizing data from sensors and cameras to promptly identify defects or anomalies (Himeur et al., 2022). This proactive approach aids in reducing defective products, heightening customer satisfaction, and minimizing waste. Efficient inventory management is a cornerstone of cost reduction and streamlined operations. Big data analytics facilitate demand forecasting (Bag et al., 2021), enabling companies to maintain optimal stock levels. This minimizes holding costs and guards against stockouts, ultimately elevating supply chain performance. Industry 4.0 extends its transformative influence beyond the factory floor. It revolutionizes supply chain management by affording real-time visibility into the movement of goods (M Kuruvilla et al., 2023). This visibility translates into more accurate delivery estimates, reduced lead times, and an overall enhancement in supply chain efficiency. The capacity to customize products according to individual customer preferences confers a competitive edge. Big data and analytics enable companies to amass data on customer behaviour (Acciarini et al., 2023), which can be harnessed to tailor products and services. This, in turn, elevates customer satisfaction and fosters loyalty. Sustainability has emerged as a pressing concern in manufacturing. Big data analytics play a pivotal role in monitoring energy consumption (Mhlanga, 2023), pinpointing areas where energy is squandered, and suggesting optimization measures. This not only reduces costs but also aligns with environmental objectives.

In a dynamic manufacturing environment, effective risk management is crucial. Big data analytics can scrutinize data from diverse sources to identify potential risks and vulnerabilities in real time. This proactive approach empowers companies to take swift corrective actions. The sheer volume of data in Industry 4.0 can be overwhelming, but analytics tools can distil this data into actionable insights (Klimczak & Petersen, 2023). Managers can make informed decisions based on data-driven recommendations, leading to improved overall decision-making. Ultimately, the adoption of big data and analytics in Industry 4.0 confers a substantial competitive advantage. Companies that harness the power of data-driven decision-making are better equipped to adapt to changing market conditions and maintain a competitive edge (Ramdurai, 2020).

In conclusion, big data and analytics are pivotal elements of Industry 4.0, significantly enhancing various aspects of manufacturing and decision-making. The capacity to collect, analyze, and act upon data in real time transforms traditional industries into more efficient, competitive, and sustainable entities. As we continue to progress in the era of Industry 4.0, the integration of big data and analytics will undoubtedly remain a cornerstone of success for organizations worldwide.

Figure 3. IIoT enabled in Industry 4.0

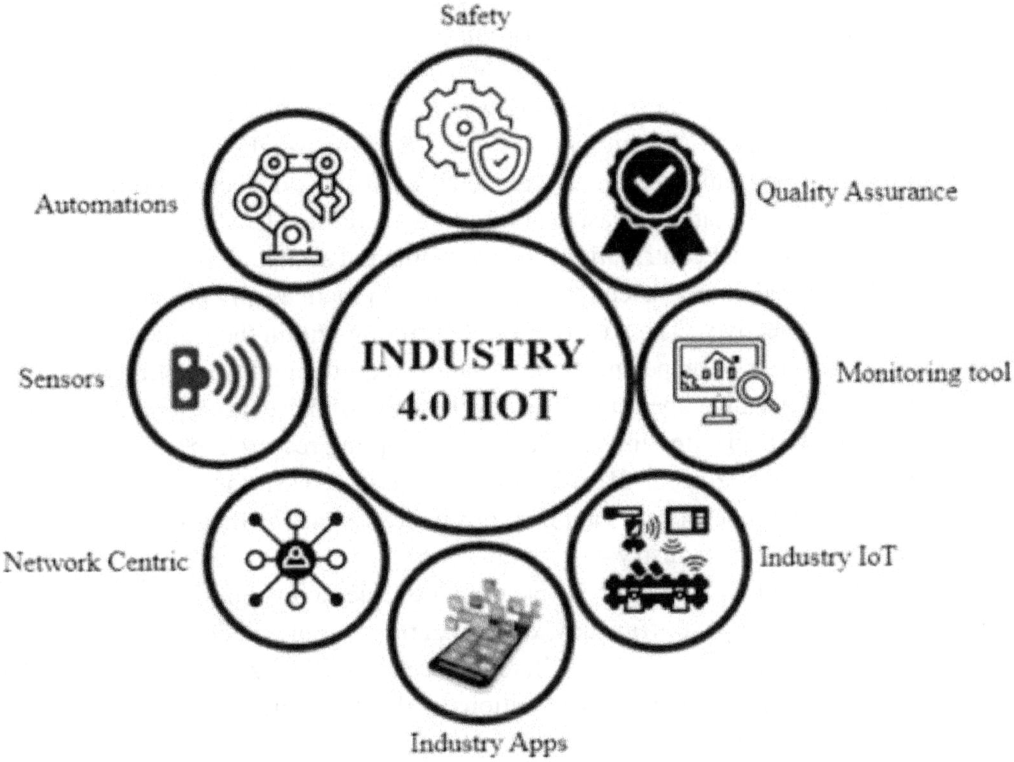

2.4 Additive Manufacturing (3D Printing) and Its Impact on Production

The rise of Industry 4.0 has brought about a profound transformation in the manufacturing sector, introducing cutting-edge technologies that elevate productivity and effectiveness. Within this realm, Additive Manufacturing, commonly referred to as 3D printing, has emerged as a game-changing innovation. 3D printing has revolutionized the production process by substantially curbing expenses and reducing material wastage. In contrast to conventional subtractive manufacturing methods like milling and cutting, which entail the removal of material from a solid block, 3D printing constructs items layer by layer, utilizing only the precise amount of material required. This results in significant cost savings and environmental advantages (Wang et al., 2023; Cabibihan et al., 2023). Industry 4.0 places a strong emphasis on customer-centric manufacturing, a goal that 3D printing adeptly facilitates. This technology enables swift and cost-effective customization of products to meet individual customer requirements (Xu & Qin, 2023). This personalization capability provides businesses with a competitive edge by delivering unique products tailored to specific customer preferences. 3D printing holds the potential to transform supply chains (Shahpasand et al., 2023) by allowing on-site or near-site production, diminishing the dependence on extensive warehousing and long-distance transportation. This leads to substantial cost reductions and enhanced supply chain adaptability, aligning with the just-in-time manufacturing principles of Industry 4.0.

One of the most remarkable advantages of 3D printing is its exceptional speed (Zhu et al., 2023). Complex components that previously required weeks or even months to manufacture can now be produced in a matter of hours. This rapid production capability empowers companies to promptly respond to market demands, resulting in shorter time-to-market and heightened agility. 3D printing grants manufacturers the ability to craft intricate and lightweight structures (Awad & Basit, 2023). This feature is especially valuable in industries such as aerospace and automotive, where reducing weight while maintaining structural integrity is of paramount importance. Complex geometries can also enhance product performance and functionality. The reduction in material wastage and the potential for localized production associated with 3D printing make substantial contributions to environmental sustainability (Oyinlola et al., 2023). In an era increasingly focused on eco-friendly manufacturing practices, 3D printing aligns seamlessly with these sustainability objectives. The adoption of 3D printing within the framework of Industry 4.0 necessitates a shift in workforce competencies. Companies require employees skilled in areas such as 3D modelling, design, and machine operation. The development of these proficiencies is pivotal to fully harnessing the potential of 3D printing in manufacturing. Ongoing research into novel printing materials continues to expand the horizons of 3D printing (Dod et al., 2023). Innovations in biocompatible materials, for instance, have unlocked fresh applications in healthcare, further broadening the impact of 3D printing within the context of Industry 4.0.

In summary, Additive Manufacturing, or 3D printing, occupies a pivotal role in the Industry 4.0 era, offering advantages in terms of cost-efficiency, customization, supply chain optimization, speed, and sustainability. However, addressing workforce skill requirements, ensuring quality control, and managing intellectual property concerns are critical considerations as this transformative technology continues to shape the future of manufacturing.

2.5 AI and ML in Smart Factories

The integration of AI and ML into the manufacturing sector, commonly known as Smart Factories Industry 4.0, has brought about a profound transformation in the operational dynamics of factories. Industry 4.0 represents the fourth industrial revolution, characterized by the convergence of digital, physical, and biological technologies. This section delves into the significant influence of AI and ML within the context of smart factories, drawing insights from various scholarly sources.

AI and ML serve as the linchpin of enhanced automation in smart factories. Machines equipped with AI can make real-time decisions, optimizing production lines and resource allocation (Mo et al., 2023). For instance, robots can adapt their movements based on data from sensors, ensuring precision and efficiency in manufacturing processes. This heightened level of automation leads to increased productivity and more efficient utilization of resources. Predictive maintenance emerges as a game-changing advancement for smart factories. By continually monitoring machine data, AI algorithms can anticipate when equipment is likely to experience failure (Dave & Patel, 2023). This allows for scheduled maintenance, preempting costly breakdowns and production stoppages. The cost savings from predictive maintenance can be substantial, as it eliminates the need for routine maintenance based on fixed schedules. AI-driven quality control systems leverage computer vision and data analytics to swiftly identify defects and anomalies in real time (Mohammad, 2023; Sankar et al., 2020). Cameras and sensors meticulously scan products for imperfections, triggering immediate corrective actions for any deviations from the desired standards. This results in higher-quality products and reduces waste and rework, ultimately enhancing customer satisfaction. Smart factories are not isolated entities; they are intricately connected with supply chains. AI and ML play pivotal roles in optimizing these supply chains by forecasting demand, managing inventory levels, and optimizing logistics routes (SOHRABI, 2023; Jazdi, 2014). This ensures that factories receive the necessary materials precisely when needed, thereby reducing inventory costs and enhancing overall operational efficiency.

AI and ML empower smart factories to efficiently produce customized products. By scrutinizing customer data and preferences, production processes can be customized to create individualized products on a large scale. This personalization significantly elevates customer satisfaction, as consumers receive products tailored to their specific requirements. Rather than replacing human workers, AI and ML complement the workforce by handling repetitive and time-consuming tasks (Appio et al., 2023; Ponnusamy et al., 2022). Robots and automation take care of routine activities, freeing human workers to concentrate on tasks that necessitate creativity, problem-solving, and decision-making. This not only enhances job satisfaction but also cultivates a more skilled workforce. AI and ML also contribute significantly to sustainability initiatives within smart factories (Othman & Yang, 2023). These technologies optimize energy consumption by adjusting machine operations in real time based on demand and energy availability. Furthermore, they minimize resource wastage by fine-tuning production processes. This alignment with global sustainability objectives reduces the environmental footprint of manufacturing.

2.6 Cloud Computing and Edge Computing in Industry 4.0

Cloud computing serves as a foundational pillar in Industry 4.0 by providing scalable and on-demand access to computing resources over the Internet. As described by Aminizadeh et al. (2023), cloud computing offers the convenience of shared computing power, storage, and applications, thereby reducing infrastructure costs and improving resource utilization. This aligns with Industry 4.0's goal of interconnected systems that optimize operations. Moreover, cloud-based solutions facilitate data storage and analysis, enabling manufacturers to harness insights for better decision-making (Bella, 2023). This centralized approach, however, comes with potential latency issues, particularly when real-time responsiveness is critical.

To address these latency concerns, edge computing has emerged as a complementary paradigm. Edge computing, according to Lu et al. (2023) involves processing data closer to the data source, at the "edge" of the network. This approach minimizes the round-trip time for data to travel to the cloud and back, resulting in improved response times and reduced network congestion. Edge computing is especially crucial in applications requiring real-time analytics, such as predictive maintenance in manufacturing equipment (Barboni, 2023). By performing computations at the edge, devices can respond instantly to local conditions, enhancing the efficiency and reliability of industrial processes. The synergy between cloud and edge computing is illustrated in various Industry 4.0 use cases. In the words of De P Biase et al. (2023) "Cloud and edge computing form a symbiotic ecosystem." Cloud resources can be leveraged for intensive data analysis, long-term storage, and centralized management of industrial data. Meanwhile, edge devices handle time-sensitive tasks like real-time monitoring, quality control, and safety systems (Shi et al., 2023). This collaborative approach optimizes the advantages of both paradigms, ensuring a balance between computational power, data storage, and low-latency responsiveness.

In conclusion, the integration of cloud computing and edge computing in Industry 4.0 presents a powerful solution to the challenges posed by modern manufacturing processes. Cloud computing provides the scalability and analytical capabilities necessary for informed decision-making, while edge computing offers real-time responsiveness, crucial for time-sensitive applications. By harnessing the strengths of both paradigms, industries can unlock the full potential of Industry 4.0, achieving increased efficiency, reduced downtime, and improved overall productivity.

2.7 Robotics and Automation Advancements for Smart Manufacturing

The emergence of Industry 4.0 marks a significant shift in manufacturing, characterized by the integration of digital technologies, automation, and robotics. This transformation is reshaping the manufacturing landscape, rendering it more streamlined, adaptable, and responsive to market dynamics. Automation and robotics assume a central role in augmenting manufacturing efficiency and productivity (Qiu & Huang, 2023). Automated systems execute repetitive tasks with precision and speed, mitigating human errors and amplifying output. Robots, including collaborative robots or cobots, work in tandem with human operators, further amplifying productivity (R et al., 2023). This synergy between humans and robots optimizes processes, leading to increased production rates. In the realm of smart manufacturing, robotics plays a critical role in maintaining consistent product quality (Hamrol et al., 2023). Robots equipped with advanced sensors and vision systems can scrutinize and identify defects with remarkable accuracy. They also excel in performing intricate tasks like welding, painting, and assembly with precision, ensuring that products adhere to stringent quality standards. Automation and robotics empower manufacturers to swiftly adapt to evolving market demands (Kazemi et al., 2023). Flexible automation systems can be reconfigured to produce diverse products, reducing downtime between production runs. This adaptability fosters efficient product customization, catering to individual customer requirements.

Figure 4. Benefits of Industry 4.0

The incorporation of robotics heightens workplace safety by automating hazardous tasks (Nof, 2023). Robots can manage heavy loads and execute tasks in perilous environments, thereby diminishing the risk of workplace accidents (Sun et al., 2023). Moreover, automation can alleviate ergonomic issues by relieving human workers of repetitive and physically demanding tasks, ultimately enhancing their well-being. Industry 4.0 heavily relies on data analytics for process optimization and decision-making (Alkaraan et al., 2023). Automation and robotics generate copious amounts of data that can be analyzed to pinpoint inefficiencies and facilitate real-time informed decision-making. This data-driven approach bolsters overall operational performance. While the initial investment in robotics and automation can be substantial, the long-term benefits encompass significant cost reductions (Ylä-Kujala et al., 2023). Automated systems curtail labour costs, diminish material wastage, and enhance resource allocation (Reza, 2023). These cost savings bolster the overall competitiveness of manufacturers. Smart manufacturing integrated with robotics and automation also aligns harmoniously with sustainability objectives (Abdullah et al., 2023). Automated systems optimize energy consumption and curtail environmental impact (Ahn et al., 2022). Additionally, they contribute to waste reduction by ensuring precise material usage. The adoption of robotics and automation stands as a pivotal factor in sustaining competitiveness on a global scale. Manufacturers embracing these technologies can efficiently produce high-quality goods, meeting global demand and maintaining a competitive edge. Figure 4 shows the benefits of Industry 4.0

The advancements in robotics and automation within the context of smart manufacturing in Industry 4.0 have ushered in an era characterized by unparalleled efficiency, quality, and adaptability. These technologies not only enhance productivity but also improve safety, cut costs, and contribute to sustainability endeavours. As manufacturers continue to embrace these innovations, they position themselves to thrive in an increasingly competitive global marketplace.

3. INDUSTRY 4.0 AND DIGITAL TRANSFORMATION

3.1 The Role of Digital Transformation in Industry 4.0

In the fast-paced contemporary world, industries are experiencing a profound transformation, with the central driving force being the concept of Industry 4.0. This fourth industrial revolution is distinguished by the seamless integration of digital technologies into all facets of industrial operations. Digital transformation assumes a pivotal role in ushering in the era of Industry 4.0, fundamentally reshaping how businesses function, manufacture goods, and provide services. This section delves into the multifaceted significance of digital transformation within the context of Industry 4.0.

Digital transformation revolves around the assimilation of technologies like the IoT and AI into industrial processes. These technologies facilitate the deployment of intelligent sensors that continually monitor the performance of equipment (Truong & Diep, 2023). These sensors collect data, transmitting it to central systems for real-time analysis. In doing so, industries can foresee potential machine breakdowns, enabling proactive maintenance that reduces downtime and bolsters overall operational efficiency and productivity. Within Industry 4.0, supply chains undergo a profound shift towards greater interconnectivity and data-driven operations (Kliestik et al., 2023). Blockchain technology ensures that each step in the supply chain is securely and transparently recorded, from the source of raw materials to the final product (Lee & Zhang, 2023). AI algorithms leverage this data to predict demand patterns, enabling companies to optimize inventory levels and embrace just-in-time production, leading to reduced waste and costs. Digital transformation empowers the transition from mass production to personalized manufacturing (Colombi & D'Itria, 2023). Through AI and data analytics, industries can amass and scrutinize consumer data to comprehend individual preferences. This invaluable information enables businesses to craft personalized products and services tailored to specific customer requirements, elevating customer satisfaction and fostering loyalty. Digital technologies like augmented reality (AR) and virtual reality (VR) equip employees with tools for enhanced decision-making and training (Kim et al., 2023). AR can overlay information onto real-world objects, aiding tasks such as equipment maintenance. VR can simulate real-life scenarios for training, enhancing employee skills and diminishing errors. Empowered employees contribute to improved overall operational efficiency. Sustainability constitutes a pivotal facet of Industry 4.0, and digital transformation assumes a significant role in attaining eco-friendly objectives (Rehman et al., 2023). Smart sensors and IoT can monitor resource consumption and emissions, while AI-driven optimizations assist in waste reduction during production processes. Together, these technologies endorse environmentally conscious practices, reducing a company's carbon footprint. The embrace of digital transformation transcends mere survival; it's about maintaining competitiveness in a global marketplace (Bansal et al., 2023; Ullah et al., 2021). Companies that adopt Industry 4.0 technologies can adapt swiftly to shifting market conditions and innovate more effectively (Turner, 2021). This agility permits them to explore new markets and extend their global reach, positioning them as industry leaders. At the core of Industry 4.0 lies data, and digital transformation facilitates data-driven decision-making (Blat, 2023; Muzammal et al., 2021). Through the collection and analysis of extensive data, businesses gain valuable insights into their operations. Predictive analytics and ML enable superior strategic planning, resource allocation, and risk management. The outcome is more informed and efficient decision-making processes.

In conclusion, digital transformation stands as the driving force propelling Industry 4.0, fundamentally reshaping industries worldwide. It enhances efficiency and productivity, optimizes supply chains, facilitates customization, empowers the workforce, promotes sustainability, and bolsters global competitiveness. By fostering data-driven decision-making, digital transformation ensures that industries remain agile and pertinent in an ever-evolving business landscape. Embracing these digital advancements is no longer a choice but an imperative for industries to thrive in the modern era. As industries continue to evolve, it becomes imperative for businesses to remain in step with digital transformation and seize the opportunities it presents. In doing so, they can not only endure but also excel in the era of Industry 4.0, delivering enhanced value to their customers while securing long-term sustainability and success.

3.2 Connectivity and Interoperability Challenges in the Manufacturing Ecosystem

Connectivity, which forms the cornerstone of Industry 4.0, revolves around linking machinery, devices, and systems to facilitate data exchange and real-time communication. In this context, the importance of a flawless and dependable network infrastructure cannot be overstated. Frequently, manufacturers encounter issues related to inconsistent network coverage and limitations in bandwidth, which can obstruct the transmission of vital data. According to research conducted by Moradeyo et al., (2023), subpar network infrastructure can lead to production process delays and disruptions. This underscores the necessity for robust, high-speed networks to enable uninterrupted communication. Interoperability presents another formidable challenge. Given the integration of diverse technologies from various providers, ensuring effective communication and collaboration among different systems and devices becomes pivotal. A study by Usmani et al., (2023) underscores that the absence of standardized communication protocols and data formats can result in compatibility problems among devices from different manufacturers. Such issues can hinder the flow of information and coordination among various elements of the manufacturing process.

Figure 5. Smart factory feature in Industry 4.0

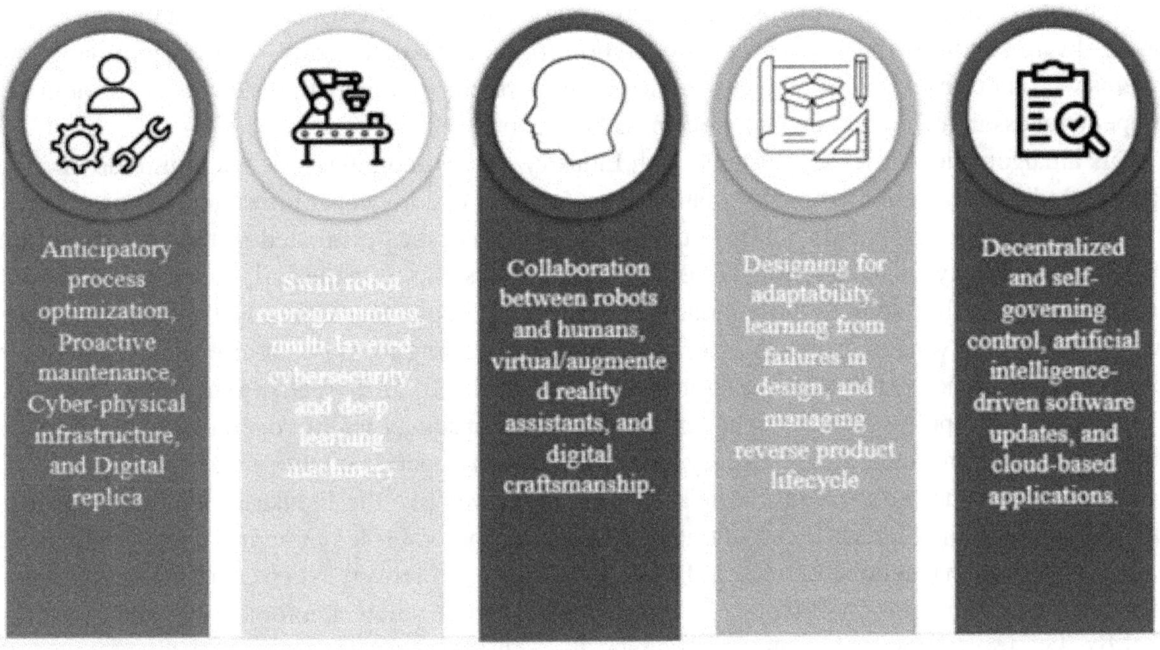

Additionally, the intricacy of merging legacy systems with contemporary technologies is a common concern. Many manufacturers still operate with outdated machinery that lacks inherent compatibility with Industry 4.0 technologies. This gives rise to a scenario of "two-speed IT," where modern and legacy systems struggle to interact seamlessly. Ensuring the alignment of these systems necessitates significant effort and financial investment. Concerns surrounding data security and privacy are closely linked to the challenges of connectivity and interoperability. As manufacturers accumulate and share extensive volumes of sensitive data, safeguarding this information takes on paramount importance. Instances of cyberattacks targeting industrial systems have been increasing, underscoring the urgency of robust cybersecurity measures to fend off potential breaches and unauthorized access. To address these challenges, collaborative initiatives involving manufacturers, technology providers, and regulatory bodies are imperative. Standardizing communication protocols and data formats can foster effortless interoperability. Furthermore, making investments in resilient, high-speed network infrastructure is essential for maintaining consistent connectivity, as emphasized by K. Wang et al. (2023). Manufacturers must also contemplate the integration of modern technologies at the design stage of new products and systems to ensure compatibility. Figure 5 shows smart factory feature in Industry 4.0.

In conclusion, despite the significant potential of Industry 4.0 to transform the manufacturing landscape, the hurdles posed by connectivity and interoperability cannot be underestimated. Establishing a sturdy network infrastructure, resolving compatibility issues, and giving priority to data security are pivotal to the successful implementation of Industry 4.0 technologies. Collaborative efforts among stakeholders are indispensable for promoting standardization and innovation in addressing these challenges.

3.3 Integration of Legacy Systems With Industry 4.0 Technologies

One of the foremost challenges currently confronting industries is the process of integrating legacy systems with cutting-edge technologies. Legacy systems are the established, often outdated, software and hardware solutions that have been in operation for an extended period. The integration of these systems with Industry 4.0 technologies is of utmost importance for companies striving to maintain their competitiveness in the swiftly evolving business landscape.

This amalgamation of legacy systems with Industry 4.0 technologies offers a multitude of advantages, including heightened efficiency, data-driven decision-making capabilities, and increased agility. This synergy empowers manufacturers to tap into the wealth of data generated by their legacy systems, which had previously been underutilized. By linking these systems with the IIoT, data can be gathered in real-time from multiple sources throughout the production process. Subsequently, this data can undergo analysis through advanced analytics and ML algorithms, leading to more precise forecasting and the development of proactive maintenance strategies (Shahin et al., 2023). To realize a successful integration, companies must grapple with several challenges. The foremost concern is interoperability between legacy systems and modern technologies. Legacy systems frequently operate on proprietary protocols that are incompatible with newer solutions. Standardization initiatives like the Industrial Internet Consortium (IIC) and the Platform Industrie 4.0 initiative have played pivotal roles in laying down guidelines for seamless integration (Javier, 2023; Ullah, Ishaq, et al., 2021). Moreover, cybersecurity holds paramount importance in the integration of legacy systems with interconnected technologies. The safeguarding of sensitive data from potential breaches necessitates the implementation of robust security measures that account for the vulnerabilities inherent in ageing systems (Al-Sherideh et al., 2023b).

Numerous strategies have emerged to facilitate this integration process. The utilization of edge computing, which entails processing data in proximity to its source, reduces latency and enhances the real-time capabilities of legacy systems (Sekonya & Sithungu, 2023). Another approach involves retrofitting legacy machines with sensor technologies. These sensors can gather data from older machines and transmit it for analysis, thereby enabling informed decision-making (Aminizadeh et al., 2023). Cloud-based solutions also play a significant role by offering scalable and cost-effective options for storing and processing data from legacy systems (Kumar & Agrawal, 2023).

In conclusion, the integration of legacy systems with Industry 4.0 technologies represents a complex yet indispensable endeavor for businesses aiming to modernize their operations. Despite the challenges related to interoperability and security, the benefits of this integration are substantial, including heightened efficiency and data-driven insights. Through the adoption of strategies such as edge computing, sensor retrofitting, and cloud-based solutions, companies can bridge the divide between their existing systems and the advanced capabilities offered by Industry 4.0. The collaborative efforts of standardization initiatives like IIC and Platform Industry 4.0 play a crucial role in guiding this integration journey. As technology continues to advance, the successful integration of these systems will determine the extent to which companies can harness the potential of Industry 4.0 and remain competitive in the global market.

3.4 Data Security and Privacy Concerns in the Era of Connected Manufacturing

The transformation ushered in by Industry 4.0 presents unprecedented opportunities for increased efficiency, reduced downtime, and improved decision-making. However, it also raises significant concerns regarding data security and privacy. These concerns are critical to ensuring the sustainable growth of this industry.

Connected manufacturing entails the interconnection of devices, machines, and systems within manufacturing environments, facilitating seamless data exchange and remote monitoring. Nevertheless, this heightened connectivity exposes manufacturing systems to a range of cyber threats. The risk of cyberattacks targeting industrial control systems (ICS) and supervisory control and data acquisition (SCADA) systems has surged. Malicious actors could exploit vulnerabilities in these systems to disrupt production, steal sensitive data, or inflict physical damage on equipment (Pottebaum et al., 2023). One major concern relates to the potential exposure of sensitive manufacturing data. With numerous devices continually collecting and transmitting data, manufacturers face challenges in ensuring the confidentiality and integrity of their proprietary information. Furthermore, the vast volume of data generated by connected manufacturing represents a treasure trove for cybercriminals seeking valuable insights for financial gain or competitive advantage (Dorn, 2023). Data privacy presents another crucial issue in connected manufacturing. The collection of extensive data, including employee information and operational data, raises ethical and legal concerns about how this data is utilized and stored. Manufacturers must navigate complex regulations like the General Data Protection Regulation (GDPR) and the California Consumer Privacy Act (CCPA) to avoid potential legal consequences stemming from mishandling sensitive information.

Supply chain vulnerabilities also emerge as a significant threat in connected manufacturing. As manufacturers collaborate with various suppliers and partners, the potential for security breaches increases. Cyberattacks targeting weaker links in the supply chain could lead to the infiltration of the entire manufacturing network (Gokkaya et al., 2023). Mitigating these challenges necessitates a comprehensive approach. Manufacturers must prioritize cybersecurity by implementing robust firewalls, and intrusion detection systems, and conducting regular security audits. The application of encryption techniques is crucial to safeguard data during both transmission and storage (Mfungo et al., 2023). Additionally, adopting a privacy-by-design approach ensures that data protection measures are seamlessly integrated into manufacturing processes from the outset (Carboni et al., 2023).

In conclusion, while connected manufacturing holds immense potential for industry transformation, the accompanying concerns about data security and privacy should not be underestimated. The threats posed by cybersecurity, data breaches, and regulatory complexities demand a proactive and multifaceted strategy to safeguard sensitive information and maintain the trust of consumers, partners, and stakeholders. By embracing robust cybersecurity practices, adhering to data privacy regulations, and fostering collaboration within the industry, manufacturers can harness the benefits of connected manufacturing while minimizing associated risks.

Figure 6. Digital transformation in Industry 4.0 (Vaswani, 2019)

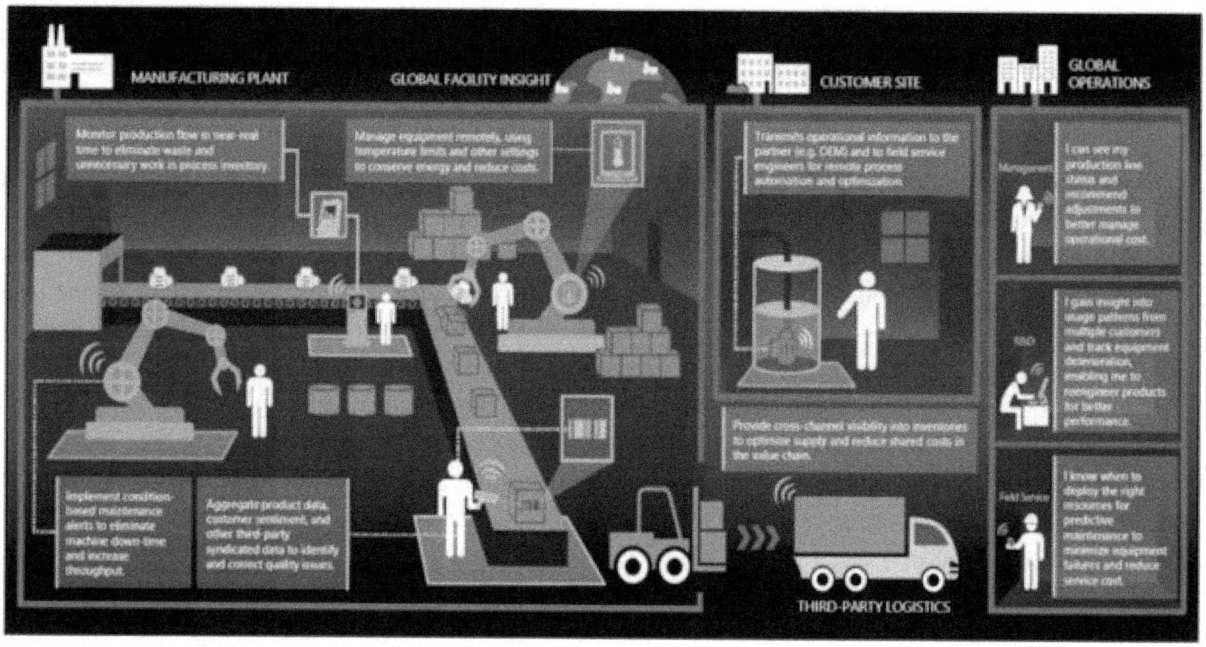

3.5 Overcoming Organizational Barriers to Embrace Industry 4.0

Resistance to change can be observed at various levels within an organization. It may manifest in front-line employees who harbour concerns about their job security amidst technological advancements. Even leadership may hesitate to disrupt established workflows and processes (Watkins & Marsick, 2023). To tackle this issue effectively, organizations should invest in change management programs. These programs should emphasize the advantages of Industry 4.0, involve employees in decision-making, and provide comprehensive training and support to facilitate a smooth transition. The shortage of digital skills can impede the successful implementation of Industry 4.0 technologies (Kee et al., 2023). To bridge this gap, organizations can form partnerships with educational institutions, offer continuous learning opportunities, and establish mentorship programs. The creation of cross-functional teams, comprising individuals with diverse skill sets, can also enhance collaboration on Industry 4.0 projects. The initial financial investment required for Industry 4.0 technologies can pose a significant challenge for many organizations (Jankowska et al., 2022b). To tackle this issue, organizations can explore financing options such as public-private partnerships, government grants, or leasing arrangements. These alternatives allow for spreading the cost over time. Moreover, conducting a thorough cost-benefit analysis can help in justifying the long-term benefits of these investments. In the interconnected Industry 4.0 ecosystem, cybersecurity is of utmost importance (Chataut, 2023). Organizations should establish comprehensive cybersecurity policies and practices. These practices should include regular risk assessments, employee training in cybersecurity best practices, and the adoption of advanced encryption and authentication methods. Engaging cybersecurity experts or consultants can also provide valuable insights. Many organizations rely on older legacy systems that may not be compatible with Industry 4.0 technologies (Spieske et al., 2023; Uygun, 2020). A gradual approach to integration is essential. This might involve building middleware to connect older systems with newer ones, prioritizing system upgrades based on criticality, or gradually phasing out legacy systems as the new technologies prove their value. Without a well-defined strategy, organizations can easily become overwhelmed by the complexities of Industry 4.0 (Frank, 2023). Creating a clear roadmap that outlines specific goals, milestones, and timelines is crucial. Additionally, organizations should establish cross-functional teams to oversee the execution of the strategy and ensure alignment with broader organizational objectives.

Beyond basic technical skills, organizations should focus on nurturing a culture of continuous learning (A. a. E. Othman & ElKady, 2021). Providing courses, workshops, and certifications in digital technologies and automation can empower employees to embrace Industry 4.0. Regular skills assessments can help customize training programs to individual needs. Pilot projects offer a secure environment for experimenting with Industry 4.0 technologies (Pozzi et al., 2021). Organizations can identify low-risk areas where automation or data analytics can make an immediate impact. Once the benefits become evident, scaling up becomes more feasible, with lessons learned from pilot projects guiding larger implementations. A robust cybersecurity framework should encompass regular security audits, intrusion detection systems, and employee training on recognizing and preventing cyber threats (Kafi & Akter, 2023). Collaborating with cybersecurity experts can help in creating a comprehensive strategy to safeguard critical assets. Organizations can adopt an incremental approach to modernize their systems (Hasan et al., 2023). Identify which legacy systems can be upgraded or augmented to work seamlessly with Industry 4.0 technologies. As newer systems are introduced, plan for a phased retirement of legacy systems. A well-structured Industry 4.0 roadmap should delineate specific objectives, budget allocations, and implementation timelines (Kilaso, 2023). Regular reviews and adjustments ensure that the organization remains on track and can adapt to evolving technology trends. Encouraging innovation involves recognizing and rewarding creative thinking, even if it results in failures (Preece et al., 2023). Provide employees with the freedom to experiment, share ideas, and collaborate across departments to drive innovation in Industry 4.0 adoption.

In conclusion, the successful adoption of Industry 4.0 necessitates organizations to proactively address these challenges. They should implement a combination of strategies tailored to their specific context, considering the unique needs and obstacles they face. This approach will enable organizations to unlock the full potential of Industry 4.0 technologies and position themselves for competitiveness and growth in the digital era.

Figure 7. Supply chain management

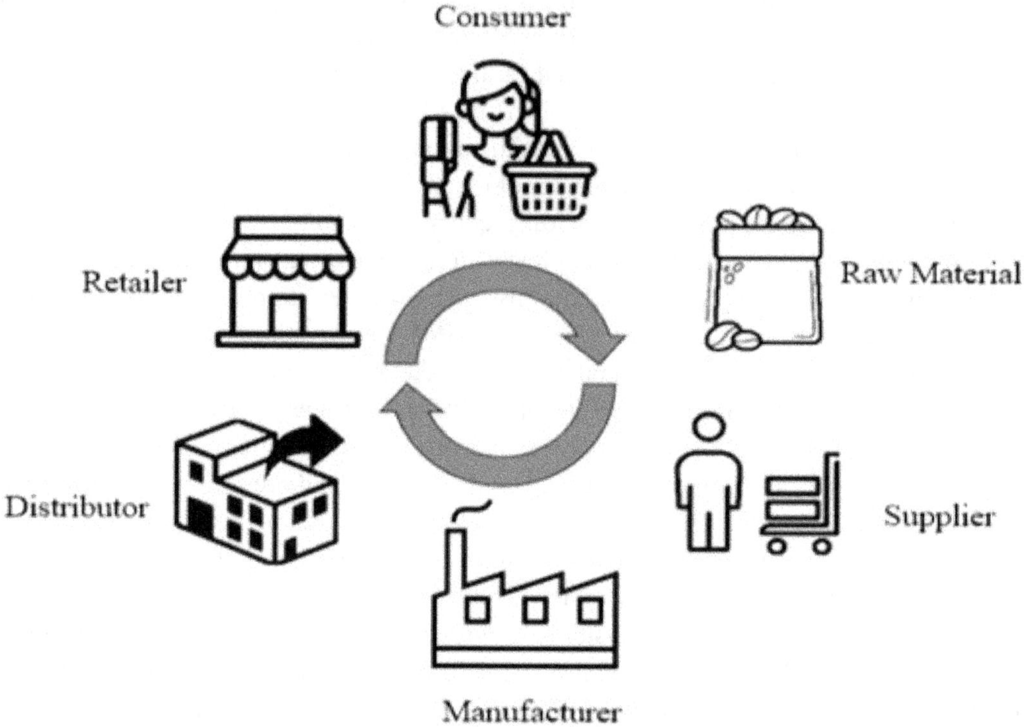

4. INDUSTRY 4.0 IN SUPPLY CHAIN MANAGEMENT

4.1 Smart and Connected Supply Chains in Industry 4.0

In the era of Industry 4.0, we witness the emergence of smart and interconnected supply chains, which are reshaping conventional manufacturing and logistics processes. This transformation is fueled by the integration of cutting-edge technologies like the IoT, AI, big data analytics, and automation into supply chain operations. This convergence of technologies has ushered in a new era characterized by heightened efficiency, visibility, and responsiveness throughout the entire supply chain ecosystem. Figure 7 shows the ecosystem of supply chain.

A fundamental characteristic of smart and interconnected supply chains is the real-time collection and sharing of data. IoT devices, integrated into production equipment, vehicles, and even products themselves, continuously generate data. This data is promptly gathered, processed, and analyzed in real time, empowering supply chain managers to make well-informed decisions swiftly (Nova, 2023). This data-driven approach reduces uncertainties and bolsters the overall agility of the supply chain. Moreover, AI and ML algorithms are playing a pivotal role in optimizing various facets of the supply chain. These algorithms can forecast demand patterns, fine-tune inventory levels, and even predict maintenance requirements for machinery (Noh, 2023). Such predictive capabilities dramatically enhance the efficiency of supply chain operations by reducing excess inventory costs and minimizing production downtimes.

The concept of smart and interconnected supply chains extends beyond individual companies. Collaborative networks and the sharing of information among supply chain partners foster improved coordination and visibility. This collaborative effort facilitates more accurate demand forecasting, efficient inventory management, and streamlined order fulfilment (Patil et al., 2023). Additionally, blockchain technology ensures transparency and traceability within complex supply chains, enabling secure and tamper-proof sharing of transaction records. The influence of Industry 4.0 on supply chains is not limited to the manufacturing sector; it also extends to logistics and distribution. Smart warehouses, equipped with autonomous robots and intelligent picking systems, optimize order fulfilment processes (Cheung et al., 2023). The integration of real-time tracking and monitoring systems into vehicles optimizes routes and enhances the accuracy of deliveries (Moumen, 2023).

In conclusion, Industry 4.0 has ushered in a new era marked by smart and interconnected supply chains. The integration of IoT, AI, big data analytics, and automation has revolutionized the way supply chains function. Real-time data sharing, predictive analytics, and collaborative networks are among the key factors driving increased efficiency and responsiveness. Despite the challenges, the advantages of embracing these technologies are substantial, promising improved operational performance and enhanced competitiveness in our increasingly interconnected global market.

4.2 Real-Time Inventory Management and Demand Forecasting

"Efficient real-time management of inventory and accurate forecasting of demand play vital roles in streamlining supply chain operations and elevating overall business effectiveness. This section examines the importance of these practices in contemporary business settings, emphasizing their advantages and primary strategies for implementation.

Inventory management encompasses the surveillance, regulation, and enhancement of a company's product stock. In the present dynamic business environment, the capability to oversee inventory in real-time has become imperative for promptly meeting customer requirements while minimizing excess inventory and its associated expenses (Kareska, 2023). Precise demand prediction serves as a foundation for proficient inventory management, enabling companies to synchronize their supply with projected customer demands. This practice aids in averting both stock shortages and overstock situations, which can negatively impact customer contentment and profit margins (Al Meslamani, 2023). Real-time inventory management relies on cutting-edge technologies like IoT sensors and Radio Frequency Identification (RFID) to furnish up-to-the-minute insights into inventory levels and movements (Kineber et al., 2023). These technologies facilitate swift data acquisition and analysis, empowering companies to make well-informed decisions instantaneously. Furthermore, ML algorithms are employed to identify patterns and trends in historical sales data, contributing to more precise demand forecasting (Taghiyeh et al., 2023). Efficient demand forecasting necessitates the integration of various data sources, encompassing historical sales records, market trends, and even external variables like weather conditions (S. M. Hassan et al., 2023). AI methods, such as neural networks and time series analysis, are employed to process these data sources and generate dependable forecasts (Alkahtani et al., 2023). The amalgamation of real-time inventory updates and AI-driven demand forecasting enables enterprises to proactively adapt their inventory levels, production schedules, and distribution strategies, resulting in reduced operational expenses and heightened customer satisfaction. The benefits of real-time inventory management and demand forecasting are multifaceted. By minimizing surplus inventory, companies can release tied-up working capital and reduce warehousing costs (Bhowal, 2023). Simultaneously, precise demand forecasting curbs the risk of inventory shortages, ensuring that products remain accessible when customers seek them, ultimately boosting sales and fostering customer loyalty. The implementation of these practices necessitates a comprehensive approach, encompassing the adoption of technology, reengineering of processes, and training of a skilled workforce (Hraiga et al., 2023). Collaborative associations with suppliers and distributors also hold a pivotal role in the exchange of information and synchronization throughout the supply chain (Zhou et al., 2023). As technology continuously evolves, businesses must remain adaptable and embrace emerging tools and techniques to sustain a competitive edge in the market.

In summary, real-time inventory management and demand forecasting are indispensable components of contemporary supply chain management. By harnessing advanced technologies and data-driven insights, companies can optimize their inventory levels, cut costs, and elevate customer satisfaction. The integration of IoT, AI, and ML empowers enterprises to swiftly respond to market fluctuations and make well-informed decisions, thus driving success in today's dynamic business landscape."

4.3 Track and Trace Technologies for Enhanced Supply Chain Visibility

"In today's globalized economy, supply chains play a pivotal role in ensuring the efficient flow of goods from manufacturers to end consumers. Nevertheless, managing these intricate networks has become progressively challenging, primarily due to factors like globalization, heightened customer expectations, and disruptions within supply chains. To counter these challenges and bolster supply chain visibility, the emergence of track and trace technologies has proven to be essential.

Track and trace technologies encompass a suite of tools and practices that enable organizations to monitor and trace product movements along the supply chain in real-time. These technologies encompass a broad spectrum of solutions, including Radio Frequency Identification (RFID), Global Positioning System (GPS), barcodes, and sensors. The implementation of these technologies offers numerous benefits, including enhanced inventory management, lowered operational expenses, improved control over product quality, and the ability to respond promptly to supply chain disruptions. One of the pivotal advantages of track and trace technologies is the capability to gain real-time insights into the whereabouts and status of products. For instance, RFID and GPS technologies enable organizations to track the journey of goods throughout various stages of the supply chain, from manufacturing facilities to distribution centres and retail outlets (GAMAL, 2023). This real-time visibility assists companies in optimizing their inventory levels, mitigating stock shortages, and reducing excess inventory, ultimately contributing to more efficient supply chain operations. Furthermore, track and trace technologies foster enhanced transparency and accountability within the supply chain. By capturing and retaining data regarding each product's journey, these technologies provide a comprehensive audit trail that proves valuable for regulatory compliance, authentication, and prevention of counterfeiting (Saxena et al., 2023). This is particularly vital in industries such as pharmaceuticals and luxury goods, where product authenticity holds paramount importance. The deployment of track and trace technologies also empowers organizations to respond swiftly to supply chain disruptions. Continuous monitoring of product movements enables companies to identify potential bottlenecks and adjust shipping routes as necessary, thereby minimizing the impact of disruptions such as natural disasters or transportation delays (Lun et al., 2023).

In conclusion, track and trace technologies present a robust solution for enhancing supply chain visibility. With benefits spanning from improved inventory management to heightened transparency and rapid response to disruptions, these technologies have evolved into indispensable tools for contemporary supply chain management. In a constantly evolving global marketplace, organizations embracing these technologies are better positioned to optimize their operations and meet the ever-growing demands of consumers."

4.4 Supply Chain Analytics and Optimization With Industry 4.0

The landscape of supply chain management has witnessed a significant transformation with the advent of Industry 4.0. This era is marked by the integration of digital technologies across various aspects of manufacturing and production. Industry 4.0 converges technologies such as the IoT, extensive data analysis, AI, and advanced robotics, effectively revolutionizing traditional supply chain practices.

Supply chain analytics involves the systematic use of data and quantitative methods to improve decision-making and enhance the performance of supply chains. It empowers organizations to gain profound insights into their supply chain operations, identify patterns, and predict future trends. Proficient supply chain analytics assists companies in optimizing inventory levels, streamlining production processes, and enhancing the accuracy of demand forecasting (Weidele et al., 2023). Analytics plays a pivotal role in identifying bottlenecks and inefficiencies within the supply chain, resulting in cost reductions and increased operational efficiency. Industry 4.0 leverages digital technologies to establish "smart" factories and interconnected supply chains. IoT-enabled sensors collect real-time data from various points in the supply chain, improving visibility and traceability. As noted by Allahloh et al. (2023), this data is used for predictive maintenance of machinery, reducing downtime and enhancing overall productivity. AI and ML algorithms analyze the collected data, offering actionable insights to decision-makers. Additionally, blockchain technology ensures both transparency and security in transactions and record-keeping (Nigmatov et al., 2023). The integration of supply chain analytics with Industry 4.0 opens up opportunities for optimization. Optimization models and algorithms contribute to improved transportation route planning, resulting in reduced delivery times and lower costs (Dorcheh & Rahbari, 2023). Furthermore, optimization enhances the precision of demand forecasting by incorporating various data sources and variables (Shen et al., 2023), leading to fewer instances of stockouts and excess inventory. Nevertheless, the integration of supply chain analytics and optimization with Industry 4.0 is not devoid of challenges. Preserving data security and privacy, managing the complexities of merging diverse technologies, and upskilling the workforce present formidable obstacles (Tarek, 2023). Nevertheless, the benefits outweigh the challenges. Ongoing technological advancements, such as edge computing, which processes data closer to its source, address some of the latency concerns associated with data processing. Figure 8 shows the benefits of Industry 4.0.

Figure 8. Benefits of Industry 4.0

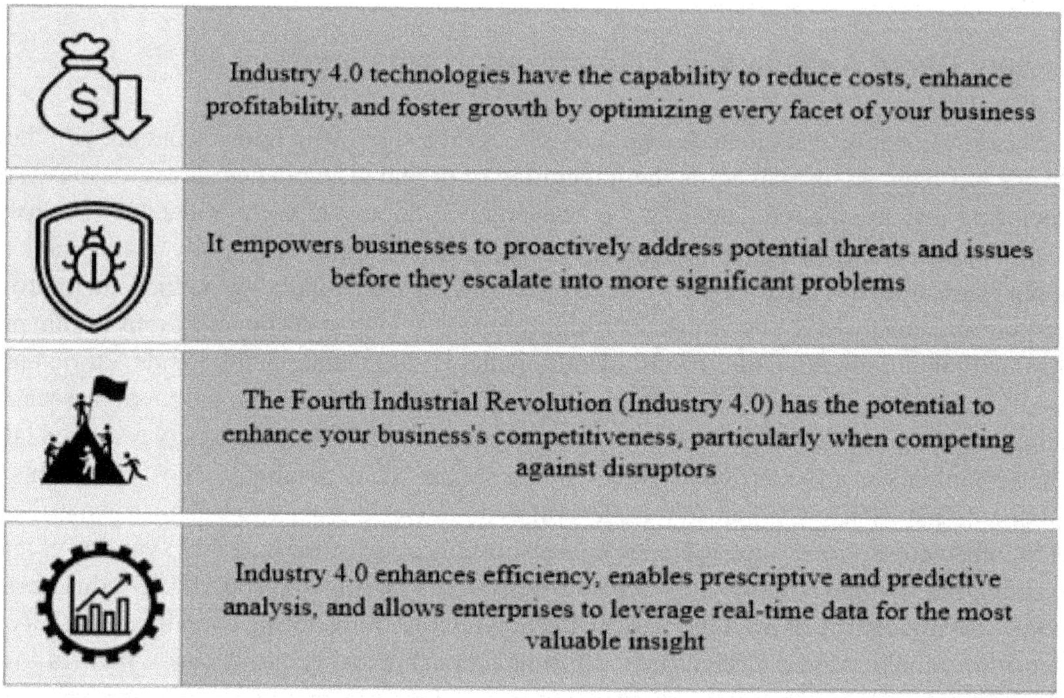

In conclusion, the combination of supply chain analytics and optimization with Industry 4.0 technologies is reshaping traditional supply chain paradigms. Through the utilization of data analytics, AI, and IoT, organizations can enhance decision-making, optimize operations, and achieve substantial cost savings. While challenges persist, ongoing technological developments and strategies like edge computing are paving the way for a more efficient and optimized supply chain ecosystem."

4.5 Collaborative and Responsive Supply Chains Enabled by Industry 4.0

Industry 4.0 has ushered in a wave of innovative technologies that promote cooperation among various participants in the supply chain. One crucial facilitator of this collaboration is the IoT, which links physical objects and devices to the Internet, enabling real-time monitoring and data exchange (Aski et al., 2023; Manchuri et al., 2024). This connectivity empowers partners in the supply chain to share precise and current information, leading to enhanced synchronization and decision-making. Additionally, technologies such as blockchain enhance trust and transparency in supply chains by offering an immutable and auditable record of transactions (Singh et al., 2023; Lee et al., 2021).

The agility seen in Industry 4.0-enabled supply chains is a result of advanced data analytics and predictive algorithms. These tools utilize vast datasets to anticipate demand patterns, optimize inventory levels, and mitigate disruptions (Mhaddolkar, 2023). ML algorithms, driven by historical data and real-time inputs, enhance the accuracy of these predictions and enable swift adjustments to evolving market conditions (Feng & Avilés, 2023; Sindiramutty, Jhanjhi, Tan, Khan, Gharib, & Yun, 2024). Collaboration within Industry 4.0 supply chains goes beyond traditional business partnerships. Crowdsourcing and open innovation, facilitated by digital platforms, enable companies to tap into a global reservoir of ideas and expertise (Sarkar & Kedas, 2022). Such collaborative efforts can yield innovative solutions, reduce time-to-market, and boost competitiveness. However, the transition to Industry 4.0-enabled supply chains comes with its set of challenges. Organizations must navigate issues related to data security and privacy, as increased connectivity exposes them to potential cyber threats (Afenyo & Caesar, 2023). Additionally, the adoption of new technologies necessitates the reskilling and upskilling of the workforce to fully harness their potential.

In summary, Industry 4.0 is reshaping the landscape of supply chain management by promoting collaborative and adaptable practices. The integration of IoT, data analytics, and automation enhances coordination among stakeholders, resulting in improved decision-making and operational efficiency. While challenges persist, the benefits of Industry 4.0-driven supply chains are evident in their ability to respond to dynamic market conditions and deliver value to customers.

5. INDUSTRY 4.0 AND WORKFORCE OF THE FUTURE

5.1 Impact of Automation on the Workforce in Industry 4.0

The advent of Industry 4.0 technologies has instigated a profound transformation in the workforce landscape. Industry 4.0, distinguished by the integration of digital technologies, the IoT, and AI, has brought about a revolution in the way industries operate (Ryalat et al., 2023). This transformation carries both positive and negative implications for the workforce.

One of the most conspicuous impacts of automation within the context of Industry 4.0 is the notable increase in efficiency. Robots and AI-driven machines exhibit tireless and precise performance, leading to heightened productivity (Heikkilä et al., 2023). Consequently, industries can achieve greater output with fewer workers, potentially reducing the demand for manual labour. However, this surge in efficiency often comes at a human cost. As automation advances, certain job roles become obsolete. For example, routine and repetitive tasks in manufacturing, such as assembly line work, are progressively being taken over by robots. This has raised concerns regarding job displacement and unemployment, particularly among low-skilled workers. On the positive side, Industry 4.0 also generates fresh employment prospects (Kamble & Gunasekaran, 2021). The technology necessitates skilled individuals to design, program, and maintain automated systems. Consequently, there is an increasing demand for professionals with expertise in AI, data analytics, and cybersecurity. Moreover, automation contributes to enhanced workplace safety. Hazardous tasks that endanger human lives can be delegated to robots. For instance, in high-risk environments like nuclear power plants or deep-sea exploration, robots can execute tasks without human safety concerns. Despite these benefits, the transition to Industry 4.0 is not without its share of challenges. There is a pressing need to upskill and reskill the existing workforce (Pradhan & Saxena, 2023). The skill sets required in the digital age differ from those in traditional industries. Workers need to adapt to effectively collaborate with machines. Furthermore, the unequal distribution of the benefits of automation raises concerns. High-skilled workers often reap the rewards of increased productivity and access to better-paying jobs, while low-skilled workers may face unemployment and stagnant wages (Urbański, 2023; Sindiramutty, Jhanjhi, Tan, Khan, Shah, & Gaur, 2024).

In conclusion, automation driven by Industry 4.0 is reshaping the workforce landscape. It enhances efficiency, creates fresh employment opportunities, and improves workplace safety. Nonetheless, it also poses challenges, including job displacement and the imperative need for workforce reskilling. Ensuring that the advantages of automation are equitably distributed among all workers stands as a pivotal challenge that policymakers and industries must address.

5.2 Skill Gaps and Workforce Training for Smart Manufacturing

The transformation brought about by Industry 4.0 is not solely about machines; it also necessitates a workforce that is skilled and adaptable. However, a substantial gap exists between the skills required for smart manufacturing and those possessed by the current workforce. This section examines the skill gaps in smart manufacturing and underscores the significance of workforce training in bridging these disparities.

Smart manufacturing requires a workforce with a diverse skill set that encompasses digital literacy, data analytics, automation, and problem-solving abilities (Telukdarie, 2023; Wen et al., 2024). Regrettably, studies indicate a significant skills gap. According to a survey conducted by Korder et al. (2023), many manufacturers have reported a shortage of qualified workers ranging from moderate to severe. This shortage can impede the adoption of smart manufacturing technologies and hinder industry growth. Several factors contribute to these skill gaps in smart manufacturing. The rapid pace of technological advancement necessitates that workers continuously update their skills (Galanti et al., 2023). Furthermore, the conventional education system often falls short of providing the requisite training in emerging technologies (Cui et al., 2023). Additionally, misconceptions about careers in manufacturing dissuade individuals from pursuing relevant education and training (Mason, 2023). Closing these skill gaps in smart manufacturing is imperative for the industry's growth and competitiveness. Skilled workers can optimize the benefits of technology adoption, such as heightened productivity and reduced operational costs (Škare et al., 2023). Furthermore, a well-trained workforce enhances product quality and fosters innovation (Sulistyaningsih & Siswanto, 2023). Investing in workforce training not only benefits individual employees but also fortifies the entire manufacturing ecosystem. To address these skill gaps, the implementation of a robust workforce training program is essential. These programs should encompass a broad spectrum of skills, ranging from basic digital literacy to advanced data analysis and machine programming (Arcadio, 2023). Moreover, these programs should be designed to meet the needs of both new entrants and current employees. Furthermore, training initiatives should be easily accessible and affordable to encourage widespread participation. Companies can collaborate with educational institutions and government bodies to create tailored training programs (Macatangay, 2023). Additionally, the promotion of continuous learning and upskilling should be facilitated through mentorship and on-the-job training (Leow et al., 2023).

The skill gaps in smart manufacturing represent a significant challenge that must be addressed to ensure the continued growth and success of the industry. Bridging these gaps requires a multifaceted approach that involves collaboration among industry stakeholders, educational institutions, and government entities. Investing in workforce training is not only a necessity but also an opportunity to empower individuals with the skills they need to thrive in the digital age of manufacturing.

5.3 Human-Robot Collaboration and Coexistence in Smart Factories

The integration of robotics and automation technologies has ushered in a new era of manufacturing, characterized by smart factories that optimize production processes through the interaction between humans and robots. This collaboration and coexistence between humans and robots in smart factories has gained significant attention due to its potential to enhance efficiency, productivity, and safety. Figure 9 shows human and robot collaboration.

Figure 9. Human and robot collaboration (Anna, 2018)

Human-robot collaboration in smart factories offers numerous advantages. Firstly, it leads to improved production efficiency by leveraging the strengths of both humans and robots. Robots excel in repetitive and precise tasks, while humans are skilled in adapting to complex and changing situations (Cressman et al., 2023). Secondly, worker safety is enhanced as robots can take on hazardous tasks. As emphasized by Kara (2023), robots can handle tasks involving toxic chemicals or extreme temperatures, reducing the risk of human accidents. Thirdly, collaboration increases overall production capacity. According to a study by Benos et al. (2023), human-robot teams outperform either humans or robots alone in terms of output. However, the implementation of human-robot collaboration in smart factories is not without challenges. One significant challenge is the need for seamless interaction between humans and robots. As highlighted by Montini et al. (2023), effective communication interfaces are required to ensure smooth coordination between human workers and their robotic counterparts. Additionally, concerns about job displacement and worker autonomy arise. Addressing these concerns requires a balance between task automation and skill enhancement to empower workers in the changing work environment. Looking ahead, the integration of AI and ML into smart factories is expected to enhance human-robot collaboration further. AI algorithms enable robots to learn from human behaviours and adapt in real time, creating a symbiotic relationship (Josphineleela, 2023). This implies that robots will not only follow pre-programmed instructions but also learn from human expertise, fostering a sense of coexistence.

In conclusion, the collaboration and coexistence of humans and robots in smart factories hold immense promise for the manufacturing industry. With careful consideration of communication interfaces, and worker empowerment, the potential benefits of increased efficiency, safety, and capacity can be harnessed. As technology continues to evolve, human-robot collaboration is poised to shape the future of manufacturing, redefining traditional notions of work and productivity.

5.4 Reshaping Job Roles and Career Paths in Industry 4.0

Industry 4.0, often hailed as the fourth industrial revolution, is reshaping the global job market landscape. This revolution is driven by the integration of digital technologies, artificial intelligence, and automation across various industries. Consequently, job roles and career trajectories are experiencing profound transformations to align with this new era.

Industry 4.0 represents a significant departure from traditional business operations, exerting a profound influence on employment dynamics. Automation and digital technologies have assumed central roles in production processes, resulting in increased productivity and efficiency (Da Silva et al., 2023). Furthermore, the application of data analytics and the IoT is optimizing decision-making, necessitating a fresh set of skills (Sasikumar et al., 2023). Perhaps the most conspicuous change lies in the evolution of job roles. Routine and repetitive tasks are progressively becoming automated, leading to a decrease in positions reliant on manual labour (George et al., 2023). Instead, there is a growing demand for professionals proficient in areas such as robotics, data science, and ML. Traditional roles, like manufacturing operators, are evolving into positions like robotics technicians and data analysts. In the Industry 4.0 era, job roles often demand interdisciplinary skills (Ying et al., 2023). Engineers are expected to grasp data analytics, and data scientists must comprehend manufacturing processes. This interconnection between fields is paving the way for professionals capable of bridging these knowledge gaps. The swift pace of technological advancement underscores the necessity of committing to continuous learning. As job roles evolve, employees must continually update their skills to remain pertinent (Lim, 2023). Companies are increasingly investing in employee training and development to ensure a workforce equipped to navigate the digital landscape. The Industry 4.0 landscape is ushering in entirely new career pathways (Luo & Zahra, 2023). For instance, there is a high demand for cybersecurity experts as companies seek to safeguard their digital assets (Nadua et al., 2023). Additionally, roles in managing big data and overseeing AI ethics are emerging. As the adoption of Industry 4.0 extends worldwide, it is also altering career pathways in terms of mobility (Turečková et al., 2023). Professionals skilled in Industry 4.0 technologies are discovering opportunities in various countries, and multinational corporations are increasingly tapping into global talent pools.

Industry 4.0 is revolutionizing job roles and career paths by emphasizing automation, interdisciplinary skills, continuous learning, and the emergence of new roles. To thrive in this era, individuals must embrace lifelong learning, while organizations must invest in the development of their workforce. As the global economy becomes more interconnected, the Industry 4.0 era offers exciting opportunities for professionals willing to adapt and evolve.

6. SUSTAINABILITY AND CIRCULAR ECONOMY IN INDUSTRY 4.0

6.1 Environmental Impact of Industry 4.0 Technologies

"Industry 4.0 innovations possess the capacity to greatly enhance energy efficiency. Through the optimization of operations and the utilization of real-time data, various sectors can curtail energy usage (Shafi et al., 2023). For instance, intelligent sensors can oversee equipment performance, facilitating prompt maintenance and minimizing energy squandering.

The adoption of Industry 4.0 also contributes to diminishing waste. Intelligent manufacturing systems can predict production errors, thus reducing the number of defective items and associated waste (Soori et al., 2023). Furthermore, real-time data analysis can bolster supply chain management, thereby lessening overproduction and resource waste (Onyeaka et al., 2023). Industry 4.0 champions sustainability by enabling circular economy practices. Using IoT devices, products can be tracked throughout their life cycle, making recycling more manageable and lessening the environmental impact of disposal (Kurniawan et al., 2023). Moreover, data-informed decision-making supports sustainable sourcing, thus shrinking the ecological footprint of raw materials. Smart factories, empowered by Industry 4.0 innovations, optimize resource utilization. Anticipatory maintenance guarantees efficient machinery operation, prolonging their lifespan and lessening the need for resource-intensive replacements. Additionally, real-time monitoring enables adjustments in production processes to minimize resource consumption (J. Wang et al., 2023). IoT-enabled logistics systems augment transportation efficiency. Real-time tracking and route optimization cut down on fuel consumption and greenhouse gas emissions (Zrigui, 2023). This is particularly noteworthy in the context of global supply chains. Nevertheless, despite these favourable impacts, Industry 4.0 innovations present challenges as well. The production and disposal of electronic components for IoT devices can lead to the generation of electronic waste (e-waste) (Farjana et al., 2023). Additionally, the energy demands of data centres supporting these technologies can be considerable.

In summary, Industry 4.0 technologies offer substantial potential for mitigating the environmental footprint of various industries using improved energy efficiency, waste reduction, sustainable practices, resource optimization, and transportation efficiency. However, it is vital to address challenges such as e-waste and the energy consumption of data centres to optimize the environmental advantages of these technologies. Striking a balance between technological progress and environmental responsibility is of utmost importance for the sustainable future of Industry 4.0."

6.2 Sustainable Practices and Green Manufacturing in Industry 4.0

The incorporation of sustainable principles and environmentally friendly manufacturing has garnered significant attention within the framework of Industry 4.0. This shift in perspective arises from the imperative to address ecological concerns while harnessing the potential of cutting-edge technologies. Industry 4.0, marked by the convergence of digital technologies and physical systems, presents a distinctive opportunity to simultaneously pursue economic growth and ecological preservation. Sustainable practices within the context of Industry 4.0 encompass a spectrum of strategies designed to minimize environmental impact. Core themes include enhancing energy efficiency, reducing waste generation, and optimizing resource utilization. These practices leverage the capabilities of technologies such as the IoT and data analytics to monitor energy consumption, identify inefficiencies, and facilitate real-time decision-making. Through the analysis of data collected by sensors embedded in manufacturing equipment, enterprises can pinpoint areas for operational streamlining and minimize energy wastage (Matin et al., 2023). Green manufacturing methods are focused on curtailing resource consumption and pollution at all stages of the production process. One prime example is additive manufacturing, commonly known as 3D printing, which allows for precise allocation of materials, thereby reducing waste in comparison to traditional subtractive techniques. Moreover, intelligent manufacturing systems can enable predictive maintenance, leading to reduced downtime and extended equipment lifespans (Qing et al., 2023). This approach not only optimizes resource utilization but also lessens the need for new equipment, consequently mitigating emissions associated with manufacturing. A circular economy approach, bolstered by Industry 4.0 technologies, champions the concept of closed-loop systems. These systems emphasize recycling, remanufacturing, and the extension of a product's lifecycle. IoT-enabled devices can monitor product usage and condition, enabling companies to provide maintenance services and upgrades instead of replacing entire products (Neligan et al., 2022). Such an approach contributes to the preservation of resources and diminishes the environmental burden associated with manufacturing.

Sustainable practices and green manufacturing are integral elements in the evolution of Industry 4.0. The fusion of advanced technologies with environmentally conscientious strategies holds the potential to create a more resource-efficient and ecologically sustainable industrial landscape. By harnessing the capabilities of IoT, data analytics, and smart manufacturing, organizations can not only enhance their operational efficiency but also make significant strides toward a more environmentally friendly future. Figure 10 shows the benefits of using IoT in industry 4.0.

Figure 10. Benefits of using IoT in Industry 4.0

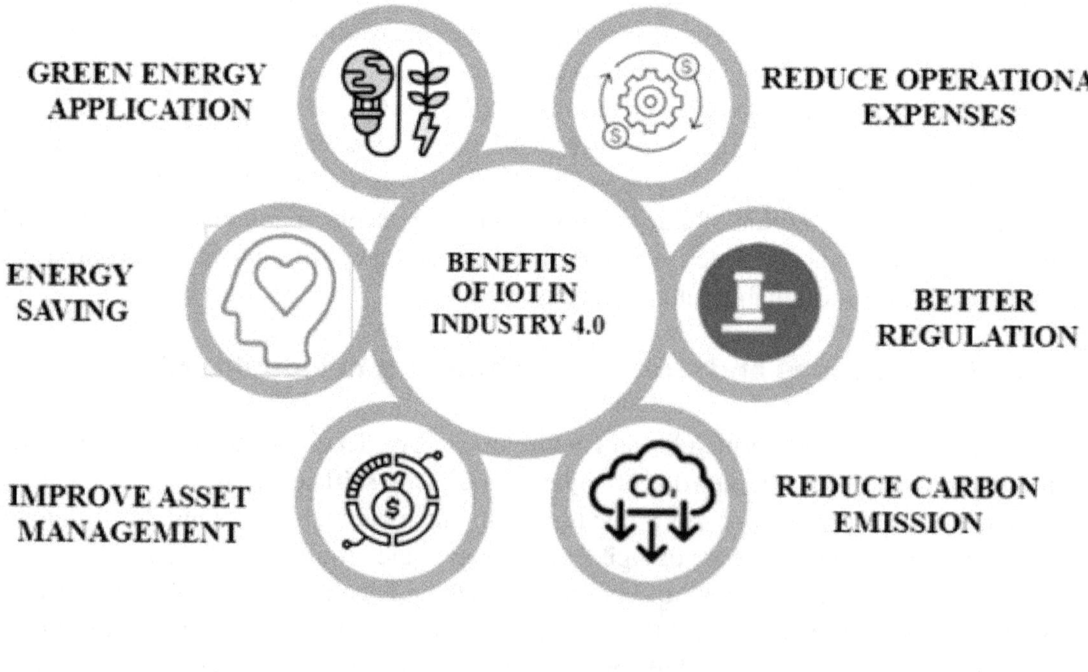

6.3 Circular Economy Principles and Their Integration in Smart Factories

The concept of a circular economy has garnered substantial attention in recent times as an environmentally sustainable approach to resource management. It advocates for a closed-loop system where resources are continually reused, recycled, and refurbished to minimize waste and mitigate the adverse environmental impacts of industrial processes. Smart factories, recognized for their incorporation of digital technologies, automation, and data-driven decision-making, are emerging as pivotal players in advancing the principles of the circular economy.

Smart factories deploy cutting-edge technologies such as IoT sensors and AI algorithms to monitor and optimize resource utilization (Sn, 2023). These technologies play a crucial role in waste reduction and energy conservation by ensuring that resources are employed efficiently and to their maximum potential. Predictive maintenance systems, underpinned by data analytics, are employed in smart factories to swiftly identify and address issues in real time, thereby extending the operational lifespan of machinery and equipment (J. Ahn et al., 2023). This aligns harmoniously with circular economy principles by curtailing the need for premature disposal. A fundamental tenet of the circular economy is designing products with their end-of-life fate in mind (Gillott et al., 2023). Smart factories incorporate these principles into their product development procedures by producing modular and easily upgradable products, consequently reducing the necessity for frequent replacements. Smart factories facilitate closed-loop supply chains by enabling the tracking of materials and products throughout their entire lifecycle (Kazancoglu et al., 2023). This traceability aids in the efficient recovery and recycling of materials, further supporting circular economy objectives. The circular economy underscores the importance of collaboration among stakeholders (Ul-Durar et al., 2023). Smart factories promote this by establishing connectivity with suppliers, customers, and partners to facilitate information exchange and optimize resource flows. Furthermore, they leverage consumer preference and behaviour data to craft customized products and services, effectively reducing overproduction and waste (P. Sun, 2023). This is in line with the circular economy's emphasis on meeting consumer needs while minimizing environmental repercussions. Smart factories also employ digital platforms to furnish consumers with information regarding a product's environmental impact and certifications, promoting transparency and informed choices. Additionally, smart factories heavily rely on data analytics for real-time decision-making (Dani et al., 2023). This data-driven approach aids in process optimization for resource efficiency and waste reduction, closely aligning with circular economy principles. Circular economy principles are fundamentally rooted in an ongoing commitment to improvement. Smart factories employ data analytics and performance metrics to continuously refine their processes and reduce their environmental footprint.

The integration of circular economy principles into smart factories represents a promising stride towards sustainable industrial practices. By harnessing digital technologies, data analytics, and automation, smart factories can not only optimize resource utilization and waste reduction but also prolong the lifespan of products, all while meeting consumer demands. Collaboration with stakeholders, eco-labelling, and a dedication to continuous improvement further solidify their alignment with circular economy principles. As the world increasingly seeks sustainable solutions, the role of smart factories in promoting circular economy practices is poised to grow significantly.

7. CHALLENGES AND BARRIERS IN IMPLEMENTING INDUSTRY 4.0

7.1 Technological Challenges and Adoption Hurdles

In the contemporary digital landscape, technological progress is reshaping our lifestyles, work environments, and social interactions. However, these advancements are accompanied by a host of challenges and obstacles that impede their smooth integration across different sectors.

In our increasingly digitalized world, the proliferation of interconnected devices and the IoT has amplified the vulnerabilities that cybercriminals can exploit. As a result, safeguarding sensitive data from cyberattacks has become a top priority for both individuals and businesses (De Azambuja et al., 2023). Cybersecurity threats have evolved into more intricate and sophisticated forms, often employing techniques such as ransomware, phishing, and exploiting zero-day vulnerabilities. As technology advances, so does the arsenal available to cyber criminals, making it an ongoing challenge to stay ahead in the cybersecurity realm. Tech companies, known for collecting vast amounts of personal data, have raised concerns regarding privacy infringement (Han & Mardani, 2023). The challenge here is to strike a delicate balance between utilizing this data for innovation and ensuring the protection of user privacy rights. Misuse of personal data can lead to surveillance, profiling, and even breaches that expose sensitive information. Consequently, there is a growing need for robust data protection regulations and ethical guidelines to govern the responsible use of personal information. Despite the promises of technology, a significant digital divide persists, disproportionately affecting underserved communities. Access to reliable internet connectivity and essential devices remains unequal (De Azambuja et al., 2023). This inequality impedes the equitable adoption of technological solutions and exacerbates existing disparities in education, job opportunities, and access to essential services. Bridging this divide is essential to ensure that the benefits of technology are accessible to all.

Technological advancements often introduce complex user interfaces that can be challenging for individuals to navigate (De Azambuja et al., 2023). Poorly designed interfaces can hinder adoption, making it difficult for users to comprehend and effectively utilize new tools. This underscores the significance of prioritizing user-centred design and adhering to user experience (UX) principles in the development of technology solutions. Human resistance to adopting new technologies poses a substantial hurdle (Haber & Carmeli, 2023). Many individuals tend to stick to familiar methods and may be hesitant to embrace new tools or processes. This resistance can stem from a fear of the unknown, concerns about job displacement, or simply a lack of motivation to change deeply ingrained habits. Effective change management strategies are crucial to address this challenge. A significant portion of the population lacks the digital literacy skills required to navigate the increasingly complex digital landscape (Chee, 2023). Without adequate digital literacy, individuals are unable to fully harness the benefits of technology, including accessing online education, finding job opportunities, or participating in the digital economy. Closing the digital literacy gap is essential to ensure that technology is an inclusive force for all. The adoption of technology often involves substantial costs (C. Qing et al., 2023). Small businesses and individuals, in particular, may find it challenging to invest in new technologies, which can impede their competitiveness. These costs encompass not only the purchase of hardware and software but also training, maintenance, and potential disruptions to existing workflows. Rapid technological advancements can sometimes outpace regulatory frameworks (Aspray & Doty, 2023). Navigating legal and ethical boundaries in the development and deployment of new technologies can be complex and time-consuming. This can lead to delays in the adoption of innovations as companies and policymakers work to establish appropriate regulations and ethical guidelines to govern emerging technologies.

The realm of technology holds immense potential for progress, but its adoption is accompanied by various challenges and obstacles. Addressing these issues is vital for creating a more inclusive and secure digital environment. Policymakers, businesses, and educators must collaborate to bridge the digital divide, enhance digital literacy, and ensure robust cybersecurity measures. Only through a concerted effort can society fully harness the benefits of technological advancements while mitigating their potential drawbacks.

7.2 Data Privacy and Security Concerns

Industry 4.0 heavily depends on gathering and analyzing extensive data from various sources such as sensors, devices, and production systems. This substantial influx of data raises serious privacy concerns. As personal and sensitive information becomes increasingly interconnected, there is a heightened risk of unauthorized access, data breaches, and inappropriate use of personal data (Marwala, 2023). Additionally, the profiling and monitoring of both employees and consumers through IoT devices pose significant threats to their privacy (El-Gendy et al., 2023).

Figure 11. Challenges in Industry 4.0

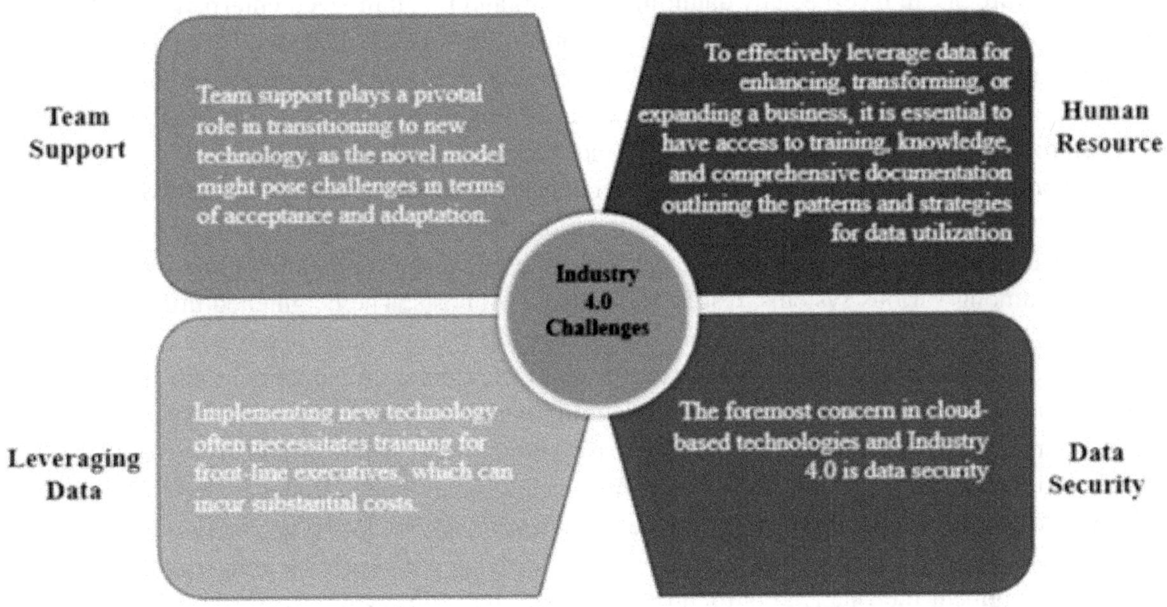

The enhanced connectivity among devices within Industry 4.0 environments also magnifies vulnerabilities in security. Malicious individuals can exploit these weaknesses to launch cyberattacks, disrupting operations, pilfering intellectual property, and compromising sensitive data. The interconnected nature of these systems makes it challenging to isolate breaches. Furthermore, the integration of older systems with modern technologies introduces security gaps that attackers can take advantage of (Jha et al., 2023). The supply chain, a critical element of Industry 4.0, is also exposed to risks related to data privacy and security. Collaborations with multiple suppliers and outsourcing expose the supply chain to potential breaches. An attack on any partner can trigger a cascading effect of data exposure across the entire supply chain network. The absence of universally accepted security standards within Industry 4.0 complicates the establishment of consistent security measures across various platforms and technologies. This lack of standardization makes it challenging to assess security risks and implement effective countermeasures. In conclusion, while Industry 4.0 presents unparalleled technological advancements, it also introduces significant challenges concerning data privacy and security. These challenges arise from the substantial data flow, interconnected devices, and integration of older systems. Addressing these concerns necessitates the development of robust security protocols, standardized practices, and adherence to data protection regulations. Collaboration among industry stakeholders is imperative to ensure that the benefits of Industry 4.0 are maximized while safeguarding sensitive information and privacy.

7.3 Economic and Financial Barriers

Although the advantages of Industry 4.0 are well-documented, there exist notable economic and financial impediments that obstruct its widespread adoption. One of the primary barriers to embracing Industry 4.0 is the substantial initial investment it demands. The incorporation of technologies like IoT sensors and automation systems necessitates a significant outlay for procuring and installing the requisite infrastructure. This financial burden can be especially daunting for small and medium-sized enterprises (SMEs) with limited financial resources. Industry 4.0 heavily relies on a workforce equipped with digital skills to operate and maintain advanced systems (Endress, 2023). However, there is a dearth of individuals possessing the necessary expertise. The process of training existing employees or recruiting specialized talent can strain a company's budget, particularly when they must compete with other industries for a limited pool of qualified professionals. Many pre-existing manufacturing systems were not originally designed with digital integration in mind. Retrofitting or integrating Industry 4.0 technologies into these legacy systems can prove intricate and expensive. This challenge is compounded when companies must ensure seamless compatibility among various systems, resulting in additional costs. The heightened utilization of data and connectivity within Industry 4.0 gives rise to considerable cybersecurity apprehensions. Safeguarding sensitive data from cyber threats demands substantial financial investments in advanced security measures, protocols, and employee training. Neglecting this aspect can lead to costly data breaches and harm to a company's reputation. Assessing the return on investment (ROI) for Industry 4.0 initiatives can pose difficulties (Sharma et al., 2023). The benefits, such as heightened efficiency and reduced downtime, may take time to fully materialize. Companies often grapple with justifying the initial expenditure, which can dissuade investment in these technologies. Complying with evolving industry regulations and standards can augment the financial burden of implementing Industry 4.0. Ensuring adherence often necessitates ongoing surveillance, adjustments, and investments in technology and personnel to meet new requirements. Access to capital is a universal constraint for businesses contemplating investments in Industry 4.0. Restricted access to loans or venture capital can impede the ability of smaller firms to compete with larger entities in adopting these technologies. In swiftly changing industries, maintaining competitiveness frequently requires continuous technological progress. Firms must persistently invest in Industry 4.0 to stay in tune with market demands. Market volatility and competition can exert pressure on companies to judiciously allocate resources. Expanding Industry 4.0 initiatives throughout a business can be intricate and costly (Kusiak, 2023). The extension of these technologies from initial pilot projects to comprehensive implementation may necessitate further investments in infrastructure and personnel.

The implementation of Industry 4.0 technologies undoubtedly offers substantial advantages, yet economic and financial barriers pose significant challenges. These hindrances, encompassing high initial expenditures, a scarcity of skilled personnel, integration complexities, concerns about data security, uncertain ROI, compliance with regulations, supplier reliability, limited financial accessibility, market unpredictability, and scalability issues, can impede progress. Overcoming these barriers requires meticulous planning, strategic investments, and a steadfast commitment to digital transformation.

7.4 Cultural and Organizational Resistance

The achievement of successful implementation of Industry 4.0 often encounters obstacles in the form of resistance within companies, both cultural and organizational in nature. Cultural resistance within organizations frequently has its origins in deep-seated traditions, beliefs, and attitudes. This resistance manifests as a reluctance to embrace novel technologies and methodologies due to apprehensions about change or a preference for familiar practices. As Chiarini et al. (2023) point out, a critical cultural barrier is the "fear of job loss" linked to automation and digitization. This fear can result in employees displaying limited enthusiasm for Industry 4.0 initiatives. Organizational resistance represents another significant hurdle in the path to implementing Industry 4.0. Companies characterized by rigid hierarchies and antiquated management approaches may grapple with adapting to the agile and collaborative essence of Industry 4.0. Resistance commonly emerges when managers are hesitant to relinquish control and empower employees to make decisions at lower levels (Mahmud et al., 2023). This hierarchical resistance can obstruct the adoption of Industry 4.0 principles, which accentuate decentralized decision-making. Cultural and organizational resistance present formidable challenges to the successful execution of Industry 4.0. Nonetheless, with the application of appropriate strategies, organizations can surmount these barriers and leverage the full potential of Industry 4.0 technologies. Effective leadership, communication, training, incentives, and change management constitute essential components of a comprehensive approach to addressing resistance. By proactively tackling these issues, companies can pave the way for a more seamless transition into the era of Industry 4.0.

8. FUTURE TRENDS AND RESEARCH DIRECTIONS IN INDUSTRY 4.0

8.1 Evolution of Industry 4.0 and Emerging Paradigms

The world of industry has witnessed a profound transformation with the emergence of Industry 4.0, representing the latest phase in the evolution of manufacturing and production. This revolution is characterized by the infusion of digital technologies into various facets of industrial processes, resulting in heightened efficiency, flexibility, and productivity. Industry 4.0 is founded on the convergence of several technological trends, including the IoT, AI, big data analytics, and advanced robotics. These technologies synergistically reshape traditional industrial practices and pave the way for emerging paradigms.

The cornerstone of Industry 4.0 lies in the concept of interconnected devices and systems, forming what is known as the IoT. According to Biswas et al. (2023), IoT enables machines and sensors to communicate and exchange data, facilitating real-time monitoring and control. This connectivity fosters predictive maintenance, where issues with machinery can be anticipated and addressed before they escalate. Moreover, AI and ML algorithms empower machines to learn from data, adapt to changes, and optimize processes autonomously. The copious amount of data generated by interconnected devices forms the bedrock of big data analytics, enabling informed decision-making and performance optimization, as highlighted by Li et al. (2023). Additionally, advanced robotics plays a pivotal role in revolutionizing production lines. Robots equipped with AI capabilities can perform intricate tasks with precision, enhancing production speed and quality. Emerging paradigms within Industry 4.0 are reshaping the industrial landscape. One such paradigm is "cyber-physical systems," where physical objects incorporate computing elements and connect to the digital realm. This integration facilitates real-time information exchange and remote control. "Smart factories" leverage data-driven insights to streamline processes and swiftly adapt to changing demands (Raufjonov, 2023). The transition to Industry 4.0 brings both challenges and opportunities. As indicated by Salahdine et al. (2022), concerns about data security and privacy arise due to increased connectivity, necessitating robust cybersecurity measures. Furthermore, there is a burgeoning demand for a skilled workforce capable of harnessing the potential of these technologies. In the pursuit of sustainability, environmental considerations have gained prominence.

In conclusion, Industry 4.0 represents a pivotal advancement in manufacturing, driven by the integration of IoT, AI, big data analytics, and advanced robotics. This evolution has given rise to emerging paradigms such as cyber-physical systems and smart factories, redefining the operational landscape of industries. Despite challenges, the potential benefits of Industry 4.0 are substantial, encompassing enhanced efficiency, improved product quality, and innovative business models. To thrive in this new era, industries must address cybersecurity concerns, invest in workforce development, and champion sustainable practices.

8.2 Impact of Quantum Computing and Neuromorphic Engineering

Quantum computing, an emerging field, harnesses the principles of quantum mechanics to revolutionize information processing fundamentally. It presents vast potential for tackling intricate optimization and simulation challenges across multiple industries. For instance, it can streamline supply chain logistics, expedite drug discovery processes, and enhance financial modelling with remarkable efficiency (L. Yang et al., 2023). The exponential speedup of quantum computers compared to classical counterparts holds substantial promise for refining manufacturing processes and product design. Furthermore, quantum computing can bolster cybersecurity by ushering in quantum-resistant encryption techniques (Gulyamov, 2023). Given that Industry 4.0 hinges on data exchange and connectivity, ensuring secure communication is of paramount importance. Quantum-resistant encryption guarantees the safeguarding of sensitive data within this interconnected ecosystem.

Neuromorphic engineering, inspired by the structural intricacies of the human brain, is centred around constructing hardware and software that emulate neural networks. This technology is a game-changer for Industry 4.0. Neuromorphic chips possess the ability to process vast volumes of data while consuming minimal power, rendering them ideal for real-time data analysis in manufacturing and the IoT (Dhanasekar et al., 2023). They empower machines to learn and adapt to shifting environments, thereby enhancing automation and decision-making processes. The impact of quantum computing and neuromorphic engineering extends across diverse industries. In the realm of healthcare, quantum computing expedites drug discovery by simulating molecular interactions (Flöther, 2023). Within manufacturing, neuromorphic sensors can bolster quality control by swiftly identifying defects in real time. The automotive sector benefits from quantum computing's optimization capabilities in supply chain management (Gupta & Sharma, 2023).

The energy sector also experiences transformation, as quantum computing aids in optimizing power grid management, leading to more efficient energy distribution. Neuromorphic engineering facilitates predictive maintenance in manufacturing, curtailing downtime and costs (Teubert, 2023). In agriculture, quantum computing can optimize crop yields through precise weather modelling and genetic analysis. Quantum computing and neuromorphic engineering are reshaping the landscape of Industry 4.0 by offering unparalleled computational power and real-time processing capabilities. Their applications span across a multitude of sectors, encompassing healthcare, manufacturing, and energy. As research advances and technology matures, these innovations hold the potential to revolutionize industries and shape the trajectory of the Fourth Industrial Revolution.

8.4 Collaborative Manufacturing and Global Industry 4.0 Ecosystems

Automation plays a crucial role in collaborative manufacturing, facilitating smooth coordination across different participants in the production process, including suppliers, manufacturers, and distributors. Automating routine tasks, such as data collection and analysis, minimizes errors and elevates operational efficiency (Aziz, 2023). This results in cost reductions and quicker time-to-market, providing a competitive advantage in today's global business landscape.

In the era of Industry 4.0, data holds significant value. Collaborative manufacturing encourages the real-time exchange of data among stakeholders, supporting well-informed decision-making. Leveraging data analytics and artificial intelligence, manufacturers can anticipate maintenance requirements, optimize production schedules, and tailor products to meet consumer demands (Bharadiya, 2023). This data-centric approach contributes to higher product quality and increased customer satisfaction. In a global context, companies can harness diverse talent pools and expertise from various geographical regions. Collaborative manufacturing networks often encompass startups, research institutions, and technology providers (Zhou & Wang, 2023). These partnerships drive the development of innovative technologies and solutions, fostering continuous improvement and adaptability to evolving market conditions. Recent global events, such as the COVID-19 pandemic, have highlighted the significance of robust supply chains. Collaborative manufacturing helps mitigate risks by diversifying suppliers and optimizing logistics. This approach bolsters supply chain resilience, ensuring that disruptions in one region have minimal impact on overall production (Zubairu, 2023). Sustainability has become a prominent concept in Industry 4.0 ecosystems. Collaborative manufacturing enables the exchange of best practices in sustainable production and resource management. Through process optimization and waste reduction, manufacturers can align with environmental regulations and meet consumer demands for eco-friendly products.

In summary, collaborative manufacturing within the global Industry 4.0 ecosystem is a transformative influence, enhancing efficiency, encouraging innovation, and strengthening supply chain resilience. The sharing of real-time data and expertise empowers manufacturers to make data-driven decisions and adapt to shifting market dynamics. Nonetheless, addressing challenges related to security, privacy, and trust remains vital for the sustained growth of collaborative manufacturing networks in the Industry 4.0 era.

9. CASE STUDIES ON INDUSTRY 4.0 IMPLEMENTATIONS

9.1 Case Study 1: Smart Factory Transformation in Automotive Industry

The notion of smart factories has attracted considerable attention across a range of industries. An illustrative instance of this concept can be found in the evolution of Tesla's manufacturing facilities into smart factories. Tesla embarked on the path toward smart factories by incorporating state-of-the-art technologies. The company adopted robotics, IoT devices, and AI systems to automate a variety of manufacturing processes. For example, they deployed robotic arms to handle tasks like assembling intricate components, reducing the reliance on human labour and ensuring precision (Karaarslan et al., 2023). Moreover, Tesla made use of IoT devices to collect real-time data from machinery and equipment, enabling the continuous monitoring of performance, predicting maintenance needs, and minimizing downtime.

A fundamental aspect of Tesla's transition into a smart factory was its unwavering focus on data-driven decision-making. The company harnessed AI algorithms to analyze vast volumes of data generated throughout the production process. This enabled predictive analysis of potential production bottlenecks, optimization of supply chain management, and a reduction in inventory costs (Pandey et al., 2023). Tesla's commitment to sustainability also extended to its smart factory practices (Jain et al., 2023). Tesla incorporated energy-efficient technologies such as solar panels and advanced lighting systems to reduce its carbon footprint. Through the optimization of energy consumption via smart grid integration, Tesla not only lower operational costs but also underscored its dedication to environmental responsibility.

The transformation of Tesla's manufacturing facilities into smart factories serves as a prominent case study, highlighting the effective utilization of advanced technologies to revolutionize manufacturing operations. By integrating robotics, AI, and IoT, Tesla streamlined its processes, reduced costs, and contributed to its sustainability objectives. This case study emphasizes the importance of embracing technological advancements to maintain a leading position in modern manufacturing, characterized by innovation and efficiency. Figure 12 shows the example of robots implementation in Automotive industry.

Figure 12. Robots in automotive Industry (Capgemini, 2023)

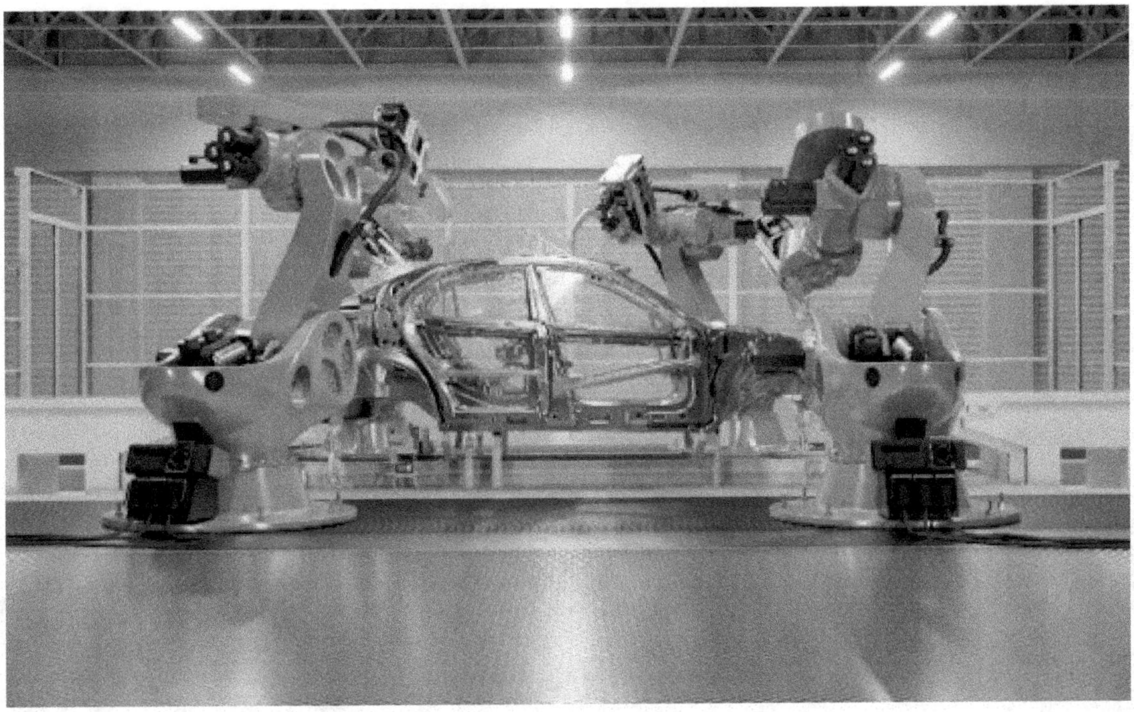

9.2 Case Study 3: AI-Driven Quality Control in Pharmaceutical Manufacturing

Quality control plays a crucial role in contemporary manufacturing, ensuring that products adhere to established standards. In the case of Prizer Company, a prominent manufacturer of appliances, the introduction of AI-powered quality control has transformed their production processes. This case study explores how AI technologies have bolstered quality control at Prizer Company, resulting in heightened product quality and operational efficiency.

Prizer Company, a leader in the realm of kitchen appliance manufacturing, grappled with the challenge of maintaining consistent product quality across its extensive product range. Traditional quality control methods proved to be time-consuming and susceptible to human errors. The adoption of AI-driven quality control sought to effectively address these issues. AI technologies, including computer vision and ML, have been seamlessly integrated into Prizer Company's production lines (Cano-Marin et al., 2023). Computer vision systems employ cameras and sophisticated algorithms to meticulously inspect products for defects. These systems have the remarkable ability to identify imperfections that could potentially escape human inspectors. The incorporation of AI has led to a substantial enhancement in efficiency. AI-powered machines can analyze products at speeds that manual inspection simply cannot match. This surge in production speed has translated into reduced lead times and improved delivery schedules. Figure 13 shows Robot Application in Pharmaceutical Manufacturing.

Figure 13. Robot application in pharmaceutical manufacturing (Schubert, n.d.)

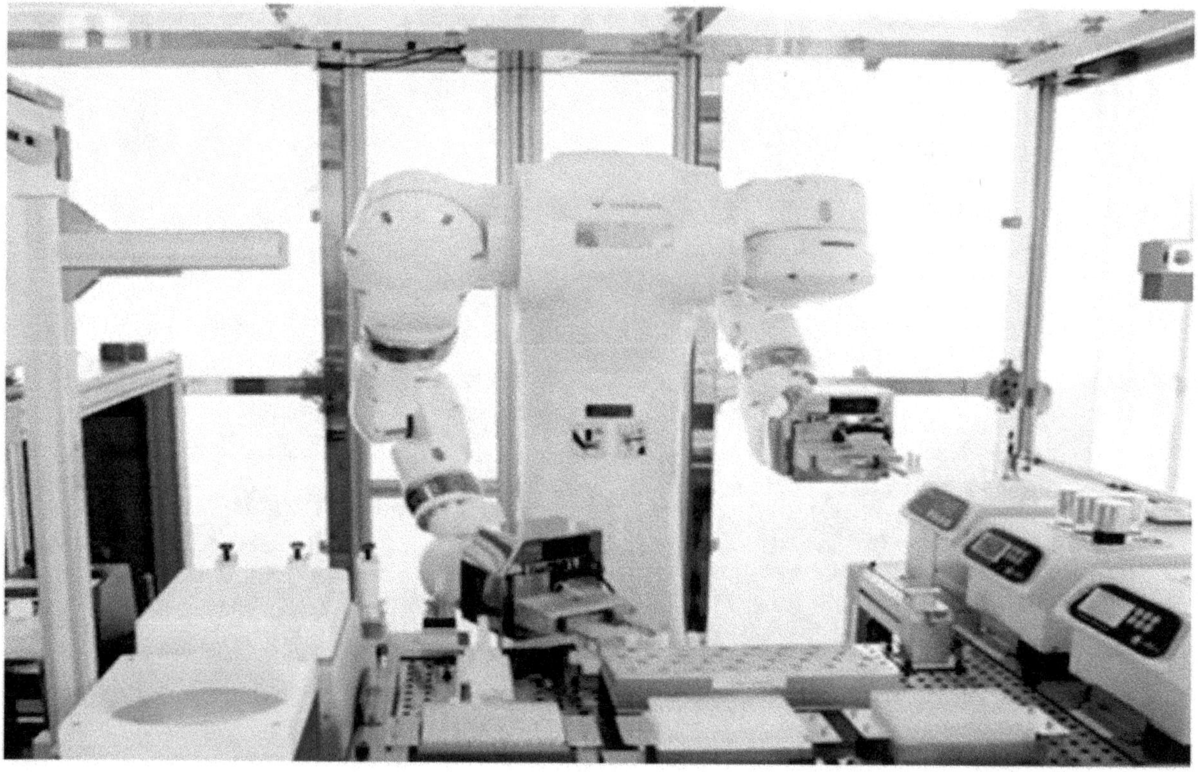

9.3 Case Study 4: Robotics and Automation in Aerospace Manufacturing

The aerospace industry has witnessed remarkable progress, with robotics and automation playing a central role in elevating manufacturing processes. This case study explores the integration of robotics and automation within the Boeing Aerospace Manufacturing Company, assessing their impact on efficiency, quality, and overall productivity. Boeing, a prominent leader in the aerospace sector, has embraced robotics and automation to streamline its manufacturing operations (Jiang et al., 2023). Robotic systems have been seamlessly incorporated at various stages of the production line, spanning assembly to quality control. These systems have taken over tasks that were previously labour-intensive and prone to errors, resulting in enhanced precision and reduced operational expenses. One of the primary advantages of employing robotics in Boeing's manufacturing processes is the substantial boost in efficiency. Robots excel at executing repetitive tasks with unwavering accuracy and speed, thereby shortening production cycle times (Guo, 2023). This, in turn, positively impacts the ability to meet delivery schedules and augments overall production capacity. Automation has also had a profound effect on the quality of aerospace components (T. Wang et al., 2023). Robots ensure that manufacturing processes adhere to precise tolerances, yielding parts that meet rigorous industry standards. This has led to a reduction in defects and the need for rework, ultimately resulting in heightened levels of customer satisfaction. Boeing has implemented collaborative robots, often referred to as "cobots," which operate alongside human workers in a shared workspace. These cobots assist in tasks that demand dexterity and decision-making, areas where human expertise is indispensable (Galizia et al., 2023). This collaborative synergy between humans and robots optimizes efficiency while simultaneously prioritizing safety in the manufacturing environment.

Figure 14. Robots in aerospace manufacturing (Edwards, 2018)

10. CONCLUSION

10.1 Recapitulation of Key Findings

1. **Enabling Technologies in Industry 4.0:** The core technologies of Industry 4.0, such as IoT, CPS, Big Data, AI, and robotics, are driving automation, data-driven decision-making, and flexible production. These technologies are interconnected and transformative, heralding the era of smart factories.
2. **Industry 4.0 and Digital Transformation:** Digital transformation is a critical driver of Industry 4.0. However, challenges like interoperability, legacy system integration, and data security need attention. Organizations must break down silos to fully embrace digital transformation.
3. **Industry 4.0 in Supply Chain Management:** Smart and connected supply chains, powered by Industry 4.0, offer real-time insights, inventory optimization, and collaborative capabilities. Supply chain analytics and visibility are central to efficiency and resilience.
4. **Industry 4.0 and Workforce of the Future:** Automation impacts jobs, requiring reskilling and upskilling efforts. Human-robot collaboration is vital, with roles evolving towards higher-level tasks. Preparing the workforce for this shift is paramount.

5. **Sustainability and Circular Economy in Industry 4.0:** Industry 4.0 technologies can promote sustainability through energy efficiency and waste reduction. Circular economy principles can be integrated into smart factories, minimizing environmental impact.
6. **Challenges and Barriers to Implementing Industry 4.0:** Barriers to adoption include technological challenges, data security concerns, regulatory issues, financial barriers, and resistance to change. Addressing these hurdles is crucial for successful implementation.
7. **Future Trends and Research Directions in Industry 4.0:** The evolution of Industry 4.0 will involve emerging paradigms, advancements in existing technologies, and the integration of quantum computing and neuromorphic engineering. Ethical considerations and collaborative global ecosystems will play a vital role.
8. **Case Studies on Industry 4.0 Implementations:** Real-world examples demonstrate the practical benefits of Industry 4.0. These include smart factory transformations in the automotive industry, AI-enabled quality control in pharmaceuticals, and advanced robotics in aerospace manufacturing.

10.2 Summary of Future Trends and Research Directions in Industry 4.0

In conclusion, Industry 4.0 stands as a transformative force that is reshaping the landscape of manufacturing and beyond. This chapter has delved into the evolution, key concepts, and profound impacts of Industry 4.0 across various sectors. The amalgamation of enabling technologies, such as IoT, CPS, big data analytics, additive manufacturing, AI, cloud computing, and robotics, has laid the foundation for smart factories and connected ecosystems. However, the journey towards Industry 4.0 is not devoid of challenges. Digital transformation has emerged as a critical driver, underlining the need for seamless connectivity, interoperability, and integration with legacy systems. Despite the promises of efficiency and innovation, concerns over data security, privacy, and the coexistence of human and automated workforce continue to pose formidable hurdles. Industry 4.0 has also cast its influence on supply chain management, workforce dynamics, and sustainability practices. Real-time inventory management, collaborative supply chains, workforce reskilling, and the integration of circular economy principles stand as essential elements in this era of transformation.

As we peer into the future, several trends and research directions beckon. The evolution of Industry 4.0 is expected to embrace emerging paradigms and technologies, with quantum computing and neuromorphic engineering potentially revolutionizing manufacturing processes. Moreover, ethical considerations and sustainability will play an even more significant role, necessitating responsible innovation and the cultivation of green manufacturing practices. Collaboration will extend beyond organizational boundaries, giving rise to global Industry 4.0 ecosystems where sharing knowledge, data, and best practices will be pivotal. The case studies presented within this report underscore the practicality and effectiveness of Industry 4.0 implementations across diverse sectors, solidifying its relevance and potential for revolutionizing traditional manufacturing. In the grand tapestry of Industry 4.0, challenges coexist with opportunities, demanding collective effort from industries, governments, and academia. The future is a canvas where innovation and adaptability will shape the trajectory of manufacturing, and the insights gathered from this report provide a compass for navigating the uncharted territory of Industry 4.0.

10.3 Implications and Recommendations for Industry, Academia, and Policymakers

The advent of Industry 4.0 has ushered in a new era of manufacturing and business processes, marked by the integration of cutting-edge technologies into various sectors. The implications of this transformation are significant for industry players, academia, and policymakers alike. Addressing these implications and proactively taking steps to navigate them will be crucial for maximizing the benefits of Industry 4.0 while mitigating potential challenges.

Industry stakeholders must recognize that embracing Industry 4.0 is not just an option but a necessity to remain competitive in the rapidly evolving market landscape. Investments in enabling technologies such as IoT, AI, and robotics should be prioritized, but a holistic approach is required. Companies should focus on workforce upskilling and reskilling initiatives to prepare employees for the changing roles and responsibilities in smart factories. Collaboration and partnerships within the industry ecosystem will be essential for sharing best practices, reducing implementation costs, and driving innovation.

Academic institutions play a pivotal role in shaping the future of Industry 4.0. They should revamp curricula to reflect the multidisciplinary nature of this transformation, emphasizing not only technical skills but also soft skills like adaptability, critical thinking, and collaboration. Research endeavours should explore novel applications and advancements in Industry 4.0 technologies, addressing challenges such as interoperability, security, and sustainability. Collaboration between academia and industry can facilitate technology transfer, foster innovation, and bridge the gap between theoretical knowledge and practical implementation.

Policymakers must formulate regulations and standards that encourage the adoption of Industry 4.0 while safeguarding data privacy, security, and ethical considerations. Incentive programs can motivate industries to invest in upgrading their manufacturing processes, ensuring a smooth transition. Addressing the potential impact of job displacement due to automation is vital; policymakers can facilitate reskilling initiatives and social safety nets to support affected workers. Moreover, international collaboration in establishing global standards will promote interoperability and facilitate seamless cross-border operations in the Industry 4.0 landscape.

In conclusion, Industry 4.0 holds immense promise for reshaping industries, economies, and societies. Industry players should proactively invest in technological adoption and human capital development. Academia must adapt to the changing educational needs, fostering innovation and research. Policymakers should create an enabling environment that balances innovation with regulation and addresses the social implications of the transformation. By working together, industry, academia, and policymakers can harness the potential of Industry 4.0 for a sustainable and technologically advanced future.

REFERENCES

Aadil, F., Mehmood, B., Hasan, N. U., Lim, S., Ejaz, S., & Jhanjhi, N. Z. (2021). Remote health monitoring using IoT-Based Smart Wireless Body Area Network. *Computers, Materials & Continua*, *68*(2), 2499–2513. doi:10.32604/cmc.2021.014647

Abdullah, F. M., Al-Ahmari, A., & Anwar, S. (2023). Analyzing Interdependencies among Influencing Factors in Smart Manufacturing. *Sustainability (Basel)*, *15*(4), 3864. doi:10.3390/su15043864

Abughazala, M., & Muccini, H. (2023). Modeling Data Analytics Architecture for IoT Applications using DAT. *2023 IEEE 20th International Conference on Software Architecture Companion (ICSA-C)*. 10.1109/ICSA-C57050.2023.00066

Acciarini, C., Cappa, F., Boccardelli, P., & Oriani, R. (2023). How can organizations leverage big data to innovate their business models? A systematic literature review. *Technovation, 123*, 102713. doi:10.1016/j.technovation.2023.102713

Afenyo, M., & Caesar, L. D. (2023). Maritime cybersecurity threats: Gaps and directions for future research. *Ocean and Coastal Management, 236*, 106493. doi:10.1016/j.ocecoaman.2023.106493

Ahn, J., Lee, Y., Kim, N. V., Park, C., & Jeong, J. (2023). Federated learning for predictive maintenance and anomaly detection using time series data distribution shifts in manufacturing processes. *Sensors (Basel), 23*(17), 7331. doi:10.3390/s23177331 PMID:37687787

Ahn, K., Du, J., Farag, M., & Rakha, H. A. (2022). Evaluating an Eco-Cooperative automated control system. *Transportation Research Record: Journal of the Transportation Research Board, 2677*(2), 1562–1578. doi:10.1177/03611981221113315

Al Meslamani, A. (2023). Applications of AI in pharmacy practice: A look at hospital and community settings. *Journal of Medical Economics, 26*(1), 1081–1084. Advance online publication. doi:10.1080/13696998.2023.2249758 PMID:37594444

Al-Sherideh, A. S., Maabreh, K., Maabreh, M., Mousa, M. R. A., & Asassfeh, M. (2023). Assessing the impact and Effectiveness of cybersecurity measures in e-Learning on students and Educators: A case study. *International Journal of Advanced Computer Science and Applications, 14*(5). Advance online publication. doi:10.14569/IJACSA.2023.0140516

Ali, I., Jhanjhi, N. Z., Amsaad, F., & Razaque, A. (2022). The role of Cutting-Edge Technologies in Industry 4.0. In Chapman and Hall/CRC eBooks (pp. 97–109). doi:10.1201/9781003203087-4

Alkahtani, H., Aldhyani, T. H. H., & Alsubari, S. N. (2023). Application of artificial intelligence model solar radiation prediction for renewable energy systems. *Sustainability (Basel), 15*(8), 6973. doi:10.3390/su15086973

Alkaraan, F., Elmarzouky, M., Hussainey, K., & Venkatesh, V. (2023). Sustainable strategic investment decision-making practices in UK companies: The influence of governance mechanisms on synergy between industry 4.0 and circular economy. *Technological Forecasting and Social Change, 187*, 122187. doi:10.1016/j.techfore.2022.122187

Allahloh, A. S., Sarfraz, M., Ghaleb, A. M., Al-Shamma'a, A. A., Farh, H. M. H., & Al-Shaalan, A. M. (2023). Revolutionizing IC Genset Operations with IIoT and AI: A Study on Fuel Savings and Predictive Maintenance. *Sustainability (Basel), 15*(11), 8808. doi:10.3390/su15118808

Allioui, H. (2023, August 16). *Unleashing the potential of AI: Investigating Cutting-Edge technologies that are transforming businesses*. https://ijceds.com/ijceds/article/view/59

Almusaylim, Z. A., & Jhanjhi, N. Z. (2018). A review on smart home present state and challenges: Linked to context-awareness internet of things (IoT). *Wireless Networks*, *25*(6), 3193–3204. doi:10.1007/s11276-018-1712-5

Alshammari, M. O., Almulhem, A. A., & Jhanjhi, N. Z. (2017). Internet of Things (IoT) : Charity automation. *International Journal of Advanced Computer Science and Applications*, *8*(2). Advance online publication. doi:10.14569/IJACSA.2017.080222

Aminizadeh, S., Heidari, A., Toumaj, S., Darbandi, M., Navimipour, N. J., Rezaei, M., Talebi, S., Azad, P. C. S., & Unal, M. (2023). The Applications of Machine Learning Techniques in Medical Data Processing based on Distributed Computing and the Internet of Things. *Computer Methods and Programs in Biomedicine*, *241*, 107745. doi:10.1016/j.cmpb.2023.107745 PMID:37579550

Anandan, R., Gopalakrishnan, S., Pal, S., & Zaman, N. (2022). *Industrial Internet of Things (IIoT): Intelligent Analytics for Predictive Maintenance*. John Wiley & Sons. doi:10.1002/9781119769026

Anna. (2018, May 3). *New research: Robots create jobs*. Robotics & Automation News. https://roboticsandautomationnews.com/2018/05/03/new-research-robots-create-jobs/17067/

Appio, F. P., La Torre, D., Lazzeri, F., Masri, H., & Schiavone, F. (2023). *Impact of artificial intelligence in business and society: Opportunities and Challenges*. Taylor & Francis.

Arcadio, R. D. (2023, July 7). *Construction workers' skills, competencies, knowledge and job satisfaction in industry 4.0 technologies*. http://www.inovatus.es/index.php/ejbsos/article/view/1854

Arguelles, P. Jr, & Polkowski, Z. (2023). Impact of Big Data on Supply Chain Performance through Demand Forecasting. *International Journal of Computations. Information and Manufacturing*, *3*(1), 19–26. doi:10.54489/ijcim.v3i1.232

Aski, V., Dhaka, V. S., Parashar, A., Kumar, S., & Rida, I. (2023). Internet of Things in healthcare: A survey on protocol standards, enabling technologies, WBAN architectures and open issues. *Physical Communication*, *60*, 102103. doi:10.1016/j.phycom.2023.102103

Aspray, W., & Doty, P. (2023). Does technology really outpace policy, and does it matter? A primer for technical experts and others. *Journal of the Association for Information Science and Technology*, *74*(8), 885–904. doi:10.1002/asi.24762

Attaran, M. (2021). The impact of 5G on the evolution of intelligent automation and industry digitization. *Journal of Ambient Intelligence and Humanized Computing*, *14*(5), 5977–5993. doi:10.1007/s12652-020-02521-x PMID:33643481

Awad, A., & Basit, A. W. (2023). 3D and 4D Printing in Digital Healthcare. In AAPS Introductions in the Pharmaceutical Sciences (pp. 1–23). doi:10.1007/978-3-031-34119-9_1

Aziz, F. (2023). *Beyond the ledger: Enhancing Global Sustainability through Data-Driven Accounting Frameworks*. Farooq Aziz.

Bach, M. P., Topalović, A., Krstić, Ž., & Ivec, A. (2023). Predictive Maintenance in Industry 4.0 for the SMEs: A Decision Support System case Study using Open-Source Software. *Designs*, *7*(4), 98. doi:10.3390/designs7040098

Bag, S., Dhamija, P., Luthra, S., & Huisingh, D. (2021). How big data analytics can help manufacturing companies strengthen supply chain resilience in the context of the COVID-19 pandemic. *International Journal of Logistics Management*, *34*(4), 1141–1164. doi:10.1108/IJLM-02-2021-0095

Balanzar Almazan, P. (2023). *Digitizing Work Instructions Through Technology using Internet of Things (IoT)* [MA Thesis]. University of Texas at El Paso.

Bansal, A., Panchal, T., Jabeen, F., Mangla, S. K., & Singh, G. (2023). A study of human resource digital transformation (HRDT): A phenomenon of innovation capability led by digital and individual factors. *Journal of Business Research*, *157*, 113611. doi:10.1016/j.jbusres.2022.113611

Barboni, L. (2023). Machine Learning and Edge Computing for Industry 4.0 Applications: Concepts and Extensive review. In EAI/Springer Innovations in Communication and Computing (pp. 3–19). doi:10.1007/978-3-031-29775-5_1

Behera, B. C., Moharana, B. R., Muduli, K., & Islam. (2023). *Smart technologies for improved performance of manufacturing systems and services*. CRC Press.

Bella, S. (2023). Enhancing financial management and accountant roles: A study on the role of technological Advancements. *Bella | SEIKO : Journal of Management & Business*. https://doi.org/ doi:10.37531/sejaman.v6i2.4842

Benos, L., Moysiadis, V., Kateris, D., Tagarakis, A. C., Busato, P., Pearson, S., & Bochtis, D. (2023). Human–Robot interaction in agriculture: A Systematic review. *Sensors (Basel)*, *23*(15), 6776. doi:10.3390/s23156776 PMID:37571559

Bharadiya, J. (2023). Machine learning and AI in Business intelligence: Trends and opportunities. *ResearchGate*. https://www.researchgate.net/publication/371902170_Machine_Learning_and_AI_in_Business_Intelligence_Trends_and_Opportunities

Bhowal, A. J. B. P. A. (2023, July 20). *Unraveling the Intricacies of Behavioral Biases: Exploring their Profound Influence on Working Capital Management Strategies of Entrepreneurs*. http://journals.kozminski.cem-j.org/index.php/pl_cemj/article/view/900

Biswas, K., Ghazzai, H., Sboui, L., & Massoud, Y. (2023). Urban Air Mobility: An IoT perspective. *IEEE Internet of Things Magazine*, *6*(2), 122–128. doi:10.1109/IOTM.001.2200237

Blat, M. O. (2023). *Enhancing big data Analytics capabilities: the influence of organisational culture and Data-Driven Orientation*. doi:10.4995/Thesis/10251/191788

Cabibihan, J., Gaballa, A., Fadli, F., Irshidat, M., Mahdi, E., Biloria, N., Mansour, Z., & Abdulrazak, H. (2023). A guided approach for utilizing concrete robotic 3D printing for the architecture, engineering, and construction industry. *Construction Robotics*, *7*(3-4), 265–278. Advance online publication. doi:10.1007/s41693-023-00103-9

Cano-Marin, E., Soriano, D. R., Mardani, A., & González-Tejero, C. B. (2023). Exploring the challenges of the COVID-19 vaccine supply chain using social media analytics: A global perspective. *Sustainable Technology and Entrepreneurship*, *100047*(3), 100047. Advance online publication. doi:10.1016/j.stae.2023.100047

Capgemini. (2023, July 13). *How automotive organizations can maximize the smart factory potential | Research & insight | Capgemini.* https://www.capgemini.com/insights/research-library/automotive-smart-factories/

Carboni, A., Russo, D., Moroni, D., & Barsocchi, P. (2023). Privacy by design in systems for assisted living, personalised care, and wellbeing: A stakeholder analysis. *Frontiers in Digital Health*, *4*, 934609. Advance online publication. doi:10.3389/fdgth.2022.934609 PMID:36860207

Chataut, R. (2023). *Unleashing the Power of IoT: A comprehensive review of IoT applications and future prospects in healthcare, agriculture, smart homes, smart cities, and industry 4.0.* MDPI. doi:10.3390/s23167194

Chee, S. Y. (2023). Age-related digital disparities, functional limitations, and social isolation: Unraveling the grey digital divide between baby boomers and the silent generation in senior living facilities. *Aging & Mental Health*, 1–12. doi:10.1080/13607863.2023.2233454 PMID:37424361

Cheung, C. F., Lee, C. K. M., Zheng, P., & Lee, W. B. (2023). Digital manufacturing systems. In Springer handbooks (pp. 805–827). doi:10.1007/978-3-030-96729-1_36

Chiarini, A., Grando, A., Venturini, S., & Borgonovo, E. (2023). Do automation and AI impact on job reduction? A study on perceived risk of losing job among white-collars in the Italian manufacturing companies. *Production Planning and Control*, 1–14. doi:10.1080/09537287.2023.2244925

Ciğerci, M. (2023). Main Effects of Big Data on Supply Chain Management. In Implementation Of Disruptive Technologies In Supply Chain Management (pp. 27–49). doi:10.59287/idtscm.68

Colombi, C., & D'Itria, E. (2023). Fashion Digital Transformation: Innovating Business Models toward Circular Economy and Sustainability. *Sustainability (Basel)*, *15*(6), 4942. doi:10.3390/su15064942

Cressman, J., Pokharna, R., & Newman, W. (2023). Compliant robotic behaviors for satellite servicing. *Frontiers in Robotics and AI*, *10*, 1124207. Advance online publication. doi:10.3389/frobt.2023.1124207 PMID:37533424

Cui, Y., Ma, Z., Wang, L., Yang, A., Liu, Q., Kong, S., & Wang, H. (2023). A survey on big data-enabled innovative online education systems during the COVID-19 pandemic. *Journal of Innovation & Knowledge*, *8*(1), 100295. doi:10.1016/j.jik.2022.100295

Da Silva, F. T., Baierle, I. C., De Faria Corrêa, R. G., Sellitto, M. A., Peres, F. P., & Kipper, L. M. (2023). Open Innovation in Agribusiness: Barriers and challenges in the transition to Agriculture 4.0. *Sustainability (Basel)*, *15*(11), 8562. doi:10.3390/su15118562

Dani, S., Rahman, A., Jin, J., & Kulkarni, A. (2023). Cloud-Empowered Data-Centric paradigm for smart manufacturing. *Machines*, *11*(4), 451. doi:10.3390/machines11040451

Dave, M., & Patel, N. (2023). Artificial intelligence in healthcare and education. *British Dental Journal*, *234*(10), 761–764. doi:10.1038/s41415-023-5845-2 PMID:37237212

De, P., Biase, L. C., Fedrecheski, G., Calcina-Ccori, P. C., De Deus Lopes, R., & Zuffo, M. K. (2023). Swarm Computing: the emergence of a collective artificial intelligence at the edge of the internet. In IntechOpen eBooks. doi:10.5772/intechopen.110907

De Azambuja, A. J. G., Plesker, C., Schützer, K., Anderl, R., Schleich, B., & Almeida, V. R. (2023). Artificial Intelligence-Based Cyber Security in the context of Industry 4.0—A survey. *Electronics (Basel), 12*(8), 1920. doi:10.3390/electronics12081920

Deivanayagampillai, N., Jacob, K., Manohar, G. V., & Broumi, S. (2023, July 29). *Investigation Of Industry 5.0 Hurdles And Their Mitigation Tactics In Emerging Economies By Todim Arithmetic And Geometric Aggregation Operators In Single Value Neutrosophic Environment.* Deivanayagampillai | Facta Universitatis, Series: Mechanical Engineering. http://casopisi.junis.ni.ac.rs/index.php/FUMechEng/article/view/11987

Ding, B., Hernández, X. F., & Agell, N. (2021). Combining lean and agile manufacturing competitive advantages through Industry 4.0 technologies: An integrative approach. *Production Planning and Control, 34*(5), 442–458. doi:10.1080/09537287.2021.1934587

Dod, G. N., Jibhakate, R., & Walke, P. V. (2023). A review on 3D printing maxillofacial surgery: Present work and future prospects. *Materials Today: Proceedings.* Advance online publication. doi:10.1016/j.matpr.2023.06.049

Dorcheh, F. R., & Rahbari, M. (2023). Greenhouse Gas Emissions Optimization for Distribution and Vehicle Routing Problem in a Poultry Meat Supply Chain in Two Phases: a Case Study in Iran. *Process Integration and Optimization for Sustainability.* doi:10.1007/s41660-023-00339-6

Dorn, T. M. (2023). *U.S. critical infrastructure: Its Importance and Vulnerabilities to Cyber and Unmanned Systems.* Page Publishing Inc.

Dutta, P., Chavhan, R., Gowtham, P., & Singh, A. (2022). The individual and integrated impact of Blockchain and IoT on sustainable supply chains:a systematic review. *Supply Chain Forum, 24*(1), 103–126. 10.1080/16258312.2022.2082851

Edwards, D. (2018, December 11). *Aerospace robotics market predicted to grow as manufacturers turn to automation to meet orders.* Robotics & Automation News. https://roboticsandautomationnews.com/2018/12/11/aerospace-robotics-market-predicted-to-grow-as-manufacturers-turn-to-automation-to-meet-orders/20102/

Ehsanifar, M., Dekamini, F., Spulbar, C., Birau, R., Khazaei, M., & Bărbăcioru, I. C. (2023). A sustainable pattern of waste management and energy efficiency in smart homes using the internet of things (IoT). *Sustainability (Basel), 15*(6), 5081. doi:10.3390/su15065081

El-Gendy, S., Elsayed, M. S., Jurcut, A. D., & Azer, M. A. (2023). Privacy preservation using machine learning in the internet of things. *Mathematics, 11*(16), 3477. doi:10.3390/math11163477

El-Haggar, N., Amouri, L., Alsumayt, A., Alghamedy, F., & Aljameel, S. S. (2023). The Effectiveness and Privacy Preservation of IoT on Ubiquitous Learning: Modern Learning Paradigm to Enhance Higher Education. *Applied Sciences (Basel, Switzerland), 13*(15), 9003. doi:10.3390/app13159003

Endress, T. (2023). *Digital project practice for new work and industry 4.0.* Auerbach Publications. doi:10.1201/9781003371397

Farjana, M., Fahad, A. B., Alam, S. E., & Islam, M. M. (2023). An IoT- and Cloud-Based E-Waste Management System for Resource Reclamation with a Data-Driven Decision-Making Process. *Iot*, *4*(3), 202–220. doi:10.3390/iot4030011

Feng, W., & Avilés, J. V. M. (2023). Enhancing operational efficiency: Integrating machine learning predictive capabilities in business intellgence for informed Decision-Making. *Frontiers in Business. Economics and Management*, *9*(1), 282–286. doi:10.54097/fbem.v9i1.8694

Flöther, F. F. (2023). The state of quantum computing applications in health and medicine. *Cornell University*, 1–21. doi:10.1017/qut.2023.4

Frank, A. G. (2023). *A journey towards Industry 4.0: The supporting role of socio-technical systems.* https://lume.ufrgs.br/handle/10183/263204

Galanti, T., De Vincenzi, C., Buonomo, I., & Benevene, P. (2023). Digital transformation: Inevitable change or sizable opportunity? The Strategic role of HR Management in Industry 4.0. *Administrative Sciences*, *13*(2), 30. doi:10.3390/admsci13020030

Galizia, F. G., Bortolini, M., & Calabrese, F. (2023). A cross-sectorial review of industrial best practices and case histories on Industry 4.0 technologies. *Systems Engineering*, *26*(6), 908–924. Advance online publication. doi:10.1002/sys.21697

Gamal, A. (2023). loT in supply chain management. In Duvar (pp. 103–132). doi:10.59287/idtscm.72

George, D., George, A., & Martin, A. (2023). ChatGPT and the Future of Work: A Comprehensive analysis of AI's impact on jobs and employment. Zenodo *(CERN European Organization for Nuclear Research)*. doi:10.5281/zenodo.8076921

Ghajar, F. G., & Reich, C. (2023). Bridge of Trust: Cross Domain Authentication for Industrial Internet of Things (IIoT) Blockchain over Transport Layer Security (TLS). *Electronics (Basel)*, *12*(11), 2401. doi:10.3390/electronics12112401

Gillott, C., Mihkelson, W., Lanau, M., Cheshire, D., & Tingley, D. D. (2023). Developing regenerate: A circular economy engagement tool for the assessment of new and existing buildings. *Journal of Industrial Ecology*, *27*(2), 423–435. Advance online publication. doi:10.1111/jiec.13377

Gokkaya, B., Aniello, L., & Halak, B. (2023). Software supply chain: review of attacks, risk assessment strategies and security controls. *arXiv (Cornell University)*. https://doi.org//arxiv.2305.14157 doi:10.48550

Gulyamov, S. (2023). Quantum Law: Navigating the legal challenges and opportunities in the age of Quantum Technologies. *irshadjournals.com*. https://doi.org/ doi:10.59022/ujldp.54

Guo, D. (2023). Fast scheduling of human-robot teams collaboration on synchronised production-logistics tasks in aircraft assembly. *Robotics and Computer-integrated Manufacturing*, *85*, 102620. doi:10.1016/j.rcim.2023.102620

Gupta, S., & Sharma, V. (2023). Effects of Quantum computing on Businesses. *2023 4th International Conference on Intelligent Engineering and Management (ICIEM)*. 10.1109/ICIEM59379.2023.10166880

Haber, L., & Carmeli, A. (2023). Leading the challenges of implementing new technologies in organizations. *Technology in Society*, *74*, 102300. doi:10.1016/j.techsoc.2023.102300

Hamrol, A., Hoffmann, M., Lisek, M., & Bozek, J. (2023). The Quality of Surgical Instrument Surfaces Machined with Robotic Belt Grinding. *Materials (Basel)*, *16*(2), 630. doi:10.3390/ma16020630 PMID:36676377

Hamzah, M., Islam, M. M., Hassan, S., Akhtar, M. N., Ferdous, M. J., Jasser, M. B., & Mohamed, A. W. (2023). Distributed control of cyber physical system on various domains: A Critical review. *Systems*, *11*(4), 208. doi:10.3390/systems11040208

Han, C., & Mardani, A. (2023). Research on the impact of consumer privacy and intelligent personalization technology on purchase resistance. *Journal of Business Research*, *161*, 113811. doi:10.1016/j.jbusres.2023.113811

Hasan, M. H., Osman, M. H., Admodisastro, N., & Muhammad, S. (2023). Legacy systems to cloud migration: A review from the architectural perspective. *Journal of Systems and Software*, *202*, 111702. doi:10.1016/j.jss.2023.111702

Hassan, S. M., Tahir, M. N., Uppal, M., Khalid, Z., Gorban, I. S., & Turki, S. (2023). STEF-DHNET: Spatiotemporal External Factors based Deep Hybrid Network for Enhanced Long-Term Taxi Demand Prediction. *arXiv (Cornell University)*. https://doi.org//arxiv.2306.14476 doi:10.48550

Heidary, R., Rao, J. P., & Fischer, O. (2023). Smart buildings in the IoT era – necessity, challenges, and opportunities. In Springer eBooks (pp. 1–21). doi:10.1007/978-3-030-72322-4_115-1

Heikkilä, S., Ghoreishi, M., & Deviatkin, I. (2023). From waste to value: enhancing circular value creation in municipal solid waste management ecosystem through artificial intelligence-powered robots. In Elsevier eBooks (pp. 415–428). doi:10.1016/B978-0-323-95278-1.00014-0

Himeur, Y., Elnour, M., Fadli, F., Meskin, N., Petri, I., Rezgui, Y., Bensaali, F., & Amira, A. (2022). AI-big data analytics for building automation and management systems: A survey, actual challenges and future perspectives. *Artificial Intelligence Review*, *56*(6), 4929–5021. doi:10.1007/s10462-022-10286-2 PMID:36268476

Hraiga, R. A., Ali, A. M., & Abbas, A. A. (2023). The role of green process reengineering in improving the performance of total productive maintenance. *Holistica*, *14*(1), 82–109. doi:10.2478/hjbpa-2023-0006

Hsu, P., Lei, H., Cheng, M., & Yuan, T. F. (2023). Applying data driven approach to cluster components for preventive maintenance. In Lecture notes in production engineering (pp. 197–205). doi:10.1007/978-3-031-18641-7_19

Hu, H., Xu, J., Liu, M., & Lim, M. K. (2023). Vaccine supply chain management: An intelligent system utilizing blockchain, IoT and machine learning. *Journal of Business Research*, *156*, 113480. doi:10.1016/j.jbusres.2022.113480 PMID:36506475

Humayun, M., Alsaqer, M., & Jhanjhi, N. Z. (2022). Energy optimization for smart cities using IoT. *Applied Artificial Intelligence*, *36*(1), 2037255. Advance online publication. doi:10.1080/08839514.2022.2037255

Humayun, M., Jhanjhi, N., & Alamri, M. Z. (2020). IoT-based Secure and Energy Efficient scheme for E-health applications. *Indian Journal of Science and Technology*, *13*(28), 2833–2848. doi:10.17485/IJST/v13i28.861

Jabeen, T., Jabeen, I., Ashraf, H., Jhanjhi, N. Z., Yassine, A., & Hossain, M. S. (2023). An intelligent healthcare system using IoT in wireless sensor network. *Sensors (Basel)*, *23*(11), 5055. doi:10.3390/s23115055 PMID:37299782

JainY.GuptaS.YalcinerS.JoglekarY. N.KhetanP.ZhangT. (2023). Overcoming complexity in ESG Investing: The role of Generative AI integration in identifying contextual ESG factors. *Social Science Research Network*. doi:10.2139/ssrn.4495647

Jamil, F., Toh, Y. P., & Chi-Tsun, C. (2023). Developing an i4.0 Cyber-Physical system to enhance efficiency and competitiveness in manufacturing. *Applied Sciences (Basel, Switzerland)*, *16*(13), 9333. Advance online publication. doi:10.3390/app13169333

Jarašūnienė, A., Čižiūnienė, K., & Čereška, A. (2023). Research on Impact of IoT on Warehouse Management. *Sensors (Basel)*, *23*(4), 2213. doi:10.3390/s23042213 PMID:36850811

Javanmard, M. E., Tang, Y., Wang, Z., & Tontiwachwuthikul, P. (2023). Forecast energy demand, CO2 emissions and energy resource impacts for the transportation sector. *Applied Energy*, *338*, 120830. doi:10.1016/j.apenergy.2023.120830

Javier, Á. C. O. (2023, August 4). *An evaluation-aware method for transforming a production system into a cyber-physical production system*. Universidad De Los Andes. https://repositorio.uniandes.edu.co/handle/1992/69519

Jazdi, N. (2014). *Cyber physical systems in the context of Industry 4.0*. CRC Cyber Physical. doi:10.1109/AQTR.2014.6857843

Jha, P. K., Teotia, F., & Saxena, A. K. (2023). Cyber Security in the Indian Electricity Distribution System: A Review. *2023 5th International Conference on Energy, Power and Environment: Towards Flexible Green Energy Technologies (ICEPE)*. 10.1109/ICEPE57949.2023.10201598

Jiang, Y., Tran, T. H., & Williams, L. (2023). Machine learning and mixed reality for smart aviation: Applications and challenges. *Journal of Air Transport Management*, *111*, 102437. doi:10.1016/j.jairtraman.2023.102437

Josphineleela, R. (2023, August 16). *Exploration Beyond Boundaries: AI-Based advancements in rover robotics for lunar Missions space like Chandrayaan*. https://www.ijisae.org/index.php/IJISAE/article/view/3318

Kafi, M., & Akter, N. (2023). Securing Financial Information in the Digital realm: Case studies in Cybersecurity for Accounting Data Protection. *American Journal of Trade and Policy*, *10*(1), 15–26. doi:10.18034/ajtp.v10i1.659

Kamble, S. S., & Gunasekaran, A. (2021). Analysing the role of Industry 4.0 technologies and circular economy practices in improving sustainable performance in Indian manufacturing organisations. *Production Planning and Control*, 1–15. doi:10.1080/09537287.2021.1980904

Kara, M. (2023). A comprehensive framework for emergency in Robotic environments. *IEEE Access : Practical Innovations, Open Solutions, 11*, 82539–82547. doi:10.1109/ACCESS.2023.3301155

Karaarslan, E., Aydin, Ö., Cali, Ü., & Challenger, M. (2023). *Digital twin driven intelligent systems and emerging metaverse*. Springer Nature. doi:10.1007/978-981-99-0252-1

KareskaK. (2023). Key factors for increasing the productivity of production organizations. *Social Science Research Network*. doi:10.2139/ssrn.4532554

Kartik, B., & P, M. (2023). IOT based Smart Helmet for Hazard Detection in mining industry. *arXiv (Cornell University)*. doi:10.48550/arxiv.2304.10156

Kazancoglu, Y., Ekinci, E., Mangla, S. K., Sezer, M. D., Choudhary, S., & Dora, M. (2023). Smart Closed-Loop food supply chain in circular economy. *IEEE Transactions on Engineering Management*, 1–18. doi:10.1109/TEM.2023.3303272

Kazemi, Z., Rask, J. K., Gomes, C., Yildiz, E., & Larsen, P. G. (2023). Movable factory—A systematic literature review of concepts, requirements, applications, and gaps. *Journal of Manufacturing Systems, 69*, 189–207. doi:10.1016/j.jmsy.2023.06.008

Kee, D. M. H., Cordova, M., & Khin, S. (2023). The key enablers of SMEs readiness in Industry 4.0: a case of Malaysia. *International Journal of Emerging Markets*. doi:10.1108/IJOEM-08-2021-1291

Keung, K. L., Lee, C., Xia, L., Liu, C., Liu, B., & Ji, P. (2023). A cyber-physical robotic mobile fulfillment system in smart manufacturing: The simulation aspect. *Robotics and Computer-integrated Manufacturing, 83*, 102578. doi:10.1016/j.rcim.2023.102578

Khan, A., Jhanjhi, N. Z., & Humayun, M. (2022). The role of cybersecurity in smart cities. In Chapman and Hall/CRC eBooks (pp. 195–208). doi:10.1201/9781003203087-9

Khan, M. A., Din, I. U., Kim, B., & Almogren, A. (2023). Visualization of remote patient monitoring system based on internet of medical things. *Sustainability (Basel), 15*(10), 8120. doi:10.3390/su15108120

Kilaso, S. (2023). *Digital Marketing And Strategic Approaches Of Electronic Component Manufacturers In The Era Of Industry 4.0*. https://doi.org/ doi:10.59670/jns.v33i.2264

Kim, J., Kim, M., Park, M., & Yoo, J. (2023). Immersive interactive technologies and virtual shopping experiences: Differences in consumer perceptions between augmented reality (AR) and virtual reality (VR). *Telematics and Informatics, 77*, 101936. doi:10.1016/j.tele.2022.101936

Kineber, A. F., Oke, A. E., Farouk, M. H., Hamed, M. M., & Kayode, F. S. (2023). Barriers to the implementation of Radio frequency identification (RFID) for sustainable building in a developing economy. *Sustainability (Basel), 15*(1), 825. doi:10.3390/su15010825

Kiradoo, G. (2023, March 6). *The prominence of IoT in enhancing business success in the context of industry 4.0*. https://papers.ssrn.com/sol3/papers.cfm?abstract_id=4387919

Klar, R., Fredriksson, A., & Angelakis, V. (2023). Digital Twins for Ports: Derived from Smart City and Supply Chain Twinning Experience. *Cornel University*. https://doi.org//arxiv.2301.10224 doi:10.48550

Kliestik, T., Nagy, M., & Valaskova, K. (2023). Global value chains and industry 4.0 in the context of lean workplaces for enhancing company performance and its comprehension via the digital readiness and expertise of workforce in the V4 nations. *Mathematics, 11*(3), 601. doi:10.3390/math11030601

Klimczak, P., & Petersen, C. (2023). *AI - Limits and Prospects of Artificial Intelligence*. Transcript Verlag.

Korder, S., Kulessa, S., Breuherr, D., Vernim, S., & Reinhart, G. (2023). The role of work system-related factors on skilled workers' turnover intentions – A study in small and medium-sized manufacturing enterprises in Southern Germany. *International Journal of Industrial Ergonomics, 93*, 103406. doi:10.1016/j.ergon.2022.103406

Kumar, R., & Agrawal, N. (2023). Analysis of multi-dimensional Industrial IoT (IIoT) data in Edge-Fog-Cloud based architectural frameworks : A survey on current state and research challenges. *Journal of Industrial Information Integration, 35*, 100504. doi:10.1016/j.jii.2023.100504

Kunhare, N., Gupta, R. K., & Sahu, Y. (2023). Role of Artificial Intelligence in the Agricultural System. *Wiley*, 227–241. doi:10.1002/9781119792161.ch12

Kurniawan, T. A., Othman, M. H. D., Liang, X., Goh, H. H., Gikas, P., Kusworo, T. D., Anouzla, A., & Chew, K. W. (2023). Decarbonization in waste recycling industry using digitalization to promote net-zero emissions and its implications on sustainability. *Journal of Environmental Management, 338*, 117765. doi:10.1016/j.jenvman.2023.117765 PMID:36965421

Kuruvilla, M., J., G. Jaspher, W. K., Kirubakaran S, S., Prem Prasad, G., & G, E. (2023). Implementation of industry 4.0 in supply chain management in the healthcare industry. *IEEE Conference Publication | IEEE Xplore*. 10.1109/ICECAA58104.2023.10212417

Kusiak, A. (2023). Smart manufacturing. In Springer handbooks (pp. 973–985). doi:10.1007/978-3-030-96729-1_45

Lampropoulos, G., & Siakas, K. V. (2022). Enhancing and securing cyber-physical systems and Industry 4.0 through digital twins: A critical review. *Journal of Software (Malden, MA), 35*(7), e2494. Advance online publication. doi:10.1002/smr.2494

Lee, K. L., & Zhang, T. (2023). Revolutionizing Supply Chains: Unveiling the power of blockchain technology for enhanced transparency and performance. *International Journal of Technology. Innovation and Management, 3*(1), 19–27. doi:10.54489/ijtim.v3i1.216

Lee, S., Abdullah, A., Jhanjhi, N. Z., & Kok, S. (2021). Classification of botnet attacks in IoT smart factory using honeypot combined with machine learning. *PeerJ, 7*, e350. doi:10.7717/peerj-cs.350 PMID:33817000

Leow, A., Chua, S., Billett, S., & Le, A. H. (2023). Employers' perspectives of effective continuing education and training in Singapore. *Higher Education, Skills and Work-based Learning, 13*(2), 217–232. doi:10.1108/HESWBL-05-2022-0115

Li, F., Laili, Y., Chen, X., Lou, Y., Wang, C., Yang, H., Gao, X., & Han, H. (2023). Towards big data driven construction industry. *Journal of Industrial Information Integration, 35*, 100483. doi:10.1016/j.jii.2023.100483

Lim, W. M. (2023). The workforce revolution: Reimagining work, workers, and workplaces for the future. *Global Business and Organizational Excellence*, *42*(4), 5–10. doi:10.1002/joe.22218

Liu, S., Lu, Y., Shen, X., & Bao, J. (2023). A digital thread-driven distributed collaboration mechanism between digital twin manufacturing units. *Journal of Manufacturing Systems*, *68*, 145–159. doi:10.1016/j.jmsy.2023.02.014

Lu, R., Zhang, W., Wang, Y., Li, Q., Zhong, X., Yang, H., & Wang, D. (2023). Auction-Based cluster federated learning in mobile edge computing systems. *IEEE Transactions on Parallel and Distributed Systems*, 1–15. doi:10.1109/TPDS.2023.3240767

Lun, Y. H. V., Lai, K., Cheng, T., & Yang, D. (2023). New technology development in the shipping industry. In Springer eBooks (pp. 257–279). doi:10.1007/978-3-031-26090-2_17

Luo, Y., & Zahra, S. A. (2023). Industry 4.0 in international business research. *Journal of International Business Studies*, *54*(3), 403–417. doi:10.1057/s41267-022-00577-9 PMID:36987430

MacatangayL. (2023). The Status, Challenges & Opportunities of Education Service Industry in the Philippines. *Social Science Research Network*. doi:10.2139/ssrn.4426082

Mahmud, H., Islam, A. K. M. N., & Mitra, R. K. (2023). What drives managers towards algorithm aversion and how to overcome it? Mitigating the impact of innovation resistance through technology readiness. *Technological Forecasting and Social Change*, *193*, 122641. doi:10.1016/j.techfore.2023.122641

Makanda, I. L. D., Jiang, P., Yang, M., & Shi, H. (2023). Emergence of collective intelligence in industrial cyber-physical-social systems for collaborative task allocation and defect detection. *Computers in Industry*, *152*, 104006. doi:10.1016/j.compind.2023.104006

Manchuri, A. R., Akhila, K., Abu Saleh, A., & Sindiramutty, S. R. (2024). Application of Supervised Machine Learning Models in Biodiesel Production Research - A Short Review. *Borneo Journal of Sciences and Technology*, *6*(1), 96–104. doi:10.35370/bjost.2024.6.1-10

Marwala, T. (2023). Data in Politics. In *Artificial Intelligence* (pp. 59–77). Game Theory and Mechanism Design in Politics. doi:10.1007/978-981-99-5103-1_5

Mason, P. (2023). *Financially Smart Career Planning For Teens: The Roadmap To Making Informed Decisions In An Uncertain Job Market, Prevent Feeling Overwhelmed & Analysis Paralysis To Achieve Affordable College Degrees*. Academic Press.

Matin, A., Islam, R., Wang, X., Huo, H., & Xu, G. (2023). AIoT for sustainable manufacturing: Overview, challenges, and opportunities. *Internet of Things : Engineering Cyber Physical Human Systems*, *100901*, 100901. Advance online publication. doi:10.1016/j.iot.2023.100901

Mfungo, D., Fu, X., Wang, X., & Xian, Y. (2023). Enhancing Image Encryption with the Kronecker xor Product, the Hill Cipher, and the Sigmoid Logistic Map. *Applied Sciences (Basel, Switzerland)*, *13*(6), 4034. doi:10.3390/app13064034

Mhaddolkar, A. V. (2023, May 1). *Optimization of warehouse inventory space using class based storage method*. http://www.dspace.dtu.ac.in:8080/jspui/handle/repository/20012

Mhlanga, D. (2023). Artificial intelligence and machine learning in making transport, safer, cleaner, more reliable, and efficient in emerging markets. In Sustainable development goals series (pp. 193–211). doi:10.1007/978-3-031-37776-1_9

Mo, F., Rehman, H. U., Monetti, F. M., Chaplin, J. C., Sanderson, D. R., Popov, A. A., Maffei, A., & Ratchev, S. (2023). A framework for manufacturing system reconfiguration and optimisation utilising digital twins and modular artificial intelligence. *Robotics and Computer-integrated Manufacturing*, *82*, 102524. doi:10.1016/j.rcim.2022.102524

Mohammad, A. (2023, August 1). *Revolutionizing Solar Energy with AI-Driven Enhancements in Photovoltaic Technology*. https://journal.mediapublikasi.id/index.php/bullet/article/view/3427

Montini, E., Cutrona, V., Dell'Oca, S., & Carpanzano, E. (2023). A framework for human-aware collaborative robotics systems development. *ResearchGate*. https://www.researchgate.net/publication/370678957_A_Framework_for_Human-aware_Collaborative_Robotics_Systems_Development

Moradeyo, A. A., Oke, A., & Muogboh, O. S. (2023). Linking supply chain disruptions and manufacturing firms' operational performance in a developing country context. *International Journal of Services and Operations Management*, *44*(4), 460. doi:10.1504/IJSOM.2023.130178

Moumen, I. (2023). Real-time GPS tracking system for IoT-Enabled connected vehicles. *E3S Web of Conferences*. doi:10.1051/e3sconf/202341201095

Muzammal, S. M., Murugesan, R. K., & Jhanjhi, N. Z. (2021). A Comprehensive Review on Secure Routing in Internet of Things: Mitigation Methods and Trust-Based Approaches. *IEEE Internet of Things Journal*, *8*(6), 4186–4210. doi:10.1109/JIOT.2020.3031162

NaduaF.EscandorL.BangayanM.VigonteF.AbanteM. V. (2023). Identifying incentives to address attrition in the government cybersecurity workforce. *Social Science Research Network*. doi:10.2139/ssrn.4382110

Neligan, A., Baumgartner, R. J., Geissdoerfer, M., & Schöggl, J. (2022). Circular disruption: Digitalisation as a driver of circular economy business models. *Business Strategy and the Environment*, *32*(3), 1175–1188. doi:10.1002/bse.3100

Nigmatov, A., Pradeep, A., & Musulmonova, N. (2023). Blockchain technology in improving transparency and efficiency in government operations. *2023 15th International Conference on Electronics, Computers and Artificial Intelligence (ECAI)*. 10.1109/ECAI58194.2023.10194154

Nof, S. Y. (2023). *Springer Handbook of Automation*. Springer Nature. doi:10.1007/978-3-030-96729-1

Noh, J. (2023). Reinforcement Learning for Optimizing Can-Order Policy with the Rolling Horizon Method. *Systems*, *11*(7), 350. doi:10.3390/systems11070350

Nova, K. (2023, June 9). *AI-Enabled Water Management Systems: An analysis of system components and interdependencies for water conservation*. https://studies.eigenpub.com/index.php/erst/article/view/12

O'Connell, E., O'Brien, W., Bhattacharya, M., Moore, D., & Penica, M. (2023). Digital Twins: Enabling interoperability in smart manufacturing networks. *Telecom*, *4*(2), 265–278. doi:10.3390/telecom4020016

Onyeaka, H., Tamasiga, P., Nwauzoma, U. M., Miri, T., Juliet, U. C., Nwaiwu, O., & Akinsemolu, A. A. (2023). Using artificial intelligence to tackle food waste and enhance the circular economy: Maximising resource Efficiency and Minimising Environmental Impact: A review. *Sustainability (Basel), 15*(13), 10482. doi:10.3390/su151310482

Ortiz, F. (2023, August 22). *Energy-Efficient On-Board radio resource management for satellite communications via neuromorphic computing.* arXiv.org. https://arxiv.org/abs/2308.11152

Othman, A. E., & ElKady, M. M. (2021). A knowledge management based framework for enhancing the learning culture in architectural design firms in developing countries. *Journal of Engineering. Design and Technology, 21*(1), 23–57. doi:10.1108/JEDT-01-2021-0027

Othman, U., & Yang, E. (2023). Human–Robot Collaborations in smart Manufacturing Environments: Review and outlook. *Sensors (Basel), 23*(12), 5663. doi:10.3390/s23125663 PMID:37420834

Oyinlola, M., Okoya, S. A., Whitehead, T., Evans, M. A., & Lowe, A. S. (2023). The potential of converting plastic waste to 3D printed products in Sub-Saharan Africa. *Resources, Conservation & Recycling Advances, 17*, 200129. doi:10.1016/j.rcradv.2023.200129

Pandey, V., Sircar, A., Bist, N., Solanki, K. P., & Yadav, K. (2023). Accelerating the renewable energy sector through Industry 4.0: Optimization opportunities in the digital revolution. *International Journal of Innovation Studies, 7*(2), 171–188. doi:10.1016/j.ijis.2023.03.003

Patil, K. R., Garg, V., Gabaldon, J., Patil, H., Niranjan, S., & Hawkins, T. G. (2023). Firm performance in digitally integrated supply chains: A combined perspective of transaction cost economics and relational exchange theory. *Journal of Enterprise Information Management.* Advance online publication. doi:10.1108/JEIM-09-2022-0335

Ponnusamy, V., Aun, Y., Jhanjhi, N. Z., Humayun, M., & Almufareh, M. F. (2022). IoT wireless intrusion detection and network Traffic Analysis. *Computer Systems Science and Engineering, 40*(3), 865–879. doi:10.32604/csse.2022.018801

Ponnusamy, V., Zaman, N., Jung, L. T., & Amin, A. H. M. (2021). *Role of IoT in green energy Systems.* IGI Global. doi:10.4018/978-1-7998-6709-8

Pottebaum, J., Rossel, J., Somorovsky, J., Acar, Y., Fahr, R., Cabarcos, P. A., Bodden, E., & Gräßler, I. (2023). Re-Envisioning industrial control systems security by considering human factors as a core element of Defense-in-Depth. *2023 IEEE European Symposium on Security and Privacy Workshops (EuroS&PW).* 10.1109/EuroSPW59978.2023.00048

Pozzi, R., Rossi, T., & Secchi, R. (2021). Industry 4.0 technologies: Critical success factors for implementation and improvements in manufacturing companies. *Production Planning and Control, 34*(2), 139–158. doi:10.1080/09537287.2021.1891481

Pradhan, I. P., & Saxena, P. (2023). Reskilling workforce for the Artificial intelligence Age: challenges and the way forward. In Emerald Publishing Limited eBooks (pp. 181–197). doi:10.1108/978-1-80455-662-720230011

Preece, C., Cappellini, B., Larsen, G., Bhogal-Nair, A., Bradshaw, A., Chatzidakis, A., Goulding, C., Keeling, D. I., Lindridge, A., Maclaran, P., Marshall, G. W., & Parsons, E. (2023). Publish or perish: Ensuring our journals don't fail us. *Journal of Marketing Management*, *39*(9-10), 1–11. doi:10.1080/0267257X.2023.2244504

Presti, C., De Santis, F., & Bernini, F. (2023). Value co-creation via machine learning from a configuration theory perspective. *European Journal of Innovation Management*, *26*(7), 449–477. doi:10.1108/EJIM-01-2023-0104

Psarommatis, F., May, G., & Azamfirei, V. (2023). Envisioning maintenance 5.0: Insights from a systematic literature review of Industry 4.0 and a proposed framework. *Journal of Manufacturing Systems*, *68*, 376–399. doi:10.1016/j.jmsy.2023.04.009

Qing, C., Zhou, W., Song, J., Deng, X., & Xu, D. (2023). Impact of outsourced machinery services on farmers' green production behavior: Evidence from Chinese rice farmers. *Journal of Environmental Management*, *327*, 116843. doi:10.1016/j.jenvman.2022.116843 PMID:36459784

Qing, F., Zhang, Y., Sun, B., Guo, X. Y., Fan, D., Ren, Y., Ye, S., & Wang, Z. (2023). Multi-level predictive maintenance of smart manufacturing systems driven by digital twin: A matheuristics approach. *Journal of Manufacturing Systems*, *68*, 443–454. doi:10.1016/j.jmsy.2023.05.004

Qiu, G., & Huang, W. (2023). Mechanical design, manufacture and automation: Research progress and fusion ant colony algorithm-based optimization. *Applied Artificial Intelligence*, *37*(1), 2219565. Advance online publication. doi:10.1080/08839514.2023.2219565

R, R., Ramamoorthy Sathya, R., V, V., S, B., & N, J. L. (2023). Industry 5.0: Enhancing Human-Robot Collaboration through Collaborative Robots – A Review. *2023 2nd International Conference on Advancements in Electrical, Electronics, Communication, Computing and Automation (ICAECA)*. doi:10.1109/ICAECA56562.2023.10201120

Ramdurai, B. (2020). *Detailed Review of Cloud based Mobile application for the stroke patient. arXiv*. Cornell University. doi:10.14445/22312803

Ranjan, A., Singh, A. N., & Kumar, A. (2023, June 16). *Transforming Judicial Systems with Blockchain: A Court Case Governance System for Tamper-Proof and Transparent Legal Processes*. IEEE Conference Publication | IEEE Xplore. https://ieeexplore.ieee.org/abstract/document/10200234

Rao, P. S., Yaqoob, S. I., Ahmed, M. A., Abdinabievna, P. S., Yaseen, S. M., & Arumugam, M. (2023). Integrated artificial intelligence and predictive maintenance of electric vehicle components with optical and quantum enhancements. *Optical and Quantum Electronics*, *55*(10), 855. Advance online publication. doi:10.1007/s11082-023-05135-7

Raufjonov, A. (2023). Industry 4.0: Integrating automation and IoT in manufacturing. *irshadjournals.com*. https://doi.org/ doi:10.59022/ibys.108

Rea, G., Sverzellati, N., Bocchino, M., Lieto, R., Milanese, G., D'Alto, M., Bocchini, G., Maniscalco, M., Valente, T., & Sica, G. (2023). Beyond Visual interpretation: Quantitative analysis and artificial intelligence in interstitial lung disease diagnosis "Expanding Horizons in Radiology." *Diagnostics (Basel)*, *13*(14), 2333. doi:10.3390/diagnostics13142333 PMID:37510077

Rehman, S. U., Giordino, D., Zhang, Q., & Alam, G. M. (2023). Twin transitions & industry 4.0: Unpacking the relationship between digital and green factors to determine green competitive advantage. *Technology in Society*, *73*, 102227. doi:10.1016/j.techsoc.2023.102227

Reza, M. (2023, June 10). *AI-Driven solutions for enhanced waste management and recycling in urban areas*. https://vectoral.org/index.php/IJSICS/article/view/9

Rosário, A. T., & Dias, J. C. (2023). How Industry 4.0 and Sensors Can Leverage product Design: Opportunities and challenges. *Sensors (Basel)*, *23*(3), 1165. doi:10.3390/s23031165 PMID:36772206

Ryalat, M., ElMoaqet, H., & AlFaouri, M. (2023). Design of a Smart Factory Based on Cyber-Physical Systems and Internet of Things towards Industry 4.0. *Applied Sciences (Basel, Switzerland)*, *13*(4), 2156. doi:10.3390/app13042156

Said, G. (2023). Adapting Legal Systems to the Development of Artificial Intelligence: Solving the Global Problem of AI in Judicial Processes. *irshadjournals.com*. https://doi.org/ doi:10.59022/ijcl.49

Sajjad, M., Hu, A., Waqar, A., Falqi, I. I., Alsulamy, S., Bageis, A. S., & Alshehri, A. (2023). Evaluation of the success of Industry 4.0 digitalization Practices for sustainable Construction Management: Chinese Construction Industry. *Buildings*, *13*(7), 1668. doi:10.3390/buildings13071668

Salahdine, F., Han, T., & Zhang, N. (2022). Security in 5G and beyond recent advances and future challenges. *Security and Privacy*, *6*(1), e271. Advance online publication. doi:10.1002/spy2.271

Sankar, S., Ramasubbareddy, S., Luhach, A. K., Deverajan, G. G., Alnumay, W. S., Jhanjhi, N. Z., Ghosh, U., & Sharma, P. K. (2020). Energy efficient optimal parent selection based routing protocol for Internet of Things using firefly optimization algorithm. *Transactions on Emerging Telecommunications Technologies*, *32*(8), e4171. Advance online publication. doi:10.1002/ett.4171

Sankarananth, S., Karthiga, M., Suganya, E., Sountharrajan, S., & Bavirisetti, D. P. (2023). AI-enabled metaheuristic optimization for predictive management of renewable energy production in smart grids. *Energy Reports*, *10*, 1299–1312. doi:10.1016/j.egyr.2023.08.005

Sarkar, S., & Kedas, S. (2022). Globally distributed talent communities: A typology of innovation problems and talent characteristics. *Thunderbird International Business Review*, *65*(1), 89–102. doi:10.1002/tie.22272

Sasikumar, A., Subramaniyaswamy, V., Kotecha, K., Indragandhi, V., Ravi, L., Selvachandran, G., & Abraham, A. (2023). Blockchain-based trust mechanism for digital twin empowered Industrial Internet of Things. *Future Generation Computer Systems*, *141*, 16–27. doi:10.1016/j.future.2022.11.002

Saxena, S., Nagpal, A., Prashar, T., Shravan, M., Al-Hilali, A. A., & Alazzam, M. B. (2023). Blockchain for Supply Chain Traceability: Opportunities and Challenges. *2023 3rd International Conference on Advance Computing and Innovative Technologies in Engineering (ICACITE)*. 10.1109/ICACITE57410.2023.10182416

Schubert, H. (n.d.). *Robots are coming and they're automating pharma research*. NNE. https://www.nne.com/techtalk/robots-are-coming-and-theyre-automating-pharma-research/

Sekonya, N., & Sithungu, S. (2023). The impact of edge computing on the industrial internet of things. *Proceedings of the . . . International Conference on Information Warfare and Security, 18*(1), 360–368. 10.34190/iccws.18.1.969

Seong, T. B., Ponnusamy, V., Jhanjhi, N. Z., Annur, R., & Talib, M. (2021). A comparative analysis on traditional wired datasets and the need for wireless datasets for IoT wireless intrusion detection. *Indonesian Journal of Electrical Engineering and Computer Science*, *22*(2), 1165. doi:10.11591/ijeecs.v22.i2.pp1165-1176

Shafi, I., Mazahir, M. F., Fatima, A., Álvarez, R. M., Miro, Y., Espinosa, J. C. M., & Ashraf, I. (2023). Deep Learning-Based real time defect detection for optimization of aircraft manufacturing and control performance. *Drones (Basel)*, *7*(1), 31. doi:10.3390/drones7010031

ShahinM.ChenF. F.HosseinzadehA. Z.ZandN. (2023). Using machine learning and deep learning algorithms for downtime minimization in manufacturing systems: an early failure detection diagnostic service. Research Square *(*Research Square*)*. doi:10.21203/rs.3.rs-2895149/v1

Shahpasand, R., Talebian, A., & Mishra, S. (2023). Investigating environmental and economic impacts of the 3D printing technology on supply chains: The case of tire production. *Journal of Cleaner Production*, *390*, 135917. doi:10.1016/j.jclepro.2023.135917

Shamsuddoha, M., Kashem, M. A., & Nasir, T. (2023). Smart Transportation Logistics: Achieving Supply Chain Efficiency with Green Initiatives. In Greening of industry networks studies (pp. 243–258). doi:10.1007/978-3-031-29823-3_10

Sharma, M., Sehrawat, R., Giannakis, M., & Dwivedi, Y. K. (2023). Learnings from Industry 4.0 for transitioning towards Industry 4.0+: Challenges and solutions for Indian pharmaceutical sector. *Annals of Operations Research*. Advance online publication. doi:10.1007/s10479-023-05391-6 PMID:37361066

Shee, H. (2023). Internet of things. In Springer eBooks (pp. 1–19). doi:10.1007/978-3-030-89822-9_78-1

Shen, X., Zhang, Z., Ma, Y., Zou, X., Zhou, F., Wang, S., & Qiu, B. (2023). Prediction of minimum ignition energy for combustible dust using graph neural networks and SMILES data augmentation. *Powder Technology*, *118876*, 118876. Advance online publication. doi:10.1016/j.powtec.2023.118876

Shi, B., Tu, X., Wu, B., & Peng, Y. (2023). Recent Advances in Time-Sensitive Network Configuration Management: A Literature Review. *Journal of Sensor and Actuator Networks*, *12*(4), 52. doi:10.3390/jsan12040052

Sindiramutty, S. R., Jhanjhi, N. Z., Tan, C. E., Khan, N. A., Gharib, A. H., & Yun, K. J. (2024). Applications of blockchain technology in supply chain management. In Advances in logistics, operations, and management science book series (pp. 248–304). doi:10.4018/978-1-6684-7625-3.ch009

Sindiramutty, S. R., Jhanjhi, N. Z., Tan, C. E., Khan, N. A., Shah, B., & Gaur, L. (2024). Securing the digital supply chain cyber threats and vulnerabilities. In Advances in logistics, operations, and management science book series (pp. 156–223). doi:10.4018/978-1-6684-7625-3.ch007

Singh, A., Kumar, V. R. P., Irfan, M., Mohandes, S. R., & Awan, U. (2023). Revealing the Barriers of blockchain technology for supply chain transparency and sustainability in the construction industry: An application of Pythagorean FAHP methods. *Sustainability (Basel), 15*(13), 10681. doi:10.3390/su151310681

Škare, M., De Las Mercedes De Obesso, M., & Ribeiro-Navarrete, S. (2023). Digital transformation and European small and medium enterprises (SMEs): A comparative study using digital economy and society index data. *International Journal of Information Management, 68*, 102594. doi:10.1016/j.ijinfomgt.2022.102594

Sn, R. B. (2023). *Industry 4.0 for pharmaceutical manufacturing; smart factories for future*. doi:10.55529/jcpp.33.17.23

Sohrabi, M. (2023). Artificial Intelligence in Logistic Industry. In Duwar (pp. 73–86). doi:10.59287/idtscm.70

Soori, M., Arezoo, B., & Dastres, R. (2023). Digital Twin for Smart Manufacturing, A Review. *Sustainable Manufacturing and Service Economics, 100017*. Advance online publication. doi:10.1016/j.smse.2023.100017

Soori, M., Arezoo, B., & Dastres, R. (2023a). Advanced virtual manufacturing systems: A review. *Journal of Advanced Manufacturing Science and Technology, 3*(3), 2023009. doi:10.51393/j.jamst.2023009

Spieske, A., Gebhardt, M., Kopyto, M., Birkel, H., & Hartmann, E. (2023). The future of industry 4.0 and supply chain resilience after the COVID-19 pandemic: Empirical evidence from a Delphi study. *Computers & Industrial Engineering, 181*, 109344. doi:10.1016/j.cie.2023.109344 PMID:37273574

Sulistyaningsih, E., & Siswanto, S. (2023). *Integrated Industrial Estate Development Strategy in increasing competitiveness through technological innovation and research*. doi:10.59890/ijmbi.v1i1.157

Sun, P. (2023). 5G+ smart Manufacturing. In Management for professionals (pp. 83–106). doi:10.1007/978-981-99-4024-0_5

Sun, Y., Jeelani, I., & Gheisari, M. (2023). Safe human-robot collaboration in construction: A conceptual perspective. *Journal of Safety Research, 86*, 39–51. Advance online publication. doi:10.1016/j.jsr.2023.06.006 PMID:37718066

Taghiyeh, S., Lengacher, D., Sadeghi, A. H., Sahebi-Fakhrabad, A., & Handfield, R. (2023). A Novel Multi-Phase Hierarchical Forecasting Approach with Machine Learning in Supply Chain Management. *Science DIrect, 100032*. Advance online publication. doi:10.1016/j.sca.2023.100032

TarekA. H. (2023). Mergers and Acquisitions: Analysing antitrust implications and Regulatory compliance. *Social Science Research Network*. doi:10.2139/ssrn.4518461

Telukdarie, A. (2023). *Industry 4.0 Technological advancement in the food and beverage manufacturing industry in South Africa—Bibliometric analysis via natural language processing*. MDPI. doi:10.3390/info14080454

Teubert, C. (2023, April 1). *An analysis of barriers preventing the widespread adoption of predictive and prescriptive maintenance in aviation*. NASA Technical Reports Server (NTRS). https://ntrs.nasa.gov/citations/20230000841

Thanigaivelan, R., Kaliappan, S., & Jegadheesan, C. (2023). *Cyber-Physical systems and supporting technologies for industrial automation*. IGI Global.

Truong, T. C., & Diep, Q. B. (2023). Technological spotlights of digital transformation in tertiary education. *IEEE Access : Practical Innovations, Open Solutions*, *11*, 40954–40966. doi:10.1109/ACCESS.2023.3270340

Turečková, K., Nevima, J., Vaňová, A., & Vitálišová, K. (2023). Society 4.0: General economic implications. *Journal of European Economy*, *22*(2), 146–157. doi:10.35774/jee2023.02.146

Ul-Durar, S., Awan, U., Varma, A., Memon, S., & Mention, A. (2023). Integrating knowledge management and orientation dynamics for organization transition from eco-innovation to circular economy. *Journal of Knowledge Management*, *27*(8), 2217–2248. Advance online publication. doi:10.1108/JKM-05-2022-0424

Ullah, A., Azeem, M., Ashraf, H., Alaboudi, A. A., Humayun, M., & Jhanjhi, N. Z. (2021). Secure healthcare Data Aggregation and Transmission in IoT—A survey. *IEEE Access : Practical Innovations, Open Solutions*, *9*, 16849–16865. doi:10.1109/ACCESS.2021.3052850

Ullah, A., Ishaq, N., Azeem, M., Ashraf, H., Jhanjhi, N. Z., Humayun, M., Tabbakh, T., & Almusaylim, Z. A. (2021). A survey on continuous object tracking and boundary detection schemes in IoT assisted wireless sensor networks. *IEEE Access : Practical Innovations, Open Solutions*, *9*, 126324–126336. doi:10.1109/ACCESS.2021.3110203

Ullah, I., Shukla, J. V., & Singh, D. K. (2023). The Applications, Opportunities and Challenges of IoT in Supply Chain Management: Insights from Literature Review. *2023 11th International Conference on Emerging Trends in Engineering & Technology - Signal and Information Processing (ICETET - SIP)*. 10.1109/ICETET-SIP58143.2023.10151507

Urbański, M. (2023). Labor Market Characteristics Pertaining to Foreigners' Employment. In Springer Link (pp. 59–98). doi:10.1007/978-981-99-3253-5_3

Usmani, U. A., Happonen, A., & Watada, J. (2023). Secure Integration of IoT-Enabled Sensors and Technologies: Engineering Applications for Humanitarian Impact. *2023 5th International Congress on Human-Computer Interaction, Optimization and Robotic Applications (HORA)*. 10.1109/HORA58378.2023.10156740

Uygun, Y. (2020). *Industry 4.0: Principles, Effects and Challenges*. Nova Science Publishers.

Vaswani, A. (2019). *Industry 4.0 : Digital transformation*. https://www.linkedin.com/pulse/industry-40-digital-transformation-arun-vaswani/

Wang, G., Wang, S., Dong, X., Zhang, Y., & Shen, W. (2023). Recent progress in additive manufacturing of ceramic dental restorations. *Journal of Materials Research and Technology*, *26*, 1028–1049. doi:10.1016/j.jmrt.2023.07.257

Wang, J., Wang, Q., & Sun, W. (2023). Quantifying flexibility provisions of the ladle furnace refining process as cuttable loads in the iron and steel industry. *Applied Energy*, *342*, 121178. doi:10.1016/j.apenergy.2023.121178

Wang, K., Jiang, W., & Zhang, M. (2023). Impact of high-speed railway on urban resilience in China: Does urban innovation matter? *Socio-Economic Planning Sciences*, *87*, 101607. doi:10.1016/j.seps.2023.101607

Wang, T., Huang, K., Guo, L., Zheng, T., & Zeng, F. (2023). An automated vacuum infusion process for manufacturing high-quality fiber-reinforced composites. *Composite Structures*, *309*, 116717. doi:10.1016/j.compstruct.2023.116717

Watkins, K. E., & Marsick, V. J. (2023). *Rethinking workplace learning and development*. doi:10.4337/9781802203776

Weidele, D. K. I., Afzal, S., Valente, A. N., Makuch, C., Cornec, O., Vu, L., Subramanian, D., Geyer, W., Nair, R., Vejsbjerg, I., Marinescu, R., Palmes, P., Daly, E., Franke, L., & Haehn, D. (2023). *AutoDOViz: Human-Centered Automation for Decision Optimization*. ACM. doi:10.1145/3581641.3584094

Wen, B. O. T., Syahriza, N., Xian, N. C. W., Wei, N., Shen, T. Z., Hin, Y. Z., Sindiramutty, S. R., & Nicole, T. Y. F. (2024). Detecting cyber threats with a Graph-Based NIDPS. In Advances in logistics, operations, and management science book series (pp. 36–74). doi:10.4018/978-1-6684-7625-3.ch002

Xia, L., Semirumi, D., & Rezaei, R. (2023). A Thorough Examination of Smart City Applications: Exploring Challenges and Solutions Throughout the Life Cycle with Emphasis on Safeguarding Citizen Privacy. *Sustainable Cities and Society*, *104771*. Advance online publication. doi:10.1016/j.scs.2023.104771

Xiao, J., Zhang, W., & Zhong, R. Y. (2023). Blockchain-enabled cyber-physical system for construction site management: A pilot implementation. *Advanced Engineering Informatics*, *57*, 102102. doi:10.1016/j.aei.2023.102102

Xu, K., & Qin, S. (2023). An Interdisciplinary Approach and Advanced Techniques for Enhanced 3D-Printed Upper Limb Prosthetic Socket Design: A literature review. *Actuators*, *12*(6), 223. doi:10.3390/act12060223

Yang, L., Sigov, A., Ratkin, L., Ivanov, L., & Zuo, M. (2023). Quantum Computing and Industrial Information Integration: A review. *Journal of Industrial Information Integration*, *100511*. Advance online publication. doi:10.1016/j.jii.2023.100511

Yang, T., Chu, Z., & Wang, B. (2023). Feasibility on the integration of passenger and freight transportation in rural areas: A service mode and an optimization model. *Socio-Economic Planning Sciences*, *88*, 101665. doi:10.1016/j.seps.2023.101665

Ying, W., Lin, X., & Philbin, S. P. (2023). Evaluating the role of the communication skills of engineering students on employability according to the Outcome-Based Education (OBE) Theory. *Sustainability (Basel)*, *15*(12), 9711. doi:10.3390/su15129711

Ylä-Kujala, A., Kedziora, D., Metso, L., Kärri, T., Happonen, A., & Piotrowicz, W. (2023). Robotic process automation deployments: A step-by-step method to investment appraisal. *Business Process Management Journal*, *29*(8), 163–187. doi:10.1108/BPMJ-08-2022-0418

Zaman, U. K. U., Siadat, A., Baqai, A. A., Naveed, K., & Kumar, A. A. (2023). Handbook of Manufacturing Systems and Design: An Industry 4.0 Perspective. Academic Press.

Zhou, J., & Wang, M. (2023). The role of government-industry-academia partnership in business incubation: Evidence from new R&D institutions in China. *Technology in Society*, *72*, 102194. doi:10.1016/j.techsoc.2022.102194

Zhou, J., Xu, T., Chiao, Y., & Fang, Y. (2023). Interorganizational systems and supply chain agility in uncertain environments: The mediation role of supply chain collaboration. *Information Systems Research*. Advance online publication. doi:10.1287/isre.2023.1210

Zhu, G., Houck, H. A., Spiegel, C. A., Selhuber-Unkel, C., Hou, Y., & Blasco, E. (2023). Introducing dynamic bonds in light-based 3D printing. *Advanced Functional Materials*, 2300456. Advance online publication. doi:10.1002/adfm.202300456

Zrigui, I. (2023). Reducing Carbon Footprint with Real-Time Transport Planning and Big Data Analytics. *E3S Web of Conferences*. doi:10.1051/e3sconf/202341201082

Zubairu, N. (2023). Application of supply chain strategies to improve the performance of SYNGAS networks. *IntechOpen*. doi:10.5772/intechopen.1002184

Compilation of References

Aadil, F., Mehmood, B., Hasan, N. U., Lim, S., Ejaz, S., & Jhanjhi, N. Z. (2021). Remote health monitoring using IoT-Based Smart Wireless Body Area Network. *Computers, Materials & Continua*, *68*(2), 2499–2513. doi:10.32604/cmc.2021.014647

Aamer, A. M., Sahara, C. R., & Al-Awlaqi, M. A. (2022). Digitalization of the supply chain: Transformation factors. *Journal of Science & Technology Policy Management*, *14*(4), 713–733. doi:10.1108/JSTPM-01-2021-0001

Abbate, S., Centobelli, P., & Cerchione, R. (2023). From Fast to Slow: An exploratory analysis of circular business models in the Italian apparel industry. *International Journal of Production Economics*, *260*, 108824. doi:10.1016/j.ijpe.2023.108824

Abdulaziz, Q. A., Kaidi, H. M., Masrom, M., Hamzah, H. S., Sarip, S., Dziyauddin, R. A., & Muhammad-Sukki, F. (2023). Developing an IoT Framework for Industry 4.0 in Malaysian SMEs: An analysis of current status, practices, and challenges. *Applied Sciences (Basel, Switzerland)*, *13*(6), 3658. doi:10.3390/app13063658

Abdullah, F. M., Al-Ahmari, A., & Anwar, S. (2023). Analyzing Interdependencies among Influencing Factors in Smart Manufacturing. *Sustainability (Basel)*, *15*(4), 3864. doi:10.3390/su15043864

Aberle, L. (2015). A comprehensive guide to enterprise IoT project success. *IoT Agenda, 1.*

Abeyratne, S. A., & Monfared, R. P. (2016). Blockchain ready manufacturing supply chain using distributed ledger. *International Journal of Research in Engineering and Technology*, *5*(9), 1–10. doi:10.15623/ijret.2016.0509001

Abikoye, O. C., Bajeh, A. O., Awotunde, J. B., Ameen, A. O., Mojeed, H. A., Abdulraheem, M., . . . Salihu, S. A. (2021). Application of internet of thing and cyber physical system in Industry 4.0 smart manufacturing. In Emergence of Cyber Physical System and IoT in Smart Automation and Robotics: Computer Engineering in Automation (pp. 203-217). Springer.

Abughazala, M., & Muccini, H. (2023). Modeling Data Analytics Architecture for IoT Applications using DAT. *2023 IEEE 20th International Conference on Software Architecture Companion (ICSA-C)*. 10.1109/ICSA-C57050.2023.00066

AbuHalimeh, A., & Ali, O. (2023). Comprehensive review for healthcare data quality challenges in blockchain technology. *Frontiers in Big Data*, 1-12.

Abulibdeh, A., Zaidan, E., & Abulibdeh, R. (2024). Navigating the confluence of artificial intelligence and education for sustainable development in the era of industry 4.0: Challenges, opportunities, and ethical dimensions. *Journal of Cleaner Production*, *437*, 140527. doi:10.1016/j.jclepro.2023.140527

Acciarini, C., Cappa, F., Boccardelli, P., & Oriani, R. (2023). How can organizations leverage big data to innovate their business models? A systematic literature review. *Technovation*, *123*, 102713. doi:10.1016/j.technovation.2023.102713

Achabou, M. A., Dekhili, S., & Hamdoun, M. (2017). Environmental Upgrading of Developing Country Firms in Global Value Chains. *Business Strategy and the Environment*, *26*(2), 224–238. doi:10.1002/bse.1911

Acharjya, D. P., Mitra, A., & Zaman, N. (2022). *Deep learning in data analytics*. Springer. doi:10.1007/978-3-030-75855-4

Achdiat, I., Mulyani, S., Azis, Y., & Sukmadilaga, C. (2022). Roles of organizational learning culture in promoting innovation. *The Learning Organization*, *30*(1), 76–92. doi:10.1108/TLO-01-2021-0013

Achibane, M., & Errahoui, A. (2023). Predicting the future value of gold: A time series approach. Zenodo *(CERN European Organization for Nuclear Research)*. doi:10.5281/zenodo.8023613

Achoki, P. M. (2023). Upskilling and reskilling for a VUCA world. *GILE Journal of Skills Development*, *3*(2), 34–52. doi:10.52398/gjsd.2023.v3.i2.pp34-52

Acioli, C., Scavarda, A., & Reis, A. (2021). Applying Industry 4.0 technologies in the COVID-19 sustainable chains. *International Journal of Productivity and Performance Management*, *70*(5), 988–1016.https://doi.org/10.1108/IJPPM-03-2020-0137

Act, R. A. M. I. (2014). *Revitalize American manufacturing and innovation act of 2014*. Retrieved from https://www.congress.gov/bill/113th-congress/house-bill/2996

Adeyemo, V. E., Abdullah, A., Jhanjhi, N. Z., Supramaniam, M., & Balogun, A. O. (2019). Ensemble and Deep-Learning Methods for Two-Class and Multi-Attack Anomaly Intrusion Detection: An Empirical study. *International Journal of Advanced Computer Science and Applications*, *10*(9). Advance online publication. doi:10.14569/IJACSA.2019.0100969

Adhikari, S., Gangopadhayay, T. K., Pal, S., Akila, D., Humayun, M., Alfayad, M., & Jhanjhi, N. (2023). A Novel Machine Learning-Based Hand Gesture Recognition Using HCI on IoT Assisted Cloud Platform. *Computer Systems Science and Engineering*, *46*(2). Advance online publication. doi:10.32604/csse.2023.034431

Adu-Gyamfi, G., Asamoah, A. N., Nketiah, E., Obuobi, B., Adjei, M., Cudjoe, D., & Zhu, B. (2023). Reducing waste management challenges: Empirical assessment of waste sorting intention among corporate employees in Ghana. *Journal of Retailing and Consumer Services*, *72*, 103261. doi:10.1016/j.jretconser.2023.103261

Adwiyah, R., Syaukat, Y., Indrawan, D., & Mulyati, H. (2023). Examining Sustainable Supply Chain Management (SSCM) Performance in the Palm Oil Industry with the Triple Bottom Line Approach. *Sustainability (Basel)*, *15*(18), 13362. doi:10.3390/su151813362

Afenyo, M., & Caesar, L. D. (2023). Maritime cybersecurity threats: Gaps and directions for future research. *Ocean and Coastal Management*, *236*, 106493. doi:10.1016/j.ocecoaman.2023.106493

Afshar, P., Mohammadi, A., & Plataniotis, K. N. (2018, October). Brain tumor type classification via capsule networks. In *2018 25th IEEE international conference on image processing (ICIP)* (pp. 3129-3133). IEEE. 10.1109/ICIP.2018.8451379

Aftab, J., Abid, N., Cucari, N., & Savastano, M. (2022). Green human resource management and environmental performance: The role of green innovation and environmental strategy in a developing country. *Business Strategy and the Environment*, *32*(4), 1782–1798. doi:10.1002/bse.3219

Agarwal, R., & Weill, P. (2012). The benefits of combining data with empathy. *MIT Sloan Management Review*, *54*(1), 35.

Agarwal, U., Rishiwal, V., Tanwar, S., Chaudhary, R., Sharma, G., Bokoro, P. N., & Sharma, R. (2022). Blockchain technology for secure supply chain management: A comprehensive review. *IEEE Access : Practical Innovations, Open Solutions*, *10*, 85493–85517. doi:10.1109/ACCESS.2022.3194319

Agbo, C., Mahmoud, Q., & Eklund, J. (2019). Blockchain Technology in Healthcare: A Systematic Review. *Health Care*. PMID:30987333

Aghahosseini, A., Solomon, A., Breyer, C., Pregger, T., Simon, S., Strachan, P. A., & Jäger-Waldau, A. (2023). Energy system transition pathways to meet the global electricity demand for ambitious climate targets and cost competitiveness. *Applied Energy*, *331*, 120401. doi:10.1016/j.apenergy.2022.120401

Agostini, L., & Nosella, A. (2020). The adoption of Industry 4.0 technologies in SMEs: Results of an international study. *Management Decision*, *58*(4), 625–643.https://doi.org/10.1108/MD-09-2018-0973

Agote-Garrido, A., Gómez, A. M. M., & Lama-Ruiz, J. R. (2023). Manufacturing System Design in Industry 5.0: Incorporating sociotechnical systems and social metabolism for Human-Centered, Sustainable, and Resilient production. *Systems*, *11*(11), 537. doi:10.3390/systems11110537

Agrawal, R., Wankhede, V. A., Kumar, A., Luthra, S., & Huisingh, D. (2022). Progress and trends in integrating Industry 4.0 within circular economy: A comprehensive literature review and future research propositions. *Business Strategy and the Environment*, *31*(1), 559–579. doi:10.1002/bse.2910

Agustian, K., Mubarok, E. S., Zen, A., Wiwin, W., & Malik, A. J. (2023). The impact of digital transformation on business models and competitive advantage. *Technology and Society Perspectives*, *1*(2), 79–93. doi:10.61100/tacit.v1i2.55

Ahmad, F., & John, B. (2023). A fuzzy quantitative model for assessing the performance of pharmaceutical supply chain under uncertainty. *Kybernetes*, *52*(3), 828–873. doi:10.1108/K-08-2021-0750

Ahmed, A. (2023). Artificial Intelligence's Integration in Supply Chain Management: A Comprehensive Review. *ResearchGate*. https://www.researchgate.net/publication/372965863_Artificial_Intelligence%27s_Integration_in_Supply_Chain_Management_A_Comprehensive_Review

Ahmed, M. M., Hassanien, E., & Hassanien, A. E. (2023). IoT-based intelligent waste management system. *Neural Computing & Applications*, *35*(32), 23551–23579. doi:10.1007/s00521-023-08970-7

Ahmed, S., Kalsoom, T., Ramzan, N., Pervez, Z., Azmat, M., Zeb, B., & Ur Rehman, M. (2021). Towards supply chain visibility using internet of Things: A dyadic analysis review. *Sensors (Basel)*, *21*(12).

Ahmed, W. A., MacCarthy, B. L., & Ahmed, W. A. (2023). Blockchain-enabled supply chain traceability – How wide? How deep? *International Journal of Production Economics*, *263*, 108963. doi:10.1016/j.ijpe.2023.108963

Ahn, J., Lee, Y., Kim, N. V., Park, C., & Jeong, J. (2023). Federated learning for predictive maintenance and anomaly detection using time series data distribution shifts in manufacturing processes. *Sensors (Basel)*, *23*(17), 7331. doi:10.3390/s23177331 PMID:37687787

Ahn, K., Du, J., Farag, M., & Rakha, H. A. (2022). Evaluating an Eco-Cooperative automated control system. *Transportation Research Record: Journal of the Transportation Research Board*, *2677*(2), 1562–1578. doi:10.1177/03611981221113315

Ahsan, M. M., & Siddique, Z. (2022). Industry 4.0 in Healthcare: A systematic review. *International Journal of Information Management Data Insights*, *2*(1), 100079. doi:10.1016/j.jjimei.2022.100079

Aitlmoudden, O., Housni, M., Safeh, N., & Namir, A. (2023). A Microservices-based Framework for Scalable Data Analysis in Agriculture with IoT Integration. *International Journal of Interactive Mobile Technologies*, *17*(19), 147–156. doi:10.3991/ijim.v17i19.40457

Ajani, Y. A. (2023). Adoption of robots in open and distance learning university libraries: A Global Overview based on review of literature. *Journal of Library & Information Services in Distance Learning*, *17*(3-4), 1–22. doi:10.1080/1533290X.2023.2234359

Akbari, M., Kok, S. K., Hopkins, J., Frederico, G. F., Nguyen, H., & Alonso, A. D. (2023). The changing landscape of digital transformation in supply chains: impacts of industry 4.0 in Vietnam. *International Journal of Logistics Management*. https://doi.org/ doi:10.1108/IJLM-11-2022-0442/FULL/XML

Akenji, L., & Bengtsson, M. (2014). Making Sustainable Consumption and Production the Core of Sustainable Development Goals. *Sustainability (Basel)*, *6*(2), 513–529. doi:10.3390/su6020513

Akhtar, M. (2022). Industry 4.0 Technologies Impact on Supply Chain Sustainability. In Recent Advances and New Perspectives in the Industry 4.0 Era. IntechOpen. doi:10.5772/intechopen.102978

Akram, M. N., & Abdul-Kader, W. (2023). Sustainable Development Goals and End-of-Life Electric Vehicle Battery: Literature Review. *Batteries*, *9*(7), 353. doi:10.3390/batteries9070353

Al Meslamani, A. (2023). Applications of AI in pharmacy practice: A look at hospital and community settings. *Journal of Medical Economics*, *26*(1), 1081–1084. Advance online publication. doi:10.1080/13696998.2023.2249758 PMID:37594444

AlAdwani, H. (2023). A Systematic Review of IoT integration on health monitoring System. *International Journal of Engineering and Management Research*, *13*(1), 50–59. doi:10.31033/ijemr.13.1.6

Alazzam, M. B., Alassery, F., & Almulihi, A. (2022). Federated deep learning approaches for the privacy and security of IoT systems. *Wireless Communications and Mobile Computing*, *2022*, 1–7.

Albach, Meffert, Pinkwart, & Ralf. (2015). *Management of Permanent Change—New Challenges and Opportunities for Change Management*. Academic Press.

Albert, M. J. (2020). The Dangers of Decoupling: Earth System Crisis and the 'Fourth Industrial Revolution.'. *Global Policy*, *11*(2), 245–254.https://doi.org/10.1111/1758-5899.12791

Albloushi, B., Alharmoodi, A., Jabeen, F., Mehmood, K., & Farouk, S. (2022). Total quality management practices and corporate sustainable development in manufacturing companies: The mediating role of green innovation. *Management Research Review*, *46*(1), 20–45. doi:10.1108/MRR-03-2021-0194

Albouq, S. S., Sen, A. A. A., Almashf, N., Yamin, M., Alshanqiti, A., & Bahbouh, N. M. (2022). A Survey of Interoperability Challenges and Solutions for Dealing With Them in IoT Environment. *IEEE Access : Practical Innovations, Open Solutions*, *10*, 36416–36428.https://doi.org/10.1109/ACCESS.2022.3162219

Alferidah, D. K., & Jhanjhi, N. Z. (2020). Cybersecurity Impact over Bigdata and IoT Growth. *2020 International Conference on Computational Intelligence (ICCI)*. 10.1109/ICCI51257.2020.9247722

Ali, A., Khan, M. R., & Ghouri, A. M. (2023). Carbon neutrality concept and progress. In Recent Developments in Green Finance, Green Growth and Carbon Neutrality (pp. 85-108). Elsevier. doi:10.1016/B978-0-443-15936-7.00003-7

Ali, I., Jhanjhi, N. Z., Amsaad, F., & Razaque, A. (2022). The role of Cutting-Edge Technologies in Industry 4.0. In Chapman and Hall/CRC eBooks (pp. 97–109). doi:10.1201/9781003203087-4

Ali, S. B. (2022). Industrial revolution 4.0 and supply chain digitization: future of supply chain management. *South Asian Journal of Social Review*, *1*(1), 21-41.

Ali, A., Al-Rimy, B. A. S., Alsubaei, F. S., Almazroi, A. A., & Almazroi, A. A. (2023). HealthLock: Blockchain-Based Privacy Preservation Using Homomorphic Encryption in Internet of Things Healthcare Applications. *Sensors (Basel)*, *23*(15), 6762. doi:10.3390/s23156762 PMID:37571545

Ali, I., Fukofuka, P. T., & Narayan, A. K. (2023). Critical reflections on sustainability reporting standard setting. *Sustainability Accounting. Management and Policy Journal*, *14*(4), 776–791. doi:10.1108/SAMPJ-01-2022-0054

Aljohani, A. (2023). Predictive analytics and machine learning for Real-Time supply chain risk mitigation and agility. *Sustainability (Basel)*, *15*(20), 15088. doi:10.3390/su152015088

Alkahtani, H., Aldhyani, T. H. H., & Alsubari, S. N. (2023). Application of artificial intelligence model solar radiation prediction for renewable energy systems. *Sustainability (Basel)*, *15*(8), 6973. doi:10.3390/su15086973

Alkaraan, F., Elmarzouky, M., Hussainey, K., & Venkatesh, V. (2023). Sustainable strategic investment decision-making practices in UK companies: The influence of governance mechanisms on synergy between industry 4.0 and circular economy. *Technological Forecasting and Social Change*, *187*, 122187. doi:10.1016/j.techfore.2022.122187

Al-Khatib, A. W. (2023). Fostering green innovation: The roles of big data analytics capabilities and green supply chain integration. *European Journal of Innovation Management*. Advance online publication. doi:10.1108/EJIM-09-2022-0491

Alkinani, M. H., Almazroi, A. A., Jhanjhi, N. Z., & Khan, N. A. (2021). 5G and IoT Based Reporting and Accident Detection (RAD) System to Deliver First Aid Box Using Unmanned Aerial Vehicle. *Sensors (Basel)*, *21*(20), 6905. doi:10.3390/s21206905 PMID:34696118

Allahloh, A. S., Sarfraz, M., Ghaleb, A. M., Al-Shamma'a, A. A., Farh, H. M. H., & Al-Shaalan, A. M. (2023). Revolutionizing IC Genset Operations with IIoT and AI: A Study on Fuel Savings and Predictive Maintenance. *Sustainability (Basel)*, *15*(11), 8808. doi:10.3390/su15118808

Allal-Chérif, O., Climent, J. C., & Berenguer, K. J. U. (2023). Born to be sustainable: How to combine strategic disruption, open innovation, and process digitization to create a sustainable business. *Journal of Business Research*, *154*, 113379. doi:10.1016/j.jbusres.2022.113379

Allioui, H. (2023, August 16). *Unleashing the potential of AI: Investigating Cutting-Edge technologies that are transforming businesses*. https://ijceds.com/ijceds/article/view/59

Almalki, F. A., Alsamhi, S. H., Sahal, R., Hassan, J., Hawbani, A., Rajput, N. S., Saif, A., Morgan, J., & Breslin, J. G. (2021). Green IoT for Eco-Friendly and Sustainable Smart Cities: Future directions and opportunities. *Mobile Networks and Applications*, *28*(1), 178–202. doi:10.1007/s11036-021-01790-w

Almoaigel, M. F., & Abuabid, A. (2023). Implementation of Cybersecurity Situation Awareness Model in Saudi SMES. *International Journal of Advanced Computer Science and Applications*, *14*(11). Advance online publication. doi:10.14569/IJACSA.2023.01411110

Almusaylim, Z. A., Jhanjhi, N. Z., & Jung, L. T. (2018). Proposing A Data Privacy Aware Protocol for Roadside Accident Video Reporting Service Using 5G In Vehicular Cloud Networks Environment. *2018 4th International Conference on Computer and Information Sciences (ICCOINS)*. 10.1109/ICCOINS.2018.8510588

Almusaylim, Z. A., & Jhanjhi, N. Z. (2018). A review on smart home present state and challenges: Linked to context-awareness internet of things (IoT). *Wireless Networks*, *25*(6), 3193–3204. doi:10.1007/s11276-018-1712-5

Alsayegh, M. F., Rahman, R. A., & Homayoun, S. (2020). Corporate Economic, Environmental, and Social Sustainability Performance Transformation through ESG Disclosure. *Sustainability (Basel)*, *12*(9), 3910. Advance online publication. doi:10.3390/su12093910

Alshammari, M. O., Almulhem, A. A., & Jhanjhi, N. Z. (2017). Internet of Things (IoT) : Charity automation. *International Journal of Advanced Computer Science and Applications*, *8*(2). Advance online publication. doi:10.14569/IJACSA.2017.080222

Al-Sherideh, A. S., Maabreh, K., Maabreh, M., Mousa, M. R. A., & Asassfeh, M. (2023). Assessing the impact and Effectiveness of cybersecurity measures in e-Learning on students and Educators: A case study. *International Journal of Advanced Computer Science and Applications, 14*(5). Advance online publication. doi:10.14569/IJACSA.2023.0140516

Alsudani, M. Q., Jaber, M. M., Ali, M. H., Khalil, S., Alkhayyat, A., Kareem, Z. H., & Mohhan, A. R. (2023). RETRACTED ARTICLE: Smart logistics with IoT-based enterprise management system using global manufacturing. *Journal of Combinatorial Optimization, 45*(2), 57. Advance online publication. doi:10.1007/s10878-022-00977-5

Althabatah, A., Yaqot, M., Menezes, B. C., & Kerbache, L. (2023). Transformative Procurement Trends: Integrating Industry 4.0 technologies for enhanced procurement processes. *Logistics, 7*(3), 63. doi:10.3390/logistics7030063

Aminizadeh, S., Heidari, A., Toumaj, S., Darbandi, M., Navimipour, N. J., Rezaei, M., Talebi, S., Azad, P. C. S., & Unal, M. (2023). The Applications of Machine Learning Techniques in Medical Data Processing based on Distributed Computing and the Internet of Things. *Computer Methods and Programs in Biomedicine, 241*, 107745. doi:10.1016/j.cmpb.2023.107745 PMID:37579550

Amjad, A., Kordel, P., & Fernandes, G. (2023). A Review on Innovation in Healthcare Sector (Telehealth) through Artificial Intelligence. *Sustainability (Basel), 15*(8), 6655. doi:10.3390/su15086655

Amosse, F., Kinshella, M. W., Boene, H., Sharma, S., Nhamirre, Z., Tchavana, C., Magee, L. A., Von Dadelszen, P., Sevene, E., Vidler, M., & Munguambe, K. (2023). The development and implementation of a community engagement strategy to improve maternal health in southern Mozambique. *PLOS Global Public Health, 3*(1), e0001106. doi:10.1371/journal.pgph.0001106 PMID:36962956

Anandan, R., Deepak, B., Suseendran, G., & Jhanjhi, N. Z. (2021). Internet of Things Platform for Smart Farming. *Human Communication Technology: Internet of Robotic Things and Ubiquitous Computing*, 337-369.

Anandan, R., Gopalakrishnan, S., Pal, S., & Zaman, N. (2022). *Industrial Internet of Things (IIoT): Intelligent Analytics for Predictive Maintenance*. John Wiley & Sons. doi:10.1002/9781119769026

Ananna, F. F., Nowreen, R., Jahwari, S. S. R. A., Costa, E., Angeline, L., & Sindiramutty, S. R. (2023). Analysing Influential factors in student academic achievement: Prediction modelling and insight. *International Journal of Emerging Multidisciplinaries Computer Science & Artificial Intelligence, 2*(1). Advance online publication. doi:10.54938/ijemdcsai.2023.02.1.254

Andreadis, I., Gioumouxouzis, C., Eleftheriadis, G., & Fatouros, D. (2022). The Advent of a New Era in Digital Healthcare: A Role for 3D Printing Technologies in Drug Manufacturing? *Pharmaceutics.*

Andrei, O. J. (2023, May 17). Blockchain technology as a driver of economic development in small economies: A dynamic capabilities framework. *Journal of Decision Systems*, 1–26. Advance online publication. doi:10.1080/12460125.2023.2214304

Angelopoulos, A., Michailidis, E. T., Nomikos, N., Trakadas, P., Hatziefremidis, A., Voliotis, S., & Zahariadis, T. (2019). Tackling faults in the industry 4.0 era—A survey of machine-learning solutions and key aspects. *Sensors (Basel), 20*(1), 109. doi:10.3390/s20010109 PMID:31878065

Anna. (2018, May 3). *New research: Robots create jobs*. Robotics & Automation News. https://roboticsandautomationnews.com/2018/05/03/new-research-robots-create-jobs/17067/

Annadurai, C., Nelson, I., Devi, K. N., Manikandan, R., Jhanjhi, N., Masud, M., & Sheikh, A. (2022). Biometric Authentication-Based Intrusion Detection Using Artificial Intelligence Internet of Things in Smart City. *Energies, 15*(19), 7430. doi:10.3390/en15197430

Annanth, K., Rao, A., & Bhaskara, L. (2021, July 23). Intelligent manufacturing in the context of industry 4.0: A case study of siemens industry. *Journal of Physics: Conference Series*, *1969*(1), 012019. Advance online publication. doi:10.1088/1742-6596/1969/1/012019

Anshari, M., Syafrudin, M., & Fitriyani, N. L. (2022). Fourth industrial revolution between knowledge management and digital humanities. *Information (Basel)*, *13*(6), 292. doi:10.3390/info13060292

Appio, F. P., La Torre, D., Lazzeri, F., Masri, H., & Schiavone, F. (2023). *Impact of artificial intelligence in business and society: Opportunities and Challenges*. Taylor & Francis.

Apte, S., & Petrovsky, N. (2016). Will blockchain technology revolutionize excipient supply chain management? *Journal of Excipients and Food Chemicals*, *7*(3), 76–78.

Aravindaraj, K., & Rajan Chinna, P. (2022). A systematic literature review of integration of industry 4.0 and warehouse management to achieve Sustainable Development Goals (SDGs). *Cleaner Logistics and Supply Chain*, *5*, 100072. https://doi.org/https://doi.org/10.1016/j.clscn.2022.100072

Arcadio, R. D. (2023, July 7). *Construction workers' skills, competencies, knowledge and job satisfaction in industry 4.0 technologies*. http://www.inovatus.es/index.php/ejbsos/article/view/1854

Arden, N., Fisher, A., Tyner, K., Yu, L., Lee, S., & Kopcha, M. (2021). Industry 4.0 for pharmaceutical manufacturing: Preparing for the smart factories of the future. *International Journal of Pharmaceutics*, *602*, 120554. doi:10.1016/j.ijpharm.2021.120554 PMID:33794326

Arguelles, P. Jr, & Polkowski, Z. (2023). Impact of Big Data on Supply Chain Performance through Demand Forecasting. *International Journal of Computations. Information and Manufacturing*, *3*(1), 19–26. doi:10.54489/ijcim.v3i1.232

Ar, I. M., Erol, I., Peker, I., Ozdemir, A. I., Medeni, T. D., & Medeni, I. T. (2020). Evaluating the feasibility of blockchain in logistics operations: A decision framework. *Expert Systems with Applications*, *158*, 113543. doi:10.1016/j.eswa.2020.113543

Arroyabe, M. F., Arranz, C. F., Arroyabe, F., Carlos, J., & Arroyabe, F. (2024). The effect of IT security issues on the implementation of industry 4.0 in SMEs: Barriers and challenges. *Technological Forecasting and Social Change*, *199*, 123051. Advance online publication. doi:10.1016/j.techfore.2023.123051

Arulkumaran, K., Deisenroth, M. P., Brundage, M., & Bharath, A. A. (2017). Deep reinforcement learning: A brief survey. *IEEE Signal Processing Magazine*, *34*(6), 26–38. doi:10.1109/MSP.2017.2743240

Asadi, S., OmSalameh Pourhashemi, S., Nilashi, M., Abdullah, R., Samad, S., Yadegaridehkordi, E., Aljojo, N., & Razali, N. S. (2020). Investigating Influence of Green Innovation on Sustainability Performance: A Case on Malaysian Hotel Industry. *Journal of Cleaner Production*, *258*, 120860. doi:10.1016/j.jclepro.2020.120860

Ashraf, H., Hanif, M., Ihsan, U., Al-Quayed, F., Humayun, M., & Jhanjhi, N. (2023). *A Secure and Reliable Supply chain management approach integrated with IoT and Blockchain*. Paper presented at the 2023 International Conference on Business Analytics for Technology and Security (ICBATS). 10.1109/ICBATS57792.2023.10111371

Aski, V., Dhaka, V. S., Parashar, A., Kumar, S., & Rida, I. (2023). Internet of Things in healthcare: A survey on protocol standards, enabling technologies, WBAN architectures and open issues. *Physical Communication*, *60*, 102103. doi:10.1016/j.phycom.2023.102103

Aspray, W., & Doty, P. (2023). Does technology really outpace policy, and does it matter? A primer for technical experts and others. *Journal of the Association for Information Science and Technology*, *74*(8), 885–904. doi:10.1002/asi.24762

Atta, K. K., Aeri, M., Grover, A., Agarwal, J., Kumar, P., & Raghu, T. (2023). Secured supply chain management system for fisheries through IoT. *Measurement. Sensors, 25*, 100632. doi:10.1016/j.measen.2022.100632

Attanasio, G., Preghenella, N., De Toni, A. F., & Battistella, C. (2022). Stakeholder engagement in business models for sustainability: The stakeholder value flow model for sustainable development. *Business Strategy and the Environment, 31*(3), 860–874. doi:10.1002/bse.2922

Attaoui, Z. E. (2023). Impact of the implementation of the Lean Six Sigma process within Moroccan environmental SMEs. *E3S Web of Conferences, 412*, 01051. doi:10.1051/e3sconf/202341201051

Attaran, M. (2020). Digital technology enablers and their implications for supply chain management. *Supply Chain Forum: An International Journal, 21*(3), 158–172. 10.1080/16258312.2020.1751568

Attaran, M. (2021). The impact of 5G on the evolution of intelligent automation and industry digitization. *Journal of Ambient Intelligence and Humanized Computing, 14*(5), 5977–5993. doi:10.1007/s12652-020-02521-x PMID:33643481

AttaranM.AttaranS.ÇelikB. G. (2023). Digital Twins and Industrial Internet of Things: Uncovering Operational Intelligence in Industry 4.0. SSRN. doi:10.2139/ssrn.4612135

Attiany, M. S., Al-Kharabsheh, S. A., Al-Makhariz, L. S., Abed-Qader, M. A., Al-Hawary, S. I. S., Mohammad, A. S., & Rahamneh, A. A. (2023). Barriers to adopt industry 4.0 in supply chains using interpretive structural modeling. *Uncertain Supply Chain Management, 11*(1), 299–306. doi:10.5267/j.uscm.2022.9.013

Awad, A., & Basit, A. W. (2023). 3D and 4D Printing in Digital Healthcare. In AAPS Introductions in the Pharmaceutical Sciences (pp. 1–23). doi:10.1007/978-3-031-34119-9_1

Awodele, O., Ngige, O., & Balogun, T. (2021). *Industry 4.0: The Impact of Technology on the Output Potentials of Skilled and Unskilled Workforce in Developing Countries.* Paper presented at the ECIAIR 2021 3rd European Conference on the Impact of Artificial Intelligence and Robotics.

Ayoubi, H., Tabaa, Y., & Kharrim, M. E. (2023). Artificial intelligence in green management and the rise of digital lean for sustainable efficiency. *E3S Web of Conferences, 412*, 01053. doi:10.1051/e3sconf/202341201053

Ayvaz, S., & Alpay, K. (2021). Predictive maintenance system for production lines in manufacturing: A machine learning approach using IoT data in real-time. *Expert Systems with Applications, 173*, 114598. doi:10.1016/j.eswa.2021.114598

Azam, H., Dulloo, M. I., Majeed, M. H., Wan, J. P. H., Xin, L. T., Tajwar, M. A., & Sindiramutty, S. R. (2023). Defending the Digital Frontier: IDPS and the Battle Against Cyber Threat. *International Journal of Emerging Multidisciplinaries: Computer Science & Artificial Intelligence, 2*(1). doi:10.54938/ijemdcsai.2023.02.1.253

Azam, H., Dulloo, M. I., Majeed, M. H., Wan, J. P. H., Xin, L. T., & Sindiramutty, S. R. (2023). Cybercrime Unmasked: Investigating cases and digital evidence. *International Journal of Emerging Multidisciplinaries Computer Science & Artificial Intelligence, 2*(1). Advance online publication. doi:10.54938/ijemdcsai.2023.02.1.255

Azam, H., Tajwar, M. A., Mayhialagan, S., Davis, A. J., Yik, C. J., Ali, D., & Sindiramutty, S. R. (2023). Innovations in Security: A study of cloud Computing and IoT. *International Journal of Emerging Multidisciplinaries Computer Science & Artificial Intelligence, 2*(1). Advance online publication. doi:10.54938/ijemdcsai.2023.02.1.252

AzamH.TanM.PinL. T.SyahmiM. A.QianA. L. W.JingyanH.UddinH.SindiramuttyS. R. (2023). Wireless Technology Security and Privacy: A Comprehensive Study. Preprints. doi:10.20944/preprints202311.0664.v1

Aziz, F. (2023). *Beyond the ledger: Enhancing Global Sustainability through Data-Driven Accounting Frameworks.* Farooq Aziz.

Bach, M. P., Topalović, A., Krstić, Ž., & Ivec, A. (2023). Predictive Maintenance in Industry 4.0 for the SMEs: A Decision Support System case Study using Open-Source Software. *Designs*, *7*(4), 98. doi:10.3390/designs7040098

Bag, S., Dhamija, P., Luthra, S., & Huisingh, D. (2021). How big data analytics can help manufacturing companies strengthen supply chain resilience in the context of the COVID-19 pandemic. *International Journal of Logistics Management*, *34*(4), 1141–1164. doi:10.1108/IJLM-02-2021-0095

Bag, S., & Pretorius, J. H. C. (2022). Relationships between industry 4.0, sustainable manufacturing and circular economy: Proposal of a research framework. *The International Journal of Organizational Analysis*, *30*(4), 864–898. doi:10.1108/IJOA-04-2020-2120

Bag, S., Rahman, M. S., Srivastava, G., Shore, A., & Ram, P. (2023). Examining the role of virtue ethics and big data in enhancing viable, sustainable, and digital supply chain performance. *Technological Forecasting and Social Change*, *186*, 122154. doi:10.1016/j.techfore.2022.122154

Bag, S., Telukdarie, A., Pretorius, J. H. C., & Gupta, S. (2018). Industry 4.0 and supply chain sustainability: Framework and future research directions. *Benchmarking*, *28*(5), 1410–1450. doi:10.1108/BIJ-03-2018-0056

Bag, S., Wood, L. C., Xu, L., Dhamija, P., & Kayikci, Y. (2020). Big data analytics as an operational excellence approach to enhance sustainable supply chain performance. *Resources, Conservation and Recycling*, *153*, 104559. doi:10.1016/j.resconrec.2019.104559

Bag, S., Yadav, G., Dhamija, P., & Kataria, K. K. (2021). Key resources for Industry 4.0 adoption and its effect on sustainable production and circular economy: An empirical study. *Journal of Cleaner Production*, *281*, 125233.https://doi.org/10.1016/j.jclepro.2020.125233

Bai, C., Dallasega, P., Orzes, G., & Sarkis, J. (2020). Industry 4.0 technologies assessment: A sustainability perspective. *International Journal of Production Economics*, *229*, 107776. doi:10.1016/j.ijpe.2020.107776

Baig, S. A. (2023, May 16). *Examining the role of diversity and inclusion in modern human resource Management: Best practices and challenges.* http://asmarapublications.com/journals/index.php/PMS/article/view/9

Bai, T., Qi, Y., Li, Z., & Xu, D. (2023). Digital economy, industrial transformation and upgrading, and spatial transfer of carbon emissions: The paths for low-carbon transformation of Chinese cities. *Journal of Environmental Management*, *344*, 118528. doi:10.1016/j.jenvman.2023.118528 PMID:37392691

Balanzar Almazan, P. (2023). *Digitizing Work Instructions Through Technology using Internet of Things (IoT)* [MA Thesis]. University of Texas at El Paso.

Balasubramanian, S., Shukla, V., & Kavanancheeri, L. (2023). Improving Supply Chain Sustainability Using Artificial Intelligence: Evidence from the Manufacturing Sector. In Environmental footprints and eco-design of products and processes (pp. 43–59). doi:10.1007/978-981-99-4894-9_4

Baltacioglu, T., Erhan, A., Kaplan, D., Yurt, M., Oznur, K., & Cem, Y. (2007, March). A new framework for service supply chains. *Service Industries Journal*, *27*(2), 105–124. doi:10.1080/02642060601122629

Bansal, A., Panchal, T., Jabeen, F., Mangla, S. K., & Singh, G. (2023). A study of human resource digital transformation (HRDT): A phenomenon of innovation capability led by digital and individual factors. *Journal of Business Research*, *157*, 113611. doi:10.1016/j.jbusres.2022.113611

Bányai, T. (2018). Real-Time Decision Making in First Mile and Last Mile Logistics: How Smart Scheduling Affects Energy Efficiency of Hyperconnected Supply Chain Solutions. *Energies*, *11*(7), 1833. doi:10.3390/en11071833

Barbhuiya, S., & Das, B. (2023). Life Cycle Assessment of construction materials: Methodologies, applications and future directions for sustainable decision-making. *Case Studies in Construction Materials*, *19*, e02326. doi:10.1016/j.cscm.2023.e02326

Barboni, L. (2023). Machine Learning and Edge Computing for Industry 4.0 Applications: Concepts and Extensive review. In EAI/Springer Innovations in Communication and Computing (pp. 3–19). doi:10.1007/978-3-031-29775-5_1

Barenji, R. V., Akdag, Y., Yet, B., & Oner, L. (2019). Cyber-physical-based PAT (CPbPAT) framework for Pharma 4.0. *International Journal of Pharmaceutics*, *567*, 118445. doi:10.1016/j.ijpharm.2019.06.036 PMID:31226474

Baroroh, D. K., & Chu, C.-H. (2022, October). Human-centric production system simulation in mixed reality: An exemplary case of logistic facility design. *Journal of Manufacturing Systems*, *65*, 146–157. doi:10.1016/j.jmsy.2022.09.005

Baroroh, D. K., Chu, C.-H., & Wang, L. (2021). Systematic literature review on augmented reality in smart manufacturing: Collaboration between human and computational intelligence. *Journal of Manufacturing Systems*, *61*, 696–711. doi:10.1016/j.jmsy.2020.10.017

Barreto, L., Amaral, A., & Pereira, T. (2017). Industry 4.0 implications in logistics: An overview. Procedia Manufacturing, 13. DOI: doi:10.1016/j.promfg.2017.09.045, 10.1016/j.promfg.2017.09.045

Barreto, L., Amaral, A., & Pereira, T. (2017). Industry 4.0 implications in logistics: An overview. *Procedia Manufacturing*, *13*, 1245–1252. doi:10.1016/j.promfg.2017.09.045

Barton, D., & Court, D. (2012). Making advanced analytics work for you. *Harvard Business Review*, *90*(10), 78–83. PMID:23074867

Bauer, W., Hämmerle, M., Schlund, S., & Vocke, C. (2015). Transforming to a Hyper-connected Society and Economy – Towards an "Industry 4.0". *Procedia Manufacturing*, *3*, 417–424. doi:10.1016/j.promfg.2015.07.200

Baweja, P., Kumar, S., & Kumar, G. (2020). Fertilizers and pesticides: Their impact on soil health and environment. In Soil biology (pp. 265–285). doi:10.1007/978-3-030-44364-1_15

Bécue, A., Praça, I., & Gama, J. (2021). Artificial intelligence, cyber-threats and Industry 4.0: Challenges and opportunities. *Artificial Intelligence Review*, *54*(5), 3849–3886. doi:10.1007/s10462-020-09942-2

Begum, K. (2023, August 30). *Health care data privacy and Compliance: Navigating Regulatory landscape*. Central Asian Journal of Medical and Natural Science - Central Asian Studies. https://cajmns.centralasianstudies.org/index.php/CAJMNS/article/view/1758

Behera, B. C., Moharana, B. R., Muduli, K., & Islam. (2023). *Smart technologies for improved performance of manufacturing systems and services*. CRC Press.

Beier, G., Ullrich, A., Niehoff, S., Reißig, M., & Habich, M. (2020). Industry 4.0: How it is defined from a sociotechnical perspective and how much sustainability it includes – A literature review. *Journal of Cleaner Production*, *259*, 120856. doi:10.1016/j.jclepro.2020.120856

Bella, S. (2023). Enhancing financial management and accountant roles: A study on the role of technological Advancements. *Bella | SEIKO : Journal of Management & Business*. https://doi.org/ doi:10.37531/sejaman.v6i2.4842

Ben-Daya, M., Hassini, E., & Bahroun, Z. (2019). Internet of things and supply chain management: A literature review. *International Journal of Production Research*, *57*(15–16), 4719–4742. doi:10.1080/00207543.2017.1402140

Benos, L., Moysiadis, V., Kateris, D., Tagarakis, A. C., Busato, P., Pearson, S., & Bochtis, D. (2023). Human–Robot interaction in agriculture: A Systematic review. *Sensors (Basel)*, *23*(15), 6776. doi:10.3390/s23156776 PMID:37571559

Benyahya, M., Collen, A., Kechagia, S., & Nijdam, N. A. (2022). Automated city shuttles: Mapping the key challenges in cybersecurity, privacy and standards to future developments. *Computers & Security*, *122*, 102904. Advance online publication. doi:10.1016/j.cose.2022.102904

Berg, H., Bendix, P., Jansen, M., Blevennec, K., Bottermann, P., & Melgar, M. M. (2021). *Unlocking the potential of Industry 4.0 to reduce the environmental impact of production.* Eionet Report.

Berman, B. (2012). 3-D printing: The new industrial revolution. *Business Horizons*, *55*(2), 155–162. doi:10.1016/j.bushor.2011.11.003

Bernal, P. (2014). *Internet privacy rights: rights to protect autonomy.* Cambridge University Press. doi:10.1017/CBO9781107337428

Bharadiya, J. (2023). Machine learning and AI in Business intelligence: Trends and opportunities. *ResearchGate.* https://www.researchgate.net/publication/371902170_Machine_Learning_and_AI_in_Business_Intelligence_Trends_and_Opportunities

Bharti, M. S., & Bharti, S. S. (2022). The EU Public Diplomacy in the Time of Virtual Reality: Political, Social and Economic Implications. In B. Olbrych (Ed.), *Life in Virtual Reality, Chances and dangers* (Vol. 2, pp. 13–25). Akademia Handlowa Nauk Stosowanych w Radomiu.

Bhattacharya, A. (2023). Achieving sustainability in supply chain operations in the interplay between circular economy and Industry 4.0. *Production Planning and Control*, *34*(10), 867–869. doi:10.1080/09537287.2021.1981032

Bhowal, A. J. B. P. A. (2023, July 20). *Unraveling the Intricacies of Behavioral Biases: Exploring their Profound Influence on Working Capital Management Strategies of Entrepreneurs.* http://journals.kozminski.cem-j.org/index.php/pl_cemj/article/view/900

Bigdeli, Z. A., Kapoor, K., Schroeder, A., & Omidvar, O. (2021). Exploring the root causes of servitization challenges: An organisational boundary perspective. *International Journal of Operations & Production Management*, *41*(5), 547–573. https://doi.org/10.1108/IJOPM-08-2020-0507

Bihani, P., & Patil, S. T. (2014). A comparative study of data analysis techniques. *International Journal of Emerging Trends in Technology and Computer Science*, *3*(2), 95–101.

Bilderback, S. (2023). Integrating training for organizational sustainability: The application of Sustainable Development Goals globally. *European Journal of Training and Development.* Advance online publication. doi:10.1108/EJTD-01-2023-0005

Binos, T., Bruno, V., & Adamopoulos, A. (2021). Intelligent agent-based framework to augment warehouse management systems for dynamic demand environments. *AJIS. Australasian Journal of Information Systems*, *25*. Advance online publication. doi:10.3127/ajis.v25i0.2845

Birkel, H. S., & Hartmann, E. (2019a). Impact of IoT challenges and risks for SCM. *Supply Chain Management*, *24*(1), 39–61. doi:10.1108/SCM-03-2018-0142

Birkel, H., & Müller, J. M. (2021). Potentials of industry 4.0 for supply chain management within the triple bottom line of sustainability – A systematic literature review. *Journal of Cleaner Production*, *289*, 125612. doi:10.1016/j.jclepro.2020.125612

Biswas, K., Ghazzai, H., Sboui, L., & Massoud, Y. (2023). Urban Air Mobility: An IoT perspective. *IEEE Internet of Things Magazine*, *6*(2), 122–128. doi:10.1109/IOTM.001.2200237

Blat, M. O. (2023). *Enhancing big data Analytics capabilities: the influence of organisational culture and Data-Driven Orientation.* doi:10.4995/Thesis/10251/191788

Blok, V. (2019). From participation to interruption: toward an ethics of stakeholder engagement, participation and partnership in corporate social responsibility and responsible innovation. *International Handbook on Responsible Innovation: A Global Resource*, 243.

Bocek, T., Rodrigues, B. B., Strasser, T., & Stiller, B. (2017, May). Blockchains everywhere-a use-case of blockchains in the pharma supply-chain. In *2017 IFIP/IEEE symposium on integrated network and service management (IM)* (pp. 772-777). IEEE.

Bo-Hu, L. I., Lin, Z., Shi-Long, W., Fei, T., Jun-wei, C. A. O., Xiao-dan, J., ... Xu-dong, C. (2010). Cloud manufacturing: a new service-oriented networked manufacturing model. *Computer Integrated Manufacturing System, 16*(1).

Bokhari, S. A. A., Duggal, K., & Myeong, S. (2023). Artificial Intelligence Application in Supply Chain Management in Government Sector of Pakistan. *Engineering Proceedings*, 37.

Bolander, T. (2019). What do we lose when machines take the decisions? *The Journal of Management and Governance*, *23*, 849–867.

Bonino, D., & Vergori, P. (2017). Agent marketplaces and deep learning in enterprises: the composition project. *IEEE 41st Annual Computer Software and Applications Conference (COMPSAC)*, 749-754. 10.1109/COMPSAC.2017.46

Borregan-Alvarado, J., Alvarez-Meaza, I., Cilleruelo-Carrasco, E., & Garechana-Anacabe, G. (2020). A bibliometric analysis in industry 4.0 and advanced manufacturing: What about the sustainable supply chain? *Sustainability (Basel)*, *12*(19), 7840. doi:10.3390/su12197840

Bosch. (2021). *Ten years of Industry 4.0.* Bosch.

Boyes, H., Hallaq, B., Cunningham, J., & Watson, T. (2018). The industrial internet of things (IIoT): An analysis framework. *Computers in Industry*, *101*, 1–12. doi:10.1016/j.compind.2018.04.015

Broadhead, J. (2023). *The role of nonprofit housing developers in addressing the affordable housing crisis: A case study of LInC Housing*. DigitalCommons@CalPoly. https://digitalcommons.calpoly.edu/cmsp/704/

BrohiS. N.JhanjhiN. Z.BrohiN. N.BrohiM. N. (2020). Key Applications of State-of-the-Art Technologies to Mitigate and Eliminate COVID-19. TechRxiv. doi:10.36227/techrxiv.12115596.v2

Brown, B., Chui, M., & Manyika, J. (2011). Are you ready for the era of 'big data'. *The McKinsey Quarterly*, *4*(1), 24–35.

Brun, A., Karaosman, H., & Barresi, T. (2020). Supply chain collaboration for transparency. *Sustainability (Basel)*, *12*(11), 4429. doi:10.3390/su12114429

Brunetti, F., Matt, D. T., Bonfanti, A., De Longhi, A., Pedrini, G., & Orzes, G. (2020). Digital Transformation Challenges: Strategies Emerging from a Multi-Stakeholder Approach. *The TQM Journal*, *32*(4), 697–724. doi:10.1108/TQM-12-2019-0309

Buonomano, A., Del Papa, G., Giuzio, G. F., Palombo, A., & Russo, G. (2023). Future pathways for decarbonization and energy efficiency of ports: Modelling and optimization as sustainable energy hubs. *Journal of Cleaner Production*, *138389*. Advance online publication. doi:10.1016/j.jclepro.2023.138389

Buonomo, I., Ferrara, B., Pansini, M., & Benevene, P. (2023). Job satisfaction and perceived structural support in Remote Working Conditions—The role of a sense of community at work. *International Journal of Environmental Research and Public Health*, *20*(13), 6205. doi:10.3390/ijerph20136205 PMID:37444053

Butt, A. S., Ali, I., & Govindan, K. (2023). The role of reverse logistics in a circular economy for achieving sustainable development goals: A multiple case study of retail firms. *Production Planning and Control*, 1–13. doi:10.1080/09537287.2023.2197851

Büyüközkan, G., & Göçer, F. (2018). Digital Supply Chain: Literature review and a proposed framework for future research. *Computers in Industry, 97*, 157–177. doi:10.1016/j.compind.2018.02.010

Cabibihan, J., Gaballa, A., Fadli, F., Irshidat, M., Mahdi, E., Biloria, N., Mansour, Z., & Abdulrazak, H. (2023). A guided approach for utilizing concrete robotic 3D printing for the architecture, engineering, and construction industry. *Construction Robotics*, *7*(3-4), 265–278. Advance online publication. doi:10.1007/s41693-023-00103-9

Caiado, R. G. G., Scavarda, L. F., Azevedo, B. D., Nascimento, D. L. de M., & Quelhas, O. L. G. (2022). Challenges and Benefits of Sustainable Industry 4.0 for Operations and Supply Chain Management—A Framework Headed toward the 2030 Agenda. *Sustainability, 14*(2), 830. doi:10.3390/su14020830

Camilleri, M. A., Troise, C., Strazzullo, S., & Bresciani, S. (2023). Creating shared value through open innovation approaches: Opportunities and challenges for corporate sustainability. *Business Strategy and the Environment, 32*(7), 4485–4502. doi:10.1002/bse.3377

Cañas, H., Mula, J., & Campuzano-Bolarín, F. (2020). A general outline of a sustainable supply chain 4.0. *Sustainability (Basel), 12*(19), 1–17. doi:10.3390/su12197978

Cano-Marin, E., Soriano, D. R., Mardani, A., & González-Tejero, C. B. (2023). Exploring the challenges of the COVID-19 vaccine supply chain using social media analytics: A global perspective. *Sustainable Technology and Entrepreneurship, 100047*(3), 100047. Advance online publication. doi:10.1016/j.stae.2023.100047

Capgemini. (2023, July 13). *How automotive organizations can maximize the smart factory potential | Research & insight | Capgemini.* https://www.capgemini.com/insights/research-library/automotive-smart-factories/

Carboni, A., Russo, D., Moroni, D., & Barsocchi, P. (2023). Privacy by design in systems for assisted living, personalised care, and wellbeing: A stakeholder analysis. *Frontiers in Digital Health, 4*, 934609. Advance online publication. doi:10.3389/fdgth.2022.934609 PMID:36860207

Carvalho, T. P., Soares, F. A., Vita, R., Francisco, R. D. P., Basto, J. P., & Alcalá, S. G. (2019). A systematic literature review of machine learning methods applied to predictive maintenance. *Computers & Industrial Engineering, 137*, 106024. doi:10.1016/j.cie.2019.106024

Casey, M. J., & Wong, P. (2017). Global supply chains are about to get better, thanks to blockchain. *Harvard Business Review, 13*, 1–6.

Cassetta, E., Dileo, I., & Pini, M. (2022). Linking external collaborations, eco-innovation and sustainable growth. An empirical analysis on the Italian manufacturing firms. *Industry and Innovation, 30*(4), 452–479. doi:10.1080/13662716.2022.2109456

Castillo, M., Monroy, R., & Ahmad, R. (2022). Scientometric analysis and systematic review of smart manufacturing technologies applied to the 3D printing polymer material extrusion system. *Journal of Intelligent Manufacturing*. Advance online publication. doi:10.1007/s10845-022-02049-1

Chamasemani, F. F., & Singh, Y. P. (2011, September). Multi-class support vector machine (SVM) classifiers--an application in hypothyroid detection and classification. In *2011 sixth international conference on bio-inspired computing: theories and applications* (pp. 351-356). IEEE.

Chan, A. (2022). GPT-3 and InstructGPT: Technological dystopianism, utopianism, and "Contextual" perspectives in AI ethics and industry. *AI and Ethics*, *3*(1), 53–64. doi:10.1007/s43681-022-00148-6

Chand, M., Jain, V., & Ajmera, P. (2023). *Data-Driven technologies and artificial intelligence in supply chain: Tools and Techniques*. CRC Press.

Chandan, A., John, M., & Potdar, V. (2023). Achieving UN SDGs in food supply chain using blockchain technology. *Sustainability (Basel)*, *15*(3), 2109. doi:10.3390/su15032109

Chandra, D., Vipin, B., & Kumar, D. (2023). A fuzzy multi-criteria framework to identify barriers and enablers of the next-generation vaccine supply chain. *International Journal of Productivity and Performance Management*, *72*(3), 827–847. doi:10.1108/IJPPM-08-2020-0419

Chang, S. E., Chen, Y. C., & Lu, M. F. (2019). Supply chain re-engineering using blockchain technology: A case of smart contract based tracking process. *Technological Forecasting and Social Change*, *144*, 1–11. doi:10.1016/j.techfore.2019.03.015

Chan, H. K., Griffin, J., Lim, J. J., Zeng, F., & Chiu, A. S. F. (2018). The impact of 3D Printing Technology on the supply chain: Manufacturing and legal perspectives. *International Journal of Production Economics*, *205*, 156–162. doi:10.1016/j.ijpe.2018.09.009

Chansamut, A. (2023). Digital model for Sugarcane Production for the Factory in Thai Supply Chain. *International Journal of Supply Chain Management*, *12*(3), 90–94. doi:10.59160/ijscm.v12i3.6133

Charfeddine, L., & Umlai, M. I. (2023). ICT sector, digitization and environmental sustainability: A systematic review of the literature from 2000 to 2022. *Renewable & Sustainable Energy Reviews*, *184*, 113482. doi:10.1016/j.rser.2023.113482

Chataut, R. (2023). *Unleashing the Power of IoT: A comprehensive review of IoT applications and future prospects in healthcare, agriculture, smart homes, smart cities, and industry 4.0*. MDPI. doi:10.3390/s23167194

Chaudhary, M., Gaur, L., Chakrabarti, A., & Jhanjhi, N. (2023). Unravelling the Barriers of Human Resource Analytics: Multi-Criteria Decision-Making Approach. *Journal of Survey in Fisheries Sciences*, 306-321.

Chauhan, S., Singh, R., Gehlot, A., Akram, S. V., Twala, B., & Priyadarshi, N. (2022). Digitalization of Supply Chain Management with Industry 4.0 Enabling Technologies: A Sustainable Perspective. *Processes, 11*(1), 96. doi:10.3390/pr11010096

Chauhan, C., Kaur, P., Arrawatia, R., Ractham, P., & Dhir, A. (2022). Supply chain collaboration and sustainable development goals (SDGs). Teamwork makes achieving SDGs dream work. *Journal of Business Research*, *147*, 290–307. doi:10.1016/j.jbusres.2022.03.044

Chauhan, M., & Shiaeles, S. (2023). An analysis of cloud security frameworks, problems and proposed solutions. *Network (Bristol, England)*, *3*(3), 422–450. doi:10.3390/network3030018

Chee, S. Y. (2023). Age-related digital disparities, functional limitations, and social isolation: Unraveling the grey digital divide between baby boomers and the silent generation in senior living facilities. *Aging & Mental Health*, 1–12. doi:10.1080/13607863.2023.2233454 PMID:37424361

Chen, D., & Zhang, R. (2022). Exploring research trends of emerging technologies in health metaverse: A bibliometric analysis. SSRN Electronic Journal, 5, 1–32.

Chen, S., Shi, R., Ren, Z., Yan, J., Shi, Y., & Zhang, J. (2017). A blockchain-based supply chain quality management framework. In *2017 IEEE 14th International Conference on E-Business Engineering (ICEBE)* (pp. 172-176). IEEE. 10.1109/ICEBE.2017.34

Chen, C., Liu, C., Wang, T., Zhang, A., Wu, W., & Cheng, L. (2023). Compound fault diagnosis for industrial robots based on dual-transformer networks. *Journal of Manufacturing Systems*, *66*, 163–178. doi:10.1016/j.jmsy.2022.12.006

Chen, J., Fu, Y., Lu, W., & Pan, Y. (2023). Augmented reality-enabled human-robot collaboration to balance construction waste sorting efficiency and occupational safety and health. *Journal of Environmental Management*, *348*, 119341. doi:10.1016/j.jenvman.2023.119341 PMID:37852080

Chen, L., Dong, T., Peng, J., & Ralescu, D. (2023). Uncertainty Analysis and Optimization Modeling with Application to Supply Chain Management: A Systematic Review. *Mathematics*, *11*(11), 2530. doi:10.3390/math11112530

Chen, M., Sinha, A., Hu, K., & Shah, M. I. (2021). Impact of technological innovation on energy efficiency in Industry 4.0 era: Moderation of shadow economy in sustainable development. *Technological Forecasting and Social Change*, *164*, 120521.

Chen, S., Su, Y., Tufail, B., Lam, V. T., Phan, T. T. H., & Ngo, T. Q. (2023). The moderating role of leadership on the relationship between green supply chain management, technological advancement, and knowledge management in sustainable performance. *Environmental Science and Pollution Research International*, *30*(19), 56654–56669. doi:10.1007/s11356-023-26304-x PMID:36920606

Chen, X. H., Tee, K., Elnahass, M., & Ahmed, R. R. (2023). Assessing the environmental impacts of renewable energy sources: A case study on air pollution and carbon emissions in China. *Journal of Environmental Management*, *345*, 118525. doi:10.1016/j.jenvman.2023.118525 PMID:37421726

Chen, X., He, C., Chen, Y., & Xie, Z. (2022). Internet of Things (IoT)—Blockchain-enabled pharmaceutical supply chain resilience in the post-pandemic era. *Frontiers of Engineering Management*, *10*(1), 82–95. doi:10.1007/s42524-022-0233-1

Chen, X., Wang, C., & Li, S. (2023). The impact of supply chain finance on corporate social responsibility and creating shared value: A case from the emerging economy. *Supply Chain Management*, *28*(2), 324–346. doi:10.1108/SCM-10-2021-0478

Chen, X., Zhou, B., Štilić, A., Stević, Ž., & Puška, A. (2023). A Fuzzy–Rough MCDM Approach for selecting green Suppliers in the furniture Manufacturing industry: A Case Study of Eco-Friendly Material Production. *Sustainability (Basel)*, *15*(13), 10745. doi:10.3390/su151310745

Chen, Y., Zhao, K., Liu, G. G., & Chen, W. (2023). Health technology assessment to inform decision making in China: Progress, challenges, and sustainability. *BMJ (Clinical Research Ed.)*, *068910*. Advance online publication. doi:10.1136/bmj-2021-068910 PMID:37321607

Chesti, I. A., Humayun, M., Sama, N. U., & Jhanjhi, N. Z. (2020). Evolution, Mitigation, and Prevention of Ransomware. *2020 2nd International Conference on Computer and Information Sciences (ICCIS)*. 10.1109/ICCIS49240.2020.9257708

Cheung, C. F., Lee, C. K. M., Zheng, P., & Lee, W. B. (2023). Digital manufacturing systems. In Springer handbooks (pp. 805–827). doi:10.1007/978-3-030-96729-1_36

Chiarini, A. (2021). Industry 4.0 technologies in the manufacturing sector: Are we sure they are all relevant for environmental performance? *Business Strategy and the Environment*, *30*(7), 3194–3207.

Chiarini, A., Grando, A., Venturini, S., & Borgonovo, E. (2023). Do automation and AI impact on job reduction? A study on perceived risk of losing job among white-collars in the Italian manufacturing companies. *Production Planning and Control*, 1–14. doi:10.1080/09537287.2023.2244925

Chkanikova, O., & Sroufe, R. (2021). Third-party sustainability certifications in food retailing: Certification design from a sustainable supply chain management perspective. *Journal of Cleaner Production*, *282*, 124344. doi:10.1016/j.jclepro.2020.124344

Chohan, I. M., Ahmad, A., Sallih, N., Bheel, N., Ali, M., & Deifalla, A. F. (2023). A review on life cycle assessment of different pipeline materials. *Results in Engineering*, *19*, 101325. doi:10.1016/j.rineng.2023.101325

Christopher, M. (1998). *Logistics and supply chain management: Strategies for reducing cost and improving service*. Financial Times Professional Limited.

Chukwu, E. (2023, June 16). *Navigating Ethical Supply chains: the intersection of diplomatic management and theological ethics*. https://jurnal.itscience.org/index.php/ijmdsa/article/view/2874

Chu, L. K., Doğan, B., Abakah, E. J. A., Ghosh, S., & Albeni, M. (2022). Impact of economic policy uncertainty, geopolitical risk, and economic complexity on carbon emissions and ecological footprint: An investigation of the E7 countries. *Environmental Science and Pollution Research International*, *30*(12), 34406–34427. doi:10.1007/s11356-022-24682-2 PMID:36512279

Ciğerci, M. (2023). Main Effects of Big Data on Supply Chain Management. In Implementation Of Disruptive Technologies In Supply Chain Management (pp. 27–49). doi:10.59287/idtscm.68

Cioffi, R., Travaglioni, M., Piscitelli, G., Petrillo, A., & De Felice, F. (2020). Artificial Intelligence and Machine Learning Applications in Smart Production: Progress, Trends, and Directions. *Sustainability, 12*(2), 492. doi:10.3390/su12020492

Cirillo, V., Rinaldini, M., Staccioli, J., & Virgillito, M. E. (2021). Technology vs. workers: The case of Italy's Industry 4.0 factories. *Structural Change and Economic Dynamics*, *56*, 166–183.https://doi.org/10.1016/j.strueco.2020.09.007

Collomb, A., & Sok, K. (2016). Blockchain/Distributed ledger technology (DLT): What impact on the financial sector? *Communications & Stratégies*, *103*, 93–111.

Colombi, C., & D'Itria, E. (2023). Fashion Digital Transformation: Innovating Business Models toward Circular Economy and Sustainability. *Sustainability (Basel)*, *15*(6), 4942. doi:10.3390/su15064942

Costa, F., Frecassetti, S., Rossini, M., & Staudacher, A. P. (2023). Industry 4.0 digital technologies enhancing sustainability: Applications and barriers from the agricultural industry in an emerging economy. *Journal of Cleaner Production*, *408*, 137208. doi:10.1016/j.jclepro.2023.137208

Cowie, M., Blomster, J., Curtis, L., Duclaux, S., Ford, I., & Fritz, F. (2016). Electronic health records to facilitate clinical research. *Clinical Research in Cardiology; Official Journal of the German Cardiac Society*. PMID:27557678

Cressman, J., Pokharna, R., & Newman, W. (2023). Compliant robotic behaviors for satellite servicing. *Frontiers in Robotics and AI*, *10*, 1124207. Advance online publication. doi:10.3389/frobt.2023.1124207 PMID:37533424

CronaB.ParlatoG.LadeS. J.FetzerI.MausV. (2023). Going beyond carbon: An "Earth System Impact" score to better capture corporate and investment impacts on the Earth system. *Social Science Research Network*. doi:10.2139/ssrn.4495331

Cui, Y., Ma, Z., Wang, L., Yang, A., Liu, Q., Kong, S., & Wang, H. (2023). A survey on big data-enabled innovative online education systems during the COVID-19 pandemic. *Journal of Innovation & Knowledge*, *8*(1), 100295. doi:10.1016/j.jik.2022.100295

Czeczot, G., Rojek, I., Mikołajewski, D., & Sangho, B. (2023). AI in IIoT Management of Cybersecurity for Industry 4.0 and Industry 5.0 Purposes. *Electronics (Basel)*, *12*(18), 3800. doi:10.3390/electronics12183800

Da Silva, F. T., Baierle, I. C., De Faria Corrêa, R. G., Sellitto, M. A., Peres, F. P., & Kipper, L. M. (2023). Open Innovation in Agribusiness: Barriers and challenges in the transition to Agriculture 4.0. *Sustainability (Basel), 15*(11), 8562. doi:10.3390/su15118562

Dadaneh, D. Z., Moradi, S., & Alizadeh, B. (2023). Simultaneous planning of purchase orders, production, and inventory management under demand uncertainty. *International Journal of Production Economics, 109012*, 109012. Advance online publication. doi:10.1016/j.ijpe.2023.109012

Dahlmann, F., & Roehrich, J. K. (2019). Sustainable supply chain management and partner engagement to manage climate change information. *Business Strategy and the Environment, 28*(8), 1632–1647. doi:10.1002/bse.2392

Daiyoub, A., Gelabert, P., Saura-Mas, S., & Vega-García, C. (2023). War and Deforestation: Using Remote Sensing and Machine Learning to Identify the War-Induced Deforestation in Syria 2010–2019. *Land (Basel), 12*(8), 1509. doi:10.3390/land12081509

Dang, V. A., Vu Khanh, Q., Nguyen, V.-H., Nguyen, T., & Nguyen, D. C. (2023). Intelligent Healthcare: Integration of Emerging Technologies and Internet of Things for Humanity. *Sensors (Basel), 23*(9), 4200. https://doi.org/10.3390/s23094200

Dani, S., Rahman, A., Jin, J., & Kulkarni, A. (2023). Cloud-Empowered Data-Centric paradigm for smart manufacturing. *Machines, 11*(4), 451. doi:10.3390/machines11040451

Daradkeh, M. (2023). Navigating the Complexity of Entrepreneurial Ethics: A Systematic Review and Future Research agenda. *Sustainability (Basel), 15*(14), 11099. doi:10.3390/su151411099

Dash, D., Farooq, R., Panda, J. S., & Sandhyavani, K. (2019). Internet of Things (IoT): The New Paradigm of HRM and Skill Development in the Fourth Industrial Revolution (Industry 4.0). *IUP Journal of Information Technology, 15*(4).

DasS. (2023). Digital Twin Technology: Enhancing efficiency and Decision-Making in Industry 4.0. *Social Science Research Network.* doi:10.2139/ssrn.4459204

Dathe, T., Dathe, R., Dathe, I., & Helmold, M. (2022). *Corporate social responsibility (CSR), sustainability and environmental social governance (ESG): Approaches to ethical management*. Springer Nature. doi:10.1007/978-3-030-92357-0

Dave, M., & Patel, N. (2023). Artificial intelligence in healthcare and education. *British Dental Journal, 234*(10), 761–764. doi:10.1038/s41415-023-5845-2 PMID:37237212

De Azambuja, A. J. G., Plesker, C., Schützer, K., Anderl, R., Schleich, B., & Almeida, V. R. (2023). Artificial Intelligence-Based Cyber Security in the context of Industry 4.0—A survey. *Electronics (Basel), 12*(8), 1920. doi:10.3390/electronics12081920

De la Peña Zarzuelo, I., Soeane, M. J. F., & Bermúdez, B. L. (2020). Industry 4.0 in the port and maritime industry: A literature review. *Journal of Industrial Information Integration, 20*, 100173. doi:10.1016/j.jii.2020.100173

De Lima, F. A., & Seuring, S. (2023). A Delphi study examining risk and uncertainty management in circular supply chains. *International Journal of Production Economics, 258*, 108810. doi:10.1016/j.ijpe.2023.108810

De Oliveira, R. T., Ghobakhloo, M., & Figueira, S. (2023). Industry 4.0 towards social and environmental sustainability in multinationals: Enabling circular economy, organizational social practices, and corporate purpose. *Journal of Cleaner Production, 430*, 139712. doi:10.1016/j.jclepro.2023.139712

De Souza Miguel, P. L., & Tonelli, M. J. (2022). Supplier diversity for socially responsible purchasing: An empirical investigation in Brazil. *International Journal of Physical Distribution & Logistics Management, 53*(1), 93–114. doi:10.1108/IJPDLM-09-2021-0407

De, P., Biase, L. C., Fedrecheski, G., Calcina-Ccori, P. C., De Deus Lopes, R., & Zuffo, M. K. (2023). Swarm Computing: the emergence of a collective artificial intelligence at the edge of the internet. In IntechOpen eBooks. doi:10.5772/intechopen.110907

Debnath, A., & Sarkar, B. (2023, January 20). Effect of circular economy for waste nullification under a sustainable supply chain management. *Journal of Cleaner Production*, *385*, 135477. doi:10.1016/j.jclepro.2022.135477

Debnath, B., Shakur, M. S., Bari, A. M., Saha, J. K., Porna, W. A., Mishu, M. J., Islam, A. R. M. T., & Rahman, M. (2023). Assessing the critical success factors for implementing industry 4.0 in the pharmaceutical industry: Implications for supply chain sustainability in emerging economies. *PLoS One*, *18*(6), e0287149. doi:10.1371/journal.pone.0287149 PMID:37319165

Deepak Kumar, S., Arun Manohar, G., Surya Teja, R., Ramana Rao, P., Mandal, A., Behera, A., & Srinivasa Rao, P. (2023). Smart Manufacturing Technologies in Industry 4.0: Challenges and Opportunities. *Intelligent Manufacturing Management Systems: Operational Applications of Evolutionary Digital Technologies in Mechanical and Industrial Engineering*, 23-57.

Deivanayagampillai, N., Jacob, K., Manohar, G. V., & Broumi, S. (2023, July 29). *Investigation Of Industry 5.0 Hurdles And Their Mitigation Tactics In Emerging Economies By Todim Arithmetic And Geometric Aggregation Operators In Single Value Neutrosophic Environment.* Deivanayagampillai | Facta Universitatis, Series: Mechanical Engineering. http://casopisi.junis.ni.ac.rs/index.php/FUMechEng/article/view/11987

Del Sarto, N., Cesaroni, F., Di Minin, A., & Piccaluga, A. (2021). One size does not fit all. Business models heterogeneity among Internet of Things architecture layers. *Technology Analysis and Strategic Management*, *34*(7), 787–202.

Deliktaş, D., Karagoz, S., Simić, V., & Aydin, N. (2023). A stochastic Fermatean fuzzy-based multi-choice conic goal programming approach for sustainable supply chain management in end-of-life buildings. *Journal of Cleaner Production*, *382*, 135305. doi:10.1016/j.jclepro.2022.135305

Despeisse, M., Johansson, B., Bokrantz, J., Braun, G., Chari, A., Chen, X., Fang, Q., Chávez, C. G., Skoogh, A., Stahre, J., Mathew, N. T., Bekar, E. T., Wang, H., & Örtengren, R. (2023). Battery production Systems: state of the art and future developments. In IFIP advances in information and communication technology (pp. 521–535). doi:10.1007/978-3-031-43688-8_36

Dessart, L., & Standaert, W. (2023). Strategic storytelling in the age of sustainability. *Business Horizons*, *66*(3), 371–385. doi:10.1016/j.bushor.2023.01.005

Dewald, J., & Bowen, F. (2010). Storm clouds and silver linings: Responding to disruptive innovations through cognitive resilience. *Entrepreneurship Theory and Practice*, *34*(1), 197–218.

Dhanpat, N., Buthelezi, Z. P., Joe, M. R., Maphela, T. V., & Shongwe, N. (2020). Industry 4.0: The role of human resource professionals. *SA Journal of Human Resource Management*, *18*(1), 1–11. doi:10.4102/sajhrm.v18i0.1302

Dharmayanti, N., Ismail, T., Hanifah, I. A., & Taqi, M. (2023). Exploring sustainability management control system and eco-innovation matter sustainable financial performance: The role of supply chain management and digital adaptability in indonesian context. *Journal of Open Innovation*, *9*(3), 100119. doi:10.1016/j.joitmc.2023.100119

DhimanB. (2023). Ethical Issues and Challenges in social Media: A current scenario. *Social Science Research Network.* doi:10.2139/ssrn.4406610

Dhirani, L. L., Mukhtiar, N., Chowdhry, B. S., & Newe, T. (2023). Ethical dilemmas and privacy issues in emerging technologies: A review. *Sensors (Basel)*, *23*(3), 1151. doi:10.3390/s23031151

Diaz Lopez, F. J., Bastein, T., & Tukker, A. (2019). Business Model Innovation for Resource-efficiency, Circularity and Cleaner Production: What 143 Cases Tell Us. *Ecological Economics, 155*, 20–35. doi:10.1016/j.ecolecon.2018.03.009

Digital twin solution from Merck offers increased traceability 2022Packaging Europe.

Ding, B. (2018). Pharma Industry 4.0: Literature review and research opportunities in sustainable pharmaceutical supply chains. *Process Safety and Environmental Protection, 119*, 115–130. doi:10.1016/j.psep.2018.06.031

Ding, B., Hernández, X. F., & Agell, N. (2021). Combining lean and agile manufacturing competitive advantages through Industry 4.0 technologies: An integrative approach. *Production Planning and Control, 34*(5), 442–458. doi:10.1080/09537287.2021.1934587

Dion, H., Evans, M., & Farrell, P. (2022). Hospitals management transformative initiatives; towards energy efficiency and environmental sustainability in healthcare facilities. *Journal of Engineering. Design and Technology, 21*(2), 552–584. doi:10.1108/JEDT-04-2022-0200

Diwaker, C., Tomar, P., Solanki, A., Nayyar, A., Jhanjhi, N. Z., Abdullah, A., & Supramaniam, M. (2019). A new model for predicting Component-Based software reliability using soft computing. *IEEE Access : Practical Innovations, Open Solutions, 7*, 147191–147203. doi:10.1109/ACCESS.2019.2946862

Dixon, L. (2024). *Unveiling The Differences Between Industry 4.0 And Industry 5.0.* Retrieved from.https://news.lineview.com/unveiling-the-differences-between-industry-4.0-and-industry-5.0#:~:text=If%20Industry%204.0's%20main,greater%20impact%20in%20innovation%2C%20productivity

Dod, G. N., Jibhakate, R., & Walke, P. V. (2023). A review on 3D printing maxillofacial surgery: Present work and future prospects. *Materials Today: Proceedings*. Advance online publication. doi:10.1016/j.matpr.2023.06.049

Doersch, C., & Zisserman, A. (2017). Multi-task self-supervised visual learning. In *Proceedings of the IEEE international conference on computer vision* (pp. 2051-2060). IEEE.

Dolzhenko, I. B., & Churakova, A. A. (2022). Environmental Responsibility of Fashion Industry Multinational Corporations (MNCs) in the Context of Industry 4.0. *Industry 4.0: Fighting Climate Change in the Economy of the Future*, 79–89. https://doi.org/ doi:10.1007/978-3-030-79496-5_7/COVER

Dorcheh, F. R., & Rahbari, M. (2023). Greenhouse Gas Emissions Optimization for Distribution and Vehicle Routing Problem in a Poultry Meat Supply Chain in Two Phases: a Case Study in Iran. *Process Integration and Optimization for Sustainability*. doi:10.1007/s41660-023-00339-6

Dorn, T. M. (2023). *U.S. critical infrastructure: Its Importance and Vulnerabilities to Cyber and Unmanned Systems*. Page Publishing Inc.

Dorsemaine, B., Gaulier, J. P., Wary, J. P., Kheir, N., & Urien, P. (2015, September). Internet of things: a definition & taxonomy. In *2015 9th International Conference on Next Generation Mobile Applications, Services and Technologies* (pp. 72-77). IEEE. 10.1109/NGMAST.2015.71

Duan, W., Khurshid, A., Khan, K., & Călin, A. C. (2024). Transforming industry: Investigating 4.0 technologies for sustainable product evolution in china through a novel fuzzy three-way decision-making process. *Technological Forecasting and Social Change, 200*, 123125. doi:10.1016/j.techfore.2023.123125

Duarte, S., Cabrita, M. D. R., & Cruz-Machado, V. (2023). Green Supply Chain Practices: Toward A Sustainable Industry Development. *E3S Web of Conferences, 409*, 01004. doi:10.1051/e3sconf/202340901004

Dubbert, C., Abdulai, A., & Mohammed, S. (2021). Contract farming and the adoption of sustainable farm practices: Empirical evidence from cashew farmers in Ghana. *Applied Economic Perspectives and Policy*, *45*(1), 487–509. doi:10.1002/aepp.13212

Dumitrascu, O., Dumitrascu, M., & Dobrotă, D. (2020). Performance Evaluation for a Sustainable Supply Chain Management System in the Automotive Industry Using Artificial Intelligence. *Processes (Basel, Switzerland)*, *8*(11), 1–20. doi:10.3390/pr8111384

Dutta, P., Chavhan, R., Gowtham, P., & Singh, A. (2022). The individual and integrated impact of Blockchain and IoT on sustainable supply chains:a systematic review. *Supply Chain Forum*, *24*(1), 103–126. 10.1080/16258312.2022.2082851

Ebinger, F., & Omondi, B. (2020). Leveraging Digital Approaches for Transparency in Sustainable Supply Chains: A Conceptual Paper. *Sustainability (Basel)*, *12*(15), 6129. Advance online publication. doi:10.3390/su12156129

Edwards, D. (2018, December 11). *Aerospace robotics market predicted to grow as manufacturers turn to automation to meet orders*. Robotics & Automation News. https://roboticsandautomationnews.com/2018/12/11/aerospace-robotics-market-predicted-to-grow-as-manufacturers-turn-to-automation-to-meet-orders/20102/

Efe, A. (2023). *An assessment on the problems and possible solutions of artificial intelligence tools and techniques on execution, monitoring and reporting of impact investments*. Girişimcilik İnovasyon Ve Pazarlama Araştırmaları Dergisi., doi:10.31006/gipad.1263598

Ehsanifar, M., Dekamini, F., Spulbar, C., Birau, R., Khazaei, M., & Bărbăcioru, I. C. (2023). A sustainable pattern of waste management and energy efficiency in smart homes using the internet of things (IoT). *Sustainability (Basel)*, *15*(6), 5081. doi:10.3390/su15065081

El-Alfy, E.-S. M., & Mohammed, S. A. (2020). A review of machine learning for big data analytics: Bibliometric approach. *Technology Analysis and Strategic Management*, *32*(8), 984–1005. https://doi.org/10.1080/09537325.2020.1732912

Elbaşi, E., Zaki, C., Topcu, A. E., Abdelbaki, W., Zreikat, A. I., Cina, E., Shdefat, A. Y., & Saker, L. (2023). Crop prediction model using machine learning algorithms. *Applied Sciences (Basel, Switzerland)*, *13*(16), 9288. doi:10.3390/app13169288

Eldem, B., Kluczek, A., & Baginski, J. P. (2022). The COVID-19 Impact on Supply Chain Operations of Automotive Industry: A Case study of Sustainability 4.0 based on Sense–ADApt–Transform Framework. *Sustainability (Basel)*, *14*(10), 5855. doi:10.3390/su14105855

El-Gendy, S., Elsayed, M. S., Jurcut, A. D., & Azer, M. A. (2023). Privacy preservation using machine learning in the internet of things. *Mathematics*, *11*(16), 3477. doi:10.3390/math11163477

El-Haggar, N., Amouri, L., Alsumayt, A., Alghamedy, F., & Aljameel, S. S. (2023). The Effectiveness and Privacy Preservation of IoT on Ubiquitous Learning: Modern Learning Paradigm to Enhance Higher Education. *Applied Sciences (Basel, Switzerland)*, *13*(15), 9003. doi:10.3390/app13159003

Emmanouilidis, C., Pistofidis, P., Bertoncelj, L., Katsouros, V., Fournaris, A., Koulamas, C., & Ruiz-Carcel, C. (2019). Enabling the human in the loop: Linked data and knowledge in industrial cyber-physical systems. *Annual Reviews in Control*, *47*, 249–265. doi:10.1016/j.arcontrol.2019.03.004

Endress, T. (2023). *Digital project practice for new work and industry 4.0*. Auerbach Publications. doi:10.1201/9781003371397

Engelenburg, S. V., Janssen, M., & Klievink, B. (2019). Design of a software architecture supporting business-to-government information sharing to improve public safety and security: Combining business rules, Events and blockchain technology. *Journal of Intelligent Information Systems, 52*(3), 595–618. doi:10.1007/s10844-017-0478-z

EpendiU.RochimA. F.WibowoA. (2023). An Assessment Model for Sustainability City Using Crowdsourced Data Based on General System Theory: A Design Science Methodology Approach. *Preprintprints.org*. doi:10.20944/preprints202309.0349.v1

Erhun, F., Kraft, T., & Wijnsma, S. (2021). Sustainable Triple-A Supply Chains. *Production and Operations Management, 30*(3), 644–655. doi:10.1111/poms.13306

Esben, H., & Østergaard, M.-A. (2018). *Welcome to Industry 5.0.* Retrieved from.https://www.isa.org/intech-home/2018/march-april/features/welcome-to-industry-5-0

Eslami, M. H., Jafari, H., Achtenhagen, L., Carlbäck, J., & Wong, A. (2021). Financial performance and supply chain dynamic capabilities: The Moderating Role of Industry 4.0 technologies. *International Journal of Production Research*, •••, 1–18.

Esmaeilian, B., Behdad, S., & Wang, B. (2016). The evolution and future of manufacturing: A review. *Journal of Manufacturing Systems, 39*, 79–100. doi:10.1016/j.jmsy.2016.03.001

Esmaeilian, B., Sarkis, J., Lewis, K., & Behdad, S. (2020). Blockchain for the future of sustainable supply chain management in Industry 4.0. *Resources, Conservation and Recycling, 163*, 105064. doi:10.1016/j.resconrec.2020.105064

Eswaran, K., Kumar, A., & Tamilarasan, K. (2024). Optimal layout planning for human robot collaborative assembly systems and visualization through immersive technologies. *Expert Systems with Applications, 241*, 122465. Advance online publication. doi:10.1016/j.eswa.2023.122465

Everritt, M., & Rundio, A. (2023). Mental Health Resources for NCAA Student-Athletes. *Case Studies in Sport Management, 12*(1), 6–10. doi:10.1123/cssm.2022-0016

Eyers, D., Lahy, A., Wilson, M., & Syntetos, A. (2019). 3D Printing for Supply Chain Service Companies. In P. Wells (Ed.), *Contemporary Operations and Logistics: Achieving Excellence in Turbulent Times* (pp. 61–79). Springer International Publishing. doi:10.1007/978-3-030-14493-7_5

Fang, B., Yu, J., Chen, Z., Osman, A. I., Farghali, M., Ihara, I., Hamza, E., Rooney, D., & Yap, P. (2023). Artificial intelligence for waste management in smart cities: A review. *Environmental Chemistry Letters, 21*(4), 1959–1989. doi:10.1007/s10311-023-01604-3 PMID:37362015

Fan, P., Song, Y., Fang, M., & Chen, X. (2023). Creating an age-inclusive workplace: The impact of HR practices on employee work engagement. *Journal of Management & Organization, 29*(6), 1–19. doi:10.1017/jmo.2023.18

Fantini, P., Pinzone, M., & Taisch, M. (2020). Placing the operator at the centre of Industry 4.0 design: Modelling and assessing human activities within cyber-physical systems. *Computers & Industrial Engineering*, •••, 139.https://doi.org/10.1016/j.cie.2018.01.025

Farahani, B., Firouzi, F., & Chakrabarty, K. (2020). Healthcare IoT. In *Intelligent Internet of Things* (pp. 515–545). Springer.

Farjana, M., Fahad, A. B., Alam, S. E., & Islam, M. M. (2023). An IoT- and Cloud-Based E-Waste Management System for Resource Reclamation with a Data-Driven Decision-Making Process. *Iot, 4*(3), 202–220. doi:10.3390/iot4030011

FarmaTrust. (n.d.). *Pharmaceutical Tracking & Data Services.* FarmaTrust.

Farziyeva, G., & Dhanik, N. (2022). *Digital Transition of Supply Chain with Industry 4.0 Applications.* Academic Press.

Fatima-Tuz-Zahra, Jhanjhi, N. Z., Brohi, S. N., Malik, N. A., & Humayun, M. (2020). Proposing a Hybrid RPL Protocol for Rank and Wormhole Attack Mitigation using Machine Learning. *2020 2nd International Conference on Computer and Information Sciences.*

Feng, W., & Avilés, J. V. M. (2023). Enhancing operational efficiency: Integrating machine learning predictive capabilities in business intellgence for informed Decision-Making. *Frontiers in Business. Economics and Management*, *9*(1), 282–286. doi:10.54097/fbem.v9i1.8694

Fernandez-Carames, T. M., & Fraga-Lamas, P. (2019). A review on the application of blockchain to the next generation of cybersecure industry 4.0 smart factories. *IEEE Access : Practical Innovations, Open Solutions*, *7*, 45201–45218. doi:10.1109/ACCESS.2019.2908780

Ferronato, N., & Torretta, V. (2019). Waste Mismanagement in Developing Countries:A Review of Global Issues. *International Journal of Environmental Research and Public Health*, 1–28. PMID:30909625

Filho, M. G., Monteiro, L., Mota, R. d., Gonella, J. d., & Campos, L. M. (2022). The Relationship between Circular Economy, Industry 4.0 and Supply Chain Performance: A Combined ISM/Fuzzy MICMAC Approach. *Sustainability.*

Fisk, R. P., Gallan, A., Joubert, A. M., Beekhuyzen, J., Cheung, L., & Russell–Bennett, R. (2022). Healing the digital divide with digital inclusion: Enabling human capabilities. *Journal of Service Research*, *26*(4), 542–559. doi:10.1177/10946705221140148

Flöther, F. F. (2023). The state of quantum computing applications in health and medicine. *Cornell University*, 1–21. doi:10.1017/qut.2023.4

Foerstl, K., Schleper, M. C., & Henke, M. (2017). Purchasing and supply management: From efficiency to effectiveness in an integrated supply chain. *Journal of Purchasing and Supply Management*, *23*(4), 223–228. doi:10.1016/j.pursup.2017.08.004

Fraboni, F., Brendel, H., & Pietrantoni, L. (2023). Evaluating organizational Guidelines for Enhancing Psychological Well-Being, Safety, and Performance in Technology Integration. *Sustainability (Basel)*, *15*(10), 8113. doi:10.3390/su15108113

Frank, A. G. (2023). *A journey towards Industry 4.0: The supporting role of socio-technical systems.* https://lume.ufrgs.br/handle/10183/263204

Fritz, M. M. (2019). *Sustainable supply chain management. In Responsible Consumption and Production. Encyclopedia of the UN Sustainable Development Goals.* Springer.

Furstenau, L. B., Sott, M. K., Kipper, L. M., MacHado, E. L., Lopez-Robles, J. R., Dohan, M. S., Cobo, M. J., Zahid, A., Abbasi, Q. H., & Imran, M. A. (2020). Link between Sustainability and Industry 4.0: Trends, Challenges and New Perspectives. *IEEE Access : Practical Innovations, Open Solutions*, *8*, 140079–140096. doi:10.1109/ACCESS.2020.3012812

Gade, S., Vagge, S., & Rathod, M. (2023). A Review on Additive Manufacturing – Methods, Materials, and its Associated Failures. *Advances in Science and Technology Research Journal*, *17*(3), 40–63.https://doi.org/10.12913/22998624/163001

Galanti, T., De Vincenzi, C., Buonomo, I., & Benevene, P. (2023). Digital transformation: Inevitable change or sizable opportunity? The Strategic role of HR Management in Industry 4.0. *Administrative Sciences*, *13*(2), 30. doi:10.3390/admsci13020030

Galeone, G., Onorato, G., Shini, M., & Dell'Atti, V. (2023). Climate-related financial disclosure in integrated reporting: What is the impact on the business model? The case of Poste Italiane. *Accounting Research Journal*, *36*(1), 21–36. doi:10.1108/ARJ-04-2022-0107

Galizia, F. G., Bortolini, M., & Calabrese, F. (2023). A cross-sectorial review of industrial best practices and case histories on Industry 4.0 technologies. *Systems Engineering*, *26*(6), 908–924. Advance online publication. doi:10.1002/sys.21697

Gamal, A. (2023). loT in supply chain management. In Duvar (pp. 103–132). doi:10.59287/idtscm.72

Gandomi, A., & Haider, M. (2015). Beyond the hype: Big data concepts, methods, and analytics. *International Journal of Information Management*, *35*(2), 137–144.https://doi.org/10.1016/j.ijinfomgt.2014.10.007

García-Alonso, R., Landeta-Manzano, B., Landín, G. A., & Laskurain-Iturbe, I. (2023). Analysing Barriers to achieving SDG 7. Managing green product development in the wind energy sector. In IFIP advances in information and communication technology (pp. 666–682). doi:10.1007/978-3-031-43688-8_46

García, S. G., & García, M. G. (2019). Industry 4.0 implications in production and maintenance management: An overview. *Procedia Manufacturing*, *41*, 415–422.

Gattullo, M., Scurati, G. W., Fiorentino, M., Uva, A. E., Ferrise, F., & Bordegoni, M. (2019). Towards augmented reality manuals for Industry 4.0: A methodology. *Robotics and Computer-integrated Manufacturing*, *56*, 276–286.https://doi.org/10.1016/j.rcim.2018.10.005

Gaur, L., Jhanjhi, N. Z., Bakshi, S., & Gupta, P. (2022). *Analyzing Consequences of Artificial Intelligence on Jobs using Topic Modeling and Keyword Extraction.* Paper presented at the 2022 2nd International Conference on Innovative Practices in Technology and Management (ICIPTM). 10.1109/ICIPTM54933.2022.9754064

Gaur, L., Singh, G., Solanki, A., Jhanjhi, N. Z., Bhatia, U., Sharma, S., & Verma, S. (2021). Disposition of youth in predicting sustainable development goals using the Neuro - fuzzy and random forest algorithms. *Human-Centric Computing and Information Sciences*. https://repository.usp.ac.fj/12807/

Gaur, L., Afaq, A., Solanki, A., Singh, G., Sharma, S., Jhanjhi, N. Z., My, H. T., & Le, D. (2021). Capitalizing on big data and revolutionary 5G technology: Extracting and visualizing ratings and reviews of global chain hotels. *Computers & Electrical Engineering*, *95*, 107374. doi:10.1016/j.compeleceng.2021.107374

Gaur, L., Solanki, A., Wamba, S. F., & Jhanjhi, N. Z. (2021). *Advanced AI techniques and applications in bioinformatics*. CRC Press. doi:10.1201/9781003126164

Gavai, A., Bouzembrak, Y., Mu, W., Martin, F., Kaliyaperumal, R., Van Soest, J., Choudhury, A., Huang, Z., Dekker, A., & Marvin, H. (2023). Applying federated learning to combat food fraud in food supply chains. *NPJ Science of Food*, *7*(1), 46. Advance online publication. doi:10.1038/s41538-023-00220-3 PMID:37658060

Gebhardt, M., Kopyto, M., Birkel, H., & Hartmann, E. (2022). Industry 4.0 technologies as enablers of collaboration in circular supply chains: A systematic literature review. *International Journal of Production Research*, *60*(23), 6967–6995.

Geiberger, P., Liu, Z., Berg, M., & Domay, C. (2023). *Monitoring energy usage of heavy-haul iron ore trains with onboard energy meter for improving energy efficiency.* Emerald Logo. doi:10.1108/RS-04-2023-0020

George, D., & George, A. (2023). Revolutionizing Manufacturing: Exploring the Promises and Challenges of Industry 5.0. Zenodo *(CERN European Organization for Nuclear Research)*. doi:10.5281/zenodo.7852124

George, D., George, A., & Martin, A. (2023). ChatGPT and the Future of Work: A Comprehensive analysis of AI's impact on jobs and employment. Zenodo *(CERN European Organization for Nuclear Research)*. doi:10.5281/zenodo.8076921

Ghadge, A., Bourlakis, M., Kamble, S., & Seuring, S. (2022). Blockchain implementation in pharmaceutical supply chains: A review and conceptual framework. *International Journal of Production Research*, 6633–6651.

Ghadge, A., Er Kara, M., Moradlou, H., & Goswami, M. (2020). The impact of Industry 4.0 on supply chains. *Journal of Manufacturing Technology Management*, *31*(4), 669–686. doi:10.1108/JMTM-10-2019-0368

Ghajar, F. G., & Reich, C. (2023). Bridge of Trust: Cross Domain Authentication for Industrial Internet of Things (IIoT) Blockchain over Transport Layer Security (TLS). *Electronics (Basel)*, *12*(11), 2401. doi:10.3390/electronics12112401

Ghasemshirazi, S., Shirvani, G., & Alipour, M. A. (2023). Zero Trust: applications, challenges, and opportunities. *arXiv (Cornell University)*. https://doi.org//arxiv.2309.03582 doi:10.48550

Ghobakhloo, M. (2018). The future of manufacturing industry: A strategic roadmap toward Industry 4.0. *Journal of Manufacturing Technology Management*, *29*(6), 910–936. doi:10.1108/JMTM-02-2018-0057

Ghobakhloo, M. (2020). Industry 4.0, digitization, and opportunities for sustainability. *Journal of Cleaner Production*, *252*, 119869. doi:10.1016/j.jclepro.2019.119869

Ghobakhloo, M., Fathi, M., Iranmanesh, M., Maroufkhani, P., & Morales, M. E. (2021). Industry 4.0 ten years on: A bibliometric and systematic review of concepts, sustainability value drivers, and success determinants. *Journal of Cleaner Production*, *302*, 127052. doi:10.1016/j.jclepro.2021.127052

Ghosh, G., Kavita, Verma, S., Jhanjhi, N. Z., & Talib, M. N. (2020). Secure surveillance system using chaotic image encryption technique. *IOP Conference Series. Materials Science and Engineering*, *993*(1), 012062. doi:10.1088/1757-899X/993/1/012062

Ghosh, S., Mandal, M. C., & Ray, A. (2023). A PDCA based approach to evaluate green supply chain management performance under fuzzy environment. *International Journal of Management Science and Engineering Management*, *18*(1), 1–15. doi:10.1080/17509653.2022.2027292

Ghouri, A. M., Khan, H., Venkatesh, M., Haq, M. A., & Jabbour, A. L. (2023). *An Artificial-Intelligence-Based Omnichannel Blood Supply Chain: A Pathway for Sustainable Development*. Academic Press.

Giallanza, A., Aiello, G., & Marannano, G. (2021). Industry 4.0: Advanced digital solutions implemented on a close power loop test bench. *Procedia Computer Science*, *180*, 93–101. doi:10.1016/j.procs.2021.01.133

Gillott, C., Mihkelson, W., Lanau, M., Cheshire, D., & Tingley, D. D. (2023). Developing regenerate: A circular economy engagement tool for the assessment of new and existing buildings. *Journal of Industrial Ecology*, *27*(2), 423–435. Advance online publication. doi:10.1111/jiec.13377

Gisi, P. J. (2024). *The Dark Factory and the future of manufacturing: A Guide to Operational Efficiency and Competitiveness*. Productivity Press. doi:10.4324/9781032688152

Glaessgen, E., & Stargel, D. (2012, April). The digital twin paradigm for future NASA and US Air Force vehicles. In *53rd AIAA/ASME/ASCE/AHS/ASC structures, structural dynamics and materials conference 20th AIAA/ASME/AHS adaptive structures conference 14th AIAA* (p. 1818). Academic Press.

Golini, R., De Marchi, V., Boffelli, A., & Kalchschmidt, M. (2018). Which governance structures drive economic, environmental, and social upgrading? A quantitative analysis in the assembly industries. *International Journal of Production Economics*, *203*, 13–23. doi:10.1016/j.ijpe.2018.05.021

Gopi, R., Sathiyamoorthi, V., Selvakumar, S., Ramesh, M., Chatterjee, P., Jhanjhi, N. Z., & Luhach, A. K. (2021). Enhanced method of ANN based model for detection of DDoS attacks on multimedia internet of things. *Multimedia Tools and Applications*, *81*(19), 26739–26757. doi:10.1007/s11042-021-10640-6

Goswami, K., Islam, M., & Evers, W. (2023). A case study on the blended reporting phenomenon: A Comparative analysis of Voluntary Reporting Frameworks and Standards—GRI, IR, SASB, and CDP. *The International Journal of Sustainability Policy and Practice, 19*(2), 35–64. doi:10.18848/2325-1166/CGP/v19i02/35-64

Gottge, S., Menzel, T., & Forslund, H. (2020). Industry 4.0 technologies in the purchasing process. *Industrial Management & Data Systems, 120*(4), 730–748. doi:10.1108/IMDS-05-2019-0304

Gottipolu, R. (2020). *Securing the Pharmaceutical Supply Chain with Full Traceability.* PharmaTech.com.

Götz, M., & Jankowska, B. (2020). Adoption of industry 4.0 technologies and company competitiveness: Case studies from a post-transition economy. *Foresight and STI Governance, 14*(4), 61–78. doi:10.17323/2500-2597.2020.4.61.78

Grabowska, S., Cagáňová, D., & Saniuk, A. (2021). Knowledge and skills of industrial employees and managerial staff for the industry 4.0 implementation. *Mobile Networks and Applications, 28*(1), 220–230. doi:10.1007/s11036-021-01788-4

Greif, T., Stein, N., & Flath, C. M. (2020). Peeking into the void: Digital twins for construction site logistics. *Computers in Industry, 121*, 103264. doi:10.1016/j.compind.2020.103264

Griggs, K. N., Ossipova, O., Kohlios, C. P., Baccarini, A. N., Howson, E. A., & Hayajneh, T. (2018). *Healthcare Blockchain System Using Smart Contracts for Secure Automated Remote Patient Monitoring.* Med Syst. doi:10.1007/s10916-018-0982-x

Grimm, J. H., Hofstetter, J. S., & Sarkis, J. (2022). Corporate sustainability standards in multi-tier supply chains – an institutional entrepreneurship perspective. *International Journal of Production Research, 61*(14), 4702–4724. doi:10.1080/00207543.2021.2017053

Guan, L., Li, W., Cheng, G. Y. M., & Huang, J. (2023). Environmental strategy for sustainable development: Role of digital transformation in China's natural resource exploitation. *Resources Policy, 87*, 104304. doi:10.1016/j.resourpol.2023.104304

Gul, I., Khan, N. R., & Ghouri, A. M. (2023). Blockchain-driven supply chain management and open innovation. In *Blockchain Driven Supply Chain Management: A Multi-dimensional Perspective* (pp. 135–154). Springer Nature Singapore. doi:10.1007/978-981-99-0699-4_9

Gul, I., Raziq, A., & Khan, M. R. (2024). Towards sustainable supply chains with blockchain. In achieving secure and transparent supply chains with blockchain technology. In *Achieving Secure and Transparent Supply Chains with Blockchain Technology* (pp. 18–37). IGI Global. doi:10.4018/979-8-3693-0482-2.ch002

Gulyamov, S. (2023). Quantum Law: Navigating the legal challenges and opportunities in the age of Quantum Technologies. *irshadjournals.com.* https://doi.org/ doi:10.59022/ujldp.54

Gu, M. H., Zhang, Y., Li, D., & Huo, B. (2023). The effect of high-involvement human resource management practices on supply chain resilience and operational performance. *Journal of Management Science and Engineering, 8*(2), 176–190. doi:10.1016/j.jmse.2022.12.001

Gunal, M. M., & Karatas, M. (2019). Industry 4.0, Digitisation in Manufacturing, and Simulation: A Review of the Literature. In M. M. Gunal (Ed.), *Simulation for Industry 4.0: Past, Present, and Future* (pp. 19–37). Springer International Publishing., doi:10.1007/978-3-030-04137-3_2

Gunasekaran, K., & Boopathi, S. (2023). Artificial intelligence in water treatments and water resource assessments. In Advances in environmental engineering and green technologies book series (pp. 71–98). doi:10.4018/978-1-6684-6791-6.ch004

Guo, D. (2023). Fast scheduling of human-robot teams collaboration on synchronised production-logistics tasks in aircraft assembly. *Robotics and Computer-integrated Manufacturing, 85*, 102620. doi:10.1016/j.rcim.2023.102620

Guo, W. (2023). Exploring the Role of Information Technology in Implementing Integrated Green Supply Chain Management in China. *DREAM*, *2*(01), 42–48. doi:10.56982/dream.v2i01.111

Guo, Y., & Liang, C. (2016). Blockchain application and outlook in the banking industry. *Financial Innovation*, *24*(1), 1–12. doi:10.1186/s40854-016-0034-9

Gupta, K. (2023, August 16). *Harnessing AI for strategic Decision-Making and business performance optimization.* https://www.ijisae.org/index.php/IJISAE/article/view/3360

Gupta, M. (2017). *E-Book: blockchain for dummies*. IBM. Available at: https://www.ibm.com/downloads/cas/36KBMBOG

Gupta, S., & Sharma, V. (2023). Effects of Quantum computing on Businesses. *2023 4th International Conference on Intelligent Engineering and Management (ICIEM)*. 10.1109/ICIEM59379.2023.10166880

Gupta, H., Dastjerdi, A. V., Ghosh, S. K., & Buyya, R. (2017). IFogSim: A Toolkit for Modeling and Simulation of Resource Management Techniques in the Internet of Things, Edge and Fog Computing Environments. *Software, Practice & Experience*, *47*(9), 1275–1296. doi:10.1002/spe.2509

Gyrard, A., Datta, S. K., Bonnet, C., & Boudaoud, K. (2015, August). Cross-domain Internet of Things application development: M3 framework and evaluation. In *2015 3rd International conference on future Internet of Things and Cloud* (pp. 9-16). IEEE.

Ha, B.-C., & Nam, H. (2016). Ethical judgments in supply chain management: A scenario analysis. *Journal of Business and Industrial Marketing*, *31*(1), 59–69. doi:10.1108/JBIM-07-2014-0148

Haber, L., & Carmeli, A. (2023). Leading the challenges of implementing new technologies in organizations. *Technology in Society*, *74*, 102300. doi:10.1016/j.techsoc.2023.102300

Habib, A., Khan, Z. A., Riaz, M., & Marinkovic, D. (2023). Performance Evaluation of Healthcare Supply Chain in Industry 4.0 with Linear Diophantine Fuzzy Sine-Trigonometric Aggregation Operations. *Mathematics*, *11*(12), 2611. doi:10.3390/math11122611

Hagendorff, T. (2020). The ethics of AI ethics: An evaluation of guidelines. *Minds and Machines*, *30*(1), 99–120. doi:10.1007/s11023-020-09517-8

Haleem, A., Javaid, M., Singh, R. P., & Suman, R. (2022). Medical 4.0 technologies for healthcare: Features, capabilities, and applications. *Internet of Things and Cyber-Physical Systems*, 12-30.

Hamad, S., Lai, F. W., Shad, M. K., Khatib, S. F. A., & Ali, S. E. A. (2022). Assessing the implementation of sustainable development goals: Does integrated reporting matter? *Sustainability Accounting. Management and Policy Journal*, *14*(1), 49–74. doi:10.1108/SAMPJ-01-2022-0029

Hamrol, A., Hoffmann, M., Lisek, M., & Bozek, J. (2023). The Quality of Surgical Instrument Surfaces Machined with Robotic Belt Grinding. *Materials (Basel)*, *16*(2), 630. doi:10.3390/ma16020630 PMID:36676377

Hamzah, M., Islam, M. M., Hassan, S., Akhtar, M. N., Ferdous, M. J., Jasser, M. B., & Mohamed, A. W. (2023). Distributed control of cyber physical system on various domains: A Critical review. *Systems*, *11*(4), 208. doi:10.3390/systems11040208

Han, C., & Mardani, A. (2023). Research on the impact of consumer privacy and intelligent personalization technology on purchase resistance. *Journal of Business Research*, *161*, 113811. doi:10.1016/j.jbusres.2023.113811

Hangl, J., Krause, S., & Behrens, V. J. (2023). Expert interviews of drivers, barriers and social considerations for AI adoption in SCM. *Technology in Society*, *74*, 102299. doi:10.1016/j.techsoc.2023.102299

Han, Y., Qamruzzaman, M., & Kor, S. (2023). Charting a Sustainable Future: The impact of economic policy, environmental tax, innovation, and natural resources on clean energy consumption. *Sustainability, 15*(18), 13591. doi:10.3390/su151813591

Han, Y., Шевченко, T., Yannou, B., Ranjbari, M., Esfandabadi, Z. S., Saidani, M., Bouillass, G., Bliumska-Danko, K., & Li, G. (2023). Exploring how digital technologies enable a circular economy of products. *Sustainability (Basel), 15*(3), 2067. doi:10.3390/su15032067

Haq, I., & Esuka, O. M. (2018). Blockchain Technology in Pharmaceutical Industry to Prevent Counterfeit Drugs. *International Journal of Computer Applications, 180*(25), 8–12. doi:10.5120/ijca2018916579

Hariadhy, R. P., Sutoyo, E., & Pratiwi, O. N. (2021). Application of K-Nearest Neighbor Algorithm for Prediction of Television Advertisement Rating. In *International Conference on Emerging Applications and Technologies for Industry 4.0 (EATI'2020) Emerging Applications and Technologies for Industry 4.0* (pp. 82-91). Springer International Publishing. 10.1007/978-3-030-80216-5_7

Hariry, R. E., Barenji, R. V., & Paradkar, A. (2021). *From Industry 4.0 to Pharma 4.0.* Academic Press.

Harris, I., Wang, Y., & Wang, H. (2015). ICT in multimodal transport and technological trends: Unleashing potential for the future. *International Journal of Production Economics, 159*, 88–103. doi:10.1016/j.ijpe.2014.09.005

Hasan, M. H., Osman, M. H., Admodisastro, N., & Muhammad, S. (2023). Legacy systems to cloud migration: A review from the architectural perspective. *Journal of Systems and Software, 202*, 111702. doi:10.1016/j.jss.2023.111702

Hasan, M., Hossain, S., Mofijur, M., Kabir, Z., Badruddin, I. A., Khan, T. M. Y., & Jassim, E. I. (2023). Harnessing solar Power: A review of photovoltaic innovations, solar thermal systems, and the dawn of energy storage solutions. *Energies, 16*(18), 6456. doi:10.3390/en16186456

Hassoun, A., Bekhit, A. E. A., Jambrak, A. R., Regenstein, J. M., Chémat, F., Morton, J. D., Guðjónsdóttir, M., Carpena, M., Prieto, M. A., Varela, P., Arshad, R. N., Aadil, R. M., Bhat, Z. F., & Ueland, Ø. (2022). The fourth industrial revolution in the food industry—part II: Emerging food trends. *Critical Reviews in Food Science and Nutrition, 64*(2), 407–437. doi:10.1080/10408398.2022.2106472 PMID:35930319

Hassoun, A., Boukid, F., Özoğul, F., Aït-Kaddour, A., Del Castillo, J. M. S., Roohinejad, S., Perestrelo, R., Galanakis, C. M., Bono, G., Bouyahya, A., Bhat, Z. F., Smaoui, S., Jambrak, A. R., & Medina, S. (2023). Creating new opportunities for sustainable food packaging through dimensions of industry 4.0: New insights into the food waste perspective. *Trends in Food Science & Technology, 142*, 104238. doi:10.1016/j.tifs.2023.104238

Hassoun, A., Prieto, M. A., Carpena, M., Bouzembrak, Y., Marvin, H., Pallarés, N., Barba, F. J., Bangar, S. P., Chaudhary, V., Ibrahim, S. A., & Boυo, G. (2022). Exploring the role of green and Industry 4.0 technologies in achieving sustainable development goals in food sectors. *Food Research International, 162*, 112068. doi:10.1016/j.foodres.2022.112068 PMID:36461323

Haval, A. M., & Rahman, F. H. (2024). Application of machine learning techniques and the Internet of Things for smart, sustainable agriculture. *BIO Web of Conferences, 82*, 05021. 10.1051/bioconf/20248205021

Hayat, A., Shahare, V., Sharma, A. K., & Arora, N. (2023). Introduction to industry 4.0. In Studies in big data (pp. 29–59). doi:10.1007/978-981-19-8730-4_2

Hazra, A., Alkhayyat, A., & Adhikari, M. (2022). Blockchain-aided integrated edge framework of cybersecurity for Internet of Things. *IEEE Consumer Electronics Magazine.*

Hearn, G., Williams, P., Rodrigues, J. H. P., & Laundon, M. (2023). Education and training for industry 4.0: A case study of a manufacturing ecosystem. *Education + Training*, *65*(8/9), 1070–1084. doi:10.1108/ET-10-2022-0407

He, B., & Mao, H. (2023). Digital Twin-Driven Product Sustainable design for low carbon footprint. *Journal of Computing and Information Science in Engineering*, *23*(6), 060805. Advance online publication. doi:10.1115/1.4062427

Hegab, H., Shaban, I. S., Jamil, M., & Khanna, N. (2023). Toward sustainable future: Strategies, indicators, and challenges for implementing sustainable production systems. *Sustainable Materials and Technologies*, *36*, e00617. doi:10.1016/j.susmat.2023.e00617

Heidary, R., Rao, J. P., & Fischer, O. (2023). Smart buildings in the IoT era – necessity, challenges, and opportunities. In Springer eBooks (pp. 1–21). doi:10.1007/978-3-030-72322-4_115-1

Heikkilä, S., Ghoreishi, M., & Deviatkin, I. (2023). From waste to value: enhancing circular value creation in municipal solid waste management ecosystem through artificial intelligence-powered robots. In Elsevier eBooks (pp. 415–428). doi:10.1016/B978-0-323-95278-1.00014-0

Heizer, J., Render, B., & Munson, C. (2020). *Operations management : sustainability and supply chain management*. https://thuvienso.hoasen.edu.vn/handle/123456789/12793

Helmiö, P. (2017). *Open source in industrial internet of things: A systematic literature review*. Academic Press.

Herath, S. K., & Joshi, P. L. (2023). Audit Data Analytics: A Game Changer for Audit Firms. *International Journal of Auditing and Accounting Studies*, *5*(1), 29–48. doi:10.47509/IJAAS.2023.v05i01.02

He, S. (2023). Do you reap what you sow? Driving mechanism of supply chain transparency on consumers' indirect reciprocity. *Frontiers in Psychology*, *14*, 1081297. Advance online publication. doi:10.3389/fpsyg.2023.1081297 PMID:36844304

Himeur, Y., Elnour, M., Fadli, F., Meskin, N., Petri, I., Rezgui, Y., Bensaali, F., & Amira, A. (2022). AI-big data analytics for building automation and management systems: A survey, actual challenges and future perspectives. *Artificial Intelligence Review*, *56*(6), 4929–5021. doi:10.1007/s10462-022-10286-2 PMID:36268476

Hlophe, M. C., & Maharaj, B. T. (2023). From Cyber–Physical Convergence to Digital Twins: A Review on Edge Computing Use Case Designs. *Applied Sciences (Basel, Switzerland)*, *13*(24), 13262. doi:10.3390/app132413262

Hoberg, K., Thornton, L., & Wieland, A. (2020). *How to deal with the human factor in supply chain management?* Emerald Publishing Limited.

Hoffmann, T., & Prause, G. (2018). On the regulatory framework for last-mile delivery robots. *Machines*, *6*(3), 33. doi:10.3390/machines6030033

Hofmann, E., & Rüsch, M. (2017). Industry 4.0 and the current status as well as future prospects on logistics. *Computers in Industry*, *89*, 23–34. doi:10.1016/j.compind.2017.04.002

Hofmann, E., Sternberg, H., Chen, H., Pflaum, A., & Prockl, G. (2019). Supply chain management and Industry 4.0: Conducting research in the digital age. *International Journal of Physical Distribution & Logistics Management*, *49*(10), 945–955. doi:10.1108/IJPDLM-11-2019-399

Holtschulte, A. (2022). Interaction of the IoT with Other Technologies. *Management for Professionals*, (Part F353), 125–147. doi:10.1007/978-3-030-89408-5_5

Hong, Z., & Guo, X. (2019). Green product supply chain contracts considering environmental responsibilities. *Omega*, *83*, 155–166. doi:10.1016/j.omega.2018.02.010

Hossain, M. I., Al Amin, M., Baldacci, R., & Rahman, M. H. (2023). Identification and Prioritization of Green Lean Supply Chain Management Factors Using Fuzzy DEMATEL. *Sustainability (Basel)*, *15*(13), 10523. doi:10.3390/su151310523

Hraiga, R. A., Ali, A. M., & Abbas, A. A. (2023). The role of green process reengineering in improving the performance of total productive maintenance. *Holistica*, *14*(1), 82–109. doi:10.2478/hjbpa-2023-0006

Hrouga, M. (2023). Towards a new conceptual digital collaborative supply chain model based on Industry 4.0 technologies: A conceptual framework. *International Journal of Quality & Reliability Management*. Advance online publication. doi:10.1108/IJQRM-07-2022-0221

Hsu, P., Lei, H., Cheng, M., & Yuan, T. F. (2023). Applying data driven approach to cluster components for preventive maintenance. In Lecture notes in production engineering (pp. 197–205). doi:10.1007/978-3-031-18641-7_19

Huang, J., & Yu, S. (2023). A study on global national green GDP accounting based on the System of Integrated Environmental-Economic Accounting. *Highlights in Business. Economics and Management*, *12*, 272–278. doi:10.54097/hbem.v12i.8362

Huang, K., Wang, K., Lee, P., & Yeung, A. C. (2023). The Impact of Industry 4.0 on Supply Chain Capability and Supply Chain Resilience: A Dynamic Resource-Based View. *International Journal of Production Economics*, *262*, 108913. doi:10.1016/j.ijpe.2023.108913

Huang, M. H., Rust, R., & Maksimovic, V. (2019). The Feeling Economy: Managing in the Next Generation of Artificial Intelligence. *California Management Review*, *61*, 43–66.

Huang, W., Shuai, B., Wang, L., & Antwi, E. (2017). Railway container station reselection approach and application: Based on entropy-cloud model. *Mathematical Problems in Engineering*, *2017*, 2017. doi:10.1155/2017/8701081

Huffman, M., Wang, Q., & Khan, F. (2023). Analysis of Sustainability Metrics from a Process Design and Operation Perspective. *Process Safety and Environmental Protection*, *177*, 1351–1365. doi:10.1016/j.psep.2023.08.001

Hu, H., Xu, J., Liu, M., & Lim, M. K. (2023). Vaccine supply chain management: An intelligent system utilizing blockchain, IoT and machine learning. *Journal of Business Research*, *156*, 113480. doi:10.1016/j.jbusres.2022.113480 PMID:36506475

Hui, C. K. C. S. H., Dan, G., Alamri, S., & Toghraie, D. (2023). Greening smart cities: An investigation of the integration of urban natural resources and smart city technologies for promoting environmental sustainability. *Sustainable Cities and Society*, *99*, 104985. doi:10.1016/j.scs.2023.104985

Hull, R., Batra, V., Chee, Y.-M., Chen, Y., Coblenz, M., Deshpande, P., & Deutsch, A. (2017). Blockchain: distributed event-based processing in a Data-Centric world. *Proceedings of the 11th ACM International Conference on Distributed and Event-Based Systems*, 2-4.

Huma, S., Siddiqui, D. A., & Ahmed, W. (2022). Understanding the impact of Green supply chain management practices on operational competitive capabilities. *The TQM Journal*. Advance online publication. doi:10.1108/TQM-08-2021-0246

Humayun, M., Hamid, B., Jhanjhi, N., Suseendran, G., & Talib, M. (2021). *5G network security issues, challenges, opportunities and future directions: A survey.* Paper presented at the Journal of Physics: Conference Series. 10.1088/1742-6596/1979/1/012037

Humayun, M. (2021). Industry 4.0 and cyber security issues and challenges. *Turkish Journal of Computer and Mathematics Education*, *12*(10), 2957–2971.

Humayun, M., Alsaqer, M., & Jhanjhi, N. Z. (2022). Energy optimization for smart cities using IoT. *Applied Artificial Intelligence*, *36*(1), 2037255. Advance online publication. doi:10.1080/08839514.2022.2037255

Humayun, M., Jhanjhi, N. Z., Alruwaili, M., Amalathas, S. S., Balasubramanian, V., & Selvaraj, B. (2020c). Privacy protection and energy optimization for 5G-Aided industrial internet of things. *IEEE Access : Practical Innovations, Open Solutions*, *8*, 183665–183677. doi:10.1109/ACCESS.2020.3028764

Humayun, M., Jhanjhi, N. Z., Hamid, B., & Ahmed, G. (2020b). Emerging smart logistics and transportation using IoT and blockchain. *IEEE Internet of Things Magazine*, *3*(2), 58–62. doi:10.1109/IOTM.0001.1900097

Humayun, M., Jhanjhi, N., & Alamri, M. Z. (2020). IoT-based Secure and Energy Efficient scheme for E-health applications. *Indian Journal of Science and Technology*, *13*(28), 2833–2848. doi:10.17485/IJST/v13i28.861

Hussain, I., Tahir, S., Humayun, M., Almufareh, M. F., Jhanjhi, N., & Qamar, F. (2022). *Health Monitoring System Using Internet of Things (IoT).* Sensing for Elderly People.

Hussain, M. N. (2023). Evaluating the impact of air transportation, railway transportation, and trade openness on inbound and outbound tourism in BRI countries. *Journal of Air Transport Management*, *106*, 102307. doi:10.1016/j.jairtraman.2022.102307

Hussain, S. J., Ahmed, U., Liaquat, H., Mir, S., Jhanjhi, N. Z., & Humayun, M. (2019). IMIAD: Intelligent Malware Identification for Android Platform. *2019 International Conference on Computer and Information Sciences (ICCIS)*. 10.1109/ICCISci.2019.8716471

Hydrogen economy. (2023). In *Elsevier eBooks*. doi:10.1016/C2021-0-01531-5

IBM. (2017a). *Maersk and IBM unveil first Industry-Wide Cross-Border supply chain solution on blockchain.* Available at: https://www-03.ibm.com/press/us/en/pressrelease/51712.wss

Ibrahimova, G., & Moog, P. (2023). Colonialism versus independence—The role of entrepreneurial ecosystems in Azerbaijan over time. *Small Business Economics*, *61*(3), 1289–1336. Advance online publication. doi:10.1007/s11187-022-00725-3

Interrante, V., Höllerer, T., & Lécuyer, A. (2018). Virtual and Augmented Reality. *IEEE Computer Graphics and Applications*.https://doi.org/10.1109/MCG.2018.02195163

Ishak, S. Z., Shaharudin, M. R., Salim, N. A., Zainoddin, A. I., & Deng, Z. (2023). The effect of supply chain adaptive strategies during the COVID-19 pandemic on firm performance in Malaysia's semiconductor industries. *Global Journal of Flexible Systems Managment*, *24*(3), 439–458. doi:10.1007/s40171-023-00347-y

IslamM. M.NayemA. I.BristyU. A.EshaS. A. (2023). Approaches to E-Waste Reduction through 4R, Public Awareness, and Design for Sustainability. *Social Science Research Network*. doi:10.2139/ssrn.4458682

Ismail, S., Reza, H., Salameh, K., Zadeh, H. K., & Vasefi, F. (2023). Toward an Intelligent Blockchain IoT-Enabled fish Supply Chain: A Review and Conceptual framework. *Sensors (Basel)*, *23*(11), 5136. doi:10.3390/s23115136 PMID:37299864

Ivanov, D., & Dolgui, A. (2021). A digital supply chain twin for managing the disruption risks and resilience in the era of Industry 4.0. *Production Planning and Control*, *32*(9), 775–788. doi:10.1080/09537287.2020.1768450

Ivanov, D., Dolgui, A., & Sokolov, B. (2019). The impact of digital technology and Industry 4.0 on the ripple effect and supply chain risk analytics. *International Journal of Production Research*, *57*(3), 829–846.https://doi.org/10.1080/00207543.2018.1488086

Jabeen, T., Jabeen, I., Ashraf, H., Jhanjhi, N. Z., Yassine, A., & Hossain, M. S. (2023). An intelligent healthcare system using IoT in wireless sensor network. *Sensors (Basel)*, *23*(11), 5055. doi:10.3390/s23115055 PMID:37299782

Jahanger, A., Ozturk, I., Onwe, J. C., Joseph, T. E., & Hossain, M. R. (2023). Do technology and renewable energy contribute to energy efficiency and carbon neutrality? Evidence from top ten manufacturing countries. *Sustainable Energy Technologies and Assessments*, *56*, 103084. doi:10.1016/j.seta.2023.103084

Jahani, H., Jain, R., & Ivanov, D. (2023). Data science and big data analytics: A systematic review of methodologies used in the supply chain and logistics research. *Annals of Operations Research*, 1–58. doi:10.1007/s10479-023-05390-7

Jain, V., & Kukreja, V. (2023). *Multidisciplinary approaches to sustainable human development*. IGI Global. doi:10.4018/978-1-6684-8223-0

JainY.GuptaS.YalcinerS.JoglekarY. N.KhetanP.ZhangT. (2023). Overcoming complexity in ESG Investing: The role of Generative AI integration in identifying contextual ESG factors. *Social Science Research Network*. doi:10.2139/ssrn.4495647

Jamil, F., Toh, Y. P., & Chi-Tsun, C. (2023). Developing an i4.0 Cyber-Physical system to enhance efficiency and competitiveness in manufacturing. *Applied Sciences (Basel, Switzerland)*, *16*(13), 9333. Advance online publication. doi:10.3390/app13169333

Jan, Z., Ahamed, F., Mayer, W., Patel, N., Großmann, G., Stumptner, M., & Kuusk, A. (2023). Artificial intelligence for industry 4.0: Systematic review of applications, challenges, and opportunities. *Expert Systems with Applications*, *216*, 119456. doi:10.1016/j.eswa.2022.119456

Jarašūnienė, A., Čižiūnienė, K., & Čereška, A. (2023). Research on Impact of IoT on Warehouse Management. *Sensors (Basel)*, *23*(4), 2213. doi:10.3390/s23042213 PMID:36850811

Javaid, M., Haleem, A., Singh, R. P., Khan, S., & Suman, R. (2021). Blockchain technology applications for Industry 4.0: A literature-based review. *Blockchain: Research and Applications*.

Javaid, M., Haleem, A., Singh, R. P., Suman, R., & Gonzalez, E. S. (2022). Understanding the adoption of Industry 4.0 technologies in improving environmental sustainability. *Sustainable Operations and Computers*, 203-217.

Javaid, M., Haleem, A., Singh, R. P., Suman, R., & Santibañez Gonzalez, E. (2022). Understanding the adoption of Industry 4.0 technologies in improving environmental sustainability. *Sustainable Operations and Computers*, *3*, 203–217.

Javaid, M., Khan, S., Haleem, A., & Rab, S. (2022). Adoption of modern technologies for implementing industry 4.0: An integrated MCDM approach. *Benchmarking*, *30*(10), 3753–3790. doi:10.1108/BIJ-01-2021-0017

Javanmard, M. E., Tang, Y., Wang, Z., & Tontiwachwuthikul, P. (2023). Forecast energy demand, CO2 emissions and energy resource impacts for the transportation sector. *Applied Energy*, *338*, 120830. doi:10.1016/j.apenergy.2023.120830

Javier, Á. C. O. (2023, August 4). *An evaluation-aware method for transforming a production system into a cyber-physical production system*. Universidad De Los Andes. https://repositorio.uniandes.edu.co/handle/1992/69519

Jayakumar, P., Brohi, S. N., & Jhanjhi, N. Z. (2021). *Artificial intelligence and military applications: Innovations, cybersecurity challenges & open research areas*. Academic Press.

Jazdi, N. (2014). *Cyber physical systems in the context of Industry 4.0*. CRC Cyber Physical. doi:10.1109/AQTR.2014.6857843

Jenneboer, L., Herrando, C., & Constantinides, E. (2022). The Impact of chatbots on Customer Loyalty: A Systematic literature review. *Journal of Theoretical and Applied Electronic Commerce Research*, *17*(1), 212–229. doi:10.3390/jtaer17010011

Jenssen, M. M., & De Boer, L. (2019). Implementing life cycle assessment in green supplier selection: A systematic review and conceptual model. *Journal of Cleaner Production*, *229*, 1198–1210. doi:10.1016/j.jclepro.2019.04.335

Jha, P. K., Teotia, F., & Saxena, A. K. (2023). Cyber Security in the Indian Electricity Distribution System: A Review. *2023 5th International Conference on Energy, Power and Environment: Towards Flexible Green Energy Technologies (ICEPE)*. 10.1109/ICEPE57949.2023.10201598

Jhanjhi, N. Z., Low, T. J., & Alghamdi, T. A. (2015). Enhancing routing energy efficiency of Wireless Sensor Networks. *2015 17th International Conference on Advanced Communication Technology (ICACT)*. 10.1109/ICACT.2015.7224928

Jhanjhi, N., Khan, M. A., Ahmad, M., & Hussain, M. (2022). The Impact of Cyber Attacks on E-Governance During the COVID-19 Pandemic. *Cybersecurity Measures for E-Government Frameworks*, 123.

Jhanjhi, N. Z., Humayun, M., & Almuayqil, S. N. (2021). Cyber security and privacy issues in industrial internet of things. *Computer Systems Science and Engineering*, *37*(3), 361–380. doi:10.32604/csse.2021.015206

Jiang, H., & Shen, H. (2020). Toward a relational theory of employee engagement: Understanding authenticity, transparency, and employee behaviors. *International Journal of Business Communication*, *60*(3), 948–975. doi:10.1177/2329488420954236

Jiang, Y., Tran, T. H., & Williams, L. (2023). Machine learning and mixed reality for smart aviation: Applications and challenges. *Journal of Air Transport Management*, *111*, 102437. doi:10.1016/j.jairtraman.2023.102437

Jin, M., Tang, R., Ji, Y., Liu, F., Gao, L., & Huisingh, D. (2017). Impact of Advanced Manufacturing on Sustainability: An Overview of the Special Volume on Advanced Manufacturing for Sustainability and Low Fossil Carbon Emissions. *Journal of Cleaner Production*, *161*, 69–74. doi:10.1016/j.jclepro.2017.05.101

Jobin, A., Ienca, M., & Vayena, E. (2019). The global landscape of AI ethics guidelines. *Nature Machine Intelligence*, *1*(9), 389–399. doi:10.1038/s42256-019-0088-2

Joseph, C., Rahmat, M., Yusuf, S. N. S., Janang, J. T., & Madi, N. (2022). The ethical value disclosure index from the lens of SDG 16 and institutional theory. *International Journal of Ethics and Systems*, *39*(3), 612–628. doi:10.1108/IJOES-05-2021-0109

Josphineleela, R. (2023, August 16). *Exploration Beyond Boundaries: AI-Based advancements in rover robotics for lunar Missions space like Chandrayaan*. https://www.ijisae.org/index.php/IJISAE/article/view/3318

Kafi, M., & Akter, N. (2023). Securing Financial Information in the Digital realm: Case studies in Cybersecurity for Accounting Data Protection. *American Journal of Trade and Policy*, *10*(1), 15–26. doi:10.18034/ajtp.v10i1.659

Kagermann, H. (2014). Change through Digitization—Value Creation in the age of industry 4.0. In Springer eBooks (pp. 23–45). doi:10.1007/978-3-658-05014-6_2

Kagermann, H., Lukas, W. D., & Wahlster, W. (2011). Industrie 4.0: Mit dem Internet der Dinge auf dem Weg zur 4. industriellen Revolution. VDI nachrichten, 13(11), 2.

Kagermann, H., Anderl, R., Gausemeier, J., Schuh, G., & Wahlster, W. (Eds.). (2016). *Industrie 4.0 in a Global Context: Strategies for Cooperating with International Partners (acatech STUDY)*. Herbert Utz Verlag.

Kamble, S. S., & Gunasekaran, A. (2021). Analysing the role of Industry 4.0 technologies and circular economy practices in improving sustainable performance in Indian manufacturing organisations. *Production Planning and Control*, 1–15. doi:10.1080/09537287.2021.1980904

Kamble, S. S., Gunasekaran, A., & Gawankar, S. A. (2018). Sustainable Industry 4.0 framework: A systematic literature review identifying the current trends and future perspectives. *Process Safety and Environmental Protection*, *117*, 408–425. doi:10.1016/j.psep.2018.05.009

Kamble, S. S., Gunasekaran, A., & Gawankar, S. A. (2020). Achieving sustainable performance in a data-driven agriculture supply chain: A review for research and applications. *International Journal of Production Economics, 219*, 179–194. doi:10.1016/j.ijpe.2019.05.022

Kamble, S. S., Gunasekaran, A., Parekh, H., Mani, V., Belhadi, A., & Sharma, R. (2022). Digital twin for sustainable manufacturing supply chains: Current trends, future perspectives, and an implementation framework. *Technological Forecasting and Social Change, 176*, 121448. doi:10.1016/j.techfore.2021.121448

Kamble, S. S., Gunasekaran, A., Subramanian, N., Ghadge, A., Belhadi, A., & Mani, V. (2021). Blockchain technology's impact on supply chain integration and sustainable supply chain performance: Evidence from the automotive industry. *Annals of Operations Research, 327*(1), 575–600. doi:10.1007/s10479-021-04129-6

Kanchana, S., Rajan, D., Mahaveerakannan, R., Sagar, K. V. D., Subramanian, P., & Rajakumar, B. R. (2024). Predictive maintenance model using hybrid procedure of improved Quantum Cat swarm optimisation for asset management in industry 4.0. In Lecture notes in networks and systems (pp. 499–515). doi:10.1007/978-981-99-6547-2_38

KanhaiyaK. (2023). Leveraging professional roles to foster sustainable development: Contributions to the sustainable development goals in the workplace. *Social Science Research Network*. doi:10.2139/ssrn.4479782

Karaarslan, E., Aydin, Ö., Cali, Ü., & Challenger, M. (2023). *Digital twin driven intelligent systems and emerging metaverse*. Springer Nature. doi:10.1007/978-981-99-0252-1

Kara, M. (2023). A comprehensive framework for emergency in Robotic environments. *IEEE Access : Practical Innovations, Open Solutions, 11*, 82539–82547. doi:10.1109/ACCESS.2023.3301155

KareskaK. (2023). Key factors for increasing the productivity of production organizations. *Social Science Research Network*. doi:10.2139/ssrn.4532554

Karmaker, C. L., Aziz, R. A., Ahmed, T., Misbauddin, S. M., & Moktadir, M. A. (2023). Impact of industry 4.0 technologies on sustainable supply chain performance: The mediating role of green supply chain management practices and circular economy. *Journal of Cleaner Production, 419*, 138249. doi:10.1016/j.jclepro.2023.138249

Karnik, N., Bora, U., Bhadr, K., Kadambi, P., & Dhatrak, P. (2022, May). A comprehensive study on current and future trends towards the characteristics and enablers of industry 4.0. *Journal of Industrial Information Integration, 27*, 2022. doi:10.1016/j.jii.2021.100294

Kartik, B., & P, M. (2023). IOT based Smart Helmet for Hazard Detection in mining industry. *arXiv (Cornell University)*. doi:10.48550/arxiv.2304.10156

Kashem, M. A., Shamsuddoha, M., Nasir, T., & Chowdhury, A. A. (2023). Supply Chain Disruption versus Optimization: A Review on Artificial Intelligence and Blockchain. *Knowledge (Beverly Hills, Calif.)*, *3*(1), 80–96. doi:10.3390/knowledge3010007

Kaya, S. K. (2023, March). A novel two-phase group decision-making model for circular supplier selection under picture fuzzy environment. *Environmental Science and Pollution Research International, 30*(12), 34135–34157. doi:10.1007/s11356-022-24486-4 PMID:36508096

Kayıkcı, Y., & Subramanian, N. (2022). Blockchain interoperability issues in Supply chain: exploration of mass adoption procedures. In *Big Data and Blockchain for Service Operations Management* (pp. 309–328). Springer International Publishing. doi:10.1007/978-3-030-87304-2_13

Kazancoglu, Y., Ekinci, E., Mangla, S. K., Sezer, M. D., Choudhary, S., & Dora, M. (2023). Smart Closed-Loop food supply chain in circular economy. *IEEE Transactions on Engineering Management*, 1–18. doi:10.1109/TEM.2023.3303272

Kazançoğlu, Y., Sağnak, M., Kazançoğlu, İ., & Dora, M. (2021). Framework for a sustainable supply chain to overcome risks in transition to a circular economy through Industry 4.0. *Production Planning and Control*, *34*(10), 902–917. doi:10.1080/09537287.2021.1980910

Kazemi, Z., Rask, J. K., Gomes, C., Yildiz, E., & Larsen, P. G. (2023). Movable factory—A systematic literature review of concepts, requirements, applications, and gaps. *Journal of Manufacturing Systems*, *69*, 189–207. doi:10.1016/j.jmsy.2023.06.008

Kee, D. M. H., Cordova, M., & Khin, S. (2023). The key enablers of SMEs readiness in Industry 4.0: a case of Malaysia. *International Journal of Emerging Markets*. doi:10.1108/IJOEM-08-2021-1291

Kegyes, T., Süle, Z., & Abonyi, J. (2021). The applicability of reinforcement learning methods in the development of industry 4.0 applications. *Complexity*, *2021*, 1–31. doi:10.1155/2021/7179374

Kelling, I., & Lawan, I. (2023). Equality, diversity and inclusion: A way forward for aquaculture in Scotland. *Frontiers*, *2*, 1151853. Advance online publication. doi:10.3389/faquc.2023.1151853

Keung, K. L., Lee, C., Xia, L., Liu, C., Liu, B., & Ji, P. (2023). A cyber-physical robotic mobile fulfillment system in smart manufacturing: The simulation aspect. *Robotics and Computer-integrated Manufacturing*, *83*, 102578. doi:10.1016/j.rcim.2023.102578

Khadem, M. (2023, August 25). *Application of artificial intelligence in supply chain revolutionizing efficiency and optimization*. http://bgsiran.ir/journal/ojs-3.1.1-4/index.php/IJIEOR/article/view/34

Khan, A., Jhanjhi, N. Z., & Humayun, M. (2022). The role of cybersecurity in smart cities. In Chapman and Hall/CRC eBooks (pp. 195–208). doi:10.1201/9781003203087-9

Khan, A., Jhanjhi, N. Z., & Sujatha, R. (2022). Emerging Industry Revolution IR 4.0 Issues and Challenges. In Cyber Security Applications for Industry 4.0 (pp. 151-169): Chapman and Hall/CRC.

Khan, M. I. (2024). Impact of Blockchain Technology on Transparency and Trust in Programmatic Advertising Supply Chain. In M. R. Khan, N. R. Khan, & A. M. Ghouri (Eds.), Achieving Secure and Transparent Supply Chains With Blockchain Technology (pp. 57-69). IGI Global. doi:10.4018/979-8-3693-0482-2.ch004

Khan, M. R., & Manzoor, A. (2021). Application and Impact of New Technologies in the Supply Chain Management During COVID-19 Pandemic: A Systematic Literature Review. *International Journal of Economics and Business Administration.*

Khan, M. R., Ali, A., & Rind, A. A. (2024). Blockchain Technology and Supply Chain Sustainability: A View From UNSDG Perspective. In Achieving Secure and Transparent Supply Chains With Blockchain Technology (pp. 1-17). IGI Global. doi:10.4018/979-8-3693-0482-2.ch001

Khan, M. R., Khan, N. R., Tufail, M., & Ali, L. (2023). A Path Towards A Greener Future Fostering Green Supply Chain, Green Marketing, And Environmental Sustainability. *LogForum, 19* (1).

Khan, N. R., Khan, M. R., & Ghouri, A. M. (2024). Industry 4.0 on the Way to Companies Performance. In Quality Management, Value Creation, and the Digital Economy (pp. 99- 120). Routledge.

Khan, N., Haq, M. A., Ghouri, A. M., Raziq, A., & Moiz, S. M. (2017). Adaptation of RFID Technology in Business Supply Chain Success: Empirical Findings from a Developing Country Logistic Industry. *Quality Management*.

Khan, A. A., Laghari, A. A., Rashid, M., Li, H., Javed, A. R., & Gadekallu, T. R. (2023). Artificial intelligence and blockchain technology for secure smart grid and power distribution Automation: A State-of-the-Art Review. *Sustainable Energy Technologies and Assessments*, *57*, 103282. doi:10.1016/j.seta.2023.103282

Khang, A., Jadhav, B., & Birajdar, S. (2023). Industry Revolution 4.0. In CRC Press eBooks (pp. 11–34). doi:10.1201/9781003357070-2

Khan, M. A., Din, I. U., Kim, B., & Almogren, A. (2023). Visualization of remote patient monitoring system based on internet of medical things. *Sustainability (Basel)*, *15*(10), 8120. doi:10.3390/su15108120

Khan, M. R., Khan, M. R., & Nallaluthan, K. (2023). Blockchain Supply Chain Management and Supply Chain Sustainability. *Management for Professionals*, (Part F539), 155–180. doi:10.1007/978-981-99-0699-4_10

Khan, M., Hussain, M., & Saber, H. M. (2016). Information sharing in a sustainable supply chain. *International Journal of Production Economics*, *181*, 208–214. doi:10.1016/j.ijpe.2016.04.010

Khan, N. R., Haq, M. A., Ghouri, A. M., Raziq, A., & Moiz, S. M. (2017). Adaptation of RFID technology in business supply chain success: Empirical findings from a developing country logistic industry. *Calitatea*, *18*(160), 93–99.

Khan, S. R., Tabish, M., & Zhang, Y. (2023). Embracement of industry 4.0 and sustainable supply chain practices under the shadow of practice-based view theory: Ensuring environmental sustainability in corporate sector. *Journal of Cleaner Production*, *398*, 136609. doi:10.1016/j.jclepro.2023.136609

Khan, S. R., Yu, Z., & Farooq, K. (2022). Green capabilities, green purchasing, and triple bottom line performance: Leading toward environmental sustainability. *Business Strategy and the Environment*. Advance online publication. doi:10.1002/bse.3234

Khatri, I., & Kjærland, F. (2023). Sustainability reporting practices and environmental performance amongst nordic listed firms. *Journal of Cleaner Production*, *418*, 138172. doi:10.1016/j.jclepro.2023.138172

Khin, S., & Ho, T. C. F. (2019). Digital Technology, Digital Capability and Organizational Performance: A Mediating Role of Digital Innovation. *International Journal of Innovation Science*, *11*(2), 177–195. doi:10.1108/IJIS-08-2018-0083

Kiangala, S. K., & Wang, Z. (2021). An effective adaptive customization framework for small manufacturing plants using extreme gradient boosting-XGBoost and random forest ensemble learning algorithms in an Industry 4.0 environment. *Machine Learning with Applications*, *4*, 100024. doi:10.1016/j.mlwa.2021.100024

Kiehle, J., Kopsakangas-Savolainen, M., Hilli, M., & Pongrácz, E. (2023). Carbon footprint at institutions of higher education: The case of the University of Oulu. *Journal of Environmental Management*, *329*, 117056. doi:10.1016/j.jenvman.2022.117056 PMID:36549059

Kilaso, S. (2023). *Digital Marketing And Strategic Approaches Of Electronic Component Manufacturers In The Era Of Industry 4.0.* https://doi.org/ doi:10.59670/jns.v33i.2264

Kilpatrick, J., Barter, L., Alexander, C., Brown, J., Calderon, R., & Carruthers, R. (2020). *Managing supply chain risk and disruption.* Deloitte.

Kim, J., Kim, M., Park, M., & Yoo, J. (2023). Immersive interactive technologies and virtual shopping experiences: Differences in consumer perceptions between augmented reality (AR) and virtual reality (VR). *Telematics and Informatics*, *77*, 101936. doi:10.1016/j.tele.2022.101936

Kineber, A. F., Oke, A. E., Farouk, M. H., Hamed, M. M., & Kayode, F. S. (2023). Barriers to the implementation of Radio frequency identification (RFID) for sustainable building in a developing economy. *Sustainability (Basel)*, *15*(1), 825. doi:10.3390/su15010825

Kiradoo, G. (2023, March 6). *The prominence of IoT in enhancing business success in the context of industry 4.0.* https://papers.ssrn.com/sol3/papers.cfm?abstract_id=4387919

Kliestik, T., Nagy, M., & Valaskova, K. (2023). Global value chains and industry 4.0 in the context of lean workplaces for enhancing company performance and its comprehension via the digital readiness and expertise of workforce in the V4 nations. *Mathematics, 11*(3), 601. doi:10.3390/math11030601

Klimczak, P., & Petersen, C. (2023). *AI - Limits and Prospects of Artificial Intelligence*. Transcript Verlag.

Koch, T., & Windsperger, J. (2017). Seeing through the Network: Competitive Advantage in the Digital Economy. *Journal of Organization Design, 6*(1), 6. Advance online publication. doi:10.1186/s41469-017-0016-z

Koh, L., Orzes, G., & Jia, F. (2019). The fourth industrial revolution (Industry 4.0): technologies disruption on operations and supply chain management. *International Journal of Operations and Production Management, 39*(6/7/8), 817–828. https://doi.org/ doi:10.1108/IJOPM-08-2019-788/FULL/PDF

Korder, S., Kulessa, S., Breuherr, D., Vernim, S., & Reinhart, G. (2023). The role of work system-related factors on skilled workers' turnover intentions – A study in small and medium-sized manufacturing enterprises in Southern Germany. *International Journal of Industrial Ergonomics, 93*, 103406. doi:10.1016/j.ergon.2022.103406

Korucuk, S., Tirkolaee, E. B., Aytekin, A., Karabašević, D., & Karamaşa, Ç. (2023). Agile supply chain management based on critical success factors and most ideal risk reduction strategy in the era of industry 4.0: application to plastic industry. *Operations Management Research*. doi:10.1007/s12063-023-00360-5

Kotsiopoulos, T., Sarigiannidis, P., Ioannidis, D., & Tzovaras, D. (2021). Machine learning and deep learning in smart manufacturing: The smart grid paradigm. *Computer Science Review, 40*, 100341. doi:10.1016/j.cosrev.2020.100341

Kouhizadeh, M., & Sarkis, J. (2018). Blockchain Practices, Potentials, and Perspectives in Greening Supply Chains. *Sustainability (Basel), 10*(10), 36–52. doi:10.3390/su10103652

Kozma, D., Varga, P., & Hegedűs, C. (2019). Supply Chain Management and Logistics 4.0 - A Study on Arrowhead Framework Integration. *Proceedings of the 8th International Conference on Industrial Technology and Management (ICITM)*. 10.1109/ICITM.2019.8710670

Krishnan, S., Thangaveloo, R., Rahman, S. B. A., & Sindiramutty, S. R. (2021). Smart Ambulance Traffic Control system. *Trends in Undergraduate Research, 4*(1), c28–c34. doi:10.33736/tur.2831.2021

Kshetri, N. (2017). Will blockchain emerge as a tool to break the poverty chain in the Global South? *Third World Quarterly, 38*(8), 1710–1732. doi:10.1080/01436597.2017.1298438

Kshetri, N. (2018). Blockchain's roles in meeting key supply chain management objectives. *International Journal of Information Management, 39*, 80–89. doi:10.1016/j.ijinfomgt.2017.12.005

Kuang, K., Li, L., Geng, Z., Xu, L., Zhang, K., Liao, B., Huang, H., Ding, P., Miao, W., & Jiang, Z. (2020). Causal inference. *Engineering (Beijing), 6*(3), 253–263. doi:10.1016/j.eng.2019.08.016

Kulkov, I., Kulkova, J., Rohrbeck, R., Menvielle, L., Kaartemo, V., & Makkonen, H. (2023). Artificial intelligence - driven sustainable development: Examining organizational, technical, and processing approaches to achieving global goals. *Sustainable Development (Bradford)*, sd.2773. Advance online publication. doi:10.1002/sd.2773

Kumar, A. A., Zaman, U. K. U., & Plapper, P. (2023). Collaborative robots. In CRC Press eBooks (pp. 90–106). doi:10.1201/9781003327523-8

Kumar, A., & Basu, R. (2023). Do eco-labels trigger green product purchase intention among emerging market consumers? *Journal of Indian Business Research, 15*(3), 466–492. doi:10.1108/JIBR-09-2022-0248

Kumar, A., Choudhary, S., Garza-Reyes, J. A., Kumar, V., Khan, S. R., & Mishra, N. (2021). Analysis of critical success factors for implementing Industry 4.0 integrated circular supply chain – moving towards sustainable operations. *Production Planning and Control, 34*(10), 984–998. doi:10.1080/09537287.2021.1980905

Kumar, D., Singh, R., Mishra, R., & Daim, T. U. (2023). Roadmap for integrating blockchain with Internet of Things (IoT) for sustainable and secured operations in logistics and supply chains: Decision making framework with case illustration. *Technological Forecasting and Social Change, 196*, 122837. doi:10.1016/j.techfore.2023.122837

Kumari, S., & Lele, V. (2023). Synergy of CRM and Industry 4.0: Advancing supply chain management and customer experience via digital innovations. *SSRG International Journal of Industrial Engineering, 10*(1), 20–25. doi:10.14445/23499362/IJIE-V10I1P104

Kumari, S., Sarkar, B., & Singh, G. (2023). Blockchain-based CRM solutions: Securing customer data in the digital transformation era. *International Journal of Computer Trends and Technology, 71*(4), 27–36. doi:10.14445/22312803/IJCTT-V71I4P105

Kumar, M., Raut, R. D., Mangla, S. K., Chowdhury, S., & Choubey, V. K. (2024). Moderating ESG compliance between industry 4.0 and green practices with green servitization: Examining its impact on green supply chain performance. *Technovation, 129*, 102898. doi:10.1016/j.technovation.2023.102898

Kumar, R., & Agrawal, N. (2023). Analysis of multi-dimensional Industrial IoT (IIoT) data in Edge-Fog-Cloud based architectural frameworks : A survey on current state and research challenges. *Journal of Industrial Information Integration, 35*, 100504. doi:10.1016/j.jii.2023.100504

Kumar, R., Singh, R. K., & Dwivedi, Y. K. (2020). Application of industry 4.0 technologies in SMEs for ethical and sustainable operations: Analysis of challenges. *Journal of Cleaner Production, 275*, 124063. doi:10.1016/j.jclepro.2020.124063 PMID:32921931

Kumar, S., & Mallipeddi, R. R. (2022). Impact of cybersecurity on operations and supply chain management: Emerging trends and future research directions. *Production and Operations Management, 31*(12), 4488–4500. doi:10.1111/poms.13859

Kumar, T., Pandey, B., Mussavi, S. H., & Jhanjhi, N. Z. (2015). CTHS based energy efficient Thermal Aware Image ALU design on FPGA. *Wireless Personal Communications, 85*(3), 671–696. doi:10.1007/s11277-015-2801-8

Kunhare, N., Gupta, R. K., & Sahu, Y. (2023). Role of Artificial Intelligence in the Agricultural System. *Wiley*, 227–241. doi:10.1002/9781119792161.ch12

Kunkel, S., Matthess, M., Xue, B., & Beier, G. (2022). Industry 4.0 in sustainable supply chain collaboration: Insights from an interview study with international buying firms and Chinese suppliers in the electronics industry. *Resources, Conservation and Recycling, 182*, 106274. doi:10.1016/j.resconrec.2022.106274

Kurniawan, T. A., Othman, M. H. D., Liang, X., Goh, H. H., Gikas, P., Kusworo, T. D., Anouzla, A., & Chew, K. W. (2023). Decarbonization in waste recycling industry using digitalization to promote net-zero emissions and its implications on sustainability. *Journal of Environmental Management, 338*, 117765. doi:10.1016/j.jenvman.2023.117765 PMID:36965421

Kuruvilla, M., J., G. Jaspher, W. K., Kirubakaran S, S., Prem Prasad, G., & G, E. (2023). Implementation of industry 4.0 in supply chain management in the healthcare industry. *IEEE Conference Publication | IEEE Xplore*. 10.1109/ICECAA58104.2023.10212417

Kusiak, A. (2023). Smart manufacturing. In Springer handbooks (pp. 973–985). doi:10.1007/978-3-030-96729-1_45

Kusi-Sarpong, S., Gupta, H., Khan, S. A., Jabbour, C. J. C., Rehman, S. T., & Kusi-Sarpong, H. (2021). Sustainable supplier selection based on industry 4.0 initiatives within the context of circular economy implementation in supply chain operations. *Production Planning and Control*, *34*(10), 999–1019. doi:10.1080/09537287.2021.1980906

Kusi-Sarpong, S., Gupta, H., & Sarkis, J. (2019). A supply chain sustainability innovation framework and evaluation methodology. *International Journal of Production Research*, *57*(7), 1990–2008. doi:10.1080/00207543.2018.1518607

Laboso, P. K., Martin, A., & Thiyagarajan, P. (2023). *Blockchain Technologies in Data Science: Challenges and Benefits.* Paper presented at the 2023 International Conference on Sustainable Computing and Data Communication Systems (ICSCDS). 10.1109/ICSCDS56580.2023.10104674

Lakner, Z., Kiss, A., Popp, J., Zeman, Z., Mate, D., & Olah, J. (2019). From Basic Research to Competitiveness: An Econometric Analysis of the Global Pharmaceutical Sector. *Sustainability (Basel)*, *11*(11), 3125. doi:10.3390/su11113125

Lamnabhi-Lagarrigue, F., & Samad, T. (2023). Social, organizational, and individual impacts of automation. In Springer handbooks (pp. 61–75). doi:10.1007/978-3-030-96729-1_3

Lampropoulos, G., & Siakas, K. V. (2022). Enhancing and securing cyber-physical systems and Industry 4.0 through digital twins: A critical review. *Journal of Software (Malden, MA)*, *35*(7), e2494. Advance online publication. doi:10.1002/smr.2494

Lando. (2017). *Digital Transformation in Journalism and News Media.* Academic Press.

Laplume, A. O., Petersen, B., & Pearce, J. M. (2016). Global value chains from a 3D printing perspective. *Journal of International Business Studies*, *47*(5), 595–609. doi:10.1057/jibs.2015.47

Laturkar, K., & Laturkar, K. (2023a). *A Blockchain-Based Approach to Revolutionizing Healthcare.*, doi:10.4018/978-1-6684-6509-7.ch003

Laturkar, K., & Laturkar, K. (2023b). *Internet of Things: Architectures.* Applications, and Challenges., doi:10.4018/978-1-6684-8145-5.ch023

Lee, C. Y., Lin, J. Y., & Chang, R. I. (2018). Improve quality and efficiency of textile process using data-driven machine learning in industry 4.0. *International Journal of Technology and Engineering Studies*, *4*(2), 4–10004.

Lee, G. G., & Rong, J. B. (2003). Organizational Mechanisms for Successful IS/IT Strategic Planning in the Digital Era. *Management Decision*, *41*(1), 32–42. doi:10.1108/00251740310445536

Lee, J. H., & Pilkington, M. (2017). How the blockchain revolution will reshape the consumer electronics industry future directions. *IEEE Consumer Electronics Magazine*, *6*(3), 19–23. doi:10.1109/MCE.2017.2684916

Lee, J., Azamfar, M., & Singh, J. (2019). A blockchain enabled Cyber-Physical System architecture for Industry 4.0 manufacturing systems. *Manufacturing Letters*, *20*, 34–39. doi:10.1016/j.mfglet.2019.05.003

Lee, J., Lapira, E., Bagheri, B., & Kao, H. A. (2013). Recent advances and trends in predictive manufacturing systems in big data environment. *Manufacturing Letters*, *1*(1), 38–41. doi:10.1016/j.mfglet.2013.09.005

Lee, J., Ni, J., Djurdjanovic, D., Qiu, H., & Liao, H. (2006). Intelligent prognostics tools and e-maintenance. *Computers in Industry*, *57*(6), 476–489. doi:10.1016/j.compind.2006.02.014

Lee, J., Wu, F., Zhao, W., Ghaffari, M., Liao, L., & Siegel, D. (2014). Prognostics and health management design for rotary machinery systems—Reviews, methodology and applications. *Mechanical Systems and Signal Processing*, *42*(1-2), 314–334. doi:10.1016/j.ymssp.2013.06.004

Lee, K. L., & Zhang, T. (2023). Revolutionizing Supply Chains: Unveiling the power of blockchain technology for enhanced transparency and performance. *International Journal of Technology, Innovation and Management, 3*(1), 19–27. doi:10.54489/ijtim.v3i1.216

Lee, S., Abdullah, A., Jhanjhi, N. Z., & Kok, S. (2021). Classification of botnet attacks in IoT smart factory using honeypot combined with machine learning. *PeerJ, 7*, e350. doi:10.7717/peerj-cs.350 PMID:33817000

Legenvre, H., Henke, M., & Ruile, H. (2020). Making sense of the impact of the internet of things on Purchasing and Supply Management:A tension perspective. *Journal of Purchasing and Supply Management, 26*(1), 100596. doi:10.1016/j.pursup.2019.100596

Le-Khac, P. H., Healy, G., & Smeaton, A. F. (2020). Contrastive representation learning: A framework and review. *IEEE Access : Practical Innovations, Open Solutions, 8*, 193907–193934. doi:10.1109/ACCESS.2020.3031549

Lele, A., & Lele, A. (2019). Artificial intelligence (AI). *Disruptive technologies for the militaries and security*, 139-154.

Leng, J., Sha, W., Lin, Z., Jing, J., Liu, Q., & Chen, X. (2023). Blockchained smart contract pyramid-driven multi-agent autonomous process control for resilient individualised manufacturing towards Industry 5.0. *International Journal of Production Research, 61*(13), 4302–4321. doi:10.1080/00207543.2022.2089929

Lenzen, M., Tzeng, M. W., Floerl, O., & Zaiko, A. (2023). Application of multi-region input-output analysis to examine biosecurity risks associated with the global shipping network. *The Science of the Total Environment, 854*, 158758. doi:10.1016/j.scitotenv.2022.158758 PMID:36113796

Leow, A., Chua, S., Billett, S., & Le, A. H. (2023). Employers' perspectives of effective continuing education and training in Singapore. *Higher Education, Skills and Work-based Learning, 13*(2), 217–232. doi:10.1108/HESWBL-05-2022-0115

Le, T. T., Vo, X. V., & Venkatesh, V. (2022). Role of green innovation and supply chain management in driving sustainable corporate performance. *Journal of Cleaner Production, 374*, 133875. doi:10.1016/j.jclepro.2022.133875

Lezoche, M., Hernandez, J. E., & Alemany Díaz, M. del M. E., Panetto, H., & Kacprzyk, J. (2020). Agri-food 4.0: A survey of the supply chains and technologies for the future agriculture. *Computers in Industry, 117*, 103187. https://doi.org/https://doi.org/10.1016/j.compind.2020.103187

Li, Z., Wu, H., King, B., Miled, Z. B., Wassick, J., & Tazelaar, J. (2017, June). On the integration of event-based and transaction-based architectures for supply chains. In *2017 IEEE 37th International Conference on Distributed Computing Systems Workshops (ICDCSW)* (pp. 376-382). IEEE.

Liao, R. (2020). *How interoperability establishes blockchain's utility and effectiveness for trade finance May 2020*. WEF. https://www.weforum.org/agenda/2020/05/blockchain-interoperability-utility-effectiveness/

Liao, Z., Yin, Q., Huang, Y., & Sheng, L. (2014). Management and application of mobile big data. *International Journal of Embedded Systems, 7*(1), 63–70.https://doi.org/10.1504/IJES.2015.066143

Liboni, B., Oranges, L., Cezarino, L., Chiappetta, J., Charbel, J., Garcia, O., ... Nelson, S. (2019). Smart industry and the pathways to HRM 4.0: Implications for SCM. *Supply Chain Management, 24*(1), 124–146. doi:10.1108/SCM-03-2018-0150

Li, C., Wang, J., Wang, S., & Zhang, Y. (2024). A review of IoT applications in healthcare. *Neurocomputing, 565*, 127017. https://doi.org/10.1016/j.neucom.2023.127017

Li, C., & Zhang, L. J. (2017). A blockchain based new secure multi-layer network model for Internet of Things. In *Proceedings of the IEEE International Congress on Internet of Things (ICIOT)* (pp. 33–41). IEEE. https://doi.org/10.1109/IEEE.ICIOT.2017.34

Li, D. X., & Duan, L. (2019). Big data for cyber physical systems in Industry 4.0: A survey. *Enterprise Information Systems, 13*(2), 148–169. doi:10.1080/17517575.2018.1442934

Li, F., Laili, Y., Chen, X., Lou, Y., Wang, C., Yang, H., Gao, X., & Han, H. (2023). Towards big data driven construction industry. *Journal of Industrial Information Integration, 35*, 100483. doi:10.1016/j.jii.2023.100483

Li, H., Wu, Y., Cao, D., & Wang, Y. (2021). Organizational Mindfulness towards Digital Transformation as a Prerequisite of Information Processing Capability to Achieve Market Agility. *Journal of Business Research, 122*(February), 700–712. doi:10.1016/j.jbusres.2019.10.036

Li, J., Wang, L., & Tan, X. (2020). Sustainable design and optimization of coal supply chain network under different carbon emission policies. *Journal of Cleaner Production, 250*, 119548. doi:10.1016/j.jclepro.2019.119548

Li, L. (2022). Reskilling and upskilling the future-ready workforce for industry 4.0 and beyond. *Information Systems Frontiers*, 1–16.

Li, L., Zheng, X., & Wang, S. (2023). The Effect of sustainability information disclosure on the cost of equity capital: An empirical analysis based on Gartner Top 50 supply chain rankings. *Journal of Risk and Financial Management, 16*(8), 358. doi:10.3390/jrfm16080358

Li, M., Li, M., Guo, D., Qu, T., & Guo, D. (2023). Real-Time Data-Driven Out-of-Order synchronization for production and intralogistics in Multiresource-Constrained assembly systems. *IEEE Transactions on Systems, Man, and Cybernetics. Systems, 53*(12), 1–13. doi:10.1109/TSMC.2023.3298927

Lim, M., Abdullah, A., Jhanjhi, N. Z., & Khan, M. K. (2020). Situation-Aware Deep Reinforcement Learning link Prediction model for evolving criminal networks. *IEEE Access : Practical Innovations, Open Solutions, 8*, 16550–16559. doi:10.1109/ACCESS.2019.2961805

Lim, W. M. (2023). The workforce revolution: Reimagining work, workers, and workplaces for the future. *Global Business and Organizational Excellence, 42*(4), 5–10. doi:10.1002/joe.22218

Li, S., Zheng, P., Liu, S., Wang, Z., Wang, X. V., Zheng, L., & Wang, L. (2023). Proactive human–robot collaboration: Mutual-cognitive, predictable, and self-organising perspectives. *Robotics and Computer-integrated Manufacturing, 81*, 102510. doi:10.1016/j.rcim.2022.102510

Li, T., Sahu, A. K., Talwalkar, A., & Smith, V. (2020). Federated learning: Challenges, methods, and future directions. *IEEE Signal Processing Magazine, 37*(3), 50–60. doi:10.1109/MSP.2020.2975749

Litke, A., Anagnostopoulos, D., & Varvarigou, T. (2019). Blockchains for supply chain management: Architectural elements and challenges towards a global scale deployment. *Logistics, 3*(1), 5. doi:10.3390/logistics3010005

Liu, B., & De Giovanni, P. (2019). Green process innovation through Industry 4.0 technologies and supply chain coordination. *Annals of Operations Research*, 1–36. doi:10.1007/s10479-019-03498-3

Liu, L., Song, W., & Liu, Y. (2023). Leveraging digital capabilities toward a circular economy: Reinforcing sustainable supply chain management with Industry 4.0 technologies. *Computers & Industrial Engineering, 178*, 109113. doi:10.1016/j.cie.2023.109113

Liu, S., Lu, Y., Shen, X., & Bao, J. (2023). A digital thread-driven distributed collaboration mechanism between digital twin manufacturing units. *Journal of Manufacturing Systems, 68*, 145–159. doi:10.1016/j.jmsy.2023.02.014

Liu, X., Cao, J., Yang, Y., & Jiang, S. (2018). CPS-Based Smart Warehouse for Industry 4.0: A Survey of the Underlying Technologies. *Computers, 7*(1), 13. doi:10.3390/computers7010013

Liu, Y., & Xu, X. (2017). Industry 4.0 and cloud manufacturing: A comparative analysis. *Journal of Manufacturing Science and Engineering*, *139*(3), 034701. doi:10.1115/1.4034667

Li, W., Fu, C., & Cheng, D. (2020). Comments on the development of blockchain technology from the perspective of patent analysis. *Frontiers of Engineering Management*, *7*(4), 615–617. doi:10.1007/s42524-020-0101-9

Li, Y., Dai, J., & Cui, L. (2020). The impact of digital technologies on economic and environmental performance in the context of Industry 4.0: A moderated mediation model. *International Journal of Production Economics*, *229*, 107777.

Li, Z., Liu, Z., Huang, J., Tang, G., Duan, Y., Zhang, Z., & Yang, Y. (2019). MV-GCN: Multi-view graph convolutional networks for link prediction. *IEEE Access : Practical Innovations, Open Solutions*, *7*, 176317–176328. doi:10.1109/ACCESS.2019.2957306

López, O. L. A., Rosabal, O. M., Ruiz-Guirola, D. E., Raghuwanshi, P., Mikhaylov, K., Lovén, L., & Iyer, S. (2023). Energy-Sustainable IoT connectivity: Vision, technological enablers, challenges, and future directions. *IEEE Open Journal of the Communications Society*, *4*, 2609–2666. doi:10.1109/OJCOMS.2023.3323832

Lubag, M., Bonifácio, J., Tan, J. M., Concepcion, R. II, Mababangloob, G. R., Galang, J. G., & Maniquiz-Redillas, M. C. (2023). Diversified impacts of enabling a Technology-Intensified agricultural supply chain on the quality of life in hinterland communities. *Sustainability (Basel)*, *15*(17), 12809. doi:10.3390/su151712809

Lun, Y. H. V., Lai, K., Cheng, T., & Yang, D. (2023). New technology development in the shipping industry. In Springer eBooks (pp. 257–279). doi:10.1007/978-3-031-26090-2_17

Luo, J., Huang, M., Bai, Y., & Li, J. (2023). Supply Chain Management during a Public Health Emergency of International Concern: A Bibliometric and Content Analysis. *Processes (Basel, Switzerland)*, *11*(3), 713. doi:10.3390/pr11030713

Luo, Y., & Zahra, S. A. (2023). Industry 4.0 in international business research. *Journal of International Business Studies*, *54*(3), 403–417. doi:10.1057/s41267-022-00577-9 PMID:36987430

Luqman, A., & Shahzadi, G. (2023, November). Multi-criteria group decision-making based on the interval-valued q-rung orthopair fuzzy SIR approach for green supply chain evaluation and selection. *Granular Computing.*, *8*(6), 1937–1954. doi:10.1007/s41066-023-00411-z

Lu, R., Zhang, W., Wang, Y., Li, Q., Zhong, X., Yang, H., & Wang, D. (2023). Auction-Based cluster federated learning in mobile edge computing systems. *IEEE Transactions on Parallel and Distributed Systems*, •••, 1–15. doi:10.1109/TPDS.2023.3240767

Lutfi, A., Alrawad, M., Alsyouf, A., Almaiah, M. A., Al-Khasawneh, A., Al-Khasawneh, A. L., Alshira'h, A. F., Alshirah, M. H., Saad, M., & Ibrahim, N. (2023). Drivers and impact of big data analytic adoption in the retail industry: A quantitative investigation applying structural equation modeling. *Journal of Retailing and Consumer Services*, *70*, 103129. doi:10.1016/j.jretconser.2022.103129

Luthra, S., & Mangla, S. K. (2018). *Evaluating challenges to Industry 4.0 initiatives for supply chain sustainability in emerging economies*. University of Plymouth. Retrieved from https://pearl.plymouth.ac.uk/bitstream/handle/10026.1/11498/SKM%20-%20Industry%204.0%20paper%20-accepted%20version.pdf;jsessionid=3560FDCF3EBDFCCB25D47A113EF5F29E?sequence=5

Luthra, S., Kumar, A., Zavadskas, E. K., Mangla, S. K., & Garza-Reyes, J. A. (2020). Industry 4.0 as an enabler of sustainability diffusion in supply chain: An analysis of influential strength of drivers in an emerging economy. *International Journal of Production Research*, *58*(5), 1505–1521. doi:10.1080/00207543.2019.1660828

Lu, Y. (2017). Industry 4.0: A survey on technologies, applications and open research issues. *Journal of Industrial Information Integration, 6*, 1–10.

Lu, Y., & Tian, Y. (2023). *Sustainability-Driven consumer experience design of an online retail system for household appliances*. ICST Transactions on Scalable Information Systems. doi:10.4108/eetsis.3331

Lv, Z., & Shang, W. (2023). Impacts of intelligent transportation systems on energy conservation and emission reduction of transport systems: A comprehensive review. *Green Technologies and Sustainability, 1*(1), 100002. doi:10.1016/j.grets.2022.100002

Ly, B. (2023). *Inclusion leadership and employee work engagement: The role of organizational commitment in Cambodian public organization*. Asia-Pacific Management Review. doi:10.1016/j.apmrv.2023.06.003

Ma, L., Zhang, Z., & Zhang, N. (2018). *Ethical dilemma of artificial intelligence and its research progress*. Paper presented at the IOP conference series: materials science and engineering. 10.1088/1757-899X/392/6/062188

Ma, B., Ni, H., Zhu, X., & Zhao, R. (2019). A Comprehensive Improved Salp Swarm Algorithm on Redundant Container Deployment Problem. *IEEE Access : Practical Innovations, Open Solutions, 7*, 136452–136470. doi:10.1109/ACCESS.2019.2933265

MacatangayL. (2023). The Status, Challenges & Opportunities of Education Service Industry in the Philippines. *Social Science Research Network*. doi:10.2139/ssrn.4426082

Machado, C. G., Winroth, M. P., & Ribeiro da Silva, E. H. D. (2020). Sustainable manufacturing in Industry 4.0: An emerging research agenda. *International Journal of Production Research, 58*(5), 1462–1484. doi:10.1080/00207543.2019.1652777

Mackey, T. K., & Nayyar, G. (2017). A review of existing and emerging digital technologies to combat the global trade in fake medicines. *Expert Opinion on Drug Safety, 16*(5), 587–602. doi:10.1080/14740338.2017.1313227 PMID:28349715

Maersk Press Release. (2018). *Maersk and IBM to form joint venture applying blockchain to improve global trade and digitise supply chains*. Available at: www.maersk.com/press/press-release-archive/maersk-and-ibm-to-form-joint-venture

Mahadevan, S., & Shah, S. L. (2009). Fault detection and diagnosis in process data using one-class support vector machines. *Journal of Process Control, 19*(10), 1627–1639. doi:10.1016/j.jprocont.2009.07.011

Maharana, M., & Lathabhavan, R. (2023). Industry 4.0 and its impact on supply chain management: An overview. *International Journal of Services. Economics and Management, 14*(2), 224–248.

Mahjoob, A., Alfadhli, Y., & Omachonu, V. (2023). Healthcare Waste and Sustainability: Implications for a Circular Economy. *Sustainability (Basel), 15*(10), 7788. doi:10.3390/su15107788

Mahmud, H., Islam, A. K. M. N., & Mitra, R. K. (2023). What drives managers towards algorithm aversion and how to overcome it? Mitigating the impact of innovation resistance through technology readiness. *Technological Forecasting and Social Change, 193*, 122641. doi:10.1016/j.techfore.2023.122641

Ma, J. Y., Shi, L., & Kang, T. W. (2022). The Effect of Digital Transformation on the Pharmaceutical Sustainable Supply Chain Performance: The Mediating Role of Information Sharing and Traceability Using Structural Equation Modeling. *Sustainability (Basel), 15*(1), 649. doi:10.3390/su15010649

Makanda, I. L. D., Jiang, P., Yang, M., & Shi, H. (2023). Emergence of collective intelligence in industrial cyber-physical-social systems for collaborative task allocation and defect detection. *Computers in Industry, 152*, 104006. doi:10.1016/j.compind.2023.104006

Makkar, S., Devi, G. N. R., & Solanki, V. K. (2020). Applications of machine learning techniques in supply chain optimization. In ICICCT 2019–System Reliability, Quality Control, Safety, Maintenance and Management: Applications to Electrical, Electronics and Computer Science and Engineering (pp. 861-869). Springer Singapore. doi:10.1007/978-981-13-8461-5_98

Malheiro, V., Duarte, J., Veiga, F., & Melo, F. M. (2023). Exploiting Pharma 4.0 Technologies in the Non-Biological-Complex Drugs Manufacturing: Innovations and Implications. *Pharmaceutics*, *15*(11), 2545. doi:10.3390/pharmaceutics15112545 PMID:38004525

Mallozzi, P. (2017, May). Combining machine-learning with invariants assurance techniques for autonomous systems. In *2017 IEEE/ACM 39th International Conference on Software Engineering Companion (ICSE-C)* (pp. 485-486). IEEE. 10.1109/ICSE-C.2017.40

Manavalan, E., & Jayakrishna, K. (2019). A review of Internet of Things (IoT) embedded sustainable supply chain for industry 4.0 requirements. *Computers & Industrial Engineering*, *127*, 925–953. doi:10.1016/j.cie.2018.11.030

Manchuri, A. R., Akhila, K., Abu Saleh, A., & Sindiramutty, S. R. (2024). Application of Supervised Machine Learning Models in Biodiesel Production Research - A Short Review. *Borneo Journal of Sciences and Technology*, *6*(1), 96–104. doi:10.35370/bjost.2024.6.1-10

Mansfield-Devine, S. (2017). Beyond Bitcoin: Using blockchain technology to provide assurance in the commercial world. *Computer Fraud & Security*, *2017*(5), 14–18. doi:10.1016/S1361-3723(17)30042-8

Manuel Maqueira, J., Moyano-Fuentes, J., & Bruque, S. (2019). Drivers and consequences of an innovative technology assimilation in the supply chain: Cloud computing and supply chain integration. *International Journal of Production Research*, *57*(7), 2083–2103. doi:10.1080/00207543.2018.1530473

Mao, W., Hu, Y., Yang, X., Ren, W., & Fang, H. (2023). ARE-Platform: An augmented Reality-Based ergonomic evaluation solution for smart manufacturing. *International Journal of Human-Computer Interaction*, 1–16. doi:10.1080/10447318.2023.2173894

Marbouh, D., Abbasi, T., Maasmi, F., Omar, I. A., Debe, M. S., Salah, K., Jayaraman, R., & Ellahham, S. (2020). Blockchain for COVID-19: Review, opportunities, and a trusted tracking system. *Arabian Journal for Science and Engineering*, *45*(12), 9895–9911. doi:10.1007/s13369-020-04950-4 PMID:33072472

Mardani, A., Kannan, D., Hooker, R. E., Ozkul, S., Alrasheedi, M., & Tirkolaee, E. B. (2020). Evaluation of green and sustainable supply chain management using structural equation modelling: A systematic review of the state of the art literature and recommendations for future research. *Journal of Cleaner Production*, *249*, 119383. doi:10.1016/j.jclepro.2019.119383

Mariani, M., & Borghi, M. (2019). Industry 4.0: A bibliometric review of its managerial intellectual structure and potential evolution in the service industries. *Technological Forecasting and Social Change*, *149*(September), 119752.https://doi.org/10.1016/j.techfore.2019.119752

Marinagi, C., Reklitis, P., Trivellas, P., & Sakas, D. (2023). The Impact of Industry 4.0 Technologies on Key Performance Indicators for a Resilient Supply Chain 4.0. *Sustainability*, *15*(6), 5185. doi:10.3390/su15065185

Martínez-Falcó, J., Sánchez-García, E., Millan-Tudela, L. A., & Marco-Lajara, B. (2023). The role of green agriculture and green supply chain Management in the Green Intellectual Capital–Sustainable Performance Relationship: A structural equation modeling analysis applied to the Spanish wine industry. *Agriculture*, *13*(2), 425. doi:10.3390/agriculture13020425

Martins, C. L., & Pato, M. V. (2019). Supply chain sustainability: A tertiary literature review. *Journal of Cleaner Production*, *225*, 995–1016. doi:10.1016/j.jclepro.2019.03.250

Marwala, T. (2023). Data in Politics. In *Artificial Intelligence* (pp. 59–77). Game Theory and Mechanism Design in Politics. doi:10.1007/978-981-99-5103-1_5

Mason, P. (2023). *Financially Smart Career Planning For Teens: The Roadmap To Making Informed Decisions In An Uncertain Job Market, Prevent Feeling Overwhelmed & Analysis Paralysis To Achieve Affordable College Degrees.* Academic Press.

Mason, S., Baines, T., Kay, J. M., & Ladbrook, J. (2005). Improving the design process for factories: Modeling human performance variation. *Journal of Manufacturing Systems*, *24*(1), 47–54. doi:10.1016/S0278-6125(05)80006-8

Masood, F., Khan, N. R., & Khan, M. R. (2024). Blockchain-based supply chain management: A challenge yet an opportunity to gauge. In *Achieving Secure and Transparent Supply Chains with Blockchain Technology* (pp. 267–285). IGI Global. doi:10.4018/979-8-3693-0482-2.ch015

Masood, T., & Egger, J. (2019). Augmented reality in support of Industry 4.0 - implementation challenges and success factors. *Robotics and Computer-integrated Manufacturing*, *58*, 181–195. doi:10.1016/j.rcim.2019.02.003

Masood, T., & Sonntag, P. (2020). Industry 4.0: Adoption challenges and benefits for SMEs. *Computers in Industry*, *121*, 103261. Advance online publication. doi:10.1016/j.compind.2020.103261

Mastos, T. D., Nizamis, A., Vafeiadis, T., Alexopoulos, N., Ntinas, C., Gkortzis, D., Papadopoulos, A., Ioannidis, D., & Tzovaras, D. (2020). Industry 4.0 sustainable supply chains: An application of an IoT enabled scrap metal management solution. *Journal of Cleaner Production*, *269*, 122377. doi:10.1016/j.jclepro.2020.122377

Mastrocinque, E., Ramírez, F. J., Honrubia-Escribano, A., & Pham, D. T. (2022). Industry 4.0 enabling sustainable supply chain development in the renewable energy sector: A multi-criteria intelligent approach. *Technological Forecasting and Social Change*, *182*, 121813. doi:10.1016/j.techfore.2022.121813

Masum, R. (2023). Cyber Security in Smart Manufacturing (Threats, Landscapes Challenges). *arXiv preprint arXiv:2304.10180.*

Matin, A., Islam, R., Wang, X., Huo, H., & Xu, G. (2023). AIoT for sustainable manufacturing: Overview, challenges, and opportunities. *Internet of Things : Engineering Cyber Physical Human Systems*, *100901*, 100901. Advance online publication. doi:10.1016/j.iot.2023.100901

McIntosh, O. B., Burnett, A. N., Feldman, I. R., Lamphere, J. A., Reuter, T., & Vital, E. (2023). The role of sustainability knowledge-action platforms in advancing multi-stakeholder engagement on sustainability. *Data & Policy*, *5*, e33. Advance online publication. doi:10.1017/dap.2023.27

McKenzie, J. (2018). *Why blockchain won't fix food safety – yet.* Available at https://thecounter.org/blockchain-food-traceability-walmart-ibm/

Meier, S., Klarmann, S., Thielen, N., Pfefferer, C., Kuhn, M., & Franke, J. (2023). A process model for systematically setting up the data basis for data-driven projects in manufacturing. *Journal of Manufacturing Systems*, *71*, 1–19. doi:10.1016/j.jmsy.2023.08.024

Melkote, S., Liang, S. Y., Ozel, T., Jawahir, I. S., Stephenson, D. A., & Wang, B. (2022). A review of advances in modeling of conventional machining processes: From merchant to the present. *Journal of Manufacturing Science and Engineering*, 1–49.

Melnyk, L., Kubatko, O., Matsenko, O., Balatskyi, Y., & Serdyukov, K. (2023). *Transformation of the human capital reproduction in line with Industries 4.0 and 5.0.* Academic Press.

Mfungo, D., Fu, X., Wang, X., & Xian, Y. (2023). Enhancing Image Encryption with the Kronecker xor Product, the Hill Cipher, and the Sigmoid Logistic Map. *Applied Sciences (Basel, Switzerland), 13*(6), 4034. doi:10.3390/app13064034

Mhaddolkar, A. V. (2023, May 1). *Optimization of warehouse inventory space using class based storage method.* http://www.dspace.dtu.ac.in:8080/jspui/handle/repository/20012

Mhlanga, D. (2023). Artificial intelligence and machine learning in making transport, safer, cleaner, more reliable, and efficient in emerging markets. In Sustainable development goals series (pp. 193–211). doi:10.1007/978-3-031-37776-1_9

Michelman, P. (2017). Seeing beyond the blockchain hype. *MIT Sloan Management Review, 58*(4), 17–19.

Milian, E. Z., Spinola, M. D. M., & De Carvalho, M. M. (2019). Fintech: A literature review and research agenda. *Electronic Commerce Research and Applications, 34*, 100833.

Milne, R. (2017). Moller-Maersk puts cost of cyber attack at up to $300m. *Financial Times*. Available at: https://www.ft.com/content/a44ede7c-825f-11e7-a4ce-15b2513cb3ff

Mindas, M., & Bednar, S. (2016). Mass customization in the context of Industry 4.0: Implications of variety induced complexity. Industry 4.0, Mass customization, Complexity, Demand, Variety, Advanced industrial engineering. *Industry, 4*(0), 21–39.

Minoofar, A., Gholami, A., Eslami, S., Haji-Zadeh, A., Gholami, A., Zandi, M., Ameri, M., & Kazem, H. A. (2023). Renewable energy system opportunities: A sustainable solution toward cleaner production and reducing carbon footprint of large-scale dairy farms. *Energy Conversion and Management, 293*, 117554. doi:10.1016/j.enconman.2023.117554

Mishra, P., & Singh, G. (2023). Energy Management Systems in Sustainable Smart Cities Based on the Internet of Energy: A Technical review. *Energies, 16*(19), 6903. doi:10.3390/en16196903

Mistarihi, M. Z., & Magableh, G. M. (2023). Unveiling Supply Chain Nervousness: A Strategic Framework for Disruption Management under Fuzzy Environment. *Sustainability (Basel), 15*(14), 11179. doi:10.3390/su151411179

Mladineo, M., Veza, I., & Gjeldum, N. (2017). Solving partner selection problem in cyber-physical production networks using the HUMANT algorithm. *International Journal of Production Research, 55*(9), 2506–2521. doi:10.1080/00207543.2016.1234084

Moavenzadeh, J., Doherty, S., Philip, R., Geiger, T., Gottfredson, M., Mattios, G., Willink, B. T., Correa, A., Hoekman, B., Jackson, S., Ferrantino, M., & Tsigas, M. (2013). *Enabling trade. Valuing growth opportunities*. World Economic Forum.

Mobarak, M. H., Islam, M. A., Hossain, N., Al Mahmud, M. Z., Rayhan, M. T., & Nishi, N. J. (2023). *Recent advances of additive manufacturing in implant fabrication A review.* Applied Surface Science Advances. doi:10.1016/j.apsadv.2023.100462

Mo, F., Rehman, H. U., Monetti, F. M., Chaplin, J. C., Sanderson, D. R., Popov, A. A., Maffei, A., & Ratchev, S. (2023). A framework for manufacturing system reconfiguration and optimisation utilising digital twins and modular artificial intelligence. *Robotics and Computer-integrated Manufacturing, 82*, 102524. doi:10.1016/j.rcim.2022.102524

Moggi, S. (2023). Sustainability reporting, universities and global reporting initiative applicability: A still open issue. *Sustainability Accounting. Management and Policy Journal, 14*(4), 699–742. doi:10.1108/SAMPJ-05-2022-0257

Mohamed, M., Sallam, K. M., & Mohamed, M. (2023). Internet of Things (IoT) in Supply Chain Management: Challenges, opportunities, and best practices. *Sustainable Machine Intelligence Journal, 2*. Advance online publication. doi:10.61185/SMIJ.2023.22103

Mohammad, A. (2023, August 1). *Revolutionizing Solar Energy with AI-Driven Enhancements in Photovoltaic Technology*. https://journal.mediapublikasi.id/index.php/bullet/article/view/3427

Mohanasundaram, T., Vetrivel, S., & Krishnamoorthy, V. (2023). *Applications of IoTSG in Smart Industrial Monitoring Environments*. Wiley. doi:10.1002/9781119812524.ch12

Mohiuddin, M., Reza, M. N. H., Jayashree, S., Al-Azad, S., & Ed-Dafali, S. (2023). The role of governments in driving industry 4.0 adoption in emerging countries. *Journal of Global Information Management, 31*(1), 1–31. doi:10.4018/JGIM.323439

Mohsen, S., Elkaseer, A., & Scholz, S. G. (2021). Industry 4.0-oriented deep learning models for human activity recognition. *IEEE Access : Practical Innovations, Open Solutions, 9*, 150508–150521. doi:10.1109/ACCESS.2021.3125733

Montini, E., Cutrona, V., Dell'Oca, S., & Carpanzano, E. (2023). A framework for human-aware collaborative robotics systems development. *ResearchGate*. https://www.researchgate.net/publication/370678957_A_Framework_for_Human-aware_Collaborative_Robotics_Systems_Development

Moradeyo, A. A., Oke, A., & Muogboh, O. S. (2023). Linking supply chain disruptions and manufacturing firms' operational performance in a developing country context. *International Journal of Services and Operations Management, 44*(4), 460. doi:10.1504/IJSOM.2023.130178

Morandini, S., Fraboni, F., De Angelis, M., Puzzo, G., Giusino, D., & Pietrantoni, L. (2023). The impact of artificial intelligence on workers' skills: upskilling and reskilling in organisations. *Informing Science the International Journal of an Emerging Transdiscipline, 26*, 39–68. doi:10.28945/5078

Mostepaniuk, A., Akalin, T., & Parish, M. R. (2023). Practices Pursuing the Sustainability of A Healthcare Organization: A Systematic Review. *Sustainability (Basel), 15*(3), 2353. doi:10.3390/su15032353

Motlagh, N. H., Mohammadrezaei, M., Hunt, J., & Zakeri, B. (2020). Internet of Things (IoT) and the energy sector. *Energies, 13*(2), 494.https://doi.org/10.3390/en13020494

Moumen, I. (2023). Real-time GPS tracking system for IoT-Enabled connected vehicles. *E3S Web of Conferences*. doi:10.1051/e3sconf/202341201095

Mridha, B., Pareek, S., Goswami, A., & Sarkar, B. (2023, February 1). Joint effects of production quality improvement of biofuel and carbon emissions towards a smart sustainable supply chain management. *Journal of Cleaner Production, 386*, 135629. doi:10.1016/j.jclepro.2022.135629

Mrozek, T., Seitz, D., Gundermann, K., & Dicke, M. (2020). *Digital supply chains: A Practitioner's Guide to Successful Digitalization*. Campus Verlag.

Mubarik, M. S., Naghavi, N., Mubarik, M., Kusi-Sarpong, S., Khan, S. A., Zaman, S. I., & Kazmi, S. H. A. (2021). Resilience and cleaner production in Industry 4.0: Role of supply chain mapping and visibility. *Journal of Cleaner Production, 292*, 126058.https://doi.org/10.1016/j.jclepro.2021.126058

Mukhlas, A., Talip, B., Mustapha, J. C., & Ismail, S. (2022). Industry 4.0 (IR 4.0) for Pharmaceutical Industry: An Exploratory Review. *International Visualization, Informatics and Technology Conference (IVIT.*

Müller, J. (2019). Assessing the barriers to Industry 4.0 implementation from a workers' perspective. *IFAC-Pap., 52*, 2189–2194.

Mumtaz, R., Amin, A., Khan, M. A., Asif, M., Anwar, Z., & Bashir, M. J. (2023). Impact of green energy transportation systems on urban air quality: A predictive analysis using spatiotemporal deep learning techniques. *Energies, 16*(16), 6087. doi:10.3390/en16166087

Munirathinam, S. (2020). Industry 4.0: Industrial Internet of Things (IIOT). In The Digital Twin Paradigm for Smarter Systems and Environments: The Industry Use Cases (pp. 129-164). Academic Press.

Muñoz-Saavedra, L., Miró-Amarante, L., & Domínguez-Morales, M. (2020). Augmented and Virtual Reality Evolution and Future Tendency. *Applied Sciences (Basel, Switzerland)*, *10*, 332.https://doi.org/10.3390/app10010332

Musamih, A., Salah, K., Jayaraman, R., Arshad, J., Debe, M., & Al Hammad, Y. (2016). A Blockchain-based Approach for Drug Traceability in Healthcare Supply Chain. *IEEE Access : Practical Innovations, Open Solutions*.

Mushafiq, M., Arisar, M. M. K., Tariq, H., & Czapp, S. (2023). Energy Efficiency and Economic Policy: Comprehensive theoretical, Empirical, and policy review. *Energies*, *16*(5), 2381. doi:10.3390/en16052381

Muzammal, S. M., Murugesan, R. K., & Jhanjhi, N. Z. (2021). A Comprehensive Review on Secure Routing in Internet of Things: Mitigation Methods and Trust-Based Approaches. *IEEE Internet of Things Journal*, *8*(6), 4186–4210. doi:10.1109/JIOT.2020.3031162

Muzammal, S. M., Murugesan, R. K., Jhanjhi, N. Z., & Jung, L. T. (2020). SMTrust: Proposing Trust-Based Secure Routing Protocol for RPL Attacks for IoT Applications. *2020 International Conference on Computational Intelligence (ICCI)*. 10.1109/ICCI51257.2020.9247818

Nadeem, K., Wong, S. I., Za, S., & Venditti, M. (2024). Digital transformation and industry 4.0 employees: Empirical evidence from top digital nations. *Technology in Society*, *76*, 102434. Advance online publication. doi:10.1016/j.techsoc.2023.102434

NaduaF.EscandorL.BangayanM.VigonteF.AbanteM. V. (2023). Identifying incentives to address attrition in the government cybersecurity workforce. *Social Science Research Network*. doi:10.2139/ssrn.4382110

Nakasumi, M. (2017). Information sharing for supply chain management based on block chain technology. *IEEE 19th Conference on Business Informatics*, 140-149. 10.1109/CBI.2017.56

Nantee, N., & Sureeyatanapas, P. (2021). The impact of Logistics 4.0 on corporate sustainability: A performance assessment of automated warehouse operations. *Benchmarking*, *28*(10), 2865–2895. doi:10.1108/BIJ-11-2020-0583

Naqvi, S. G., Sheraz, S., Mehmood, I., & Yasin, M. (2023). Cyber-physical Systems and Artificial Intelligence: The Role of Cyber Security, Machine Learning, Threats and benefits to Modern Economies and Industries. *Pakistan Journal of Humanities and Social Sciences, 11*(2), 1513–1522.

Narula, R. (2019). Enforcing higher labor standards within developing country value chains: Consequences for MNEs and informal actors in a dual economy. *Journal of International Business Studies*, *50*(9), 1622–1635. doi:10.1057/s41267-019-00265-1

Nascimento, D. L. M., Alencastro, V., Quelhas, O. L. G., Caiado, R. G. G., Garza-Reyes, J. A., Lona, L. R., & Tortorella, G. (2019). Exploring Industry 4.0 technologies to enable circular economy practices in a manufacturing context: A business model proposal. *Journal of Manufacturing Technology Management*, *30*(3), 607–627.https://doi.org/10.1108/JMTM-03-2018-0071

Naseem, M. H., & Yang, J. (2021). Role of Industry 4.0 in Supply Chains Sustainability: A Systematic Literature Review. *Sustainability (Basel)*, *13*(17), 9944. doi:10.3390/su13179544

Naseem, M. H., Yang, J., Zhang, T., & Alam, W. (2023). Utilizing Fuzzy AHP in the Evaluation of Barriers to Blockchain Implementation in Reverse Logistics. *Sustainability (Basel)*, *15*(10), 7961. doi:10.3390/su15107961

Negri, M., Cagno, E., Colicchia, C., & Sarkis, J. (2021). Integrating sustainability and resilience in the supply chain: A systematic literature review and a research agenda. *Business Strategy and the Environment*, *30*(7), 2858–2886. doi:10.1002/bse.2776

Neligan, A., Baumgartner, R. J., Geissdoerfer, M., & Schöggl, J. (2022). Circular disruption: Digitalisation as a driver of circular economy business models. *Business Strategy and the Environment*, *32*(3), 1175–1188. doi:10.1002/bse.3100

Ness, D. (2008). Sustainable Urban Infrastructure in China: Towards a Factor 10 Improvement in Resource Productivity through Integrated Infrastructure Systems. *International Journal of Sustainable Development and World Ecology*, *15*(4), 288–301. doi:10.3843/SusDev.15.4:2a

Neumann, W. P., Winkelhaus, S., Grosse, E. H., & Glock, C. H. (2021). Industry 4.0 and the human factor - A systems framework and analysis methodology for successful development. International Journal of Production Economics, 233(November 2020), 107992.

News, I. (2021). *Novartis' Industry 4.0 Tech Transforms Cell Therapy Manufacturing*. LogiPharma.

Nguyen, A. T., Ha, V. D., Ngo, H. K., Le, N., Khong, P. M., Thi, N. T., Trinh, M. T., Nguyen, T. D., Ngo, T. Q. K., Vu, L. C., Thi, M. L., Le, A. H. T., Tran, B. M., & Nguyen, V. T. (2023). Understanding the importance of Eco-Labeling for organic foods at UNESCO Biosphere Reserves: A case study of the cocoa powder at the Dong Nai, Vietnam. *Sustainability (Basel)*, *15*(12), 9603. doi:10.3390/su15129603

Nguyen, G. N., Mani, V., Kha, M. K., & Papadopoulos, T. (2023). Supply chain social responsibility in labour-intensive industries: A practitioner's perspective. *Production Planning and Control*, *34*(4), 371–390. doi:10.1080/09537287.2021.1925172

Nguyen, T. T., Grote, U., Neubacher, F., Rahut, D. B., Hung, M. D. O., & Paudel, G. P. (2023). Security risks from climate change and environmental degradation: Implications for sustainable land use transformation in the Global South. *Current Opinion in Environmental Sustainability*, *63*, 101322. doi:10.1016/j.cosust.2023.101322

Nicolosi, A., Laganà, V. R., & Di Gregorio, D. (2023). Habits, Health and Environment in the Purchase of Bakery Products: Consumption Preferences and Sustainable Inclinations before and during COVID-19. *Foods*, *12*(8), 1661. doi:10.3390/foods12081661 PMID:37107456

Nigmatov, A., Pradeep, A., & Musulmonova, N. (2023). Blockchain technology in improving transparency and efficiency in government operations. *2023 15th International Conference on Electronics, Computers and Artificial Intelligence (ECAI)*. 10.1109/ECAI58194.2023.10194154

Nir, K. (2017). Can blockchain strengthen the internet of things? *IT Professional*, *19*(4), 68–72. doi:10.1109/MITP.2017.3051335

Niyommaneerat, W., Suwanteep, K., & Chavalparit, O. (2023). Sustainability indicators to achieve a circular economy: A case study of renewable energy and plastic waste recycling corporate social responsibility (CSR) projects in Thailand. *Journal of Cleaner Production*, *391*, 136203. doi:10.1016/j.jclepro.2023.136203

Nkanu, W. O. (2010). Digital Divide: Bridging the Gap through ICT in Nigerian Libraries. *Library Philosophy and Practice*.

Nof, S. Y. (2023). *Springer Handbook of Automation*. Springer Nature. doi:10.1007/978-3-030-96729-1

Noh, J. (2023). Reinforcement Learning for Optimizing Can-Order Policy with the Rolling Horizon Method. *Systems*, *11*(7), 350. doi:10.3390/systems11070350

Norgren, A., & Janzon Hägglund, W. (2023). Implementing Artificial Intelligence in Supply Chain Management: A Qualitative Study of How Manufacturing Companies Can Implement AI to Improve Supply Chain Management. Academic Press.

Nova, K. (2023, June 9). *AI-Enabled Water Management Systems: An analysis of system components and interdependencies for water conservation.* https://studies.eigenpub.com/index.php/erst/article/view/12

Novitasari, M., Wijaya, A. L., Agustin, N. M., Gunardi, A., & Dana, L. P. (2023). Corporate social responsibility and firm performance: Green supply chain management as a mediating variable. *Corporate Social Responsibility and Environmental Management, 30*(1), 267–276. doi:10.1002/csr.2353

Nozari, H., & Edalatpanah, S. A. (2023). Smart Systems Risk management in IoT-Based supply chain. In Industrial and applied mathematics (pp. 251–268). doi:10.1007/978-981-19-9909-3_11

Nugroho, A. (2023). *The effect of household income and consumption on family welfare with lifestyle as a moderating variable.* https://doi.org/ doi:10.35335/ijafibs.v11i2.96

Nwabueze & Ozioko. (2011). Information and Communication Technology for Sustainable Development in Nigeria. *Library Philosophy and Practice.*

Nyarko, D. A., & Fong, R. C. (2023). Cyber security compliance among remote workers. In Advanced sciences and technologies for security applications (pp. 343–369). doi:10.1007/978-3-031-20160-8_18

Nydrioti, I., & Grigoropoulou, H. (2022). Using the water footprint concept for water use efficiency labelling of consumer products: The Greek experience. *Environmental Science and Pollution Research International, 30*(8), 19918–19930. doi:10.1007/s11356-022-23573-w PMID:36242669

O'Connell, E., O'Brien, W., Bhattacharya, M., Moore, D., & Penica, M. (2023). Digital Twins: Enabling interoperability in smart manufacturing networks. *Telecom, 4*(2), 265–278. doi:10.3390/telecom4020016

Oborski, P., & Wysocki, P. (2022). Intelligent Visual Quality Control System Based on Convolutional Neural Networks for Holonic Shop Floor Control of Industry 4.0 Manufacturing Systems. *Advances in Science and Technology. The R Journal, 16*(2), 89–98.

Ocelik, V., Kolk, A., & Ciulli, F. (2023). Multinational enterprises, Industry 4.0 and sustainability: A multidisciplinary review and research agenda. *Journal of Cleaner Production, 413*, 137434. doi:10.1016/j.jclepro.2023.137434

Oe, H., Yamaoka, Y., & Duda, K. (2022). How to Sustain Businesses in the Post-COVID-19 Era: A focus on innovation, sustainability and leadership. *Business Ethics and Leadership, 6*(4), 1–9. doi:10.21272/bel.6(4).1-9.2022

Ogbuke, N. J., Yusuf, Y. Y., Dharma, K., & Mercangoz, B. A. (2022). Big data supply chain analytics: Ethical, privacy and security challenges posed to business, industries and society. *Production Planning and Control, 33*(2-3), 123–137. doi:10.1080/09537287.2020.1810764

Okogwu, N. C., Agho, N. M. O., Adeyinka, N. M. A., Odulaja, N. B. A., Eyo-Udo, N. N. L., Daraojimba, N. C., & Banso, N. A. (2023). Exploring the integration of sustainable materials in supply chain management for environmental impact. *Engineering Science & Tecnology Journal, 4*(3), 49–65. doi:10.51594/estj.v4i3.546

Okoli, C. (2015). A Guide to Conducting a Standalone Systematic Literature Review. *Communications of the Association for Information Systems, 37.* Advance online publication. doi:10.17705/1CAIS.03743

Olabi, A., Abdelghafar, A. A., Maghrabie, H. M., Sayed, E. T., Rezk, H., Radi, M. A., Obaideen, K., & Abdelkareem, M. A. (2023). Application of artificial intelligence for prediction, optimization, and control of thermal energy storage systems. *Thermal Science and Engineering Progress, 39*, 101730. doi:10.1016/j.tsep.2023.101730

Oláh, J., Aburumman, N., Popp, J., Khan, M. A., Haddad, H., & Kitukutha, N. (2020). Impact of Industry 4.0 on Environmental Sustainability. *Sustainability, 12*(11), 4674. doi:10.3390/su12114674

Onyeaka, H., Tamasiga, P., Nwauzoma, U. M., Miri, T., Juliet, U. C., Nwaiwu, O., & Akinsemolu, A. A. (2023). Using artificial intelligence to tackle food waste and enhance the circular economy: Maximising resource Efficiency and Minimising Environmental Impact: A review. *Sustainability (Basel), 15*(13), 10482. doi:10.3390/su151310482

Organization, W. T. (2017). *Global Value Chain Development Report 2019.* WTO. doi:10.30875/6b9727ab-en

Ortiz, F. (2023, August 22). *Energy-Efficient On-Board radio resource management for satellite communications via neuromorphic computing.* arXiv.org. https://arxiv.org/abs/2308.11152

Othman, A. E., & ElKady, M. M. (2021). A knowledge management based framework for enhancing the learning culture in architectural design firms in developing countries. *Journal of Engineering. Design and Technology, 21*(1), 23–57. doi:10.1108/JEDT-01-2021-0027

Othman, U., & Yang, E. (2023). Human–robot collaborations in smart manufacturing environments: Review and outlook. *Sensors (Basel), 23*(12), 5663. doi:10.3390/s23125663

Ouedraogo, K. E., Ekim, P. O., & Demirok, E. (2023). Feasibility of low-cost energy management system using embedded optimization for PV and battery storage assisted residential buildings. *Energy, 271*, 126922. doi:10.1016/j.energy.2023.126922

OumaW. N. (2023). Africa's renewable energy dilemma. *Social Science Research Network.* doi:10.2139/ssrn.4477421

Oyinlola, M., Okoya, S. A., Whitehead, T., Evans, M. A., & Lowe, A. S. (2023). The potential of converting plastic waste to 3D printed products in Sub-Saharan Africa. *Resources, Conservation & Recycling Advances, 17*, 200129. doi:10.1016/j.rcradv.2023.200129

Ozkan-Ozen, Y. D., & Kazancoglu, Y. (2021). Analyzing workforce development challenges in the Industry 4.0. *International Journal of Manpower.*https://doi.org/10.1108/IJM-03-2021-0167

Oztemel, E. (2010). Intelligent manufacturing systems. *Artificial intelligence techniques for networked manufacturing enterprises management*, 1-41.

Oztemel, E., & Gursev, S. (2020). Literature review of Industry 4.0 and related technologies. *Journal of Intelligent Manufacturing, 31*(1), 127–182. doi:10.1007/s10845-018-1433-8

Pacaux-Lemoine, M.-P., & Trentesaux, D. (2019). Ethical risks of human-machine symbiosis in industry 4.0: Insights from the human-machine cooperation approach. *IFAC-PapersOnLine, 52*(19), 19–24. doi:10.1016/j.ifacol.2019.12.077

Pacchini, A. P. T., Lucato, W. C., Facchini, F., & Mummolo, G. (2019). The degree of readiness for the implementation of Industry 4.0. *Computers in Industry, 113*, 103125.

Pachouri, V., Singh, R., Gehlot, A., Pandey, S., Shaik, V. A., & Abbas, M. (2024, March). Empowering sustainability in the built environment: A technological Lens on industry 4.0 Enablers. *Technology in Society, 76*, 102427. Advance online publication. doi:10.1016/j.techsoc.2023.102427

Palsodkar, M., Yadav, G., & Nagare, M. (2023). Integrating Industry 4.0 and agile new product development practices to evaluate the penetration of sustainable development goals in manufacturing industries. *Journal of Engineering, Design and Technology.* doi:10.1108/JEDT-02-2022-0101

Pamucar, D., Torkayesh, A. E., & Biswas, S. (2023). Supplier selection in healthcare supply chain management during the COVID-19 pandemic: A novel fuzzy rough decision-making approach. *Annals of Operations Research, 328*(1), 977–1019. doi:10.1007/s10479-022-04529-2 PMID:35039705

Pandey, S., Singh, R. K., & Gunasekaran, A. (2021). Supply chain risks in Industry 4.0 environment: Review and analysis framework. *Production Planning and Control, 34*(13), 1275–1302. doi:10.1080/09537287.2021.2005173

Pandey, V., Sircar, A., Bist, N., Solanki, K. P., & Yadav, K. (2023). Accelerating the renewable energy sector through Industry 4.0: Optimization opportunities in the digital revolution. *International Journal of Innovation Studies, 7*(2), 171–188. doi:10.1016/j.ijis.2023.03.003

Panetto, H., Iung, B., Ivanov, D., Weichhart, G., & Wang, X. (2019). Challenges for the cyber-physical manufacturing enterprises of the future. *Annual Reviews in Control, 47*, 200–213. doi:10.1016/j.arcontrol.2019.02.002

Pan, Y. (2016). Heading toward artificial intelligence 2.0. *Engineering (Beijing), 2*(4), 409–413. doi:10.1016/J.ENG.2016.04.018

Pan, Y., & Froese, F. J. (2023). An interdisciplinary review of AI and HRM: Challenges and future directions. *Human Resource Management Review, 33*(1), 100924. doi:10.1016/j.hrmr.2022.100924

Papetti, A., Ciccarelli, M., Scoccia, C., Palmieri, G., & Germani, M. (2022). A human-oriented design process for collaborative robotics. *International Journal of Computer Integrated Manufacturing, 36*(12), 1760–1782. doi:10.1080/0951192X.2022.2128222

Park, B. I., Xiao, S. S., Shi, Y. P., Wang, M., Wang, B., & Luo, C. (2023). *Future opportunities in supply chain management 4.0*. SAGE.

Pata, U. K., Caglar, A. E., Kartal, M. T., & Depren, S. K. (2023). Evaluation of the role of clean energy technologies, human capital, urbanization, and income on the environmental quality in the United States. *Journal of Cleaner Production, 402*, 136802. doi:10.1016/j.jclepro.2023.136802

Patel, D., Bothra, J., & Patel, V. (2017, January). Blockchain exhumed. In *2017 ISEA Asia Security and Privacy (ISEASP)* (pp. 1-12). IEEE.

Patil, K. R., Garg, V., Gabaldon, J., Patil, H., Niranjan, S., & Hawkins, T. G. (2023). Firm performance in digitally integrated supply chains: A combined perspective of transaction cost economics and relational exchange theory. *Journal of Enterprise Information Management*. Advance online publication. doi:10.1108/JEIM-09-2022-0335

Patil, P. S., Patil, M. S., Tamhankar, S. G., & Patil, S. S. (2020). Ensembles of ensemble machine learning approach for fault detection of bearing. *Solid State Technology, 63*(6), 14442–14455.

Patil, S. M., Baramati, P., Dhone, N. C., & Chourasiya, R. H. (2023). Industry 4.0 technologies in the context of Supply Chain Management 4.0. *The Online Journal of Distance Education and e-Learning : TOJDEL, 11*(2).

Pauceanu, A. M., Rabie, N., & Moustafa, A. (2020). Employability in the fourth industrial revolution. *Economia e Sociologia, 13*(3), 269–283. doi:10.14254/2071- 789X.2020/13-3/17

Pavloudakis, F., Karlopoulos, E., & Roumpos, C. (2023). Just transition governance to avoid socio-economic impacts of lignite phase-out: The case of Western Macedonia, Greece. *The Extractive Industries and Society, 14*, 101248. doi:10.1016/j.exis.2023.101248

Payton, T., & Claypoole, T. (2023). *Privacy in the age of Big data: Recognizing threats, defending your rights, and protecting your family*. Rowman & Littlefield. doi:10.5771/9781538167830

Peake, B., Braund, R., Tremblay, L., & Tong, A. (2016). Impact of pharmaceuticals on the environment. *The Life-Cycle of Pharmaceuticals in the Environment.*

Pearce, C. L., & Locke, E. A. (2023). *Principles of organizational behavior: The Handbook of Evidence-Based Management*. John Wiley & Sons.

Pelaez, R. M., Brust, A. O., Rivera, S., Felix, V., Ostos, R., & Brito, H. (2023). Role of Digital Transformation for Achieving Sustainability: Mediated Role of Stakeholders, Key Capabilities, and Technology. *Sustainability*, 1–27.

Peña, J., & Caruajulca, P. (2022). Industry 4.0 Evolutionary Framework: The Increasing Need to Include the Human Factor. *Journal of Technology Management & Innovation*, *17*(3).http://dx.doi.org/10.4067/S0718-27242022000300070

Peng, Y., Ahmad, S. F., Irshad, M. I., Al-Razgan, M., Ali, Y. A., & Awwad, E. M. (2023). Impact of Digitalization on Process Optimization and Decision-Making towards Sustainability: The Moderating Role of Environmental Regulation. *Sustainability (Basel)*, *15*(20), 15156. doi:10.3390/su152015156

Penumuru, D. P., Muthuswamy, S., & Karumbu, P. (2020). Identification and classification of materials using machine vision and machine learning in the context of industry 4.0. *Journal of Intelligent Manufacturing*, *31*(5), 1229–1241. doi:10.1007/s10845-019-01508-6

Peres, R. S., Azevedo, M., Araújo, S. O., Guedes, M., Miranda, F., & Barata, J. (2021). Generative adversarial networks for data augmentation in structural adhesive inspection. *Applied Sciences (Basel, Switzerland)*, *11*(7), 3086. doi:10.3390/app11073086

Peres, R. S., Barata, J., Leitao, P., & Garcia, G. (2019). Multistage quality control using machine learning in the automotive industry. *IEEE Access : Practical Innovations, Open Solutions*, *7*, 79908–79916. doi:10.1109/ACCESS.2019.2923405

Perifanis, N.-A., & Kitsios, F. (2023). Investigating the Influence of Artificial Intelligence on Business Value in the Digital Era of Strategy: A Literature Review. *Information (Basel)*, *14*(2), 85. https://doi.org/10.3390/info14020085

Pessot, E., Zangiacomi, A., Marchiori, I., & Fornasiero, R. (2023). Empowering supply chains with Industry 4.0 technologies to face megatrends. *Journal of Business Logistics*, *44*(4), 609–640. doi:10.1111/jbl.12360

Pfaff, Y. M. (2023). Agility and digitalization: Why strategic agility is a success factor for mastering digitalization – evidence from Industry 4.0 implementations across a supply chain. *International Journal of Physical Distribution & Logistics Management*, *53*(5/6), 660–684. doi:10.1108/IJPDLM-06-2022-0200

Pham, Q. V., Dev, K., Maddikunta, P. K. R., Gadekallu, T. R., & Huynh-The, T. (2021). Fusion of federated learning and industrial internet of things: a survey. *arXiv preprint arXiv:2101.00798.*

Phuyal, S., Bista, D., & Bista, R. (2020). Challenges, opportunities and future directions of smart manufacturing: A state of art review. *Sustainable Futures : An Applied Journal of Technology, Environment and Society*, *2*, 100023. doi:10.1016/j.sftr.2020.100023

Pianykh, O. S., Langs, G., Dewey, M., Enzmann, D. R., Herold, C. J., Schoenberg, S. O., & Brink, J. A. (2020). Continuous learning AI in radiology: Implementation principles and early applications. *Radiology*, *297*(1), 6–14. doi:10.1148/radiol.2020200038 PMID:32840473

Picasso, F. G., Biazzin, C., Paiva, E. L., & Partyka, R. B. (2021). Socially responsible supply chain initiatives and their outcomes: A taxonomy of manufacturing companies. *Supply Chain Management*, *28*(1), 90–106. doi:10.1108/SCM-11-2020-0578

Picavet, M. E. B., De Macedo, L. S. V., Bellezoni, R. A., & De Oliveira, J. P. (2022). How can Transnational Municipal Networks foster local collaborative governance regimes for environmental management? *Environmental Management, 71*(3), 505–522. doi:10.1007/s00267-022-01685-w PMID:35906346

Pivoto, D. G. S., De Almeida, L. F. F., Da Rosa Righi, R., Rodrigues, J. J. P. C., Lugli, A. B., & Alberti, A. M. (2021). Cyber-physical systems architectures for industrial internet of things applications in Industry 4.0: A literature review. *Journal of Manufacturing Systems, 58*, 176–192. doi:10.1016/j.jmsy.2020.11.017

Pochiraju, K., Patnaik, A., & Basu, A. (2019). A novel method to optimize energy and productivity in Industry 4.0 enabled smart factories. *Journal of Manufacturing Systems, 53*, 113–124.

Polim, R., Hu, Q., & Kumara, S. (2017). Blockchain in megacity logistics. In *IIE Annual Conference. Proceedings* (pp. 1589-1594). Institute of Industrial and Systems Engineers (IISE).

Ponnusamy, V., Aun, Y., Jhanjhi, N. Z., Humayun, M., & Almufareh, M. F. (2022). IoT wireless intrusion detection and network Traffic Analysis. *Computer Systems Science and Engineering, 40*(3), 865–879. doi:10.32604/csse.2022.018801

Ponnusamy, V., Zaman, N., Jung, L. T., & Amin, A. H. M. (2021). *Role of IoT in green energy Systems*. IGI Global. doi:10.4018/978-1-7998-6709-8

Popkova, E. G., Ragulina, Y. V., & Bogoviz, A. V. (2019). Fundamental differences of transition to industry 4.0 from previous industrial revolutions. *Studies in Systems. Decision and Control, 169*, 21–29. doi:10.1007/978-3-319-94310-7_3/COVER

Pottebaum, J., Rossel, J., Somorovsky, J., Acar, Y., Fahr, R., Cabarcos, P. A., Bodden, E., & Gräßler, I. (2023). Re-Envisioning industrial control systems security by considering human factors as a core element of Defense-in-Depth. *2023 IEEE European Symposium on Security and Privacy Workshops (EuroS&PW)*. 10.1109/EuroSPW59978.2023.00048

Pournader, M., Kach, A., & Talluri, S. (2020). A Review of the Existing and Emerging Topics in the Supply Chain Risk Management Literature. *Decision Sciences, 51*(4), 867–919. doi:10.1111/deci.12470 PMID:34234385

Pozzi, F. A., & Dwivedi, D. N. (2023). ESG and IoT: Ensuring Sustainability and Social Responsibility in the Digital Age. In Communications in computer and information science (pp. 12–23). doi:10.1007/978-3-031-47997-7_2

Pozzi, R., Rossi, T., & Secchi, R. (2021). Industry 4.0 technologies: Critical success factors for implementation and improvements in manufacturing companies. *Production Planning and Control, 34*(2), 139–158. doi:10.1080/09537287.2021.1891481

Pradhan, I. P., & Saxena, P. (2023). Reskilling workforce for the Artificial intelligence Age: challenges and the way forward. In Emerald Publishing Limited eBooks (pp. 181–197). doi:10.1108/978-1-80455-662-720230011

Prakash, C., Singh, L., Gupta, A., & Lohan, S. K. (2023). Advancements in smart farming: A comprehensive review of IoT, wireless communication, sensors, and hardware for agricultural automation. *Sensors and Actuators. A, Physical, 362*, 114605. doi:10.1016/j.sna.2023.114605

Pranata, M., & Adhariani, D. (2023). Analysis of the potential implementation of Material Flow Cost Accounting (MFCA) in muslim fashion SMEs Y. *International Journal of Financial, Accounting, and Management, 5*(1), 97–111. doi:10.35912/ijfam.v5i1.1512

Preece, C., Cappellini, B., Larsen, G., Bhogal-Nair, A., Bradshaw, A., Chatzidakis, A., Goulding, C., Keeling, D. I., Lindridge, A., Maclaran, P., Marshall, G. W., & Parsons, E. (2023). Publish or perish: Ensuring our journals don't fail us. *Journal of Marketing Management, 39*(9-10), 1–11. doi:10.1080/0267257X.2023.2244504

Presti, C., De Santis, F., & Bernini, F. (2023). Value co-creation via machine learning from a configuration theory perspective. *European Journal of Innovation Management*, *26*(7), 449–477. doi:10.1108/EJIM-01-2023-0104

procureport. (n.d.). *Components of SCM*. Retrieved from https://blog.procureport.com/components-of-supply-chain-management/

Psarommatis, F., May, G., & Azamfirei, V. (2023). Envisioning maintenance 5.0: Insights from a systematic literature review of Industry 4.0 and a proposed framework. *Journal of Manufacturing Systems*, *68*, 376–399. doi:10.1016/j.jmsy.2023.04.009

Puhlmann, N., Vidaurre, R., & Kummerer, K. (2024). Designing greener active pharmaceutical ingredients: Insights from pharmaceutical industry into drug discovery and development. *European Journal of Pharmaceutical Sciences*, *192*, 106614. doi:10.1016/j.ejps.2023.106614 PMID:37858896

Qahtan, S., Yatim, K., Zulzalil, H., Osman, M. H., Zaidan, A. A., & Alsattar, H. A. (2023). Review of healthcare industry 4.0 application-based blockchain in terms of security and privacy development attributes: Comprehensive taxonomy, open issues and challenges and recommended solution. *Journal of Network and Computer Applications*, *209*, 103529. doi:10.1016/j.jnca.2022.103529

Qayyum, F., Jamil, H., & Ali, F. (2023). A review of smart Energy Management in Residential Buildings for Smart Cities. *Energies*, *17*(1), 83. doi:10.3390/en17010083

Qing, C., Zhou, W., Song, J., Deng, X., & Xu, D. (2023). Impact of outsourced machinery services on farmers' green production behavior: Evidence from Chinese rice farmers. *Journal of Environmental Management*, *327*, 116843. doi:10.1016/j.jenvman.2022.116843 PMID:36459784

Qing, F., Zhang, Y., Sun, B., Guo, X. Y., Fan, D., Ren, Y., Ye, S., & Wang, Z. (2023). Multi-level predictive maintenance of smart manufacturing systems driven by digital twin: A matheuristics approach. *Journal of Manufacturing Systems*, *68*, 443–454. doi:10.1016/j.jmsy.2023.05.004

Qiu, G., & Huang, W. (2023). Mechanical design, manufacture and automation: Research progress and fusion ant colony algorithm-based optimization. *Applied Artificial Intelligence*, *37*(1), 2219565. Advance online publication. doi:10.1080/08839514.2023.2219565

Quarshie, A. M., Salmi, A., & Leuschner, R. (2016). Sustainability and corporate social responsibility in supply chains: The state of research in supply chain management and business ethics journals. *Journal of Purchasing and Supply Management*, *22*(2), 82–97. doi:10.1016/j.pursup.2015.11.001

R, R., Ramamoorthy Sathya, R., V, V., S, B., & N, J. L. (2023). Industry 5.0: Enhancing Human-Robot Collaboration through Collaborative Robots – A Review. *2023 2nd International Conference on Advancements in Electrical, Electronics, Communication, Computing and Automation (ICAECA)*. doi:10.1109/ICAECA56562.2023.10201120

Rad, F. F., Oghazi, P., Palmie, M., Chirumalla, K., Pashkevich, N., Patel, P. C., & Sattari, S. (2022). Industry 4.0 and supply chain performance: A systematic literature review of the benefits, challenges, and critical success factors of 11 core technologies. *Industrial Marketing Management*, *105*, 268–293. doi:10.1016/j.indmarman.2022.06.009

Rahanu, H., Georgiadou, E., Siakas, K., Ross, M., & Berki, E. (2021). *Ethical issues invoked by industry 4.0.* Paper presented at the Systems, Software and Services Process Improvement: 28th European Conference, EuroSPI 2021, Krems, Austria. 10.1007/978-3-030-85521-5_39

Rahman, A. U., Alballa, T., Alqahtani, H., & Khalifa, H. A. E. W. (2023). A Fuzzy Parameterized Multiattribute Decision-Making Framework for Supplier Chain Management Based on Picture Fuzzy Soft Information. *Symmetry*, *15*(10), 1872. doi:10.3390/sym15101872

Rahwan, I. (2018). Society-in-the-loop: Programming the algorithmic social contract. *Ethics and Information Technology, 20*, 5–14.

Raizada, A. (2023, July 12). From automation to digital transformation: the evolution of Industry 4.0. *Copper Digital.* https://copperdigital.com/blog/industry-4-0-evolution-automation-digital-transformation/

Raj, A., Dwivedi, G., Sharma, A., de Sousa Jabbour, A. B. L., & Rajak, S. (2020). Barriers to the adoption of industry 4.0 technologies in the manufacturing sector: An inter-country comparative perspective. *International Journal of Production Economics, 224*, 107546. doi:10.1016/j.ijpe.2019.107546

Raj, A., Dwivedi, G., Sharma, A., Lopes de Sousa Jabbour, A. B., & Rajak, S. (2020). Barriers to the adoption of Industry 4.0 technologies in the manufacturing sector: An inter-country comparative perspective. *International Journal of Production Economics*, •••, 224.https://doi.org/10.1016/j.ijpe.2019.107546

Rajmohan, R., Kumar, T. A., Pavithra, M., & Sandhya, S. (n.d.). *Blockchain: Next-generation technology for industry 4.0.* Academic Press.

Raj, P. V. R. P., Jauhar, S. K., Ramkumar, M., & Pratap, S. (2022). Procurement, traceability and advance cash credit payment transactions in supply chain using blockchain smart contracts. *Computers & Industrial Engineering, 167*, 108038. doi:10.1016/j.cie.2022.108038

Raman, R., Sreenivasan, A., Ma, S., Patwardhan, A., & Nedungadi, P. (2023). Green Supply Chain Management Research Trends and Linkages to UN Sustainable Development Goals. *Sustainability (Basel), 15*(22), 15848. doi:10.3390/su152215848

Ramdurai, B. (2020). *Detailed Review of Cloud based Mobile application for the stroke patient. arXiv.* Cornell University. doi:10.14445/22312803

RaneN.ChoudharyS.RaneJ. (2023). Sustainable tourism development using leading-edge Artificial Intelligence (AI), Blockchain, Internet of Things (IoT), Augmented Reality (AR) and Virtual Reality (VR) technologies. *Social Science Research Network.* doi:10.2139/ssrn.4642605

Rane, S. B., Potdar, P. R., & Aware, S. (2023). *Strategies for development of smart and green products using Blockchain-IoT integrated architecture.* Operations Management Research. doi:10.1007/s12063-023-00398-5

Rani, S., Bhambri, P., Kataria, A., Khang, A., & Sivaraman, A. K. (2023). *Big data, cloud computing and IoT: Tools and Applications.* CRC Press. doi:10.1201/9781003298335

Ranjan, A., Singh, A. N., & Kumar, A. (2023, June 16). *Transforming Judicial Systems with Blockchain: A Court Case Governance System for Tamper-Proof and Transparent Legal Processes.* IEEE Conference Publication | IEEE Xplore. https://ieeexplore.ieee.org/abstract/document/10200234

Rao, P. S., Yaqoob, S. I., Ahmed, M. A., Abdinabievna, P. S., Yaseen, S. M., & Arumugam, M. (2023). Integrated artificial intelligence and predictive maintenance of electric vehicle components with optical and quantum enhancements. *Optical and Quantum Electronics, 55*(10), 855. Advance online publication. doi:10.1007/s11082-023-05135-7

Rashid, A. A. (2018). The Fourth Industrial Revolution impact on the future of sustainable urban development in Malaysia. Urbanice Malaysia. Academia.edu. Accessed from (https://www.academia.edu/36382024/THE_FOURTH_INDUSTRIAL_REVOLUTION_IMPACT_TO_THE_FUTURE_OF_SUSTAINABLE_URBAN_DEVELOPMENT_IN_MALAYSIA).

Rath, M., Satpathy, J., & Oreku, G. S. (2021). Artificial Intelligence and Machine Learning Applications in Cloud Computing and Internet of Things. *Artificial Intelligence to Solve Pervasive Internet of Things Issues*, 103–123. doi:10.1016/B978-0-12-818576-6.00006-X

Rathod, S. (2023, July 16). *Ensuring Optimized Storage with Data Confidentiality and Privacy-Preserving for Secure Data Sharing Model Over Cloud.* https://www.ijisae.org/index.php/IJISAE/article/view/3140

Raufjonov, A. (2023). Industry 4.0: Integrating automation and IoT in manufacturing. *irshadjournals.com.* https://doi.org/ doi:10.59022/ibys.108

Ravi, D., Ramachandran, S., Vignesh, R., Falmari, V. R., & Brindha, M. (2022). *Privacy preserving transparent supply chain management through Hyperledger Fabric.* Academic Press.

Rawindaran, N. (2023). Legal Considerations and Ethical Challenges of Artificial Intelligence on Internet of Things and Smart Cities. In Data Protection in a Post-Pandemic Society: Laws, Regulations, Best Practices and Recent Solutions (pp. 217-239): Springer. doi:10.1007/978-3-031-34006-2_8

Rayar, P., & Kumar, K. N. V. (2023). Triple bottom line Sustainability and Industry 4.0 implementation in Indian MSMEs: a Conceptual model. In Smart innovation, systems and technologies (pp. 425–432). doi:10.1007/978-981-19-8497-6_39

RayhanA.GrossD. (2023). Sustainable Business Ideas: The Ultimate guide to starting and running a profitable and Eco-Friendly business. *ResearchGate.* doi:10.13140/RG.2.2.35344.99847

Ray, P. P., Dash, D., De, D., Salah, K., & Kumar, N. (2020). Blockchain for IoT-Based Healthcare: Background, Consensus, Platforms, and Use Cases. *IEEE Systems Journal.*

Razak, G. M., Hendry, L. C., & Stevenson, M. (2023). Supply chain traceability: A review of the benefits and its relationship with supply chain resilience. *Production Planning and Control, 34*(11), 1114–1134. doi:10.1080/09537287.2021.1983661

Razzak, M. R. (2023, March 7). Mediating effect of productivity between sustainable supply chain management practices and competitive advantage: Evidence from apparel manufacturing in Bangladesh. *Management of Environmental Quality, 34*(2), 428–445. doi:10.1108/MEQ-01-2022-0022

Rea, G., Sverzellati, N., Bocchino, M., Lieto, R., Milanese, G., D'Alto, M., Bocchini, G., Maniscalco, M., Valente, T., & Sica, G. (2023). Beyond Visual interpretation: Quantitative analysis and artificial intelligence in interstitial lung disease diagnosis "Expanding Horizons in Radiology." *Diagnostics (Basel), 13*(14), 2333. doi:10.3390/diagnostics13142333 PMID:37510077

Ream, J., Chu, Y., & Schatsky, D. (2016). Upgrading blockchains: smart contract use cases in industry. *Deloitte insights.* Available at: https://www2.deloitte.com/us/en/insights/focus/signals-for-strategists/using-blockchain-for-smart-contracts.html

Reddy, T. T., Devi, Y. R., & Kavita, G. (2023). Logistics, traceability in food supply chain management. *E3S Web of Conferences, 391,* 01075. doi:10.1051/e3sconf/202339101075

Reddy, K. R. K., Gunasekaran, A., Kalpana, P., Sreedharan, V. R., & Kumar, S. A. (2021). Developing a blockchain framework for the automotive supply chain: A systematic review. *Computers & Industrial Engineering, 157,* 107334. doi:10.1016/j.cie.2021.107334

Reddy, K., Chandu, V., Srilakshmi, S., Thagaram, E., Sahyaja, C., & Osei, B. (2023). Consumers perception on green marketing towards eco-friendly fast moving consumer goods. *International Journal of Engineering Business Management, 15,* 18479790231170962. Advance online publication. doi:10.1177/18479790231170962

Rehman, O. U., & Ali, Y. (2022). Enhancing healthcare supply chain resilience: Decision-making in a fuzzy environment. *International Journal of Logistics Management, 33*(2), 520–546. doi:10.1108/IJLM-01-2021-0004

Rehman, S. U., Giordino, D., Zhang, Q., & Alam, G. M. (2023). Twin transitions & industry 4.0: Unpacking the relationship between digital and green factors to determine green competitive advantage. *Technology in Society*, *73*, 102227. doi:10.1016/j.techsoc.2023.102227

Reis, F., Bastos, Camargo, J., & Salles, A. (2024). Industry 4.0: An investigation of benefits and barriers with managers of Brazilian manufacturers adopters. *Journal of Engineering and Technology Management, 71*. doi:10.1016/j.jengtecman.2023.101786

Rejeb, A., Keogh, J. G., Wamba, S. F., & Treiblmaier, H. (2021). The potentials of augmented reality in supply chain management: A state-of-the-art review. *Management Review Quarterly*, *71*(4), 819–856. doi:10.1007/s11301-020-00201-w

Rendtorff, J. D. (2023). Responsible Business and Integrated Stakeholder Reporting: towards a stakeholder model for integrated reporting of ESG and SDG. In Ethical economy (pp. 49–59). doi:10.1007/978-3-031-26959-2_6

Renugadevi, N., Saravanan, S., & Sudha, C. N. (2023). IoT based smart energy grid for sustainable cites. *Materials Today: Proceedings*, *81*, 98–104. doi:10.1016/j.matpr.2021.02.270

Reza, M. (2023, June 10). *AI-Driven solutions for enhanced waste management and recycling in urban areas.* https://vectoral.org/index.php/IJSICS/article/view/9

Riaz, M., Farid, H. M. A., Jana, C., Pal, M., & Sarkar, B. (2023). Efficient city supply chain management through spherical fuzzy dynamic multistage decision analysis. *Engineering Applications of Artificial Intelligence*, *126*, 106712. doi:10.1016/j.engappai.2023.106712

Rijal, S., & Saranani, F. (2023). The role of blockchain technology in increasing economic transparency and public trust. *Technology and Society Perspectives*, *1*(2), 56–67. doi:10.61100/tacit.v1i2.51

Rikhardsson, P., & Yigitbasioglu, O. (2018). Business intelligence & analytics in management accounting research: Status and future focus. *International Journal of Accounting Information Systems*, *29*, 37–58.

Rind, Y. M., Raza, M. H., Zubair, M., Mehmood, M. Q., & Massoud, Y. (2023). Smart energy meters for smart grids, an internet of things perspective. *Energies*, *16*(4), 1974. doi:10.3390/en16041974

Rivas, A., Fraile, J. M., Chamoso, P., González-Briones, A., Sittón, I., & Corchado, J. M. (2020). A predictive maintenance model using recurrent neural networks. In *14th International Conference on Soft Computing Models in Industrial and Environmental Applications (SOCO 2019) Seville, Spain, May 13–15, 2019, Proceedings 14* (pp. 261-270). Springer International Publishing.10.1007/978-3-030-20055-8_25

Rivera, L., Ortíz, N. R., Moreno, G., & Páez-Gabriunas, I. (2023). The effect of company ownership on the environmental practices in the supply chain: An Empirical approach. *Sustainability (Basel)*, *15*(16), 12450. doi:10.3390/su151612450

Robson, G. J., & Tsou, J. Y. (2023). *Technology Ethics: A Philosophical Introduction and Readings*. Taylor & Francis. doi:10.4324/9781003189466

Rocha, C. F., Mamédio, D. F., & Quandt, C. O. (2019). Startups and the innovation ecosystem in Industry 4.0. *Technology Analysis and Strategic Management*, *31*(12), 1474–1487.

Roman, R., Alcaraz, C., Lopez, J., & Sakurai, K. (2023). Current Perspectives on Securing Critical Infrastructures' Supply Chains. *IEEE Security and Privacy*, *21*(4), 29–38. doi:10.1109/MSEC.2023.3247946

Rosado, D. G., Santos-Olmo, A., Sánchez, L. E., Serrano, M. A., Blanco, C., Mouratidis, H., & Fernández-Medina, E. (2022). Managing cybersecurity risks of cyber-physical systems: The MARISMA-CPS pattern. *Computers in Industry*, *142*, 103715. Advance online publication. doi:10.1016/j.compind.2022.103715

Rosário, A. T., & Dias, J. C. (2023). How Industry 4.0 and Sensors Can Leverage product Design: Opportunities and challenges. *Sensors (Basel), 23*(3), 1165. doi:10.3390/s23031165 PMID:36772206

Roth, L., Lowitzsch, J., & Yildiz, Ö. (2023). Which (co-)ownership types in renewables are associated with the willingness to adopt energy-efficient technologies and energy-conscious behaviour? Data from German households. *Energy Policy, 180*, 113683. doi:10.1016/j.enpol.2023.113683

Rousseau, D., Manning, J., & Denyer, D. (2008). Evidence in Management and Organizational Science Assembling the Field's Full Weight of Scientific Knowledge Through Syntheses. *The Academy of Management Annals, 2*(1), 475–515. doi:10.5465/19416520802211651

Rupp, M., Schneckenburger, M., Merkel, M., Börret, R., & Harrison, D. K. (2021). Industry 4.0: A Technological-Oriented Definition Based on Bibliometric Analysis and Literature Review. *Journal of Open Innovation, 7*(1), 68.https://doi.org/10.3390/joitmc7010068

Ryalat, M., ElMoaqet, H., & AlFaouri, M. (2023). Design of a smart factory based on cyber-physical systems and internet of things towards Industry 4.0. *Applied Sciences (Basel, Switzerland), 13*(4), 2156.

Ryalat, M., ElMoaqet, H., & AlFaouri, M. (2023). Design of a Smart Factory Based on Cyber-Physical Systems and Internet of Things towards Industry 4.0. *Applied Sciences (Basel, Switzerland), 13*(4), 2156. doi:10.3390/app13042156

Saarika, P. S., Sandhya, K., & Sudha, T. (2017). Smart transportation system using IoT. In *Proceedings of the International Conference on Smart Technologies for Smart Nation (SmartTechCon)* (pp. 1104-1107).

Saberi, S., Kouhizadeh, M., Sarkis, J., & Shen, L. (2019). Blockchain technology and its relationships to sustainable supply chain management. *International Journal of Production Research, 57*(7), 2117–2135. doi:10.1080/00207543.2018.1533261

Sabu, S., Ramalingam, H. M., Vishaka, M., Swapna, H. R., & Hegde, S. (2021). Implementation of a Secure and privacy-aware E-Health record and IoT data Sharing using Blockchain. *Global Transitions Proceedings, 2*(2), 429–433. doi:10.1016/j.gltp.2021.08.033

Saccani, N., Bressanelli, G., & Visintin, F. (2023). Circular supply chain orchestration to overcome Circular Economy challenges: An empirical investigation in the textile and fashion industries. *Sustainable Production and Consumption, 35*, 469–482. doi:10.1016/j.spc.2022.11.020

Sadiku, M. N., Ajayi-Majebi, A. J., & Adebo, P. O. (2023). Smart Manufacturing. In *Emerging Technologies in Manufacturing* (pp. 49–66). Springer. doi:10.1007/978-3-031-23156-8_4

Saeed, M. A., & Kersten, W. (2019). Drivers of Sustainable Supply Chain Management: Identification and Classification. *Sustainability, 11*(4), 1137. doi:10.3390/su11041137

Sahal, R., Breslin, J. G., & Ali, M. I. (2020). Big data and stream processing platforms for Industry 4.0 requirements mapping for a predictive maintenance use case. *Journal of Manufacturing Systems, 54*, 138–151.

Sahoo, S., Kumar, S., Sivarajah, U., Lim, W. M., Westland, J., & Kumar, A. (2022). Blockchain for sustainable supply chain management:trends and ways forward. *Electronic Commerce Research*. Advance online publication. doi:10.1007/s10660-022-09569-1

Said, G. (2023). Adapting Legal Systems to the Development of Artificial Intelligence: Solving the Global Problem of AI in Judicial Processes. *irshadjournals.com*. https://doi.org/ doi:10.59022/ijcl.49

Saidakhrarovich, G. S., & Tursunovich, K. O. (2022). Digital Future & Cyber Security Necessity. *World Bulletin of Management and Law, 10*, 31–45.

Saidani, M., Bayless, J. R., Huey, D., Kim, H. M., & Anderson, K. L. (2023). Life cycle assessment and circular economy indicators to design sustainable electric outboards: results from workshops with industrial experts. *Proceedings of the Design Society*, *3*, 2445–2454. doi:10.1017/pds.2023.245

Sajjad, M., Hu, A., Waqar, A., Falqi, I. I., Alsulamy, S., Bageis, A. S., & Alshehri, A. (2023). Evaluation of the success of Industry 4.0 digitalization Practices for sustainable Construction Management: Chinese Construction Industry. *Buildings*, *13*(7), 1668. doi:10.3390/buildings13071668

Salahdine, F., Han, T., & Zhang, N. (2022). Security in 5G and beyond recent advances and future challenges. *Security and Privacy*, *6*(1), e271. Advance online publication. doi:10.1002/spy2.271

Saleem, J., Tahir, F., Baig, M. Z. K., Al-Ansari, T., & McKay, G. (2023). Assessing the environmental footprint of recycled plastic pellets: A life-cycle assessment perspective. *Environmental Technology & Innovation*, *32*, 103289. doi:10.1016/j.eti.2023.103289

Salim, S. (2023). Promoting firm performance via board of directors effectiveness: A study of financial services companies. . . *ResearchGate*. https://www.researchgate.net/publication/373777145_PROMOTING_FIRM_PERFORMANCE_VIA_BOARD_OF_DIRECTORS_EFFECTIVENESS_A_STUDY_OF_FINANCIAL_SERVICES_COMPANIES_IN_NEW_ORLEANS

Sanders, N. R., Boone, T., Ganeshan, R., & Wood, J. D. (2019). Sustainable Supply Chains in the Age of AI and Digitization: Research Challenges and Opportunities. *Journal of Business Logistics*, *40*(3), 229–240. doi:10.1111/jbl.12224

Sankarananth, S., Karthiga, M., Suganya, E., Sountharrajan, S., & Bavirisetti, D. P. (2023). AI-enabled metaheuristic optimization for predictive management of renewable energy production in smart grids. *Energy Reports*, *10*, 1299–1312. doi:10.1016/j.egyr.2023.08.005

Sankar, S., Ramasubbareddy, S., Luhach, A. K., Deverajan, G. G., Alnumay, W. S., Jhanjhi, N. Z., Ghosh, U., & Sharma, P. K. (2020). Energy efficient optimal parent selection based routing protocol for Internet of Things using firefly optimization algorithm. *Transactions on Emerging Telecommunications Technologies*, *32*(8), e4171. Advance online publication. doi:10.1002/ett.4171

Santhi, A. R., & Muthuswamy, P. (2023). Industry 5.0 or industry 4.0S? Introduction to industry 4.0 and a peek into the prospective industry 5.0 technologies. *International Journal on Interactive Design and Manufacturing*, *17*(2), 947–979. doi:10.1007/s12008-023-01217-8

Santhi, R. A., & Muthuswamy, P. (2023). Industry 5.0 or Industry 4.0S? Introduction to Industry 4.0 and a peek into the prospective industry 5.0 technologies. *International Journal of Interactive Design and Manufacturing*, *17*, 947–979. https://doi.org/10.1007/s12008-023-01217-8

Santos, E. (2023). From Neglect to Progress: Assessing social sustainability and decent work in the tourism sector. *Sustainability (Basel)*, *15*(13), 10329. doi:10.3390/su151310329

Saqib, N., Durán, I. A., & Ozturk, I. (2023). Unraveling the Interrelationship of Digitalization, Renewable Energy, and Ecological Footprints within the EKC Framework: Empirical Insights from the United States. *Sustainability (Basel)*, *15*(13), 10663. doi:10.3390/su151310663

Sarkar, B. D., Shankar, R., & Kar, A. K. (2022). Port logistic issues and challenges in the Industry 4.0 era for emerging economies: An India perspective. *Benchmarking*, *30*(1), 50–74. doi:10.1108/BIJ-08-2021-0499

Sarkar, S., & Kedas, S. (2022). Globally distributed talent communities: A typology of innovation problems and talent characteristics. *Thunderbird International Business Review*, *65*(1), 89–102. doi:10.1002/tie.22272

Sarker, I. H. (2021). Machine learning: Algorithms, real-world applications and research directions. *SN Computer Science*, *2*(3), 160. doi:10.1007/s42979-021-00592-x PMID:33778771

Sarpong, F. A., Sappor, P., Nyantakyi, G., Ahakwa, I., Agyeiwaa, O. E., & Cobbinah, B. B. (2023). From traditional roots to digital bytes: Can digitalizing ESG improves Ghanaian rural banks' brand equity through stakeholder engagement, and customer loyalty? *Cogent Business & Management*, *10*(2), 2232159. Advance online publication. doi:10.1080/23311975.2023.2232159

Sasikumar, A., Subramaniyaswamy, V., Kotecha, K., Indragandhi, V., Ravi, L., Selvachandran, G., & Abraham, A. (2023). Blockchain-based trust mechanism for digital twin empowered Industrial Internet of Things. *Future Generation Computer Systems*, *141*, 16–27. doi:10.1016/j.future.2022.11.002

Sawant, R., Thomas, B., & Kadlag, S. (2022). Reskilling and upskilling: To stay relevant in today's industry. *International Review of Business and Economics*, *7*(1). Advance online publication. doi:10.56902/IRBE.2022.7.1.4

Saxena, S., Nagpal, A., Prashar, T., Shravan, M., Al-Hilali, A. A., & Alazzam, M. B. (2023). Blockchain for Supply Chain Traceability: Opportunities and Challenges. *2023 3rd International Conference on Advance Computing and Innovative Technologies in Engineering (ICACITE)*. 10.1109/ICACITE57410.2023.10182416

Schleich, B., Anwer, N., Mathieu, L., & Wartzack, S. (2017). Shaping the digital twin for design and production engineering. *CIRP Annals*, *66*(1), 141–144. doi:10.1016/j.cirp.2017.04.040

Schneider, J., Abraham, R., Meske, C., & Brocke, J. V. (2022). Artificial Intelligence Governance For Businesses. *Information Systems Management*, 1–21. doi:10.1080/10580530.2022.2085825

Schoenherr, T., Mena, C., Vakil, B., & Choi, T. Y. (2023). Creating resilient supply chains through a culture of measuring. *Journal of Purchasing and Supply Management*, *29*(4), 100824. doi:10.1016/j.pursup.2023.100824

Schubert, H. (n.d.). *Robots are coming and they're automating pharma research*. NNE. https://www.nne.com/techtalk/robots-are-coming-and-theyre-automating-pharma-research/

Schuster, A., Zoll, M., Otto, I. M., & Stölzel, F. (2023). The unjust just transition? Exploring different dimensions of justice in the lignite regions of Lusatia, Eastern Greater Poland, and Gorj. *Energy Research & Social Science*, *104*, 103227. doi:10.1016/j.erss.2023.103227

Schwab, K. (2016). The Fourth Industrial Revolution: What it means and how to respond. World Economic Forum. Retrieved from https://www.weforum.org/agenda/2016/01/thefourth-industrial-revolution-what-it-meansand-how-to-respond [Accessed September 2023]

Seele, P. (2016). Digitally Unified Reporting: How XBRL-Based Real-Time Transparency Helps in Combining Integrated Sustainability Reporting and Performance Control. *Journal of Cleaner Production*, *136*, 65–77. doi:10.1016/j.jclepro.2016.01.102

Sekonya, N., & Sithungu, S. (2023). The impact of edge computing on the industrial internet of things. *Proceedings of the . . . International Conference on Information Warfare and Security*, *18*(1), 360–368. 10.34190/iccws.18.1.969

Sellitto, M. A., Hermann, F. F., Blezs, A. E. Jr, & Barbosa-Póvoa, A. P. (2019). Describing and organizing green practices in the context of Green Supply Chain Management: Case studies. *Resources, Conservation and Recycling*, *145*, 1–10. doi:10.1016/j.resconrec.2019.02.013

Sen, A. A. A., Eassa, F. A., Jambi, K., & Yamin, M. (2018). Preserving privacy in Internet of Things: A survey. *International Journal of Information Technology : an Official Journal of Bharati Vidyapeeth's Institute of Computer Applications and Management*, *10*(2), 189–200.

Senapati, T., & Yager, R. R. (2020). Fermatean fuzzy sets. *Journal of Ambient Intelligence and Humanized Computing, 11*(2), 663–674. doi:10.1007/s12652-019-01377-0

Senghor, K., Partelow, S., Herrera, C. G., & Osemwegie, I. (2023). Conflicting governance realities: Aligning historical and cultural practices with formal marine protected area co-management in Senegal. *Marine Policy, 155*, 105706. doi:10.1016/j.marpol.2023.105706

Seong, T. B., Ponnusamy, V., Jhanjhi, N. Z., Annur, R., & Talib, M. (2021). A comparative analysis on traditional wired datasets and the need for wireless datasets for IoT wireless intrusion detection. *Indonesian Journal of Electrical Engineering and Computer Science, 22*(2), 1165. doi:10.11591/ijeecs.v22.i2.pp1165-1176

Seyedghorban, Z., Samson, D., & Tahernejad, H. (2020). Digitalization opportunities for the procurement function: Pathways to maturity. *International Journal of Operations & Production Management, 40*(11), 1685–1693. doi:10.1108/IJOPM-04-2020-0214

Shabir, I., Dash, K. K., Dar, A. H., Pandey, V. K., Fayaz, U., Srivastava, S., & Nisha, R. (2023). Carbon footprints evaluation for sustainable food processing system development: A comprehensive review. *Future Foods : a Dedicated Journal for Sustainability in Food Science, 7*, 100215. doi:10.1016/j.fufo.2023.100215

Shafi, I., Mazahir, M. F., Fatima, A., Álvarez, R. M., Miro, Y., Espinosa, J. C. M., & Ashraf, I. (2023). Deep Learning-Based real time defect detection for optimization of aircraft manufacturing and control performance. *Drones (Basel), 7*(1), 31. doi:10.3390/drones7010031

Shah, I. A., Sial, Q., Jhanjhi, N. Z., & Gaur, L. (2023). The role of the iot and digital twin in the healthcare digitalization process: Iot and digital twin in the healthcare digitalization process. In Digital Twins and Healthcare: Trends, Techniques, and Challenges (pp. 20-34). IGI Global.

Shah, H., Gardas, B. B., Narwane, V. S., & Mehta, H. S. (2021). The contemporary state of big data analytics and artificial intelligence towards intelligent supply chain risk management: A comprehensive review. *Kybernetes, 52*(5), 1643–1697. doi:10.1108/K-05-2021-0423

Shah, I. A., Jhanjhi, N., & Laraib, A. (2023). Cybersecurity and Blockchain Usage in Contemporary Business. In *Handbook of Research on Cybersecurity Issues and Challenges for Business and FinTech Applications* (pp. 49–64). IGI Global.

ShahinM.ChenF. F.HosseinzadehA. Z.ZandN. (2023). Using machine learning and deep learning algorithms for downtime minimization in manufacturing systems: an early failure detection diagnostic service. Research Square *(*Research Square*)*. doi:10.21203/rs.3.rs-2895149/v1

Shahpasand, R., Talebian, A., & Mishra, S. (2023). Investigating environmental and economic impacts of the 3D printing technology on supply chains: The case of tire production. *Journal of Cleaner Production, 390*, 135917. doi:10.1016/j.jclepro.2023.135917

Shahzad, M., Du, J., & Junaid, M. (2023). Impact of green HRM practices on sustainable performance: Mediating role of green innovation, green culture, and green employees' behavior. *Environmental Science and Pollution Research International, 30*(38), 88524–88547. doi:10.1007/s11356-023-28498-6 PMID:37438507

Shahzad, M., Qu, Y., Zafar, A. U., Rehman, S. U., & Islam, T. (2020). Exploring the Influence of Knowledge Management Process on Corporate Sustainable Performance through Green Innovation. *Journal of Knowledge Management, 24*(9), 2079–2106. doi:10.1108/JKM-11-2019-0624

Shamsuddoha, M., Kashem, M. A., & Nasir, T. (2023). Smart Transportation Logistics: Achieving Supply Chain Efficiency with Green Initiatives. In Greening of industry networks studies (pp. 243–258). doi:10.1007/978-3-031-29823-3_10

Shao, X.-F., Liu, W., Li, Y., Chaudhry, H. R., & Yue, X.-G. (2021). Multistage implementation framework for smart supply chain management under industry 4.0. *Technological Forecasting and Social Change*, *162*, 120354. doi:10.1016/j.techfore.2020.120354

Sharma, H., Garg, R., Sewani, H., & Kashef, R. (2023). Towards A Sustainable and Ethical Supply Chain Management: The Potential of IoT Solutions. *arXiv preprint arXiv:2303.18135.*

Sharma, A., Kosasih, E., Zhang, J., Brintrup, A., & Calinescu, A. (2022). Digital Twins: State of the art theory and practice, challenges, and open research questions. *Journal of Industrial Information Integration*, *30*, 100383. doi:10.1016/j.jii.2022.100383

Sharma, C. (2023). Security and Privacy Aspects of Cyber Physical Systems. In *Cyber Physical Systems* (pp. 53–66). Chapman and Hall/CRC.

Sharma, D., Pate, P., & Shah, M. (2023). A comprehensive study on Industry 4.0 in the pharmaceutical industry for sustainable development. *Environmental Science and Pollution Research International*, *30*(39), 90088–90098. doi:10.1007/s11356-023-26856-y PMID:37129827

Sharma, I., & Tiwari, V. (2023). Modeling the impact of techno-stress and burnout on employees' work-life balance and turnover intention: A job demands-resources theory perspective. *Global Business and Organizational Excellence*, *43*(1), 121–134. doi:10.1002/joe.22206

Sharma, M., Kamble, S., Mani, V., Sehrawat, R., Belhadi, A., & Sharma, V. (2021). Industry 4.0 adoption for sustainability in multi-tier manufacturing supply chain in emerging economies. *Journal of Cleaner Production*, *281*, 125013. doi:10.1016/j.jclepro.2020.125013

Sharma, M., Sehrawat, R., Giannakis, M., & Dwivedi, Y. K. (2023). Learnings from Industry 4.0 for transitioning towards Industry 4.0+: Challenges and solutions for Indian pharmaceutical sector. *Annals of Operations Research*. Advance online publication. doi:10.1007/s10479-023-05391-6 PMID:37361066

Sharma, V., Raut, R. D., Hajiaghaei-Keshteli, M., Narkhede, B. E., Gokhale, R., & Priyadarshinee, P. (2022). Mediating effect of industry 4.0 technologies on the supply chain management practices and supply chain performance. *Journal of Environmental Management*, *322*, 115945. doi:10.1016/j.jenvman.2022.115945

Shayganmehr, M., Kumar, A., Garza-Reyes, J. A., & Moktadir, M. A. (2021). Industry 4.0 enablers for a cleaner production and circular economy within the context of business ethics: A study in a developing country. *Journal of Cleaner Production*, *281*, 125280. doi:10.1016/j.jclepro.2020.125280

Shee, H. (2023). Internet of things. In Springer eBooks (pp. 1–19). doi:10.1007/978-3-030-89822-9_78-1

Shehada, D., Gawanmeh, A., Yeun, C. Y., & Zemerly, M. J. (2022). Fog-based distributed trust and reputation management system for internet of things. *Journal of King Saud University. Computer and Information Sciences*, *34*(10), 8637–8646.

Shen, X., Zhang, Z., Ma, Y., Zou, X., Zhou, F., Wang, S., & Qiu, B. (2023). Prediction of minimum ignition energy for combustible dust using graph neural networks and SMILES data augmentation. *Powder Technology*, *118876*, 118876. Advance online publication. doi:10.1016/j.powtec.2023.118876

Shi, B., Tu, X., Wu, B., & Peng, Y. (2023). Recent Advances in Time-Sensitive Network Configuration Management: A Literature Review. *Journal of Sensor and Actuator Networks*, *12*(4), 52. doi:10.3390/jsan12040052

Shi, H., Feng, T., & Zhu, Z. (2023). The impact of big data analytics capability on green supply chain integration: An organizational information processing theory perspective. *Business Process Management Journal*, *29*(2), 550–577. doi:10.1108/BPMJ-08-2022-0411

Shirazi, H., Muramudalige, S. R., Ray, I., & Jayasumana, A. P. (2020, November). Improved phishing detection algorithms using adversarial autoencoder synthesized data. In *2020 IEEE 45th conference on local computer networks (LCN)* (pp. 24-32). IEEE. 10.1109/LCN48667.2020.9314775

Shi, Z., Xie, Y., Xue, W., Chen, Y., Fu, L., & Xu, X. (2020). Smart factory in Industry 4.0. *Systems Research and Behavioral Science*, *37*(4), 607–617. doi:10.1002/sres.2704

Shneiderman, B. (2020). Bridging the gap between ethics and practice: Guidelines for reliable, safe, and trustworthy human-centered AI systems. *ACM Transactions on Interactive Intelligent Systems*, *10*(4), 1–31. doi:10.1145/3419764

Shojaeshafiei, M., Etzkorn, L., & Anderson, M. (2020). Analytic hierarchy process-based fuzzy measurement to quantify vulnerabilities of web applications. *International Journal of Computer Networks and Communications*, *12*(4), 105–123. doi:10.5121/ijcnc.2020.12407

Sibhensana, B., & Maistry, S. (2023). Conceptualising public-private partnerships for social innovation through community engagement in higher education institutions. *South African Journal of Higher Education*, 1–21. doi:10.20853/37-1-5669

Siems, E., Seuring, S., & Schilling, L. (2022). Stakeholder roles in sustainable supply chain management: A literature review. *Journal of Business Economics*, *93*(4), 747–775. doi:10.1007/s11573-022-01117-5

Silva, P. M., Moreira, A. C., & Mota, J. (2022). Employees' perception of corporate social responsibility and performance: The mediating roles of job satisfaction, organizational commitment and organizational trust. *Journal of Strategy and Management*, *16*(1), 92–111. doi:10.1108/JSMA-10-2021-0213

Simon, C. G. K., Jhanjhi, N. Z., Goh, W. W., & Sukumaran, S. (2022). Applications of machine learning in knowledge management system: A comprehensive review. *Journal of Information & Knowledge Management*, *21*(02), 2250017. doi:10.1142/S0219649222500174

Sindiramutty, S. R., Jhanjhi, N. Z., Ray, S. K., Jazri, H., Khan, N. A., & Gaur, L. (2024). Metaverse: Virtual Meditation. In Advances in medical technologies and clinical practice book series (pp. 93–158). IGI Global. doi:10.4018/978-1-6684-9823-1.ch003

Sindiramutty, S. R., Jhanjhi, N. Z., Ray, S. K., Jazri, H., Khan, N. A., Gaur, L., Gharib, A. H., & Manchuri, A. R. (2024). Metaverse: Virtual Gyms and Sports. In Advances in medical technologies and clinical practice book series (pp. 24–92). IGI Global. doi:10.4018/978-1-6684-9823-1.ch002

Sindiramutty, S. R., Jhanjhi, N. Z., Tan, C. E., Khan, N. A., Gharib, A. H., & Yun, K. J. (2024). Applications of blockchain technology in supply chain management. In Advances in logistics, operations, and management science book series (pp. 248–304). doi:10.4018/978-1-6684-7625-3.ch009

Sindiramutty, S. R., Jhanjhi, N. Z., Tan, C. E., Khan, N. A., Shah, B., & Gaur, L. (2024). Securing the digital supply chain cyber threats and vulnerabilities. In Advances in logistics, operations, and management science book series (pp. 156–223). doi:10.4018/978-1-6684-7625-3.ch007

Sindiramutty, S. R., Jhanjhi, N. Z., Tan, C. E., Tee, W. J., Lau, S. P., Jazri, H., Ray, S. K., & Zaheer, M. A. (2024). IoT and AI-Based Smart Solutions for the Agriculture Industry. In Advances in Explainable AI Applications for Smart Cities (pp. 317–351). doi:10.4018/978-1-6684-6361-1.ch012

Sindiramutty, S. R., Tan, C., Lau, S. P., Thangaveloo, R., Gharib, A. H., Manchuri, A. R., Khan, N. A., Tee, W. J., & Muniandy, L. (2024). Explainable AI for Cybersecurity. In Advances in Explainable AI Applications for Smart Cities (pp. 31–97). doi:10.4018/978-1-6684-6361-1.ch002

Sindiramutty, S. R., Tan, C., Tee, W. J., Lau, S. P., Balakrishnan, S., Kaur, S. D. A., Jazri, H., & Aslam, M. (2024). Modern Smart Cities and Open Research Challenges and Issues of Explainable Artificial Intelligence. In Advances in Explainable AI Applications for Smart Cities (pp. 389–424). doi:10.4018/978-1-6684-6361-1.ch015

Sindiramutty, S. R., Tee, W. J., Balakrishnan, S., Kaur, S., Thangaveloo, R., Jazri, H., Khan, N. A., Gharib, A. H., & Manchuri, A. R. (2024). Explainable AI in Healthcare Application. In Advances in Explainable AI Applications for Smart Cities (pp. 123–176). doi:10.4018/978-1-6684-6361-1.ch005

Singh, U. P. (2023, July 22). *Development of sustainable and biodegradable materials for packaging*. http://jsrt.innovascience.uz/index.php/jsrt/article/view/246

Singh, A., Kumar, V. R. P., Irfan, M., Mohandes, S. R., & Awan, U. (2023). Revealing the Barriers of blockchain technology for supply chain transparency and sustainability in the construction industry: An application of Pythagorean FAHP methods. *Sustainability (Basel)*, *15*(13), 10681. doi:10.3390/su151310681

Singh, A., Kumar, V., Verma, P., & Kandasamy, J. (2023). Identification and severity assessment of challenges in the adoption of industry 4.0 in Indian construction industry. *Asia Pacific Management Review*, *28*(3), 299–315. doi:10.1016/j.apmrv.2022.10.007

Singh, A., Kumar, V., Verma, P., & Ramtiyal, B. (2022). Can suppliers be sustainable in construction supply chains? Evidence from a construction company using best worst approach. *Management of Environmental Quality*. Advance online publication. doi:10.1108/MEQ-03-2022-0057

Singh, A., Madaan, G., Hr, S., & Kumar, A. (2022). Smart manufacturing systems: A futuristics roadmap towards application of industry 4.0 technologies. *International Journal of Computer Integrated Manufacturing*, *36*(3), 411–428. doi:10.1080/0951192X.2022.2090607

Singhal, V., Jain, S. P., Anand, D., Singh, A., Verma, S., Kavita, Rodrigues, J. J. P. C., Jhanjhi, N. Z., Ghosh, U., Jo, O., & Iwendi, C. (2020). Artificial Intelligence Enabled Road Vehicle-Train Collision Risk Assessment Framework for Unmanned railway level crossings. *IEEE Access : Practical Innovations, Open Solutions*, *8*, 113790–113806. doi:10.1109/ACCESS.2020.3002416

Singh, D., & Singh, B. (2020). Investigating the impact of data normalization on classification performance. *Applied Soft Computing*, *97*, 105524. doi:10.1016/j.asoc.2019.105524

Singh, P. K., & Kumar, A. (2023). Cyber Physical Systems in Supply Chain Management. In *Cyber Physical Systems* (pp. 85–110). Chapman and Hall/CRC.

Singh, S. K., Rathore, S., & Park, J. H. (2020). Blockiotintelligence: A blockchain-enabled intelligent IoT architecture with artificial intelligence. *Future Generation Computer Systems*, *110*, 721–743. doi:10.1016/j.future.2019.09.002

Sivaraman, P., Ilakiya, P., Prabhu, M., & Ajayan, A. (2023). Real-Time gearbox defect detection using IIOT-Based Condition Monitoring System. *SAE Technical Paper Series*. doi:10.4271/2023-01-5057

Škare, M., De Las Mercedes De Obesso, M., & Ribeiro-Navarrete, S. (2023). Digital transformation and European small and medium enterprises (SMEs): A comparative study using digital economy and society index data. *International Journal of Information Management*, *68*, 102594. doi:10.1016/j.ijinfomgt.2022.102594

Skordilis, E., & Moghaddass, R. (2020). A deep reinforcement learning approach for real-time sensor-driven decision making and predictive analytics. *Computers & Industrial Engineering*, *147*, 106600. doi:10.1016/j.cie.2020.106600

Sn, R. B. (2023). *Industry 4.0 for pharmaceutical manufacturing; smart factories for future*. doi:10.55529/jcpp.33.17.23

Sobb, T., Turnbull, B., & Moustafa, N. (2020). Supply chain 4.0: A survey of cyber security challenges, solutions and future directions. *Electronics (Basel)*, *9*(11), 1864. doi:10.3390/electronics9111864

Sohrabi, M. (2023). Artificial Intelligence in Logistic Industry. In Duwar (pp. 73–86). doi:10.59287/idtscm.70

Soltani, S., Maxwell, D., & Rashidi, A. (2023). The State of Industry 4.0 in the Australian Construction Industry: An examination of industry and academic point of view. *Buildings*, *13*(9), 2324. doi:10.3390/buildings13092324

Song, W., Ma, Y., Fan, X., & Peng, X. (2023). Corporate environmental ethics and employee's green creativity? The perspective of environmental commitment. *Corporate Social Responsibility and Environmental Management*, *30*(4), 1856–1868. doi:10.1002/csr.2459

Song, Y., Li, Y., & Liu, T. (2023). Carbon asset remolding and potential benefit measurement of machinery products in the light of lean production and low-carbon investment. *Technological Forecasting and Social Change*, *186*, 122166. doi:10.1016/j.techfore.2022.122166

Soni, R. G., & Soni, B. (2019). *Evolution of supply chain management: Ethical issues for leaders.* Paper presented at the Competition Forum.

Soori, M., Arezoo, B., & Dastres, R. (2023). Digital Twin for Smart Manufacturing, A Review. *Sustainable Manufacturing and Service Economics*, *100017*. Advance online publication. doi:10.1016/j.smse.2023.100017

Soori, M., Arezoo, B., & Dastres, R. (2023a). Advanced virtual manufacturing systems: A review. *Journal of Advanced Manufacturing Science and Technology*, *3*(3), 2023009. doi:10.51393/j.jamst.2023009

Soori, M., Arezoo, B., & Dastres, R. (2023a). Internet of things for smart factories in industry 4.0, a review. *Internet of Things and Cyber-Physical Systems*, *3*, 192–204. doi:10.1016/j.iotcps.2023.04.006

Soori, M., Arezoo, B., & Dastres, R. (2023b). Optimization of energy consumption in industrial robots, a review. *Cognitive Robotics*, *3*, 142–157. doi:10.1016/j.cogr.2023.05.003

Sordi, A., Tate, W. L., & Huang, F. (2022). Going beyond supplier diversity to economic Inclusion:Where are we now and where do we go from here? *Journal of Purchasing and Supply Management*, *28*(2), 100751. doi:10.1016/j.pursup.2022.100751

Soydaner, D. (2022). Attention mechanism in neural networks: Where it comes and where it goes. *Neural Computing & Applications*, *34*(16), 13371–13385. doi:10.1007/s00521-022-07366-3

Spieske, A., Gebhardt, M., Kopyto, M., Birkel, H., & Hartmann, E. (2023). The future of industry 4.0 and supply chain resilience after the COVID-19 pandemic: Empirical evidence from a Delphi study. *Computers & Industrial Engineering*, *181*, 109344. doi:10.1016/j.cie.2023.109344 PMID:37273574

Srhir, S., Jaegler, A., & Montoya-Torres, J. R. (2023). Introducing a framework toward sustainability goals in a supply chain 4.0 ecosystem. *Journal of Cleaner Production*, *418*, 138111. doi:10.1016/j.jclepro.2023.138111

Srhir, S., Jaegler, A., & Montoya-Torres, J. R. (2023). Uncovering Industry 4.0 technology attributes in sustainable supply chain 4.0: A systematic literature review. *Business Strategy and the Environment*, *32*(7), 4143–4166. doi:10.1002/bse.3358

Stadnicka, D., Sęp, J., Amadio, R., Mazzei, D., Tyrovolas, M., Stylios, C., Carreras-Coch, A., Merino, J. A., Żabiński, T., & Navarro, J. (2022). Industrial needs in the fields of artificial intelligence, internet of things and edge computing. *Sensors (Basel)*, *22*(12), 4501. doi:10.3390/s22124501 PMID:35746287

Stanley, A. O., Ovie, E. A., Ughovero, B. A., & Ijoyah, C. T. (2022). Sustainable Production Strategy and Product Availability: A Study of Unilever Nigeria PLC. *Lafia Journal of Economics and Management Sciences, 7*(1), 44–65. https://lajems.com/index.php/lajems/article/view/201

Steinwandter, V., Borchert, D., & Herwing, C. (2019). Data science tools and applications on the way to Pharma 4.0. *Drug Discovery Today, 24*(9), 1795–1805. doi:10.1016/j.drudis.2019.06.005 PMID:31207205

Stock, T., & Seliger, G. (2016). Opportunities of Sustainable Manufacturing in Industry 4.0. *Procedia CIRP, 40*, 536–541. doi:10.1016/j.procir.2016.01.129

Straub, E. T. (2009). Understanding Technology Adoption: Theory and Future Directions for Informal Learning. *Review of Educational Research, 79*(2), 625–649. doi:10.3102/0034654308325896

Subramaniam, N., Akbar, S., Situ, H., Ji, S., & Parikh, N. (2023). Sustainable development goal reporting: Contrasting effects of institutional and organisational factors. *Journal of Cleaner Production, 411*, 137339. doi:10.1016/j.jclepro.2023.137339

Sucar, L. E. (2015). Probabilistic graphical models. *Advances in Computer Vision and Pattern Recognition. London. Springer London., 1*. Advance online publication. 10(978)

Su, D., Zhang, L., Hua, P., Saeidi, P., & Tirkolaee, E. B. (2023). Technical challenges of blockchain technology for sustainable manufacturing paradigm in Industry 4.0 era using a fuzzy decision support system. *Technological Forecasting and Social Change, 188*, 122275. doi:10.1016/j.techfore.2022.122275

Sugiawan, Y., Kurniawan, R., & Managi, S. (2023). Assessing the United Nations sustainable development goals from the inclusive wealth perspective. *Scientific Reports, 13*(1), 1601. Advance online publication. doi:10.1038/s41598-023-28540-0 PMID:36709239

Sujatha, R., Prakash, G., & Jhanjhi, N. Z. (2022). *Cyber Security Applications for Industry 4.0*. CRC Press. doi:10.1201/9781003203087

Sulistyaningsih, E., & Siswanto, S. (2023). *Integrated Industrial Estate Development Strategy in increasing competitiveness through technological innovation and research*. doi:10.59890/ijmbi.v1i1.157

Sun, P. (2023). 5G+ smart Manufacturing. In Management for professionals (pp. 83–106). doi:10.1007/978-981-99-4024-0_5

Sundarakani, B., Kamran, R., Maheshwari, P., & Jain, V. (2021). Designing a hybrid cloud for a supply chain network of Industry 4.0: A theoretical framework. *Benchmarking, 28*(5), 1524–1542. doi:10.1108/BIJ-04-2018-0109

Sun, L., Zhao, Y., Sun, W., & Liu, Z. (2020). Study on supply chain strategy based on cost income model and multi-access edge computing under the background of the Internet of Things. *Neural Computing & Applications, 32*(19), 15357–15368. doi:10.1007/s00521-019-04125-9

Sunmola, F., & Burgess, P. (2023). Transparency by design for Blockchain-Based supply chains. *Procedia Computer Science, 217*, 1256–1265. doi:10.1016/j.procs.2022.12.324

Sun, Y., Jeelani, I., & Gheisari, M. (2023). Safe human-robot collaboration in construction: A conceptual perspective. *Journal of Safety Research, 86*, 39–51. Advance online publication. doi:10.1016/j.jsr.2023.06.006 PMID:37718066

Suppipat, S., Chotiratanapinun, T., Teachavorasinskun, K., & Hu, A. H. (2022). Designer's guide for life cycle Assessment. In Springer eBooks (pp. 15–29). doi:10.1007/978-3-031-15060-9_2

Svensson, G. (2009). The transparency of SCM ethics: Conceptual framework and empirical illustrations. *Supply Chain Management, 14*(4), 259–269. doi:10.1108/13598540910970090

Taghiyeh, S., Lengacher, D., Sadeghi, A. H., Sahebi-Fakhrabad, A., & Handfield, R. (2023). A Novel Multi-Phase Hierarchical Forecasting Approach with Machine Learning in Supply Chain Management. *Science DIrect, 100032*. Advance online publication. doi:10.1016/j.sca.2023.100032

Taj, S., Imran, A. S., Kastrati, Z., Daudpota, S. M., Memon, R. A., & Javed, A. (2023). IoT-based supply chain management: A systematic literature review. *Internet of Things : Engineering Cyber Physical Human Systems, 24*, 100982. doi:10.1016/j.iot.2023.100982

Tao, F., Cheng, J., Qi, Q., Zhang, M., Zhang, H., & Sui, F. (2018). Digital twin-driven product design, manufacturing, and service with big data. *International Journal of Advanced Manufacturing Technology, 94*(9-12), 3563–3576. doi:10.1007/s00170-017-0233-1

Tao, F., Zhang, L., Venkatesh, V. C., Luo, Y., & Cheng, Y. (2011). Cloud manufacturing: A computing and service-oriented manufacturing model. *Proceedings of the Institution of Mechanical Engineers. Part B, Journal of Engineering Manufacture, 225*(10), 1969–1976. doi:10.1177/0954405411405575

Tao, F., Zhang, M., Cheng, J., & Qi, Q. (2017). Digital twin workshop: A new paradigm for a future workshop. *Jisuanji Jicheng Zhizao Xitong, 23*, 1–9.

TarekA. H. (2023). Mergers and Acquisitions: Analysing antitrust implications and Regulatory compliance. *Social Science Research Network*. doi:10.2139/ssrn.4518461

Tariq, S., Nisar, Q. A., Mahmood, K., & Moeen, R. (2023). *Supply Chain Strategies and Competitive Advantage: A Roadmap to Achieving Sustainable Performance*. Academic Press.

Tashtoush, Y. M., Darweesh, D. A., Husari, G., Darwish, O. A., Darwish, Y., Issa, L. B., & Ashqar, H. I. (2022). Agile Approaches for Cybersecurity Systems, IoT and Intelligent Transportation. *IEEE Access : Practical Innovations, Open Solutions, 10*, 1360–1375. doi:10.1109/ACCESS.2021.3136861

Tavanti, M. (2023). Assessing and measuring sustainability impact. In Sustainable development goals series (pp. 453–473). doi:10.1007/978-3-031-36907-0_17

Tayyab, M., Marjani, M., Jhanjhi, N., Hashem, I. A. T., Usmani, R. S. A., & Qamar, F. (2023). A Comprehensive Review on Deep Learning Algorithms: Security and Privacy Issues. *Computers & Security, 131*, 103297. doi:10.1016/j.cose.2023.103297

Tekinerdogan, B., Köksal, Ö., & Çelik, T. (2023). System architecture design of IoT-based smart cities. *Applied Sciences (Basel, Switzerland), 13*(7), 4173.

Telukdarie, A. (2023). *Industry 4.0 Technological advancement in the food and beverage manufacturing industry in South Africa—Bibliometric analysis via natural language processing*. MDPI. doi:10.3390/info14080454

Terziyan, V., Gryshko, S., & Golovianko, M. (2021). Taxonomy of generative adversarial networks for digital immunity of Industry 4.0 systems. *Procedia Computer Science, 180*, 676–685. doi:10.1016/j.procs.2021.01.290

Teubert, C. (2023, April 1). *An analysis of barriers preventing the widespread adoption of predictive and prescriptive maintenance in aviation*. NASA Technical Reports Server (NTRS). https://ntrs.nasa.gov/citations/20230000841

Thakur, A. (2021). Supply Chain Sustainability in Food and Beverage Industry. In Driving Innovation and Productivity Through Sustainable Automation (pp. 173–189). doi:10.4018/978-1-7998-5879-9.ch008

Thanigaivelan, R., Kaliappan, S., & Jegadheesan, C. (2023). *Cyber-Physical systems and supporting technologies for industrial automation*. IGI Global.

The History Of Pharmaceutical Manufacturing: Industry 1.0 To Pharma 4.0 2017LWS 40 Years.

The Importance of Environmental Awareness When Running a Business 2019Maryville University.

Thramboulidis, K., Vachtsevanou, D. C., & Kontou, I. C. (2019). PuS-IoT: A Cyber-Physical Microservice and IoT-Based Framework for Manufacturing Assembly Systems. *Annual Reviews in Control*, *2019*(47), 237–248. doi:10.1016/j.arcontrol.2019.03.005

Tiago, F., Gil, A., Stemberger, S., & Borges-Tiago, T. (2021). Digital Sustainability Communication in Tourism. *Journal of Innovation and Knowledge*, *6*(1), 27–34. doi:10.1016/j.jik.2019.12.002

Tian, F. (2016). An agri-food supply chain traceability system for China based on RFID & blockchain technology. In *2016 13th international conference on service systems and service management (ICSSSM)* (pp. 1-6). IEEE.

Tian, F. (2017). A supply chain traceability system for food safety based on HACCP, blockchain & Internet of things. In *2017 International conference on service systems and service management* (pp. 1-6). IEEE.

Tian, L., & Wang, Q. (2024). Improving mineral mining enterprises environmental performance through corporate social responsibility practices in China: Implications for minerals policymaking. *Resources Policy*, *88*, 104442. doi:10.1016/j.resourpol.2023.104442

Tiwari, S., Sharma, P., Choi, T.-M., & Lim, A. (2023). Blockchain and third-party logistics for global supply chain operations: Stakeholders' perspectives and decision roadmap. *Transportation Research Part E, Logistics and Transportation Review*, *170*, 103012. doi:10.1016/j.tre.2022.103012

Toktaş-Palut, P. (2022). Analyzing the effects of Industry 4.0 technologies and coordination on the sustainability of supply chains. *Sustainable Production and Consumption*, *30*, 341–358. doi:10.1016/j.spc.2021.12.005

Tortorella, G. L., Prashar, A., Antony, J., Fogliatto, F. S., Gonzalez, V., & Filho, M. G. (2023). Industry 4.0 adoption for healthcare supply chain performance during COVID-19 pandemic in Brazil and India: the mediating role of resilience abilities development. *Operations Management Research*.

Tortorella, G. L., Miorando, R., Caiado, R., Nascimento, D., & Portioli Staudacher, A. (2021). The mediating effect of employees' involvement on the relationship between Industry 4.0 and operational performance improvement. *Total Quality Management & Business Excellence*, *32*(1-2), 119–133.https://doi.org/10.1080/14783363.2018.1532789

Tortorella, G., Fogliatto, F. S., Kumar, M., Gonzalez, V., & Pepper, M. (2023). Effect of Industry 4.0 on the relationship between socio-technical practices and workers' performance. *Journal of Manufacturing Technology Management*, *34*(1), 44–66. doi:10.1108/JMTM-04-2022-0173

towardsdatascience. (n.d.). *Cousins for Artificial Intelligence*. Retrieved from https://towardsdatascience.com/cousins-of-artificial-intelligence-dda4edc27b55

Toyoda, K., Mathiopoulos, P. T., Sasase, I., & Ohtsuki, T. (2017). A novel blockchain-based product ownership management system (POMS) for anti-counterfeits in the post supply chain. *IEEE Access : Practical Innovations, Open Solutions*, *5*, 17465–17477. doi:10.1109/ACCESS.2017.2720760

Tracxn. (2023). *Blockchain in Healthcare Startups in India*. Author.

Tranfield, D., Denyer, D., & Smart, P. (2003). Towards a Methodology for Developing Evidence-Informed Management Knowledge by Means of Systematic Review. *British Journal of Management*, *14*(3), 207–222. doi:10.1111/1467-8551.00375

Tran, M. Q., Elsisi, M., Mahmoud, K., Liu, M. K., Lehtonen, M., & Darwish, M. M. (2021). Experimental setup for online fault diagnosis of induction machines via promising IoT and machine learning: Towards industry 4.0 empowerment. *IEEE Access : Practical Innovations, Open Solutions*, *9*, 115429–115441. doi:10.1109/ACCESS.2021.3105297

Truong, T. C., & Diep, Q. B. (2023). Technological spotlights of digital transformation in tertiary education. *IEEE Access : Practical Innovations, Open Solutions*, *11*, 40954–40966. doi:10.1109/ACCESS.2023.3270340

Tsao, M., Yang, K., Zoepf, S., & Pavone, M. (2022). Trust but Verify: Cryptographic Data Privacy for Mobility Management. *IEEE Transactions on Control of Network Systems*, *9*(1), 50–61. doi:10.1109/TCNS.2022.3141027

Tschentscher, T., Chege, N., & Remaury, H. (2023). An Integrated Seascape Approach to Revitalise Ecosystems and Livelihoods in Shimoni-Vanga, Kenya. In Springer Link (pp. 179–202). doi:10.1007/978-981-99-1292-6_10

Tsolakis, N., Schumacher, R., Dora, M., & Kumar, M. (2022). Artificial intelligence and blockchain implementation in supply chains: A pathway to sustainability and data monetisation? *Annals of Operations Research*, *327*(1), 157–210. doi:10.1007/s10479-022-04785-2 PMID:35755830

Tunca, T., & Cansu, Y. (2019). The development of servitization concept in the era of industry 4.0 through SCM perspective. Handbook of Research on Strategic Fit and Design in Business Ecosystems, 593 - 615. doi:10.4018/978-1-7998-1125-1.ch026

Turečková, K., Nevima, J., Vaňová, A., & Vitálišová, K. (2023). Society 4.0: General economic implications. *Journal of European Economy*, *22*(2), 146–157. doi:10.35774/jee2023.02.146

Turner, C. J., Oyekan, J., Stergioulas, L., & Griffin, D. (2021). Utilizing Industry 4.0 on the Construction Site: Challenges and Opportunities. *IEEE Transactions on Industrial Informatics*, *17*(2), 746–756.https://doi.org/10.1109/TII.2020.3002197

Ueda, D., Kakinuma, T., Fujita, S., Kamagata, K., Fushimi, Y., Ito, R., Matsui, Y., Nozaki, T., Nakaura, T., Fujima, N., Tatsugami, F., Yanagawa, M., Hirata, K., Yamada, A., Tsuboyama, T., Kawamura, M., Fujioka, T., & Naganawa, S. (2023). Fairness of artificial intelligence in healthcare: Review and recommendations. *Japanese Journal of Radiology*. Advance online publication. doi:10.1007/s11604-023-01474-3 PMID:37540463

Ugvekar, N., Kamath K, K., Subramanyam, E., & Shabaraya, A. (2021). A Review on Change Management System in Pharmaceutical Industry. *International Journal of Drug Regulatory Affairs*.

Uhlemann, T. H. J., Lehmann, C., & Steinhilper, R. (2017). The digital twin: Realizing the cyber-physical production system for industry 4.0. *Procedia CIRP*, *61*, 335–340. doi:10.1016/j.procir.2016.11.152

Ul-Durar, S., Awan, U., Varma, A., Memon, S., & Mention, A. (2023). Integrating knowledge management and orientation dynamics for organization transition from eco-innovation to circular economy. *Journal of Knowledge Management*, *27*(8), 2217–2248. Advance online publication. doi:10.1108/JKM-05-2022-0424

Ullah, I., Shukla, J. V., & Singh, D. K. (2023). The Applications, Opportunities and Challenges of IoT in Supply Chain Management: Insights from Literature Review. *2023 11th International Conference on Emerging Trends in Engineering & Technology - Signal and Information Processing (ICETET - SIP)*. 10.1109/ICETET-SIP58143.2023.10151507

Ullah, A., Azeem, M., Ashraf, H., Alaboudi, A. A., Humayun, M., & Jhanjhi, N. Z. (2021). Secure healthcare Data Aggregation and Transmission in IoT—A survey. *IEEE Access : Practical Innovations, Open Solutions*, *9*, 16849–16865. doi:10.1109/ACCESS.2021.3052850

Ullah, A., Ishaq, N., Azeem, M., Ashraf, H., Jhanjhi, N. Z., Humayun, M., Tabbakh, T., & Almusaylim, Z. A. (2021b). A survey on continuous object tracking and boundary detection schemes in IoT assisted wireless sensor networks. *IEEE Access : Practical Innovations, Open Solutions*, *9*, 126324–126336. doi:10.1109/ACCESS.2021.3110203

Unhelkar, B., Joshi, S. K., Sharma, M., Prakash, S., Mani, A. K., & Prasad, M. (2022). Enhancing supply chain performance using RFID technology and decision support systems in the industry 4.0–A systematic literature review. *International Journal of Information Management Data Insights*, *2*(2), 100084. doi:10.1016/j.jjimei.2022.100084

Urbański, M. (2023). Labor Market Characteristics Pertaining to Foreigners' Employment. In Springer Link (pp. 59–98). doi:10.1007/978-981-99-3253-5_3

Usmani, U. A., Happonen, A., & Watada, J. (2023). Secure Integration of IoT-Enabled Sensors and Technologies: Engineering Applications for Humanitarian Impact. *2023 5th International Congress on Human-Computer Interaction, Optimization and Robotic Applications (HORA)*. 10.1109/HORA58378.2023.10156740

Ustundag, A., Cevikcan, E., & Karacay, G. (2018). Talent development for Industry 4.0. *Industry 4.0: Managing the digital transformation*, 123-136.

Uygun, Y. (2020). *Industry 4.0: Principles, Effects and Challenges*. Nova Science Publishers.

Valilai, O. F., & Houshmand, M. (2013). A collaborative and integrated platform to support distributed manufacturing system using a service-oriented approach based on cloud computing paradigm. *Robotics and Computer-integrated Manufacturing*, *29*(1), 110–127. doi:10.1016/j.rcim.2012.07.009

Vara, R. C., Prieto, J., Prieta, F., & Corchado, J. M. (2018). How blockchain improves supply chain: The case study alimentary supply chain. *Procedia Computer Science*, *134*, 393–398. doi:10.1016/j.procs.2018.07.193

Vărzaru, A. A. (2022). Assessing the Impact of AI Solutions' Ethical Issues on Performance in Managerial Accounting. [DOI: 10.3390/electronics11142221]. *Electronics (Basel)*, *11*, 2221.

Vasanthraj, K., Kaur, A., Potdar, V., & Agrawal, H. (2023). Industry 4.0 adoption in food Supply Chain to Improve Visibility and Operational Efficiency—A content analysis. *IEEE Access : Practical Innovations, Open Solutions*, *11*, 73922–73958. doi:10.1109/ACCESS.2023.3295780

Vassakis, K., Petrakis, E., & Kopanakis, I. (2018). Big data analytics: applications, prospects and challenges. *Mobile big data: A roadmap from models to technologies*, 3-20.

Vaswani, A. (2019). *Industry 4.0 : Digital transformation*. https://www.linkedin.com/pulse/industry-40-digital-transformation-arun-vaswani/

Vazifeh, Z., Bensebaa, F., Shadbahr, J., Gonzales-Calienes, G., Mafakheri, F., Benali, M., Ebadian, M., & Vézina, P. L. (2023). Forestry based products as climate change solution: Integrating life cycle assessment with techno-economic analysis. *Journal of Environmental Management*, *330*, 117197. doi:10.1016/j.jenvman.2022.117197

Ventura, M., & Coeli, C. M. (2018). *Beyond privacy: the right to health information, personal data protection, and governance*. Sci ELO Brazil.

Verma, N. S., Kuldeep, D. K., Chouhan, M., Prajapati, R., & Singh, S. K. (2023). A review on Eco-Friendly pesticides and their rising importance in sustainable plant protection practices. *International Journal of Plant and Soil Science*, *35*(22), 200–214. doi:10.9734/ijpss/2023/v35i224126

Verma, S., Kaur, S., Rawat, D. B., Chen, X., Alex, L. T., & Jhanjhi, N. Z. (2021). Intelligent framework using IoT-Based WSNs for wildfire detection. *IEEE Access : Practical Innovations, Open Solutions*, *9*, 48185–48196. doi:10.1109/ACCESS.2021.3060549

Villegas-Galaviz, C., & Martin, K. (2023). Moral distance, AI, and the ethics of care. *AI & Society*, 1–12. doi:10.1007/s00146-023-01642-z

Vizcaino, N. (2023). *How do the Female Attitudes Towards Sustainable Branding Influence Purchase Intention in the Sportswear Industry : A qualitative study of women aged 20-50*. DIVA. https://www.diva-portal.org/smash/record.jsf?pid=diva2%3A1763924&dswid=-4010

Volkov, B. B., Ragon, B., Doyle, J. M., & Bredella, M. A. (2022). Adaptive capacity and preparedness of Clinical and Translational Science Award Program hubs: Overview of an environmental scan. *Journal of Clinical and Translational Science*, *7*(1), e31. Advance online publication. doi:10.1017/cts.2022.400 PMID:36845304

Voukkali, I., Papamichael, I., Loizia, P., Lekkas, D., Rodríguez-Espinosa, T., Pedreño, J. N., & Zorpas, A. A. (2023). Waste metrics in the framework of circular economy. *Waste Management & Research*, *41*(12), 1741–1753. Advance online publication. doi:10.1177/0734242X231190794 PMID:37602734

Wagner, M., Van Phu, N., Azomahou, T., & Wehrmeyer, W. (2002). The Relationship between the Environmental and Economic Performance of Firms: An Empirical Analysis of the European Paper Industry. *Corporate Social Responsibility and Environmental Management*, *9*(3), 133–146. doi:10.1002/csr.22

Wang, B., Tao, F., Fang, X., Liu, C., Liu, Y., & Freiheit, T. (2021). Smart manufacturing and intelligent manufacturing: A comparative review. *Engineering (Beijing)*, *7*(6), 738–757. doi:10.1016/j.eng.2020.07.017

Wang, G., Wang, S., Dong, X., Zhang, Y., & Shen, W. (2023). Recent progress in additive manufacturing of ceramic dental restorations. *Journal of Materials Research and Technology*, *26*, 1028–1049. doi:10.1016/j.jmrt.2023.07.257

Wang, H., Feil, J., & Yu, X. (2023). Let the data speak about the cut-off values for multidimensional index: Classification of human development index with machine learning. *Socio-Economic Planning Sciences*, *87*, 101523. doi:10.1016/j.seps.2023.101523

Wang, H., Hu, C., Li, Y., & Tang, J. (2022). Deep reinforcement learning for Industry 4.0: A comprehensive review. *Journal of Manufacturing Systems*, *63*, 429–444.

Wang, J., & Feng, T. (2023). Supply chain ethical leadership and green supply chain integration: A moderated mediation analysis. *International Journal of Logistics*, *26*(9), 1145–1171. doi:10.1080/13675567.2021.2022640

Wang, J., Ma, Y., Zhang, L., Gao, R. X., & Wu, D. (2018). Deep learning for smart manufacturing: Methods and applications. *Journal of Manufacturing Systems*, *48*, 144–156. doi:10.1016/j.jmsy.2018.01.003

Wang, J., Wang, Q., & Sun, W. (2023). Quantifying flexibility provisions of the ladle furnace refining process as cuttable loads in the iron and steel industry. *Applied Energy*, *342*, 121178. doi:10.1016/j.apenergy.2023.121178

Wang, J., Wu, P., Wang, X., & Shou, W. (2017). The outlook of blockchain technology for construction engineering management. *Frontiers of Engineering Management*, *4*(1), 67–75. doi:10.15302/J-FEM-2017006

Wang, K., Jiang, W., & Zhang, M. (2023). Impact of high-speed railway on urban resilience in China: Does urban innovation matter? *Socio-Economic Planning Sciences*, *87*, 101607. doi:10.1016/j.seps.2023.101607

Wang, L. (2019). From intelligence science to intelligent manufacturing. *Engineering (Beijing)*, *5*(4), 615–618. doi:10.1016/j.eng.2019.04.011

Wang, L., Törngren, M., & Onori, M. (2015). Current status and advancement of cyber-physical systems in manufacturing. *Journal of Manufacturing Systems*, *37*, 517–527. doi:10.1016/j.jmsy.2015.04.008

Wang, S., Wan, J., Zhang, D., Li, D., & Zhang, C. (2016). Towards smart factory for Industry 4.0: A self-organized multi-agent system with big data based feedback and coordination. [DOI: 10.1016/j.comnet.2015.12.017]. *Computer Networks*, •••, 101.

Wang, S., Wan, J., Zhang, D., Li, D., & Zhang, C. (2016). Towards smart factory for industry 4.0: A self-organized multi-agent system with big data based feedback and coordination. *Computer Networks*, *101*, 158–168. doi:10.1016/j.comnet.2015.12.017

Wang, T., Huang, K., Guo, L., Zheng, T., & Zeng, F. (2023). An automated vacuum infusion process for manufacturing high-quality fiber-reinforced composites. *Composite Structures*, *309*, 116717. doi:10.1016/j.compstruct.2023.116717

Wang, X. E., Su, X., & Bi, K. (2023). Achieving synergies of carbon emission reduction, cost savings, and asset investments in China's industrial sector: Towards sustainable practices. *Sustainability (Basel)*, *15*(14), 10956. doi:10.3390/su151410956

Wasiq, M., Kamal, M., & Ali, N. (2023). Factors influencing green innovation adoption and its impact on the sustainability performance of Small- and Medium-Sized Enterprises in Saudi Arabia. *Sustainability (Basel)*, *15*(3), 2447. doi:10.3390/su15032447

Wasumwa, N. S. A. (2023). Safeguarding the future: A comprehensive analysis of security measures for smart grids. *World Journal of Advanced Research and Reviews*, *19*(1), 847–871. doi:10.30574/wjarr.2023.19.1.1387

Watkins, K. E., & Marsick, V. J. (2023). *Rethinking workplace learning and development*. doi:10.4337/9781802203776

Waxin, M. (2023). *Environmental management systems in public sector*. https://dspace.aus.edu/xmlui/handle/11073/25241

Weber, I., Xu, X., Riveret, R., Governatori, G., Ponomarev, A., & Mendling, J. (2016). Untrusted business process monitoring and execution using blockchain. *Business Process Management: 14th International Conference, BPM 2016, Rio de Janeiro, Brazil, September 18-22, 2016 Proceedings*, *14*, 329–347.

Weidele, D. K. I., Afzal, S., Valente, A. N., Makuch, C., Cornec, O., Vu, L., Subramanian, D., Geyer, W., Nair, R., Vejsbjerg, I., Marinescu, R., Palmes, P., Daly, E., Franke, L., & Haehn, D. (2023). *AutoDOViz: Human-Centered Automation for Decision Optimization*. ACM. doi:10.1145/3581641.3584094

Wen, B. O. T., Syahriza, N., Xian, N. C. W., Wei, N., Shen, T. Z., Hin, Y. Z., Sindiramutty, S. R., & Nicole, T. Y. F. (2024). Detecting cyber threats with a Graph-Based NIDPS. In Advances in logistics, operations, and management science book series (pp. 36–74). doi:10.4018/978-1-6684-7625-3.ch002

West, S., & Schill, C. (2022). Negotiating the ethical-political dimensions of research methods: A key competency in mixed methods, inter-and transdisciplinary, and co-production research. *Humanities & Social Sciences Communications*, *9*(1), 1–13. doi:10.1057/s41599-022-01297-z

White, C. M. (2022). *Dangerous Counterfeit Drugs are Putting Millions at Risk, a New Study Says*. UConn Today.

Whitehead, B., Andrews, D., Shah, A., & Maidment, G. (2015). Assessing the environmental impact of data centres part 2: Building environmental assessment methods and life cycle assessment. *Building and Environment*, *93*, 395–405. doi:10.1016/j.buildenv.2014.08.015

Widder, D. G., & Wong, R. (2023). Thinking Upstream: Ethics and Policy Opportunities in AI Supply Chains. *arXiv preprint arXiv:2303.07529*.

Widianingsih, I., Abdillah, A., Herawati, E., Dewi, A. U., Miftah, A. Z., Adikancana, Q. M., Pratama, M. N., & Sasmono, S. (2023). Sport Tourism, Regional Development, and Urban Resilience: A focus on regional economic development in Lake Toba District, North Sumatra, Indonesia. *Sustainability (Basel)*, *15*(7), 5960. doi:10.3390/su15075960

Widodo, R. E., & Napitupulu, T. A. (2023). Exploring The Impact Of Live Streaming For Ecommerce Business A Systematic Literature Review. *ResearchGate*. https://www.researchgate.net/publication/373572273_Exploring_The_Impact_Of_Live_Streaming_For_Ecommerce_Business_A_Systematic_Literature_Review

Williams, L. (2014). *The Real Impact of Counterfeit Medications*. US Phamacist.

Wolniak, N. (2023). Functioning of real-time analytics in business. *Zeszyty Naukowe, 2023*(172). doi:10.29119/1641-3466.2023.172.40

World Trade Organization. (2019). *World trade statistical review 2019, 31 May 2019*. Author.

Wu, D., Rosen, D. W., Wang, L., & Schaefer, D. (2015). Cloud-based design and manufacturing: A new paradigm in digital manufacturing and design innovation. *Computer Aided Design, 59*, 1–14. doi:10.1016/j.cad.2014.07.006

Wu, D., & Xie, L. (2023). From concept to reality: Leveraging green innovation and supply chain management for sustainable corporate performance. *Environmental Science and Pollution Research International, 30*(46), 102574–102585. Advance online publication. doi:10.1007/s11356-023-29351-6 PMID:37668785

Wu, L., Subramanian, N., Abdulrahman, M. D., Liu, C., Lai, K., & Pawar, K. (2015). The Impact of Integrated Practices of Lean, Green, and Social Management Systems on Firm Sustainability Performance-Evidence from Chinese Fashion Auto-Parts Suppliers. *Sustainability (Basel), 7*(4), 3838–3858. doi:10.3390/su7043838

Xia, J., Li, H., & He, Z. (2023). The Effect of Blockchain Technology on Supply Chain Collaboration: A Case Study of Lenovo. *Systems, 11*(6), 1–25. doi:10.3390/systems11060299

Xia, L., Semirumi, D., & Rezaei, R. (2023). A Thorough Examination of Smart City Applications: Exploring Challenges and Solutions Throughout the Life Cycle with Emphasis on Safeguarding Citizen Privacy. *Sustainable Cities and Society, 104771*. Advance online publication. doi:10.1016/j.scs.2023.104771

Xiao, J., Zhang, W., & Zhong, R. Y. (2023). Blockchain-enabled cyber-physical system for construction site management: A pilot implementation. *Advanced Engineering Informatics, 57*, 102102. doi:10.1016/j.aei.2023.102102

Xing, K., Qian, W., & Zaman, A. U. (2016). Development of a cloud-based platform for footprint assessment in green supply chain management. *Journal of Cleaner Production, 139*, 191–203. doi:10.1016/j.jclepro.2016.08.042

Xu, B., Liu, W., & Li, J. (2023). Resilience Regulation Strategy for Container Port Supply Chain under Disruptive Events. *Journal of Marine Science and Engineering, 11*(4), 732. doi:10.3390/jmse11040732

Xu, K., & Qin, S. (2023). An Interdisciplinary Approach and Advanced Techniques for Enhanced 3D-Printed Upper Limb Prosthetic Socket Design: A literature review. *Actuators, 12*(6), 223. doi:10.3390/act12060223

Xu, M., Cui, Y., Hu, M., Xu, X., Zhang, Z., Liang, S., & Qu, S. (2019). Supply chain sustainability risk and assessment. *Journal of Cleaner Production, 225*, 857–867. doi:10.1016/j.jclepro.2019.03.307

Xu, X. (2012). From cloud computing to cloud manufacturing. *Robotics and Computer-integrated Manufacturing, 28*(1), 75–86. doi:10.1016/j.rcim.2011.07.002

Xu, X., Lu, Y., Vogel-Heuser, B., & Wang, L. (2021). Industry 4.0 and Industry 5.0—Inception, conception and perception. *Journal of Manufacturing Systems, 61*, 530–535. doi:10.1016/j.jmsy.2021.10.006

Yacob, P., Wong, L. S., & Khor, S. C. (2019). An Empirical Investigation of Green Initiatives and Environmental Sustainability for Manufacturing SMEs. *Journal of Manufacturing Technology Management, 30*(1), 2–25. doi:10.1108/JMTM-08-2017-0153

Yadav, G., Luthra, S., Jakhar, S. K., Mangla, S. K., & Rai, D. P. (2020). A framework to overcome sustainable supply chain challenges through solution measures of industry 4.0 and circular economy: An automotive case. *Journal of Cleaner Production, 254*, 120112. doi:10.1016/j.jclepro.2020.120112

Yaiprasert, C., & Hidayanto, A. N. (2023). AI-driven ensemble three machine learning to enhance digital marketing strategies in the food delivery business. *Intelligent Systems With Applications*, *18*, 200235. doi:10.1016/j.iswa.2023.200235

Yang, L., Sigov, A., Ratkin, L., Ivanov, L., & Zuo, M. (2023). Quantum Computing and Industrial Information Integration: A review. *Journal of Industrial Information Integration*, *100511*. Advance online publication. doi:10.1016/j.jii.2023.100511

Yang, T., Chu, Z., & Wang, B. (2023). Feasibility on the integration of passenger and freight transportation in rural areas: A service mode and an optimization model. *Socio-Economic Planning Sciences*, *88*, 101665. doi:10.1016/j.seps.2023.101665

Yao, Y. L., Cheng, G. J., Rajurkar, K. P., Kovacevic, R., Feiner, S., & Zhang, W. (2005). Combined research and curriculum development of nontraditional manufacturing. *European Journal of Engineering Education*, *30*(3), 363–376. doi:10.1080/03043790500114581

Yap, K. Y., Chin, H. H., & Klemeš, J. J. (2023). Blockchain technology for distributed generation: A review of current development, challenges and future prospect. *Renewable & Sustainable Energy Reviews*, *175*, 113170. doi:10.1016/j.rser.2023.113170

Yaqoob, I., Salah, K., Jayaraman, R., & Al-Hammad, Y. (2021). Blockchain for healthcare data management: Opportunities,challenges, and future recommendations. *Neural Computing & Applications*.

Yenugula, M., Sahoo, S. K., & Goswami, S. S. (2023). Cloud computing in supply chain management: Exploring the relationship. *Management Science Letters*, *13*(3), 193–210. doi:10.5267/j.msl.2023.4.003

Ying-Jun, F., Lai, K., & Zhu, Q. (2022). Green supply chain innovation: Emergence, adoption, and challenges. *International Journal of Production Economics*, *248*, 108497. doi:10.1016/j.ijpe.2022.108497

Ying, W., Lin, X., & Philbin, S. P. (2023). Evaluating the role of the communication skills of engineering students on employability according to the Outcome-Based Education (OBE) Theory. *Sustainability (Basel)*, *15*(12), 9711. doi:10.3390/su15129711

Ylä-Kujala, A., Kedziora, D., Metso, L., Kärri, T., Happonen, A., & Piotrowicz, W. (2023). Robotic process automation deployments: A step-by-step method to investment appraisal. *Business Process Management Journal*, *29*(8), 163–187. doi:10.1108/BPMJ-08-2022-0418

Yosef, F. A., Jum'a, L., & Alatoom, M. (2023). Identifying and categorizing sustainable supply chain practices based on triple bottom line dimensions: Evaluation of practice implementation in the cement industry. *Sustainability (Basel)*, *15*(9), 7323. doi:10.3390/su15097323

Yuan, Y., & Wang, F. Y. (2016). Towards blockchain-based intelligent transportation systems. In *2016 IEEE 19th international conference on intelligent transportation systems (ITSC)* (pp. 2663-2668). 10.1109/ITSC.2016.7795984

Yuan, J., & Tian, Y. (2019). An intelligent fault diagnosis method using GRU neural network towards sequential data in dynamic processes. *Processes (Basel, Switzerland)*, *7*(3), 152. doi:10.3390/pr7030152

Zadeh, S. B. I., & Garay-Rondero, C. L. (2023). Enhancing Urban Sustainability: Unravelling Carbon Footprint Reduction in Smart Cities through Modern Supply-Chain Measures. *Smart Cities*, *6*(6), 3225–3250. doi:10.3390/smartcities6060143

Zadeh, S. B. I., Pérez, M. D. E., Gutiérrez, J. S. L., & Fernández-Sánchez, G. (2023). Optimizing smart energy infrastructure in smart ports: A Systematic Scoping Review of carbon Footprint Reduction. *Journal of Marine Science and Engineering*, *11*(10), 1921. doi:10.3390/jmse11101921

Zahari, M. K., Zakuan, N., Yusoff, M. F. M., Saman, M. Z. M., Khan, M. N. A., Muharam, F. M., & Yaacob, T. Z. (2023). Viable Supply Chain Management toward Company Sustainability during COVID-19 Pandemic in Malaysia. *Sustainability (Basel), 15*(5), 3989. doi:10.3390/su15053989

Zakari, N., Al-Razgan, M., Alsaadi, A., Alshareef, H., Al saigh, H., Alashaikh, L., Alharbi, M., Alomar, R., & Alotaibi, S. (2022). Blockchain technology in the pharmaceutical industry: A systematic review. *PeerJ. Computer Science, 8*, 1–26. doi:10.7717/peerj-cs.840 PMID:35634106

Zaman, U. K. U., Siadat, A., Baqai, A. A., Naveed, K., & Kumar, A. A. (2023). Handbook of Manufacturing Systems and Design: An Industry 4.0 Perspective. Academic Press.

Zamiela, C., Ibne Hossain, N., & Jaradat, R. (2022). Enablers of resilience in the healthcare supply chain: A case study of U.S healthcare industry during COVID-19 pandemic. *Research in Transportation Economics, 93*, 101174. doi:10.1016/j.retrec.2021.101174

Zarei, H., Rasti−Barzoki, M., Altmann, J., & Egger, B. (2023). Cooperation, coordination, or collaboration? A structured review of buyers' partnerships to support sustainable sourcing in supply chains. *Environmental Science and Pollution Research International, 30*(31), 76491–76514. doi:10.1007/s11356-023-27541-w PMID:37280495

Zezulka, A., Kaczmarczyk, M., & Schroeder, B. (2018). Implementing Industry 4.0 in Discrete Manufacturing. *IFAC-PapersOnLine, 51*(6), 473–478. doi:10.1016/j.ifacol.2018.07.106

Zhang, G., Yang, Y., & Yang, G. (2023). Smart supply chain management in Industry 4.0: The review, research agenda and strategies in North America. *Annals of Operations Research, 322*(2), 1075–1117. doi:10.1007/s10479-022-04689-1 PMID:35531562

Zhang, J., & Wang, J. S. (2020). Improved Salp Swarm Algorithm Based on Levy Flight and Sine Cosine Operator. *IEEE Access : Practical Innovations, Open Solutions, 8*, 99740–99771. doi:10.1109/ACCESS.2020.2997783

Zhang, L., Luo, Y., Tao, F., Li, B. H., Ren, L., Zhang, X., Guo, H., Cheng, Y., Hu, A., & Liu, Y. (2014). Cloud manufacturing: A new manufacturing paradigm. *Enterprise Information Systems, 8*(2), 167–187. doi:10.1080/17517575.2012.683812

Zhao, H., Zhao, Q. H., & Ślusarczyk, B. (2019). Sustainability and Digitalization of Corporate Management Based on Augmented/Virtual Reality Tools Usage: China and Other World IT Companies' Experience. *Sustainability, 11*(17), 4717. doi:10.3390/su11174717

Zhao, R., Zhang, Y., Zhu, Y., Lan, R., & Hua, Z. (2022). Metaverse: Security and Privacy Concerns. arXiv, arXiv:2203.03854.

Zhao, J. L., Fan, S., & Yan, J. (2016). Overview of business innovations and research opportunities in blockchain and introduction to the special issue. *Financial Innovation, 2*(1), 1–7. doi:10.1186/s40854-016-0049-2

Zhao, N., Hong, J., & Lau, K. H. (2023). Impact of supply chain digitalization on supply chain resilience and performance: A multi-mediation model. *International Journal of Production Economics, 259*, 108817. doi:10.1016/j.ijpe.2023.108817 PMID:36852136

Zhao, R., Liu, Y., Zhang, N., & Huang, T. (2017). An optimization model for green supply chain management by using a big data analytic approach. *Journal of Cleaner Production, 142*, 1085–1097. doi:10.1016/j.jclepro.2016.03.006

Zheng, Y., Yang, S., & Cheng, H. (2019). An application framework of digital twin and its case study J. *Journal of Ambient Intelligence and Humanized Computing, 10*(3), 1141–1153. doi:10.1007/s12652-018-0911-3

Zhong, R. Y., Xu, X., Klotz, E., & Newman, S. T. (2017). Intelligent manufacturing in the context of Industry 4.0: A review. *Engineering (Beijing), 3*(5), 616–630. doi:10.1016/J.ENG.2017.05.015

Zhong, Y., & Cheol, M. H. (2023). Investigating the Impact of Industry 4.0 Technology through a TOE-Based Innovation Model. *Systems, 11*(6), 277. doi:10.3390/systems11060277

Zhou, J., Li, P., Zhou, Y., Wang, B., Zang, J., & Meng, L. (2018). Toward new-generation intelligent manufacturing. *Engineering (Beijing), 4*(1), 11–20. doi:10.1016/j.eng.2018.01.002

Zhou, J., & Wang, M. (2023). The role of government-industry-academia partnership in business incubation: Evidence from new R&D institutions in China. *Technology in Society*, *72*, 102194. doi:10.1016/j.techsoc.2022.102194

Zhou, J., Xu, T., Chiao, Y., & Fang, Y. (2023). Interorganizational systems and supply chain agility in uncertain environments: The mediation role of supply chain collaboration. *Information Systems Research*. Advance online publication. doi:10.1287/isre.2023.1210

Zhu, G., Houck, H. A., Spiegel, C. A., Selhuber-Unkel, C., Hou, Y., & Blasco, E. (2023). Introducing dynamic bonds in light-based 3D printing. *Advanced Functional Materials*, 2300456. Advance online publication. doi:10.1002/adfm.202300456

Zhu, S., Yu, T., Xu, T., Chen, H., Dustdar, S., Gigan, S., Gündüz, D., Hossain, E., Jin, Y., Lin, F. H., Liu, B., Wan, Z., Zhang, J., Zhao, Z., Zhu, W., Chen, Z., Durrani, T., Wang, H., Wu, J., ... Pan, Y. (2023). Intelligent Computing: The latest advances, challenges, and future. *Intelligent Computing*, *2*, 0006. Advance online publication. doi:10.34133/icomputing.0006

Zimek & Baumgartner. (2017). Corporate Sustainability Activities and Sustainability Performance of First and Second Order. *Researchgate.Net*.

Zong, J., Zhang, X., Yang, Y., Li, H., & Yuan, H. (2023). Guideline for Green Design of Computer Products. *SHS Web of Conferences, 155*, 03025. 10.1051/shsconf/202315503025

Zozaya, N., Alcala, B., & Galindo, J. (2019). *The offset effect of pharmaceutical innovation: A review study*. Global & Regional Health Technology Assesment.

Zrigui, I. (2023). Reducing Carbon Footprint with Real-Time Transport Planning and Big Data Analytics. *E3S Web of Conferences*. doi:10.1051/e3sconf/202341201082

Zubairu, N. (2023). Application of supply chain strategies to improve the performance of SYNGAS networks. *IntechOpen*. doi:10.5772/intechopen.1002184

About the Contributors

Muhammad Rahies Khan has a working Experience of 16 years in Government Health care Org. Sound administrative skills, Personal development/management, procurement experience, Teaching and training skills. Certification of safety and security, health care softwares and electromechanical equipment, Learning management systems and strong communication skills.

Naveed R. Khan received his PhD in Human Resource Management from University Pendidikan Sultan Idris, a public sector university in Malaysia. Later, he was selected for a post-doctoral fellowship. He have been teaching for the last 14 years in higher education institutions. Throughout his career, he has taught graduate and post-graduate levels, both qualification and non-qualification bearing programs. Besides teaching, he is an enthusiastic trainer. He has designed training modules and conducted several pieces of trainings for Corporate employees and University faculty. He won two research grants from USAID and UPSI and have supervised to completion five PhD scholars. The main themes of his research interest, largely reflected in his research publications, have been Green HRM, Firm Competitiveness, Sustainable Performance, and Gender in Management. One of his latest research papers have been published in European Management Journal. He has been a member of British Academy of Management, UK. Currently, he has been affiliated with the Faculty of Business and Management, UCSI University, Malaysia.

Noor Zaman Jhanjhi (N.Z Jhanjhi) is currently working as a Professor in Computer Science (Cybersecurity and AI), Program Director for the Postgraduate Research Degree Programmes in computer science, Director of the Center for Smart Society (CSS5) at the School of Computer Science at Taylor's University, Malaysia. He has been nominated as the world's top 2% research scientist globally consecutive for 2022, and 2023; he is among the top five computer science researchers in Malaysia and was nominated as an Outstanding Faculty Member by the MDEC Malaysia for the year 2022. He has highly indexed publications in WoS/ISI/SCI/Scopus, and his collective research Impact factor is more than 1000 plus points. His Google Scholar H index is 60, and I-10 Index is close to 277, and his Scopus H index is 39, with more than 600 publications on his credit. He has several international patents on his account, including Australian, German, UK, and Japanese patents. He edited/authored over 50 research books published by world-class publishers, including Springer, IGI Global USA, Taylors and Frances, IET, Willeys, Intech Open, etc. He has excellent experience supervising and co-supervising postgraduate students, and more than 38 Postgraduate scholars graduated under his supervision. Prof. Jhanjhi serves as Associate Editor and Editorial Assistant Board for several reputable journals, such as PeerJ Computer Science, CMC Computers, Materials & Continua, Computer Systems Science and Engineering

CSSE, Frontier in Communication and Networks, etc. He received the Outstanding Associate Editor award for IEEE ACCESS. Active reviewer for a series of top-tier journals has been awarded globally as a top 1% reviewer by Publons (Web of Science). He is an external Ph.D./Master thesis examiner/evaluator for several universities globally and has evaluated 60 plus theses. He has completed more than 40 internationally funded research grants successfully. He has been a keynote/invited speaker for over 60 international conferences and has chaired international conference sessions. He has vast experience in academic qualifications, including ABET, NCAAA, and NCEAC, for 10 years. His research areas include Cybersecurity, IoT security, Wireless security, Data Science, Software Engineering, and UAVs. .

* * *

Rehan Akbar has over 22 years of experience in teaching and research in Computer Science and Information Systems. Throughout his career, he has been working at academic, research, and management positions at various levels. Currently, he is working as Associate Teaching Professor at School of Computing and Information Sciences, Florida International University, Miami, Florida. Before joining FIU, Dr. Rehan was working as Associate Professor in the Department of Computer and Information Sciences at Universiti Teknologi PETRONAS, Malaysia. He also served as Associate Professor and Head of Department in the Department of Information Systems, Faculty of Information & Communication Technology, Universiti Tunku Abdul Rahman, Malysia for about 10 years. Moreover, he has been working in the software industry as Project Manager of software projects. Dr. Rehan is a Senior Member of IEEE (SMIEEE), Member of Association for Information Systems (AIS), and Professional Technologist with Malaysian Board of Technologists (MBOT), Malaysia.

Nitesh Behare is an accomplished author with a wealth of knowledge and 15 years of experience in the academic field. He currently holds the position of Associate Professor at the Balaji Institute of International Business (BIIB), Sri Balaji University Pune (SBUP). Throughout his career, Dr. Behare has made significant contributions to the academic world through the publication of numerous research papers and book chapters, establishing himself as a recognized authority in his field.

Mukesh Shankar Bharti is a research scholar with a research background in foreign policy analysis and social science research. The author holds a PhD degree in International Relations with a specialization in East and Central Europe. His research area includes democracy, political institutions, European Union and South Asia.

Loveleen Gaur, Program Director (Artificial Intelligence and Data Analytics), Senior IEEE member, and Series Editor. For over 18 years she served in India and abroad in different capacities. Prof. Gaur has significantly contributed to enhancing scientific understanding by participating in over three hundred scientific conferences, symposia, and seminars, by chairing technical sessions and delivering plenary and invited talks. She has specialized in the fields of Artificial Intelligence, Machine Learning, Information Sciences, IoT, Data Analytics. Prof. Gaur pursued research in truly inter-disciplinary areas and authored and co-authored many books with renowned International and National publishers like Elsevier, Springer, Taylor and Francis. She has been invited as Guest Editor for reputed Q1, ABDC, SCI journals. She has also published various research papers in SCI and Q1 Journals. She is actively involved in various professional activities and has chaired various positions in International Conferences of repute and is a reviewer with IEEE, SCI, and ABDC Journals. She is currently involved in various projects of the Government of India and abroad.

Abdalla Hassan Gharib earned his Ph.D. and M.Sc. in Computer Science from Universiti Malaysia Sarawak, Malaysia. Currently, he serves as a lecturer and Quality Assurance Coordinator within the Faculty of Engineering at Zanzibar University, located in Zanzibar, Tanzania. In 2022, he was honored to be appointed as a council member of the Karume Institute of Science and Technology (KIST) by the Minister of Education and Vocational Training, Zanzibar, Tanzania. With numerous research articles to his name and supervision of eight Master's degree students by the end of 2023, Dr. Abdalla Gharib has emerged as a dedicated scholar in the realm of Mobile Communication Networks. His research specialization lies in communication protocols and information dissemination within Opportunistic Networks, addressing scenarios where traditional network infrastructures may be limited or absent. Beyond his core focus, he displays versatility and a wide array of interests, encompassing Artificial Intelligence (AI), Internet of Things (IoT), Quality Assurance, Digital Transformation, Cybersecurity and Graphic Design.. Driven by a profound passion for innovation and technology, his ultimate goal is to assist organizations and communities in harnessing technology ethically for competitive advantage and sustainable societal progress.

Wei Wei Goh is the Programme Director of the Dual Awards program in the School of Computing and IT, Faculty of Innovation and Technology in Taylor's University. Her expertise is in e-Learning Technologies. Her research interests includes E-Learning technologies, emerging web technologies, critical thinking skills, learning theories, MOOC, ontological based webpage segmentation, tools and applications, social media marketing and communications as well as persuasive messages and communications in social media. Some of her professional affiliations includes the International Association of Computer Science and Information Technology (IACSIT) and IEEE.

Norhidayah Hamzah is a seasoned professional with a 13-year career spanning from Systems Engineer to Project Manager, specializing in system implementation, troubleshooting, and project management for medium to high-level complexity projects. Her transition to academia as a lecturer reflects her commitment to sharing practical insights gained from industry experience. With a focus on project management, requirement engineering, software quality, UI/UX, HCI, and XAI, she contributes significantly to both industry and academia.

Laksitha M. Herath earned her Master of Science in Accounting degree at New York University's Stern School of Business and works at Pricewaterhouse Coopers (PwC). Prior to her current endeavor, she gained valuable experience as a program accountant at Enstar Group Limited, a well-known global insurance company, and at Deloitte, a Big Four accounting firm, in Atlanta and New York. Laksitha holds a Bachelor of Arts degree in Accounting from Clark Atlanta University, where she held executive positions in its Toastmasters Club and she and a team of selected classmates won the Deloitte Regional Case Study Competition. She also published two book chapters and an article in a reputable journal. In her leisure time, she enjoys photography, cooking, and quality time with her family and friends.

Siriyama Kanthi Herath is an Associate Professor of Accounting at Clark Atlanta University's School of Business (CAU) and was a Renwick Faculty Fellow at New York University's Stern School of Business in 2022. She earned a Bachelor of Commerce Honors and an MBA from the University of Colombo in Sri Lanka, as well as a Ph.D. and a Master of Commerce Honors in Accounting from the University of Wollongong in Australia. She worked at the University of Lynchburg, Georgia State University and Georgia Institute of Technology before joining CAU. Prior to relocating to the United States, Dr. Herath worked in Australia at the University of Wollongong and Western Sydney University and in Sri Lanka at the University of Ruhuna and the University of Colombo. She holds positions on the editorial boards of multiple academic journals and has contributed over 70 publications to a diverse range of journals. Her research areas include Accounting Education, Management Control and Outsourcing, Cost Management, Corporate Governance, Data Analytics, and Sustainability Accounting. She is a Distinguished Toastmaster and served as the President and Treasurer of the Georgia Institute of Technology Toastmasters International Club from 2019 to 2020, the Treasurer of the Emory University Toastmasters International Club from 2019 to 2020, and as an Area Director from 2020 to 2021 in Georgia, United States. Additionally, she possesses the TESOL Professional Certificate from Arizona State University and the Professional Certificate in Google Data Analytics. In her leisure time, she enjoys traveling and gardening.

H. Jazri is a professor of cybersecurity at the Taylor's University. Prior to that he was also a serving professor at the Namibia University of Science and Technology (NUST), Asia Pacific University Malaysia (APU), and University of Computing and Engineering (UniMY). He is the founder of Cybersecurity Malaysia and OIC-CERT Team. Prof Jazri is the recipient of the Harold Tipton Award by ISC2 in 2010 and serves cybersecurity field for more than 30 years. He is a certified CISSP since 2002 until today.

Mustafa Rehman Khan has been associated with UCSI University, Malaysia. He received PhD in Management Sciences from Universiti Pendidikan Sultan Idris, Malaysia. He has published in several esteemed international journals such as the IEEE Transactions on Engineering Management, Management of Environmental Quality, and the International Journal of Productivity and Performance Management.

Kasturi Laturkar is currently working as a Validation Engineer for Validation Associates LLC. She graduated with a M.S. in Chemical Engineering from Syracuse University and a B.Tech in Chemical Engineering from Guru Gobind Singh Indraprastha University, Delhi, India. She has more than 5 years of experience working in commissioning, qualification and validation of upstream and downstream bioprocessing equipment and critical utilities.

Kaustubh Laturkar is currently working as an engineer at the Facility for Rare Isotope Beams which is a US-DOE project in Michigan after completing his M.S in chemical engineering from University of Florida and B.E. in Chemical Engineering from Panjab University, Chandigarh, India. He has more than 10 years of experience working in the field of process engineering, refinery operations, utility systems design and operation with a special focus on design and commissioning of engineering systems.

Sei Ping Lau is a senior lecturer at Faculty of Computer Science & Information Technology (FCSIT), Universiti Malaysia Sarawak (UNIMAS). He received his Doctor of Philosophy (PhD) from University of Southampton, UK at 2015. His in-depth knowledge in computer science had given him the trust to handle wide varieties of course in UNIMAS including commercial postgraduate program courses. Besides the teaching and learning activities, he also actively participates and had more than 10 years experience in research and development (R&D) activities. The area of interests includes wireless sensor networks, applied computing, and cybersecurity.

Rashmi Mahajan is a triple post graduate and is a Masters of Computer Management, Post Graduate Diploma in Business Management [Marketing] & Masters of Business Studies [Marketing]. She has completed her PhD in Marketing Management and a Diploma in Training & Development from Indian Society for Training & Development, Pune Chapter. She has around 19+ years of experience teaching undergraduate as well as post graduate students and has 3 PhD scholars pursuing their PhD under her. She has published various papers in National as well as International journals and has 2 patents and 1 copyright credited to her name. She also has 2 Chapter Published. She is a Professor, Head of Department of International Business & Dy. Director of BIIB in Sri Balaji University Pune (SBUP).

Fazeelat Masood is an Assistant Professor at Bahria Business School, Bahria University. Her research interests are wellbeing, soft HRM, quality of life, sustainable HR practices, organizational behavior and social entrepreneurship. Dr. Masood has published in a few esteemed research journals. One of her research papers was accepted for presentation in the British Academy of Management Conference 2019 and another in the Asian Academy of Management Conference 2021.

Ilyas Masudin is a Professor of Logistics and Supply Chain at the Department of Industrial Engineering, University of Muhammadiyah Malang. He is currently the Dean of Engineering Faculty of the University of Muhammadiyah Malang.

Lalitha Muniandy is an Assistant Professor in the Department of Computing and Information Technology at Tunku Abdul Rahman University of Management and Technology (TARUMT). She has been teaching at TARUMT since 2001 – present. She completed her undergraduate degree in Computer Science in 2001, received her Master of Computer Science in 2003, and her PhD in 2017 from Universiti Sains Malaysia. Her research interests include cyber security and human-computer interaction.

Raja Kumar Murugesan is an Associate Professor of Computer Science, and Head of Research for the Faculty of Innovation and Technology at Taylor's University, Malaysia. He has a PhD in Advanced Computer Networks from the Universiti Sains Malaysia. His research interests include IPv6, Future Internet, Internet Governance, Computer Networks, Network Security, IoT, Blockchain, Machine Learning and Deep Learning Algorithms. He is a Senior Member of the IEEE and IEEE Communications Society, member of the Internet Society (ISOC), member of the Malaysia Data Science Association and associated with the IPv6 Forum, Asia Pacific Advanced Network Group (APAN), Internet2, and Malaysia Network Operator Group (MyNOG) member's community. Talks about IoT, Blockchain, AI, Machine learning, IPv6, Internet Governance, Digital Transformation in the context of Industry 4.0 (IR4.0) and Sustainable Development Goals (SDG's), and Futurist Thinking at various international conferences, forums, and events. Obtained substantial research funds locally and internationally, and actively engages in research, consultancy, and outreach activities in Advanced Computer Networks.

Anandhi R. J. did her BE in Computer Science, M.Tech in Computer Science and Ph.D in Computer Science with a specialization in SpatialData Mining. She is associated with New Horizon college of Engineering, Bengaluru since 2018. She has a rich experience of 26 years in teaching and industry.

A recognized PhD guide under VTU, she has numerous publications under her name and has attended many conferences, workshops and symposiums. She has been awarded for the best publication in the International conference held at Singapore. Under her guidance various project proposals have been approved by the Secretary, Karnataka State Council for Science and Technology (KSCST) under the "Student Project Programme-38th, 39th and 40th Series". She has chaired many international conferences as resource person. She was the coordinator and member, of Board of Examination, VTU and External Examiner for PhD at VTU and Anna University.

Dian Palupi Restuputri is a lecturer and researcher in the Industrial Engineering department at the University of Muhammadiyah Malang. Her research interests are in the area of ergonomics and human factor engineering. She received his bachelor's degree in Industrial Engineering from Diponegoro University (2007). She holds a master's degree in Industrial Engineering from Institute of Technology Bandung (2012).

Archana Sharma has a Ph.D (Computer Science) in Mobile Database, is distinguished Academician with overall 27+ years of experience of different hierarchy levels in Institutes/Organizations and having successfully covered various work areas in academics and excelling in each with commendations as Star Performer and Distinguished Academician & Researcher Award. Her area of expertise includes Database, IoT, Cloud and Blockchain. Further, she has authored Text Book for UG/PG Students and published/presented more than 50 research papers and several Book Chapters in reputed Journals indexed in Scopus. She has participated and successfully completed various FDPs as well.

Pritesh Pradeep Somani is an Academician with over 11 years of teaching experience with a keen interest across research. With a keen interest towards S.P.S.S. and data crunching, open to collaboration across Qualitative and Quantitative Research.

Chong Eng Tan, an Associate Professor at Universiti Malaysia Sarawak (UNIMAS), has been a dedicated member of the Faculty of Computer Science and Information Technology since 1999. He earned his Ph.D. from the University of Cambridge in 2004, specializing in wireless networks and broadband access technology. With over 25 years of research experience, Dr. Tan has focused his research on connecting remote areas to the internet. Notably, he designed the pilot long-range wireless system in 2010 in Bario and played a pivotal role in establishing Telecentres in remote locations in Malaysia. Dr. Tan is a senior member of the IEEE and a graduate member of IEM, and he currently leads the 5G& Connectivity Keylab, contributing significantly to technology advancements in connectivity and rural ICT solutions. His notable research achievements include the development of the Virtual Telecentre concept and innovative solar power solutions for ICT systems.

Arunadevi Thirumalraj did her BE in Computer Science Engineering in Government college of Engineering, Bodinayakanur and she has worked as a Research associate in various industrial and academic research institutes for past 6 years. Now she is pursing ME Computer Science Engineering in K. Ramakrishnan College of Technology, (KRCT), Tiruchirappalli. She is actively involved in the field of innovative teaching and Learning. She has publishing a good number of papers in indexed journals.

Revathi V. did her M.Sc., M.Phil (Materials Sciences) from Madurai Kamaraj University and completed her Ph.D from SRM university, Chennai. She is associated with New Horizon college of Engineering, Bengaluru since 2001 and currently heading department of Applied Sciences - Physics. She is actively involved in R&D and has published good number of papers in indexed journals and is a recognized research guide under Visveswaraya Technological University.

Index

A

B

C

D

www.ingramcontent.com/pod-product-compliance
Lightning Source LLC
LaVergne TN
LVHW062105300926
849161LV00010B/2378